Handbook of Cross-Cultural and Multicultural Personality Assessment

The LEA Series in Personality and Clinical Psychology
Irving B. Weiner, Editor

Handbook of Cross-Cultural and Multicultural Personality Assessment

Edited by

Richard H. Dana
Portland State University

LAWRENCE ERLBAUM ASSOCIATES, PUBLISHERS

2000   Mahwah, New Jersey   London

Lawrence Erlbaum Associates, Inc., Publishers
10 Industrial Avenue
Mahwah, NJ 07430

Cover design by Kathryn Houghtaling Lacey

Library of Congress Cataloging-in-Publication Data

Handbook of cross-cultural and multicultural personality
assessment / edited by Richard H. Dana.
     p. cm.
Includes bibliographical references and index.
ISBN 0-8058-2789-7 (cloth : alk. paper)
1. Minorities—Psychological testing. 2. Personality
assessment. 3. Ethnopsychology. I. Dana, Richard H.
(Richard Henry), 1927– .
RC473.P79H36   1999
616.89′075′089 —dc21   99-30954
                                       CIP

Printed in the United States of America
10 9 8 7 6 5 4 3 2

This handbook is dedicated to the legion of multicultural persons in the United States and other countries who, as assessees (i.e., clients, patients, or research participants), have been subjected to indignities and frustrations during assessment proceedings and outcomes using standard Anglo-American instruments. I hope this volume serves to remind practitioners of the labor, knowledge, responsibility, and devotion required to provide competent cross-cultural and multicultural assessment as a prerequisite and foundation for quality mental health care.

Contents

Foreword

Irving B. Weiner
University of South Florida

How do people resemble and differ from each other? These two questions have long been basic to theory and research concerning the nature and implications of personality characteristics. When expanded to include groups of people, these questions define the essential issues in cross-cultural personality study: How do groups of people resemble or differ from each other on the basis of their national, racial, or ethnic origins? In what ways do similar personality characteristics have different implications for adaptation in diverse cultures? Conversely, in what ways do different personality characteristics have similar implications in diverse cultures? To what extent is there as much variability within national, racial, and ethnic groups on certain personality characteristics as there are differences among them? What if any personality characteristics are sufficiently unique to and homogenous within an cultural group to define a distinct national, racial, or ethnic characteristic?

To explore these questions effectively, researchers studying groups of people and practitioners examining individual persons must have at their disposal adequate methods of personality assessment. These personality assessment methods should be psychometrically sound with established reliability and validity. They should be culturally sensitive by virtue of comprising stimulus content and language usage tailored to help test-takers from diverse backgrounds feel comfortable and communicate clearly. The original contributions that Richard Dana has assembled for this handbook address these considerations extensively in light of current thinking and presently available information concerning cross-cultural and multicultural personality assessment.

   Authored by a distinguished international group of assessment psychologists, the various chapters of this book discuss conceptual and definitional
issues, methodological considerations in research design, observed personality differences among ethnic and racial groups in many different parts
of the world, the teaching and practice of responsible personality assessment in working with diverse groups and individuals, and cross-cultural
application of such widely used assessment instruments as the Minnesota
Multiphasic Personality Inventory (MMPI), the Thematic Apperception
Test (TAT), and the Rorschach.
   Assessment psychologists engaged in cross-cultural research or practice
will appreciate the breadth of coverage in this volume and benefit from the
abundance and quality of the information it provides. Beyond being a wel-
come new addition to the current literature in cross-cultural assessment,
Dr. Dana's handbook is likely to play an important future role in stimulating interest in the cultural diversity of personality assessment and suggesting new avenues of research into its clinical implications.

Preface

Persons of color now include approximately 40% of mental health patients and will represent over half of the U.S. population early in the next century. At present, 65% of Asians and 70% of Hispanics in the United States speak English as a second language, and many retain a traditional cultural orientation as well. These persons have not often received the quality mental health services that competent assessment of personality and psychopathology can make possible (Dana, 1998c). Instead, there has been a history of misdiagnosis and distortion of personality by stereotype, caricature, and dehumanization.

Hall (1997) has indicted psychology for "cultural malpractice" during a period of rapid changes in the racial/ethnic population. Cultural malpractice occurs as a result of unintentional, often unconscious, but unremitting bias from a variety of sources (see Dana, in press). Bias is predicated on a Euro-American worldview and ethnocentrism that minimizes cultural/racial differences among persons. The consequences of bias can permeate the assessment process, and the outcomes of assessment in psychological reports and treatment recommendations are frequently demeaning and damaging.

Cultural malpractice is evidenced by bias in providing services for these populations. It begins with the scientific methodology and statistics used to make group comparisons from the perspective of a Euro-American worldview. Assessors display bias not only by minimizing group differences, but by stereotyping clients and failing to have adequate information resources on the cultural/racial groups they serve. Bias is also apparent in culture-specific Anglo emic standard tests used as universal measures or genuine etics and as pseudoetics without adequate demonstrations of equivalence for other populations. The outcomes of cultural malpractice are chronicled in a history of misdiagnosis and pathologization using the diagnostic and statistical manuals published by the American Psychiatric Association. Finally, chronic underutilization of mental health services by multicultural groups strongly suggests deficiencies in the proffered mental health services, including assessments and how these services have been made available to clients during the service delivery process.

Professional psychologists have expressed their dissatisfaction with training for culturally competent practice with multicultural populations and their discomfort in attempting to provide services for these individuals (Allison, Crawford, Echemendia, Robinson, & Kemp, 1994; Allison, Echemendia, Crawford, & Robinson, 1996). The professional psychologists surveyed by Allison et al. (1994) had sound reasons for their feelings of distress when encountering clients who differ from themselves in cultural/racial origins: Their training included neither a model for practice nor the cultural information, language skills, and experience required for cultural competence with these populations.

This handbook was designed to remediate bias by presenting information relevant to components of a practice model described in chapter 1. The model includes the development of both universal and culture-specific instruments, acculturation measures, cultural formulations for personality description and clinical diagnosis, and the goodness-of-fit between assessment outcomes and potentially more effective interventions than have been available in the immediate past. The seven sections and 28 chapters herein address specific points in this model where questions need to be asked of the research literature from other informed sources (Dana, 1998c). Research findings can constitute exemplar data points within an assessment-intervention model where available information can increase the reliability of the entire assessment process and provide incremental validity for personality conceptualizations or clinical diagnoses. These data points are formalized by a series of relevant questions involving culture-specific information that can lead to more effective matching of any subsequent interventions with specific client problems and personality dilemmas.

An examination of ingredients for practice models and the description of a specific assessment-intervention model formalizes an introduction to a new generation of research and practice with cultural/racial populations in the United States and a perspective from which to evaluate the research history of assessment. Diagnosis of psychopathology is included as are problems in living such as acculturative stress, discrimination, culture-specific dilemmas, and cultural identity issues. This dovetailing of assessment and intervention requires not only culture-specific models of psychological intervention (Dana, 1998c), but also suggests the kind and number of culture-specific elements to incorporate into interventions for particular psychopathologies or problems in living.

In addition to methodology and reviews of research findings, this handbook describes both standard and new objective tests and projective methods for personality assessment. Historically, the usage of standard instruments represented professional practice applications of shared reality perceptions, ideology, and ethics; these were dichotomized by factors of experimentalism and social concern discovered among graduate students by Lipsey (1974) and also reported in many other samples (Dana, 1982, 1998a, 1998b). Experimentalism refers to confidence in psychological methodology for problem solving with reliance on objective tests, whereas social concern invoked a personal responsibility for promoting human welfare using personal intuition and projective methods.

This dichotomy of values was fostered by the training of professional psychologists in programs deliberately designed to nourish students who represented either the objective or intuitive extremes on various research scales. Professional psychology matured as a legitimate area of social science. Training programs increasingly favored those students who espoused psychological methodology and experienced a concomitant preference for low-inference interpretation in dealing with reliable scores from their assessment instruments.

Consequently, the use of the Rorschach increased with the adoption of the Rorschach Comprehensive System, whereas the use of the Thematic Apperception Test decreased to become what has been described as a *projective interview* because there were no comparative objective scores and normative data to transform the interpretation process from high inference to low inference. The Minnesota Multiphasic Personality Inventory (MMPI) prospered and increased in popularity to become the most frequently used assessment measure as a majority of professional psychologists applied their scientific training in their assessment practices.

This handbook recognizes and honors assessor preferences for either low- and/or high-inference interpretation procedures because both of these approaches are legitimate and necessary to fully comprehend the richness and complexity of human personality and psychopathology. Although I practice as an assessor with equal comfort using both approaches, I am aware that Scylla and Charybdis are contributors to cultural malpractice. The Scylla of low-inference interpretation is a failure to appreciate the assessee outside of the context provided by available test scores and normative data. When standard Anglo-American emic tests and methods are used with culturally diverse populations, low-inference interpretation may be faulty for new populations due to deficiencies in cross-cultural equivalence. The Charybdis of high-inference interpretation is eisegesis—a commingling and confounding of assessor and assessee in the reporting of test results (see Dana, 1966). Remediation occurs by training assessors to recognize their own eisegesis in their psychological reports and by attention to check points during interpretation to increase reliability. Instruments dependent on high-inference interpretation can place assessees in jeopardy of dehumanization if their emotional experiences as a cultural being, first languages, and history of contact and living in the United States are not sufficiently understood and accepted within an ethnorelativistic perspective.

Four professional obligations or ground rules to resolve these dilemmas were invoked in preparation of this handbook. First, all tests and methods require a research foundation to provide a database that is adequate for responsible low-inference interpretation. Second, cogent demonstrations of cross-cultural equivalence are necessary before tests are applied routinely in practice with new populations underrepresented or misrepresented in available norms. Third, projective methods lacking in formal scores and normative data (e.g., Thematic Apperception Test [TAT]) require reliable high-inference interpretation procedures that can be communicated to students and practitioners. These methods should be provided with formal scoring systems as a basis for collection and use of normative data to facilitate the use of low-inference interpretation (see chap. 20). Fourth, by fostering both low- and high-inference interpretation and providing guidelines for research, training, and practice, the reliability and validity of interpretation with diverse cultural and national populations can be increased.

The information in this handbook has been provided by 35 contributing authors in sections that (a) provide an overview and one non-Euro-American perspective, (b) examine bias and methodological remediations in research technology and assessment instruments, (c) articulate acculturation theory and measurement, and (d) present objective tests and projective methods as well as their applications in assessment practice. An informed commentary on how to teach and learn culturally competent personality assessment is also included. Many of these authors are from outside the United States either by birth or nationality, with five from Latin America (Brazil, Chile, Columbia, Mexico, Venezuela), five from Europe (France, The Netherlands, Portugal, Spain), one from Israel, and one from Canada. This international representation enables the presentation of information on how tests developed in the United States have been applied in Europe and Latin America. It also provides readers with exposure to tests developed in other countries that have bona fide applications in the United States. Many of these authors also represent their own cultural/racial groups in the United States. They have exercised their voice to articulate assessment contributions that can describe with fidelity the experience of persons in their own cultural/racial groups. As a consequence of personal and professional experiences, they are also familiar with the impact of constructing their personalities, psychopathologies, and problems in living from a Euro-American perspective. These contributors have specialized in methodology, development of specific tests, or applications of these tests in assessment practice. How these assessment issues can affect individual clients by disrupting their lives and personal well-bing has been clearly described from an advocacy stance in three chapters (23, 24, 25). It is also embedded in many other chapters that address general research issues, research with particular tests, and new approaches to practice or teaching.

ACKNOWLEDGMENTS

This book was made possible by the Regional Research Center (RRI), of Portland State University. Specifically, Dr. Nancy Korloff, Director RRI, and Ron Talarico, Assistant to the Director, provided me with a scholar's shelter, collegial privileges, and a supportive context. Without their indulgences and computer help from many persons, including Jeff Allworth, Lynne Chase, Shad Jessen, Denise Schmit, Paul Koren, Darey Shell, and Ron Talarico, I would have floundered.

I also wish to acknowledge the good will, enthusiasm, and perseverance of the contributing authors, particularly those outside of the United States who suffered my unremitting editorial scrutiny of their translated sentences. I am grateful for their understanding that translations from Portuguese and Spanish—a transformation from a more literary and literate style into psychologized English—is a profound and unsettling cross-cultural experience. Finally, I would like to thank a number of nameless journal and book editors who tolerated my enthusiastic citation of these chapters by handbook authors prior to their publication.

As the last sentence suggests, despite the repeated citations by contributors to my own work, I am certain I have learned more from their chapters than they could possibly have learned from me. Editing a handbook is a daunting experience. As Irv Weiner warned me, 12 chapters per editor is more than a sufficient test of task orientation and endurance. I designed this handbook to encourage expression of my advocacy and beliefs in the more credible idioms of these contributors. Not only has this occurred, but, in this process, I have experienced their passion, knowledge, and greater familiarity with what is entailed in research and assessment practice with multicultural populations. For these gifts, I will always be indebted.

Finally, I would like to acknowledge Lawrence Erlbaum for his initial receptiviity to this project and Irv Weiner for his enthusiastic and unremitting support as the reader of the initial prospectus and later throughout the entire publication process as series editor.

REFERENCES

Allison, K. W., Crawford, I., Echemendia, R., Robinson, L., & Kemp, D. (1994). Human diversity and professional competence: Training in clinical and counseling psychology revisited. *American Psychologist, 49*, 792-796.

Allison, K. W., Echemendia, R., Crawford, I., & Robinson, W. L. (1996). Predicting cultural competence: Implications for practice and training. *Professional Psychology: Research and Practice, 27*, 386-393.

Dana, R. H. (1962). The validation of projective tests. *Journal of Projective Techniques, 26*, 182-186.

Dana, R. H. (1966). Eisegesis and assessment. *Journal of Projective Techniques and Personality Assessment, 30*, 215-222.

Dana, R. H. (1982). *A human science model for personality assessment with projective techniques.* Springfield, IL: Thomas.

Dana, R. H. (1993). *Multicultural assessment perspectives for professional psychology.* Boston: Allyn & Bacon.

Dana, R. H. (1998a). *A humanistic science of personality assessment: History, practice, methodology.* Unpublished manuscript.

Dana, R. H. (1998b). *Psychological assessment of cultural identity and psychopathology.* Thousand Oaks, CA: Sage.

Dana, R. H. (1998c). *Understanding cultural identity in intervention and assessment.* Thousand Oaks, CA: Sage.

Dana, R. H. (in press). Multicultural assessment of adolescent and child personality and psychopathology. In A. L. Cominian and U. P. Gielen (Eds.), *Human development in an international perspective.* Lengerich, Germany: Pabst Scientific Publishers.

Hall, C. I. J. (1997). Cultural malpractice: The growing obsolescence of psychology with the changing U. S. population. *American Psychologist, 52*, 642-651.

Lipsey, M. (1974). Research and relevance: A survey of graduate students and faculty in psychology. *American Psychologist, 29*, 541-555.

I

OVERVIEW AND A NON-EURO-AMERICAN PERSPECTIVE

Part I (see chap. 1) provides a brief description of the assessment-intervention process that subsequent chapters flesh out for substance, clarification, examples, and increased credibility. This model is neonate and tentative, open to a questioning of specific steps or addition of new steps, revisions, and replacement by alternative models. I hope this handbook serves to inform the model. Assessment has become part and parcel of intervention, with inextricable components fused to compose one fluid process and subject to demands for predictive validation of diagnostic and therapeutic outcomes. Chapter 2 provides an example of only one of a number of recent culture-specific perspectives critical of the efficacy of the Euro-American mental health establishment with non-Anglo clients. The perspectives of the various cultural/racial groups in the United States all differ remarkably from a Euro-American perspective, but they share common concerns with being heard and understood by the mainstream mental health establishment. Other chapters in the handbook provide vivid glimpses of Hispanic, American Indian/Alaska Native, and Asian American perspectives, but these perspectives have not been articulated in detail comparable with the Africentric perspective.

Chapter 2, an Africentric perspective, begins with an examination of ethics as codified by the American Psychological Association (APA). Carolyn Payton (1994) described the 1992 ethics code as "downgrading in importance of psychologists' declaration of respect for the dignity and worth of the individual" (p. 317) consumer of services in favor of pro-

1

tecting psychologists. Ethical practice with African Americans includes cultural knowledge from literature, clinical expertise predicated on culture-specific sensitivity, and diagnostic conceptualizations from experience with etic and emic tools. This vision of ethical practice and these specific objectives, although rational and absolutely necessary, were not verbalized in the 1992 code. Ethical decision making requires a process that is described by a series of steps: identification of the problem in a cultural setting, identification of potential conflicting ethical issues, consultation, and review of possible actions and their consequences. Professional and cultural competence were not distinguished in the ethical code; as a result, the umbrella for protection from harm does not cover multicultural consumers of psychological services.

By juxtaposing Eurocentric and Africentric worldviews, the magnitude of potential differences in cultural/ethnic/racial perspectives becomes apparent. What is understood by *services* and *service delivery*, by *roles* of providers, and the construction of reality that undergirds these client expectations differs immensely. These differences in expectations persist despite the clear understanding among many educated, bicultural individuals of the ingredients that compose establishment mental health services. However, such understanding can strengthen the desire to receive services that have a more comfortable fit with their own culture-specific expectations.

An Africentric perspective functions for self-understanding and a cultural construction of reality. This perspective is communicated by means of the seven principles of Nguzo Saba that emphasize core humanistic values and the integrity of African-American culture. These principles are elaborated in detail to provide a portrait of the cultural self, the role of the individual in society, the responsible, cooperative interface with the community and community goals, as well as wholehearted belief that community persons will cherish and foster these principles.

When ethnic or racial comparisons are made against a standard provided by the dominant or mainstream Euro-American group, the outcomes are always prejudicial and demeaning because of the erroneous assumption that the measures used are universal. Although there has been a recent history of good intentions to provide fairness in using assessment instruments, the level of intentionality on the part of the assessment establishment has not been sufficient to foster cross-cultural equivalence. The effects of racism have been cumulative across generations on Anglo as well as African Americans. Anglo Americans have not understood racism and discrimination because few have experienced a daily presence of denigration or experience expectations for a continuation of this process. A strong quality of involuntary servitude still remains when acceptability of persons who are designated non-White is predicated on assuming the values, behaviors, and affect of the mainstream Euro-American society. This recognition was the impetus for Nigrescence theories, descriptions of pathologies attending emulation of the White mainstream, and later for articulating Africentrism as a source of pride in self and group so vital to physical, mental, and spiritual health.

REFERENCE

Payton, C. R. (1994). Implications of the 1992 Ethics Code for diverse groups. *Professional Psychology: Research and Practice, 25,* 317–320.

An Assessment-Intervention Model for Research and Practice With Multicultural Populations

Richard H. Dana
Portland State University

An assessment-intervention model was designed to illustrate how assessment research and practice can move in the direction of cultural competence. This model was initially proposed in a basic multicultural assessment text (Dana, 1993) and subsequently was expanded to incorporate culture-specific intervention strategies for African Americans, American Indians/Alaska Native, Asian Americans, and Hispanic Americans that contained culturally relevant components (Dana, 1998e). Whenever the format, structure, substance, service providers, and service delivery styles of interventions for multicultural clients met client expectations and conformed to their health–illness beliefs, these interventions were more likely to be accepted and responded to positively with beneficial outcomes. The history of mental health services provided by culture-specific mental health agencies had suggested many ingredients of cultural competence that were found to be credible to clients and necessary for quality care (Isaacs & Benjamin, 1991). Similarly, characteristics of agencies, programs, and personnel were identified in research literature and operationalized in an Agency Cultural Competence Checklist (Dana, 1998a; Dana, Behn, & Gonwa, 1992; Dana & Matheson, 1992). Finally, the impact of matching language and ethnicity of clients and providers was associated with increased retention rates and more beneficial outcomes of interventions for multicultural clients (Takeuchi, Sue, & Yeh, 1995). These several avenues of research and practice evidence were influential in the development of this model, as described in earlier papers (Dana,

1997, 1998c). The description offered in this chapter includes additional research evidence and cites other handbook chapters for additional documentation, illustrations, and examples.

The model assumes differences in human behavior, including personality variables and symptomatology suggestive of dysfunction, on the basis of cultural identifications. Culture is considered to be of major importance unless specific cultural issues can be ruled out by information provided in the responses to a series of seven questions posed at different points during the entire assessment process (Fig. 1.1). The initial phase of the assessment process serves to establish whether the magnitude of cultural differences is sufficient to require either culture-specific modifications and/or corrections for culture in standard instruments or the use of culture-specific instruments. This information can increase the reliability of the assessment process and lead to more valid diagnostic statements. Following this model can also result in subsequent interventions that are more likely to be well received and effective. When individuals are assimilated or bicultural and cultural issues are minimal, standard assessment and standard interventions can be used to meet criteria of acceptability and fairness. However, the presence of cultural self-identification and/or presenting issues related to culture, ethnicity, or race suggests that standard services may be ineffective and should either be applied with caution or not used at all. Instead, culture-specific interventions should be provided, if available, or referral to another provider for these services may be necessary.

PREMISE

The model begins with the premise that universal or culture-general instruments called *etics* may become feasible in the future but are not sufficiently developed at the present time for meaningful applications in clinical assessment practice. The initial question pertains to the availability of these etic instruments, and the answer is negative. There has been a prolonged search for universals, and a taxonomy of possible psychological universals is available (Lonner, 1980), but there are few genuine etic tests available for clinical assessment purposes. If these etics were available, their use would lead to an etic diagnostic formulation and interventions that were culturally universal, as Fig. 1.1 indicates. Similarly, culture-specific or emic instruments were developed historically for research purposes and more recently for clinical assessment. A combined etic–emic approach for use with particular constructs has been suggested (Triandis et al., 1972) and applications have been completed (e.g., Davidson, Jaccard, Morales, Triandis, & Diaz-Guerrero, 1976; Triandis et al., 1993). In chapter 18, Ephraim describes another etic–emic rationale developed by De Vos

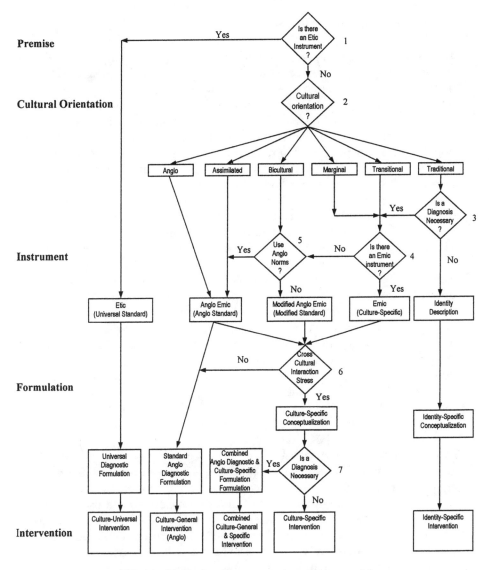

FIG. 1.1. Multicultural assessment-intervention model.

for cross-cultural interpretation of the Thematic Apperception Test (TAT) that has stimulated interesting research. It provides clinical examples for sensitization of students to the potential of this approach for understanding persons from many countries. Similarly, in chapter 12, Holden presents several newer tests for personality and psychopathology that have potential as genuine etics, but their status as etics is neither sufficient nor conclusive at present.

CULTURAL ORIENTATIONS

The second question in Fig. 1.1 invokes culture specifically by asking for information concerning the relationship between an original cultural identification and acculturation to a host culture. I have suggested the cultural orientation status categories of *traditional, marginal, bicultural,* and *assimilated* included in Fig. 1.1 (Dana, 1992). A transitional category for American Indians/Alaska Natives contains bilingual persons who question traditional values and religion (LaFromboise, Trimble, & Mohatt, 1990); it is also included in Fig. 1.1 together with a sixth orientation, *Anglo.* These orientations are nominal categories for providing a reasonably good fit between clients and tests. Four of these cultural orientations are similar to those developed by Berry (1989) in response to questions of the relative value of maintaining cultural identity and relationships to other groups. These acculturation outcomes have been measured in linear terms as the extent of transition from a traditional cultural orientation status to an assimilated status. However, most recent research has focused on the development of two separate and independent or orthogonal scales measuring psychological activity for each culture to provide an index of balance between two cultures. In chapter 6, Cuéllar indicates that linear measures are limited in the amount of information provided about personality constructs and acculturation while orthogonal measures can generate additional information including two types of bicultural individuals. Cuéllar also provides a selected chronology of acculturation/ethnicity measurement between 1955 and 1995. Sodowsky and Maestas have an appendix in chapter 7 describing non-Hispanic acculturation and ethnic identity instruments. An examination of major Hispanic acculturation instruments is also available (Dana, 1996). Burlew and her colleagues review and describe racial identity measures for African Americans in chapter 8. Good psychometric measures of acculturation now exist in abundance for a large number of cultural groups, but practitioners have not used them routinely in clinical assessment. The APA ethics committee provided a negative response to the published recommendation that acculturation evaluation was an ethical necessity (Dana, 1994).

Acculturation information in response to Question 2 has several major uses: (a) determine the suitability of standard tests, with or without modifications, for multicultural clients; (b) help in developing cultural formulations for *Diagnostic and Statistical Manual of Mental Disorders* (4th ed. [DSM–IV]); (c) encourage an examination of the contents and boundaries of the cultural self; and (d) provide some of the ingredients for culture- and identity-specific conceptualizations leading to culture- and identity-specific interventions. This information can be gathered using linear and/or orthogonal scales and by judicious use of interview content. Although there have been many single-item, several-item, or brief instruments developed for research purposes, these research tools are not suitable for clinical assessment purposes because the information provided may not be reliable and leads to a label rather than a selection among cultural orientation status categories. Research to identify salient components across instruments suggests that these consensual items may eventually be used in an interview format to evaluate cultural orientation status. However, only the item selection and analysis phase of research has been completed (Tanaka-Matsumi, 1998). The information resulting from Question 2 is used to determine selection or modification of the instruments used in assessment.

Cultural formulations and conceptualizations for purposes of diagnosis or intervention require considerably more detailed knowledge of culture. Question 3 pertains to the necessity of diagnosis. If a diagnosis is not required (e.g., when identity problems are presented), then an identity description can lead to an identity-specific conceptualization as the basis for an identity-specific intervention (e.g., Phillips, 1990; Ruiz, 1990). Additional information may be required from culture-specific tests. In chapter 24, Morris includes a listing of African-American emics described in detail in edited volumes (Jones, 1996).

Whenever a diagnosis is required, the *DSM–IV* outline for cultural formulations (American Psychiatric Association, 1994) calls for information in five areas, including cultural identity, particularly from orthogonal instruments that describe involvement with the culture of origin and the host culture as well as language abilities and preference. A cultural explanation of the individual's illness contains idioms of distress, the meaning and severity of the illness described using cultural reference norms, and any local categorization for illness as well as causes and explanations. Cultural factors related to the psychosocial environment and levels of function as well as cultural elements in the relations with the clinician are also included. The outline concludes with an overall cultural assessment for diagnosis and cure. Chapters 25 and 26 describe the preparation of cultural formulations and present examples (e.g., Hispanics and American Indians/Alaska Natives). As these chapters suggest, providing this information entails in-depth cultural knowledge and may require an emic instrument for supplemental content whenever available (see Question 4). There are relatively few emic instruments at the present time, except for African Americans, as noted earlier. However, some emic instruments for several different populations have been developed to measure acculturative stress. Examples include the Hispanic Stress Inventory (Cervantes, Padilla, & Salgado de Snyder, 1991); the Societal, Attitudinal, Familial, and Environmental Stress Scale (Chavez, Moran, Reid, & Lopez, 1997); and the Cultural Mistrust Inventory (Terrell & Terrell, 1981) recently used by Whaley (1998) with African–American psychiatric patients. However, measures of acculturation and cultural identity are not sufficient in the absence of explicit assessor knowledge, language skills, and culturally relevant experiences. Some professional training programs now have various requirements for increasing cultural knowledge, and there are several available measures of cultural competence that include awareness of self, beliefs/attitudes, and several kinds of cultural knowledge and skills (Pope-Davis & Dings, 1995). There is also one description of emic and etic sources of personality-psychopathology information for students learning to be assessors (Dana, 1998d).

INSTRUMENTS

Four classes of instruments are recognized in this model in addition to etic or universal instruments that have already been discussed (see Fig. 1.1). Standard or Anglo-American emic instruments are culture specific but are applied as if they were etics and are labeled as pseudoetics to suggest their unproved authenticity as universal instruments. These standard instruments may be modified, adjusted, or corrected for use with multicultural populations. Emic instruments are developed for culture-specific populations in the United States. Instruments for identity description are not standard assessment instruments but special purpose measures for particular populations.

The selection of tests on the basis of cultural orientation status begins with our present knowledge concerning base rates for these categories. Traditional persons compose approximately 20% of the entire multicultural population in the United States, with this percentage rising sharply to include almost all immigrants, refugees, sojourners, and foreign students (Dana, 1998e). Traditional persons may not speak English or have only modest amounts of English as a second language. Many of these persons have meager educational histories and low socioeconomic status (SES). The use of translated paper-and-pencil tests is often necessary and any examiner-administered testing should be accomplished in the client's first language. Translations of standard tests have major problems of linguistic equivalence (Dana, 1993). Even the MMPI/MMPI–2, which has been translated into a large number of different languages including many Spanish versions using recognized systematic procedures, has major unresolved translation problems. These translation deficiencies are discussed in chapters 5 and 11. Of even greater problematic significance, these standard tests are interpreted using normative data collected in the United States and are called *Anglo norms* in Fig. 1.1. These norms ordinarily reflect social class/education, gender, and representativeness of each cultural population. These norms are entirely suitable for assimilated individuals from multicultural populations and for some biculturals.

Question 5 probes the legitimacy of using these Anglo or standard norms with multicultural populations. Typically such norms pathologize traditional and marginal clients. However, it is possible to reinterpret these norms based on extensive cultural information (see chaps. 13, 15, and 23 for Iberoamerican examples), but this information has not been systematically prepared and made available to assessors and students. Moreover, few Anglo Americans have sufficient cultural knowledge for responsible reinterpretation, although when assessors and clients are matched for ethnicity such reinterpretation is feasible and bias is minimized. Chapter 23 presents a practitioner perspective on the magnitude of bias in the MMPI/MMPI–2 when used with Hispanic clients.

The development of cultural orientation status norms is feasible, however, and this approach has been demonstrated for Hispanics using selected Halstead–Reitan neuropsychological tests (Arnold, Montgomery, Castanada, & Longoria, 1994). Acculturation status norms for all standard tests would be cost-effective. Such norms could avoid reduction or obliteration of intragroup differences (e.g., among Mexican Americans, Cuban Americans, Puerto Ricans, and other Latin Americans) that would occur if overinclusive, culture-specific norms were developed. A focus on traditional cultural orientation as a major moderating variable for generating additional norms for standard tests would result in fewer diagnostic misclassifications, particularly with the MMPI/MMPI–2. Local norms are also feasible and sometimes necessary for the MMPI/MMPI–2, particularly for isolated cultural entities including some Indian tribes and communities (e.g., Charles, 1988).

It has been estimated that marginal persons may include 30% to 60% of multicultural populations (Dana, 1998e). Some of the characteristics of these persons have been described by Pinderhughes (1982). Marginal individuals have adopted values and behaviors from both an original culture and the host society; in this process, a considerable degree of traditionality can be retained. Marginal persons who have adequate English language skills, as demonstrated by assessor evaluations (see chaps. 23 and 28 for examples), can usually be administered standard tests. Although these standard tests are often assumed to be useful for cross-cultural or multicultural populations, as pseudoetics they were constructed and standardized in the United States on assimilated populations that differ on many relevant variables from these target groups. As a consequence, standard tests require corrections or adjustments for nonequivalence whenever applied to persons of marginal cultural orientation status (Dana, 1998b). As described earlier, these corrections include adjustments for acculturation measures, use of systematically developed translations as adaptations, and modified interpretations using practice guidelines, research-based documentation, and specific cultural knowledge. In chapter 6, Cuéllar describes several statistical corrections for culture that examine the impact of moderators on a criterion (e.g., slope bias, intercept bias, and the Index for Correction for Culture). In the absence of cross-cultural construct validation, such corrections are needed to dispel the mythology (e.g., that T-score difference of five points or less on the MMPI/MMPI–2 indicate no cultural difference).

FORMULATIONS

Cultural formulations are used to relate assessment and interview contents to psychiatric diagnoses by asking Question 6 regarding cross-cultural interaction stress. This question is only asked if the multicultural client is traditional, marginal, or bicultural and stressors such as oppression, prejudice, discrimination, acculturation stress, and associated problems in living are present. An affirmative answer to Question 6 requires a culture-specific conceptualization. This culture-specific conceptualization only becomes a cultural formulation after Question 7 asks whether a clinical diagnosis is required and the response is affirmative. The cultural formulation then becomes the modus operendi for using *DSM–IV* in a culturally sensitive manner with a possible outcome in a combined culture-general and culture-specific intervention. However, in some instances, the cultural formulation may also suggest a culture-specific intervention for a culture-bound *DSM–IV* glossary condition. Referral should be made to an indigenous healer for culture-specific interventions. However, when the answer to Question 7 is negative, no clinical diagnosis is required. In this instance, assisted problem solving using a culture-specific intervention is necessary, and this intervention will most likely be carried out by an ethnically similar professional provider regardless of whether English or another language is used to provide service.

INTERVENTIONS

Figure 1.1 includes five classes of interventions: culture-universal, culture-general, combined culture-general and culture-specific, culture-specific, and identity-specific. There is no clear assessment path at present to culture-universal interventions. However, the assessment paths to these other categories of interventions are described in the model. Culture-general interventions have origins in the Euro-American mainstream and include behavioral-cognitive, humanistic-existential, and psychodynamic approaches among others. Culture-general interventions are frequently applicable for multicultural clients, although cultural considerations should never be ignored. Whenever used with multicultural clients, there should be therapist role flexibility, a culturally credible and appropriate service delivery style (Atkinson, Thompson, & Grant, 1993), as well as awareness that there may be conflict with specific cultural values (Suinn, 1985). Culture-general interventions may be used as preferred whenever English is the first language or when bilinguality or biculturality is present.

Combined approaches adapt or modify culture-general interventions by an infusion of cultural values as some components of the interventions. A relatively large number of combined interventions are available and have been described in detail for each major cultural group in the United States (Dana, 1998e). Combined interventions are often used with bicultural or marginal clients when the client's second language is English or the clinician is competent in the client's first language. A cultural conceptualization and/or cultural formulation based on cultural orientation status categorization is a recommended assessment outcome. Ethnic and/or language match may be required for successful application.

Culture-specific interventions are used when English is not spoken at all or a client is lacking in English fluency. Traditional health–illness beliefs, as well as a cultural formulation leading to diagnosis of a culture-bound disorder, are required for referral to indigenous healers for these interventions. Language and ethnicity matching with the designated healer is preferable. Cultural elements are used exclusively in these interventions.

DISCUSSION

This assessment-intervention model for professional practice with multicultural populations in the United States provides a format for training assessors to become more culturally competent by asking relevant questions at various stages during the assessment process. This format is not a substitute for immersion in any culture over a long period of time that is representative of an assessor's clients and including proficiency in the language, familiarity with literature, and close ties to persons in the cultural community of interest. The assessment-intervention model provides an introduction to the process of reducing bias in cross-cultural and multicultural assessment. This model has been juxtaposed with the contents from chapters in this handbook to illustrate the range and quality of knowledge required for cultural competence in assessment.

Sue (1998) described three orthogonal ingredients of cultural competence as scientific mindedness, dynamic sizing, and culture-specific elements. Scientific mindedness has been a reiterated theme in many handbook chapters and was particularly emphasized in chapter 28 as the major tool for teaching cultural competence to students. Dynamic sizing refers to skills that enable generalization inclusivity and individualization exclusivity. Dynamic sizing also involves learning to switch cognitive styles as needed with clients. Such skills can reduce stereotyping of clients by assessors. These skills are particularly recognizable among bicultural/bilingual assessors who are able to apply dynamic sizing with apparent ease perhaps because they share a common cultural blanket and have experienced many of the same problems, including discrimination, as their clients. Chapter 23 exemplifies how these skills may be used. These skills are most difficult for Anglo-American assessors to learn to use consistently and effectively with their multicultural clients. Such expertise is the product of personal lifelong learning about a culture. It would be helpful to have sustained experience providing assessment reports and recommendations for these clients in an atmosphere permitting glimpses of predictive validity by knowledge of how reports were used and whether recommendations were heeded or ignored. An example of such learning within a clinical research and practice context with adolescents was an effective stimulus for my own learning and clinical development (Dana, Hannifin, Lancaster, Lore, & Nelson, 1963). Culture-specific expertise includes an understanding of one's own worldview, in-depth knowledge of one's clients' cultural groups within a sociopolitical framework, as well as the kinds of technical assessment information and applications informing the handbook chapters.

REFERENCES

American Psychiatric Association. (1994). *Diagnostic and statistical manual of mental disorders* (4th ed.). Washington, DC: Author.

Arnold, B. R., Montgomery, G. T., Castanada, J., & Longoria, R. (1994). Acculturation and performance of Hispanics on selected Halstead–Reitan neuropsychological tests. *Assessment, 1*, 239–248.

Atkinson, D. R., Thompson, C. E., & Grant, S. K. (1993). A three-dimensional model for counseling racial-ethnic minorities. *The Counseling Psychologist, 21*, 257–277.

Berry, J. W. (1989). Psychology of acculturation. *Nebraska Symposium on Motivation, 39*, 201–234.

Cervantes, R. C., Padilla, A. M., & Salgado de Snyder, N. (1991). The Hispanic Stress Inventory: A culturally relevant approach to psychosocial assessment. *Psychological Assessment, 3*, 438–447.

Charles, K. (1988). *Culture-specific MMPI norms for a sample of Northern Ontario Indians.* Unpublished master's thesis, Lakehead University, Thunder Bay, Ontario, Canada.

Chavez, D. V., Moran, V. R., Reid, S. L., & Lopez, M. (1997). Acculturative stress in children: A modification of the SAFE scale. *Hispanic Journal of Behavioral Sciences, 19*, 34–44.

Dana, R. H. (1992). Assessment of cultural orientation. *SPA Exchange, 2*(2), 14–15.

Dana, R. H. (1993). *Multicultural assessment perspectives for professional psychology*. Thousand Oaks, CA: Allyn & Bacon.

Dana, R. H. (1994). Testing and assessment ethics for all persons: Beginning and agenda. *Professional Psychology: Research and Practice, 25*, 349–354.

Dana, R. H. (1996). Assessment of acculturation in Hispanic populations. *Hispanic Journal of Behavioral Sciences, 18*, 317–328.

Dana, R. H. (1997). Multicultural assessment and cultural identity: An assessment-intervention model. *World Psychology, 3*(1–2), 121–141.

Dana, R. H. (1998a). Cultural competence in three human service agencies. *Psychological Reports, 83*, 107–112.

Dana, R. H. (1998b). Cultural identity assessment of culturally diverse groups: 1997. *Journal of Personality Assessment, 70*, 1–16.

Dana, R. H. (1998c). Multicultural assessment in the United States, 1997: Still art, not yet science, and controversial. *European Journal of Personality Assessment, 14*, 62–70.

Dana, R. H. (1998d). Personality and the cultural self: Emic and etic contexts as learning resources. In L. Handler & M. Hilsenroth (Eds.), *Teaching and learning personality assessment* (pp. 325–345). Mahwah, NJ: Lawrence Erlbaum Associates.

Dana, R. H. (1998e). *Understanding cultural identity in intervention and assessment*. Thousand Oaks, CA: Sage.

Dana, R. H., Behn, J. D., & Gonwa, T. (1992). A checklist for examination of cultural competence in social service agencies. *Research on Social Work Practice, 2*, 220–233.

Dana, R. H., Hannifin, P., Lancaster, C., Lore, W., & Nelson, D. (1963). Psychological reports and juvenile probation counseling. *Journal of Clinical Psychology, 19*, 352–355.

Dana, R. H., & Matheson, L. (1992). An application of the Agency Cultural Competence checklist to a program serving small and diverse ethnic communities. *Psychosocial Rehabilitation Journal, 15*(4), 101–105.

Davidson, A. R., Jaccard, J. I., Morales, M. L., Triandis, H. C., & Diaz-Guerrero, R. (1976). Cross-cultural model testing: Toward a solution of the etic-emic dilemma. *International Journal of Psychology, 11*(1), 1–13.

Isaacs, M. R., & Benjamin, M. P. (1991). *Toward a culturally competent system of care* (Vol. 2). Washington, DC: CAASP Technical Assistance Center, Georgetown University Child Development Center.

Jones, R. L. (Ed.). (1996). *Handbook of tests and measurements for Black populations* (Vols. 1–2). Hamptom, VA: Cobb & Henry.

LaFromboise, T. D., Trimble, J. E., & Mohatt, G. V. (1990). Counseling intervention and American Indian tradition: An integrative approach. *The Counseling Psycholgist, 18*, 628–654.

Lonner, W. J. (1980). The search for psychological universals. In H. C. Triandis & W. W. Lambert (Eds.), *Handbook of cross-cultural psychology: Perspectives* (Vol. 1, pp. 143–204). Boston: Allyn & Bacon.

Phillips, F. B. (1990). NTU psychotherapy. *Journal of Black Psychology, 17*, 55–74.

Pinderhughes, E. (1982). Afro-American families and the victim system. In M. McGoldrick, J. K. Pierce, & J. Giordino (Eds.), *Ethnicity and family therapy* (pp. 108–122). New York: Guilford.

Pope-Davis, D. B., & Dings, J. G. (1995). The assessment of multicultural counseling competencies. In J. G. Ponterotto, J. M. Casas, L. A. Suzuki, & C. M. Alexander (Eds.), *Handbook of multicultural counseling* (pp. 287–311). Thousand Oaks, CA: Sage.

Ruiz, A. S. (1990). Ethnic identity: Crisis and resolution. *Journal of Multicultural Counseling and Development, 18*, 29–40.

Sue, S. (1998). In search of cultural competence in psychotherapy and counseling. *American Psychologist, 53*, 440–448.

Suinn, R. M. (1985). Research and practice in cross-cultural counseling. *The Counseling Psychologist, 13,* 673–684.

Takeuchi, D. T., Sue, S., & Yeh, M. (1995). Return rates and outcomes from ethnicity-specific mental health programs in Los Angeles. *American Journal of Public Health, 85,* 638–643.

Tanaka-Matsumi, L. (1998, August). *Measurement of acculturation: An examination of psychometric properties.* Paper presented at the XIV Congress of the International Association of Cross-Cultural Psychology, Western Washington University.

Terrell, F., & Terrell, S. L. (1981). An inventory to measure cultural mistrust among Blacks. *Western Journal of Black Studies, 5,* 180–184.

Triandis, H. C., McCusker, C., Betancourt, H., Iwao, S., Leung, K., Salazar, J. M., Setiadi, B., Sinha, J. B. P., Touzard, H., & Zaleski, Z. (1993). An etic-emic analysis of individualism-collectivism. *Journal of Cross-Cultural Psychology, 24,* 366–383.

Triandis, H. C., Vassilou, V., Vassilou, G., Tanaka, Y., & Shanmugam, A. V. (1972). *The analysis of subjective culture.* New York: Wiley.

Whaley, A. L. (1998, August). *Acculturative stress in people of African descent in the U.S.A.: A study of cultural mistrust in Black psychiatric patients.* Paper presented at the XIV Congress of the International Association of Cross-Cultural Psychology, Western Washington University, Bellingham, WA.

2

An Africentric Perspective for Clinical Research and Practice

Edward F. Morris
George Fox University

The demographic composition of the United States has undergone dramatic changes during the past several decades. In fact, it is estimated that before the end of the millennium, Euro-Americans will no longer be the dominant culture within this country (U.S. Bureau of the Census, 1995). The demographic shift has been attributed to several factors, including increased migration of African, Asian, and Latin Americans to the United States (Portes & Rumbaut, 1990), fewer babies born during the past decade compared with previous decades, more ethnic-minority children born than Euro-American children, and different birth mortality rates among the various cultural groups (National Center for Health Statistics, 1994). The demographic data also suggest that non-Euro-Americans are more economically and socially diverse, less concentrated in specific geographic areas, and representative of a continuum of worldviews (Wallen, 1992). Thus, suburban as well as rural communities are increasingly finding themselves with ethnic-minority residents from a variety of diverse backgrounds. The physical and economic boundaries that once separated communities are becoming more diffuse as the various ethnic populations grow and migrate across the country. When these sociocultural changes are examined from a clinician's perspective, it appears that the current conceptual models are ill equipped to address the diverse cultural needs and demands of different ethnic groups. Compared to Euro-Americans, most ethnic-minorities' worldviews tend to be incongruent, historical experiences tend to be different, and enculturation process tends to be more difficult. African Americans have a unique place within the ethnic-minority subgroup. Within this country, their history has been more violent, their experiences have been more debilitating, and their tribulations have been more insidious and ongoing. As service providers working with African Americans, these historical and current experiences need to serve as a background for understanding their adaptive styles and coping strategies. More important, these experiences need to serve as a cultural context in developing a conceptual model for research, clinical intervention, and diagnostic differentiation.

This chapter's goal is to provide a synthesized review of the literature as it pertains to current clinical and research practices with African Americans. Through this process, this author presents an integrated approach to conceptualizing and evaluating African Americans that is sensitive to the cultural uniqueness of this particular group. Using an Africentric perspective as the theoretical underpinning, this chapter examines various issues that may impact the credibility of psychologists who work with African-American clients.

ETHICAL CONSIDERATIONS IN PROVIDING RESPONSIBLE SERVICES TO AFRICAN AMERICANS

According to the American Psychological Association (APA), the Ethical Principles of Psychologists and Code of Conduct (i.e., Ethics Code) is intended to provide standards of professional conduct for psychologists and any other professional organization that chooses to adopt its principles. According to the Preamble, the standards are intended to provide both the general principles and the decision rules to cover most situations encountered by psychologists. Therefore, its primary goal is to protect the welfare of individuals and groups with whom psychologists work. Also according to the Preamble, it is the individual psychologist's responsibility to (a) aspire to the highest possible standard of ethical conduct within his or her area of expertise, and (b) take any steps necessary to resolve conflicts that prevent him or her from upholding the ethical standards. If a conflict does occur that violates an ethical code, it is the individual psychologist's primary responsibility to cease the unethical behavior. If he or she fails to uphold the highest possible standard with all individuals or cultural groups, or commits an ethical violation, the psychologist is at risk for reprimand, remediation, or censorship. However, if the psychologist commits an act that does not necessarily violate an ethical code, but is professionally questionable, then he or she may be required by the Ethics Board to seek consultation from other professionals, obtain supervision, or review pertinent literature (American Psychological Association, 1992).

The principles of the Ethics Code appear simple and straightforward. Psychologists have a responsibility to uphold the highest standards in activities, a professional responsibility to recognize competency boundaries and limitations, and an ethical obligation to provide services only within areas of education, training, and experience. Psychologists also have a moral obligation to avoid activities that passively or actively perpetuate cultural biases, a social responsibility to advocate for services that would advance the welfare of underserved cultural groups, and a personal responsibility to be sensitive to personal values, needs, and limitations and how they may inadvertently impact others with culturally different backgrounds. Given the stated expectations of the Ethics Code, psychologists who work with African-American clients may be practicing unethically if they lack the (a) cultural knowledge that comes with familiarity of African-American literature, (b) clinical expertise that comes with sensitivity to the cultural nuances that distinguish this particular cultural group, and (c) diagnostic conceptualization that comes with experience with multicultural evaluation tools. If psychologists fail to obtain the necessary conceptual knowledge of the African-American culture, clinical skills with African-American clients, and assessment expertise with both etic and emic diagnostic tools, their actions are professionally questionable, if ethical. Thus, they violate the most basic mandates of the Ethics Code: to aspire to the highest standards of conduct and protect the welfare of individuals and groups with whom psychologists work.

Sue and Sue (1990) indicated that one of the major ethical challenges that psychologists must address in multicultural counseling is understanding and accepting the complex role that cultural diversity plays within our professional activities. They further indicated that psychology has failed to meet the unique mental health needs of ethnic minorities. Numerous studies have reported that ethnic-minority clients frequently felt that the services they received were antagonistic or inappropriate to their life experiences, the treatment lacked sensitivity and understanding of their unique cultural pressures, and the providers were patronizing or condescending (Adebimpe, 1984; Carter, 1991; Dana, 1994, 1998b; Sue & Sue, 1990). Pedersen (1995) contended that the Ethics Code is culturally encapsulated and lacks ethical guidelines for psychologists to work with multicultural clients. He also added that the present guidelines are based on stereotyped values from a Euro-American perspective.

Despite empirical evidence of the poor fit between Eurocentric psychology and African-American clients' issues, the APA has failed to delineate specific cultural competencies that would begin to rectify this ethical dilemma. By default, its reticence in establishing a standard of cultural competence within the profession further perpetuates ethnocentric thinking, possible misinterpretation of clinical data, and potential misdiagnoses of culturally diverse individuals. In fact, the APA's insensitivity to African-American issues was one of the major reasons that a significant number of African-American psychologists left the organization almost 30 years ago and began a separate association. The goal of this organization—The Association of Black Psychologists—is to promote a more constructive and proactive approach to understanding and working with African Americans and to fill the clinical and diagnostic gap created by the APA (Williams, 1999).

Ethical decision making is not always an easy task. The issues involved are often complex, multifaceted, and defy simplistic solutions. The process entails not only learning information about ethical standards, but also learning how to define and work with a variety of difficult situations. When working with African Americans, the psychologist must juxtapose knowledge that he or she has about this particular cultural group and hope that the way in which he or she interprets the clinical or diagnostic data is comprehensive, sensitive, and accurate. The Ethical Codes provide guidelines and few exact answers. Unfortunately, changes in ethical codes tend to be reactive and emerge from what has occurred rather than anticipating what may occur. Unfortunately, most ethical violations are subtle and usually committed out of personal ignorance. Should our reactive tendencies within the profession dictate the speed with which we equip ourselves to function as competent psychologists within this multicultural society? Should our cultural unfamiliarity be the cause of inadequate performance with African Americans? Should our rationalization in using inappropriate assessment and clinical techniques be sufficient to justify using measures that could do more harm than good to clients who are culturally different from the normative population? Should we continue to blame African-American clients for their pattern of being premature terminators of sessions? If we commit any of these *shoulds*, then we are potentially committing an unethical act.

Pedersen and Marsella (1982) indicated that the Ethics Code is not a blueprint that removes all need for the use of judgment and sound reasoning. Being a competent clinician or diagnostician sometimes warrants an active, deliberate, and creative approach to meeting ethical responsibilities. When working with African Americans or any other ethnic-minority groups, such an approach becomes essential if not imperative. Ethical Codes cannot be applied in a rote manner because each client's situation is unique and calls for a different solution. The African-American culture is uniquely different from the Euro-American culture. Thus, techniques, measures, and clinical conceptualizations that work with Euro-American clients may not necessarily work with African-American clients.

Both clients and psychologists bring to their relationship attitudes, values, and behaviors that can vary widely. Under normal conditions, sorting the degrees of variance can be difficult. When one introduces cultural factors that have been mitigated by a history of racism, stereotypes, and ethnocentricity, the task becomes unyielding. To deny the importance of these cultural variables would be a serious mistake with far-reaching implications for the client as well as the psychologist. Regardless of their racial background, psychologists need to become aware of how their own culture, life experiences, attitudes, and values have influenced them personally and professionally. They must also go beyond their cultural encapsulation and correct any of their biases before they adversely impact the client–psychologist relationship. Lorion and Parron (1987) contended that mental health professionals need to respond to the needs of ethnic-minority groups whose social, psychological, and behavioral disorders are accentuated by realities such as economic hardship, racism, discrimination, and environmental stress. Similarly, Ibrahim (1985), Arrendondo-Dowd (1985), and LaFromboise and Foster (1989) noted that many ethnic-minority groups do share similarities with Euro-Americans. However, they also have unique belief systems, values, assumptions, and coping strategies that are different and therefore should be conceptualized differently.

If we think of the development of ethical standards as a process instead of a product, the prognosis for the field of psychology to be more culturally responsive to African-American clients is hopeful. However, its hopefulness hinges on Euro-American psychologists' ability to engage in ongoing dialogue with African-American psychologists and others who are sensitive to multicultural issues. The prognosis is also contingent on our ability as a collective body of professionals to (a) be aware of and deal with the biases, stereotypes, and assumptions that undergird our practices; (b) develop appropriate intervention strategies that take into account the social, cultural, historical, and environmental influences of culturally different clients; and (c) understand and actualize cultural pluralism within our conceptualization processes. If we begin the process of understanding African Americans by being students of the culture, then we begin a step in the right direction. Such a step would allow sufficient dialogue between Euro-American and African-American psychologists, increase understanding of the impact of sociocultural influences on African-American personality dynamics, and development of more culturally sensitive assessment measures. Once we begin this process, we are able to act more in accord with the Ethics Code's intent.

Several writers have developed models for ethical decision making (Jordan & Meara, 1990; Keith-Spiegel & Koocher, 1985; Kitchener, 1984; Loewenberg & Dolgoff, 1988; Smith, McGuire, Abbott, & Blau, 1991;

Stadler, 1986) that could assist in the process of helping clinicians and diagnosticians be more in compliance with ethical standards for all ethnic-minority groups. The following is a list of steps that may assist psychologists in thinking through potential ethical dilemmas that may arise when working with African Americans:

• *Identify the problem within a cultural context.* When working with an African-American client and confronted with a potential ethical dilemma, collect as much background information from the client and other collateral sources as you can so that you can make an informed decision. Do not limit yourself to information presented during the session. Obtain consent from the client so that you may consult with other members of the African-American community who might be able to provide additional information that would help you consider the issues within an appropriate cultural context. Such collateral information may come from pastors, other African-American clinicians and/or professionals, relatives of the client, and professional associations (i.e., Association of Black Psychologists, National Association of Black Social Workers).

• *Identify the potential conflicting ethical issues.* After collecting sufficient information to allow consideration of issues within an appropriate cultural context, review the Ethics Code to see how it compares to the established ethical standard. Based on the collected information, if the results of your actions constitute an ethical or legal violation, it would be ill-advised to act in that direction. Conversely, if the results of your actions do not constitute an ethical or legal violation, be sure that the actions are consistent with clinical goals.

• *Seek consultation.* When in doubt or when confronted with an ambiguous dilemma, consultation with the Ethics Board and/or attorney is indicated. If you begin in this direction, be sure that you have a paper trail and, if possible, the support of your supervisor and/or administrator. If you act in a way that protects the welfare of the client, you will probably be on safer grounds. However, there is always the risk that by making that decision you will be violating one or several of the other ethical codes. As a general rule and before seeking consultation, review relevant cultural issues that create the potential ethical conflict and clearly identify the competing ethical, legal, and/or moral principles. If the cultural issues are sufficient mitigating factors that warrant further actions, evaluate the rights and welfare of all those who will be impacted by your decision. If there are still no alternative options that would protect the rights of all concerned parties as well as uphold the intent of the affected ethical principles, seek consultation from state ethics board, the American Psychological Association, or legal counsel.

- *Review possible courses of actions.* At this point in the process, it is strongly advisable to review your concerns and potential actions with supervisor(s), colleagues, and members of the African-American community. Brainstorming is a useful exercise at this stage of the decision-making process. You have all of the relevant clinical and/or diagnostic data, you know the legal and ethical parameters as determined by ethics board and legal counsel, and you have considered the relevant cultural issues that are involved in the case. All that is left is a methodical review of the issues. By considering a variety of courses of action, you may come up with options that you had not considered that may be unorthodox, but legal, ethical, and culturally relevant.

- *Review the consequences of various decisions with the client and decide on the best course of action.* As part of the decision-making team, the client and/or his or her guardian should be involved in each stage of the process. You will need the person's support as well as his or her consent. At this stage of the process, review the various decision options with the client. With each of the options, be sure to explain the advantages and disadvantages. Finally, make a collateral decision with the client. If both you and the client are in agreement with the decision, the issue is resolved. If you are at odds with the client, then negotiate with him or her so that you can also feel morally, legally, and ethically comfortable with the decision. If you are still at odds with the client and are unable to negotiate a mutually acceptable action, consider referring the case. At this point, you have probably explored all acceptable options. To be ethical at this point may require you to refer or close the case.

The Ethics Code provides several principles regarding professional behaviors and competence. However, it does not make a distinction between professional and cultural competence. They are not the same. The former focuses on generalized expectations within one's discipline or specialty area. Conversely, the latter focuses on specific cultural knowledge that transcends disciplines or specialty areas. According to Dana (1998a), without delineating specific competencies required for services to various ethnic-minority groups, the Ethics Code falls short of being able to protect the welfare of non-Euro-American clients. Placing the burden of responsibility for cultural self-awareness on the individual psychologist assumes that he or she is aware of his or her own cultural identity and issues as well as those of other ethnic-minority groups. However, several studies on racial identity (Carter, 1991, 1995; Helms, 1990, 1994; Parham & Helms, 1981) indicate that Euro-Americans are the least sensitive group to cultural identity issues. Racism, discrimination, and cultural disparity force African-American and other ethnic-minority groups to address race-based issues on a regular basis. For most Euro-Americans, such issues have only become a concern during recent years when various socioeconomic events have more directly impacted their lives. Thus, the expectation that psychologists must assume responsibility for their own cultural sensitivity is unrealistic. If the best predictor of future behavior is past behavior, then the likelihood of there being a groundswell of cultural sensitivity and heightened awareness within the field of psychology without the overt prompting of the APA is unrealistic and doubtful.

AFRICENTRIC PERSPECTIVE

The need for cross-cultural dialogue within psychology has been espoused for nearly three decades. During the early period of this dialogue, the more critics of the Eurocentric worldview became vocal, the more members of both the African-American and Euro-American communities became frustrated. Both communities wanted an articulated description of African-American experiences that could be incorporated into the theoretical literature, clinical experiences, and diagnostic measures. Both communities also recognized that the Eurocentric perspective did not represent the experiences of African Americans within this country. Both communities admitted that there was a serious lack of empirical literature that described African Americans and their experiences. When the Africentric perspective was first articulated by professionals within the African-American community, it was met with criticisms from both Euro-American as well as African-American intellectuals. The former group thought that it was too culturally divisive, whereas the latter group thought that it did not represent the array of worldviews within the African-American community. These criticisms were probably prompted by fears of having culturally divisive communities, of losing separate intracultural identities, and of having to choose a particular cultural affiliation.

The Africentric perspective provided a first step in the development of a paradigm that began to capture the exemplars of the African-American culture and experiences. As a paradigm, it provides a template that can be used to understand the philosophical premises of individuals and groups within the African-American culture. Not all African Americans adhere to this particular paradigm. In fact, not all African Americans place their primary identity with Africa. Some African Americans believe that they are primarily and secondarily American. For these individuals, Africa is a place from whence their foreparents came hundreds of years ago—an event in time with little relevance for current experiences. Despite common stereotypes, African Americans do not represent a culturally monolithic group. There is considerable intragroup as well as intercultural variation. For this reason alone, the Africentric perspective represents an evolving effort to capture the total experiences of African Americans.

Several authors (Baldwin & Hopkins, 1990; Katz, 1985; Sue & Sue, 1990) have attempted to articulate the differences between Eurocentric values and Africentric values (Table 2.1). Such a description provides clinicians and diagnosticians with an empirically based delineation of the predominant values and behavioral indicators of these two worldviews.

Africentricism and Eurocentricism as theoretical worldviews do not represent monolithic orientations. They can represent a continuum of thoughts within a particular cultural group as well as a variety of racial affiliations. Thus, Euro-Americans can have an Africentric orientation and African Americans can have a Eurocentric orientation. Therefore, it is necessary for the clinician or diagnostician to have information on the client's level of acculturation and worldview prior to the onset of any assessment or intervention procedure. Such information is imperative because not all clients who appear to belong to a particular cultural group in terms of appearance and surname will share the same worldviews, values, and perceptions. To avoid stereotyping, the service provider should gather information on the client's cultural orientation from the interview, or assessment measures, prior to formulating treatment conceptualization or diagnostic considerations. According to Dana (1992), the information should reflect the relative contributions from the dominant and nondominant cultures in the client's cultural orientation. Such information can assist the clinician or diagnostician in the determination of appropriate assessment measures, clinical formulation, and intervention strategies. As service providers, clinicians and diagnosticians should be

TABLE 2.1
Eurocentric and Africentric Differences

Eurocentricism	*Africentricism*
Values	
1. Emphasis on individual rights	Emphasis on group and relationships
2. Authoritative orientation	Democratic orientation
3. Nuclear family structure	Extended family structure
4. Emphasis on youthfulness	Emphasis on maturity
5. Independence oriented	Interdependence oriented
6. Assertive and competitive	Compliant and cooperative
7. Thrive under conflict	Thrive under harmony
8. Freedom oriented	Security oriented
9. Written tradition	Verbal tradition

(Continued)

TABLE 2.1
(Continued)

Eurocentricism	Africentricism
Guiding principles of action	
1. Fulfillment of individual needs	Achievement of collective or cultural goals
2. Individual responsibility	Group or culture responsibility
Behavior orientation	
1. Self-actualization	Collective actualization
2. Projection of feelings	Expression of feelings
Time orientation	
1. Future oriented	Here-and-now oriented
2. Time determined	Event determined
Ethical orientation	
1. Morality anchored in person	Morality anchored in relationships
Language usage	
1. Standard English	Standard and nonstandard English
Client–therapist communication	
1. Ambiguous approach	Concrete, tangible approach
2. Cause–effect orientation	Environmentally influenced
3. Physical and mental health distinction	Combined physical and mental health
4. Long-term goals	Immediate and short-range goals
Communication style	
1. Speak fast to control listener	Speak with affect
2. Greater eye contact when listening	Direct/prolonged eye contact when speaking; less when listening
3. Nonverbal markers (head nods)	Interrupt when can (turn taking)
4. Quick responding	Quicker responding
5. Objective, task oriented	Affective, emotional, interpersonal oriented
History	
1. Based on immigrants' experience	Based on slavery experience
2. Romanticize war	Avoidance of conflict
Status and power	
1. Measured by economic possessions	Measured by noneconomic possessions
2. Credentials, titles, and positions	Status in the community
3. Believe better than other systems	Believe as good as other systems
Aesthetics	
1. Music/art based on European cultures	Music/art based on multiple cultures, primarily African American
2. Females: blonde, thin, young	Females: multiple personal and personality
3. Males: athletic ability, power, status	Males: personal and personality qualities
Religion	
1. No tolerance for deviation (monodeity)	Tolerant of other's religion/interpretations of God

ever vigilant of their own values and worldviews. They should also be willing to examine the potential impact of their values on African-American clients. Their understanding of this group's cultural values and idiosyncracies would be greatly enhanced if they resist making value judgments before adequate sociocultural information has been collected, challenge stereotypes and assumptions, and avoid imposing their own worldviews onto clients.

The Africentric perspective—or Africentricism—is an ideological model that serves two major functions. Foremost, it is a culturally consistent frame of reference for African Americans that allows them to gain a better understanding of themselves, their culture, and Euro-American society. As a model of self-understanding, Africentricism provides a conceptual framework that is based on African culture and not on standards constructed by the Euro-American culture. With this paradigm shift, African Americans are able to develop a more functional and positive self-concept. Without the shift, African Americans continue to be plagued with roles, prejudices, and functions determined by the Euro-American culture. Most of the roles are derogatory, most of the functions are subservient, most of the prejudices are emotionally debilitating, and most of the perceptions are based more on media portrayals than on personal experiences with African Americans. Africentricism is not a panacea that promises instant relief from the myriad of social and psychological ills that plague African Americans. However, it does have the potential of enhancing African Americans' self-image and sense of pride in their unique heritage.

The Africentric perspective places an emphasis on the humanistic value of human beings. The seven principles of Nguzo Saba (Karenga, 1989) exemplify this core value as well as the integrity of the African-American culture:

- The first principle, *Umoja* (unity), means to strive for and maintain unity in the family, community, and culture. Within the African-American community, *family* has a much broader definition than what is usually ascribed within the Euro-American community. For many African Americans, the family includes biological and adopted siblings, stepbrothers and stepsisters, churches members, close friends and neighbors, and elders within the community. The common defining thread that defines family for many African Americans is the emotional connection between its members and their willingness to protect the integrity of the family structure, community, and cultural values. The concept of *family* transcends geographic origin, prior interpersonal experiences, socioeconomic status, educational background, and reference groups. Despite numerous negative sociocultural experiences and hurdles that have affected African Americans individually and collectively, there appears to be an indomitable spirit that has prompted its members to encourage each other to progress, use the strength and sacrifices of African-American foreparents and sociopolitical martyrs, and maintain one's cultural identity and pride regardless of achieved status. It is the collective goodwill of the African-American community from which individual members draw strength to overcome daily struggles and hardships. It is the individual member's accomplishments from which the collective community draws its pride. Shared cultural values, struggles, and pain have forged African-American communities within various academic, social, professional, and political arenas. It is their culturally inherent sense of family that has fostered a sense of collective goodwill and groupness within a community that has endured the psychological and physical assaults of oppression, discrimination, and racial biases. Because of this shared experience of broad-based families and communities, re-creation of the dynamics becomes a natural process whenever African-American individuals convene.

• The second principle, *Kujichagulia* (self-determination), means to define and speak for oneself rather than being defined, and spoken for, by others. Historically, African Americans were seen as a cultural group without a voice. This perception was based on stereotypes, prescribed attributes, and unfounded cultural assumptions. Unfortunately, it was the Eurocentric perspective that fed this perception. Based on this worldview, African Americans were too inarticulate to speak for themselves, too divided to have a unified voice, too cognitively limited to articulate a theoretical or philosophical position, or too uneducated to know anything that is worth publishing. Fortunately, the many accomplishments of numerous African Americans in various fields provided data that disputed these perceptions. With the emergence of professional organizations that are predominantly African American, more culturally consistent perspectives are being presented within various academic and professional domains. Thus, African-American experiences are being presented by individuals who are familiar with the culture, who have lived within the culture, and who understand the impact of the Euro-American experience on the psychological development of African Americans. Information that is presented by representatives of the cultural group will have more reliability than reports and data presented by non-African-American researchers and academicians who may lack the intuitive knowledge of the African-American experience.

For African Americans, representation can be a "double-edged sword." As a group, they only want what Euro-Americans want—appropriate representation without the extraneous pressures that come with one's racial orientation. Unfortunately, it does not work that way. The more African-American individuals advocate for themselves as cultural beings, the more organizations look to them to represent the "Black view" on various issues. The desired information is sought independent of the African-American individual's personal thoughts, feelings, or desire. What was once considered an opportunity to present a different cultural perspective can easily become a burden that their Euro-American counterparts do not have to assume. For African Americans, this ordeal is juxtaposed on their already difficult burdens that go along with being cultural beings within a race-conscious society.

• The third principle, *Ujima* (collective work and responsibility), means to build and maintain a community and share problems and accomplishments. The African-American experience within this country has been fraught with frustrations, agony, and pain. It is beyond the mission of this chapter to explore these cultural atrocities. It is within the purview of this description, however, to examine the positive impact of these experiences on the African-American culture. Because of the tentative socioeconomic base of most African-American communities, many individuals have had to make do with nothing. Consequently, they had to be creative with their limited finances and resources, compartmentalize their pride to not react to discriminatory acts and behaviors, sacrifice their own comfort so that their children will do better, and develop a cultural belief that the future will be better than the past. More important, African Americans who have *made it* have had to endure the maintenance of dual roles within a society that is ethnocentric and passively against the development of cultural pride. For those individuals who have *made it* and for those who are *making it*, they are doing so on the collective shoulders of those who are still struggling. Except for major sporting events, African Americans represent a minuscule percentage of those who are successful by Euro-American standards. Compared with Euro-Americans, there is a greater proportion of African Americans who are below the poverty line, below the average education level, and below the upwardly mobile standard. Conversely, there are proportionately more African Americans who are in prison, illiterate, and *reported* substance abusers (Gallo, Marino, Ford, & Anthony, 1995).

Just as problems are shared and processed as a group, the accomplishments are enjoyed and celebrated as a group. When an individual member within the African-American community achieves a certain accomplishment, the community celebrates. When an individual member experiences sorrow, the community grieves. Currently, the community is exuberant at the significant increase of first- and second-generation professionals with advanced degrees. It was not all that long ago that African Americans were banned from many of the universities within this country. The community is also joyful at the number of key positions that African Americans are assuming within various public and private organizations. It was not all that long ago that African Americans were banned from having anything but servant type positions. However, the community is grieving at the significant number of African Americans who are dying or being killed, incarcerated or at risk for incarceration, or paying the price for their professional status with culture-specific health problems. The community is also grieving at the sociocultural changes that are fostering a sense of apathy and helplessness among the African-American youth. It is the collective cultural ownership of problems and accomplishments that has helped the African-American community survive in the face of cultural adversity. It is also the collective ownership and the sacrifices of African-American foreparents and sociopolitical martyrs that have provided the internal cultural strength for individuals to use to rise above the daily struggles of being a cultural being within a Eurocentric society.

- The fourth principle, *Ujamaa* (cooperative economics), means to build and maintain resources and businesses within the African-American community and to profit from them together. As a cultural group, African Americans have not been able to establish the financial base that many Euro-Americans have been able to achieve. Consequently, most African-American businesses within the African-American community are struggling. The resources as well as the product selections are insufficient, the external support from traditional financial institutions is inadequate, and the perceptions of the businesses are racially skewed. Singularly, these issues may be easily resolved. Concurrently, however, they contribute to the continued struggles that many African-American communities experience in their attempts to be semicapable of handling the indigenous needs of its community members. Until sufficient sociocultural changes occur at a broader level within this country, which would help rectify these issues, many African Americans will continue to be victimized by discriminatory practices within the housing, financial, and product industries. As a goal, the African-American community continues to strive for cooperative economics. As a reality, at this point in history, the institutional barriers are too burdensome to overcome without continued sacrifice by members within the African-American community and faith in the cooperative struggle by individuals outside of the community.

- The fifth principle, *Nia* (purpose), means to collectively build and develop the community to restore African Americans to their highest level. With the proliferation of stereotypes, racial biases, and discrimination in this country, African Americans as a collective group have carried the burdens of this country's greatest sin—racism. Despite the significant progress that African Americans have made over the past several decades, they are still perceived as second-class citizens, still discriminated overtly and covertly in the many institutions of society, and are still fighting for basic human rights. Despite economic and educational advancements in most areas, African-American accomplishments are downplayed, ignored, or rationalized in a derogatory manner. Despite these adversities, African Americans have learned to collectively build and rebuild their sense of community, political empowerment, and spiritual groundedness. The African-American purpose lies in its fervent desire to not only survive everyday struggles, but to surpass the accomplishments of their cultural foreparents. The list of these accomplishments is staggering and goes back to the earliest days of recorded history. Because information is such a powerful weapon, such data have been kept from African Americans. The more African Americans learn about themselves and their culture, the more empowered they can become—which, in turn, can lead to a rejuvenated sense of purpose. The more Euro-Americans know about African Americans and their culture, the more sensitive they can be to cultural issues and embracing of a multicultural society.

• The sixth principle, *Kuumba* (creativity), means to do as much as possible in the way that leaves the community more beautiful and beneficial to others. African Americans may have been deprived of many things of the years, yet they remain notably creative in many areas. Their cultural creativity is exemplified in the expansive behaviors when they interact with each other, in the expressiveness of their music and art forms, in the boundless energy of their activities, and in the depth of their intellectual thought. It is often asserted that creativity is part of the African heritage. Since being in this country, African Americans have learned to explore the many forms of cultural creativity and integrate it in multiple arenas. As a result of this creative expansion, some of the most gifted sporting heros are African American; some of the most gifted artists, musicians, and dancers are African American; and some of the most gifted analytical thinkers are African American. As increasingly more African Americans become involved in areas that have been historically denied to them, their presence will become increasingly more formidable.

• The final principle, *Imani* (faith), means to believe with all of one's heart in other African Americans, parents, teachers, and our community leaders. According to the Life Application Bible (1988), *faith* is "the confident assurance that something we want is going to happen. It is the certainty that what we hope for is waiting for us, even though we cannot see it up ahead" (Hebrews 11:1). The first premise of this particular scripture suggests unquestionable belief of future opportunities and promises; the second premise of this scripture suggests unquestionable belief that the past is not necessarily predictive of the future. Combined, they suggest that the words of wisdom, encouragement, faith, and faithfulness of our collective cultural mentors (i.e., parents, teachers, leaders, loved ones) must be "held close to the heart" during the difficult times. During those periods of adversity, African Americans must not focus on the visible obstacles that have been placed by the obstructionists (of which can come from any racial or cultural group) to deter dreams and hopes. Rather, they should focus on the promises of which every wise person within the African-American community believes to be forthcoming. Maybe the promises were not actualized during their generation, maybe they will not be actualized during the current generation. However, the peace, affirmation, and comfort that these elders and foreparents possessed could serve the same strengthening function during present-day struggles of African Americans.

As African-American elders would say, "God never promised that life would be easy or fair. He only promised that righteousness will prevail in the end." For those of us who are more present-day oriented, these words of wisdom become difficult to grasp at times. It is difficult to focus on future hopes when one is struggling with present challenges. Therefore, it appears that *Imani* may be one of the most important goals of self- and cultural actualization. One of the primary functions of African-American elders has been to remind younger generations of the historical context of their accomplishments as well as their frustrations. As community touchstone, elders have helped individuals within the African-American community to keep things in perspective and strive for the betterment of the African-American community.

The second primary function of Africentricism is what Dana (1998a) called a "cultural construction of reality" (p. 16). As such, Africentricism serves as an insider's perception of the world—a perception that is based on the juxtaposition of a horrid historical past and the realities of the here and now. The past consisted of a reality that all but obliterated the strength of the African social, political, and family structure—a past that all but determined the future of generations of African Americans within the sociopolitical, educational, and economic structure of this society and a past that still creates a racial barrier between the two dominant races in this country.

The here and now is probably best exemplified by Parham (1995) in a report that he presented at a meeting of the Council of the National Psychological Associations for the Advancement of Ethnic-Minority Interests. In the report, Parham presented a concept that characterizes the African-American experience. The concept, MAAFA, is a Kiswahili word that describes "a great disaster and misfortune of death and destruction which are beyond human comprehension and convention" (p. 20). According to Parham, the disparate experiences of African-Americans represent more than a single historical event. It is an ongoing, sophisticated, and insidious process that supports the dehumanization of African-Americans and the denial and validity of their humanity. Once the validity of their humanity is questioned, then any and every inhumane behavior or opinion is allowable or goes unchallenged. (p. 21)

Evidence of these inhumane experiences would include the inexcusable Rodney King beating, brutal Yosef Hawkins interrogation, resurgence of hate crimes against African Americans, disproportionate number of African Americans within the prison system, and unjust treatment of African Americans within various segments of the judicial, social, and economic community. These incidents, taken singularly, point to discriminatory and insensitive behavior. When considered as a contemporary version of a historical pattern, however, they provide compelling evidence of a pattern of dehumanization that has been thoroughly integrated into the fabric of society and its institutions.

Africentricism, as an ideological worldview, is different from Eurocentricism. The Eurocentric perspective is central to traditional (i.e., Western) psychology. It is based on Euro-American cultural norms, values, and philosophical views. It assumes that the Euro-American cultural norms and behavioral standards appropriately define the normative behavior of most people within this country (Akbar, 1984; Baldwin, 1976, 1979, 1985; Nobles, 1976, 1980). Within this perspective, there is an emphasis on control over people and nature, survival of the fittest, competition and aggression, individual achievement, and emotional control. Although the Eurocentric perspective purports to represent cross-cultural thoughts, it does not accomplish such a task. Instead, it projects a negative and pathological picture of non-Westernized cultures and, in particular, the African-American culture (Baldwin, 1979; Nobles, 1980).

The Eurocentric perspective makes several assumptions. It assumes that cultural homogeneity exists between Euro-Americans and African Americans. It assumes that any behavioral and value variances that exist between these two cultural groups are the result of slavery and racial discrimination rather than basic cultural differences that can coexist within our society. It assumes that African Americans' enculturated experiences within this country should eliminate most of the aberrant African cultural traits (Miller & Dreger, 1973; Thomas & Sillen, 1972). As indicated by these assumptions, the Eurocentric perspective minimizes the existence of substantive cultural differences between African Americans and Euro-Americans. If there are differences, they are usually associated with some type of psychopathological condition within the individual and/or the culture. Typically the pathology exists within African Americans or within their culture. The Eurocentric perspective fosters a parent–child, or superior–inferior, relationship with other cultures. Thus, it fails to recognize the legitimacy of a distinct and independent African-American culture. The major conclusions that are derived from this relationship disequilibrium are: African Americans are culturally disadvantaged or deprived relative to Euro-Americans, and their culture is a subsidiary and reactive phenomenon that grew out of the American slavery experience (Baldwin, Brown, & Hopkins, 1989). Most of the research supporting the Eurocentric perspective has focused primarily on African Americans with Euro-American cultural norms as the basis or standard for assessing cross-cultural differences (Baldwin, 1979; Miller & Dreger, 1973). Criticisms of this approach to research and normative standardization has been fervent over the years. Such comments against this approach suggest that Eurocentricism is (a) too ethnocentric in its conceptualization, (b) too superficial in its analysis of culture and cultural differences, (c) too insensitive to the cultural deep structure or worldview of African Americans relative to Euro-Americans, and (d) too ignorant of cultural relativism and cross-cultural paradigms when attempting to assess cultural differences (Nobles, 1986; Nobles & Goddard, 1984).

Evidence of the ill effects of inappropriate racial comparisons are seen in standardized tests, educational screening measures, and personality inventories (Hui & Triandis, 1985, 1989; Sattler, 1992). On both standardized and educational screening tests, African Americans generally score lower than Euro-Americans (Boykin, 1983; Irvine & Carroll, 1980; Kaufman, 1973). On personality inventories, African Americans generally appear more emotionally or behaviorally dysfunctional than Euro-Americans (Adebimpe, 1984; Linton, 1945; Walters et al., 1983). Jensen (1981) attributed the differences to some intellectual deficits that are unique to African Americans. Other researchers have since attributed the discrepancy to culturally specific environmental differences (Marsella, 1987; Marsella & Kameoka, 1989). Numerous researchers and psychometricians attributed differences in personality attributes to personality styles, where African Americans are more aggressive, defensive, and prone to certain personality disorder traits than Euro-Americans (Dahlstrom, Lachar, & Dahlstrom, 1986; Somervell et al., 1989). Still other researchers have since attributed the personality discrepancies to test biases, unrepresentative normative data, and cultural insensitivities of the test items (Akbar, 1991, 1984; Helms, 1992; Mercer, 1976; Okazaki & Sue, 1995). Despite discrepancies in the literature, most clinicians and diagnosticians act as if there is no alternative explanation that could account for the cultural differences between African Americans and Euro-Americans on various cognitive and personality tests. Consequently, educational, administrative, and clinical decisions are made based on assumed individual deficiencies rather than on possible test biases and/or evaluators' cultural insensitivities.

For Euro-Americans, being an individual in our society is a *no brainer*. Except under extreme circumstances, such individuals do not have to think about it, process it, worry about it, or experience the ill effects of their particular racial status on a daily basis. For Euro-Americans, their racial status does not necessarily correspond with their self-esteem. Conversely, for African Americans, the acceptance of one's racial identity is crucial to the development of a functional self-esteem. Much of the pre-1960s literature emphasized the self-hatred and self-rejection of African-American children. The Clark studies (Clark & Clark, 1939, 1950) high-lighted the self-esteem issues that many African-American children experienced within this society. The Helm's racial identity studies (Helms, 1990, 1992, 1994) continued the illumination of the correlation of racial identity and self-concept. As Woodson (1990) indicated, "the thought of inferiority of the African-American is drilled into him in almost every class he enters and in almost every book he studies" (p. 98). The common thread that is woven throughout these sources is the suggestion that African Americans have poor self-concepts because they belong to a racial group that is perceived negatively within a Eurocentric paradigm.

The reality of most African Americans is undeniably sobering. If the field of psychology hopes to diversify its profession, this reality needs to be kept at the forefront of all discussions regarding policy, program development, test construction, research initiatives, and administrative composition. If the profession fails to attend to the sociocultural needs of its African-American constituents, then any attempts to integrate its professional organizations, graduate programs, and training sites will be for naught. Literature written by non-African Americans provides one aspect of this reality. At times it is skewed; at other times it is written through the conceptual or empirical lens of Eurocentrism. Literature written by African Americans who have a more intimate understanding of its cultural dynamics provides a different and hopefully more reliable perspective of African Americans and their culture. The wealth of literature that is readily available to educators, clinicians, diagnosticians, and researchers can provide an objective and culturally congruent understanding of African Americans and their culture. The Africentric perspective provides a conceptual worldview that individuals working with such clients can use to develop assessment protocols and treatment strategies that are more congruent with the cultural lifestyle of African Americans.

Understanding African Americans from a multicultural perspective requires a level of intentionality that goes beyond clinicians' and researchers' usual role and function. First, it requires that they assume that their intimate knowledge of African-American clients and their culture is inadequate especially if they are not from this particular cultural group. Adopting this position would help service providers and social researchers listen more carefully to clients' issues and needs with fewer cultural filters. Because these filters tend to bend and blend their perceptions of the clients' experiences in a way that is more comfortable intellectually and emotionally, there is a high probability of misinterpretation that is prompted by their cultural shortsightedness. Such a position would also allow clinicians and researchers to be in a better listening mode with African Americans so that they can interpret information from within the context of the clients' cultural experiences. Understanding clients from within their cultural contexts would help them be more adaptable in their theoretical orientation, flexible with their skills and strategies, and sensitive to clients' cultural idiosyncrasies. More important, such a position would help them be less ethnocentric in their orientation and interactions with African Americans. Cultural intentionality requires not only the given skills of being a competent clinician or researcher, but also necessitates a flexibility with ever-changing clients who may come from widely varying intra- and intercultural backgrounds. Not all African Americans come from the same cultural mindset, not all African Americans have the same worldviews, and not all African Americans are at the same stage of identity development. However, all African Americans have similar cultural roots and have experienced, to varying degrees, the effects of racism and the divergent impact of Eurocentric thinking on their psychosocial development. Because clients live within a social context, the awareness of the African-American environment and their surrounding cultural context becomes as important as the individuals themselves.

Development of a conceptual orientation is an ongoing process. Typically the process begins in graduate school when the developing psychologist learns about various theoretical perspectives in more than a superficial manner. It is also during graduate school when most students start to emulate supervisors or mentors with whom they respect. Early in the process, the graduate student memorizes theoretical tenets, testing protocols, and research designs. With more experience, practice, and supervision, the graduate student becomes better able to synthesize the material and integrate theory with his or her experiences in the field. Eventually the graduate student becomes a practicing psychologist and begins to integrate personal style and idiosyncrasies into his or her professional activities. Because the clinician or researcher is a conglomeration of personal and professional experiences, supervisors' wisdom and intervention, and formal education, it is conceivable that his or her theoretical orientation is influenced by his or her cultural worldview as well as that of his or her supervisors and mentors. If the worldview is Eurocentric, one set of assumptions will be made about clients and their sociocultural experiences. Similarly, if the worldview is Africentric, another set of assumptions will be made about clients and their sociocultural experiences.

The categories *Africentric* and *Eurocentric* are more than geographic designates. They represent an individual's social, political, and cultural worldview. They consist of the presumptions and assumptions that an individual holds about the makeup of his or her world (Kearney, 1975; Sue, 1978). Horner and Vandersluis (1981) wrote that it is a "culturally based variable that influences the relationship between the helper and the client" (p. 33). Similarly, Dana (1998a) noted that it contains the collective wisdom that a person uses to make sense of life experiences. Therefore, it is imperative that clinicians and researchers understand, or try to understand, clients' presumptions and assumptions. Such knowledge can make a difference, for the client, between effective and efficacious intervention or disappointment and dissatisfaction. If the service provider and client's worldviews coincide, the person–environment fit will be good. Therapy will progress, and the client will feel satisfied with the treatment. Conversely, if the worldviews clash, the fit will not be productive. Consequently, the services will become unacceptable or underutilized, with the client feeling frustrated, misunderstood, and defensive (Ibrahim, 1985; Sue & Zane, 1987) .

Because traditional clinical practice is grounded in Western assumptions, there is a high probability that many clinicians and researchers are *operating in the dark* when working with African-American clients. Because of limited cultural information, there is the potential for service providers to make faulty assumptions, inaccurate diagnoses, incongruous treatment plans, and inappropriate assessment protocols. To avoid these errors, clinicians and researchers need to understand the philosophical premises of African Americans as individuals and as a cultural group. Such an awareness will assist them in developing the skills necessary for effective cross-cultural therapy and assessment evaluations. The Africentric perspective provides service providers with a foundation for understanding the philosophical premises of this particular cultural group. Once this particular worldview is understood, the challenge becomes finding a way to integrate elements of Africentricism with Eurocentricism. Bennett (1986) offered the concept of *ethnorelativism* as a means to reconcile the differences of the two worldviews. He contended that, for service providers to be cross cultural within their professional orientation, they should strive for the following goals: They must accept that different worldviews can coexist, they must adapt their skills and abilities so they would be applicable with other cultures, and they must integrate the different worldviews to be comfortable in *both worlds* as a therapist or diagnostician.

REFERENCES

Adebimpe, V. R. (1984). American Blacks and psychiatry. *Transcultural Psychiatric Research*, *21*, 83–111.

Akbar, N. (1984). Africentric social sciences for human liberation. *Journal of Black Studies*, *14*, 395–414.

Akbar, N. (1991). Mental disorders among African-Americans. In R. G. Jones (Ed.), *Black psychology* (3rd ed., pp. 339–351). Berkeley, CA: Cobb & Henry Press.

American Psychological Association. (1992). Ethical principles of psychologists and code of conduct. *American Psychologist*, *47*, 1597–1611.

Arrendondo-Dowd, P. (1987). Cross-cultural counselor education and training. In P. B. Pedersen (Ed.), *Handbook of cross-cultural counseling and therapy* (pp. 281–289). Westport, CT: Greenwood.

Baldwin, J. A. (1976). Black psychology and Black personality: Some issues for consideration. *Black Books Bulletin*, *4*, 6–11.

Baldwin, J. A. (1979). Theory and research concerning the notion of Black self-hatred: A review and reinterpretation. *Journal of Black Psychology*, *5*, 51–77.

Baldwin, J. A. (1985). Psychological aspects of European cosmology in American society. *The Western Journal of Black Studies*, *9*, 216–223.

Baldwin, J. A., Brown, R., & Hopkins, R. (1989). The Black self-hatred paradigm revisited: An Africentric analysis. In R. L. Jones (Ed.), *Black psychology* (3rd ed., pp. 141–165). Berkeley: Cobb & Henry.

Baldwin, J. A., & Hopkins, R. (1990). African-American and European-American cultural differences as assessed by the worldviews paradigm: An empirical analysis. *The Western Journal of Black Studies*, *14*(1), 38–52.

Bennett, M. J. (1986). Toward ethnorelativism: A developmental model of intercultural sensitivity. In R. M. Paige (Ed.), *Cross-cultural orientation: New conceptualizations and applications* (pp. 27–69). Lanham, MD: University Press of America.

Carter, R. T. (1991). Cultural values: A review of empirical research and implications for counseling. *Journal of Counseling and Development*, *70*, 164–173.

Carter, R. T. (1995). *The influence of race and racial identity in psychotherapy: Toward a racially inclusive model*. New York: Wiley.

Clark, K. B., & Clark, M. K. (1939). The development of consciousness of self and the emergence of racial identification in Negro preschool children. *Journal of Social Psychology*, *10*, 591–599.

Clark, K. B., & Clark, M. P. (1950). Emotional factors in racial identification and preference in Negro children. *Journal of Negro Education*, *19*, 341–350.

Dahlstrom, W. G., Lachar, D., & Dahlstrom, L. E. (1986). *MMPI patterns of American minorities*. Minneapolis: University of Minnesota Press.

Dana, R. (1992). A commentary on assessment training in Boulder and Vail model programs: In praise of differences. *Journal of Training and Practice in Professional Psychology*, *6*(2), 19–26.

Dana, R. H. (1994). Testing and assessment ethics for all persons: A beginning and an agenda. *Professional Psychology: Research and Practice*, *25*, 349–354.

Dana, R. H. (1998a). Multicultural assessment of personality and psychopathology in the United States: Still art, not yet science, and controversial. *European Journal of Psychological Assessment*, *14*(1), 62–70.

Dana, R. H. (1998b). *Understanding cultural identity in intervention and assessment*. Thousand Oaks, CA: Sage.

Gallo, J. J., Marino, S., Ford, D., & Anthony, J. C. (1995). Filters on the pathway to mental health care: Sociodemographic factors. *Psychological Medicine, 25,* 1149–1160.

Helms, J. E. (1990). *Black and White racial identity: Theory, research, and practice.* New York: Greenwood.

Helms, J. E. (1992). Why is there no study of cultural equivalence in standardized cognitive ability testing? *American Psychologist, 9,* 1083–1101.

Helms, J. E. (1994). How multiculturalism obscures facial factors in the therapy process: Comments on Ridley et al. (1994), Sodowsky et al. (1994), Ottavi et al. (1994), and Thompson et al. (1994). *Journal of Counseling Psychology, 41*(2), 162–165.

Horner, D., & Vandersluis, B. (1981). Cross-cultural counseling. In G. Althen (Ed.), *Learning across cultures.* Washington, DC: National Association of Foreign Student Affairs.

Hui, C. H., & Triandis, H. C. (1985). Measurement in cross-cultural psychology: A review and comparison of strategies. *Journal of Cross-Cultural Psychology, 20,* 296–309.

Hui, C. H., & Triandis, H. C. (1989). Effects of culture and response format on extreme response style. *Journal of Cross-Cultural Psychology, 20,* 296–309.

Ibrahim, F. A. (1985). Effective cross-cultural counseling and psychotherapy. *Counseling Psychologist, 13,* 625–638.

Irvine, S., & Carroll, W. (1980). Testing and assessment across cultures: Issues in methodology and theory. In H. Triandis & J. Berry (Eds.), *Handbook of cross-cultural psychology: Methodology.* Boston: Allyn & Bacon.

Jensen, A. R. (1981). *Straight talk about mental tests.* New York: The Free Press.

Jordan, A. E., & Meara, N. M. (1990). Ethics and the professional practice of psychologists: The role of virtues and principles. *Professional Psychology: Research and Practice, 21*(2), 107–114.

Karenga, M. (1989). *The African-American holiday of Kwanzaa.* Los Angeles: University of Sankore Press.

Katz, J. H. (1985). The sociopolitical nature of counseling. *The Counseling Psychologist, 13*(4), 615–624.

Kaufman, A. (1973). Comparison of the performance of matched groups of Black children and White children on the Wechsler Preschool and Primary Scale of Intelligence. *Journal of Consulting and Clinical Psychology, 41*(2), 186–191.

Kearney, M. (1975). Worldview theory and study. In B. J. Siegel (Ed.), *Annual review of psychology* (Vol. 4, pp. 247–270). Palo Alto, CA: Annual Reviews.

Keith-Spiegel, P., & Koocher, G. (1985). *Ethics in psychology: Professional standards and cases.* New York: Random House.

Kitchener, K. S. (1984). Intuition, critical evaluation and ethical principles: The foundation for ethical decisions in counseling psychology. *The Counseling Psychologist, 12*(3), 43–55.

LaFromboise, T. D., & Foster, S. L. (1989). Ethics in multicultural counseling. In P. B. Pedersen, J. G. Draguns, W. J. Lonner, & J. E. Trimble (Eds.), *Counseling across cultures* (3rd ed., pp. 115–136). Honolulu: University of Hawaii.

Life Application Bible. (1988). Wheaton, IL: Tyndale House.

Linton, R. (1945). *The culture background of personality.* New York: Appleton-Century-Crofts.

Loewenberg, F., & Dolgoff, R. (1988). *Ethical decisions for social work practice* (3rd ed.). Itasca, IL: F. E. Peacock.

Lorion, R., & Parron, D. (1987). Countering the countertransference: A strategy for treating the untreatable. In P. Pedersen (Ed.), *Handbook of cross-cultural counseling and therapy* (pp. 79–86). Westport, CT: Greenwood Press.

Marsella, A. J. (1987). The measurement of depressive experience and disorders across cultures. In A. J. Marsella, R. Hirschfeld, & M. Katz (Eds.), *The measurement of depression: Biological, psychological, behavioral, and social aspects* (pp. 376–397). New York: Guilford.

Marsella, A. J., & Kameoka, V. (1989). Ethnocultural issues in the assessment of psychopathology. In S. Wetzler (Ed.), *Measuring mental illness: Psychometric assessment for clinicians* (pp. 231–256). Washington, DC: American Psychiatric Press.

Mercer, J. R. (1976). Pluralistic diagnosis in the evaluation of Black and Chicano children: A procedure for taking sociocultural variables into account in clinical assessment. In C. A. Hernandez, M. J. Haug, & N. N. Wagner (Eds.), *Chicanos: Social and psychological perspectives* (pp. 183–195). St. Louis: Mosby.

Miller, K. S., & Dreger, R. M. (1973). *Comparative studies of Blacks and Whites in the United States.* New York: Seminar Press.

National Center for Health Statistics. (1994). *Division of vital statistics.* Washington, DC: Public Health Service.

Nobles, W. W. (1976). Black people in White insanity: An issue for Black community mental health. *Journal of Afro-American Issues, 4,* 21–27.

Nobles, W. W. (1980). Extended self: Rethinking the Negro self-concept. In R. L. Jones (Ed.), *Black psychology* (3rd ed., pp. 295–304). New York: Harper & Row.

Nobles, W. W. (1986). *African psychology: Toward its reclamation, reascension and revitalization.* Oakland, CA: Institute of Black Family Life and Culture.

Nobles, W. W., & Goddard, L. L. (1984). *Understanding the Black family: A guide for scholarship and research.* Oakland, California: Institute of Black Family Life and Culture.

Okazaki, S., & Sue, S. (1995). Methodological issues in assessment research with ethnic minorities. *Psychological Assessment, 7,* 367–375.

Parham, T. A. (1995). American violence: Our challenges. *Psych Discourse, 26*(3), 7–9.

Parham, T. A., & Helms, J. E. (1981). The influence of Black students' racial identity attitudes on preference for counselor's race. *Journal of Counseling Psychology, 28,* 250–257.

Pedersen, P., & Marsella, A. J. (1982). The ethical crisis for cross-cultural counseling and therapy. *Professional Psychology, 13*(4), 494–500.

Pedersen, P. B. (1995). Culture-centered ethical guidelines for counselors. In J. G. Ponterotto, J. M. Casas, L. A. Suzuki, & C. M. Alexander (Eds.), *Handbook of multicultural counseling* (pp. 34–49). Thousand Oaks, CA: Sage.

Portes, A., & Rumbaut, R. G. (1990). *Immigrant America: A portrait.* Berkeley: University of California Press.

Sattler, J. M. (1992). *Assessment of children* (3rd ed.). San Diego, CA: Jerome Sattler.

Smith, T. S., McGuire, J. M., Abbott, D. W., & Blau, B. I. (1991). Clinical ethical decision making: An investigation of the rationales used to justify doing less than one believes one should. *Professional Psychology: Research and Practice, 22*(3), 235–239.

Somervell, P. D., Leaf, P. J., Weissman, M. M., Blazer, D. G., & Bruce, M. L. (1989). The prevalence of major depression among Black and White adults in five U.S. communities. *American Journal of Epidemiology, 130,* 725–735.

Stadler, H. A. (1986). Making hard choices: Clarifying controversial ethical issues. *Counseling and Human Development, 19*(1), 1–10.

Sue, D. W. (1978). World views and counseling. *Personnel and Guidance Journal, 56,* 458–462.

Sue, D. W., & Sue, D. (1990). *Counseling the culturally different: Theory and practice.* New York: Wiley.

Sue, S., & Zane, N. (1987). The role of culture and cultural techniques in psychotherapy: A critique and reformulation. *American Psychologist, 42,* 37–45.

Thomas, A., & Sillen, (1972). *Racism and psychiatry.* Secaucus, NJ: Citadel Press.

U.S. Bureau of the Census (1995). *Statistical abstract of the United States.* Washington, DC: Government Printing Office.

Wallen, J. (1992). Providing culturally appropriate mental health services for minorities. *Journal of Mental Health Administration, 19*(3), 288–295.

Walters, G. D., Greene, R. L., Jeffrey, T. B., Kruzich, D. J., & Haskin, J. J. (1983). Racial variations on the MacAndrew Alcoholism Scale of the MMPI. *Journal of Consulting and Clinical Psychology, 51,* 947–948.

Williams, R. (1999). The purposes and missions of the ABPsi: A history. *Psych Discourse, 30*(4), 4–6.

Woodson, C. G. (1990). *The mis-education of the Negro.* Trenton, NJ: Africa World Press.

MINIMIZING BIAS IN ASSUMPTIONS, METHODOLOGY, AND RESEARCH STUDIES

Personality tests constructed in the United States have been standardized primarily on persons of European cultural backgrounds and ethnic identities. In addition to the routine use of these tests with populations of non-European origins in the United States, worldwide exportation has occurred despite limited cross-cultural research on the personality constructs represented in these tests.

Chapter 3 argues convincingly that bias begins in the research literature—the presumably informed source for reliable information to inform professional psychology research and practice. This literature is predicated on statistical analysis of data. The null hypothesis is the capstone of these analyses.

Four myths concerning the null hypothesis are described: (a) Some null hypotheses are true, (b) We must pose no-difference null hypotheses, (c) We cannot accept the null hypothesis, and (d) Statistical significance is either/or. These myths have become ambiguous, contradictory, and misleading statistical ground rules; their fragility has been discussed frequently, but their parameters continue to remain inflexible among researchers and practitioners. Malgady unravels the structure and functions of this mythology to conclude that significance conventions need to be increasingly flexible to provide what he calls "affirmative action for null hypothesis testing in ethnic minority populations."

Because value judgments always inform decisions in the interpretation of significance levels, chapter 3 considers the relative seriousness of Type I and Type II errors. The traditional null hypothesis of no cultural bias means that Type I errors support the validity of ethnic group differences, whereas Type II errors deny individuals culturally competent services. An alternative null hypothesis of cultural bias would reverse the relative seriousness of Type I and Type II errors.

I would go one step further to suggest that the null hypothesis exemplifies the Anglo-American assumption of similarity that minimizes differences and results in belief in a palpable homogeneity among persons. Minimizing differences, as Bennett (1986) has indicated, is a hallmark of ethnocentrism. As a direct consequence, all the informed and searching examinations of the inflexibility and limitations of statistical decision making using the null hypothesis have not prevailed on professional psychologists to reexamine the research literature providing a basis for practice. This is particularly apparent among the majority of professional psychologists who prefer low-inference interpretation and demand a research basis for providing responsible clinical services.

Cultural competence among professional service providers is ultimately dependent on awareness of the limits of cultural knowledge to be gained using the null hypothesis. Because an outdated and limited technology has been replaced by a flexible and powerful computer technology, it is now feasible to address the professional and social impact of continuing the status quo in statistical decision making using the null hypothesis. Malgady cites some early signs of recognizing the limits of null hypothesis testing in the 1985 APA *Standards for Educational and Psychological Testing*, the 1992 *DSM–IV*, the 1994 APA *Publication Manual*, and three practice reforms advocated in 1996.

In chapter 4, the focus is on construct-oriented approaches to validation of tests for use with cultural/racial populations in the United States and for assessment applications in other countries. However, construct validation—the measurement of a construct underlying a test variable for purposes of test construction and test interpretation evaluation—has always been difficult to demonstrate. In fact, Shneidman (1959) described the construct validation as analogous to "attempting to measure a floating cloud with a rubber band in a shifting wind" (p. 261). Despite a variety of relevant construct validation methods (Dana, 1962, 1993), construct status has always been difficult to establish unequivocally even within a homogeneous population. Chapter 4 indicates how difficult it is to screen a given construct prior to beginning serious validation research. Nonetheless, cross-cultural construct validity should also be demonstrated by methods used to develop translations for linguistic equivalency, metric fidelity, and constancy of meaning across different populations.

Three underutilized statistical procedures are proposed; these can be applied prior to any significant investment in cross-cultural construct validation. The first procedure, confirming factor analysis or cross-validation of the factor structure across groups, examines the nomological network based on internal or external relationships. Internal equivalence is established by demonstrating invariance in the factor structure of a standard test with a cultural group of interest. Confirmatory factor analysis also provides replication by examining the goodness of fit between a theoretical model of the factor structure derived from the original sample and a new sample. A more powerful statistical test for cross-cultural application examines multiple groups simultaneously for invariance in common factor loadings.

In a second procedure, test scores are related either to culture-relevant variables or measures of cultural identification using regression analysis. These statistical techniques permit an examination of relationship among a dependent variable, the construct, and a set of independent variables or predictors. Measurement equivalence is supported whenever prediction is not confirmed using these culture-relevant measures. A green light is then indicated for subsequent construct validation. If equivalence is not supported, several options are available to the researcher. A psychopathology construct is deemed equivalent if the same regression equation is found with an external correlate in both the original and new groups. Because the assumptions for this statistic are considered to be problematic, cultural identification measures or culturally related psychological variables can also be used as predictors.

A third procedure, item response theory (IRT) modeling, has had relatively little application with measures of personality and psychopathology. IRT uses a response pattern instead of a linear combination for an estimate of construct level. Three common types of IRT models for single and multiple parameters are described to identify items susceptible to change across groups.

This chapter not only describes these statistical approaches, but has identified their assumptions, required sample sizes, and critical limitations. Caveats for interpreting research using these approaches provide the reader with guidelines for evaluation of specific studies. Details are provided primarily on the generalizability aspect of construct validity. Some attention is also given to item content relevance and item engagement with culture-related processes. The importance of an investigation of internal structure as well as demonstrations of relationships with external variables are also recognized. Nonetheless, a construct-driven approach to equivalence is purely quantitative and unfortunately ignores methodologies that incorporate qualitative approaches. The logic of hypothesis disconfirmation has been used exclusively for the purpose of deciding on the feasibility of more intensive construct validation research. Construct validation independent of evidence from linguistic and metric equivalence studies is not sufficient.

These authors have convincingly argued that even a test with demonstrated cross-cultural construct validity must meet other desiderata for interpretation that are derived from a comprehensive framework for construct validation. Ultimately the testing procedure should be meaningful for an individual assessee. To meet this standard, the test must also be perceived as an appropriate task administered in a recognizable setting using a credible social etiquette.

Chapter 5 provides an international and cross-cultural perspective on bias in projective assessment from a methodological standpoint. *Bias* always has a culture-specific meaning and is defined as "a lack of similarity of psychological meaning of test scores across cultural groups." A discussion of the adequacy of test scores and interpretations is tantamount to an examination of bias. Test scores can be affected by construct, item, and method sources of bias. Each of the sources of bias is carefully defined and described using research examples. Construct and method bias are global in their effects, whereas item bias is local.

Bias in a construct can be minimized by specifying all emic parameters in each comparison culture necessary for definition prior to cross-cultural comparisons. Whenever an underlying universal structure has omitted some aspects of a construct because the etic rationale has been developed independently of the construct definition in different cultures, the culture-specific aspects of psychological functioning may be omitted as well. For example, one of the merits of a combined etic–emic approach to the TAT, as presented in chapter 18, is that the likelihood of omitting aspects of a construct in any particular emic content is reduced.

Method bias is apparent in samples, instruments, and procedures or administration. Truly representative samples are extraordinarily difficult to obtain and, to some extent, all samples of populations are samples of convenience or opportunity. Faithful rendition of social class representation is handicapped in the United States (e.g., by differences in numbers and relative sizes of social class structures in African-American and White groups). Language proficiency may also differ for various cultural samples taking the same test as a function of differences in first languages and/or educational levels.

Instrument bias occurs whenever the test stimuli are not equally familiar to different samples. For example, in picture–story methods, the pictures should be recognizable as familiar scenes for persons in different populations. The outdated clothing, decor, and furnishings in many Murray TAT cards depicting Anglo individuals is a case in point. Even the degree to which these pictures are ambiguous or literal may be inhibiting to persons who require more or less structure to stimulate fantasy and storytelling. Instrument bias is also found in inadequacy of scoring rules that not only reduce reliability of scoring responses, but may not have been examined for their validity with particular groups.

For example, administration or procedure bias occurs as a function of examiner gender, at least as demonstrated with intelligence tests. It is also seen on the Rorschach and TAT as suggested by Card IV responses with authority connotations and use of examiner-selected TAT cards, as well as TAT card 7GF stories that incorporate attitudes and feelings toward the examiner. Familiarity with the examiner as well as examiner gender have effects on response productivity and probably quality of responses as well. Eisegesis is also an example of bias on the part of the assessor in the absence of any safeguards for use of high-inference interpretation procedures (Dana, 1966).

Item bias, also called *differential item functioning* or the likelihood of unequal item endorsement across groups, has not been explicitly studied in projective methods. This chapter suggests that the frequencies of responses to the Rorschach blots could be examined in different cultural groups. This has been done without any intention of examining differential item functioning, but for clinical or local normative assessment research purposes. For example, samples of Rorschach Comprehensive System scores have been obtained in various countries (see chaps. 13–16). These samples do in fact demonstrate bias in the form of differential item functioning. Adequacy of translation, another example of potential item bias, could also be examined by available methods. Translations are generally assumed to be useful for responsible research or assessment practice if they have followed standard rules. However, these standard procedures do not necessarily render the items free from bias.

REFERENCES

Bennett, M. J. (1986). Toward ethnorelativism: A developmental model of intercultural sensitivity. In R. M. Paige (Ed.), *Cross-cultural orientation: New conceptualizations and applications* (pp. 27–69). Lanham, MD: University Press of America.

Dana, R. H. (1962). The validation of projective tests. *Journal of Projective Techniques, 26,* 182–186.

Shneidman, E. S. (1959). Suggestions for the delineation of validation studies. *Journal of Projective Techniques, 23,* 259–263.

Myths About the Null Hypothesis and the Path to Reform

Robert G. Malgady
New York University

Cultural bias in the delivery of mental health services has many faces, ranging from the very definition of *DSM–IV* psychiatric symptomatology to services utilization, psychological assessment and diagnosis, and treatment (Rogler, Malgady, & Rodriguez, 1989). Underlying the issue of culturally competent or unbiased mental health practice is a more fundamental issue of potential bias in the research literature, presumably on which culturally competent services are predicated. Research, in turn, invariably is based on the statistical analysis of empirical data leading to pragmatic decisions such as whether one ethnic group is utilizing services less than another, whether an assessment instrument is culturally biased, or whether ethnic minorities have differential treatment outcomes relative to their nonminority counterparts. All statistical hypothesis testing is premised on the notion of the null hypothesis.

The purpose of this chapter is to discuss some issues of bias in null hypothesis testing, which is the root of research that informs clinical practice. It begins by discussing some of the myths surrounding null hypothesis folklore, which are widely shared beliefs and practices that are not scientifically valid. It concludes with recent attempts to reform traditional null hypothesis testing practices and discusses the implications for cross-cultural psychological research.

MYTH 1 OF THE NULL HYPOTHESIS: SOME NULL HYPOTHESES ARE TRUE

Traditionally in statistical hypothesis testing, the null hypothesis is a presumption of no difference. For example, a null hypothesis might be a statement that a particular diagnostic assessment tool has equal validity for African Americans and Whites. This tradition—namely, posing no bias as the null hypothesis—prevails in cross-cultural mental health research. Historically, this can be traced to Sir Ronald Fisher's (1925) work in agriculture early in the 20th century.

According to statistical logic, if a researcher cannot reject the null hypothesis, it prevails as the status quo governing our actions. In the present context, this would lead to a belief that the ethnic groups being compared are not different. Type I versus Type II errors refer to the consequences attending incorrect statistical decisions regarding the null hypothesis. According to conventional standards of risk, Type I errors (incorrectly rejecting the null hypothesis of no bias) are permitted a maximum probability of .05; Type II errors (failure to reject a false null hypothesis in favor of a conclusion of bias) are afforded a maximum probability of .20 (Cohen, 1988). Thus, it might appear superficially that there is a bias in our statistical conventions because we are more likely to conclude no bias than bias. In other words, we are more liberal in our risk tolerance toward the bias hypothesis than we are to the no bias hypothesis.

Paradoxically, however, in research, the opposite is true. Whether a researcher rejects or fails to reject the null hypothesis is largely a function of two factors: the magnitude of the difference between groups and the sample size. Cohen (1994) eloquently argued that, in his and others' estimation, Type II errors (i.e., concluding no bias when in fact there is bias) occur about 50% of the time in social science research. Cohen and others (e.g., Malgady, 1998) have also argued that indeed no null hypotheses of this sort are true—all groups are different; it is merely a question of whether the difference is consequential to mental health practice. Thus, one myth that needs to be dispelled about the null hypothesis, particularly as it pertains to cross-cultural research, is that it is never true and all ethnic groups are different.

MYTH 2 OF THE NULL HYPOTHESIS: WE MUST POSE NO DIFFERENCE NULL HYPOTHESES

Regardless of Myth 1, one may question the traditional statistical practice of posing no difference or no bias as the null hypothesis. As originally conceived, the null hypothesis—not necessarily no difference, but more generally the proposition to be nullified—dictates the nature of the particular statistical distribution that is used to determine the probability of observed data. Fisher (1925) conceived of this procedure at a time when advanced computational technology was not available. Before the advent

error, the latter is rarely reported in the behavioral science literature (Cohen, 1990, 1994).

According to Hays (1973), an a priori decision should be made regarding which of the two types of errors is more serious. Then the corresponding hypothesis risking this error would play the null role or hypothesis to be nullified. Such a decision preceding scientific hypothesis testing is predicated on what may be an unscientific and subjective value judgement (Malgady, 1996).

Even in the philosophy of science, the scientific method requires value judgments to verify a theory. According to Rudner (1961), value judgments are required in the process of validating scientific hypotheses. Rudner pointed out that, in making probabilistic decisions, the choice of a significance level, such as the conventional .05 level, is a value judgment. Indeed, our conventional significance level of .05 stems from Fisher's (1935) quite arbitrary choice to use the 1/20 risk of error in agricultural experiments. Rudner emphasized the need for researchers to be conscious of the intrinsic value judgments they make during the course of scientific validation.

This suggests that cross-cultural researchers should first decide which of the two types of statistical decision errors is more serious (i.e., false conclusion of no cultural bias or false conclusion of cultural bias). Then the null hypothesis can be formulated so that the more serious error would be Type I.

Malgady (1996) proposed the following scenario. In Table 3.1, the null hypothesis specifies no bias. A Type I error would mean that ethnic group differences are believed to be valid when in fact they are not. This would suggest that new culturally competent standards for mental health care should be developed (e.g., Dana, 1997), but in fact they would eventually prove to be no more effective than mainstream services. A Type I error in this scenario means that culturally competent services do not really improve the mental health care of ethnic minorities. Therefore, fiscal resources will be misspent and mental health services possibly misdi-

TABLE 3.1
Comparison of Consequences of Type I and Type II
Errors From Traditional Null Hypotheses

Traditional Null Hypothesis: No Cultural Bias		
	Type I Error	Type II Error
Truth	No Bias	Bias
Decision	Difference	No Difference
Burden	Mental Health System	Minority Client
Value Judgment	Less Serious	More Serious

rected. This type of error would burden the mental health care system. Today this would exacerbate the system's present struggle to deliver culturally competent mental health services within the context of managed care (Dana, 1998).

However, if a Type II error is committed (i.e., no cultural bias is incorrectly concluded), the conclusion would be that there is no need for culturally competent services for ethnic minorities in the mental health care system (see Table 3.1). In this scenario, they might be deterred from utilizing services because of institutional barriers to health care that are culturally insensitive (Rogler, Malgady, & Rodriguez, 1989). Similarly, ethnic minority clients might be evaluated by biased assessment techniques (Costantino, Malgady, & Rogler, 1994), misdiagnosed (Marcos, 1994), and ultimately receive less than effective treatment plans (Sue, 1988).

In the alternate scenario, cultural bias would be formulated as the null hypothesis. Hence, the nature of Type I and Type II errors would be reversed (see Table 3.2). The more serious Type I errors would be client centered, and system-centered errors would be the less serious Type II errors. In other words, "mainstream mental health services procedures would be presumed guilty of bias against other cultures, unless proven innocent" (Malgady, 1996, p. 76).

Clearly an unscientific value judgment must be made regarding which type of error is more serious: client-centered or service system-centered error. Siding with the client, Dana (1998) lamented the particular lack of concern for culturally competent client-centered care within the current dominating climate of managed care by insurance providers.

Similarly, Hays (1973) stated that the choice of which error to risk ". . . depends upon the value . . . of the various outcomes" (p. 344). Hays (1988) provided an example in economics that quantifies the value of the two errors in terms of expected loss. He also provided various methods for choosing decision rules that minimize expected loss. However, Hays offered the caveat that such methods are rare in psychological research because the impact of Type I and Type II errors are qualitatively different,

TABLE 3.2
Comparison of Consequences of Type I and Type II
Errors From Alternate Null Hypotheses

	Alternate Null Hypothesis: Cultural Bias	
	Type I Error	*Type II Error*
Truth	Bias	No Bias
Decision	No Difference	Difference
Burden	Minority Client	Mental Health System
Value Judgment	More Serious	Less Serious

such as erring about a client's health care versus the cost to the mental health care system. As Dana emphasized, this presents a compelling challenge with today's emphasis on insurance reimbursement control over mental health care.

Perhaps one of the strongest diatribes against null hypothesis testing was boldly stated two decades ago by Meehl (1978):

> I believe that the almost universal reliance on merely refuting the null hypothesis as the standard method for corroborating substantive theories in . . . social science . . . is a terrible mistake, is basically unsound, poor scientific strategy, and one of the worst things that ever happened in the history of psychology. (p. 817)

He elaborated that: "the whole business is so radically defective as to be scientifically almost pointless" (p. 823).

Other statisticians have been highly critical of traditional no difference null hypothesis testing, or what Cohen (1994) referred to as *nil hypothesis* testing, but they have not suggested its abandonment (American Psychological Association, 1997; Thompson, 1996). Consistent with Malgady's (1996) proposal to reverse the null and alternate hypothesis in cross-cultural research, Thompson (1996) suggested that practice would be improved by eschewing no difference null hypotheses "in favor of tests postulating particular parameters based on previous research or theory" (p. 28). Dana (1997) adopted this paradigm in the development of a multifaceted model of assessment and intervention. The model assumes differences in behavior, personality, and psychiatric symptomatology. His assessment strategy seeks to determine whether the cultural difference between groups is "sufficient to require culture specific assessment and to implement that assessment as needed." These culturally sensitive assessments are linked, then, to interventions based on cultural elements embedded within the minority client's presenting symptomatology. Thus, Dana sought to increase the reliability and validity of psychological assessment by taking cultural differences as a preliminary assumption (which may be rejected) and thus improving the efficacy of psychotherapeutic interventions that are tailored to the assessment outcomes.

HUMAN DIVERSITY AND NULL HYPOTHESIS REFORM

Historically, a major focus in the field of psychology has been on the study of individual differences. Similarly, a significant cornerstone of statistical analysis is the concept of variance and the explanation or prediction of differences between people. Thus, it is ironic that scientific researchers continue to pose null hypotheses, all too often accepted according to Cohen (1994), that suggest we ignore human diversity. In the context of this discussion about cross-cultural mental health issues, it is estimated that, by the year 2000, ethnic minorities will comprise 40% of the clients in the mental health services system in the United States (Cross et al., 1989). This is a formidable sector of the mental health services system—certainly not diversity that can be ignored.

It is only within the last decade that formal professional standards and editorial policies have explicitly addressed cultural diversity. Thompson (1996) emphasized the importance of professional and editorial policy formally sanctioning acceptable hypothesis testing practices because

> we must understand the bad implicit logic of persons who misuse statistical tests if we are to have any hope of persuading them to alter their prac- tices—it will not be sufficient to merely tell researchers not to use statistical tests, or to use them judiciously. (p. 26)

The implication is that, because researchers fail to heed the message about the limits of null hypothesis testing, professional associations and journals should establish new policies or encourage reform in conformity with certain standards.

For the first time in the history of the American Psychiatric Associa- tion's *Diagnostic and Statistical Manuals,* the publication of the fourth edition (*DSM–IV*; American Psychiatric Association, 1994) reflects an un- precedented recognition of the importance of the cultural diversity of clients in psychiatric evaluations. Despite the importance of accurate psychodiagnosis in the delivery of clinical services, empirical research on this topic has been historically equivocal, whereas theoretical formulations have been limited (Malgady & Costantino, 1998). Attention is given to the consideration of cultural and linguistic diversity in the formulation of diagnostic criteria in the *DSM–IV* (e.g., "ethnic and cultural considera- tions," p. xxxiv) and its glossary of "culture-bound syndromes." The *DSM–IV* imposes cultural boundaries on many psychiatric disorders, which were previously conceived of as biologically invariant. The spirit of these caveats is consistent with the notion of abandoning the traditional null hypothesis and proceeding as if diagnostic procedures are not rou- tinely valid with members of diverse ethnic populations.

Similarly, the American Psychological Association's (1985) revised *Stan- dards for Educational and Psychological Testing* includes numerous cautions against using testing norms, item content, reliability, and validity estimates with demographically, linguistically, and culturally diverse populations.

With growing awareness of what can and cannot be learned from null hypothesis testing (e.g., Cohen, 1990, 1994; Hagen, 1996), the Board of Scientific Affairs of the American Psychological Association recently convened a Task Force on Statistical Inference (1997). The Task Force was convened to discuss the role of null hypothesis testing in psychological research and the modification of current practice in the quantitative treatment of data in scientific psychology. The Task Force did not support banning null hypothesis testing, but it explored ways to broaden our understanding through other statistical means such as Baysian methods, focusing more attention on descriptive indexes of differences (as opposed to significance testing), and encouraging the use of graphic techniques. The Task Force also stressed the need for hypothesis testing to be theoretically informed because: "The premature formulation of theoretical models has often led to the worst problems seen in the use of null hypothesis testing" (p. 3).

The *Diagnostic and Statistical Manual* (American Psychiatric Association, 1994) has taken on an unprecedented stance regarding editorial policy on research studies based on null hypothesis testing. Referring to Type I and Type II error rates, the *Manual* states that "Neither of the two types of probability values reflects the importance or magnitude of an effect because both depend on sample size" (p. 18). The new editorial policy encourages authors to provide "effect size information" to describe the meaningfulness of findings.

In the same context, Thompson (1996) suggested three reforms regarding statistical null hypothesis testing. Thompson referred to the *file drawer* problem or the editorial practice of only publishing articles with statistically significant findings, with extreme prejudice against publishing studies that do not have significant findings. As the latter accumulate in our files—and we all must admit to having a few—this creates a bias toward covert Type II errors in behavioral science research. Conversely, as more and more studies with significant findings are published, this biases the behavioral science literature by increasing the probability of Type I errors.

Thompson's (1996) solution is to implement three reforms for *best practice*, which he argued should constitute editorial policy: use of better language, emphasis on effect-size interpretation, and evaluation of result replicability. Regarding language, the first recommendation is that results should always be reported as statistically significant rather than merely significant to avoid the common misconception that *significance* is a synonym for *importance*. (As mentioned earlier, historically the term derives from Fisher's, 1925, use of the phrase that the differences in a sample were "significant of" a difference in the population. In other words, the sample results signified something about the population.)

Thompson's second reform was that editorial policy should require the report of effect sizes, including such indexes as Cohen's d (i.e., mean difference relative to the standard deviation), r^2, R^2, eta^2, odds ratios, and confidence intervals.

The third suggested reform concerns replicability of scientific findings. Ironically, Fisher developed statistical hypothesis testing so one did not have to conduct, say, 100 actual experiments and find out empirically the number of failures and successes. Rather, through a single, inferential, no difference null hypothesis test, one could more economically predict the outcome of future replications with, of course, his standard .05 risk of error. Today, contrary to this tradition, statisticians are emphasizing the need for replication of findings. Modern statistical techniques cheat a bit by quasireplication procedures such as cross-validation, jackknifing, and bootstrapping. All these techniques take place within the single sample at hand nonetheless. Obviously the best strategy would be to repeat a cross-cultural study over and over, from culture to culture. Replication of findings is a major task that faces the reformation of no difference null hypothesis testing, and it is not unique to cross-cultural research.

HOW DO WE PROCEED FROM HERE?

Anyone who has studied philosophy knows that if one can fault the premise of a particular argument, or in mathematics the assumptions of any proof, the remaining logical or mathematical conclusion is not valid. At the least, the conclusion is a non sequitur, although it might be valid by fiat. The premise underlying empirical psychological research, and not just cross-cultural research, is the formulation of a no difference (no bias) hypothesis to be nullified. Through a double negative, saying "no" to no difference—and perhaps this is a source of confusion—we all too often conclude that human diversity does not exist.

Clinicians are charged with the prevention and treatment of mental disorders. Culturally competent clinicians are faced with special adaptations of psychotherapeutic modalities and diagnostic procedures in accordance with their ethnic-minority clientele's cultural values and beliefs. To better inform culturally sensitive or competent clinical practice, researchers and practitioners require preventive intervention regarding the limits of knowledge that can be gained from null hypothesis testing, which is so deeply ingrained in our professional training. I have attempted to summarize some of the myths of null hypothesis testing and have suggested efforts at reform. Clearly, researchers and practitioners who are the consumers of research need to be demystified of statistical hypothesis testing practices. We need to reverse the traditional null hypothesis to specify hypotheses of clinical, not statistical, significance; we need to reexamine our conventions regarding our decision rule governing statistical significance. Clinicians will be happy to hear that we need *arm chair* interpretations of data in conjunction with p values. Even if all these preventive intervention criteria are eventually satisfied, publication policies of the major professional organizations need to reconsider standards for the publication of behavioral science research.

REFERENCES

American Psychiatric Association. (1994). *Diagnostic and statistical manual* (4th ed.). Washington, DC: Author.

American Psychological Association. (1985). *Standards for educational and psychological testing.* Washington, DC: Author.

American Psychologial Association. (1997). *Task force on statistical inference. Board of scientific affairs.* Washington, DC: Author.

Baken, D. (1966). The test of significance in psychological research. *Harvard Educational Review, 66,* 423–437.

Carver, R. (1993). The case against statistical significance testing, revisited. *Journal of Experimental Education, 61,* 287–292.

Cohen, J. (1988). *Statistical power analysis in the behavioral sciences.* Hillsdale, NJ: Lawrence Erlbaum Associates.

Cohen, J. (1990). Things I have learned (so far). *American Psychologist, 45,* 1304–1312.

Cohen, J. (1994). The earth is round ($p < .05$). *American Psychologist, 49,* 997–1003.

Costantino, G., Malgady, R. G., & Rogler, L. H. (1994). Storytelling-through-pictures: Culturally sensitive psychotherapy for Hispanic children and adolescents. *Journal of Clinical Child Psychology, 23,* 13–20.

Cronbach, L. J. (1975). Beyond the two disciplines of psychology. *American Psychologist, 30,* 116–127.

Cross, R., Bazron, B., Dennis, K., & Ísaacs, M. (1989). *Towards a culturally competent system of care: A monograph on effective services for minority children who are severely emotionally disturbed.* (Available from CAASP Technical Assistance Center, Georgetown University Child Development Center, 3800 Reservoir Road NW, Washington, DC 20007).

Dana, R. H. (1997). Multicultural assessment and cultural identity: An assessment intervention model. *World Psychology, 3,* 121–141.

Dana, R. H. (1998). Problems with managed mental health care for multicultural populations. *Psychological Reports, 83,* 283–294.

Falk, R., & Greenbaum, C. (1995). Significance tests die hard. *Theory and Psychology, 5,* 75–98.

Fisher, R. A. (1925). *Statistical methods for research workers.* London: Oliver & Boyd.

Fisher, R. A. (1935). *The design of experiments.* London: Oliver & Boyd.

Hagen, R. L. (1996). In praise of the null hypothesis statistical test. *American Psychologist, 52,* 15–23.

Hays, W. (1973). *Statistics for the social sciences.* New York: Holt, Rinehart & Winston.

Hays, W. (1988). *Statistics.* New York: Holt, Rinehart & Winston.

Kanekar, S. (1990). Statistical significance as a continuum. *American Psychologist, 45,* 296.

Kuhn, T. (1970). *The structure of scientific revolutions.* Chicago: University of Chicago Press.

Levenson, R. L. (1990). Comment on Harcum. *American Psychologist, 45,* 295–296.

Malgady, R. G. (1996). The question of cultural bias in assessment and diagnosis of ethnic minority clients: Let's reject the null hypothesis. *Professional Psychology: Research and Practice, 27,* 73–77.

Malgady, R. G. (1998). In praise of value judgements . . . and of "accepting" the null hypothesis. *American Psychologist, 53,* 797–798.

Malgady, R. G., & Costantino, G. (1998). Symptom severity in bilingual Hispanics as a function of interviewer ethnicity and language of interview. *Psychological Assessment, 10,* 379–387.

Marcos, L. (1994). The psychiatric examination of Hispanics across the language barrier. In R. Malgady & O. Rodriguez (Eds.), *Theoretical and conceptual issues in Hispanic mental health* (pp. 143–154). Melbourne, FL: Krieger.

Meehl, P. (1978). Theoretical risks and tabular asterisks: Sir Karl, Sir Ronald, and the slow progress of soft psychology. *Journal of Consulting and Clinical Psychology, 46,* 806–834.

Rogler, L., Malgady, R., & Rodriguez, O. (1989). *Hispanics and mental health: A framework for research.* Melbourne, FL: Krieger.

Roseboom, W. (1960). The fallacy of the null hypothesis significance test. *Psychological Bulletin, 57,* 416–428.

Rosnow, R., & Rosenthal, R. (1989). Statistical procedures and the justification of knowledge in psychological science. *American Psychologist, 44,* 1276–1284.

Rudner, R. (1961). Value judgments in the acceptance of theories. In P. Frank (Ed.), *The validation of scientific theories* (pp. 31–35). New York: First Collier Books. (originally published by the American Association for the Advancement of Science, 1954).

Sue, S. (1988). Psychotherapeutic services for ethnic minorities. *American Psychologist, 43,* 301–308.

Thompson, B. (1996). AERA editorial policies regarding statistical significance testing: Three suggested reforms. *Educational Researcher, 26,* 29–30.

Tryon, W. W. (1998). The inscrutable null hypothesis. *American Psychologist, 53,* 796.

4

A Construct-Based Approach to Equivalence: Methodologies for Cross-Cultural/Multicultural Personality Assessment Research

James Allen
University of Alaska Fairbanks

James A. Walsh
University of Montana

Psychological assessment in the United States is undergoing a significant shift in context. This shift results from dramatic, ongoing social changes in the United States; the ethnic and cultural makeup of the United States is changing. For some time, people of European backgrounds have comprised the majority ethnic and cultural group in the United States. Given current trends, in 2010, there will be no dominant ethnic or cultural group in the United States (Sue, 1991). Instead, more than half the population will include members of visible racial and ethnic groups who do not share this European ethnic and cultural background. However, aside from some notable exceptions (e.g., TEMAS; Constantino, Malgady, & Rogler, 1988), most of the standardized personality tests currently used in the United States were developed using samples composed predominately of Euro-American individuals. Over half a century ago, Guilford (1942) emphasized, as did other writers, that validity is not a general characteristic of a test, thus, a test could be highly valid for one purpose or setting, but not at all valid for another.

Changes similar to those in the United States are occurring elsewhere in the world—the direct consequence of cross-immigration and globalization of the economy. Given the magnitude of this change in the social context of personality assessment, there has been surprisingly limited research on the application of standardized personality tests developed with a sample in which one ethnic and cultural group predominates to other groups. In addition, the existing research on assessment instruments has had a controversial history, plagued by methodological problems (Okazaki & Sue, 1995). Currently, scant consensus exists regarding appropriate methodologies for screening instruments for possible cross-cultural/multicultural adaptation.

This chapter attempts to address this deficiency. It provides a nontechnical introduction to selected methods to research the appropriateness of a psychological assessment instrument, developed and standardized with a group in which one ethnic or cultural group predominates, for potential use among people from a different ethnic or cultural groups. We argue that much of the multicultural critique regarding the application of standardized personality instruments with ethnic minorities, although at times controversial and at odds with the viewpoints of many within mainstream personality assessment, is entirely consistent with the viewpoints articulated by many of the methodologists who advanced theory-based or construct approaches to test construction and validation beginning in the 1950s. We present a brief review of this approach, relevant to cross-cultural and multicultural research, to provide some guidelines for a construct-based approach to multicultural and cross-cultural assessment research on standardized personality and clinical psychodiagnostic instruments. We briefly discuss the concept of test bias from the perspective of construct validity. We also touch on the lack of construct specificity regarding ethnicity as a variable in much of the current assessment research. In doing this, we present specific statistical methodologies that are currently underutilized in studies of the equivalence of measures across cultures and ethnic groups. We also briefly overview potential uses of more recent approaches to test validation—most notably item response theory—in cross-cultural/multicultural assessment research. We conclude with a discussion of the limitations of these approaches, including a consideration of the potential limitations of the psychometric-statistical approach in cross-cultural and multicultural research.

TYPES OF EQUIVALENCE

The primary issue in the use of assessment measures cross-culturally and multiculturally concerns equivalence. We refer to application of tests across cultural groups, often internationally, as *cross-cultural application*. We refer to application with ethnic minorities within a specific nation as *multicultural application* while recognizing the frequent overlap inherent between culture and minority group status.

Brislin (1993) described translation, metric, and conceptual equivalence as the three most important areas of concern in cross-cultural research methodology. Okazaki and Sue (1995) asserted that these same concerns are relevant to research with ethnic minorities, providing a review of selected research demonstrating these factors operating on standardized tests with U.S. ethnic minorities.

Translation equivalence is concerned with the accuracy of the translation of items of a test from one language, or dialect of a language, to another. Okazaki and Sue noted that the issue of linguistic equivalence of a test is also of significant importance for ethnic–minority people in any particular country, even when they speak the dominant language(s) of a particular society. In the United States, for example, people from ethnic–minority backgrounds may be functionally English speaking, but bilingual, or may have exposure to White English and, in the case of many African Americans, also have exposure to Black English (Helms, 1992; Lindsay, 1998)—or, for many American Indians, exposure to reservation English (Allen, 1998). In these and other cases, a potentially complex interaction emerges between language or dialect, specific word meanings therein, and the nature of specific test items or assessment tasks. Because most standardized assessment instrument items and task instructions used in the United States are in White English, important questions remain regarding whether items retain the same meaning across groups. Dunnigan, McNall, and Mortimer (1993) showed how a group of Hmong adolescents living in the United States, although capable of meeting high school academic requirements in English, displayed different understandings of the meanings and situational uses of common metaphors for emotions, attitudes, and personality characteristics than adolescents in the general population. This metaphorical nonequivalence was reflected in poor reliability and validity coefficients on standardized personality and psychopathology instruments for the Hmong, but not general population adolescents.

Brislin (1993) described a multistage translation–back translation procedure wherein translation of an instrument into a new language or different dialect is then followed by a second translator's translation back into the original language. Next, inconsistencies in the resultant back translation are identified through comparison, and revision occurs in an iterative process until resolution of these inconsistencies is achieved. Geisinger (1994) recommended use of an editorial board as a more effective alternative to back translation. The editorial board is composed of a group meeting the same qualifications as the original translator. The board carefully reviews the translation or adaption. This could occur in the form of a group meeting or through individual reviews, followed by a discursive process wherein the translator and panel reconcile any differences or concerns.

Metric equivalence relates to whether the same metric can be used to measure the same attribute among people from two or more groups or cultures. In an example from the intellectual assessment literature, Lopez and Romero (1988) analyzed differences in score conversion, administration, and content between the Weschler Adult Intelligence Scale (WAIS) and its Spanish translation/adaptation, *Escala de Inteligencia Weschler para Adultos* (EIWA). They concluded that scores between the two should not be viewed as quanitatively comparable or metrically equivalent.

Brislin (1993) recognized a third form of equivalence, which he termed *conceptual equivalence*. This refers to whether the underlying psychological construct tapped by an assessment instrument holds the same meaning in the new group to which the instrument is to be applied as was the case with the group with whom the test was originally developed. A number of authors have described a fourth type of equivalence, termed *functional equivalence* (Berry, 1980; Butcher & Han, 1996; Helms, 1992). A specific overt behavior can have different functions or meaning across cultures. In personality assessment, the underlying construct measured by one culture could be measured by another scale in a different culture. Although the scales were designed for different purposes, they are functionally equivalent (Butcher & Han, 1996). With regard to personality assessment, we consider functional equivalence a special case of conceptual equivalence. This chapter focuses on methodologies associated with tests of this third type of equivalence—conceptual equivalence in the underlying psychological construct between ethnic or cultural groups.

CONSTRUCT EQUIVALENCE

The construct approach to test construction developed during the 1950s. As originally formulated by Cronbach and Meehl (1955), a psychological construct is an attribute of people that is not operationally defined, but assumed reflected in test performance. Relevant to our discussion here, constructs occur within a nomological network—an interlocking system of laws constituting theory. This nomological network may relate to observables or different theoretical constructs, but some of these laws, or relations, must involve observables to be scientific. Study of the construct involves elaboration of its nomological network, which is justified if it adds elements confirmed by observables or if it reduces elements (nomologicals) required to predict behavior. "Test operations . . . overlap or measure the same thing" (Cronbach & Meehl, 1955, p. 291) if their positions in the nomological network tie them to the same construct variable.

During this same decade, a method for evaluation of the interpretation of a test as a measure of a psychological construct was also developed. Through their development of a method of systematic examination of a test's convergent and discriminant validity using multiple measures of traits and multiple methods of measurement, Campbell and Fiske (1959) provided a procedure to evaluate the adequacy of a test as a measure of a construct.

In efforts to adopt an existing standardized assessment instrument for use with a culture or group different than the group with whom the instrument was developed, we are interested in adopting the nomological network of the instrument developed in the original culture or group (Ben-Porath, 1990). Conceptual equivalence refers to whether the underlying construct tapped by a particular personality assessment instrument is equivalent across cultures or groups. If the instrument in question taps the same underlying construct among people of the new culture or group, as with the culture or group of its origin, then the nomological network can be adopted for interpretation of the instrument. The remainder of this chapter focuses on selected methodologies useful for screening measures for further study into the appropriateness of such an adoption of a nomological net. These approaches study measurement issues that must hold true for a particular personality assessment instrument to tap an equivalent underlying construct across cultures.

CONCEPTUALIZING BIAS IN PERSONALITY TESTS FROM THE PERSPECTIVE OF CONSTRUCT VALIDITY

The term *test bias* has multiple meanings (Flaugher, 1978): It encompasses definitions as disparate as any group difference on a test as evidence of test bias, to bias inherent in the wording or meaning of individual items, to statistical measures of differential relations between predictor and criterion variables (Hunter & Schmidt, 1976). In one formulation, Van de Vijver and Poortinga (1997) summarized three sources of bias: method bias, related to the form of test administration; item bias, related to item content/wording; and construct bias. In multicultural and cross-cultural personality assessment, one way to conceptualize many of the commonly described types of biases is through the logic of construct validation. Test bias exists, from this viewpoint, when an existing test does not measure the equivalent underlying psychological construct in a new group or culture, as was measured within the original group in which it was standardized. One reason for this difference, especially if the test or test adaptation is of demonstrated linguistic equivalence, may be that the underlying construct may differ between groups. In such a case, an existing measure will not accurately tap the construct of interest when applied to the new group. For example, the experience of depression varies in important ways between ethnic and cultural groups (Manson, 1994). Manson (1995) reviewed research with the Center for Epidemiological Studies–Depression Scale (CES–D; Radloff, 1977)—a standardized, widely used composite measure of depressive symptomatology developed by researchers at the National Institute of Mental Health for epidemiological studies. It includes items from several previously established depression scales. The factor analytic studies he reviewed show important changes in the internal structure of the instrument across Chinese-American, Mexican-American, and American Indian groups, which he interpreted as reflective of a change in the underlying patterning of affect in depression (e.g., the construct). These changes led to an internal structure that differed from that of the standardization sample with the CES–D.

In the case where the underlying construct tapped by an instrument differs across ethnic and cultural groups, the interpretation of the assessment instrument has also necessarily changed. Significant misunderstanding can result from a confusion regarding the purposes and intent of test validation. From the perspective of the developers of construct-based approaches to test development and validation, tests are not valid or invalid:

> The phrase *validation of a test* is a source of much misunderstanding. One validates, not a test, but an *interpretation of data arising from a specified procedure*. A single instrument may be used in many different ways. . . . Since each application is based on a different interpretation, the evidence that justifies one application may have little relevance to the next. Because every interpretation has its own degree of validity, one can never reach the simple conclusion that a particular test "is valid." (Cronbach, 1971, p. 447; italics original)

Validity is properly understood in relation to a test's intended use. Cook and Campbell (1979) described this as the *generalizability* aspect of construct validity. The validity of an interpretation for a particular test can change with different uses, including uses with different ethnic and cultural groups:

> Note that it is not the test that has validity, but rather *the inferences* made from test scores. Thus before we can assess a test's validity, we must know the purposes to which it is to be put. (Wainer & Braun, 1988, p. xvii; italics original)

Malgady (1996) argued that the directionality of the null hypothesis in assessment research should be changed from that of no cultural difference to cultural nonequivalence, on the basis of social and ethical concerns regarding the magnitude of the potential negative impact on consumers of services. Many researchers (e.g., Rogler, Malgady, & Rodriguez, 1989) have noted that differences on personality measures among members of ethnic groups and different cultures are often interpreted negatively from Western perspectives. This multicultural critique of the application of standardized personality instruments for the purpose of assessment among cultures and groups different than the group predominate in its normative sample and validation, in the absence of data on the validity of these interpretations for this new purpose, is consistent with this methodologically conservative construct-based approach to test validity. A construct-based approach also has important implications regarding the manner in which cultural or ethnic group membership is specified in research on multicultural and cross-cultural application of personality instruments.

Specificity of the Variable of Interest

Much of the research studying multicultural and cross-cultural application of personality assessment instruments does not make explicit the underlying assumptions regarding ethnicity or cultural group membership. Okazaki and Sue (1995) noted that ethnicity as a variable embodies assumptions regarding some shared psychological characteristics that are related to personality or psychopathology. Therefore, they contended that ethnicity specified as a demographic variable is not the variable of psychological interest in assessment research. Instead, underlying psychological variables associated with culture and ethnicity, hypothesized to produce ethnic group or cultural differences, are more directly relevant to this inquiry. They asserted that the failure to clarify assumptions about ethnicity and the imprecision in ethnic and cultural group categorizations when they are used as a demographic variable have caused significant confusion and problems in cross-cultural and multicultural assessment research. A construct-based approach to understanding these potential differences among cultural and ethnic groups dictates that these constructs of interest can and should be directly measured. Clark (1987), Betancourt and Lopez (1993), and Okazaki and Sue (1995) all argued strongly that cross-cultural and multicultural research must specify and measure directly the constructs associated with culture theorized to produce differences. Dana (1993, 1998) provided reviews of a wide array of measures of cultural orientation status and other measures of constructs associated with culture for groups in the United States.

METHODOLOGICAL APPROACHES
TO TEST CONSTRUCT EQUIVALENCE

Construct validation procedures were first systematically elaborated in the conceptual and empirical testing elaborated by Campbell and Fiske (1959) through a logic of strong relationships with other measures of the same construct and weak relationships with measure of other constructs. Generalization of a construct to a new cultural or ethnic group through the process of construct validation is a lengthy and involved process. The following methodological approaches describe three statistical procedures that hold particular promise, but are currently underutilized, in cross-cultural and multicultural personality assessment research. These methodologies are intended to screen measures for potential cross-cultural and multicultural adoption or adaptation. They can provide a first step prior to the significant investment required by the intensive process of validation of an adapted instrument with a new cultural or ethnic group. These approaches include cross-validation of the factor structure across groups using confirmatory factor analytic techniques, regression using culture-specific construct and cultural identity status measures as predictor variables, and item response theory (IRT) modeling.

Factor Analytic Approaches to Equivalence

In the case of adoption of an instrument from one ethnic or cultural group to another, we are interested in adopting the nomological network of the underlying construct tapped by the instrument, as established in the original culture or ethnic group. Relevant to the issue of multicultural and cross-cultural adaptation, this nomological network can be understood as based on two sets of relationships: (a) the internal network of empirical relationships within the factor structure of the assessment instrument, and (b) the relationship of the instrument with external correlates associated with the construct of interest that the instrument is intended to tap (Ben-Porath, 1990). To establish the cross-cultural or multicultural validity of an adopted instrument, both internal and external sets of relationships must be demonstrated to be invariant across cultural or ethnic groups. Cross-validation of the instrument's factor structure from previous research with a sample of participants from the ethnic minority or cultural group to which it is being adapted, by providing a test of equivalence of the internal structure of the instrument across groups, indicates whether the more involved research with external correlates is worth pursuing.

Ben-Porath (1990) described the logic behind this procedure, which he termed *replicatory factor analysis*. He delineated a methodology for studying the invariance of factor structure across groups using exploratory factor analysis (EFA). In this procedure, a representative sample of the group with whom the instrument is to be adopted completes the assessment instrument; the data is then factor analyzed using the same EFA techniques for extraction, estimation of communalities, and rotation, as were used in the original development and validation of the instrument.

In this new analysis, the number of factors extracted is constrained to the number of factors identified in the research with the instrument in its culture of origin. He recommended use of several different indices of comparison common to the literature (e.g., Gorush, 1983). This procedure provides a test of the factorial invariance, or internal structure, of the instrument across cultural or ethnic groups. If the two structures vary significantly in these comparisons, this indicates that a qualitative change has occurred in what is measured by the instrument when it is used with the new cultural or ethnic group. This being the case, it is most likely that the external correlates of the instrument have also changed. Such a finding suggests either adaptation of a different instrument or development of a culture-specific instrument to tap the construct of interest. If the factor structure proves invariant across samples, the investigator may then proceed with the more laborious task of validation of the instrument, having used this procedure to screen the instrument for possible adoption.

In the ensuing years since Ben-Porath described this methodology, newer confirmatory factor analytic (CFA) techniques have become widely used in psychology and psychological assessment research as a way to study the underlying structure of data. Floyd and Widaman (1995) termed this procedure of replicating factor structure *cross-validation* and described this application of CFA as the study of *measurement invariance*. We briefly review a few of the issues relevant to the use of CFA techniques in the study of cross-cultural and multicultural studies of measurement invariance. A number of excellent general sources on CFA provide more detailed explanations (e.g., Bollen, 1989; Bollen & Long, 1993; Byrne, 1989, 1994; Loehlin, 1992). These sources, along with Crowley and Fan (1997), also provide discussion of some of the advantages and disadvantages of the three most widely used computer programs for CFA: LISREL (Jöreskog & Sörbom, 1989), EQS (Bentler, 1992), and PROC CALIS of SAS (SAS Institute, Inc., 1990).

CFA allows hypothesis testing. In tests of cross-cultural/multicultural measurement invariance, CFA allows testing of a theoretical model regarding the factor structure of the adopted instrument, as found in the sample with which it was developed, using data collected from the new group of interest. Using CFA, the parameters of the factor coefficients for each item of a personality assessment instrument in research with data from a new cultural or ethnic group can either be constrained in cross-validation to a value, as specified by the factor structure found in previous research, or fixed to zero on factors on which the item should not load. Once the coefficients are specified, the data from the new sample can be used to test the fit of the model. The parameter estimates set by the researcher are then used in CFA to reconstruct the covariance or correlation matrix of the observed data. This matrix constructed from the parameter estimates is then compared to the actual covariance or correlation matrix produced by the new sample data. If the difference between the two matrices is small, the factor structure identified in the original research with the instrument fits the data well with the new ethnic or cultural group. This indicates that the internal structure of the instrument remains similar with the new group, suggesting it is feasible to move on to study of external correlates of the test with the new group. If the difference between the matrices is large, the goodness of fit of the model identified through previous research to the current data produced by the new sample is poor. This indicates that the factor structure varies between samples; the internal relations of the items in the personality instrument have changed when used with the new cultural or ethnic group. This being the case, it would be advisable to select a different instrument for possible adoption or develop a new instrument specific to the cultural or ethnic group.

CFA techniques provide a variety of goodness of fit indices (cf. Bentler, 1990; Bentler & Bonnet, 1980; Bollen, 1990; Tanaka, 1993, for an explanation and evaluation of many of the most common indices). These indices provide a gauge of how well the observed data collected from the new group fits the factor structure found with the sample of the instrument's origin. In EFA, results may capitalize on such factors as sampling errors and idiosyncracies of the sample data. In contrast, CFA avoids many of these problems by fitting the data to the factor structure prespecified through earlier work with the instrument in its sample of origin.

An alternative, more laborious, but more powerful strategy for testing measurement invariance using CFA involves collecting data on multiple groups simultaneously, including data from participants from the group that predominated in the sample in which the structure was identified originally, along with data from the new cultural or ethnic group(s) of interest. Such an approach would be an excellent procedure to employ in instrument development if the instrument is intended for use with different ethnic or cultural groups. Jöreskog and Sörbom (1989) described extensions of CFA for use with multiple samples allowing for assessment of measurement invariance across groups. The procedure in this approach is to constrain all common factor loadings to be invariant across groups.

Three issues warrant brief discussion here regarding limitations in the use of CFA with personality assessment research in general (Crowley & Fan, 1997) and with cross-cultural/multicultural CFA cross-validation procedures in particular. First, many CFA procedures, including the most widely used maximum likelihood estimation procedure, assume multivariate normality, and the procedure is quite sensitive to violations of this assumption (Bentler, 1982). Given that distributions of the data produced by standardized instruments can change quite markedly when applied with new cultural and ethnic groups, assessment for multivariate normality is an important first step in CFA cross-validation research. Byrne (1994) described estimation procedures that do not require this assumption and alternate test statistics that allow for correction to take into account non-normality if present. Second, although correlation matrices are easier to obtain for many standardized instruments, the researcher should be aware that many of the estimation models used in CFA were originally developed for covariance matrices. Cudek (1989) described a number of potential problems that can arise when using correlation instead of covariance matrices, including inaccurate standard errors for estimates of parameters and inaccurate fit indicators. Because of these concerns, use of the covariance matrix from the original factor structure research with the instrument is recommended whenever feasible. Finally, the CFA literature generally notes that large sample sizes (e.g., 10 participants per item; Jöreskog & Sörbom, 1989) are recommended as necessary for stable parameter estimates. This can potentially create serious problems for cross-cultural and multicultural researchers, who often study groups with small population sizes (Okazaki & Sue, 1995). Guadagnoli and Velicer (1988) challenged hard and fast rules for large sample sizes. Their Monte Carlo work with EFA suggests that variable saturation with factors and number of indicators (items) per factor covaries with sample size in determining the stability of a solution. With loadings of .80, solutions were quite stable with samples as small as 50, regardless of the number of indicators. This work suggests that with standardized instruments possessing clear, well-defined factor structures, stable coefficients in CFA with samples smaller than 200 may be possible. Similar Monte Carlo work with CFA techniques is greatly needed.

Regression Approaches to Equivalence

A second important question when considering adoption of an instrument in a new culture involves an investigation of the relation of test scores from the instrument to direct measures of cultural identification and underlying variables associated with culture that are hypothesized to produce potential cultural or ethnic group differences. At issue here is the following question: Is variation in the test score predicted by psychological variables associated with identification with a particular cultural or ethnic group? This becomes an important issue for an assessment instrument that measures psychopathology.

Regression analysis is a set of statistical techniques that allow the assessment of the relationship between one dependent variable and a set of independent, or predictor, variables. Regression analysis produces an equation that provides the best prediction of a dependent variable from a group of continuous or dichotomous variables.[1] This equation takes the form:

$$Y' = \beta_o + B_1X_1 + B_2X_2 \ldots + B_kX_k$$

where Y' is the predicted value for the dependent variable and β_o is the regression constant, or the value of Y when all X values are zero. The Xs are the independent, or predictor, variables, of which there can be one to k values depending on the number of variables used by the researcher. The Bs are the regression coefficients assigned to the respective independent variable. The goal of regression is to develop a set of regression coefficients for each independent variable that leads to prediction, using the regression equation, of a value for the dependent variable (the Y value), for each case that is as close as possible to the actual value obtained on the dependent variable.[2] As applied to personality assessment research, regression is most often used to test the ability of scores on a particular assessment instrument to predict an external correlate of behavior or to use other external correlates of behavior and/or test scores from measures of similar or related constructs to predict test scores on the instrument.

Regression has been most commonly used in cross-cultural/multicultural assessment research in questions of test bias through the Cleary Rule (Cleary, 1968), which states that a test developed for use in measurement of a construct is equivalent if it has the same regression equation with some external correlate of behavior in the new cultural or ethnic group as with the group with which it was developed.[3] Although courts have used this rule heavily in determinations of test bias, the approach embodies at least three problematic assumptions (Nunnally & Bernstein, 1994): (a) the distribution of scores on the external correlate of behavior in the new cultural or ethnic group is similar to the group with which the test was validated, (b) the groups are matched on relevant third variables such as socioeconomic status; and most importantly, (c) the external correlate of behavior is equivalent across groups.

---

[1]Although some classical inferences may not be appropriate if dichotmous variables are employed.

[2]This is a rough approximation of the goal of regression because it is the average squared error that is in practice what regression uses in its estimates (cf. Pedhazur, 1982).

[3]Most often the Cleary Rule has been used in court cases to address the issue of criterion validity, which is a different form of validity than construct validity. *Criterion validity* refers to how well a test accurately predicts some other observation of behavior or ability. This observation serves as a criterion. In this use of the Cleary Rule, the behavior or ability that the test is intended to accurately predict is termed the *criterion variable*, and a similar regression equation must predict this variable for both groups to demonstrate an absence of test bias.

An alternative use for regression becomes particularly important with a measure of a construct that does not reflect mainstream behaviors, practices, beliefs, and worldviews within the culture or ethnic group, such as constructs related to psychopathology. In this application, regression is used to examine the relationship of scores on the instrument to measures of cultural identification, or ideally, to direct measures of psychological variables underlying cultural identification that are hypothesized to impact the test score. This approach is an extension of regression methodologies presented by Van de Vivjer and Poortinga (1991) for the investigation of what they termed *context variables* in cross-cultural research. One of the major concerns when adapting a measure of psychopathology to a new cultural group is that of pathologizing differences. Symptom formation and illness behavior can vary immensely among groups (Dinges & Cherry, 1995; Kleinman, 1988a). Rogler, Malgady, and Rodriguez (1989) noted that differences on personality measures among members of ethnic groups and different cultures are often interpreted negatively from Western perspectives.

If scores on tests of psychopathology are not predicted by measures of cultural identification or culture-related psychological variables in the regression analysis, this suggests measurement equivalence with regard to this area of concern. In this case, the investigator may cautiously proceed with research to validate the construct tapped by this test with the new group. If scores on tests of psychopathology are predicted by measures of cultural identification or culture-related psychological variables in the regression analysis, this suggests that mainstream, nondeviant behaviors, practices, or beliefs within the group may be pathologized by the test. From the perspective of construct equivalence, this suggests that the underlying construct has changed across cultural or ethnic groups and that the instrument is not measuring equivalent constructs across the groups. In such a case, the investigator has three options: choose a different instrument to adopt or adapt that taps the construct differently, develop a new culture-specific instrument to more accurately tap the construct as indigenously defined within the culture, or investigate the item pool for items that display differential functioning across groups. This final approach has potential in cases when the construct, in general, may hold equivalent across groups. In such cases, a single or restricted set of items on an instrument may tap normative signs, symptoms, traits, or behaviors within a cultural or ethnic group, which the instrument pathologizes.

Item Response Theory Approaches to Equivalence

Item response theory (IRT) has enjoyed prominent usage within educational testing (Hambleton, Swaminathan, & Rogers, 1991), but has only been sporadically applied in research with personality and psychopathology assessment instruments (Panter, Swygert, Dahlstrom, & Tanaka, 1997). In contrast to classical test theory, which estimates the level of a personality trait as a linear combination, usually the sum, sometimes weighted, of individual test item responses, IRT conceptualizes in terms of a response pattern. Underlying this idea of the response pattern is an assumed relationship between the person's responses and the personality trait, attitude, or attribute of interest, called θ.

IRT can be used to study personality instruments, or factor scales from personality instruments, that tap a single underlying dimension of personality thought to generate a set of dichotomous item responses (Hambleton, Swaminathan, & Rogers, 1991). However, variants of the model (e.g., the Samejima model) are designed to work with ordered response scaling approaches such as Likert scales (Nunnally & Bernstein, 1994). In the case of a unidimensional, dichotomous (e.g., true–false) scale intended to measure depression, the probability of endorsing any particular item in this scale as true, or self-descriptive, is assumed to be a function of two components: (a) item parameters, or characteristics of the particular item; and (b) a single parameter related to the person and his or her level of the personality trait or attribute, or θ—in this case, level of depression. The relationship between the probabilities of response to an item, as a function of its item parameters, and different levels of the trait being measured is a nonlinear function termed the *item characteristic curve* (ICC; Lord, 1952); it takes the form of an S-shaped curve. The graphed ICC is a line that is tracing the probability (Lazarsfeld, 1950) of endorsement of the item as self-descriptive as a function of θ, hence ICCs are often referred to as *trace lines*.

There are three common types of IRT models. The Rasch, or one-parameter IRT model (Rasch, 1960), is the most simple. A single parameter, b, describes the probability of endorsing an item. This parameter, which in personality research may be termed *item threshold*, reflects the point of the trace line where the probability of endorsing an item as self-descriptive is .5. The lower the value of b, the higher the rate of endorsement for an item at a given level of the latent trait, or θ. Figure 4.1 graphs two trace lines for two items from a hypothetical unidimensional dichotomous depression scale with different rates of endorsement, or b values. As can be seen in the S-shaped curve for $b = 1$, higher b values shift the curve along the horizontal axis, measuring the latent trait of depression, to the right, whereas lower b values, as seen through the $b = -1$ value, shift the curve to the left.

There are limitations in the ability of a single parameter model to describe actual item functioning (Hambleton, Swaminathan, & Rogers, 1991). Therefore, a two-parameter model (Birnbaum, 1968) conceptualizes the probability that an individual will endorse an item, given their level

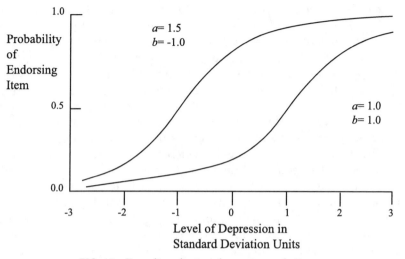

FIG. 4.1.   Trace lines for two depression scale items.

on θ or the underlying trait, as a function of b or the item threshold parameter, along with a second parameter, a, termed *item discrimination*. Item discrimination is a function of the slope of the item response curve at the item threshold point. Returning to Fig. 4.1, the two items differ in terms of item discrimination. As can be seen in the trace line for $a = 1.5$, higher positive scores on a lead to steeper slopes. This reflects stronger relations of the item to the underlying trait, θ, and greater differentiation of the item at corresponding points along the trait dimension. The lower score on the other item trace line ($a = 1$) reflects less differentiation.

Three-parameter IRT models attempt to describe the actual responses of items in standardized testing situations even more accurately by including a third parameter, the *lower asymptote parameter*. In educational research, this is often referred to as the pseudoguessing parameter. Even low-ability test takers on a test of ability or achievement have a probability of getting the item correct by guessing. This parameter, labeled c, as applied to personality instruments indicates the probability of a person with a low level of the trait θ (in our example, someone who is not depressed) still endorsing the item as self-descriptive. In personality research, most investigators have focused on two-parameter models, although theoretically this three-parameter model is conceptually plausible. Several computer programs now allow researchers to model both dichotomous and Likert scale data using IRT. Hambleton, Swaminathan, and Rogers (1991) provided a more detailed description of IRT, as well as a review of the features, strengths, and weaknesses of BILOG (Mislevy & Block, 1986) and MULTILOG (Thissen, 1991)—two of the more widely used IRT modeling programs.

Use of IRT in cross-cultural and multicultural research has focused on identifying items whose parameters change across cultural or ethnic groups. When item parameters change, the item displays differential item functioning (DIF; Thissen, Steinberg, & Wainer, 1988). To review, from the perspective of IRT, a test is intended to provide a measure of a latent trait, θ, and the ICC represents the probability of endorsing an item at any given level of the trait of interest. Hence, IRT defines DIF in terms of the item trace line: If the trace line for an item is similar between two groups, its function is equivalent across groups; if the item trace lines differ between two groups, this is evidence of DIF. Figure 4.2 displays trace lines for a hypothetical depression scale that functions differently between two cultural groups. At any level of θ, it is less likely that a member of Group 1, the original group with whom the assessment instrument was developed, will endorse the depression scale item as self-descriptive, as compared with an individual from Group 2, the new cultural group with whom the measure is to be adopted. Holland and Wainer (1993) provided a detailed examination of DIF.

The item parameters in IRT are a numerical description of these trace lines. This means that hypothesis testing with the item parameters is equivalent to testing the lines themselves. As a result, a number of chi-square procedures were originally proposed to test the hypothesis that item parameters differ across groups (cf. Holland & Thayer, 1988). Beginning with Lord's (1977, 1980) procedure that used the Mahalanobis distance between parameters, more recent authors have proposed procedures that are more based within the context of IRT. These procedures analyze

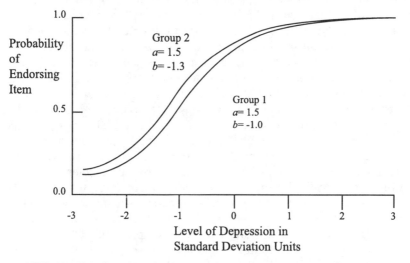

FIG. 4.2. Trace lines for a depression scale item displaying differential item functioning.

differences between the trace lines or make use of item factor analysis procedures. Thissen, Steinberg, and Wainer (1988) provided a brief discussion of DIF, a brief review of these procedures, and a detailed explanation and evaluation of two recent procedures that directly test hypotheses concerning item parameters: Lord's Mahalanobis distance procedure and their own marginal maximum likelihood procedure.

A number of important limitations exist regarding IRT procedures in tests of item equivalence. Two important assumptions must be met for the use of IRT with personality instruments. First, the set of items to be analyzed is assumed to be unidimensional, as demonstrated empirically, through factor analysis. Many personality instruments intended to measure a particular construct are multidimensional. Drasgow and Parsons (1983) suggested that IRT is relatively robust to violations of unidimensionality. However, others (e.g., Panter, Swygert, Dahlstrom, & Tanaka, 1997) have asserted that IRT is best used with empirically identified factor scales to ensure that properties of the IRT model are maintained in the analysis. Second, local independence must hold for the item set, that is, item responses must depend or be based on their common association with θ, the underlying personality trait or attribute, rather than other external variables related to the items themselves, such as the potential effects of item order, content carryover from other items, or use of common stem. Another limitation of IRT involves the relatively large sample sizes needed for stable parameter estimation—a major disadvantage for researchers who study small overall population groups. Finally, IRT yields findings regarding item equivalence, not conceptual equivalence of the construct.

This is an important distinction. Item equivalence on a test indicates that individual items function similarly across cultures or ethnic groups and that the observed score metrics are equivalent with regard to translation or word meaning. Item equivalence does not imply construct or conceptual equivalence. IRT does not provide a test of whether it may be appropriate to adopt the nomological network of the construct of interest to the new cultural or ethnic group. Further, these applications of IRT cannot provide information regarding the source of DIF, which may be the result of factors such as translation difficulty or cultural difference related to a specific cultural variable.

New developments in IRT modeling of dichotomous variables that extend the model to include external variables hold promise to address some of the limitations in the use of IRT to study DIF. Muthen (1988a) proposed the use of structural equation modeling (a larger set of procedures of which CFA is one application) as a means to extend IRT. This allows the researcher to explain DIF in terms of context variables, which could include measures of such variables as cultural identity and culture-specific processes hypothesized to influence test item functioning. The procedure allows for estimation of item parameters, the detection of DIF, the potential explanation of DIF through various culturally related variables, and relaxation of potentially problematic assumptions regarding unidimensionality and conditional independence. Muthen provided a detailed explanation and an example of the application of this procedure using LISCOMP software (Muthen, 1988b).

LIMITATIONS TO A CONSTRUCT APPROACH
TO EQUIVALENCE

Many important limitations exist regarding the construct-based approach to studying the equivalence of personality assessment instruments across cultural and ethnic groups. Directly relevant to the methodology is that these methods employ the logic of hypothesis disconfirmation. In other words, they do not establish cross-cultural or multicultural conceptual equivalence of the underlying construct tapped by the instrument. The methods reviewed only provide evidence to disconfirm equivalence. They test for measurement problems in the instrument that are incompatible with construct equivalence. Investigation of measurement invariance, the impact of culture-related variables, and differential item functioning provide methods to screen tests for the purpose of adoption with a new group. These steps are performed before embarking on careful research validating the measure with the new cultural or ethnic group. In addition, other forms of equivalence, including linguistic and metric equivalence, must also be attended to in adaptation of an instrument.

It is also important to bear in mind, as part of an evaluation of construct equivalence, the context within which a test may be used. Many people from varying cultural backgrounds have markedly different expectations regarding the nature of psychological services and, in particular, the service delivery style for assessment practice. Without attention and competence in these important skill areas of service delivery style, even use of a well-validated, culture-specific test as part of an assessment will not provide meaningful information regarding the individual. Okazaki and Sue (1995) pointed to a number of additional ways in which the conceptual equivalence of a construct can be dependent on context. For example, a measure for adolescents may be valid in a school setting wherein members of an ethnic group share the same environmental space and ecological context with members of other ethnic groups. However, the same construct may not be equivalent when the context shifts from the more mainstream cultural setting of the school to the more traditional setting of the family at home—or to other settings, such as street culture.

This chapter on methodological approaches, and much of personality assessment research in general, is rooted in the psychometric tradition and quantitative approaches. Many authors (e.g., Brink, 1994; Kleinman, 1988b) have argued that purely quantitative approaches are insufficient to adequately assess the depth and nuance of cultural factors. Methodologies that integrate qualitative approaches with assessment research are sorely needed.

Helms (1992) cautioned that the quantitative approach has also been used without regard to how cultural factors may impact the statistics and their assumptions. In particular, she noted that important assumptions regarding equal range, variance, and independence of groups have generally been unexamined in much of the cross-cultural and multicultural research on assessment.

CONSEQUENTIAL ASPECTS OF CONSTRUCT VALIDITY

Messick (1965, 1975, 1980, 1995) developed a comprehensive approach to construct validation over the course of three decades of work; it elevates a consideration of values and meaning as integral to the test validation process. Within this framework, he described six aspects of construct validity. This chapter focuses almost exclusively on only one aspect of construct validity—generalizability. It presents selected methodologies that can be used to screen personality assessment instruments for potential generalization of their interpretations across groups. As part of this consideration, we have touched on four other aspects of validation: content, or the item/material relevance; substantive, or whether the items/tasks actually engage processes tapped by the construct; structural, or investigation of the internal structure of the instrument; and external, which includes convergent and discriminant validation.

One final aspect of construct validity that this chapter has not yet touched on is the consequential aspect of validity. Use of any test should be appraised in light of the probable consequences of the testing. In this way, all test validation is rooted in values and meaning:

> One must inquire whether the potential and actual social consequences of test interpretation and use are not only supportive of the intended testing purposes, but also at the same time consistent with other social values. . . . Anticipation of likely outcomes may guide one where to look for side effects and toward what kinds of evidence are needed to monitor consequences; second, such anticipation may alert one to take timely steps to capitalize on positive effects and to ameliorate or forestall negative effects. (Messick, 1995, p. 744)

Multicultural and cross-cultural personality assessment research must concern itself with both generalizability and consequential aspects of construct validity. Messick (1995) described a progressive matrix unified validity approach to construct validation that begins with the evidential bases for validity of test interpretations and then integrates these with a consideration of the consequential basis of test interpretation. With regard to cross-cultural and multicultural personality assessment, we would add to this a consideration of context, including the ecological setting of the assessment, the cultural appropriateness of the assessment task, and the service delivery style expectations for the provider.

Much of the multicultural critique regarding current use of standardized personality instruments, and the existing research base to support such usage, is entirely consistent with the approaches to test validation proposed by many of construct theory's major architects. The current state of affairs and set of developments regarding testing controversies was not entirely unforseen by the early proponents of construct approaches to validation, who viewed construct validation as a continuing and unfinished process: ". . . fresh challenges follow shifts in social power or social philosophy. *So validation is never finished*" (Cronbach, 1988, p. 5; italics original).

REFERENCES

Allen, J. (1998). Personality assessment with American Indians and Alaska Natives: Instrument considerations and service delivery style. *Journal of Personality Assessment, 70*, 17–42.

Ben-Porath, Y. S. (1990). Cross-cultural assessment of personality: The case for replicatory factor analysis. In J. N. Butcher & C. D. Spielberger (Eds.), *Advances in personality assessment* (Vol. 8, pp. 27–48). Hillsdale, NJ: Lawrence Erlbaum Associates.

Bentler, P. M. (1982). Confirmatory factor analysis via noniterative estimation: A fast, inexpensive method. *Journal of Marketing Research, 19*, 417–424.

Bentler, P. M. (1990). Comparative fit indices in structural models. *Psychological Bulletin, 107*, 238–246.

Bentler, P. M. (1992). *EQS: Structural equations program manual.* Los Angeles: BMDP Statistical Software.

Bentler, P. M., & Bonnet, D. G. (1980). Significance test and goodness of fit in the analysis of covariance structures. *Psychological Bulletin, 88*, 588–606.

Berry, J. W. (1980). Introduction to methodology. In H. C. Triandis & J. W. Berry (Eds.), *Handbook of cross-cultural psychology: Vol 2* (pp. 1–28). Boston: Allyn & Bacon.

Betancourt, H., & Lopez, S. R. (1993). The study of culture, ethnicity, and race in American psychology. *American Psychologist, 48*, 629–637.

Birnbaum, A. (1968). Some latent trait models and their use in inferring an examinee's ability. In F. M. Lord & M. R. Novick (Eds.), *Statistical theories of mental test scores* (pp. 392–479). Reading, MA: Addison-Wesley.

Bollen, K. A. (1989). *Structural equations with latent variables.* New York: Wiley.

Bollen, K. A. (1990). Overall fit in covariance structure models: Two types of sample size effects. *Psychological Bulletin, 107*, 256–259.

Bollen, K. A., & Long, J. S. (Eds.). (1993). *Testing structural equation models.* Newbury Park, CA: Sage.

Brink, T. L. (1994). The need for qualitative research on the mental health of elderly Hispanics. *International Journal of Aging and Human Development, 38*, 279–291.

Brislin, R. W. (1993). *Understanding culture's influence on behavior.* New York: Harcourt Brace.

Butcher, J. N., & Han, K. (1996). Methods of establishing cross-cultural equivalence. In J. N. Butcher (Ed.), *International adaptations of the MMPI–2: Research and clinical applications* (pp. 44–63). Minneapolis, MN: University of Minnesota Press.

Byrne, B. M. (1989). *A primer of LISREL: Basic applications and programming for confirmatory factor analytic models.* New York: Springer.

Byrne, B. M. (1994). *Structural equation modeling with EQS and EQS/Windows: Basic concepts, applications, and programming.* Newbury Park, CA: Sage.

Campbell, D. T., & Fiske, D. W. (1959). Convergent and discriminant validation by the multitrait-multimethod matrix. *Psychological Bulletin, 56*, 81–105.

Cleary, T. A. (1968). Test bias: Prediction of grades of Negro and white students in integrated colleges. *Journal of Educational Measurement, 10*, 43–56.

Clark, L. A. (1987). Mutual relevance of mainstream and cross-cultural psychology. *Journal of Consulting and Clinical Psychology, 55*, 461–470.

Constantino, G., Malgady, R. G., & Rogler, L. H. (1988). *Technical manual: The TEMAS thematic apperception test.* Los Angeles: Western Psychological Services.

Cook, T. D., & Campbell, D. T. (1979). *Quasi-experimentation: Design and analysis issues for field settings.* Chicago: Rand McNally.

Cronbach, L. J. (1971). Test validation. In R. L. Thorndike (Ed.), *Educational measurement* (2nd ed., pp. 433–507). Washington, DC: American Council on Education.

Cronbach, L. J. (1988). Five perspectives on validity argument. In H. Wainer & H. I. Braun (Eds.), *Test validity* (pp. 3–17). Hillsdale, NJ: Lawrence Erlbaum Associates.

Cronbach, L. J., & Meehl, P. E. (1955). Construct validity in psychological tests. *Psychological Bulletin, 52*, 281–302.

Crowley, S. L., & Fan, X. (1997). Structural equation modeling: Basic concepts and applications in personality assessment research. In J. A. Schinka & R. L. Greene (Eds.), *Emerging issues and methods in personality assessment* (pp. 285–307). Mahwah, NJ: Lawrence Erlbaum Associates.

Cudek, R. (1989). Analysis of correlation matrices using covariance structure models. *Psychological Bulletin, 105*, 317–327.

Dana, R. H. (1993). *Multicultural assessment perspectives for professional psychology.* Boston: Allyn & Bacon.

Dana, R. H. (1998). Cultural identity assessment of culturally diverse groups: 1997. *Journal of Personality Assessment, 70*, 1–16.

Dinges, N., & Cherry, D. (1995). Symptom expression and the use of mental health services among American ethnic minorities. In J. E. Aponte, R. Y. Rivers, & J. Wohl (Eds.), *Psychological interventions and cultural diversity* (pp. 40–56). Needham Heights, MA: Allyn & Bacon.

Drasgow, F., & Parsons, C. K. (1983). Application of unidimensional item response models to multidimensional data. *Applied Psychological Measurement, 7*, 189–199.

Dunnigan, T., McNall, M., & Mortimer, J. T. (1993). The problem of metaphorical nonequivalence in cross-cultural survey research: Comparing the mental health statuses of Hmong refugee and general population adolescents. *Journal of Cross-Cultural Psychology, 24*, 344–365.

Flaugher, R. J. (1978). The many definitions of test bias. *American Psychologist, 33*, 671–679.

Floyd, F. J., & Widaman, K. F. (1995). Factor analysis in the development and refinement of clinical assessment instruments. *Psychological Assessment, 7*, 286–299.

Geisinger, K. F. (1994). Cross-cultural normative assessment: Translation and adaptation issues influencing the normative interpretation of assessment instruments. *Psychological Assessment, 6*, 304–312.

Gorush, R. L. (1983). *Factor analysis* (2nd ed.). Hillsdale, NJ: Lawrence Erlbaum Associates.

Guadagnoli, E., & Velicer, W. F. (1988). Relation of sample size to the stability of component patterns. *Psychological Bulletin, 103*, 265–275.

Guilford, J. P. (1942). *Fundamental statistics in psychology and education.* New York: McGraw-Hill.

Hambleton, R. K., Swaminathan, H., & Rogers, H. J. (1991). *Fundamentals of item response theory.* Newbury Park, CA: Sage.

Helms, J. E. (1992). Why is there no study of cultural equivalence in standardized cognitive ability testing? *American Psychologist, 47*, 1083–1101.

Holland, P. W., & Thayer, D. T. (1988). Differential item performance and the Mantel–Haenszel procedure. In H. Wainer & H. I. Braun (Eds.), *Test validity* (pp. 129–145). Hillsdale, NJ: Lawrence Erlbaum Associates.

Holland, P. W., & Wainer, H. (Eds.). (1993). *Differential item functioning.* Hillsdale, NJ: Lawrence Erlbaum Associates.

Hunter, J. E., & Schmidt, F. L. (1976). Critical analysis of the statistical and ethical implications of various definitions of test bias. *Psychological Bulletin, 83*, 1053–1071.

Jöreskog, K. G., & Sörbom, D. (1989). *LISREL 7: User's reference guide.* Mooresville, IN: Scientific Software.

Kleinman, A. (1988a). *Illness narratives.* New York: Basic Books.

Kleinman, A. (1988b). *Rethinking psychiatry: From cultural category to personal experience.* New York: The Free Press.

Lazarsfeld, P. F. (1950). The logical and mathematical foundation of latent structure analysis. In S. A. Stouffer, L. Guttman, E. A. Suchman, P. F. Lazarsfeld, S. A. Star, & J. A. Clausen (Eds.), *Measurement and prediction* (pp. 362–472). New York: Wiley.

Lindsay, M. L. (1998). Culturally competent assessment of African-American clients. *Journal of Personality Assessment, 70*, 43–44.

Loehlin, J. C. (1992). *Latent variable models: An introduction to factor, path, and structural equations analysis.* Hillsdale, NJ: Lawrence Erlbaum Associates.

Lopez, S. R., & Romero, A. (1988). Assessing the intellectual functioning of Spanish-speaking adults: Comparison of the EIWA and the WAIS. *Professional Psychology: Research and Practice, 19*, 263–270.

Lord, F. M. (1952). A theory of test scores. *Psychometric Monographs*, Whole Monographs No. 7.

Lord, F. M. (1977). A study of item bias using item characteristic curve theory. In Y. H. Poortinga (Ed.), *Basic problems in cross-cultural research* (pp. 19–29). Amsterdam: Swets & Zeitlinger.

Lord, F. M. (1980). *Application of item response theory to practical testing problems.* Hillsdale, NJ: Lawrence Erlbaum Associates.

Malgady, R. G. (1996). The question of cultural bias in assessment and diagnosis of ethnic minority clients: Let's reject the null hypothesis. *Professional Psychology: Research and Practice, 27*, 33–73.

Manson, S. M. (1994). Culture and depression: Discovering variations in the experience of illness. In W. J. Lonner & R. S. Malpass (Eds.), *Psychology and culture* (pp. 285–290). Boston, MA: Allyn & Bacon.

Manson, S. M. (1995). Culture and major depression: Current challenges in the diagnosis of mood disorders. *Psychiatric Clinics of North America, 18*, 487–501.

Messick, S. (1965). Personality measurement and the ethics of assessment. *American Psychologist, 20,* 136–142.

Messick, S. (1975). The standard problem: Meaning and values in measurement and education. *American Psychologist, 30,* 955–966.

Messick, S. (1980). Test validity and the ethics of assessment. *American Psychologist, 35,* 1012–1027.

Messick, S. (1995). Validity of psychological assessment: Validation of inferences from persons' responses and performances as scientific inquiry into score meaning. *American Psychologist, 50,* 741–749.

Mislevy, R. J., & Bock, R. D. (1986). *BILOG I maximum likelihood item analysis and test scoring with binary logistic models* [Computer program]. Mooresville, IN: Scientific Software.

Muthen, B. (1988a). Some uses of structural equation modeling in validity studies: Extending IRT to external variables. In H. Wainer & H. I. Braun (Eds.), *Test validity* (pp. 213–238). Hillsdale, NJ: Lawrence Erlbaum Associates.

Muthen, B. (1988b). *LISCOMP. Analysis of linear structural equations using a comprehensive measurement model. User's guide.* Mooresville, IN: Scientific Software.

Nunnally, J. C., & Bernstein, I. H. (1994). *Psychometric theory* (3rd ed.). New York: McGraw-Hill.

Okazaki, S., & Sue, S. (1995). Methodological issues in assessment research with ethnic minorities. *Psychological Assessment, 7,* 367–375.

Panter, A. T., Swygert, K. A., Dahlstrom, W. G., & Tanaka, J. S. (1997). Factor analytic approaches to personality item-level data. In J. A. Schinka & R. L. Greene (Eds.), *Emerging issues and methods in personality assessment* (pp. 285–307). Mahwah, NJ: Lawrence Erlbaum Associates.

Pedhazur, E. J. (1982). *Multiple regression in behavioral research* (2nd ed.). New York: Holt, Rinehart & Winston.

Radloff, L. S. (1977). A CES-D scale: A self-report scale for research in the general population. *Applied Psychological Measurement, 1,* 385–401.

Rasch, G. (1960). *Probabilistic models for some intelligence and attainment tests.* Copenhagen: Danish Institute for Educational Research.

Rogler, L. H., Malgady, R. G., & Rodriguez, O. (1989). *Hispanics and mental health: A framework for research.* Malabalar, FL: Krieger.

SAS Institute, Inc. (1990). *SAS/STAT user's guide* (Version 6, 4th ed., Vol. 1). Cary, NC: Author.

Sue, S. (1991). A conceptual model for cultural diversity. *Journal of Counseling and Development, 70,* 99–105.

Tanaka, J. S. (1993). Multifaceted conceptions of fit in structural equations models. In K. A. Bollen & J. S. Long (Eds.), *Testing structural equation models* (pp. 10–39). Newbury Park, CA: Sage.

Thissen, D. (1991). *MULTILOG* [Computer program]. Mooresville, IN: Scientific Software.

Thissen, D., Steinberg, L., & Wainer, H. (1988). Use of item response theory in the study of group differences in trace lines. In H. Wainer & H. I. Braun (Eds.), *Test validity* (pp. 213–238). Hillsdale, NJ: Lawrence Erlbaum Associates.

Van de Vijver, F. J. R,. & Poortinga, Y. H. (1991). Testing across cultures. In R.K. Hambleton & J. N. Zaal (Eds.), *Advances in educational and psychological testing* (pp. 214–230). Boston: Kluwer.

Van de Vijver, F. J. R., & Poortinga, Y. H. (1997). Towards an integrated analysis of bias in cross-cultural assessment. *European Journal of Psychological Assessment, 13,* 29–37.

Wainer, H., & Braun, H. I. (Eds.). (1988). *Test validity.* Hillsdale, NJ: Lawrence Erlbaum Associates.

5

The Nature of Bias

Fons Van de Vijver
Tilburg University, The Netherlands

The nature of the migration in the United States has changed. Until recently, the predominant acculturation mode was the *melting pot*—an assimilationist model of unidirectional movement from the original cultures to mainstream ones (Gordon, 1964). However, it has become increasingly clear that complete absorption into American culture, with the inherent loss of the original culture and language, is not pursued by all immigrants (see Berry & Sam, 1997; Choney, Berryhill-Paapke, & Robbins, 1995, for recent overviews of acculturation research). Many immigrants either want to develop a bicultural identity or retain their original culture without making extensive adjustments to American society. These trends are not restricted to the United States. As an example, both children and adults of Turkish descent in the Netherlands prefer to develop a bicultural identity (e.g., Van de Vijver, Helms-Lorenz, & Feltzer, in press).

This global change is probably fueled by two factors. The first is the sheer magnitude of migration. According to Sue (1991), in 2010, more than half of the U.S. population will be composed of visible racial and ethnic groups. Second, the Zeitgeist of the assimilationist doctrine is gradually giving way. For a mixture of reasons, ranging from humanitarian to economic, the *melting pot* doctrine is slowly being replaced by more variegated perspectives on acculturation.

These developments provide impetus to the development of culture-informed assessment practices (e.g., APA Office of Ethnic Minority Affairs, 1993). According to Dana (1996), these practices lead to changes in various aspects of assessment: (a) cultural orientation/acculturation, (b)

culturally appropriate styles of service delivery, (c) assessment methodology, and (d) feedback to the client. The present chapter focuses on the
third aspect, although occasionally references are made to the other aspects (e.g., acculturation).

The present chapter mainly deals with methodological issues of projective assessment in a cross-cultural and multicultural context. Current
cross-cultural research with projective tests is scarce (Lonner & Ibrahim,
1989). Psychological anthropologists in the 1940s and 1950s had more
interest in projective tests. They assumed that such tests would give them
access to the basic personality of non-Western cultures. This expectation
was short-lived. In Piker's (1998) words,

> the early optimism about the prospects of the Rorschach quickly faded,
> . . . as serious questions developed about the reliability and replicability of
> scoring procedures with western subjects, the absence of statistical norms
> for virtually all nonwestern cultures in which the test was employed, and
> the culture-bound nature of the testing situation, regardless of how culture-
> free the ink blots themselves might be. (p. 25)

Psychological anthropologists have ceased to apply projective tests ever
since.

Multicultural testing is a more promising area for the employment of
projective techniques in the coming decades, particularly in the United
States. The combination of the popularity of projective techniques among
clinicians and the expected increase in demand for their services by
cultural and ethnic groups makes an increased usage likely. There are no
comparative studies of projective tests in a multicultural setting (cf.
Costantino, Malgady, & Rogler, 1988). Yet like all other psychological
instruments, projective tests should be psychometrically adequate. The
culturally blind application of an instrument and foreign norms is inde-
fensible. The present chapter attempts to formulate a theoretical background to studies and applications of projective instruments in a cross-
cultural and multicultural setting.

The next section describes the concept of bias, followed by a taxonomy
of bias that is relevant for projective assessment in a multicultural and
cross-cultural context. The fourth section describes ways of dealing with
bias. Conclusions are drawn in the final section.

BIAS

The key concept in evaluating the adequacy of a multicultural or cross-
cultural assessment procedure is bias. *Bias* is a lack of similarity of psychological meaning of test scores across cultural groups. Bias can emanate

from various sources. For example, it has been argued that classical Western personality measures do not cover salient aspects of non-Western personality. In developing a Chinese personality measure, Cheung et al. (1996) found that common Western personality measures did not contain measures of culturally salient dimensions of Chinese personality such as *face* and *harmony*. In other cases, bias sources are more mundane. In the development of a culturally appropriate Thematic Apperception Test (TAT) for India, faces and dresses were *Indianized* to facilitate identification (cf. Misra, Sahoo, & Puhan, 1997).

In addition to bias, *equivalence* is often defined as an essential feature of cross-cultural and multicultural assessment. The two concepts are strongly related, but have a somewhat different connotation. Bias refers to the presence or absence of validity-threatening factors in such assessment, whereas equivalence involves the consequences of these factors on the comparability of test scores. For reasons of brevity, equivalence is not further considered here. For a fuller description of equivalence (and its statistical methodological meaning), the reader is referred to Poortinga (1989) and Van de Vijver and Leung (1997a, 1997b).

Various studies have examined bias in mental tests and objective personality measures (e.g., Church & Lonner, 1998; Holland & Wainer, 1993; Jensen, 1980). However, bias in projective tests has never been the subject of empirical scrutiny (Costantino, Flanagan, & Malgady, 1995; Dana, 1998b). Regular psychometric conditions, such as reliability, validity, and absence of bias, also apply to projective tests (Dana, 1962). Empirical studies are needed to show the suitability of such applications to gain scientific credibility. The need for such studies is underscored by the widespread usage of projective instruments and their popularity in clinical teaching programs (Weiner, 1997), especially in Spanish- and Portuguese-speaking countries (Fagulha & Dana, 1997). If they support the adequacy of an instrument and its scoring, these studies would serve a double purpose. First, they provide counterevidence against critiques often leveled at projective tests. Second, such studies help improve the quality of professional services delivered to ethnic groups by adding culturally validated instruments.

A TAXONOMY OF BIAS IN PROJECTIVE INSTRUMENTS

The transition from recorded responses to scores on previously defined categories, such as Exner's (1986, 1991) system of Rorschach scoring, and the subsequent interpretation require extensive training. In particular, the latter aspect demands specialized expertise. In Groth-Marnat's (1997) words: "the same number of C responses in two protocols can easily have quite different meanings, depending on the implications from, and interactions with, other aspects of the Rorschach data" (p. 422). To clinicians, such a freedom of interpretation may constitute a major asset of projective tests. However, psychometricians are more likely to see this as a liability of the procedure. They point to the need to specify conditions when which interpretation should be chosen. Interpretation problems are an even greater challenge in multicultural and cross-cultural applications. Without a good knowledge of the patient's cultural background, it becomes tempting for the diagnostician to apply common standards of interpreting a protocol, which may be partly or even wholly inadequate for interpreting the responses of a person from a different cultural background. Without precaution, the strength of projective tests, the freedom to generate and interpret responses, can easily become their Achilles heel.

How can we decide about the adequacy of an instrument, the test score, and its interpretation for an individual? Determining the adequacy of a measure amounts to addressing its bias. When an item, subtest, or test does not measure the same psychological construct across cultural groups, bias is said to occur. Biased scores have a meaning that is culture-specific. Hence, they cannot be compared across cultures. Following Van de Vijver and Leung (1997a, 1997b) and Van de Vijver and Poortinga (1997), three types of bias are distinguished depending on whether the bias is engendered by the theoretical construct (construct bias), the method of assessment such as the form of test administration (method bias), or the item content (item bias).

As a fairly arbitrary example in projective tests, consider the *suicide constellation* of the Rorschach, in which various category scores are combined in an attempt to identify individuals at risk for committing suicide (Exner, 1986). Since Durkheim's work, we have known that suicide rates vary across cultural groups. It is doubtful whether these variations are effectively gauged by a scoring system that has been developed for an Anglo-American group. The contribution of the different categories may well vary across cultural groups, especially for a taboo topic like suicide. The TAT shows similar problems. The conversion of responses to scores is not always straightforward. As a consequence, there is considerable room for bias. In general, the adequacy of the scoring categories for a particular cultural group cannot be merely assumed; reliability and validity of the scoring schemes should be established.

Construct Bias

A measure shows construct bias if the construct measured is not identical across cultural groups. Lack of identity could be induced by a lack of overlap in behaviors associated with the construct in the cultures studied (see Table 5.1). Ho (1996) examined the concept of *filial piety* in China. The concept refers to the behaviors associated with being a good son or daughter. Nonmaterial aspects turned out to be shared by Western and Chinese subjects, such as obedience and respect. However, the Chinese conceptualization also included material aspects, such as taking care of one's parents and conforming to their requests.

Another example comes from work on depression among Native Americans and Alaska Natives. Factor analyses of Radloff's (1977) Center for Epidemiological Studies Depression scale have been carried out on data obtained among these groups. Radloff reported four independent factors among Anglo-Americans, whereas applications among Native Americans/Alaska Natives tend to find highly correlated Depressed Affect and Somatic Complaint factors (Allen, 1998). There is more evidence that cultures differ in their relative contribution and distinctiveness of psychological and somatic complaints in depression. For instance, Tanaka-

TABLE 5.1
Typical Sources for the Three Types of Bias in
Multicultural and Cross-Cultural Projective Assessment
(modified after Van de Vijver & Poortinga, 1997)

Type of Bias	Source of Bias
Construct Bias	Only partial overlap in the definitions of the construct across cultures
	Differential appropriateness of the behaviors associated with the construct (e.g., skills do not belong to the repertoire of a cultural group)
	Poor sampling of all relevant behaviors (e.g., short instruments)
	Incomplete coverage of all relevant aspects/facets of the construct (e.g., not all relevant domains are sampled)
Method Bias	Incomparability of individuals from different ethnic and cultural groups (e.g., caused by differences in education, motivation)[a]
	Differential knowledge of testing language[a]
	Differential familiarity with stimulus material and response procedures[b]
	Differential response styles (e.g., social desirability, extremity scoring, acquiescence)[b]
	Inappropriate scoring of responses[b]
	Differences in environmental administration conditions, physical (e.g., recording devices), or social (e.g., class size)[c]
	Ambiguous instructions for clients/respondents and/or guidelines for administrators[c]
	Differential expertise of administrators[c]
	Tester/counselor effects (e.g., eisegesis)[c]
	Communication problems between client/respondent and tester/counselor[c]
Item Bias	Poor item translation or differential expression of essential aspects of pictorial material
	Nuisance factors (e.g., item or picture may invoke different psychological functions)
	Cultural specifics (e.g., accidental differences in connotative meaning and/or appropriateness of the item or picture content)

[a]Sample bias. [b]Instrument bias. [c]Administration bias.

Matsumi and Marsella (1976) found that when Japanese and Americans were asked to generate words associated with depression, the latter group referred more often to mood states, whereas the former gave more somatic responses. Similarly, Kleinman (1977), working with depressive students in Taiwan, found that most patients came to him with somatic complaints. In service delivery to cultural and ethnic groups in the Netherlands, the high frequency with which somatic complaints are expressed is considered to constitute a major problem for physicians and psychologists, who often experience difficulty in getting to the *real* problem. Acculturation processes or, more generally, cultural change may affect this pattern. Hutschemaekers (1990) carried out a large-scale study of files from Dutch psychiatric institutions from the end of last century to the 1960s. Symptoms expressed to the psychiatrists were examined. He found an almost uninterrupted decrease of somatic complaints and an increase of psychological complaints throughout the entire period.

Construct bias has major implications for assessment. Suppose that, as part of a study of the immensely popular individualism–collectivism dimension (e.g., Triandis, 1995), we want to compare filial piety in the United States and China. If we include nonmaterial aspects, the measure will be adequate for the United States but not for China. In contrast, if material aspects are also included, the measure will only measure the intended construct in China. The problem can be solved by explicitly defining the behavioral domain that is included in the measure, such as "immaterial aspects of filial piety." Such a specification avoids sweeping, invalid generalizations about cross-cultural differences.

Assessment in multicultural populations may often be troubled by construct bias. Incomplete coverage of psychological constructs may be fairly common. In delivering clinical services to a relatively small cultural group, a psychologist may not have an instrument that is known to be a reliable and valid measure of the construct of interest. He or she can then decide to rely on instruments, such as the NEO–PI–R or other instruments, that are known to have a cross-culturally robust factor structure. However, as shown by Cheung et al. (1996) with regard to the Big Five, these broad instruments may leave out aspects of psychological functioning that are deemed salient by a specific cultural and ethnic group. Thus, the application of instruments with a presumably universal underlying structure may inadvertently not touch on locally salient aspects of the construct. These aspects may be relevant for clinical practice.

Method Bias

Method bias refers to the presence of nuisance variables due to method-related factors. The term was coined because such factors are usually described in the method section of empirical papers. A further subdivision of method bias types is based on the common triplet of sample, instruments, and procedure. These are labeled *sample, instrument,* and *administration bias,* respectively.

Sample Bias. Cross-cultural comparisons can yield misleading results when samples in which the data are obtained differ in test-relevant background characteristics, such as level of education, motivation, or knowledge of the testing language.

Sample bias is a recurrent problem in the assessment of heterogeneous populations. From a psychological perspective, the distinction between mainstream and migrant groups is a misnomer. Cultural variation among migrants is immense in most Western countries. Okazaki (1998) aptly pointed out that, even within the population of Asian and Pacific Islander Americans, 25 countries are represented, each with their own language, cultural background, and migration history.

Weiner (1995) pointed to the problem of volunteer bias. Particularly in the case of uncommon clinical groups, it may be difficult to obtain truly representative samples. In these cases, researchers show an understandable, although regrettable, tendency of "recruiting previously untested volunteers who happen to be conveniently available in one particular setting at some particular time" (p. 331). Dana (1998a) cited studies in which social class effects in projective data were found.

As another example, language problems may arise in a multicultural context. Cultural and ethnic groups may differ in their mastery of the testing language. In projective tests, individuals have considerable latitude in how they choose to respond. Level of proficiency of the testing language may be a good predictor of the number of responses generated. Invalid conclusions are likely to be drawn when the nature and quantity of an individual's response are limited by knowledge of the testing language. In all these examples, we may be inclined to infer that we have observed valid cross-cultural differences where it would be more appropriate and prudent to conclude that the samples differ in a test-relevant background characteristic.

Instrument Bias. This type of bias involves instrument characteristics that induce cross-cultural score differences that are unrelated to the construct studied. The most important sources of instrument bias are cultural and ethnic group differences in stimulus familiarity in mental testing and response styles and social desirability in personality and attitude questionnaires (e.g., Arvey, Strickland, Drauden, & Martin; 1990; Deregowksi & Serpell, 1971; Hui & Triandis, 1989; Nkaya, Huteau, & Bonnet, 1994; Oakland, Gulek, & Glutting, 1996; Ross & Mirowsky, 1984; Serpell, 1979).

The unfamiliarity of pictorial material, as used in many projective techniques, may be a source of unwanted cross-cultural differences. The testing situation in which the individual is asked to start talking about a vague stimulus with a moderate ecological validity at best may not be conducive to the response-generating process in which the psychologist is interested. In particular, poorly educated individuals may find such a situation difficult to deal with. Regrettably, no empirical studies of the influence of these factors in multicultural contexts have been carried out despite their obvious relevance. An example can be found in a study by Bleuler and Bleuler (1935; cited in Lindzey, 1961). Working with the Rorschach, they found that Moroccans gave many Small Detail responses—a sign of schizophrenia. It is likely that this tendency is due to the lack of experience of Islamic individuals with this type of pictorial material. It is well known from cross-cultural research that persons who have never been exposed to pictures may have a tendency to describe details rather than the picture as a whole (such as naming legs and a head instead of the whole animal; e.g., Deregowski, Muldrow, & Muldrow, 1972).

Scoring rules of responses to projective instruments may constitute a final source of instrument bias. For some projective tests, there is no agreed on procedure to assign scores to categories. However, even if such rules exist, their validity for a particular cultural and ethnic group may not have been shown. These problems, which can trouble intracultural usage of an instrument, can only be exacerbated when an instrument is employed in a multicultural or cross-cultural context.

Administration Bias. A final source of method bias stems from personal characteristics of the psychologist and his or her interaction with the respondent/client. Dana (1966) introduced the term *eisegesis* to refer to all "interpretive inferences from projective data that are prone to contamination by unacknowledged assessor fantasy, personalization and/or bias" (Dana, 1998b, p. 171). Tacit views toward cultural groups or the multicultural society held by assessors may have an uncontrolled influence on the outcome of projective assessment, irrespective of the nature of these views.

Empirical studies have reported administration bias. Thus, Masling (1997) mentioned a study (Masling & Harris, 1969) that found that

> male clinicians use the four sexual-romantic cards (of the Thematic Apperception Test) more frequently with female clients than with men . . . whereas female clinicians either used these cards with both male and female clients or did not use them at all. (p. 260)

As another example, Weiner (1995) reported that

both children and adults give more responses and embellish their responses more fully when they are tested by someone they know than when they are given the Rorschach by an unfamiliar examiner. (p. 331)

The influence of the administrator has been examined in various studies using objective tests. With a few notable exceptions, neither interviews (Singer & Presser, 1989) nor mental tests (Jensen, 1980) tend to be strongly influenced by administrator characteristics, such as gender, age, and ethnic group. Future studies should determine how these conclusions hold for projective instruments. Such a generalizability should be demonstrated and not merely assumed.

Self-disclosure is another characteristic that may have a bearing on the interaction of tester and testee and the observed responsivity. Cross-cultural research has pointed to the existence of salient differences between cultural and ethnic groups in the tendency to disclose private information to strangers (such as a tester or counselor). According to Smith and Bond (1993), persons from individualist cultures are less reluctant to communicate private matters to strangers than are persons from collectivist cultures. The United States has a high score on individualism. As a consequence, Anglo-American psychologists who serve in multicultural groups will often work with clients who are less inclined to share personal matters with strangers than are clients of their own cultural group.

Item Bias

An item of an anxiety scale is said to be biased if persons with the same trait anxiety, but coming from different cultures, are not equally likely to endorse the item. As a hypothetical example, the item "Are you afraid when you walk alone on the street in the middle of the night?" may be responded to differently by persons depending on the safety of their neighborhood, even when the persons would have equal total scores on the questionnaire.

Reasons for such differential response patterns may be, among other things, differential applicability of a picture across cultural contexts, inadequate adaptations of pictures that make particular aspects less or more salient, and the depiction of persons or objects with a different connotation. This type of bias, also known as *differential item functioning* (Berk, 1982; Holland & Wainer, 1993), has been extensively studied by psychometricians.

Item bias in projective tests has never been studied. Yet it would be interesting to apply statistical procedures—aimed to identify biased items—to projective tests. Such a study could address questions such as: Do the same Rorschach inkblots give rise to pure form responses in various cultural and ethnic groups? Do persons with the same score on some category, such as anxiety, show the same pattern of high and low scores on the various inkblots? From a statistical perspective, such a study would be straightforward.

Influence of Bias on Test Scores

The three types of bias do not all have the same influence on test scores. Construct and method bias have a global influence on test scores. Let us return to our example of filial piety. A comparison of Chinese and American scores on a test of filial piety will reveal a difference on all aspects of the concept. Because it is impossible to design an instrument that adequately covers all aspects in both countries, scores cannot be compared across countries. The only solution involves reformulation of the target construct of the instrument (e.g., nonmaterial aspects of filial piety).

Method bias also has a global influence on test scores. For example, if persons from a particular cultural group have a low self-disclosure or are not familiar with working with pictorial stimuli, scores on all items will be affected. Method bias leads to an increase or decrease in average scores of a cultural group, which cannot be attributed to the construct measured. Method bias invalidates interpretations of responses to projective tests because it gives rise to score differences, which are induced by methodological aspects of the study.

As its name already suggests, item bias exerts a less global and more local influence on test scores than the other forms of bias. An item that is inadequately translated may measure different psychological constructs in the two languages. An example can be found in the European Value Survey (L. Halman, personal communication, April 21, 1998). This scale of value orientations contained an item about loyalty. The Spanish language version yielded cross-cultural differences that were highly different from those on other items. On closer examination, it appeared that, unlike in other languages, the Spanish word for *loyalty* that was used has the connotation of sexual faithfulness.

It can be concluded that bias always invalidates cross-cultural comparisons. To compare scores across cultures, the absence of any type of bias has to be confirmed. There is no rationale for the often observed practice to compare scores across cultural and ethnic groups without any concern for the occurrence of bias.

HOW TO DEAL WITH BIAS

In this section, various ways to deal with bias are described. Two types of approaches are discussed: (a) the pros and cons of developing culture-specific tests and norms, and (b) the ways to address construct, method, and item bias.

Scores on instruments in which one or more items are biased cannot be compared across cultures. To make scores comparable across cultures, the biased items should be left out of the comparison. Despite these methodological concerns, the observation that an item is biased may be interesting from a psychological perspective and may provide the beginning of a fruitful exploration of cross-cultural differences.

As an example, Spielberger (1988) distinguished in his State–Trait Anger Expression Inventory three styles of anger expression: Anger Out as expression of anger toward other people or objects, Anger In as holding in or the suppression of angry feelings, and Anger Control as an attempt to control the expression of anger (cf. Van de Vijver & Tanzer, 1997). The postulated three-factor structure of the original English anger expression items was confirmed in several countries, such as Germany, Norway, and Singapore. However, in some studies, the item "I am secretly quite critical of others" shifted from Anger In to Anger Out. This item could be interpreted as either privately holding grudges, which would then be an Anger-In expression, or as "talking negatively behind someone's back," which would convey a covert Anger-Out expression. Depending on cultural norms on the freedom to communicate such emotions, either interpretation may be chosen and the item may appear on one or the other factor. Although such an item may well challenge the comparability of the scales, it also provides interesting information about the expression of anger in different societies.

Culture-Specific Tests and Norms

If a projective test would turn out to show bias, it is prudent to refrain from all cross-cultural comparisons. The actual or suspected bias may be the starting point of efforts to develop culture-specific norms or instruments. Examples of such instruments are the Hispanic Stress Inventory (Cervantes, Padilla, & Salgado de Snyder, 1990, 1991), the Holtzman Inkblot Test (Holtzman, Thorpe, & Herron, 1981), and TEMAS—a projective test for which test versions and validation data exist for various cultural and ethnic groups in the United States (Costantino, Malgady, & Rogler, 1988). Major assets of culture-specific tests are the high ecological validity of the instrument and the allowance to delve into culture-specific aspects of a particular construct. Such tools may be useful or even indispensable for high-quality service delivery to these groups.

Despite the obvious need to develop more culture-specific tests, both in non-Western cultures and multicultural societies, their usage requires attention to the following issues. First, culture-specific tests cannot be used for cross-cultural comparisons. Sattler (1992; cited in Lindsey, 1998) argued that pluralistic norms "provide a basis for invidious comparisons among different ethnic groups" (p. 45). The present writer agrees. Cross-cultural score comparisons based on culture-specific instruments or norms are invalid due to the presence of bias.

Second, cultures are continuously changing, and this maxim holds a fortiori for acculturating groups in multicultural societies (Okazaki, 1998). Moreover, most acculturating groups show a large variation of cultural adjustment to the original and main culture. It may be difficult to answer the question of which cultural group an acculturating individual belongs (Lonner & Ibrahim, 1989). Should we rely on self-reports (e.g., self-declared ethnic identity, proficiency in the languages of the original and main culture), demographic variables (e.g., length of residence, educational history), or still other criteria (e.g., judgments by peers)? Some criteria may be unreliable and not all criteria will show convergent information (Dana, 1998a). Depending on their acculturation status, members of cultural and ethnic groups may be more adequately assessed using instruments or norms made for their original culture or for the main culture.

It can be concluded that it is not fruitful to answer the question of whether culture-specific instruments or norms should be developed. Rather, it makes more sense to delineate conditions in which such tests or norms can add to the validity and quality of assessment. The delivery of psychological services in which there is no culture-comparative element, such as counseling, may profit from the development and application of culture-specific tests. A complete coverage of psychological constructs is essential in clinical assessment; it is immaterial whether an instrument has a universal or culture-specific applicability. However, when there is an interest in comparing psychological constructs across cultures, culture-specific instruments do not provide a legitimate basis for comparison. These measures can only help demonstrate the (in)validity of other instruments used for cross-cultural comparisons. In summary, the question vis-à-vis culture-specific tests is not whether they should be developed, but when they should be applied.

Construct Bias

The remainder of this section describes approaches to deal with bias in studies, in which the same instrument is employed in different cultural and ethnic groups. There are various ways to address construct bias (Table 5.2). For example, if one is interested in comparing anxiety across various ethnic groups in the United States, one could form a group of researchers from all intended cultural groups. When so much cultural expertise is invested in the development of an instrument, construct bias is likely to be detected even before the instrument is applied for the first time.

Other effective means of addressing construct bias (and/or method bias) are the use of local informants and bilingual subjects. These persons

TABLE 5.2
Strategies for Identifying and Dealing With Bias
(after van de Vijver & Tanzer, 1997)

Type of Bias	Strategies
Construct Bias	Decentering (i.e., simultaneously developing the same instrument in several cultures)
	Convergence approach (i.e., independent within-culture development of instruments and subsequent cross-cultural administration of all instruments)
Construct Bias and/or Method Bias	Use of informants with expertise in local culture and language
	Use of bilingual subjects
	Use of local surveys (e.g., content analyses of free-response questions)
	Nonstandard instrument administration (e.g., "thinking aloud")
	Cross-cultural comparison of nomological networks (e.g., convergent/discriminant validity studies, monotrait-multimethod studies, connotation of key phrases)
Method Bias	Extensive training of test administrators (e.g., increasing cultural sensitivity)
	Detailed manual/protocol for administration, scoring, and interpretation
	Detailed instructions (e.g., with sufficient number of examples and/or exercises)
	Use of subject and context variables (e.g., educational background)
	Use of collateral information (e.g., test-taking behavior or test attitudes)
	Assessment of response styles
	Use of stability studies
Item Bias	Judgmental methods of item bias detection (e.g., linguistic and psychological analysis)
	Psychometric methods of item bias detection (e.g., differential item functioning analysis)

may yield valuable information about the target culture. In addition, it is informative to administer the instrument to them in a nonstandard way to learn whether the instrument is perceived as intended.

Method Bias

There is an established tradition to apply common standards of objective tests, such as reliability and validity, to projective techniques (e.g., Dana, 1955, 1975, 1998b; Exner, 1986, 1991; Weiner, 1995, 1996, 1997). Many of the recommendations proposed by these authors can be seen as ways to address method bias, such as (among other things) a plea for the use of fixed scoring rules, the importance of a standardized administration, the need to view the administration as a structured interview (with its inherent bias sources), and the need to carry out stability studies.

A thorough training of test administrators is also required. In addition to the usual clinical skills, test administrators of projective instruments in a multicultural or cross-cultural context need good intercultural communication skills. Sue (1998) recently described three qualities that are needed for effective intercultural counseling: culture-specific expertise, scientific mindedness, and dynamic sizing (i.e., flexible use of generalization and individualization). When psychologists and testees are of the same cultural group, these requirements are likely to be met; such a person can administer an instrument in the testee's first language and their shared cultural background will presumably rule out communication failures due to cultural differences. Sue's qualities require more scrutiny when there is no common background between tester and testee. In these cases, a fourth requirement can be added: cultural sensitivity—a general awareness of the "cultural factor in human behavior" and awareness of areas of potential differences of both cultures (e.g., conventions in communication and communication styles; Asante & Gudykunst, 1989; Coupland, Giles, & Wiemann, 1991; Ting Toomey & Korzenny, 1991).

Cultural groups tend to differ in various characteristics that, as argued before, often provide alternative interpretations to observed differences. If two cultural populations show different scores on a depression measure, the most obvious interpretation is that one group is more depressed than the other. However, score differences may also be due to, among other things, population differences in social desirability, acquiescence, self-disclosure, or accidental differences in background characteristics of the samples studied.

How can these alternative interpretations be ruled out? According to methodology textbooks, there are two ways to control for test-relevant background differences in quasi-experimental research: matching and statistical control. Matching amounts to the sampling of subjects on the basis of test-relevant background characteristics, such as education. If the group differences are fairly small, matching may provide the researcher with a valuable tool to rule out an alternative explanation. If group differences are large, it may be naive to attempt to match them. With some luck and persistence, it may be possible to find matched samples in a highly and a poorly educated cultural group, but neither group may constitute an adequate representation of their respective populations.

In such cases, statistical control may do a better job. Poortinga and Van de Vijver (1987; cf. Van de Vijver & Leung, 1997a, 1997b) outlined an approach in which cross-cultural score differences are primarily treated as differences in test-relevant subject or environment characteristics, which they called *context variables*. Information on context variables should be included in a study; the variables should be measured at an individual or a group level. Using an analysis of covariance (ANCOVA) or hierarchical regression procedure, the impact of context variables on the size of observed score differences of cultural and ethnic groups is evaluated and statistically corrected for. Suppose that a researcher hypothesizes that differences in scores on a depression scale of Asian Americans and An-glo-Americans are due to differential self-disclosure. Measures of self-disclosure and social desirability are administered to samples of both groups. If the reasoning would be correct, statistical correction for intergroup differences in self-disclosure should then decrease or even eliminate these differences.

Item Bias

Two kinds of procedures have been developed for identifying item bias: judgmental and statistical. The latter is described on the basis of a hypothetical example of a cross-cultural application of the Thematic Apperception Test (TAT) here. The most relevant approach may be to examine a particular scoring system, such as Bellak's (1993). We focus on the conversion of responses to underlying aspects such as defense mechanisms. The hypothesis is examined as to whether persons from different cultures with the same number of, say, reaction-formation responses across all plates show this defense mechanism in response to the same drawings. Unbiased plates will trigger the same amount of reaction formation from individuals who have the same total number of responses pointing to reaction formation but belong to different cultural and ethnic groups. Pictures are biased when they yield a pattern of responses for persons with the same standing on the underlying construct (reaction formation) that systematically differs across cultural and ethnic groups.

Other procedures may be followed for different projective tests. For example, in the Rorschach, it is possible to examine the cross-cultural similarity of responses elicited by the stimuli. It can be examined to what extent persons with an equal number of pure form responses, but coming from different cultural and ethnic groups, show their form responses on the same items. If the stimuli were unbiased, persons from different cultural groups who are equally likely to give such responses should show their form responses on the same inkblots.

In judgmental item bias procedures, a content analysis of an item content is made using the help of experts in the target group for which the bias is examined. As an example, Van Leest (1997) asked members of various ethnic groups in the Netherlands to judge the suitability of common Dutch personality measures for their original groups. According to these experts, various items were inappropriate due to ethnocentric content.

A disturbing feature of item bias procedures is the frequently observed lack of agreement of judgmental and statistical procedures. For example,

Van Leest found no relationship between outcomes of statistical checks of item bias and expert judgments about item appropriateness.

Translating and Adapting Tests

The advent of multicultural and cross-cultural testing has been accompanied by a heightened interest in translation issues. This interest has led to the formulation of guidelines for proper test translations (e.g., Geisinger, 1994; Van de Vijver & Hambleton, 1996). In the past, linguistic equivalence has been emphasized. An example is the well-known and widely employed translation–back-translation procedure (Werner & Campbell, 1970). The procedure consists of a translation followed by an independent back translation. Similarity of the original and back-translated test is seen as evidence of appropriate translation. Although useful in many cases, the procedure has lost popularity in the last years because it capitalizes on literal translations, thereby ignoring possible differences in readability, comprehensibility, and natural flow of the test of both language versions. Translators who know that their work will be back translated often find it easy to produce a test that, after back translation, will give a verbatim reproduction of the original. However, their translation may use an awkward and stilted language that is easily recognized as coming from some other language. Moreover, a translation–back-translation procedure does not provide any guarantee that construct and method bias do not jeopardize the test. There is an increased awareness in the literature on test translations that a good translation requires the combined expertise of linguistic experts who take care of the linguistic equivalence and psychological experts who ensure psychological equivalence as well as psychometric adequacy.

CONCLUSION

This chapter discussed various methodological issues in multicultural and cross-cultural application of projective tests. The major themes of the chapter are brought together here in seven conclusions:

1. Multicultural and cross-cultural testing have become more widespread in the last decades. This trend will continue. Projective testing in a multicultural context will become increasingly important.

2. Multicultural and cross-cultural projective assessment creates new challenges to psychology.

3. Bias (dissimilarity of psychological meaning of a test or score in different cultural groups) is germane to multicultural and cross-cultural

testing. Construct, method, and item bias can constitute threats to score comparability.

4. There are various ways to deal with bias. Common methods were described in this chapter.

5. Assessment of acculturation status is essential in multicultural research.

6. Empirical studies of the suitability of projective instruments in various cultural and ethnic groups are badly needed. Ethical and legal considerations prevent us from using nonvalidated instruments.

7. Projective tests were not popular in research with non-Western groups in the last decades. This is not surprising because there was little ground for the lofty initial expectations of the enterprise. With more realistic expectations and with the achievements of the last decades in mind (e.g., well-established scoring systems for some tests, more experience in administering tests to non-Western groups, and a framework to study bias), we may try again to embark on cross-cultural research with projective tests.

Almost 40 years ago, Lindzey (1961)—in a book on the use of projective tests in non-Western societies—argued that, "However valid projective techniques may be within our own society, it remains *a task for the future to demonstrate* that they possess *cross-cultural validity*" (p. 191; italics original). When cross-cultural is interpreted as referring both to multicultural and transnational, Lindzey's remark is still up to date. Compared with the anthropologists of some decades ago, we are now in a much better position to examine this validity. We can learn from the experiences of the last decades of multicultural and cross-cultural research, and we have a better theoretical, methodological, and statistical framework to study bias and validity in this research. Hopefully this chapter can stimulate the interest and perceived need for research of projective instruments in a multicultural and cross-cultural context and help contribute to the framework of these studies.

REFERENCES

Allen, J. (1998). Personality assessment with American Indians and Alaska Natives: Instrument considerations and service delivery style. *Journal of Personality Assessment*, 70, 17–42.

APA Office of Ethnic Minority Affairs. (1993). Guidelines for providers of psychological services to ethnic, linguistic, and culturally diverse populations. *American Psychologist*, 48, 45–48.

Arvey, R. D., Strickland, W., Drauden, G., & Martin, C. (1990). Motivational components of test taking. *Personnel Psychology*, 43, 695–716.

Asante, M. K., & Gudykunst, W. B. (Eds.). (1989). *Handbook of international and intercultural communication*. London: Sage.

Bellak, L. (1993). *The TAT, CAT, and SAT in clinical use* (5th ed.). New York: Grune & Stratton.

Berk, R. A. (Ed.). (1982). *Handbook of methods for detecting item bias*. Baltimore: Johns Hopkins University Press.

Berry, J. W., & Sam, D. (1997). Acculturation and adaptation. In J. W. Berry, M. H. Segall, & C. Kagitcibasi (Eds.), *Handbook of cross-cultural psychology* (2nd ed., Vol. 3, pp. 291–326). Boston: Allyn & Bacon.

Cervantes, R. C., Padilla, A. M., & Salgado de Snyder, N. (1990). Reliability and validity of the Hispanic Stress Inventory. *Hispanic Journal of Behavioral Sciences, 12,* 76–82.

Cervantes, R. C., Padilla, A. M., & Salgado de Snyder, N. (1991). The Hispanic Stress Inventory: A culturally relevant approach toward psychological assessment. *Psychological Assessment, 3,* 438–447.

Cheung, F. M., Leung, K., Fan, R. M., Song, W. Z., Zhang, J. X., & Chang, J. P. (1996). Development of the Chinese Personality Assessment Inventory. *Journal of Cross-Cultural Psychology, 27,* 181–199.

Choney, S. K., Berryhill-Paapke, E., & Robbins, R. R. (1995). The acculturation of American Indians: Developing frameworks for research and practice. In J. G. Ponterotto, J. M. Casas, L. A. Suzuki, & C. M. Alexander (Eds.), *Handbook of multicultural counseling* (pp. 73–92). Thousand Oaks, CA: Sage.

Church, A. T., & Lonner, W. J. (Eds.). (1998). Personality and its measurement in cross-cultural perspective [Special Issue]. *Journal of Cross-Cultural Psychology, 29* (Whole No. 1).

Costantino, G., Flanagan, R., & Malgady, R. G. (1995). The history of the Rorschach: Overcoming bias in multicultural projective assessment. *Rorschachiana, 20,* 148–171.

Costantino, G., Malgady, R. G., & Rogler, L. H. (1988). *TEMAS (Tell-Me-a-Story) manual*. Los Angeles: Western Psychological Services.

Coupland, N., Giles, H., & Wiemann, J. M. (Eds.). (1991). *Miscommunication and problematic talk*. Newbury Park, CA: Sage.

Dana, R. H. (1955). The objectification of projective techniques: Rationale. *Psychological Reports, 39,* 93–102.

Dana, R. H. (1962). The validation of projective techniques. *Journal of Projective Techniques, 26,* 182–186.

Dana, R. H. (1966). Eisegesis and assessment. *Journal of Projective Techniques and Personality Assessment, 30,* 215–222.

Dana, R. H. (1975). Ruminations on teaching projective assessment: An ideology, specific usages, teaching practices. *Journal of Personality Assessment, 39,* 563–572.

Dana, R. H. (1996). Culturally competent assessment practice in the United States. *Journal of Personality Assessment, 66,* 472–487.

Dana, R. H. (1998a). Cultural identity assessments of culturally diverse groups: 1997. *Journal of Personality Assessment, 70,* 1–16.

Dana, R. H. (1998b). Projective assessment of Latinos in the United States: Current realities, problems, and prospects. *Cultural Diversity and Mental Health, 4,* 165–184.

Deregowski, J., Muldrow, E. S., & Muldrow, W. F. (1972). Pictorial recognition in a remote Ethiopian population. *Perception, 1,* 417–425.

Deregowski, J. B., & Serpell, R. (1971). Performance on a sorting task: A cross-cultural experiment. *International Journal of Psychology, 6,* 273–281.

Exner, J. E. (1986). *The Rorschach: A comprehensive system: Vol. 1. Basic foundations* (2nd ed.). New York: Wiley.

Exner, J. E. (1991). *The Rorschach: A comprehensive system: Vol. 2. Interpretation* (2nd ed.). New York: Wiley.

Fagulha, T., & Dana, R. H. (1997). Professional psychology in Portugal. *Psychological Reports, 81,* 1211–1222.

Geisinger, K. F. (1994). Cross-cultural normative assessment: Translation and adaptation issues influencing the normative interpretation of assessment instruments. *Psychological Assessment, 6,* 304–312.

Gordon, M. M. (1964). *Assimilation in American life: The role of race, religion, and national origins.* New York: Oxford University Press.

Groth-Marnat, G. (1997). *Handbook of psychological assessment* (2nd ed.). New York: Wiley.

Ho, D. Y. F. (1996). Filial piety and its psychological consequences. In M. H. Bond (Ed.), *Handbook of Chinese psychology* (pp. 155–165). Hong Kong: Oxford University Press.

Holland, P. W., & Wainer, H. (Eds.). (1993). *Differential item functioning.* Hillsdale, NJ: Lawrence Erlbaum Associates.

Holtzman, W. H., Thorpe, J. D., & Herron, E. W. (1961). *Inkblot perception and personality: Holtzman Inkblot Technique.* Austin, TX: Hogg Foundation for Mental Health, University of Texas Press.

Hui, C. H., & Triandis, H. C. (1989). Effects of culture and response format on extreme response style. *Journal of Cross-Cultural Psychology, 20,* 296–309.

Hutschemaekers, G. J. M. (1990). *Neurosen in Nederland: Vijfentachtig jaar psychisch en maatschappelijk onbehagen* [Neuroses in the Netherlands: Eighty-five years of psychic and societal distress]. Nijmegen, The Netherlands: SUN.

Jensen, A. R. (1980). *Bias in mental testing.* New York: The Free Press.

Lindsey, M. L. (1998). Culturally competent assessment of African American clients. *Journal of Personality Assessment, 70,* 43–53.

Lindzey, G. (1961). *Projective techniques and cross-cultural research.* New York: Appleton-Century-Crofts.

Lonner, W. J., & Ibrahim, F. A. (1989). Assessment in cross-cultural counseling. In P. B. Pedersen, J. G. Draguns, W. J. Lonner, & J. E. Trimble (Eds.), *Counseling across cultures* (3rd ed., pp. 299–333). Honolulu: University of Hawaii Press.

Jensen, A. R. (1980). *Bias in mental testing.* New York: The Free Press.

Kleinman, A. M. (1977). Depression, somatization and the new cross-cultural psychiatry. *Social Science and Medicine, 11,* 3–10.

Masling, J. M. (1997). On the nature and utility of projective tests and objective tests. *Journal of Personality Assessment, 69,* 257–270.

Masling, J. M., & Harris, S. (1969). Sexual aspects of TAT administration. *Journal of Consulting and Clinical Psychology, 33,* 166–169.

Misra, G., Sahoo, F. M., & Puhan, B. N. (1997). Cultural bias in testing: India. *European Review of Applied Psychology, 47,* 309–316.

Nkaya, H. N., Huteau, M., & Bonnet, J. (1994). Retest effect on cognitive performance on the Raven-38 Matrices in France and in the Congo. *Perceptual and Motor Skills, 78,* 503–510.

Oakland, T., Gulek, C., & Glutting, J. (1996). Children's test-taking behaviors: A review of literature, case study, and research of children. *European Journal of Psychological Assessment (Bulletin of the International Test Commission), 12,* 240–246.

Okazaki, S. (1998). Psychological assessment of Asian Americans: Research agenda for cultural competency. *Journal of Personality Assessment, 70,* 54–70.

Piker, S. (1998). Contributions of psychological anthropology. *Journal of Cross-Cultural Psychology, 29,* 9–31.

Poortinga, Y. H. (1989). Equivalence of cross-cultural data: An overview of basic issues. *International Journal of Psychology, 24,* 737–756.

Poortinga, Y. H., & Van de Vijver, F. J. R. (1987). Explaining cross-cultural differences: Bias analysis and beyond. *Journal of Cross-Cultural Psychology, 18,* 259–282.

Radloff, L. S. (1977). A CES-D scale: A self-report scale for research in the general population. *Applied Psychological Measurement, 1,* 385–401.

Ross, C. E., & Mirowsky, J. (1984). Socially-desirable response and acquiescence in a cross-cultural survey of mental health. *Journal of Health and Social Behavior, 25*, 189–197.

Serpell, R. (1979). How specific are perceptual skills? *British Journal of Psychology, 70*, 365–380.

Singer, E., & Presser, S. (1989). The interviewer. In E. Singer & S. Presser (Eds.), *Survey research methods: A reader* (pp. 245–246). Chicago: University of Chicago Press.

Smith, P. B., & Bond, M. H. (1993). *Social psychology across cultures*. New York: Harvester Wheatsheaf.

Spielberger, C. D. (1988). *State–Trait Anger Expression Inventory research edition. Professional manual*. Odessa, FL: Psychological Assessment Resources.

Sue, D. W. (1991). A conceptual model for cultural diversity. *Journal of Counseling and Development, 70*, 99–105.

Sue, S. (1998). In search of cultural competence in psychotherapy and counseling. *American Psychologist, 53*, 440–448.

Tanaka-Matsumi, J., & Marsella, A. J. (1976). Cross-cultural variations in the phenomenological experience of depression: I. Word association studies. *Journal of Cross-Cultural Psychology, 7*, 379–396.

Ting Toomey, S., & Korzenny, F. (Eds.). (1991). *Cross-cultural interpersonal communication*. Newbury Park, CA: Sage.

Triandis, H. C. (1995). *Individualism & collectivism*. Boulder, CO: Westview Press.

Van de Vijver, F. J. R., & Hambleton, R. K. (1996). Translating tests: Some practical guidelines. *European Psychologist, 1*, 89–99.

Van de Vijver, F. J. R., Helms-Lorenz, M., & Feltzer, M. F. (in press). Acculturation and cognitive performance of migrant children in the Netherlands. *International Journal of Psychology*.

Van de Vijver, F. J. R., & Leung, K. (1997a). Methods and data analysis of comparative research. In J. W. Berry, Y. H. Poortinga, & J. Pandey (Eds.), *Handbook of cross-cultural psychology* (2nd ed., Vol. 1, pp. 257–300). Boston: Allyn & Bacon.

Van de Vijver, F. J. R., & Leung, K. (1997b). *Methods and data analysis for cross-cultural research*. Newbury Park, CA: Sage.

Van de Vijver, F. J. R., & Poortinga, Y. H. (1997). Towards an integrated analysis of bias in cross-cultural assessment. *European Journal of Psychological Assessment, 13*, 29–37.

Van de Vijver, F. J. R., & Tanzer, N. K. (1997). Bias and equivalence in cross-cultural assessment: An overview. *European Review of Applied Psychology, 47*, 263–280.

Van Leest, P. F. (1997). Bias research in the Netherlands. *European Review of Applied Psychology, 47*, 319–327.

Weiner, I. B. (1995). Methodological considerations in Rorschach research. *Psychological Assessment, 7*, 330–337.

Weiner, I. B. (1996). Some observations on the validity of the Rorschach Inkblot Method. *Psychological Assessment, 8*, 206–213.

Weiner, I. B. (1997). Current status of the Rorschach Inkblot Method. In J. A. Schinka & R. L. Greene (Eds.), *Emerging issues and methods in personality assessment* (pp. 3–17). Mahwah, NJ: Lawrence Erlbaum Associates.

Werner, O., & Campbell, D. T. (1970). Translating, working through interpreters, and the problem of decentering. In R. Naroll & R. Cohen (Eds.), *A handbook of cultural anthropology* (pp. 398–419). New York: American Museum of Natural History.

III

ACCULTURATION AND CULTURAL/RACIAL IDENTITY

Part III explores acculturation and cultural/racial identity. This part begins with a scholarly review in chapter 6 of the concept of *culture* as an introduction to acculturation measurement and acculturation measures, leading to a description of an Index of Correction for Culture. Chapter 7 provides a focus on Asian-American acculturation and ethnic identities by reviewing selected instruments. Chapter 8 describes racial identity measures for African Americans and provides a new classification system. Chapter 9 explores American Indian/Alaska Native self-identifications and cites recent research findings in this area.

Chapter 6 examines culture as an antecedent to behavior, a mediator variable accounting for relationships between a predictor and a criterion as well as a moderator that controls the direction or strength of the relationship. Culture has been construed in many ways, by macro and micro definitions that provide a basis for examining contact between cultures, acculturation phenomena, and the measurement of acculturation as a moderator that is the focus in this chapter.

Acculturation measurement history is reviewed in terms of content areas of psychological functioning, exemplified by Acculturation Balance Scale methodology as a precursor to an orthogonal approach with separate scales for the original and host cultures. Thirty-one major acculturation scales are tabularized and identified chronologically from 1955 to 1995 to demonstrate multidimensional measurement. Relationships between acculturation and psychopathology variables are also tabularized chronologically. Scales for clinical diagnosis are more sensitive to acculturation status than are personality traits, and persons who are less Anglo-acculturated, particularly in a context of lower social class and minimal education, will appear more pathological. The Acculturation Rating Scale for Mexican Americans (ARSMA–II) is a linear measure that provides an index of balance between two cultures as well as an orthogonal measure. Linear acculturation measurement minimizes the complexity of multidomain constructs, whereas orthogonal measures can generate a larger number of categories. This distinction is relevant to the assessment purpose in using acculturation measures. If it is necessary to decide whether or not to use standard tests that are pseudoetic by definition, with or without corrections, or to consider the possibility of using available emic measures, then a linear acculturation measure may suffice. However, if a *DSM–IV* clinical diagnosis is required, cultural formulations (see chaps. 25 and 26) are necessary and can be derived partially from orthogonal measures because they are enriched sources of culturally relevant information. A linear model only registers deviance from a host culture, whereas an orthogonal model is expanded for greater understanding of identity and requires extra-test data as well. As a consequence, enriched cultural data becomes available as well as an expanded rationale for interpretation of standard tests. These data are useful in the absence of demonstrated cross-cultural equivalence of standard tests and can document different meanings of group differences for each cultural/racial group. Orthogonal measures also provide information for describing cultural identity that is essential for a more complete understanding of cultural identity. When clinical diagnosis is not an assessment objective, the information from orthogonal measures may be helpful for problems arising from acculturation, discrimination, or confusion with regard to personal identity. Acculturation practice should recognize that deviations from standard test norms can be interpreted as standard deviation units representing degrees of exposure to nonmainstream cultural influences rather than degrees of difference from whatever the particular scores measures. The use of acculturation status measurement as a moderator is a legitimate approach to understanding changes in cultural identity or acquisition of a new cultural identity.

Chapter 6 continues by discussing the mechanics of using moderators in clinical assessment practice to enable "corrections" to be applied in the interpretation of standard tests. Slope bias and intercept bias are introduced as statistical methodologies for examining the influence of a moderator on a criterion. Slope or intercept corrections provide refined estimates of the magnitude of bias. Such statistical corrections are needed in the absence of cross-cultural construct validation to understand the meaning of group differences whenever a test is used with individuals or groups who differ from the normative population. In other words, even when the means and predictive validities of coefficients are similar, it cannot be assumed that meanings are equivalent across groups. Nor can it be assumed that group differences between T-scores of less than five points, for example, may be interpreted as no difference. Only by use of a statistical correction such as the Index for Correction for Culture, described in this chapter, can more accurate T-scores or T-score differences be obtained.

Chapter 6 has taken an important step toward further research on corrections by presenting a rationale for slope and intercept bias as well as the moderator and statistical ingredients for an Index of Correction for Culture. This step indicates some consequences of a reversal of the Null Hypothesis (see chap. 3). Moreover, some mechanics are made available for exploring the implications of continuing to ask relevant questions during the assessment process as a direct consequence of being dissatisfied with the historic bias of no difference imposed by the Null Hypothesis. At this point in time, standardized procedures for moderating scores are sorely needed. Clinical judgment must still be used to estimate the acculturation difference between an assessee and the standardization sample. Essentially this procedure involves using interview data within a context of experience with a particular assessee and adequate cultural knowledge as a context for judgment. However, clinical judgment is prone to error and statistical corrections are required for culturally competent assessment practice as well as for training student assessors.

Chapter 7 examines the mediation of orthogonal constructs, acculturation, and ethnic identity by acculturative stress and intercultural competence at both individual and group levels with a focus on Asian Americans. To facilitate empirical differentiation of these two constructs, literature is reviewed, acculturation trends are chronicled, and the psychometric properties of selected instruments are presented in tabular format. *Acculturation* is viewed here as various adoptions from White culture, whereas *ethnic identity* refers to functional aspects of shared affective/cathectic attachment and beliefs.

This chapter deals with two important issues: differences across generations in acculturation issues and the relationship between acculturation and adjustment. First-generation immigrants learn what is necessary for survival during acculturation, experiencing a variety of intense stressors during the process, but essentially maintaining intact cultural identities. Incursions to self-esteem are common, but acculturative stress is mediated by the ideology of the dominant society, the nature of the acculturating group, the mode of acculturation selected, as well as the individual's demographics. Second-generation persons are preoccupied with keeping what is relevant to who they are, or their ethnic identities, and balancing two worlds simultaneously. Third-generation persons may sometimes find it necessary to rediscover their ethnic and cultural origins. Interpersonal conflicts are frequent, although overall adjustment improves in this generation particularly when biculturalism is the preferred acculturation orientation status. Although many Asian Americans have preferred biculturalism, this socialization can also contribute to acculturation stress as well as foster the maintenance of ethnic identity resources important for mental health. A centralized core of bicultural integrated identity is accompanied by temporal and situational externally induced movements across all acculturation outcomes. This has been examined by the Sodowsky et al. Internal–External Ethnic Identity measure of bicultural competencies, which includes internal components (i.e., morally obligated attachment and family-related values) and external components (i.e., practices, behaviors and festivities). Isajiw's Ethnic Identity Retention Model separates cognitive, affective, and moral aspects of internal identity from the observables of sociocultural behavior, within-group friendships, language, and participation in traditional group activities. Measurement of bicultural competencies leads to the description of several development and retention models for ethnic identity. These models serve to describe the anticipated contents of cultural alienation, cultural confusion, bicultural, and gender role and cultural conflicts. This provides guidelines for identity-specific interventions. This linkage of research-based models to psychological practice technologies is an important outcome of instrument development and subsequent literature review.

Ethnic identity is less important for Euro-Americans than for cultural/racial groups in the United States, who require an integrated ego identity predicated on pride, a sense of belongingness, and enhanced security to cope with cultural conflicts and discrimination. It is relevant that important residues of cultural identity persist across five or six generations and provide ingredients that have been increasingly identified in research studies as conducive to emotional stability and mental health.

Chapter 8 describes racial identity as a complex concept overlapping with ethnic identity. It has been operationalized by a variety of measuring instruments for identity formation, cultural connectedness, multicultural experiences, and multidimensional measures. Identity formation has been examined by three measures (i.e., Developmental Inventory of Black Consciousness, Racial Identity Attitude Scale, and Black Personality Questionnaire). The first two instruments have been used with the MMPI as corrections for the potential confound with psychopathology resulting from arousal of emotions associated with an emerging racial identity. These measures have not been adopted for routine assessment with African Americans, but their use would provide important diagnostic avenues leading to identity-specific interventions designed to facilitate the process of developing a comfortable racial identity.

Cultural connectedness has been measured by six instruments eliciting group-specific affiliation preferences and traditional values. Several of these instruments have immediate application for routine assessment. For example, the Africentrism Scale describes the extent of endorsement of Kwanza principles (see chap. 2) and can serve as an introduction to interventions using these principles. The African Self-Consciousness Scale may be used to examine the outcome of a racial identity developmental process. The African-American Acculturation Scale assesses cultural beliefs and practices, or cultural identity, and is a useful precursor to culture-specific interventions.

Six measures of multicultural experience focus on racism. A common core of dimensions includes exposure to racism, appraisal of emotional effects, and emotional responses and behavioral strategies examined in academic, employment, and public arenas. The impact of racism often contributes or is directly responsible for distress that may be unrecognized by standard assessment procedures that demonstrate the emotional effects of racism without pinpointing the sources. Moreover, Anglo-American assessors who have never experienced discrimination on a personal basis may overlook this area of experience that can be evidenced by Posttraumatic Stress Disorder (PTSD), for example. Measures such as the Schedule of Racist Events can provide greater awareness among assessors that prejudice and discrimination not only occur to persons of color, often on a daily basis, but can have pervasive effects on physical and psychological well-being.

Four multidimensional measures tap more than one dimension of the classification system presented in this chapter. One of these measures, the Multigroup Ethnic Identity Measure, examines group membership in all three dimensions using scales for Affirmation and Belonging, Ethnic Identity Achievement, Ethnic Behaviors, and Other Group Orientation. This instrument has applications for cultural identity assessment in the absence of emic measures for particular cultural/racial groups. Many of the racial identity measures have had only infrequent research use, and the authors recommend that a wider range of measures be employed in this area. Both racial and ethnic identity measures are required as well as measures that can be used with several different groups. Furthermore, many of these measures have only been standardized on college samples. In addition, it is imperative to incorporate some of these instruments into assessment practice to provide information on racial and cultural identity, the impact of discrimination, and the information required for culture- and identity-specific interventions. These interventions serve to depathologize problems of acculturation, identity development, and identity confusion as well as to identify effects of discrimination and racism that also require specialized interventions.

Chapter 9 approaches American Indian/Alaska Native self-identification by examining the conditions responsible for an ethnic group, the elements of the categorical term *ethnic identity*, and the more complex qualitative and quantitative term *ethnic identification*. The ethnic glosses *American Indian* and *Alaska Native* are sociopolitical labels that can mask heterogeneity, provide invidious or deficit-related comparisons, and convey moral evaluation. The term *American Indian* is described as "an imposed, invented ethnic category." Tribes have their own self-designations and have been subjected to a legal blood quantum definition by the U.S. government as well as to eligibility-for-services criteria developed by government agencies. In addition to these definitions, ethnic affiliation information is shared among strangers in a conversational process of *common basing*, often tribe-specific in content, to determine a potential for relationships among individuals. Ethnic self-identification is described in this chapter by natal measures, subjective measures, behavioral measures, and situation settings.

The question of why people identify themselves as American Indians is explored but not answered definitely because of an absence of objective criteria. Conventional explanations include "the Indian windfall syndrome" of something to gain, an identity that promises pride and new learning, family solidarity, or family obligations to retain Indian identity and as a defense against prejudice and discrimination. Several ethnic identity models are described that assume the identification process is related to ego development and self-esteem. The Cross model in particular is cited as germane to American Indian identity development.

The measurement of ethnic identity/ethnic identification has been attempted using single items and dimensional scales. Identity structure analysis is introduced as a more sophisticated measure that can provide indexes for self-image, values, and role models among other identity domains. An interview schedule of over 100 questions is also described. These two approaches should be examined by assessors as potentially useful information resources for identity description and cultural formulations. A two-item interview measure used in large-scale surveys presented in this chapter may also be unfamiliar to assessors.

A recent study of 846 self-identified American Indian youth is reported. Although a large majority identified themselves as American Indians, some were also self-identified with Anglo-White and Spanish-Mexican groups, and 11% said they did not identify as American Indian although they self-identified nominally as American Indian. This study supports orthogonal identification theory discussed in this chapter while indicating identification with other groups as well, which is influenced by geographic location, reference groups, socialization, and perceived tolerance.

6

Acculturation As a Moderator of Personality and Psychological Assessment

Israel Cuéllar
University of Texas—Pan American

The study of culture and personality, as well as their interactions, has been of much interest in the fields of psychology, anthropology, and cross-cultural psychology. As aptly stated by Lonner and Adamopoulos (1997), the basic idea is that one's personality and culture are inextricably intertwined. As Suarez-Orozco, Spindler, and Spindler (1994) pointed out, the phenomenological, existential conception of the relation among human minds, environment, and culture has probably been a preoccupation of intellectuals for centuries and probably since the first stirrings of human consciousness.

CULTURE AS ANTECEDENT TO BEHAVIOR

Among the various models conceptualizing culture as antecedent to human thought and behavior reviewed by Lonner and Adamopoulus (1997), culture is viewed as either having a direct or an indirect effect on thought and behavior. In one perspective, culture is seen as a mediator variable or set of variables; in another perspective, culture is seen as a moderator. Mediator variables influence both the predictor and criterion; as such, they account for the relations between a psychological predictor variable and a criterion variable, whereas moderator variables control and potentially alter the strength or direction of the relationship between a predictor and a criterion variable (Lonner & Adamopoulos, 1997). A theoretical example of culture as a mediator variable is provided by a regression model in which a personality trait (e.g., traditionalism) is used to predict willingness to accept change in gender roles (e.g., caring for young infants by males). In this example, culture, a third variable, indirectly moderates the criterion variable (caring or not caring for infants by males) through its influence on traditionalism—the predictor variable. In this example, culture mediates by indirectly influencing the criterion variable but directly influencing the predictor variable (traditionalism). Because culture has influences on both the predictor and the criterion in this theoretical example, culture is a mediator variable. Thus, culture mediates both traditionalism and willingness to care for infants. Traditionalism may predict, to some degree, willingness to care for young infants by males. In doing so, it moderates the criterion variable, but both traditionalism and the criterion variable are mediated by culture in this example.

In the prior example, traditionalism was the moderator variable and culture was the mediator variable. Culture can be either a moderator or mediator variable. If a predictor variable moderates a criterion and the predictor is largely a measure of culture, it could be said that culture moderates the criterion. An example of culture as a moderator variable using a similar example of childrearing practice follows. In a theoretically homogeneous cultural group, the number of doctor visits (criterion variable) may be predicted by hypochondriasis (predictor variable). Culture manifests itself in this example primarily through its interaction with the predictor variable (personality characteristic of hypochondriasis). That is, to the extent that culture moderates the predictor variable, it (culture) influences (moderates) the criterion variable. However, in this example, as well as most, there is always the theoretical possibility that culture could directly or indirectly influence the criterion (number of doctor visits) as well. Whether culture is a mediator or moderator variable is an empirical question that can be answered using regression analysis, path analysis, or some other appropriate statistical technique on the variables of interest within a given ecocultural context.

Culture, defined as a set of contextual variables, can and often does moderate what responses take place at any given time. In behavioral terms, stimulus conditions moderate responses by determining what responses take place at any given time. For example, if the traffic light is green, we press on the accelerator; if the traffic light is red, we press on the break pedal. To the extent that our environments are a reflection of our culture, we are continuously moderating our thoughts and actions by cultural influences. Although both mediating and moderating influence of culture are equally important, this chapter focuses on the latter to keep matters simple. In this respect, this chapter is largely concerned with the accuracy with which psychological test scores predict behavior for individuals who are poorly represented or excluded from standardization samples. This perspective holds as its basic premise that many predictors in the behavioral sciences are moderated by culture. That prediction is enhanced to the extent that cultural variance is controlled, understood, and/or included in the equation.

MODELS OF CULTURAL INFLUENCE ON PERSONALITY

To have a good understanding of cultural influences on personality, it is necessary to have some understanding of the overarching role of culture on human behavior in general. The psychosocial model places culture at the periphery. It is an extension of the medical model—a model that starts, naturally, with a biological focus. A more centralized role of culture is provided by Marsella and Kameoka (1989) in their General Interactional Model of human behavior. In their model, there is an interaction between internal/external variables and contexts, environments, and situations having omnipresence at the site of the interaction that produces behavior. As Angel (1994) stated, culture is not like any other variable because culture comprises the context for the operation of all other variables. In his model, culture is provided a centralized role in understanding behavior, as much of our behavior is shared, learned behavior transmitted from one generation to the next, constituting Linton's (1945) definition of *culture*. Berry, Poortinga, Segall, and Dasen (1992) described the ecological context as the setting in which human organisms and the physical environment interact. They describe the central feature of this setting as *economic activity*. Their ecocultural framework is presented not as a theory, but as a heuristic device to help researchers develop hypotheses about specific interrelationships among culture, ethnicity, ecology, and behavior. This framework is similar to Bandura's (1986) *reciprocal determinism*, in which there is a continual three-way interaction among situation, person, and behavior. It is a dynamic interaction and changes to one part of the equation causes probabilistic changes to the other two components, characterizing an ecosystem. In the ecocultural framework (Berry et al. 1992), individual psychological outcomes are influenced by culture via ecological context, cultural adaptation, acculturation, and cultural transmission.

Psychologists have been postulating behavior as a function of person and environment interaction for a long time (Lewin, 1935). Likewise, personality has been postulated by Lewin as developing at least in part from person–environment interactions. Culture clearly plays an important role in many of the more prominent macrotheories of human development, such as the Ecological Systems Theory, Sociocultural Theory, Social Learning Theory (see Beck, 1998), and the Ecocultural Model (Berry, 1994). In each of these models, psychological outcomes, both positive and negative, are influenced by culture in highly complex, interactive, and dynamic ways. In Marsella and Kameoka's (1989) General Interactional Model, human behavior is a function of a variety of determinants (biological, psychological, cultural, and environmental) that are in simultaneous interaction. They also distinguish between the physical and cultural environments.

There appears to be little or no doubt that culture influences psychological outcome including personality. The major disagreement with regard to culture is the prominence, complexity, or centrality of its role in human development. In more recent formulations, each component of the three-way interaction (situation, person, and behavior) has a cultural component.

Recent advances in the measurement of culture have led to a better understanding of cultural influences on behavior, development, and psychological adjustment. Kroeber and Kluckholm (1952) compiled 167 different definitions of culture, and the number of definitions appears to be expanding. Culture has gone from something out there at the macrolevel to something inside the head—a conceptual structure or system of ideas (Geertz, 1984). Poortinga (1990/1992) contended that culture becomes manifest in shared constraints that limit the behavior repertoire available to its members in a way different from individuals from other cultural groups.

Redfield, Linton, and Herskovitz (1936) defined *acculturation* as encompassing those phenomena that result when "groups of individuals having different cultures come into continuous first-hand contact, with subsequent changes in the original cultural patterns of either or both groups" (p. 149). This definition provided a framework for the empirical measurement of acculturation. Acculturation phenomena include both macro- and microlevel phenomena. Acculturation phenomena include a full range of human behavior at the social and individual levels. Berry (1980) identified six areas of psychological functioning that are directly impacted by the process of acculturation: (a) language, (b) cognitive styles, (c) personality, (d) identity, (e) attitudes, and (f) acculturative stress. Among the areas that are impacted by acculturation, in addition to those at the psychological level, are social and macrolevel changes. Among some of the many components of culture that are subject to acculturative changes are language, values, beliefs, ideas, customs, practices, music, architecture, foods, and many more, including views of illness and health. At the individual psychological level, cognitive referents of culture and acculturation phenomena most commonly studied include values, behaviors,

language, and beliefs. Even affective referents of culture have been identified (Kitayama & Markus, 1994).

EMPIRICAL MEASUREMENT OF ACCULTURATION

The first empirically developed instrument used to measure psychological
acculturation per se was developed by Pierce, Clark, and Kiefer (1972).
Pierce et al. developed a scale that measures how oriented a person is to
one or more cultures. Their scale, called the Acculturative Balance Scale
(ABS), utilized a scaling technique referred to as the *bootstrap technique* to
get the process of acculturation measurement started. The ABS essentially
measures knowledge of culture of origin and compares it with knowledge
of adopted culture. The ABS yields an index measuring the extent to
which an individual is bicultural with respect to two cultures. It was
developed for Asian Americans and Mexican Americans living in the
United States.

The Pierce et al. technique is simple, explicit, and empirical. It measures
knowledge or awareness of cultural items. Unfortunately, the ABS is now
an outdated instrument in terms of much of its content. It is also unidimensional and covers a much too narrow range of acculturation phenomena. However, it demonstrates considerable validity and, perhaps more
important, provided a methodology for the development of many acculturation measures that followed. Its methodology later became known as
the *orthogonal* approach when measuring psychological activity for each
culture on a separate scale. By measuring the amount of orientation,
involvement, participation, knowledge, and so on toward each of two
cultures independently, an index of balance between the two competing
cultures is derived.

Prior to the development of the ABS, measurement of different aspects
of culture focused primarily on values and ideologies that served as
referents of cultural orientations. Researchers debated the relative value
of using values versus behavioral referents of culture in its measurement
(Olmedo, 1979).

The omnidimensional aspects of acculturation phenomena have generated a multitude and variety of acculturation measures. In the 1970s
and 1980s, there was a boom in the development of acculturation measures. Some of the more relevant scales accessing different behavioral and
cognitive aspects of acculturation developed between 1955 and 1995 are
listed in Table 6.1. Table 6.1 shows a limited chronology, but one that
nonetheless demonstrates the growth of acculturation measures and the
multidimensionality of cultural phenomena and its measurement.

TABLE 6.1
Select Chronology of Acculturation/Ethnicity
Measurement Between 1955 and 1995

Scale	Authors	Year
The Traditional Family Ideology Scale	D. J. Levinson & P. E. Huffman	1955
Values Orientation Scale	F. R. Kluckholm & F. L. Strodtbeck	1961
Diaz–Guerrero's Scale of Mexican Family Values	R. Diaz-Guerrero	1968
The Acculturative Balance Scale	R. C. Pierce, M. M. Clark, & C. W. Kiefer	1972
The Bicultural Inventory (BI)	M. Ramirez III; A., Castaneda, & B. G. Cox	1977
Measure of Acculturation for Chicano Adolescents	E. L. Olmedo, J. L. Martinez, & S. R. Martinez	1978
Value Orientations Scale	J. Szapocznik, M. A. Scopetta, M. A. Aranalde, & W. Kurtines	1978b
Measure of Acculturation for Mexican Americans	E. L. Olmedo & A. Padilla	1978
Behavioral Acculturation Scale	J. Szapocznik, M. A. Scopetta, & M. A. Aranalde	1978a
Bicultural Involvement Questionnaire	J. Szapocznik, M. A. Scopetta, M. A. Aranalde, & W. Kurtines	1978b
Tradition Family Ideology Scale	R. A. Montemayor	1979
Sociocultural Scales	J. Mercer	1979
Cuban Behavioral Identity Questionnaire	M. Garcia & L. I. Lega	1979
Padilla's Acculturation Scale	A. M. Padilla	1980
Acculturation Rating Scale for Mexican Americans (ARSMA)	I. Cuéllar, L. C. Harris, & R. Jasso	1980
Short Acculturation Scale for Hispanics	G. Marin, F. Saboqal, B. VanOss Marin, R. Otero-Saboqal, & E. J. Perez-Stable	1986
Racial Identity Attitude Scale	J. E. Helms	1986
Scale to Assess World Views	F. A. Ibrahim & H. Kahn	1987
Suinn–Lew Acculturation Scale	R. M. Suinn, K. Richard-Figueroa, S. Lew, & S. Vigil	1987
Los Angeles ECA Acculturation Scale	M. A. Burnam, C. A. Telles, M. Karno, & J. Escobar	1987
Cultural Awareness and Ethnic Loyalty Scale	S. E. Keefe & A. M. Padilla	1987
Individualism-Collectivism Scale	C. H. Hui	1988
Cultural Lifestyle Inventory	R. H. Mendoza	1989
Comfort with Acculturation Scale	G. T. Montgomery & S. Orozco	1992
The Multigroup Ethnic Identity Scale (MEIM)	J. S. Phinney	1992
Na-Mea-Hawaii—A Hawaiian Acculturation Scale	W. C. Rezentes	1993
The African American Acculturation Scale	H. Landrine & E. A. Klonoff	1994

(Continued)

TABLE 6.1
(Continued)

Scale	Authors	Year
A Multidimensional Measure of Cultural Identity for Latino and Latina Adolescents	M. Felix-Ortiz, M. D. Newcomb, & H. Myers	1994
Acculturation Scale for Mexican Americans–II (ARSMA–II)	I. Cuéllar, B. Arnold, & R. E. Maldonado	1995
Multicultural Assessment of Cultural Constructs (MACC–SF)	I. Cuéllar, B. Arnold, & G. Gonzalez	1995
Bidimensional Acculturation Scale for Hispanics	G. Marin & R. J. Gamba	1996

THE RELATIONS OF ACCULTURATION AND PERSONALITY

An increasing number of studies show a significant relationship between acculturation and personality variables (see Table 6.2). It is premature to draw any definite conclusions based on overall convergence of findings across the varied studies. However, some aspects of the findings to date are of interest and suggestive of the relations between the two. Clinical scales seem to be more sensitive than normal personality traits to the influence of acculturation. The Pd, Pa, and Sc scales of the MMPI seem to be among the more sensitive scales to the moderating influences of acculturation, particularly the Pd scale. In their attempt to understand personality and human behavior, Butcher, Narikiyo, and Vitouset (1993) noted the great commonalities and differences among cultural groups. Not all personality traits are equally moderated by culture nor are they all equally malleable to the influences of culture. Personality is part heritability, part environmental, and part interactive.

Acquiescence, quiet submissiveness, or the tendency to answer in the affirmative is clearly a trait that is subject to influences from authoritarian, sociopolitical, socioeconomic, and ecocultural contextual transactions. It might be expected to be found in some groups but, due to cultural influences, is more pronounced in some groups than in others. However, within-group variance may be more dramatic than between groups due to changes in the sociopolitical climate in a given cultural context. For this reason, it is not always advisable to generalize findings beyond a specific group. To say, for example, that Hispanics tend to score higher on acquiescence is obviously a gross overgeneralization, yet it may be true for some Hispanics living within a given ecocultural context.

One of the more common behavioral measures used to assess acculturation is the Acculturation Rating Scale for Mexican Americans

TABLE 6.2
Select Research Studies Showing Relations
of Acculturation and Personality

Personality Trait/Scale Administered	Year	Study	Scores Moderated by Ethnicity or Acculturation
California Personality Inventory (CPI)	1980	A. Arrey	13 of 18 scales moderated
MMPI	1980	D. Pollack & J. H. Shore	Pd, Pa, & Sc
Shortened version of The Marlowe–Crown Social Desirability Scale; Rotter's Internal–External Locus of Control Scale	1984	C. E. Ross & J. Mirowsky	Social Desirability & Acquiescence
MMPI	1985	G. T. Montgomery & S. Orozco	10 of 13 MMPI were moderated by acculturation
MMPI	1985	T. Hoffmann, R. H. Dana, & B. Bolton	D, Pd, Pt, Sc, and Si scores were moderated by acculturation for Native Americans
Hopkins Symptom Checklist 90	1986	J. E. Escobar, E. T. Randolph, & M. Hill	Hispanic veterans reported more somatization than a comparison Anglo sample
Rosenberg's Self-Esteem Scale	1987	V. N. Salgado de Snyder	The more Mexican-oriented females had lower Self-Esteem scores
MMPI	1990	G. T. Montgomery, B. R. Arnold, & S. Orozco	8 of 13 Wiggins Content Scales and 17 of 28 Harris–Lingoes Scales were moderated by acculturation
MMPI	1993	S. Sue	Pd, Pa, and Si moderated by acculturation; Hy, D, Pt, and 8 moderated by Asian identity ethnicity
MMPI and MMPI–2	1993	R. H. Whitworth & D. D. McBlaine	L, K, Hy, and Pd moderated by Hispanic ethnicity
Psychological Screening Inventory	1993	C. Negy & D. J. Woods	Alienation, Defensiveness Social Nonconformity, and Expression
MMPI–2	1995	L. H. Lessenger	Pd, Pa, PT, and Si Scales moderated by cultural identity
Millon Clinical Multiaxial Inventory (MCMI–II)	1994	B. Arnold	Social Desirability
Multicultural Assessment of Cultural Constructs–Short Form (MACC–SF)	1995	I. Cuéllar, B. Arnold, & G. Gonzalez	Fatalism, Machismo Familism (Traditionalism)

(ARSMA) and ARSMA–II (Cuéllar, Arnold, & Maldonado, 1995). ARSMA–II provides both linear and orthogonal measures of acculturation. ARSMA–II is composed of two subscales: An Anglo Orientation Subscale (AOS) and a Mexican Orientation Subscale (MOS). In its linear form, an acculturation score is obtained from ARSMA–II, which can serve as an acculturative balance scale (Acculturation Score = AOS – MOS); this indicates deviations from an equal balance between two cultures. Positive acculturation scores on ARSMA–II are indicative of the degree of acculturation toward the Anglo culture.

Increases in acculturation have been found to have differential effects on different personality traits and characteristics. Sometimes the moderating effects of ARSMA–II acculturation scores increase normal and/or psychopathology scores on etic measures, sometimes they have the opposite effect, and still other times there is no noticeable effect at all. A general conclusion that can be drawn about the relationship between acculturation and personality tests scores seems to be that less acculturated persons, particularly when accompanied by lower socioeconomic status (SES) and education, have elevated scores in the direction of greater psychopathology.

Linear acculturation measurement is not always helpful in discerning the more complex relations characterizing multidomain constructs such as personality and acculturation. The newer acculturation measures are orthogonal and generate, among other categories, two distinct types of biculturals that have opposite psychological features (Cuéllar, Roberts, Romero, & Leka, 1998). On a linear measure, these two types of biculturals cannot be differentiated because their scores would be identical (i.e., on a linear scale of 1 to 5, both types of biculturals would obtain a 3). ARSMA–II is able to separate both types because ARSMA–II is both a linear and an orthogonal acculturation measure. Each type of acculturation measurement, linear versus orthogonal, has advantages and disadvantages. Orthogonal acculturation scores, unlike linear acculturation scores, cannot be correlated directly with psychological measures and require nonparametric correlational coefficients.

ACCULTURATION AND ASSESSMENT PRACTICES

Although it is well understood that acculturation is not unidirectional, it is sometimes convenient to frame acculturation as reflecting an implied direction—namely, toward American mainstream (White Euro-American culture). That is, as one acculturates, one moves in the direction of becoming Americanized. With this frame of reference in mind, it is possible to understand deviations from U.S. standardized test score norms as possible reflections of degrees of exposure to other than mainstream U.S. cultural influences. As individuals such as minorities acculturate in this model, they acquire the behaviors, customs, attitudes, and values among other characteristics of the host culture. Of course, they may retain, give up, or integrate traditional culture as they acquire (acculturate) U.S. mainstream culture. This unidirectional, linear, and heuristic model of acculturation, although not entirely correct, is helpful from a statistical point of view in understanding acculturation variance as standard deviation units from the mean (U.S. culture). Using this model, the more assimilated the person is to mainstream U.S. culture, the greater the likelihood that standardized norms can be applied with confidence for that individual. This is the basis of Mercer's (1979) Sociocultural Scale, which serves as a moderator of intelligence test scores. It is also the basis for understanding the use of acculturation as a moderator variable in clinical practice. As an individual acculturates, he or she is believed to be acquiring and changing his or her worldview, perceptions, attitudes, identity, personality features, as well as other behaviors and cognition already discussed. The application of moderator variables may provide the only defensible rationale when using psychological measures on individuals who are culturally different from standardization populations (Dana, 1993a). Both confidence and validity are enhanced with their use in such cases and should be required with imposed etic measures.

It is important to assess not only commonalities but differences as well in competent professional practices (Dana, 1993a). The prior linear model of acculturation helps in understanding deviance from mainstream culture, but it does not go far enough. It does not yield an understanding of the specific cultural beliefs, worldviews, attitudes, identities, behaviors, and so on of individuals being assessed. To gather cultural identity information for individuals who do not fit the standard U.S. norms, an orthogonal approach is required (Oetting & Beauvais, 1991). The orthogonal approach, when applied to clinical practice, requires gathering information on how acculturated an individual is as well as how traditional he or she is with respect to his or her culture of origin. As Dana (1993a) noted, the assessment paradigm in multicultural practice is expanded from the role of individual tests to encompassing other informants, other sources of data, observation of behavior in several settings, the goodness of fit between persons, and a variety of environmental demands. Assessment of cultural components such as language, worldview, identity, group sanctioned behaviors, perceptions of health/illness, spirituality, and other cultural domains provides a better understanding of the person, as well as a basis for interpretation of imposed etic measures of both personality and psychopathology. Dana (1993b) noted that the use of corrections using moderator variables contributes to cultural competence in assessment practice.

Misclassification in clinical practice increases proportionally to the differences that exist between the consumer and provider. This is also true for differences between the test taker and the standardization sample for any given test. An assessment is considered to be a cross-cultural assessment when the person taking the test is racially or ethnically different from the examiner. It can also be defined when the test taker's demographic, sociocultural, or other psychological characteristics are sufficiently distinct from those of the standardization sample for that test (Cuéllar, 1998). Butcher (1995) reminded us that personality test results do not always mean what we think they mean. When differences are noted between two groups (e.g., between two ethnic groups) on a psychological test, it cannot be assumed that the scores have the same meaning for each group. Cultural equivalence for a given test needs to be established before the test can be used meaningfully cross-culturally. Until cross-cultural equivalence for a given test and group is established, all cross-cultural applications should be qualified by a statement such as the following: "Group differences may, and most likely have, different meaning for each group."

The Mechanics of Moderating Test Scores

There is little written on how to utilize moderator variables in making needed corrections. Nonetheless, there is precedent for making adjustment to minority scores upward to lessen disparate impact in the field of personnel psychology. Adjustments are calculated based on race-specific norms or on a test's level of predictive validity (Gottfredson, 1994). Less has been written on clinical and personality scale adjustments (see Dana, 1993b).

However, there is a statistical analyses methodology for examining test bias that may be helpful in understanding the influence of a moderator variable on a given criterion. Anastasi and Urbina (1997) described slope bias and intercept bias and provided some decision models for the fair use of tests. Slope bias occurs when a test has differential validity for two groups. Validity coefficients are used to assess slope bias. When both test and criterion scores are expressed as standard scores ($SD = 1.0$), the slope of the regression line equals the validity coefficient obtained for each group. It is important to keep in mind that the number of cases used to obtain the validity coefficient will make a difference as to whether any given correlation is significant. Thus, it is necessary to take into account the magnitude of a correlation coefficient and its significance as well.

However, even where predictive validity coefficients are equal for two groups, the scores may have differential construct validity. Butcher (1995) stated that meaning of scores may vary even when scores are equal for two groups. It cannot be assumed that the meaning of scores is the same for two groups just because both groups obtained similar means. This suggests that, in some cases, it may be necessary to moderate scores even when no quantitative differences exist between groups.

The second type of bias mentioned by Anastasi and Urbina is intercept bias. Even when a test yields the same validity coefficient for two groups, it may still show intercept bias—systematic under- or overprediction of criterion performance for a particular group. In intercept bias, the validity coefficients for two groups may be equal. However, because one group has a regression line that intersects the Y axis at a higher point than the other, the same score obtained by members of the two groups has different predictive meaning for the two groups.

When acculturation scores are used to moderate performance for a given ethnic group on a personality trait or clinical test, the score on the personality scale/test is either increased or decreased by some index of correction for culture. One method that can be used to arrive at an Index of Correction for Culture (ICC) is to determine via acculturation how deviant the testee is from the standardization sample. The greater the cultural deviance of the testee from the standardization sample, the greater the ICC. The direction is determined by the direction of the correlation between acculturation and the criterion variable for a specific ethnic group.

What the ICC does is address the following question: If the testee were culturally similar to the standardization sample, how would the testee have scored? The ICC provides a quantitative glimpse of the influence of a given culture on a given personality trait or possibly state. To be specific, let's say we obtain a significant negative correlation of −.35 between ARSMA–II and the Pd scale on the MMPI. Let's also say that a correlation coefficient (actually Multiple R) of −.20 is obtained on a White Euro-American sample when drug abuse is regressed by the Pd scale (i.e., the Pd scale is the predictor and drug use is the criterion variable). Let's also say that a given Mexican American takes the Pd scale of the MMPI and obtains a T-score of 75. If the Mexican American is very traditional or not very acculturated, a downward correction for acculturation would be required. The lower the level of acculturation of the Mexican American, the greater the correction (adjustment downward) required to the Pd score.

Before making this correction, it would be most helpful to determine what the mean score for Mexican Americans is on the Pd scale. Corrections for culture might be made in several ways. The simplest is to compare mean scores for the standardization sample with the minority group and then add or subtract average point differences for the minority group to equalize means. In the example provided, this would most likely entail subtracting a given number of T-score points from the obtained Pd T-score because there are some data to suggest Mexican Americans obtain higher Pd scores.

A more exact method for making corrections entails correcting the known slope of the regression line for Pd and drug abuse for the non-Hispanic sample. A third method of correction would entail correcting the intercept of the regression of drug abuse by Pd. The latter two options require specific knowledge of the regression of drug abuse by Pd for Mexican Americans. If both the slope and intercept are known, a regression line specific for each ethnic group can be obtained—the ultimate in prediction. Rarely is such knowledge known; if it were known, corrections would not be required. In the absence of such knowledge, less exacting corrections such as those suggested later have to be employed.

The previous statistical procedures require knowledge of validity coefficients as well as influences of culture via acculturation to determine test bias and moderate scores for a particular group accordingly. In clinical practice, such information is often simply not available. Use of majority regression line for ethnic minorities could result in over- or underprediction of the criterion. In clinical practice, this could translate into risk of either over- or underdiagnosis. Validity cannot and should not be assumed in the absence of a minority, group-specific, regression line for a given psychological test and criterion. Yet psychologists commonly assume there are no differences among groups instead of assuming the opposite—that ethnic and other group differences are most likely significantly different from the standardization sample.

Tests scores often need to be moderated when normative data for a given group are not available. As it became better known that males and females had distinct profiles, gender-specific norms became commonplace. Besides gender, there are numerous demographic, socioeconomic, educational, and ethnocultural variables whose influence on scores also warrant group-specific norms. For example, individuals with lower SES tend to do worse on psychological tests, and minority groups tend to score lower on some measures (e.g., cognitive abilities tests) and higher on others (e.g., Pd scale of MMPI). All of these differences work in conjunction as subtractive and/or additive factors with respect to any given criterion. The following is a regression model that is suggested as a checklist when considering the need to moderate a given score: Gender + SES (income and education) + group-specific validity coefficient + intercept for a given group + acculturation differences between the subject and the standardized population = ICC.

As noted by the length of this equation, acculturation is only one of numerous variables that may impact a criterion variable. Arriving at some ICC is challenging, but should be utilized in lieu of the assumption that group differences are not significant. Unfortunately, there are no stan-

dardized procedures currently in place for moderating scores. It is possible
for a clinician to make a clinical judgment based on the information that
is available at any point in time. A short-cut regression formula is simply
to examine the acculturation differences between the person taking the
test and the standardization sample. The greater the differences, the
greater the moderation required. The direction of the moderation would
depend on the direction of any known correlation coefficients between
acculturation and the criterion measure.

Given the current state of knowledge, quantitative moderation techniques are not always possible. An estimate of the acculturation level of
the subject, the acculturation differences between the subject and the
group on which the test was standardized, and the degree and direction
of moderation are all variables that can be derived via clinical judgment.
This judgment should be based on a quantifiable science whenever or
wherever possible.

In the absence of objective quantifiable data, a clinical judgment can
still be rendered. Clinical judgments can be based on a number of factors,
including but not limited to: knowledge or experience with the predictor
variable, the criterion, familiarity with the subject, the subject's culture,
and the context of testing. Not taking moderating influences into account
when assessing personality can result in errors—those that come about
from the false assumption that there is no need to moderate.

REFERENCES

Anastasi, A., & Urbina, S. (1997). *Psychological testing*. Englewood Cliffs, NJ: Prentice-Hall.
Angel, R. (1994). The impact of culture and social class on health status and medical care
    usage. In S. K. Hoppe & Wayne H. Holtzman (Eds.), *Search for a common language in
    psychiatric assessment*. The University of Texas, Texas-World Health Organization
    Collaborating Center. Austin: Hogg Foundation for Mental Health, University of Texas
    at Austin.
Arnold, B. (1994, November). *Performance of Mexican Americans on the Millon Clinical Multiaxial
    Inventory–II*. Paper presented at the annual Texas Psychological Association conference,
    Houston, Texas.
Arrey, A. (1980). *Performance of Anglo-American and Chicano males and females on a measure of
    acculturation and the California Personality Inventory*. Unpublished master's thesis, the
    University of Texas Health Science Center at Dallas.
Bandura, A. (1986). *Social foundation of thought and action: A social cognitive theory*. Englewood
    cliffs, NJ: Prentice-Hall.
Beck, L. (1998). *Development through the lifespan*. Boston: Allyn & Bacon.
Berry, J. W. (1980). Acculturation as varieties of adaptation. In A. M. Padilla (Ed.), *Theory,
    models and some new findings* (pp. 9–25). Boulder, CO: Westview.
Berry, J. W. (1994). An ecological perspective on cultural and ethnic psychology. In E. J.
    Trickett, R. J. Watts, & D. Birman (Eds.), *Human diversity: Perspectives on people in context*
    (pp. 115–141). San Francisco: Jossey-Bass.
Berry, J. W., Poortinga, Y. H., Segall, M. H., & Dasen, P. R. (1992). *Cross-cultural psychology:
    Research and applications*. Cambridge, England: Cambridge University Press.

Burnam, M. A., Telles, C. A., Karno, M., & Escobar, J. (1987). Measurement of acculturation in a community population of Mexican Americans. *Hispanic Journal of Behavioral Sciences, 9*, 105–130.

Butcher, J. N. (1995). Clinical personality assessment: An overview. In J. N. Butcher (Ed.), *Clinical personality assessment* (pp. 3–9). New York: Oxford University Press.

Butcher, J. N., Narikiyo, T., & Vitouset, K. B. (1993). Understanding abnormal behavior in cultural context. In P. B. Sutker & H. E. Adams (Eds.), *Comprehensive handbook of psychopathology* (pp. 83–105). New York: Plenum.

Cuéllar, I. (1998). Cross-cultural clinical psychological assessment of Hispanic Americans. *Journal of Personality Assessment, 70*(1), 71–86.

Cuéllar, I., Arnold, B., & Gonzalez, G. (1995). Cognitive referents of acculturation: Assessment of cultural constructs in Mexican Americans. *Journal of Community Psychology, 23,* 339–356.

Cuéllar, I., Arnold, B., & Maldonado, R. (1995). The Acculturation Rating Scale for Mexican Americans–II (ARSMA–II): A revision of the original ARSMA scale. *The Hispanic Journal of Behavioral Science, 17*(3), 275–304.

Cuéllar, I., Harris, L. C., & Jasso, R. (1980). The acculturation rating scale for Mexican Americans. *Hispanic Journal of Behavioral Sciences, 2,* 197–217.

Cuéllar, I., Roberts, R. E., Romero, A. J., & Leka, G. (1998). *Acculturation and marginalization: A test of Stonequist's hypothesis.* Manuscript submitted for publication.

Dana, R. H. (1993a). *Multicultural assessment perspectives for professional psychology.* Boston: Allyn & Bacon.

Dana, R. H. (1993b, November). *Can "corrections" for culture using moderator variables contribute to cultural competence in assessment?* Paper presented at the annual convention of the Texas Psychological Association, Austin, Texas.

Diaz-Guerrero, R. (1968). *Psychology of the Mexican: Culture and personality.* Austin, TX: University of Texas Press.

Escobar, J. E., Randolph, E. T., & Hill, M. (1986). Symptoms of schizophrenia in Hispanic and Anglo veterans. *Culture, Medicine and Psychiatry, 10,* 259–276.

Felix-Ortiz, M., Newcomb, M. D., & Myers, H. (1994). A multidimensional measure of cultural identity for Latino and Latina adolescents. *Hispanic Journal of Behavioral Sciences, 16*(2), 99–115.

Garcia, M., & Lega, L. I. (1979). Development of a Cuban Ethnic Identity Questionnaire. *Hispanic Journal of Behavioral Sciences, 1*(3), 247–261.

Geertz, C. (1984). Comment, in preview: A colloquy of cultural theorists. In R. A. Shweder & R. A. LeVine (Eds.), *Culture theory* (pp. 1–24). Cambridge, England: Cambridge University Press.

Gottfredson, L. S. (1994). The science and politics of race-norming. *American Psychologist, 49*(11), 955–963.

Helms, J. E. (1986). Expanding racial identity theory to cover the counseling process. *Journal of Counseling Psychology, 33,* 62–64.

Hoffmann, T., Dana, R. H., & Bolton, B. (1985). Measured acculturation and MMPI-168 performance of Native Americans. *Journal of Cross-Cultural Psychology, 16*(2), 243–256.

Hui, C. H. (1988). Measurement of individualism-collectivism. *Journal of Research in Personality, 22,* 17–36.

Ibrahim, F. A., & Kahn, H. (1987). Assessment of world view. *Psychological Reports, 60,* 163–176.

Keefe, S. E., & Padilla, A. M. (1987). *Chicano ethnicity.* Albuquerque: University of New Mexico Press.

Kitayama, S., & Markus, H. R. (1994). Introduction to cultural psychology and emotions. In S. Kitayama & H. R. Markus (Eds.), *Emotions and culture: Empirical studies of mutual influence.* Washington, DC: American Psychologial Association.

Kluckholm, F. R., & Strodtbeck, F. L. (1961). *Variations in value orientations.* Homewood, IL: Dorsey.

Kroeber, A. L., & Kluckholm, C. (1952). *Culture: A critical review of concepts and definitions.* Cambridge, MA: Peabody Museum of American Archaeology and Ethnology.

Landrine, H., & Klonoff, E. A. (1994). The African American Acculturation Scale: Development, reliability, and validity. *Journal of Black Psychology, 20*(2), 104–127.

Lessenger, L. H. (1995). *The relationship between cultural identity and MMPI–2 scores of Mexican American Substance Abuse patients.* Unpublished doctoral dissertation, California School of Professional Psychology, Fresno.

Levinson, D. J., & Huffman, P. E. (1955). Traditional Family Ideology Scale. *Journal of Personality, 23,* 251–273.

Lewin, K. (1935). *A dynamic theory of personality.* New York: McGraw-Hill.

Linton, R. (1945). *The cultural background of personality.* New York: Appleton-Century-Crofts.

Lonner, W. J., & Adamopoulos, J. (1997). Culture as antecedent to behavior. In J. W. Berry, Y. H. Poortinga, & J. Pandey (Eds.), *Handbook of cross-cultural psychology* (2nd ed., Vol. 1., pp. 43–83). Boston: Allyn & Bacon.

Marin, G., & Gamba, R. J. (1996). A new measurement of acculturation for Hispanics: The Bidimensional Acculturation Scale for Hispanics. *Hispanic Journal of Behavioral Sciences, 18*(3), 297–316.

Marin, G., Sabogal, F., VanOss Marin, B., Otero-Sabogal, R., & Perez-Stable, E. J. (1986). Development of a short acculturation scale for Hispanics. *Hispanic Journal of Behavioral Sciences, 9,* 183–205.

Marsella, A. J., & Kameoka, V. A. (1989). Ethnocultural issues in the assessment of psychopathology. In S. Wetzler (Ed.), *Measuring mental illness: Psychometric assessment for clinicians* (pp. 229–256). Washington, DC: American Psychiatric Press.

Mendoza, R. H. (1989). Am empirical scale to measure type and degree of acculturation in Mexican American adolescents and adults. *Journal of Cross-Cultural Psychology, 20,* 372–385.

Mercer, J. (1979). *System of Multicultural Pluralistic Assessment (SOMPA): Technical Manual.* San Antonio, TX: Psychological Assessment Corporation.

Montemayor, R. A., & Becker, R. E. (1979, December). *Study of intergenerational differences in a three generation Mexican American family.* Unpublished research pilot study. Warden School of Social Work, Our Lady of the Lake University, San Antionio, TX.

Montgomery, G. T., Arnold, B. R., & Orozco, S. (1990). MMPI supplemental scale performance of Mexican Americans and level of acculturation. *Journal of Personality Assessment, 54*(1 & 2), 328–342.

Montgomery, G. T., & Orozco, S. (1985). Mexican American's performance on the MMPI as a function of level of acculturation. *Journal of Personality Assessment, 54*(1–2), 328–342.

Montgomery, G. T., & Orozco, S. (1992). Comfort with Acculturation Status among students from south Texas. *Hispanic Journal of Behavioral Sciences, 14*(2), 201–223.

Negy, C., & Woods, D. J. (1993). Mexican-American and Anglo-American differences on the Psychological Screening Inventory. *Journal of Personality Assessment, 60*(3), 543–553.

Oetting, E. R., & Beauvais, F. (1991). Orthogonal cultural identification theory: The cultural identification of minority adolescents. *The International Journal of the Addictions, 25*(5a–6a), 655–685.

Olmedo, E. L. (1979). Acculturation: A psychometric perspective. *American Psychologist, 34,* 1061–1070.

Olmedo, E. L., Martinez, J. L., & Martinez, S. R. (1978). Measure of acculturation for Chicano adolescents. *Psychological Reports, 42,* 159–170.

Olmedo, E. L., & Padilla, A. (1978). Empirical and construct validation of a measure of acculturation for Mexican Americans. *The Journal of Social Psychology, 105,* 179–187.

Padilla, A. M. (1980). The role of cultural awareness and ethnic loyalty in acculturation. In A. M. Padilla (Ed.), *Acculturation: Theory, models and some new findings* (pp. 47–84). Boulder, CO: Westview.

Phinney, J. S. (1992). The Multigroup Ethnic Identity Measure: A new scale for use with diverse groups. *Journal of Adolescent Research, 7*, 156–176.

Pierce, R. C., Clark, M. M., & Kiefer, C. W. (1972). *Human Organization, 31*(4), 403–410.

Pollack, D., & Shore, J. H. (1980). Validity of the MMPI with Native Americans. *American Journal of Psychiatry, 137*, 946–950.

Poortinga, Y. H. (1990/1992). Towards a conceptualization of culture for psychology. *Cross-Cultural Psychology Bulletin, 24*(3), 2–10.

Ramirez, M., Castaneda, A., & Cox, B. G. (1977). *A biculturalism inventory for Mexican-Americans* (Technical Report). Office of Naval Research: Organizational Effectiveness Research Program, March 1977.

Redfield, R., Linton, R., & Herskovitz, M. J. (1936). Memorandum for the study of acculturation. *American Anthropologist, 38*, 149–152.

Rezentes, W. C. (1993). Na-Mea-Hawaii—A Hawaiian Acculturation Scale. *Psychological Reports, 73*(2), 383–393.

Ross, C. E., & Mirowsky, J. (1984). Socially-desirable response and acquiescence in a cross-cultural survey of mental health. *Journal of Health and Social Behavior, 25*, 189–197.

Salgado de Snyder, V. N. (1987). Factors associated with acculturation stress and depressive symptomatology among married Mexican immigrant women. *Psychology of Women Quarterly, 11*, 477–488.

Suarez-Orozco, M. M., Spindler, G., & Spindler, L. (Eds.). (1994). *The making of psychological anthropology II.* Fort Worth, TX: Harcourt Brace.

Sue, S. (1993, September). *Measurement, testing and ethnic bias: Can solutions be found?* Paper presented at the Ninth Buros-Nebraska Symposium on Measurement and Testing, Lincoln, Nebraska.

Suinn, R. M., Richard-Figueroa, K., Lew, S., & Vigil, S. (1987). The Suinn-Lew Asian Self-Identity Acculturation Scale: An initial report. *Educational and Psychological Measurement, 47*, 401–407.

Szapocznik, J., Scopetta, M. A., & Aranalde, M. A. (1978a). Theory and measurement of acculturation. *Interamerican Journal of Psychology, 12*, 113–130.

Szapocznik, J., Scopetta, A., Aranalde, M. A., & Kurtines, W. (1978b). Cuban value structure: Treatment implications. *Journal of Consulting and Clinical Psychology, 46*(5), 961–970.

Whitworth, R. H., & McBlaine, D. D. (1993). Comparison of the MMPI and MMPI–2 administered to Anglo-American and Hispanic-American University students. *Journal of Personality Assessment, 61*(1), 19–27.

Acculturation, Ethnic Identity, and Acculturative Stress: Evidence and Measurement

Gargi Roysircar-Sodowsky
Michael Virgil Maestas
University of Nebraska–Lincoln

The changing racial and ethnic composition of U.S. society has prompted research attention to the acculturation and ethnic identity of visible ethnic minority groups. The collective understanding among investigators working closely within this area (e.g., Berry, 1980; Isajiw, 1990; Phinney, 1991; Smith, 1991; Sodowsky, Kwan, & Pannu, 1995) is that ethnic minority individuals living in the U.S. pluralistic society must contend with four critical issues: (a) experiences of racism and discrimination owing to their immigrant and minority status, (b) relationship with the dominant culture, (c) retention of ethnic or cultural heritage, and (d) stress that results from the previously mentioned experiences. The constraints of this chapter do not allow us to address ethnic minorities' racism experiences and their consequent development of racial consciousness. The three remaining issues studied within three broad research domains of acculturation, ethnic identity, and acculturative stress are addressed along with generational status, which has been shown to cause differences in the three said domains (Sodowsky, 1998).

In surveying the recent multicultural literature (e.g., Casas & Pytluk, 1995; Choney, Berryhill-Paapke, & Robbins, 1995; Osvold & Sodowsky, 1995), it appears that researchers have increasingly come to recognize that all ethnic minority individuals can, at some level, identify with issues relating to their acculturation and retention of ethnic identity in the mainstream White society. This is evidenced by the development of several multidimensional acculturation measures (see this chapter's appendix for a review of the psychometrics of seven such measures for non-Hispanics/-Latinos; see also Table 7.1 for an analysis of trends in acculturation instruments), ethnic identity measures (see a review of the psychometrics of three such measures in the Appendix), and related theoretical models and empirical inquiries.

Acculturation and ethnic identity researchers have underscored the need to recognize the heterogeneity both between and within Asian-American ethnic groups. Factors by which Asian Americans have shown

TABLE 7.1
Trends in Acculturation Instrumentation

Trends from the late 1970s to the early 1980s:
- A focus on instruments for Hispanic/Latino populations (7 of 7)
- An emphasis on assessing language (5 of 7)
- An interest in generational issues and differences (3 of 7)
- Some attention on cultural exposure (3 of 7), behavioral (2 of 7), and relational (3 of 7) dimensions of acculturation
- Participants were more often exclusively recruited than randomly sampled (5 of 7)
- Geographic locations included 3 California samples, 2 Texas samples, 2 Florida samples, and 1 New Jersey sample
- 4 of the 7 instruments also included White Americans in instrument development studies

Trends from 1987 to present:
- Development of acculturation instruments and validation studies on other diverse populations, including Asian Americans (7 of 15), Native Americans (1 of 15), African Americans (1 of 15), and International people (2 of 15); Hispanics/Latinos continue to be a focus of studies (10 of 15) and White Americans were included in 4 of the 15 studies
- Language continues to be of importance (11 of 15)
- Still some attention on cultural exposure and behavioral dimensions of acculturation
- More of an emphasis on the social/relational dimensions than previously (12 of 15)
- Inclusion of "perceived prejudice" as a subscale (4 of 15)
- New participants most often recruited (9 of 15) and often from populations of convenience rather than general population (6 of 15)
- Geographic locations included 4 Nebraska samples, 4 California samples, 3 Texas samples, 2 Colorado samples, 1 Hawaiian sample, 1 Ohio sample, and 1 Oklahoma sample

Other comments:
- Many of the samples were recruited and not random; therefore the results may not be generalizable to a general ethnic population
- Most scales had fairly high reliabilities and many had criterion-related and convergent validity
- Overall, sample sizes were quite large, ranging from 62 to 2,885 participants
- Subscales labeled as Ethnic Identity are precursors of the current development of more comprehensive ethnic identity conceptual models and measurement instruments

---

Note. Some of this analysis is based on information provided by Lai and Sodowsky's (1996) Acculturation Instrumentation in G. R. Sodowsky and J. C. Impara (Eds.), *Multicultural assessment in counseling and clinical psychology.* Lincoln, NE: Buros Institute of Mental Measurements.

wide variations include interethnic variables (i.e., among Asian ethnic groups), such as country of ancestry, pre-immigration (e.g., voluntary immigration vs. political refugee status) and immigration history, ethnic language, religion, sociopolitical relationship with the White American society, and degree of acculturation. Asian Americans also differ on intraethnic variables (i.e., within an Asian ethnic group), including migration and relocation experiences, degree of acculturation and cultural ethnic identity retention, ethnic and English language proficiency, ethnic dialect, socioeconomic status (SES), family composition and intactness, adherence to religious beliefs, and generational status. Some of these sociodemographic/cultural variables, as well as acculturation and cultural ethnic identity, influence both inter- and intraethnic variations.

ACCULTURATION VERSUS ETHNIC IDENTITY

Acculturation issues are more befitting of first-generation immigrant minority groups who go through the continuous process of adapting to the mainstream White culture. Ethnic identity issues related to a reverse acculturation to one's original cultural group are more relevant and meaningful to U.S.-born minorities—the children of immigrants. Sodowsky and Lai (1997) distinguished between the two constructs, stating that "Acculturation adaptation is a response to the dominant group, and ethnic identity is a response to one's ethnic group" (p. 213). Whereas first-generation immigrants who arrived in the United States at an older age must struggle with their acculturation to the mainstream society after having been socialized in their culture, second- and later generation individuals are likely to question what aspects of their ethnic cultures are most relevant to them and, thus, to be retained. Through exposure, experience, and both involuntary and voluntary learning, the immigrant gains acculturation to the dominant society. However, the need to attach to a reference or social group (i.e., to a secure base) drives the descendants of immigrants to recognize their ethnic identity. Velez (1995), studying first- and second-generation Puerto Rican and Chinese-American college students throughout New York City, indicated that second-generation subjects had higher acculturation scores than the first generation, but ethnic identity was not inversely correlated with level of acculturation. Bufka's (1998) study showed that first-generation Asian Indian adolescents were less acculturated than their second-generation peers. They also perceived more prejudice and used an Indian language more than their second-generation peers. However, the two generations did not show any differences in various components of ethnic identity. Cuéllar, Roberts, Nyberg, and Maldonado (1997) found in a sample of Mexican-American freshman college students that those students who were classified as High-Bicultural acculturative type scored higher on a measure of ethnic identity than those students classified as Low-Bicultural acculturative type. Thus, acculturation and ethnic identity are relatively independent phenomena, both being experienced by ethnic minorities. Ethnic identity formation is possible only in the context of both the dominant and ethnic minority societies, but loses its relevance in a monocultural society. Conceptually, the relationship between acculturation and ethnic identity can be described as a push-and-pull psychological phenomenon: One feels both the push to acculturate to the dominant society and the pull toward one's ethnic group. The tension between the push and pull could be described as acculturative stress and bicultural stress.

A weakness noted in measurement studies on acculturation and ethnic identity is that the two constructs have not been sufficiently differentiated empirically. We suggest that, for the measurement of acculturation, one needs to study the adoptions of White American ways of doing things in language usage, cultural exposure, social behaviors, and relational acts. For the measurement of ethnic identity, one needs to study an affective/cathectic attachment that values connecting with one's ethnic group members, believes in the importance of one's ethnicity, and seeks to retain certain aspects of an ethnic cultural heritage that are relevant and functional in a given context. In certain acculturation measures (see the appendix), subscales labeled as *Ethnic Identity* are precursors of the current development of more comprehensive ethnic identity conceptual models and measurement instruments.

According to Berry (1993), *enculturation*, as opposed to acculturation, refers to the ethnic socialization process "by which developing individuals acquire (either by generalized learning in a particular cultural milieu, or as a result of specific instruction and training) the host of cultural and psychological qualities that are necessary to function as a member of one's group" (p. 272). In a descriptive model of cultural transmission, Berry distinguished three ways by which culture is transmitted: (a) vertical transmission through the learning and influence of one's parents, (b) horizontal transmission involving peer interactions, and (c) oblique transmission through interactions with adults and institutions in one's society or community. For Asian Americans, particularly those who immigrated to the United States in adolescence as well as second-generation Asian Americans who are likely to have immigrant parents who adhere to the traditional Asian culture, this enculturation process is complicated by the need to unlearn and learn two opposing, but equally significant, cultural systems simultaneously (Sung, 1985). As stated by Sung, "Even though they [immigrant Chinese] may find some aspects of the old culture obsolete, they are loathe to give up that which is part of them. . . . How much of the new must they take on to function adequately? . . . How much of the old culture do they retain?" (p. 255). For some, biculturalism may be the answer to the problem. For instance, Chabbra (1994) showed that Asian-Indian subjects in Southern California who indicated bilingual scores on the language subscale of the Sodowsky et al. (1991) acculturation instrument showed the most adaptive acculturation: integration.

In terms of Berry's cultural transmission model, one's ethnic culture is likely to be transmitted vertically by the parents (Sodowsky & Lai, 1997). Yet the culture of the dominant society is learned horizontally through peer interactions as well as obliquely through interactions with White adults (e.g., teachers) and institutions (e.g., school system). Minority groups undergoing a dual socialization process are thoroughly accultur-ated to the dominant culture by mainstream institutions, including mass media advertisements, the entire experience of public schooling, and widespread exposure to national holidays, fashions, and heroes. Thus, enculturation into one's ethnic society has less overt reinforcements than acculturation into the dominant society.

BIDIMENSIONAL ACCULTURATION MODEL

Acculturation is generally viewed as a process of change that occurs as a consequence of a continuous, first-hand contact of two or more distinct cultural groups. Sodowsky, Lai, and Plake (1991) defined *acculturation* as the adaptation of minority groups to the culture of the dominant group. Berry and colleagues (e.g., 1980, 1987, 1989, 1993) proposed a two-dimen-sional model of acculturation that provides a framework to understand the effect of the two-way interaction between a majority group and a minority group to determine the acculturation of ethnic groups. According to the model, ethnic minorities must confront two general issues: the maintenance and development of one's ethnic distinctiveness by retaining one's cultural identity, and the desire to seek interethnic contact by valu-ing and maintaining positive relations with the dominant society. These two general issues represent the dimensions of acculturation, and they can be assessed by two central questions (Berry, 1980): (a) Is it considered to be of value to maintain cultural identity and characteristics?, and (b) Is it considered to be of value to maintain relationships with other groups? The combination of answers results in four acculturation attitudes: inte-gration (yes/yes), assimilation (no/yes), separation (yes/no), and mar-ginalization (no/no). The integration adaptation mode is characterized by an allegiance to cultural identity and involvement in the dominant culture. Those who use the assimilation mode relinquish their cultural identity and prefer to interact only with members of the dominant society.

In contrast, a separation involves the exclusive identification with and retention of one's cultural values and an avoidance of contact with the dominant society. Individuals who become marginal "lose cultural and psychological contact with both their culture and the larger society" (Berry, Kim, Power, Young, & Bujaki, 1989, p. 188). Similar to Berry's second question regarding how one relates to the dominant society, Sodowsky and her colleagues (Osvold & Sodowsky, 1995; Sodowsky & Lai, 1997; Sodowsky et al., 1991, 1995; Sodowsky & Plake, 1992) understand acculturation as a U.S. minority group's conflict-reduction process of behavioral adaptation as it attempts to reduce the majority–minority group conflict over cultural value and power differences. This bidirectional adaptation process creates a multidimensional profile of factors related to acculturation (see the Appendix for a description of measures that assess some of these factors).

Studies on Acculturation

First generations have consistently shown differences in acculturation when compared with later generations. The appendix reports the differences as indicated by acculturation measures. *Generation* is defined according to one's country of birth or one's parents' country of birth. For example, *first generation* is defined as foreign-born, U.S. immigrants; *second generation* is defined as U.S.-born offspring of first-generation immigrant parent(s); and *third generation* is defined as offspring of second-generation, U.S.-born parent(s). In other words, third-generation individuals have grandparent(s) who were foreign-born immigrants. Abe and Zane (1990) found that foreign-born Asian Americans were significantly more other directed or highly attuned to the desires and needs of others than American-born Asian Americans.

In regard to Asian cultural values, Sodowsky et al. (1995) stated that family bonds are central to the experiences of Asian Americans and, thus, are expected to contribute the most variation among Asian Americans from different generational levels. For example, many first-generation, less acculturated Asian immigrants are likely to sacrifice their personal desires and independence for the sake of maintaining their family obligations, avoiding loss of face, and bringing honor to the family name. Second-generation, more acculturated Asian Americans may seek more personal independence and feel conflicted by the value placed on family expectations. Because individual achievement is believed to reflect on the family as a whole in many Southeast and South Asian cultures, failure to meet high expectations of first-generation parents may cause emotional distress for the second-generation student. Aldwin and Greenberger (1987) indicated that for Korean science college majors, having parents with higher standards for doing well, adhering to modern values, and perceiving parents as endorsing traditional values were positively related to depression. In contrast, for White students, adherence to modern values, regardless of parental endorsement, was associated significantly with lower depression. In another study, Greenberger and Chen (1996) found that late adolescent (undergraduates) Asian Americans reported more depressive symptoms and a less favorable view of their family relationships than White college students, and early adolescent (seventh and eighth graders) Asian Americans reported less maternal warmth and acceptance than White early adolescents. Murthy's (1998) quasiethnographic interviews with second-generation Asian Indians indicated that the interviewees felt that their parents' attention was focused primarily on their children's economic future, rather than their overall psychological development. Murthy (1998) suggested that inadequate communication in many Asian Indian immigrant households may lead to severe tension. The young Asian Indians in Murthy's study wanted freedom with regard to dating and making their own choice in marriage, without imposition of traditional marriage values of parents. Mok (1994) articulated the types of Asian Americans (Chinese Americans, Korean Americans, and Japanese Americans) who would most likely date persons outside of or within their own race. An Asian American likely to date a White American is likely to be highly acculturated, find Whites more attractive than Asians, have some prior interracial dating experience, have more White friends than Asian friends, perceive little parental influence over dating behavior, and have grown up around relatively few Asians. In contrast, the reverse of these correlates were noted for Asian Americans who would most likely date an Asian American.

Family acculturation conflicts refer to problems that are attributed to the different rates of acculturation between parents and children. In one early study, Connor (1977) described the attenuation of acculturation conflicts across three generations in Japanese-American families. Chambon (1989) also identified family acculturation conflicts as a serious problem in Southeast Asian refugee families. Ying and Chao (1996) described intercultural conflicts among Iu Mien American families. In a comparative study, Rumbaut (1994) reported that Asian-American immigrant adolescents (Filipino, Vietnamese, Cambodian) had higher amounts of family acculturation conflict than Hispanic/Latino immigrant adolescents. Using their recently developed Family Acculturation Conflicts and Tactics Scale (FACT), Lee, Choe, Kim, and Ngo (1998) measured typical family conflicts related to acculturation differences between U.S.-raised children and their Asian immigrant parents. This scale revealed that recent immigrant families experience more family acculturation conflicts. In other words, children's perceptions of their parents' level of acculturation played a significant role in their amount of family acculturation conflict. There were significant negative correlations of family acculturation conflicts with parental freedom, mutual understanding, and quality time spent together, which are family relationship qualities more typical in families in which parents adopt Westernized parenting styles.

At the same time, immigrant Asian parents who bring *traditional* Asian cultural values with them are not identical to their sedentary Asian counterparts (Sodowsky, 1991; Sodowsky et al., 1995). For instance, based on the finding that first-generation Chinese immigrants showed marked acculturation to Western cultures, Feldman, Mont-Reynaud, and Rosenthal (1992a) postulated that Chinese families who emigrated from Hong Kong might have differed in important cultural dimensions from those who remained in Hong Kong. They suggested that immigrant Chinese families may be less traditional and more educated, individualistic, and proactive in seeking new opportunities than nonimmigrant Chinese families. Ethnic cultures are also commonly perceived to be dynamic and evolving rather than static (Feldman, Mont-Raynaud, & Rosenthal, 1992b; Sodowsky et al., 1995). Thus, Asian immigrants and Asian Americans in the United States tend to form unique ethnic cultures (i.e., different from their home country's and different by generations in the United States) that are influenced and moderated by their ongoing experiences in the United States. Likewise, the mainstream culture is also influenced by the diversity of ethnic cultures in the United States (Sodowsky & Lai, 1997).

ACCULTURATIVE STRESS

Acculturative stress stems from the stressors in the context of acculturation and is "mildly pathological and disruptive to the individual and the group" (Berry, 1980, p. 21). Berry, Kim, Minde, and Mok (1987) defined this stress as a "generalized physiological and psychological state . . . brought about by the experience of stressors in the environment, and which requires some reduction . . . through a process of coping until some satisfactory adaption to the new situation is achieved" (p. 492). Dressler and Bernal (1982) stated that acculturative stress occurs "when an individual's adaptive resources are insufficient to support adjustment to a new cultural environment" (p. 34). The stress is elicited by drastically new life events and cues the acculturating individual to possible dangers or opportunities. Although a certain amount of stress may be necessary or helpful in alerting the individual to respond to new situations, too much stress can threaten healthy adaptation. Thus, Berry et al. (1987) stated that acculturative stress could be a "reduction in health status (including psychological, somatic, and social aspects) of individuals who are undergoing acculturation, and for which there is evidence that these health phenomena are related systematically to acculturation phenomena" (p. 491). For instance, studies have related frequent, high-maximum alcohol consumption of Mexican-American men to level of acculturation and acculturative stress (Zimmerman & Sodowsky, 1993). Higher acculturated African-American and Native-American women in a predominantly White midwestern society indicated problematic eating attitudes (Osvold & Sodowsky, 1995).

However, individuals undergoing acculturation do not necessarily experience mental health problems. The level of acculturative stress can vary considerably depending on four individual and group characteristics. According to Berry and Kim (1988), the first mediating variable includes the nature of the dominant society, which includes factors such as its pluralistic or assimilationist ideology. Acculturative stress is less predominant in multicultural societies than in unicultural societies. The second mediating variable refers to the nature of the acculturating group. Berry and Kim identified five groups that varied in degree of voluntariness, movement, and permanence of contact: immigrants, refugees, native peoples, ethnic groups, and sojourners. The third mediating variable is the mode of acculturation adaptation chosen: assimilation, integration, rejection, or deculturation. Berry (1980) found that among nine groups of *Amerindians* in northern Canada, those communities with the highest stress levels were those (a) with the least cultural similarity to the dominant group, (b) who had some contact, and (c) who preferred the rejection mode of adaptation. Conversely, those minorities in Canada with the least amount of stress had more initial cultural similarity to the dominant group, had experienced more contact, and preferred the integration mode of adaptation. The fourth factor includes the demographic (see Sodowsky & Carey, 1988; Sodowsky et al., 1991; Sodowsky & Plake, 1992), social (see Sodowsky & Lai, 1997), and psychological characteristics (see Kwan & Sodowsky, 1997) of the acculturating individual that can mediate the acculturation and stress relationship. Some of these characteristics also include coping strategies, education, age, gender, cognitive styles, prior intercultural experiences, and contact experiences.

Acculturative stress is a common experience of first-generation immigrants. On the other hand, U.S.-born second- and later generation ethnic minorities experience acculturative stress owing to the conflicts that arise out of their bicultural socialization. Asian Americans undergoing a bicultural socialization process must negotiate between two disparate cultures: the ethnic culture and the White dominant culture. There is vast disparity between Asian and Western cultures. Some of the more salient cultural values and beliefs of the Asian culture include emphasis on family kinship, reciprocal duty and obligation (i.e., filial piety), hierarchical roles and social status, and respect and deference to authority figures or persons of higher social status (Sodowsky, 1991; Sodowsky et al., 1995). In contrast, Western cultures tend to value rugged individualism or autonomy, personal rights and privileges, egalitarian relationships, assertiveness, and self-expression. Studies of worldviews (Sodowsky, Maguire, Johnson, Ngumba, & Kohles, 1994; Ihle, Sodowsky, & Kwan, 1996) have found significant differences between White Americans and Chinese international students. For example, White Americans were more individualistic in their approach to relationships, focusing on personal needs and issues, whereas Chinese students were more likely to conceptualize relationships as collective in nature, where social roles are arranged in a linear and hierarchical fashion.

Given the disparity between Asian and Western cultures, acculturative stress is a particularly relevant issue for Asian Americans. Such cultural adjustment difficulties of Asian Americans, particularly first-generation immigrants, have been predominantly studied within the framework of acculturation. However, ethnic identity studies on later generation ethnic minorities have been concerned with the mental health correlate of self-esteem measures (Phinney, 1991) and specific sources of stress associated with ethnic identity formation such as cultural alienation, cultural confusion, cultural conflict, and bicultural identity conflict (Kiefer, 1974; Kim, 1981; Kwan & Sodowsky, 1997; Sodowsky & Lai, 1997).

S. Sue and D. W. Sue (1971) contended that peer group influences, along with the constant bombardment of White societal values and standards by the educational system and mass media, are likely to erode parental authority and, hence, the retention of ethnic cultures. However, because family kinship is a core value in Asian cultures, Asian Americans who attempt to relinquish their ethnic ties are likely to experience intergenerational conflict with their parents. At the individual level, disidentification with their Asian ethnic identity is likely to be experienced as ego dystonic. Thus, bicultural conflict involves reconciling two opposing, but equally significant, cultures.

Kiefer (1974) identified three types of bicultural conflict experienced by later generation Asian Americans: cultural alienation, cultural confusion, and cultural conflict. *Cultural alienation* refers to a sense of personal discontinuity that occurs across time and as a result of disruption in cultural patterns. It is associated with a weak or poorly developed self-image. Kim (1981) added that cultural alienation experienced by Asian Americans is compounded by racial and ethnic stereotypes that deny one's individuality. *Cultural confusion* occurs as a result of being confronted with multiple norms (e.g., norms of Asian cultures and Western cultures) and the inability to identify and associate with a definite norm within a given context. Thus, there is an incongruence between one's experiences and one's assumptions. *Cultural conflict* occurs when one's values and beliefs are perceived to be incompatible with a given social interaction. Sodowsky and Lai (1997) stated that, as a result of living with two sets of opposing norms and attitudes with regard to interpersonal behaviors, Asian immigrants' sense of self-efficacy in how to be socially poised may be negatively impacted.

Kim (1981) defined *identity crisis* of later generation Asian Americans as "a situation where an individual perceives certain aspects of him/herself which s/he rejects simultaneously" (p. 153). This occurs because, despite their attempts to be White identified or fully assimilated with the White culture, they cannot completely rid themselves of their Asian physical traits and of the core Asian values and ways of conducting life. As stated by Wong (1995),

> No matter how Americanized they become, no matter how similar to Whites in values, aspirations, mannerism, or actions, Chinese Americans will always be perceived as different. Ethnic identity and consciousness among Chinese Americans, therefore, regardless of the extent of their acculturation, are not likely to fully disappear. (p. 87)

Thus, the *marginal person* is conceptualized as living "between the margin of two different cultural traditions" (D. W. Sue & D. Sue, 1990, p. 202). In addition to the psychological stress of identity crisis, the marginal person's over-Westernized attitude and behaviors are frequently in conflict with the Asian values of his or her parents. The marginal person is likely to deny or minimize experiences of personal and institutional racism because admitting widespread racism by the White society would conflict with his or her desire to be White identified. Consequently, marginal persons attribute blame to their own group for their lack of success in the U.S. society. They see Asian values as maladaptive and responsible for their group's rejection by the host society.

Bicultural conflict appears to involve two dimensions: the interpersonal, measured as Intercultural Competence Concerns, and intrapersonal, measured as Acculturative Distress (Sodowsky & Lai, 1997). The interpersonal dimension involves having cultural conflicts with one's own ethnic group (e.g., second-generation's conflicts with first-generation parents) and/or with members of the dominant culture (Sodowsky & Lai, 1997). The intrapersonal dimension includes identity crisis, a personal sense of inferiority as a member of one's cultural group, lack of ethnic ego differentiation due to feeling marginalized from both cultural groups, and feelings of anger and guilt toward one or both cultural groups (Sodowsky & Lai, 1997). In addition, extreme bicultural conflict leaves the individual vulnerable to experiences of bicultural stress, which is

manifested by feelings of emotional turmoil and alienation (D. W. Sue &
D. Sue, 1990), cultural marginality (Masuda, Matsumoto, & Meridith, 1970;
Sodowsky, 1988; Sodowsky et al., 1995), poor self-concept (Padilla, Wagatsuma, & Lindholm, 1985), depression (Draguns, 1996), anxiety (S. Sue,
1996), disordered eating attitudes and behaviors (Osvold & Sodowsky,
1995), and career-choice indecision (Sodowsky, 1991). Sung (1985) identified bicultural conflicts in aggressiveness, sexuality, loyalty, physical
affection, education, finances, autonomy, and respect for authority and
heroes/heroines for Chinese immigrant children.

Studies of Acculturative Stress

In a study of Asian immigrants, Sodowsky and Lai (1997) found a number
of moderating variables that contribute to acculturative stress. The variables that were demonstrated to be related to Acculturative Distress and
Interactional Intercultural Competence included: traditional Asian cultural orientation, young age such as adolescence, immigration at an older
age, social network that excludes White Americans, limited family kinship, low income, and higher levels of perceived prejudice. These findings
were supported by Mehta's (1998) study of Asian-Indian immigrants. The
data show that feeling accepted by the dominant society (i.e., having
lower levels of perceived prejudice), more years of U.S. residence, higher
educational attainment and family income, higher level of pre-immigration adjustment, and being involved with both the U.S. culture as well
as with White Americans were related to better mental health. With regard
to within-group differences, Sodowsky et al. (1991) found that Asian
political refugees experienced more stress than voluntary Asian immigrants. Yeh, Chiang, and Wang (1998) showed that middle-school Chinese
immigrant students self-reported serious psychological problems on the
Symptom Checklist–90–R that were associated with low acculturation,
cultural adjustment difficulties, and low cross-cultural adaptability.

Among a multiethnic group (Asian, African American, Hispanic, and
White Americans) of high school and college students, Phinney, Chavira,
and Williamson (1992) studied the relationship between acculturation and
self-esteem. The results show that (with the exception of African Americans and foreign-born Asian Americans), for both high school and college
students, having an integrated or bicultural attitude was related to higher
levels of self-esteem. In contrast, assimilation attitudes were negatively
correlated with self-esteem for both school samples and across all ethnic
groups (with the exception of White high school and African-American
college students). This latter finding is of particular importance for Asian
Americans because they had endorsed assimilation more than African
and Hispanic Americans. However, foreign-born Asian high school stu-

dents had relatively higher separation scores (separation from White Americans), thus pointing to the significant difference between foreign-born first-generation and U.S.-born second-generation Asians. Likewise, Rotheram-Borus (1990) found that Asian Americans, along with the White group, reported significantly less ethnic pride than the Hispanic and African-American groups. Compared with other groups, Asian Americans perceived their ethnic group as having less power and they had significantly less cross-ethnic contact. Moreover, regardless of whether Asian Americans identified as being mainstream, bicultural, or strongly ethnically identified, the Asian-American group reported significantly more behavioral problems than all other groups.

Kim, O'Neal, and Owen (1996) investigated how acculturation levels were related to gender-role conflict for a group of Asian-American men. The study was based on the assumption that bicultural individuals may experience confusion and conflict as they attempt to redefine and integrate notions of masculine and feminine roles of the dominant culture and of one's ethnic culture. Although Japanese-, Chinese-, and Korean-American men did not differ in their acculturation level (most of the participants were bicultural), acculturation accounted for 18% of the variance on subscales of gender-role conflict. Specifically, for this sample of Asian Americans, higher acculturation scores predicted higher levels of gender-role conflict over issues of success, power, and competition and lower levels of gender-role conflict over issues of restrictive emotionality. Kim et al. (1996) concluded that the acculturation of Asian-American men to the values of the U.S. mainstream society may have costs related to their striving for success, power, and competition. Conversely, as Asian-American men become more acculturated, they are more relaxed with regard to their emotional expressions, which is in contrast to the traditional Asian value of emotional restraint.

Studies of Acculturative Stress and Generational Status

Several studies have found that first-generation Asian Americans experience significantly more acculturative stress than second or later generations. The Sodowsky et al. (1991) study of a diverse group of Asians (e.g., Asians from the Indian subcontinent, Chinese, Japanese, Koreans, and Vietnamese) showed that first-generation Asian immigrants experienced higher levels of adaptation difficulties than second and third generations. Similar findings were indicated in a study of three generations of Japanese Americans. Padilla, Wagatsuma, and Lindholm (1985) found that first-generation Japanese immigrants reported significantly more stress and were more externally controlled than second and later generations. Additionally, compared with the third and later generations, first-generation immigrants scored significantly lower on self-esteem. Interestingly, second-generation Japanese Americans' scores on stress and self-esteem resembled those of first-generation immigrants more than later generations (third and later). Padilla et al. (1985) explained that, because the first-generation individuals are likely to be low in acculturation, their greater experience of stress may be due to difficulties in interpersonal relationships. Further, they stated the second generation's "higher stress scores, as compared to third and later generation, may be a result of being caught between the cultural values of their parents and the dominant society" (p. 304). The researchers noted that the pattern of cultural values scores, which varied systematically across the three generational groups from first, second, and third/later generations, is indicative of the second generation being in transition from their traditional values to those held by the dominant culture. For all three groups, acculturation level, generational status, and self-esteem were the best predictors of stress.

Experiences of acculturative stress were also found to vary by generational level among a multiethnic group of college students (Mena, Padilla, & Maldonado, 1987). Mena et al. (1987) divided the participants into four generational groups: early immigrants (immigrated before age 12), late immigrants (immigrated after 12), second generation, and third generation. The results show that, although first-generation individuals scored significantly higher on stress and lower on self-esteem than second and third generations, late immigrants experienced greatest stress compared with all other groups.

Similarly, Padilla, Alvarez, and Lindholm (1986) divided their multiethnic college sample into early immigrants (immigrated before age 14), late immigrants (immigrated after 14), second generation, and third/later generation. The late-immigrant group experienced the most stress and scored lowest on self-esteem and locus of control. The second-generation group had the second highest stress levels. The third/later generation group, as well as early immigrants, scored lowest on stress and were most likely to score high on self-esteem. Both immigrant groups were more likely to score low on internal locus of control; the second and third/later generations were much more likely to score higher on internality. With generational status, locus of control, and introversion–extraversion taken into account, self-esteem was the best predictor of stress. However, for the late-immigrant group, generational status alone was a significant predictor of stress.

S. Sue and Zane (1985) found that, compared with American-born Chinese students, foreign-born Chinese students exhibited greater socioemotional distress as evidenced by their scores on: (a) single-item measure of happiness and satisfaction, (b) the Dimensions of Self-Concept (DOSC) measure, and (c) the Omnibus Personality Inventory (OPI). Similarly, Abe and Zane (1990) reported that, on the Personal Integration subscale of the OPI, foreign-born Asian Americans reported greater levels of interpersonal and intrapersonal distress compared with U.S.-born Asian Americans and White Americans.

Generational differences in the experience of stress were also found in an early study of Japanese Americans. Masuda et al. (1970) reported that both first- and second-generation Japanese Americans in Seattle experienced acculturative stress. However, whereas the first generation's stress arose from their tendency to segregate themselves from the mainstream society (i.e., cultural alienation), the second generation experienced stress in terms of cultural marginality. Yu (1984) made a similar conclusion regarding the stress experienced by second-generation Chinese adults. The results of Yu's study indicate that, although higher acculturation was related to less stress among immigrant Chinese, high acculturation, as indicated by place of birth (e.g., American-born), was associated with greater stress. Yu suggested that American-born Chinese may have experienced greater stress due to a loss of group identity and having to face double rejection (i.e., rejection by White Americans due to racism and rejection by immigrant Chinese Americans who tend to perceive American-born Chinese individuals as *bananas*—a derogatory term to describe Chinese Americans who are *yellow* on the outside and *white* on the inside).

In summary, acculturative stress studies reveal that there are a host of moderating variables in the experiences of bicultural conflict and stress among Asian Americans. One theme across these studies is that individuals who have a bicultural orientation tend to report positive psychological adjustment. In contrast, U.S.-born Asian Americans who are highly acculturated or assimilated or who have low acculturation or are separated from the White American society tend to experience greater psychological problems. In regard to generational differences, first-generation Asian Americans tend to report greater stress than second-generation Asian Americans. However, as suggested by several studies, American-born Asians are not free of acculturative stress. This review of studies appears to suggest that the stress of first-generation immigrants arises from struggling with acculturation issues; the stress of second-generation individuals involves having to adjust to two worlds at the same time.

MODELS OF ETHNIC IDENTITY

Although researchers differ in their operationalization of ethnic identity, investigators generally share a broad understanding of ethnic identity. According to Tajfel and Turner (1979), *ethnic identity* refers to that aspect of an individual's self-concept that is derived from his or her knowledge of membership of a social group (or groups), together with the value and emotional significance attached to that membership. Similarly, Smith (1991) stated that ethnic identity is the "sum total of group members' feelings about those values, symbols, and common histories that identify them as a distinct group" (p. 183). In regard to social group, Smith defined an ethnic reference group as:

> people who share a common history and culture, who may be identifiable because they share similar physical features and values and who, through the process of interacting with each other and establishing boundaries with others, identify themselves as being a member of that group. (p. 181)

According to DeVos and Romanucci-Ross (1975), central to ethnic identity is a "subjective symbolic or emblematic use of any aspect of culture" (p. 16). On the basis of definitions, we suggest that the issues of ethnic identity tend to be affectively and cathectically related, whereas issues of acculturation tend to be behaviorally related.

Phinney's Ethnic Identity Development Model

Phinney's (1993) model of ethnic identity development is based on the ego-identity literature—specifically, the theoretical models of Erickson and Marcia. It is proposed to be a process model of ethnic identity formation and is applicable to all ethnic groups. The model posits three stages of ethnic identity development: unexamined ethnic identity, ethnic identity search, and achieved ethnic identity. The unexamined ethnic identity stage is characterized by a lack of exploration of ethnicity. There are two possible subtypes: diffused identity, in which there is a lack of interest in or concern with ethnicity, and foreclosed identity, where an individual's view of ethnicity is based on opinions of others. Individuals in the ethnic identity search stage are actively involved in exploring and seeking to understand what their ethnicity means to them. In the final achieved ethnic identity stage, individuals hold a clear and confident sense of their own ethnicity. They have resolved racial and ethnic issues, and they accept themselves as members of a minority group. See the appendix for a summary on the psychometrics of Phinney's (1992) Multigroup Ethnic Identity Measure (MEIM).

Smith's Ethnic Identity Model

Smith (1991) proposed a model of ethnic identity that is applicable to both minority and majority groups. The term *ethnic identity* rather than *racial identity* is used because the former term is broader in scope. Additionally, the term *ethnic identity* also suggests that, for certain groups (e.g., Anglo group, European ethnic groups), ethnic group membership rather than race is a determining factor in identity formation. Smith's model of ethnic identity extends beyond the issue of oppression; it focuses on the status inequality that exists between majority and minority members. The central tenet of Smith's model is that the minority or majority status is what affects one's movement toward ethnic identity formation. Ethnic identity involves a process of continual boundary line drawing, where individuals decide which groups will be included in their inner group and which groups will be considered their outer boundary groups.

Ethnic identity development is conceptualized as the degree to which an individual identifies with his or her ethnic reference group. *Ethnic reference group* refers to one's psychological relatedness to a particular group. It serves as "a self-anchoring point for structuring his or her values, morals, and perceptual fields" (Smith, 1991, p. 185). Smith asserted that individuals with *embeddedness* in their culture are more likely to be ethnically hardy (i.e., their identities are less vulnerable to the pressures of the social environment as compared with those who do not identify with their ethnic reference group).

Smith's (1991) model describes four phases that individuals go through as they experience ethnic identity conflict. In the first phase, preoccupation with self, or preservation of ethnic self-identity, an individual's ethnic self-equilibrium is challenged by positive or negative contact experience with an outside group. The second phase is the preoccupation with the ethnic conflict and with the salient ethnic outer boundary group. In this phase, individuals who have significant contact with an outgroup experience strong feelings that motivate them to seek safety and support from their own ingroup. In the third phase, resolution of conflict, the individual restores his or her ethnic self-equilibrium by seeking a solution to the ethnic identity conflict. This involves making decisions about how to avoid similar ethnic conflicts. Finally, the fourth phase, integration, is characterized by an integration of current and previous experiences of ethnic contact. Individuals attempt to balance a negative or positive ethnic contact experience with the totality of past ethnic contact experiences. Smith posited that a lack of resolution of ethnic identity conflict will predispose a person to ethnic identity confusion and diffusion.

Models of Cultural Ethnic Identity Retention

The process of ethnic identification begins in early childhood; parents or family play a significant role in the ethnic socialization of minority children (Casas & Pytluk, 1995; Sodowsky & Lai, 1997). Among Asian Americans, family kinship is a primary socializing agent in which core Asian values such as obedience, discipline, and self-restraint are instilled (Sodowsky & Carey, 1987; Sodowsky et al., 1995; Sodowsky & Lai, 1997). Consequently, it can be argued that one's ethnic identity, which was inculcated by the family during early developmental years, becomes eroded as one becomes acculturated into the mainstream culture. Thus, inherent in the process of ethnic identity development, ethnic minorities must deal with the fundamental issue of which aspects and to what degree of one's ethnic identity must be retained (Isajiw, 1990; Kwan & Sodowsky, 1997; Sodowsky et al., 1995). Three models that deal with the retention of one's cultural identification are presented next.

Sodowsky's Multidimensional Ethnic Identity Retention Model

Sodowsky and colleagues (1995) expanded Berry's (1980) bidimensional model of acculturation to address the complex dynamics of ethnic identity. They proposed that the ethnic identity process is bidirectional, involving two orthogonal dimensions: degree of adoption of Whiteness and degree of retention of one's Asianness. These two dimensions create a multidimensional ethnic identity model in which ethnic minority individuals must face two basic ethnic identity questions: (a) Is my ethnic identity of value and to be retained? and (b) Is the White identity of U.S. dominant identity to be sought? The "yes" or "no" response to each question leads to a model with a two-by-two design. The combination of responses to the two questions—yes–yes, yes–no, no–yes, and no–no—result in four ethnic identity orientations: (a) bicultural identity, where the individual identifies with both groups; (b) strong ethnic identity, where the individual values retaining one's ethnic identity over White identity; (c) strong U.S. White identity, which suggests that the individual is not ethnically identified; and (d) identity of cultural marginalization, which characterizes individuals who do not identify with either cultural group. Although there are four ethnic identifications, it is possible to have variations in a particular orientation. For example, in the bicultural orientation, there could be high identification with one culture and medium identification with another.

Sodowsky and colleagues conceptualized the ethnic identity process as nonlinear (i.e., one's ethnic identity orientation often varies over time and across different situations). An individual with one ethnic identity orientation can move to another depending on the time and context. Thus, an individual can move back and forth among four orientations. The movement between two orientations is a transitional ethnic identity orientation. This transitional movement across different ethnic identity orientations is a consequence of

the ethnic individual's adaptive principle of flexibility and openness to possibilities, which has been conditioned through exposure to the effects

of the White society and the ethnic society, both societies being necessary
for the formation of an ethnic identity. (Sodowsky et al., 1995, p. 145)

Although having to constantly negotiate two ethnic identities due to
variations in one's ethnic identity orientation may pose difficulties, it can
also be an enriching and rejuvenating experience for the individual
(Sodowsky et al., 1995).

However, Sodowsky and colleagues pointed out that the individual
has a predominant internalized ethnic identity (e.g., a bicultural integrated
identity) and that other potential ethnic identities (e.g., a marginalized
identity) could become salient when the individual responds to specific
majority–minority intersections that put pressure on the individual to
change (e.g., those concerning Western vs. Eastern religions, traditional
vs. feminist gender-role attitudes, and issues of sexuality, such as homosexuality, heterosexuality, or liberal sexual behaviors—contexts that are characterized by values and cause value-based bicultural conflict for U.S.
Asians). In a review of the literature on the psychological impact of being
bicultural, LaFromboise, Coleman, and Gerton (1993) concluded that "the
more an individual is able to maintain active and effective relationships
through alternation between both cultures, the less difficulty he/she will
have in acquiring and maintaining competency in both cultures" (p. 402).

Sodowsky and Kwan's Internal–External Ethnic Identity Measure
(INT–EXT ID; Kwan & Sodowsky, 1997) is intended for Asian immigrants
and Asian Americans. It includes ethnic practices, behaviors, and festivities that the authors considered as external aspects of ethnic identity. Item
contents also include internal aspects such as attachment (e.g., a sense of
moral obligation) to family-related cultural values, which is central to the
ethnic identity of U.S. Asians. Items indicate that this implicit attachment
is also manifested behaviorally. In addition, the INT–EXT ID covers ethnic
pride and attachment and a sense of belonging to an ethnic group. Although Phinney (1990) did not distinguish between ethnic identity and
African-American racial identity, Sodowsky and Kwan's measure specifically demonstrates the cultural aspects of ethnic identity. Studying Chinese immigrants and second-generation Chinese Americans, Kwan and
Sodowsky (1997) found that perception of ethnicity salience and fear of
loss of face predicted internal ethnic identity but not external ethnic
identity. This could have been due to the inner-directed focus of internal
ethnic identity, which may "perceive, analyze, and reflect on issues of
physical salience and visibility more" and "may be more threatened by
the core values of shame and guilt, which most Asians are socialized to
monitor in their interpersonal relationships" (Kwan & Sodowsky, 1997,
p. 65). External ethnic identity and socioenvironmental variables (salience
of ethnicity, income, and loss of face) contributed 32% of the variance of
acculturative stress. The Chinese Americans could be divided into three

significantly different ethnic identity groups: internal, external, and un-differentiated internal–external, showing the heterogeneity among the U.S. Chinese. In a study on the correlates of ethnic identity retention, Suthakaran and Sodowsky (in press) found that Asian Muslims had a higher internal ethnic identity than Asian Hindus. Also, the Asian Muslims' higher intrinsic religious motivation than the Hindus contributed large variance to their internal ethnic identity, whereas Asian Hindus' higher extrinsic religious motivation than the Muslims was the only significant predictor of their external ethnic identity.

Isajiw's Ethnic Identity Retention Model

Isajiw's (1990) ethnic identity retention model concerns the retention of cultural aspects across generations. Specifically, *ethnic identity retention* is defined as the extent to which characteristics of an ethnic group are present among second or subsequent generations. In this model, Isajiw stated that ethnic identity retention and, inversely, ethnic identity loss are independent of one's level of assimilation to the host society. In other words, ethnic identity loss does not necessarily indicate greater assimilation because both do not necessarily take place simultaneously. For example, a marginalized person may show both loss of ethnic identity as well as a low degree of assimilation.

Isajiw (1990) posited that ethnic identity is composed of internal, psychological aspects and external, social aspects. The internal aspects of ethnic identity encompass three dimensions: cognitive (e.g., ethnic self-image and cultural knowledge), moral (e.g., sense of obligation to one's ethnic group), and affective (e.g., sense of belonging or attachment and comfort with one's ethnic group). Isajiw asserted that the moral dimension involving group obligation represents the core of one's subjective, internal ethnic identity. The external aspects of ethnic identity refer to observable sociocultural behaviors such as having ethnic group friendships, speaking the ethnic language, and participating in ethnic traditions and festivals.

Although the internal and external aspects of ethnic identity may be complementary to each other, Isajiw (1990) stated that these two aspects should not be assumed to be dependent. Isajiw identified four forms of ethnic identity that are distinguished by what aspects of ethnic identity are retained. A ritualistic ethnic identity is one in which there is a higher retention of the external aspects and a lower retention of internal aspects. For instance, a person with a ritualistic identity may be highly involved in ethnic practices and traditions, yet may not have a strong sense of group obligation. Sodowsky et al. (1995) suggested that second-generation Asian Americans and first-generation immigrants living in a predominantly White setting (i.e., a monocultural society) are likely to have a ritualistic identity. In contrast to a ritualistic identity, an ideological ethnic identity is characterized by a strong sense of group obligation and a low level of involvement in ethnic practices. Racially conscious Asian Americans who are politically active are likely to have an ideological ethnic identity (Sodowsky et al., 1995). A rebelling ethnic identity may be the characteristic of those individuals who have internalized negative images of their ethnic group and, consequently, are entirely disidentified with their ethnic group. Conversely, one who has an ethnic rediscovery identity will hold positive images of one's ethnic group, feel a sense of group obligation, be involved in ethnic practices, and seek support from other ethnic group members. Sodowsky et al. (1995) suggested that this may be the case of later generation Asian Americans who are motivated to rediscover their cultural roots.

Empirical Studies on Ethnic Identity

To understand the role of ethnic identity and mental health, a number of studies have investigated the relationship between ethnic identity and various indexes of psychological adjustment among different racial and ethnic groups. In a study of Israeli adolescents, Tzuriel and Klein (1977) reported that ethnic group identification was significantly related to ego identity for individuals from developing nations (e.g., from North Africa, Middle East, and South Asian) but not for Western ethnic groups. They concluded that ethnic group identification was more important for minority ethnic groups than for European groups because it provides the former with a sense of pride, belonging, and security. A strong ethnic identity enables minority group members to better cope with cultural conflicts and it facilitates the formation of an integrated ego identity.

Phinney (1989) reported similar findings among a sample of American-born adolescents. A positive relationship was found between level of ethnic identity and psychological adjustment. Specifically, ethnic identity-achieved participants had higher scores on a measure of ego identity as well as other measures of adjustment (e.g., sense of mastery, social and peer relations). In another study of second-generation college students, Phinney and Alipuria (1990) found that ethnic identity search, or "the extent to which participants thought about and resolved issues involving their ethnicity," (p. 171) was highest among African Americans, followed by Mexican Americans, Asian Americans, and Whites (in that order). Interestingly, ethnic identity search was positively related to self-esteem for African and Mexican Americans, but not for Asian and White Americans. Compared with the other minority groups, Asian Americans scored the lowest in ethnic identity search, and their scores on this variable had the weakest correlation with self-esteem. However, Kwan (1996) showed that Chinese-American immigrants indicated a significant relationship between their cultural ethnic identity retention and collective self-esteem. This finding points to the strong Asian awareness of a collective Asian ingroup rather than self-esteem related to a personal ego.

Studies of Ethnic Self-Labels Among Asian Americans. In one line of research, investigators examined the relationship between ethnic self-labels and ethnic behaviors and attitudes of Asian Americans. Hutnik (1986) found that the majority (35.9%) of second-generation, adolescent, Asian-Indian girls living in Britain self-identified as British only, followed by those who self-identified as Indian only (26.2%), both British and Indian (24.3%), and neither British nor Indian (13.6%). Interestingly, these ethnic self-identifications were found to be unrelated to the participants' acculturation behavior (e.g., assimilation vs. separation from the dominant group). For example, among the participants who self-identified as *Indian only,* merely 4% were separated or low in their acculturation behavior and 60% were highly acculturated. Hutnik contended that ethnic identity in the second generation may become functionally autonomous from the individual's acculturated behavior within two cultural contexts. Thus, a person may be strongly identified with his or her ethnic culture, yet be entirely acculturated in his or her behaviors. Likewise, those who exhibit highly acculturated behaviors may also have a positive sense of their ethnic identity.

Rotheram-Borus (1990) found that 46% of the Asian-American adolescents (most of whom were Filipino Americans) self-reported that they were bicultural, whereas 27% perceived themselves as White or strongly ethnic. Despite these differences, a majority of the participants (91%) selected the *Filipino* label exclusively. Using the Twenty Statements Test (TST) to study ethnic self-identification, Uleman, Uleman, Lee, and Roman (1995) compared the spontaneous self-descriptions of Asian Americans, White Americans, and Koreans in Seoul, Korea. The Asian-American sample consisted of Chinese, Indian, and Korean Americans who were mostly first and second generations. The Asian Americans were classified into three groups: (a) unidentified Asian Americans who did not identify themselves in ethnic-related terms (33%), (b) singly identified Asian Americans who identified themselves either by ethnicity (e.g., Asians or Asian Americans) or nationality (e.g., Chinese, Indian, or Korean, 54%), and (c) doubly identified Asian Americans who identified themselves by both ethnicity (e.g., Asian or Asian American) and nationality (e.g., Chinese, Indian, or Korean, 13%). In terms of self-concept, (a) unidentified Asian Americans resembled the self-concepts of White Americans, (b) singly identified (e.g., Asian American, Chinese, Indian, or Korean) Asian

Americans' self-concept resembled both (i.e., fell somewhere in between) the White Americans' and the Koreans' in Seoul, and (c) doubly identified (Asian American and Indian) Asian Americans had self-concepts that resembled the Koreans' in Seoul. The investigators also found that the unidentified Asian Americans were more extreme than White Americans on several categories of self-concept. They concluded that "it is as though they 'bent over backwards' to adopt a Euro-American perspective in their self-descriptions and, in the process, 'over-shot' the norm of the dominant culture" (p. 151). Sodowsky (1988) made a similar point about marginalized first-generation Asian-Indian immigrants who are exclusively attentive to adopting White American ways.

In the previously mentioned study, Uleman et al. (1995) found that the three Asian-American groups did not differ on acculturation variables of generational status, socioeconomic status, and bilingualism. However, significant differences were found among the three groups in terms of the age at which they learned English and whether English was their first language. It should be noted that English language usage is a variable used consistently to measure acculturation (the appendix on acculturation measures indicates this). Unidentified Asian Americans learned English at the mean age of 3, singly (Asian American, Chinese, Indian, Korean) identified Asian Americans learned English at the mean age of 5, and doubly identified Asian Americans (Asian American and Indian) learned English at the mean age of 6. Eighty-three percent of the unidentified Asian Americans learned English as their first language, followed by 45% of singly identified Asian Americans and 26% of doubly identified Asian Americans.

Ethnic Identity Retention: Differences Across Generations. A series of studies have been conducted to test Hansen's third-generation return or third-generation interest hypothesis. This hypothesis states that, "What the son [daughter] wishes to forget the grandson [granddaughter] wishes to remember." Hansen believed that, although first-generation immigrants must struggle with acculturational issues while surviving economically (which is an acculturation issue), the problem of the second generation is to adapt to two worlds at same time. The third generation, however, is perceived to be a successful and secure group that is motivated to rediscover its ancestral roots. In other words, the second generation attempts to remove itself or rebel against its ethnic group, whereas the third generation returns to it. Research findings do not clearly support Hansen's specific assumptions about the second and third generations. Generally studies show a decline in ethnic identity across generations. However, even fifth- and sixth-generation U.S.-born Asian Americans acknowledge those aspects of their ethnicity that are meaningful to them in the context of their time and history.

Ting-Toomey (1981) found that first-generation Chinese Americans mainly identified themselves with the Chinese culture and the second- and third-generation groups mainly identified themselves as bicultural (i.e., both American and Chinese). An overwhelming majority (78%) of third-generation Chinese Americans had identified themselves as bicultural, suggesting that the retention of Chinese identity was of significance to them. Interestingly, two thirds of the fourth-generation Chinese Americans maintained their Chinese identity and only one third identified themselves as mainly American. Ting-Toomey concluded that ethnic identity for this sample was a cyclical rather than a linear process, where the fourth-generation Chinese Americans returned to search their ancestral roots.

Uyeki (1960) found that, despite the Nisei's (Japanese second generation) rapid assimilation to the host society, they were also strongly identified with other Nisei (e.g., the majority of their friendships were Nisei). In comparing three generations of Japanese Americans in Seattle and Honolulu, Matsumoto, Meredith, and Masuda (1970) found a gradual erosion of ethnic identity for the Seattle group from Nisei to Sansei (Japanese third generation). Although no significant differences were found between Nisei and Sansei in the Honolulu group, the Honolulu Sansei showed both a steady decline and a considerable degree of ethnic identity. It should be noted that Matsumoto et al. acknowledged that a limitation of their study was the confounding of age with generational status (e.g., first generations were older in age than second generation).

In a study of Japanese Americans in Sacramento, California, Connor (1977) found that the Issei (Japanese first generation) obtained significantly higher ethnic identity scores than the Nisei and the Sansei; no significant differences were found between the Nisei and Sansei groups. However, the author noted that the Sansei differed from the Nisei in that they reported a greater interest in retaining their symbolic ethnic identity rather than the external, behavioral aspects. Wooden, Leon, and Toshima (1988) found that, although third- and fourth-generation Japanese-American youths did not differ in their level of ethnic identity, ethnic identity was maintained in both groups. Moreover, they noted that participants in their study had endorsed similar ethnic identity items (on the same measure) as those reported in a previous study (Connor, 1977). This suggests that certain aspects of Japanese ethnicity remain important to Japanese Americans even after two generations.

Newton, Buck, Kunimura, Colfer, and Scholesbert (1988) noted that their sample of Nisei and Sansei both obtained higher ethnic identity scores on the same measure of ethnic identity than those reported in earlier studies (Masuda et al., 1970). The authors suggested that the ethnic renaissance experienced by their participants may be a reaction to the contemporary increase in ethnic and racial consciousness of the society. Newton et al. (1988) concluded that ethnic identities are invariably influenced by larger societal issues.

In a study of ethnic identity retention among Chinese-American and Chinese-Australian youths, Rosenthal and Feldman (1992) found that, despite the expected moderate overlap among separate components of ethnic identity (e.g., ethnic knowledge and behavior, ethnic evaluation, and ethnic importance), there was a substantial amount of noncommon variance (e.g., low intercorrelations) for these components. Their findings demonstrate that first- and second-generation Chinese adolescents only differed significantly on the ethnic behavior and knowledge components of ethnic identity, but not on their sense of importance in maintaining ethnic practices and their positive evaluation of their ethnic group. The researchers concluded that, although the most external aspects of ethnic identity may be more readily relinquished as immigrant groups acculturate to the host country, those that are more internal appear to be more resistant to change over time.

Similar results were found in a study of Pilipino Americans in which separate components of ethnic identity were assessed (Revilla, 1993). The study found that, regardless of ethnic labels preferences (e.g., Pilipino, Pilipino American, American of Pilipino descent) and generational status (first and second generation), the majority of Pilipino Americans strongly embraced Pilipino values and enjoyed Pilipino food and dances. However, Pilipino music, television, and media elicited neutral and negative responses. There was also a decreasing trend in Pilipino language usage. Revilla concluded that certain aspects of the Pilipino culture such as ethnic loyalty are important to many second-generation Pilipino Americans, and thus are more likely to be retained.

In summary, the empirical studies of ethnic identity suggest that (a) ethnic identity is related to psychological adjustment, (b) Asian Americans as a group are less ethnically identified compared with other minority groups, (c) most Asian Americans identify themselves as bicultural regardless of generational status, (d) generation status is a significant predictor of ethnic identity retention for Asian Americans particularly between the first and second or later generations, (e) Asian Americans retain different aspects of their ethnic culture depending on generational status, and (f) internal aspects of ethnic identity (pride and sense of belonging) as opposed to external aspects of ethnic identity (ethnic practices and behavior) are more likely to be retained across generational levels. It should be noted here that the psychological conflict and stress involved in the process of ethnic identity formation represents one form of bicultural conflict.

CONCLUSION

Although it would appear that acculturation and ethnic identity are relatively independent constructs and processes, the two are mediated—both at the group and individual levels—by acculturative stress and intercultural competence (Sodowsky, 1998). While acculturation has been variously operationalized, its core concept involves the change and adaptation that takes place as a result of contact between two or more different cultural groups. We have learned that, for the most part, acculturation is most salient for first-generation ethnic minority immigrants. Notwithstanding the host of evidence for this generational difference, acculturation differentially impacts second and later generations to a lesser degree.

Acculturative stress is the direct result of the adaptation process of acculturation for first-generation ethnic minority immigrants and a response to the pulls of maintaining ethnic ties in second and later generations. Although this stress can be pathological in nature, it is not necessarily so and is mediated by a number of variables in first and subsequent generations. As with acculturation, the experience and nature of acculturative stress also vary by generational level.

Conversely, ethnic identity is the force that pulls an individual to his or her ethnic group. It is understood to entail sociocultural heritage and a sense of belonging and cathectic attachment to a reference group. Models that describe the development of ethnic identity as well as how it is retained have been proposed and studied. The effects of generational status on ethnic identity indicate an overall decline across generations. However, this decline only appears to affect the behavioral aspects of ethnic identity and not its internal, affective state.

ACKNOWLEDGMENTS

For Nepal Chandra Rai Sircar and Amita Rai Sircar, immigrants from Bangladesh to India, transmigrants across all regions of India, and late immigrants in their 70s to the United States of America so that they could be grandparents to their U.S.-born, second-generation grandchildren; Para mis padres—Reinaldo E. y Sandra D. Maestas—De la cosecha del betabel y el algodón viene una cosecha nueva y más dadivosa—Los amo.

APPENDIX: NON-HISPANIC/-LATINO ACCULTURATION, ACCULTURATIVE STRESS, AND ETHNIC IDENTITY INSTRUMENTS

Acculturation Instruments

Authors*	Ethnicity	Size	Age	Sampling
1. Sodowsky & Plake (1991, 1992) AIRS N of items = 34	International people (Africans, Asians, South Americans, & Europeans)	941	M = 26	Recruitment
Geographic Location	*Characteristics*		*Scale Development*	
Nebraska & Texas	College students, faculty, & staff		Factor analysis Internal consistency test Content analysis Subscales: 1) Perceived Prejudice 2) Social Customs 3) Language	
Reliability (rel.)			*Validity*	
For pilot study Coefficient alphas = .77 & .87 and Spearman–Brown split half rel. = .75 to .82 For final study coefficient alphas = .89 (full scale), .88, .79, & .82			Similar factor analysis results for both studies Respective factor variances = 20.6%, 8.1%, & 5.6% Factor loadings = .33 to .83 Criterion-related validity: Differentiation by nationality groups, residence status, years of residence, & religion	

(Continued)

APPENDIX (Continued)

Authors*	Ethnicity	Size	Age	Sampling
2. Wong-Rieger & Quintana (1987) MAS N of items = 21	Southeast Asians, Hispanics, & Anglos	434	not reported	Recruitment
Geographic Location	*Characteristics*		*Scale Development*	
Oklahoma	General population		Pilot study Subscales: 1) Voluntary Behavior 2) Involuntary Behavior 3) Cognitions 4) Self-Identity	
Reliability (rel.)		*Validity*		
not reported		Criterion-related validity: Differentiation between Canadian and foreign-born students Convergent validity: Correlation with two acculturation scales (information unpublished)		

Authors*	Ethnicity	Size	Age	Sampling
3. Sodowsky et al. (1991) MMRS N of items = 38	Hispanics/Latinos, Asian Americans (Vietnamese, Koreans, Indian subcontinent, Chinese, Japanese)	282	$M = 24$	Recruitment
Geographic Location	*Characteristics*		*Scale Development*	
Nebraska	College students, faculty, & staff		Confirmatory factor analysis Test of generalizability Internal consistency test	

158

Subscales: 1) Perceived Prejudice 2) Social Customs 3) Language		

Reliability (rel.)
Coefficient alphas = .95 (full scale), .92, .89, & .94

Validity
For generalizability study, coefficients of factor congruence between MMRS & AIRS = .86, .54, & .80
Goodness of fit index of confirmatory factor analysis = .73
Criterion-related validity:
Differentiation by ethnic group, Asian ethnic groups, immigration status, religion, & generation

Size	Age	Sampling
62	M = 25	Recruitment

*Authors**
4. Osvold & Sodowsky (1993)
MMRS
N of items = 38

Ethnicity
Native Americans & African Americans

Geographic Location
Nebraska

Characteristics
High school students, human service professionals, & homemakers

Reliability (rel.)
Coefficient alphas = .82, .77, & .70

Scale Development
Internal consistency test
Same subscales as above

Validity
Criterion-related validity:
Differences between more and less acculturated women on problematic eating attitudes and behaviors

Size	Age	Sampling
150	18–86	Recruitment

Authors
5. Rezentes (1993)
NMHS
N of items = 34

Ethnicity
Hawaiian, Caucasian, & Japanese

(Continued)

Geographic Location	Characteristics	Scale Development
Hawaii	General population	A priori Pilot study Structured interviews Item analysis Items were retained based on ability to differentiate Hawaiians from Japanese and Caucasians

Reliability (rel.)	Validity	Sampling
not reported	not reported	not reported

Authors	Ethnicity	Age	Size
6. Ranieri et al. (1994) SIAS N of items = 1	Vietnamese	13–25 $M = 18.2$	177

Geographic Location	Characteristics	Scale Development
Australia	adolescents & young adults	"To what extent have (/has) you (your mother/your father) adopted Australian ways of doing things?"

Reliability (rel.)	Validity
not reported	Predictive and convergent validity: differentiation by gender, length of residence in Australia, Adolescent Independence Values, Traditional Vietnamese Family Values, Hold Strongly to Traditions, physical identification as Vietnamese, Vietnamese Culture and Language, Australian Culture and Language, Vietnamese Cultural Participation, Australian Cultural Participation

Authors*	Ethnicity	Size	Age	Sampling
7. Suinn et al. (1987) SL-ASIA N of items = 21	Asian Americans	82	M = 19	Recruitment
Geographic Location	Characteristics		Scale Development	
Colorado & California	College students		Internal consistency test Subscales: 1) Language 2) Ethnic Identity & Generation 3) Cultural Heritage & Exposure 4) Ethnic Interaction	
Reliability (rel.)		Validity		
Coefficient alpha = .88 (full scale) Subscales not scored separately		Criterion-related validity: Differentiation by generation, length of residence in United States, and self-rating		

Authors*	Ethnicity	Size	Age	Sampling
8. Suinn et al. (1992) SL-ASIA N of items = 26	Asian Americans	284	M = 24.4	Recruitment
Georaphic Location	Characteristics		Scale Development	
Colorado	College students		Internal consistency test Principal Components Factor analysis 1) Reading/Writing/Cultural Preference 2) Ethnic Identity 3) Affinity for Ethnic Identity and Pride 4) Generational Identity 5) Food Preferences	

(Continued)

161

APPENDIX: (Continued)

Reliability (rel.)

Coefficient alpha = .91 (full scale)
Factors not scored separately

Validity

Concurrent validity:
  Significant correlations with years in U.S. school, age of entering
  U.S. school, length of residence in United States, years lived in non-
  Asian neighborhood, significant effect of English as first language
Factorial validity:
  Factors 1, 2, & 4 similar to ARSMA factors 2, 3, & 4
  Self-rated acculturation related to language preferences and
  ethnicity of friends
  Large sample factor analysis with new 26-item SL-ASIA has not
  been done
  Studies lacking on this revised version

Authors	*Ethnicity*	*Size*	*Age*	*Sampling*
9. Kodama & Canetto (1995) SL-ASIA (Suinn et al. 1987) N of items = 21	Japanese temporary residents	62	19–44	recruitment

Geographic Location	*Characteristics*	*Scale Development*
Colorado	College students	same as above Internal consistency test Factor analysis 1) Cultural/Language Preference 2) Ethnic Identity 3) Written Language 4) Ethnic Involvement & Pride 5) Ethnicity of Friends 6) Food Preference 7) Spoken Language

Reliability (rel.)	Authors	Geographic Location	Validity	Size	Age	Characteristics	Ethnicity	Sampling	Scale Development
Coefficient alpha = .72 (full scale)	10. Iwamasa (1996) SL-ASIA (Suinn-Lew et al. 1987) N of items = 21	Indiana	Convergent validity: significant correlation with self-ratings of acculturation Respective factor variances = 20.1%, 15.6%, 9.8%, 9.0%, 7.4%, 5.6%, & 5.5%	87	M = 20.1	College students	Asian Americans	Recruitment	Same as above Internal consistency test
Cronbach's alpha = .87 (full scale)	11. Anderson et al. (1993) ASSA N of items = 13	Ohio	Concurrent validity: Significant correlations with generational status, length of residence in U.S., self-identification, and self-ratings of cultural values	1,126	18-89	General population	Cambodian, Laotian, & Vietnamese	Convenience	Factor analysis Internal consistency test Subscales: 1) English & Language of Origin Proficiency (2-factor composite) 2) LSF (language, social, & food)

(Continued)

Reliability (rel.)	Validity
Coefficient alphas = .98, .81, & .79	Criterion-related validity: Significant correlations with current age, years in USA, total years of education, percentage of lifetime in USA, & age on entering USA Respective factor variances = 62.2%, 36.2%, & 2.2%

Acculturative Stress Instruments

Authors	Ethnicity	Size	Age	Sampling
1. Sandhu & Asrabadi (1994) ASSIS N of items = 36	International students	Men = 86 Women = 42	M = 23.6 W = 22.8	Random

Geographic Location	Characteristics	Scale Development
10 regions across the United States	Graduate & undergraduate students	Factor analysis Subscales: 1) Perceived Discrimination 2) Homesickness 3) Perceived Hate 4) Fear 5) Stress Due to Change/Culture Shock 6) Guilt

Reliability (rel.)	Validity
not reported	Respective factor variances = 38.3%, 9%, 7.2%, 6.1%, 3.7%, & 3.2% Factor loadings ranged from .58 to .91

Authors*	Ethnicity	Size	Age	Sampling
2. Sodowsky & Lai (1997) CADC N of items = 48	Asian Americans	200	M = 27	Recruitment

Geographic Location

Nebraska

Characteristics

College students, faculty, & staff

Scale Development

Factor analysis
Internal consistency test
Subscales:
1) Acculturative Distress
2) Intercultural Competence Concerns
Confirmatory factor analysis on an Asian sojourner sample; GFI = .85 & Adj GFI = .82; Pearson correlations of the factor structures of the two samples = .92 & .94

Reliability (rel.)

Full scale coefficient alpha = .92
Respective subscale coefficient alphas = .90 & .88

Validity

Structural equation modeling:
GFI = .87; Adj GFI = .85
nonsignificant chi square (as required); significant path coefficients and t scores for extent of ethnic friendships, years of U.S. residence, and age at immigration, with acculturation as dependent variable (used MMRS; see above); significant path coefficient and t score for acculturation (MMRS), with acculturative distress as dependent variable
Respective factor variances = 21% & 8.4% for Acculturative Distress & Intercultural Competence Concerns

Ethnic Identity Instruments

Authors	Ethnicity	Size	Age	Sampling
1. Isajiw (1990) EII N of items = 3	Majority Canadian, English, German, Italian, Jewish, & Ukranian	not reported	not reported	not reported

(Continued)

Geographic Location
Toronto, Canada

Characteristics
not reported

Scale Development
Factor analysis
Scale:
Internal Ethnic Identity
lack of information

Sampling
Convenience

Reliability (rel.)
not reported

Validity
not reported

Authors
2. Kwan & Sodowsky (1997)
INT-EXT ID
N of items = 35

Ethnicity
Chinese immigrants & second-generation Chinese Americans

Age
M of males = 32.7
M of females = 29.2

Size
224

Scale Development
Expert rating
Internal consistency test
Subscales:
1) Internal Ethnic Identity
2) External Ethnic Identity

Geographic Location
Lincoln, NE; west coast, midwest, east coast, & southwest

Characteristics
Students and nonstudents

Reliability (rel.)
Full scale r = .90
Respective subscale
r = .79 & .86

Validity
Content validity:
Grand Phi coefficient = .582,
significant relationship between instrument developers' and each independent rater's assignment of items to respective hypothesized dimensions
Criterion-related validity:
subjects could be separated into Internal Ethnic Identity group, External Ethnic Identity group, & Internal-External Ethnic Identity group; salience of ethnicity predicted Internal Ethnic Identity; Internal Ethnic Identity predicted fear of loss of face; income, salience of ethnicity, External Ethnic Identity, & loss of face predicted acculturative stress

Authors	Ethnicity	Size	Age	Sampling
3. Phinney (1992) MEIM N of items = 20	Asian Americans, African Americans, Hispanics, American Indians, & Whites	T = 553 136 College 417 High School	M for High School = 16.5 M for College = 20.2	Convenience

Geographic Location

southern California

Characteristics

High school and college students

Scale Development

Pilot study
Expert analysis
Factor analysis
Internal Consistency test
Subscales:
1) Affirmation/Belonging (5 items)
2) Ethnic Identity Achievement (7 items)
3) Ethnic Behaviors (2 items)
Separate Scale:
1) Other-group Orientation (6 items)

Reliability (rel.)

High School sample:
Full scale Cronbach's alpha = .81
subscales 1 & 2 Cronbach's alphas = .75 & .69
Subscale Ethnic Practice not tested for alpha
Separate scale Cronbach's alpha = .71
College sample:
Full scale Cronbach's alpha = .90
Subscales 1 & 2 Cronbach's alphas = .86 & .80
Separate scale Cronbach's alpha = .74

Validity

High School sample:
Factor 1 variance (all items designed to assess ethnic identity) = 20%
Factor 2 variance (other-group orientation) = 9.1%
Factor loadings ranged from –.19 to .72
College Sample:
Factor 1 variance (all items designed to assess ethnic identity) = 30.8%
Factor 2 variance (other-group orientation) = 11.4%
Factor loadings ranged from –.18 to .77

*Adapted from Lai & Sodowsky (1996)
**AIRS = American International Relations Scale, ASSA = Acculturation Scale, ASSIS = Acculturative Stress Scale for International Students, CADC = Cultural Adjustment Difficulties Checklist, EII = Ethnic Identity Index, INT-EXT ID = Internal-External Ethnic Identity Measure, MEIM = Multigroup Ethnic Identity Measure, MMRS = Minority-Majority Relations Scale, NMHS = Na Mea Hawai'i Scale, SIAS = Single Item Acculturation Scale, and SL-ASIA = Suinn-Lew Asian Self-Identity Acculturation Scale.

REFERENCES

Abe, J. S., & Zane, N. W. S. (1990). Psychological maladjustment among Asian and White American college students: Controlling for confounds. *Journal of Counseling Psychology, 37*(4), 437–444.

Aldwin, C., & Greenberger, E. (1987). Cultural differences in the predictors of depression. *American Journal of Community Psychology, 15*(6), 789–813.

Anderson, J., Moeschberger, M., Chen, Jr, M. S., Kunn, P., Wewers, M. E., & Guthrie, R. (1993). An acculturation scale for Southeast Asians. *Social Psychiatry and Psychiatric Epidemiology, 28,* 134–141.

Berry, J. W. (1980). Acculturation as varieties of adaptation. In A. M. Padilla (Ed.), *Acculturation: Theory, models and some new findings* (pp. 9–25). Boulder, CO: Westview.

Berry, J. W. (1993). Ethnic identity in pluralistic societies. In M. E. Bernal & G. P. Knight (Eds.), *Ethnic identity: Formation and transmission among Hispanics and other minorities* (pp. 271–296). Albany, NY: State University of New York Press.

Berry, J. W., & Kim, U. (1988). Acculturation and mental health. In P. R. Dasen & J. W. Berry (Eds.), *Health and cross-cultural psychology: Toward applications* (pp. 207–236). Newbury Park, CA: Sage.

Berry, J. W., Kim, U., Minde, T., & Mok, D. (1987). Comparative studies of acculturative stress. *International Migration Review, 21,* 491–511.

Berry, J. W., Kim, U., Power, S., Young, M., & Bujaki, M. (1989). Acculturation attitudes in plural societies. *Applied Psychology: An International Review, 38*(2), 158–206.

Bufka, L. F. (1998, August). *Family factors, acculturation, and identity in second generation Asian Indians.* Paper presented at the 106th annual convention of the American Psychological Association, San Francisco, CA.

Casas, J. M., & Pytluk, S. D. (1995). Hispanic identity development: Implications for research and practice. In J. Ponterotto, M. Casas, L. Suzuki, & C. Alexander (Eds.), *Handbook of multicultural counseling* (pp. 155–180). Newbury Park, CA: Sage.

Chambon, A. (1989). Refugee families experiences: Three family themes—family disruption, violent trauma, and acculturation. *Journal of Strategic and Systemic Therapies, 8,* 3–13.

Chabbra, S. (1994). Acculturation, personality, and adjustment: A study of Asian Indians in the United States (Doctoral dissertation, California School of Professional Psychology, San Diego, 1994). *Dissertation Abstracts International, 55*(06).

Choney, S. K., Berryhill-Paapke, E., & Robbins, R. R. (1995). The acculturation of American Indians: Developing frameworks for research and practice. In J. C. Ponterotto, J. M. Casas, L. A. Suzuki, & C. A. Alexander (Eds.), *Handbook of multicultural counseling* (pp. 73–92). Thousand Oaks, CA: Sage.

Connor, J. W. (1977). *Tradition and change in three generations of Japanese Americans.* Chicago: Nelson-Hall.

Cuéllar, I., Roberts, R. E., Nyberg, B., & Maldonado, R. E. (1997). Ethnic identity and acculturation in a young adult Mexican-origin population. *Journal of Community Psychology, 25*(6), 535–549.

DeVos, G., & Romanucci-Ross, L. (1975). *Ethnic identity.* Palo Alto, CA: Mayfield.

Draguns, J. G. (1996). Multicultural and cross-cultural assessment: Dilemmas and decisions. In G. R. Sodowsky & J. C. Impara (Eds.), *Multicultural assessment in counseling and clinical psychology* (pp. 37–84). Lincoln, NE: Buros Institute of Mental Measurements.

Dressler, W. W., & Bernal, H. (1982). Acculturation and stress in a low-income Puerto Rican community. *Journal of Human Stress, 8*(3), 32–38.

Feldman, S. S., Mont-Reynaud, R., & Rosenthal, D. A. (1992a). The acculturation of Chinese immigrants: Perceived effects on family functioning of length of residence in two cultural contexts. *The Journal of Genetic Psychology, 151,* 495–514.

Feldman, S. S., Mont-Reynaud, R., & Rosenthal, D. A. (1992b). When east moves west: The acculturation of values of Chinese adolescents in the U.S. and Australia. *Journal of Research on Adolescence, 2*, 147–173.

Greenberger, E., & Chen, C. (1996). Perceived family relationships and depressed mood in early and late adolescence: A comparison of European and Asian American. *Developmental Psychology, 32*(4), 707–716.

Hutnik, N. (1986). Patterns of ethnic minority identification and modes of social adaptation. *Ethnic and Racial Studies, 2*, 150–167.

Ihle, G. M., Sodowsky, G. R., & Kwan, K. L. (1996). Worldviews of women: Comparisons between White American clients, White American counselors, and Chinese international students. *Journal of Counseling and Development, 74*(3), 300–306.

Isajiw, W. W. (1990). Ethnic-identity retention. In R. Breton, W. W. Isajiw, W. E. Kalbach, & J. G. Reitz (Eds.), *Ethnic identity and equality* (pp. 34–91). Toronto: University of Toronto Press.

Iwamasa, G. Y. (1996). Acculturation of Asian American university students. *Assessment, 3*(1), 99–102.

Kiefer, C. W. (1974). *Changing cultures, changing lives: An ethnographic study of three generations of Japanese Americans.* San Francisco: Jossey & Bass.

Kim, E. J., O'Neil, J. M., & Owen, S. V. (1996). Asian American men's acculturation and gender-role conflict. *Psychological Reports, 79*, 95–104.

Kim, J. (1981). *The process of Asian American identity development: A study of Japanese American women's perceptions of their struggle to achieve positive identities.* Unpublished doctoral dissertation, University of Massachusetts.

Kodama, K., & Canetto, S. S. (1995). Reliability and validity of the Suinn–Lew Asian Self-Identity Acculturation Scale with Japanese temporary residents. *Psychologia, 38*, 17–21.

Kwan, K.-L. K. (1996). *Ethnic identity and cultural adjustment difficulties of Chinese Americans.* Unpublished doctoral dissertation, University of Nebraska–Lincoln.

Kwan, K.-L. K., & Sodowsky, G. R. (1997). Internal and external ethnic identity and their correlates: A study of Chinese American immigrants. *Journal of Multicultural Counseling and Development, 25*(1), 51–67.

LaFromboise, T., Coleman, H. L. K., & Gerton, J. (1993). Psychological impact of biculturalism. Evidence and theory. *Psychological Bulletin, 114*, 395–412.

Lai, E. W., & Sodowsky, G. R. (1996). Acculturation instrumentation. In G. R. Sodowsky & J. C. Impara (Eds.), *Multicultural assessment in counseling and clinical psychology* (pp. 347–352). Lincoln, NE: Buros Institute of Mental Measurements.

Lee, R. M., Choe, J., Kim G., & Ngo, V. (1998, August). *Construction of the Family Acculturation Conflicts and Tactics Scale.* Paper presented at the 106th annual convention of the American Psychological Association, San Francisco, CA.

Masuda, M., Matsumoto, G. H., & Meridith, G. M. (1970). Ethnic identity in three generations of Japanese Americans. *Journal of Social Psychology, 81*(2), 199–207.

Matsumoto, G. H., Meridith, G. M., & Masuda, M. (1970). Ethnic identification: Honolulu and Seattle Japanese Americans. *Journal of Cross-Cultural Psychology, 1*, 63–76.

Mehta, S. (1998). Relationship between acculturation and mental health for Asian Indian immigrants in the United States. *Genetic, Social, and General Psychology Monographs, 124*(1), 61–78.

Mena, F. J., Padilla, A. M., & Maldonado, M. (1987). Acculturative stress and specific coping strategies among immigrant and later generation college students. *Hispanic Journal of Behavioral Sciences, 9*, 207–225.

Mok, T. A. (1994, August). Looking for love: Factors influencing Asian Americans' choice of dating partners. In J. Y. Fong (Ed.), *Proceedings of the Asian American Psychological Association 1994 convention*, Los Angeles, CA.

Murthy, K. (1998, August). *Implications for counseling Asian Indians: Second generation perceptions of the American milieu.* Paper presented at the 106th annual convention of the American Psychological Association, San Francisco, CA.

Newton, B. J., Buck, E. G., Kunimura, D. T., Colfer, C. P., & Scholesbert, D. (1988). Ethnic identity among Japanese Americans in Hawaii: A critique of Hansen's third-generation return hypothesis. *International Journal of Intercultural Relations, 12*, 305–315.

Osvold, L. L., & Sodowsky, G. R. (1993). Eating disorders of White American, racial and ethnic minority American, and international women. *Journal of Multicultural Counseling and Development, 21*(3), 143–154.

Osvold, L. L., & Sodowsky, G. R. (1995). Eating attitudes of Native American and African American women: Differences by race and acculturation. *Explorations in Ethnic Studies, 18*, 187–210.

Padilla, A. M., Alvarez, M., & Lindholm, K. J. (1986). Generational and personality factors as predictors of stress in students. *Hispanic Journal of Behavioral Sciences, 8*, 275–288.

Padilla, A. M., Wagatsuma, Y., & Lindholm, K. J. (1985). Acculturation and personality as predictors of stress in Japanese and Japanese-Americans. *Journal of Social Psychology, 125*(3), 295–305.

Phinney, J. S. (1989). Stages of ethnic identity development in minority group adolescents. *Journal of Early Adolescence, 6*(1–2), 34–49.

Phinney, J. S. (1990). Ethnic identity in adolescents and adults: Review of research. *Psychological Bulletin, 108*(3), 499–514.

Phinney, J. S. (1991). Ethnic identity and self-esteem: A review and integration. *Hispanic Journal of Behavioral Sciences, 13*(2), 193–208.

Phinney, J. S. (1992). The multigroup ethnic identity measure: A new scale for use with diverse groups. *Journal of Adolescent Research, 7*(2), 156–176.

Phinney, J. S. (1993). A three-stage model of ethnic identity development in adolescence. In A. J. Marsella & P. B. Perdersen (Eds.), *Ethnic identity: Formation and transmission among Hispanics and other minorities* (pp. 61–79). Albany: State University of New York Press.

Phinney, J. S., & Alipuria, L. L. (1990). Ethnic identity in college students from four ethnic groups. *Journal of Adolescence, 13*, 171–183.

Phinney, J. S., Chavira, V., & Williamson, L. (1992). Acculturation attitudes and self-esteem among high school and college students. *Youth and Society, 23*, 299–312.

Ranieri, N. F., Klimidis, S., & Rosenthal, D. A. (1994). Validity of a single-item index of acculturation in Vietnamese immigrant youth. *Psychological Reports, 74*, 735–738.

Rezentes, W. C., III. (1993). Na mea Hawai'i: A Hawaiian acculturation scale. *Psychological Reports, 73*, 383–393.

Revilla, L. A. (1993). Brown and proud: The ethnic identity of Pilipino American college students. In L. A. Revilla, G. M. Nomura, S. Wong, & S. Hune (Eds.), *Bearing dreams, shaping visions: Asian Pacific perspectives* (pp. 107–124). Pullman, WA: Washington State University Press.

Rosenthal, D. A., & Feldman, S. S. (1992). The nature and stability of ethnic identity in Chinese youth: Effects of length of residence in two cultural contexts. *Journal of Cross-Cultural Psychology, 23*(2), 214–227.

Rotheram-Borus, M. J. (1990). Adolescents' reference-group choices, self-esteem, and adjustment. *Journal of Personality and Social Psychology, 59*(5), 1075–1081.

Rumbaut, R. G. (1994). The crucible within: Ethnic identity, self-esteem and segmented assimilation among children of immigrants. *International Migration Review, 28*, 748–794.

Sandhu, D. S., & Asrabadi, B. R. (1994). Development of an acculturative stress scale for international students: Preliminary findings. *Psychological Reports, 75*, 435–448.

Smith, E. J. (1991). Ethnic identity development: Toward the development of a theory within the context of majority/minority status. *Journal of Counseling and Development, 70*, 181–188.

Sodowsky, G. R. (1988). Marginality of ethnic immigrants. *Zone: A Feminist Journal for Women and Men, 2*, 123–129.

Sodowsky, G. R. (1991). Effects of culturally consistent counseling tasks on American and international student observers' perception of counselor credibility: A preliminary investigation. *Journal of Counseling and Development, 69*, 253–256.

Sodowsky, G. R. (1998, August). *Acculturation, ethnic identity, and acculturative stress of Asian Indians: A path analysis.* Paper presented at the 106th annual convention of the American Psychological Association, San Francisco, CA.

Sodowsky, G. R., & Carey, J. C. (1987). Asian Indians immigrants in America: Factors related to adjustment. *Journal of Multicultural Counseling and Development, 15*, 129–141.

Sodowsky, G. R., & Carey, J. C. (1988). Relationship between acculturation related demographics and cultural attitudes of Asian Indian immigrants. *Journal of Multicultural Counseling and Development, 16*, 117–136.

Sodowsky, G. R., Kwan, K. L. K, & Pannu, R. (1995). Ethnic identity of Asians in the United States: Conceptualization and illustrations. In J. Ponterotto, M. Casas, L. Suzuki, & C. Alexander (Eds.), *Handbook of multicultural counseling* (pp. 123–154). Newbury Park, CA: Sage.

Sodowsky, G. R., & Lai, E. W. M. (1997). Asian immigrant variables and structural models of cross-cultural distress. In A. Booth, A. C. Crouter, & N. Landale (Eds.), *Immigration and the family: Research and policy on U.S. immigrants* (pp. 211–234). Mahwah, NJ: Lawrence Erlbaum Associates.

Sodowsky, G. R., Lai, E. W. M., & Plake, B. S. (1991). Moderating effects of sociocultural variables on acculturation attitudes of Hispanics and Asian Americans. *Journal of Counseling and Development, 70*, 194–204.

Sodowsky, G. R., Maguire, K., Johnson, P., Ngumba, W., & Kohles, R. (1994). World views of White American, mainland Chinese, Taiwanese, and African students: An investigation into between-group differences. *Journal of Cross-Cultural Psychology, 25*(3), 309–324.

Sodowsky, G. R., & Plake, B. S. (1991). Psychometric properties of the American-International Relations Scale. *Educational and Psychological Measurement, 51*(1), 207–216.

Sodowsky, G. R., & Plake, B. S. (1992). A study of acculturation differences among international people and suggestions for sensitivity to within group differences. *Journal of Counseling and Development, 71*(1), 53–59.

Sue, D. W., & Sue, D. (1990). *Counseling the culturally different: Theory and practice* (2nd ed.). New York: Wiley.

Sue, S. (1996). Measurement, testing, and ethnic bias: Can solutions be found? In G. R. Sodowsky & J. C. Impara (Eds.), *Multicultural assessment in counseling and clinical psychology* (pp. 7–36). Lincoln, NE: Buros Institute of Mental Measurements.

Sue, S., & Sue, D. W. (1971). Chinese American personality and mental health. *Amerasia Journal, 1*, 36–49.

Sue, S., & Zane, N. W. S. (1985). Academic achievement and socioemotional adjustment among Chinese university students. *Journal of Counseling Psychology, 32*(4), 570–579.

Suinn, R. M., Ahuna, C., & Khoo, G. (1992). The Suinn-Lew Asian self-identity acculturation scale: Concurrent and factorial validation. *Educational and Psychological Measurement, 52*(4), 1041–1046.

Suinn, R. M., Rickard-Figueroa, K., Lew, S., & Vigil, P. (1987). The Suinn-Lew Asian Self-Identity Acculturation Scale: An initial report. *Educational and Psychological Measurement, 47*(2), 401–407.

Sung, B. L. (1985). Bicultural conflicts in Chinese immigrant children. *Journal of Comparative Family Studies, 26*, 255–269.

Suthakaran, V. & Sodowsky, G. R. (in press). Ethnic identity and religious orientation. A study of Asian Hindus and Muslims in the U.S. Midwest. *Journal of Multicultural Counseling and Development.*

Tajfel, H., & Turner, J. C. (1979). An integrative theory group conflict. In W. G. Austin & S. Worchel (Eds.), *The social psychology of intergroup relations* (pp. 33–47). Monterey, CA: Brooks/Cole.

Ting-Toomey, S. (1981). Ethnic identity and close relationship in Chinese-American college students. *International Journal of Intercultural Relations, 5,* 383–406.

Tzuriel, D., & Klein, M. M. (1977). Ego identity: Effects of ethnocentrism, ethnic identification, and cognitive complexity in Iraeli, Oriental, and Western ethnic groups. *Psychological Reports, 40,* 1099–1110.

Uleman, E. R., Uleman, J. S., Lee, H. K., & Roman, R. J. (1995). Spontaneous self-descriptions and ethnic identities in individualist and collectivistic cultures. *Journal of Personality and Social Psychology, 69*(1), 142–152.

Uyeki, E. (1960). Correlates of ethnic identification. *American Journal of Sociology, 65,* 468–474.

Velez, M. (1995). The relationship between ethnic identity and acculturation in a sample of Puerto Rican and Chinese college students (Doctoral dissertation, Long Island University, 1994). *Dissertation Abstracts International, 55*(11).

Wong, M. G. (1995). Chinese Americans. In P. G. Min (Ed.), *Asian Americans: Contemporary trends and issues* (pp. 58–94). Thousand Oaks, CA: Sage.

Wong-Rieger, D., & Quintana, D. (1987). Comparative acculturation of Southeast Asian and Hispanic immigrants and sojourners. *Journal of Cross-Cultural Psychology, 18,* 345–362.

Wooden, W., Leon, J., & Toshima, M. (1988). Ethnic identity among Sansei and Yonsei church-affiliated youth in Los Angeles and Honolulu. *Psychological Reports, 62,* 268–270.

Yeh, C., Chiang, L., & Wang, Y.-W. V. (1998, August). *Cultural adjustment and mental health of Chinese immigrant adolescents.* Paper presented at the 106th annual convention of the Asian American Psychological Association, San Francisco, CA.

Ying, Y.-W., & Chao, C. C. (1996). Intergenerational relationship in Iu Mien American families. *Amerasia Journal, 22.*

Yu, L. C. (1984). Acculturation and stress within Chinese American families. *Journal of Comparative Family Studies, 15,* 77–94.

Zimmerman, J., & Sodowsky, G. R. (1993). The influence of acculturation on Mexican American drinking practices and implications for counseling. *Journal of Multicultural Counseling and Development, 21,* 22–35.

Racial Identity Measures:
A Review and Classification System

A. Kathleen Burlew
Shana Bellow
Marilyn Lovett
University of Cincinnati

According to some estimates, racial minorities will constitute nearly 50% of the U.S. population by 2050 (American Psychological Association, 1997). The changing ethnic composition may intensify the controversy over the generalizability of research findings based on White samples to individuals whose values and beliefs may be shaped as much by their own subcultures as by the mainstream culture. For this reason, it may be unwise to ignore important differences between these groups and the mainstream culture.

It may be equally unwise to assume that all members of a specific subculture endorse the unique values and beliefs of that subculture to the same degree. Racial identity may represent one way to account for within-group variability. *Racial identity* refers to "a sense of collective identity based on one's perception that he or she shares a common heritage with a particular racial group" (Helms, 1990, p. 3). Individual racial identity may range from total immersion within the subculture to total acculturation into the mainstream culture. Hence, it may be quite beneficial to include racial identity rather than just race as a variable whenever appropriate in future research.

Clearly racial identity is a multifaceted concept. Some of the more salient features include identity formation, involvement with one's group, and perceptions about and strategies used to deal with the dominant group (Phinney, 1990). The multidimensional nature of racial identity is quite evident in the diverse group of theoretical perspectives present in the literature. In fact, Helms (1990) identified 11 different theoretical perspectives about the nature of racial identity. Moreover, Sellers and his colleagues proposed that the inconsistent findings in the literature on the relationship between racial identity and other variables may be attributable to the use of multiple conceptualizations and measurements of racial identity (Sellers, Rowley, Chavous, Shelton, & Smith, 1997).

The differences among these theoretical perspectives are striking and important. Accordingly, it may advance our understanding of both between- and within-group differences to encourage such a multifaceted approach to conceptualizing racial identity rather than limit the field to any one perspective. However, to facilitate that goal, appropriate measures must be available that tap various dimensions of racial identity.

Several alternative classification systems for depicting the multidimensional perspectives of racial identity have already been proposed. Kohatsu and Richardson (1996) reasoned that racial identity models can be classified into two types: stage and typology. The stage models are process-oriented; they typically describe how individuals move from a state of less healthy identity through a series of stages, each with its unique attitudes and emotions, ultimately to arrive at a state of healthier resolution of the role of race in their lives. Typology models classify individuals according to various personality and psychological characteristics that presumably shape response to environmental racial oppression.

Most definitions of racial and ethnic identity overlap except that ethnic identity is concerned with the enculturation of intergenerational values and beliefs from one's cultural heritage. However, the connection is not necessarily based on race (Spencer & Markstrom-Adams, 1990). Nevertheless, some of the models for conceptualizing ethnic identity may also be useful for categorizing dimensions of racial identity. For example, Bernal and Knight (1993) proposed that the various conceptualizations of ethnic identity can be classified into two general approaches. One approach includes models that focus on the extent to which individuals are shaped by the cultural teachings or enculturation that occur within the ethnic community. The other approach focuses on models that describe the cultural change or acculturation that occurs during the course of adaptation to the dominant culture.

Phinney (1990) proposed three conceptual frameworks for organizing the study of ethnic identity: social identity, acculturation, and ethnic identity formation. Social identity includes the sense of belonging to a specific group, the evaluation of that group, and the potential inner conflict from participation in two cultures. Phinney's concept of acculturation is similar to that posed by Bernal and Knight (1993). However, Phinney's notion of acculturation also examines how an individual perceives his or her group as a subgroup of the larger society. Ethnic identity addresses the dynamic movement from a state in which ethnicity is relatively unexamined to a state characterized by appreciation or regard for one's own ethnicity.

The racial identity measures also differ in the dimension of racial identity they are tapping. However, the models were developed for classifying the theoretical frameworks. These models are not completely applicable to the available racial identity measures because not all measures are associated with a particular theoretical perspective. Therefore, a separate classification system is needed specifically for classifying the various measures.

Burlew and Smith (1993) first proposed four dimensions for classifying the measures of racial identity available at that time. The dimensions included (a) Developmental, (b) Africentric, (c) Group-based, and (d) Racial stereotypes. Numerous measures are now available that were not available when this classification system was first presented. For that reason, it is time to consider what adjustments to that model are required to classify the current measures of racial identity. The objectives of this chapter are twofold. First, an alternative classification system is described for conceptualizing the various assumptions about the nature of racial identity implicit in the current set of measures. Second, recent and established measures are described that appear to tap the various dimensions of racial identity.

NEW DIRECTIONS IN ASSESSING RACIAL IDENTITY

The current set of measures has altered our understanding of alternative methods of assessing racial identity in several important ways. First, the earlier measures associated with the developmental approach focus almost exclusively on a stage theory approach. At least one of the more recent measures construes identity formation as something other than a stage process. Moreover, even several stage theorists have argued against using their scale to assign respondents to one specific stage due to the reality that an individual may simultaneously manifest attitudes characteristic of more than one stage (Helms & Parham, 1996). Accordingly, we have expanded what was formerly the developmental dimension in the earlier article to include this new perspective. This dimension is now called *identity formation*.

In our earlier conceptualization (Burlew & Smith, 1993), scales tapping a preference to affiliate with other members of one's own racial group were grouped together into a category named *group-based approaches*. Other scales that assessed the endorsement of culturally specific values and attitudes were placed together in the Africentric category. Treating these two groups as separate dimensions ignores that attachment to one's racial group is at the core of both these dimensions. Accordingly, we have opted for a broader term—*cultural connectedness*—to represent the alter-

native ways that individuals can conceivably demonstrate their attachment to their cultural group or background. However, within this broader
category, the measures are subdivided according to whether they are
tapping group affiliation or adherence to traditional values.

A third set of measures (Multicultural Experiences/Ractial Attitudes)
assesses racial attitudes and perceptions of experiences with other racial
groups. Some might question whether attitudes about or experiences with
other groups are actually dimensions of racial identity. However, we
decided to include these areas for several reasons. First, although neither
racial attitudes nor multicultural experiences are evident among the theoretical perspectives, a number of the actual measures of racial identity
focus on attitudes and/or experiences about other groups. Furthermore, to
the extent that individuals develop perceptions about their own racial group
in the context of their perceptions about and interactions with other groups,
it is important to have measures that facilitate research in this area.

Finally, several measures include various dimensions in a single measure. For example, the dimensions of the Scale for the Effects of Ethnicity
and Discrimination (SEED) measure identity formation and multicultural
experiences. Measures that tap more than one of our dimensions have
been placed in a separate category now termed *multidimensional measures*.

The study of racial and ethnic identity is growing so fast that it would
not be feasible to review every available measure. Therefore, the following
guidelines were used to select measures to review in this chapter. First, a
number of the early measures, especially those not frequently used since
1980, are not reviewed here. The reader can refer to Burlew and Smith (1993)
for a description of these measures. Second, this presentation is limited to
measures useful for assessing racial identity among adults. However,
several adolescent measures that can be used with adult populations are
discussed. Finally, the focus of this chapter is on measures of racial identity.
Measures that are only useful for ethnic identity are not reviewed here.
However, several measures of ethnic identity that have been used by
researchers to assess racial as well as ethnic identity are included.

In summary, an alternative method of conceptualizing measures of
racial identity is being presented in this chapter. The dimensions include
(a) Identity Formation, (b) Cultural Connectedness, and (c) Multicultural
Experiences. A set of multidimensional measures is also included. Each
dimension and the specific measures that capture that dimension are
described in Table 8.1 and in the sections that follow.

IDENTITY FORMATION

Some instruments grouped in the identity-formation category assess individual progress through a series of stages in which views about the

self, other African Americans, and other ethnic groups undergo substantial change. Thomas (1971) and Cross (1971) performed pioneering work by delineating the first developmental models of Black consciousness. These key theorists described a stagelike progression often fueled by a racist encounter from an unexamined and unhealthy racial identity to a secure and healthy manifestation of racial identity. Other instruments in this section are based on assumptions about personality or psychological characteristics. Williams (1981) proposed a reconstruction of stage theory models of Black identity and inferred that the behavioral tendencies of Black awareness coexist in varying levels depending on individual and environmental factors. He also stated that response to oppression is manifested in different ways throughout the developmental stages of Cross and Thomas (Wright & Isenstein, 1978).

Milliones (1980) and Parham and Helms (1981) developed inventories that identify specific racial attitudes associated with various stages. Williams (1981) proposed a scale assessing personality traits that would be predictive of racial identity response styles. These measures that conceptualize racial identity as identity formation are reviewed here.

Developmental Inventory of Black Consciousness

Milliones (1980) based his construction of the Developmental Inventory of Black Consciousness (DIB–C) on the models of Black identity formulated by Cross (1971) and Thomas (1971), as well as changes in Black consciousness evidenced in autobiographies of notable African-American revolutionaries. The DIB–C assesses the progression from negative views of what it means to be African American to a more mature level of Black consciousness. This 84-item scale postulates that individuals advance through four stages: Preconscious, Confrontation, Internalization, and Integration. The reader is referred to Milliones (1980) for a more complete description of the theory and the four stages.

The DIB–C is scored on an 11-point scale ranging from *agree not at all* (1) to *entirely agree* (11). Denton (1985) reported acceptable alpha coefficients for the Preconscious, Confrontation, and Internalization scales. However, the internal consistency for the Integration scale was lower. Split-half reliabilities range from .66 to .88 and .58 to .83 (Milliones, 1980). Construct validity was supported by demonstrating correlations between scores on the DIB–C and the Taylor Nadinolization Scale (Milliones, 1980). Denton (1985) provided further evidence of the validity by demonstrating support for three of the existing four factors and found the DIB–C to be correlated with measures of Black nationalism and internalized racism. In a review article, Sabnani and Ponterotto (1992) described a shortened form consisting of 65 items and scored on a 7-point Likert scale.

TABLE 8.1
Characteristics of Racial Identity Measures

Instrument	Number of Items	Subscales	Demonstrated Reliability*	Validity	Validation Sample
Identity Formation					
Developmental Inventory of Black Consciousness (Milliones, 1980)	84	Preconscious Confrontation Internalization Integration	Split-half Internal consistency	Construct	African-American college men
Racial Identity Attitude Scale (Parham & Helms, 1981)	Long Form-50 Short Form-30	Pre-encounter Encounter Immersion Internalization	Internal consistency	Construct	African-American college students
Black Personality Questionnaire (Williams, 1981)	50	Pro-White Anti-Black Anti-White Pro-Black Pan-African Third World	Split-half	Construct	African-American college students
Cultural Connectedness					
Black Identification Scale (Whittler, Calantone, & Young, 1991)	13	**N/A	Internal consistency	Criterion-related	African-American college students
Multidimensional Racial Identification Scale (Sanders-Thompson, 1992)	30	Physical Sociopolitical Sociocultural Psychological	Internal consistency	Convergent	Community sample of African Americans

178

Scale	Items	Subscales	Reliability	Validity	Sample
Africentrism Scale (Grills & Longshore, 1996)	Form A-17 Form B-13 Form C-15	**N/A	Internal consistency	Construct	Community sample of African Americans
African Self Consciousness Scale (Baldwin & Bell, 1985)	42	Personal Identification Reinforcement Against Racism Racial and Cultural Awareness Value for African Culture	Internal consistency Test–retest	Construct	African-American college students
African-American Acculturation Scale (Landrine & Klonoff, 1994)	Long Form-74 Short Form-33	Preference for African-American Things Traditional Family Practices/Values Traditional Health Beliefs/Practices Traditional Socialization Traditional Foods/Practices Religious Beliefs/Practices Interracial Attitudes Superstitions	Split-half	Criterion-related Concurrent	Community sample of African Americans
Belief System Analysis Scale (Montgomery, Fine, & Edwards, 1990)	31	**N/A	Internal consistency Test–retest	Construct	Introductory Psychology students

Multicultural Experiences/Racial Attitudes

Scale	Items	Subscales	Reliability	Validity	Sample
Perceived Racism Scale (McNeily et al., 1996)	51	Exposure to Racism Emotional Coping Strategies Behavioral Strategies	Internal consistency Test–retest	Discriminant Convergent Concurrent	Community sample of African Americans
Schedule of Racist Events (Landrine & Klonoff, 1986)	18	Frequency of Exposure (Lifetime) Frequency of Exposure (Past Year) Appraisal of Racist Events	Internal consistency Split-half	Concurrent	African University students, faculty & staff

(Continued)

TABLE 8.1
(Continued)

Instrument	Number of Items	Subscales	Demonstrated Reliability*	Validity	Validation Sample
Acculturative Stress Scale (Williams-Flournoy & Anderson, 1996)	9	**N/A	Internal consistency	Concurrent	African-American college students
Cultural Mistrust Inventory (Terrell & Terrell, 1981)	48	Education and Training Law and Politics Work and Business Interpersonal and Social Settings	Internal consistency Test-retest	Discriminant Concurrent	African-American college men
Institutional Racism Scale (Barbarin & Gilbert, 1981)	72	Indexes of Racism Effectiveness of Strategies to Reduce Racism Use of Strategies to Reduce Racism Agency Climate for Racism Administrative Efforts to Reduce Racism Personal Efforts to Reduce Racism	Internal consistency Test-retest	Concurrent	African-American college students & community sample
Prejudice Perception Assessment Scale (Martinez, in press)	5	**N/A	Internal consistency	Convergent Discriminant	African-American college students

Measure	Items	Subscales	Reliability	Validity	Sample
Multidimensional Schema Based (Allen, Dawson & Brown, 1989)	25	African-American Autonomy Closeness to African-American Masses Closeness to African-American Elites Positive Beliefs About African Americans Negative Beliefs About African Americans	***NA	Construct	Community sample of African Americans
Multigroup Ethnic Identity Measure (Phinney, 1992)	24	Affirmation and Belonging Ethnic Identity Achievement Ethnic Behaviors Other Group Orientation	Internal consistency	Construct	Ethnically diverse college students
Scale for the Effects of Ethnicity and Discrimination (Cardo, 1994)	35	Valence of Ethnicity for Self Valence of Ethnicity for Others Perception of Discrimination	Item total	Construct	**NA
Multidimensional Inventory of Black Identity (Sellers, Rowley, Chavous, Shelton, & Smith, 1997)	51	Centrality Ideology Regard	Internal consistency	Predictive	African-American college students

*Reliability values of .70 and above are considered acceptable (Nunnally, 1978)
**N/A = Not Applicable
***NA = Not Available

Racial Identity Attitude Scale

The Racial Identity Attitude Scale (RIAS) was developed by Parham and Helms (1981) to measure attitudes and beliefs consistent with the stages of racial identity development originally postulated by Cross (1971). The scale assesses movement through these four stages: Pre-encounter, Encounter, Immersion-Emersion, and Internalization.

The RIAS is scored using a 5-point Likert scale ranging from *strongly agree* (1) to *strongly disagree* (5). Three forms of the RIAS are available: a 50-item long form (RIAS–L) and two short forms (RIAS–A and RIAS–B) consisting of 30 items (Helms, 1990). Cronbach alpha reliability coefficients ranged from .37 to .80 (Parham & Helms, 1981; Pomales, Claiborne & LaFromboise, 1986; Ponterroto & Wise, 1987; Sabnani & Ponterroto, 1992) for the four subscales of the long form. For the short forms, Cronbach alpha reliability coefficients ranged from .49 to .79 (Helms, 1990; Parham & Helms, 1981).

Factor analytic studies support four factors consistent with Black identity (Brookins, 1994; Helms, 1990). However, Ponterroto and Wise (1987) accounted for the Pre-encounter, Immersion-Emersion, and Internalization stages but found little support for the Encounter stage. Evidence for construct validity is found in the correlation of the RIAS with the DIB–C (Grace, 1984) and the Belief Systems Analysis Scale (Brookins, 1994). Speight, Vera, and Derrickson (1996) reported that higher immersion scores were associated with self-identification as African American.

Black Personality Questionnaire

Williams (1981) constructed the Black Personality Questionnaire (BPQ) to assess a theory of Black personality based on an African-American culturally specific conceptual framework. In his conceptualization, Williams (1981) discarded stage theory notions in favor of identifying diverse behavioral styles for responding to racial oppression. All items for the BPQ were based on Williams' theory of Black awareness (Azibo, 1996). Four of of the six subscales (Anti-White, Pro-Black, Pan-African, and Third World) measure the endorsement of various Africentric response styles. The other two subscales (Pro-White and Anti-Black) measure the endorsement of Eurocentric response styles.

Respondents indicate whether they agree, disagree, or cannot say to each of 50 statements. The response to each statement is used to calculate a subscale score and a total score for either the Africentric or Eurocentric domain. A split-half reliability coefficient of .99 has been reported by Davis (1979). Williams (cited in Azibo, 1996) established construct validity for the scale in a factor analysis yielding six factors consistent with the six proposed constructs of Black awareness. Additional evidence of construct validity has been suggested by the correlation of the BPQ with the African Self-Consciousness Scale (Baldwin & Bell, 1985). Content validity has also been reported as adequate (Azibo, 1996).

CULTURAL CONNECTEDNESS

Some racial/ethnic identity measures are concerned with the affinity for one own's culture. Actually cultural connectedness involves two components. The first component, affiliation, measures the extent to which African Americans express either a preference for associating with other African Americans or a sense of belonging to their own racial group. The degree to which African Americans endorse the traditions and values of the African-American heritage is the second component. The two scales that focus on affiliation are the Black Identification Scale (BIS) and the Multidimensional Racial Identification Scale (MRIS). The four measures that assess the endorsement of traditions and values are the Africentrism scale, the African Self-Consciousness Scale, the African-American Acculturation Scale, and the Belief Systems Analysis Scale.

Black Identification Scale

The Black Identification Scale (BIS; Whittler, Calantone, & Young, 1991) assesses adherence to the group. Overall, the scale measures strength of ethnic affiliation. The major elements focus on cross-race attraction and political/social relations. The BIS has 13 items. The scale was first standardized on African-American college students and later generalized to other African Americans. An alpha coefficient of .82 and adequate criterion validity have been reported.

Multidimensional Racial Identification Scale

The Multidimensional Racial Identification Scale (MRIS; Sanders-Thompson, 1992) assesses the sense of connection between self and other African Americans. The researcher's conceptualization is consistent with Hilliard's (1985) four parameters of racial identity: color (comfort with physical attributes), caste (sociopolitical or economic attitudes), culture (acceptance of traditions), and consciousness (group membership awareness). The MRIS has 30 items and was standardized on African-American adults of various ages and socioeconomic levels. Factor analyses confirmed four dimensions of identity that account for 78% of the variance (Myers & Sanders-Thompson, 1994; Sanders-Thompson, 1992). These dimensions as well as the alpha coefficients reported for each subscale were: physical (.53), sociopolitical (.39), sociocultural (.53), and psychological (.63). Although the sociocultural component assesses endorsement of traditions, most of the items measure group affiliation. High scores indicate an African-American orientation and low scores represent predominant mainstream influences.

Africentrism Scale

The Africentrism scale (ACS; Grills & Longshore, 1996; Longshore, Grills, Anglin, & Annon, 1998) was conceived to assess endorsement of the Nguzo Saba (Seven Principles of Kwanzaa), such as self-determination (Kujichagulia) and purpose (Nia) (Karenga, 1980). The authors of this scale view the endorsement of these particular values as evidence of ethnic identity. There are three forms: Form A (17 items with an alpha coefficient of .74), Form B (13 items with an alpha coefficient of .62), and Form C (15 items with an alpha coefficient of .79). Forms A and C were highly correlated (.98). Acceptable construct validity has been reported. Likert responses range from *strongly disagree* (1) to *strongly agree* (5).

African Self-Consciousness Scale

The African Self-Consciousness Scale (ASCS; Baldwin & Bell, 1985) is based on Baldwin's (1981) ideas about the African-American personality. African self-consciousness includes an awareness and appreciation of the African cultural heritage, an endorsement of the priorities and institutions necessary for affirming African life, active participation in the development of African people, and a resistance to racial oppression. The ASCS includes 42 items based on a Likert-type scale system ranging from *strongly disagree* (1–2) to *strongly agree* (7–8). A test–retest reliability of .90 and adequate internal consistency (.78–.92) have been reported. A factor analysis performed by Stokes, Murray, Peacock, and Kaiser (1994) confirmed the authors' four dimensions: Personal Identification, Self-Reinforcement Against Racism, Racial and Cultural Awareness, and Value for African Culture. Myers and Sanders-Thompson (1994) found seven factors. The additional three were Group Self-Concept, Sociocultural/Educational Aspects of Black Identity, and Black Political Orientation. A factor analysis of data collected from a clinical sample of African-American crack-addicted men yielded two factors: value for African-centered institutions and relationships and value against affirmative Africanity. The scale was first standardized on African-American college students and later generalized to other African Americans.

African American Acculturation Scale

The African American Acculturation Scale (AAAS; Landrine & Klonoff, 1994) measures eight dimensions of African-American traditional practices. The AAAS focuses on the extent to which African Americans endorse traditional African-American cultural practices and beliefs. The scale classifies an African American as either traditional or acculturated (subscribing to mainstream practices). The dimensions and associated alpha coefficients reported for each were: Preference for African-American Things (.90), Traditional Family Practices/Values (.71), Traditional Health Beliefs/Practices (.78), Traditional Socialization (.81), Traditional Foods/Practices (.81), Religious Beliefs/Practices (.76), Interracial Attitudes (.79), and Superstitions (.72). Family Practices, Health Beliefs/Practices, and Traditional Socialization correlated highest with the total score. The long form has 74 items and a split-half reliability of .93. An individual with high scores on the AAAS is considered more traditional in his or her orientation; low scores reflect more mainstream thinking. The scale is based on a Likert-type format ranging from *totally disagree* (1) to *totally agree* (7). Both criterion-related and concurrent validity have been reported.

The short form (AAAS–II; Landrine & Klonoff, 1995) consists of 10 dimensions. The eight dimensions of the AAAS are included. However, the Traditional Family Practices/Values scale on the long form was separated into two separate scales on the short form. Moreover, a Traditional Games subscale was also added. The Traditional Childhood scale on the short form assesses what is Traditional Socialization on the long form; the Falling Out scale on the short form measures what is Health Beliefs/Practices on the long form. Internal consistencies ranged from .42 to .89. The AAAS–II has 33 items, and a split-half reliability of .78 has been reported. The correlation between the AAAS and AAAS–II is .94. Concurrent validity has been demonstrated.

Belief Systems Analysis Scale

The Belief Systems Analysis Scale (BSAS; Montgomery, Fine, & Myers, 1990) is based on an Africentric worldview. Myers' (1988) notion of an optimal worldview is derived from ancient African cultures and includes an emphasis on harmony, interpersonal relationships, communalism, and knowledge through experience. The BSAS has 31 items. A Cronbach alpha of .80 and a test–retest reliability of .63 have been reported. The authors of the BSAS demonstrated acceptable construct validity by correlating the BSAS with the Social Interest Scale (.50), Symptom Checklist–90–R (–.38 for the global severity index), and the Dogmatism scale (–.51). Although the BSAS was standardized on introductory psychology students at a private midwestern university, Brookins (1994) found a relationship between the BSAS and the RIAS in a sample of African-American college students.

MULTICULTURAL EXPERIENCES

The scales in this category are all concerned with racial attitudes and experiences or perceptions regarding other cultural groups (primarily Whites). A theme common to at least four of the scales is exposure to racism. Beyond exposure to racism, various scales consider (a) emotional response to racism, (b) behavioral strategies used to cope with racist events, (c) the appraisal of the emotional effects of racial events, and (d) more general perceptions about other groups.

Perceived Racism Scale

McNeilly et al. (1996) reported that many of the earlier racism measures only addressed exposure to racism and failed to include individual response to racism. The Perceived Racism Scale (PRS), a 51-item scale, was developed to provide a more comprehensive instrument that would include behavioral and emotional coping methods along with exposure to racism. The scale includes separate subscales (called *dimensions*) for Exposure, Emotional Coping Strategies, and Behavioral Strategies. Each dimension is assessed across four domains—employment, academic, public, and general exposure to racist statements.

Forty-three of the 51 items explore exposure to racism. Using a five-point scale ranging from *almost never* (1) to *several times a day* (5), the respondent is asked to indicate how frequently each of the 43 situations has happened over the past year and over his or her entire lifetime. Four of the remaining items ask the respondent about experiencing anger, frustration, powerlessness, hopelessness, or other emotions when exposed to racism across the four domains. The other four items ask the respondent to report behavioral strategies he or she has used when experiencing racism across the four domains.

Coefficient alphas ranging from .88 to .96 and test–retest reliabilities ranging from .71 to .80 have been reported for Dimension I and from .51 to .78 for Dimensions II and III. Acceptable test–retest reliability has been reported. Confirmatory factor analyses supported the three dimensions. Construct validity (both convergent and discriminant) and concurrent validity have been demonstrated (McNeilly et al., 1996).

Schedule of Racist Events

Landrine and Klonoff (1996) conceptualized racist events as analogous to other stressful events. Hence, *racist events* refer to culturally specific, negative life events. The Schedule of Racist Events (SRE) is modeled after the PERI–LES (Dohrenwend, Krasnoff, Askenasy, & Dohrenwend, 1978), a measure of the frequency of experiencing stressful events, and the Perceived Stress Scale, a measure of the appraisal of stressful events (Cohen, Kamarck, & Mermelstein, 1983). These two dimensions are both represented in the SRE. Each of the 18 items of the SRE asks the respondent for three ratings that are summed to yield three separate subscale scores. Two of these three subscales involve the frequency of experiencing a specific racist event either over the course of one's entire life or during the past year. Respondents indicate the frequency on a six-point rating scale ranging from *never* (1) to *almost all the time* (6). A third subscale, the Appraisal scale, asks about the degree of stress that each racist event created for that person. These responses are also on a six-point scale but the response choices range from *not at all* (1) to *extremely stressful* (6).

Strong evidence of internal consistency reliability has been obtained, including .95 for both recent and lifetime racist events and .94 for the appraisal of racist events (Landrine & Klonoff, 1996). Split-half reliability on all three subscales exceeded .90 (Landrine & Klonoff, 1996). Concurrent validity was established in studies of the relationship between the SRE and stress-related psychiatric symptoms (Landrine & Klonoff, 1996).

Acculturative Stress Scale

The Acculturative Stress Scale (ACS; Williams-Flournoy & Anderson, 1996) is based on a theoretical perspective that individuals will cope with the discomfort associated with acculturation by either withdrawing from uncomfortable social situations or changing behaviors to facilitate social interaction. The nine-item scale includes items that consider exposure to racism (perceived or received) and appraisal (racial anxiety) along with several items on ethnocentrism. However, these areas are not treated as separate factors or subscales. Therefore, it may be more accurate to describe the scale as a global measure of the psychological discomfort associated with assimilation. The format includes a five-point Likert scale. A Cronbach alpha coefficient of .86 and adequate concurrent validity have also been reported (Williams-Flournoy & Anderson, 1996)

Cultural Mistrust Inventory

Terrell and Terrell (1981) constructed the Cultural Mistrust Inventory (CMI) to measure the extent to which African Americans mistrust Whites and White-related organizations. The authors postulated that African-American suspiciousness of Whites develops as a result of exposure to racism or other discriminatory treatment (Terrell & Terrell, 1981). The 48-item scale includes four subscales in which the cultural mistrust of

Whites may exist: Education and Training, Law and Politics, Work and Business, and Interpersonal and Social Settings.

The CMI is scored on a seven-point scale ranging from *strongly disagree* (1) to *strongly agree* (7). Terrell and Terrell (1981) reported a 2-week test–retest reliability of .82 and provided evidence for discriminant validity (e.g., low correlations between subscales). A Cronbach alpha of .89 has been reported by Nickerson, Helms, and Terrell (1994). Evidence of concurrent validity was demonstrated by correlating the CMI with the Racial Discrimination Index (Terrell & Terrell, 1981).

Institutional Racism Scale

The Institutional Racism Scale (IRS) was designed to evaluate perceptions of racism on a personal as well as organizational level (Barbarin & Gilbert, 1981). The authors defined *institutional racism* as racial differences in outcome due to discriminatory "institutional practices, policies, processes, and interpersonal climates" (Barbarin, 1996, p. 375). The 72-item scale consists of six subscales that assess the following dimensions of racism in specific settings: Indexes of Racism, Effectiveness of Strategies to Reduce Racism, Use of Strategies to Reduce Racism, the Agency Climate for Racism, Administrative Efforts to Reduce Racism, and Personal Efforts to Reduce Racism.

The six areas of the IRS have distinct scoring criteria. For example, the Indexes of Racism subscale is scored on a seven-point scale ranging from *not at all* (1) to *most sensitive* (7), whereas the Climate for Racism domain ranges from *mildly agree* (1) to *disagree* (7). For a further description of the scale and scoring criteria, the reader is referred to Barbarin (1996). Internal consistency reliabilities ranged from .72 to .94, and 2-month test–retest reliabilities ranged from .55 to .70 (Barbarin, 1996). Concurrent validity for the scale has been demonstrated by the correlation between the IRS and the number of reported racist incidents occurring within an agency (Barbarin, 1996).

Prejudice Perception Assessment Scale

The Prejudice Perception Assessment Scale (PPAS; Martinez, 1998) is theoretically grounded in attribution theory, which asserts that people seek meaning for the events that occur in their lives. The scale was developed to examine individual differences among African Americans in the attribution of negative events to prejudice. Respondents are asked to assess the extent to which they believe that prejudice is responsible for the negative outcomes presented in five hypothetical ambiguous vignettes. Focus groups with college students were used to develop the final version of the vignettes. The response options for the five items range from *extremely likely* to *extremely unlikely*. A Cronbach alpha of .84 has been reported along with item-total correlations ranging from .61 to .70 for the five vignettes. Convergent validity was established by demonstrating that individuals who attributed more prejudice to the scenarios on the PPAS reported higher levels of distrust on a composite of the Education and Training and Interpersonal and Social Settings scales of the Cultural Mistrust Inventory (Terrell & Terrell, 1981). Discriminant validity was supported by demonstrating a low correlation between scores on the PPAS and scores on the Marlowe Crown Social Desirability Scale (Crowne & Marlowe, 1960). Principal components factor analysis revealed only one factor of stigma vulnerability; that factor accounted for 62.1% of the overall variance. All of the vignettes involve situations that might happen to college students.

MULTIDIMENSIONAL MEASURES

Several measures tap more than one of the three dimensions. These are grouped together based on these criteria and are referred to here as multidimensional measures.

African-American Racial Belief System: Schema-Based Approach

The schema-based approach to modeling an African-American racial belief system (Allen, Dawson, & Brown, 1989) is based on the authors' theory that there are three major components of racial consciousness: Black autonomy, closeness to other Blacks, and internalization of positive and negative stereotypes. According to our categorizations, the schema-based approach captures the dimensions of Cultural Connectedness and Multicultural Experiences. The scale examines affiliation toward other African Americans and espoused values of African-American culture, as well as perceptions regarding the influence of the dominant society on views about oneself and other African Americans. The 25-item measure consists of five cognitive constructs of a racial belief system: Black Autonomy, Closeness to the Black Masses, Closeness to Black Elites, Propensity to Adopt Positive Beliefs About African Americans, and Propensity to Adopt Negative Stereotypical Beliefs About African Americans. The instrument also measures socioeconomic status, religion, and the extent to which exposure to the Black media influences African-American racial beliefs.

Each of the constructs has distinct scoring criteria. For example, religiosity and Black media exposure are scored based on a five-point frequency of contact scale (e.g., frequency of reading religious books and frequency of watching Black television programs). For a further description of the scale and scoring criteria, the reader is referred to Allen, Dawson, and Brown (1989). Based on statistically significant factor loadings, the authors found support for the following constructs: Black Autonomy, Propensity to Adopt Positive Beliefs About African Americans, and Propensity to Adopt Negative Beliefs About African Americans (Allen, Dawson, & Brown, 1989). The scale was developed from data provided by the 1980 National Survey of Black Americans conducted by the Program for Research on Black Americans at the Survey Research Center at the University of Michigan.

Multigroup Ethnic Identity Measure

The Multigroup Ethnic Identity Measure (MEIM) was developed by Phinney (1992) to capture aspects of ethnic identity that are relevant across cultural groups. The author describes ethnic identity as an aspect of social identity that is also a component of self-concept and results from membership in a social group, together with the value and emotional significance attached to that involvement (Tajfel, 1981). Phinney's (1992) 24-item measure has four subscales: Affirmation and Belonging, Ethnic Identity Achievement, Ethnic Behaviors, Other-Group Orientation. Based on our classification system, this scale taps the following areas of racial identity: cultural connectedness, multicultural experiences, and identity formation. More specifically, the instrument assesses feelings of belonging and attachment to the cultural group, involvement with ethnic practices and cultural traditions, level of ethnic identity development, and attitudes and interactions with other ethnic groups.

Items are scored on a four-point Likert scale ranging from *strongly agree* (1) to *strongly disagree* (4). Results of a principal axis factor analysis supported the existence of an ethnic identity and other-group orientation factor (Phinney, 1992). Overall reliability coefficients ranging from .80 to .92 have been reported, and Cronbach alphas for the individual subscales have ranged from .69 to .86 (Birnbaum, 1991; Phinney, 1992). Evidence of construct validity has been shown in research relating ethnic identity to self-esteem, ego-identity development, and tolerance for diversity (Phinney, 1992; Rothery, 1992; Taylor, 1990).

Scale for the Effects of Ethnicity and Discrimination

The Scale for the Effects of Ethnicity and Discrimination (SEED; Cardo, 1994) is primarily based on Banks' (1981) stages of ethnicity. This theoretical perspective includes six nonsequential stages of ethnicity that range from "ethnic psychological captivity and encapsulation through identity clarification to bi-ethnicity, multiethnicity, and globalism" (Cardo, 1994, p. 51). This 35-item scale is classified as a multidimensional measure because it assesses two of our proposed areas of racial identity: identity formation and multicultural experiences. Separate scores can be calculated for each subscale. The Valence of Ethnicity for Self (VES) assesses identity formation that can range from ethnic rejection, as described in the early stages of either the Banks (1981) or Cross (1978) model, to the internalized positive attitudes in the later stages of these two models. The Valence of Ethnicity for Others (VEO) measures attitudes about other groups. Scores tap positive attitudes about other groups as well as outgroup rejection and feelings of inferiority or superiority. The Perception of Discrimination (PD) subscale assesses perceptions about differential treatment due to race and appears to evaluate multicultural experiences.

Moderate to high correlations have been obtained in studies of item to total reliability. Construct validity of the VES and PD subscales was demonstrated in a study correlating the scores of these dimensions with a measure of self-esteem (Mirage, 1987). The subscales appear to have been rationally derived.

Multidimensional Inventory of Black Identity

Sellers, Rowley, Chavous, Shelton, and Smith (1997) developed the Multidimensional Inventory of Black Identity (MIBI) to assess African-American beliefs about the significance of race. The three stable components in the Sellers theoretical model are Centrality, Ideology, and Regard. The fourth dimension, Identity Salience, is viewed as situational and is not included in the MIBI. The MIBI taps two of our dimensions: cultural connectedness and multicultural experiences. The scale is composed of items from the ASCS (Baldwin & Bell, 1985), DIB–C (Milliones, 1980), MEIM (Phinney, 1992), and the CMI (Terrell & Terrell, 1981) as well as original items developed by the authors. This 51-item measure has a seven-point Likert type format ranging from *strongly disagree* (1) to *strongly agree* (7). Alpha coefficients for the Centrality and Regard subscales have been reported as .74 and .60, respectively. The Ideology scales consists of four separate domains: Nationalist, Oppressed Minority, Assimilationist, and Humanist, with reliability estimates ranging from .80 to .67. The Public Regard subscale was not included in the revised MIBI. Predictive validity has been demonstrated by correlating appropriate subscales with the race of the best friend, enrollment in Black Studies courses, and reported interracial contact. The scale was standardized on African-American college students.

SUMMARY AND CONCLUSIONS

As mentioned earlier, a variety of measures are required to facilitate research on alternative facets of racial identity. This review clearly illustrates that psychometrically sound measures addressing alternative aspects of racial identity are available. Moreover, new options within each of the categories are now available to potential researchers.

All three of the identity formation measures (DIB–C, RIAS, and BPQ) have been widely used in research with African Americans, and adequate to exceptional psychometric properties have been demonstrated. Six measures of cultural connectedness were identified. Two (MRIS and BIS) assess affiliation and four (ASCS, AAAS, BSAS, and the Africentrism Scale) measure endorsement of traditions/values. Most of the measures of cultural connectedness were standardized in community samples of African Americans. Sound psychometric properties have been demonstrated in five of the six Multicultural Experiences scales (SRE, ACS, CMI, IRS, and the PPAS) among college students or university personnel. However, the psychometric properties of the PRS have been demonstrated in a community sample. Adequate reliability and validity have been demonstrated for three of the four multidimensional measures (MEIM, SEED, and MIBI). However, little published research is available on the psychometric properties of the schema-based approach.

It was beyond the scope of this chapter to provide a comprehensive critique of the current state of research on racial identity. Nevertheless, several comments seem appropriate that are relevant to this review of available measures.

First, most of the research on racial identity has been conducted using just a few of the measures—especially the RIAS, the ASCS, and the DIB–C. Because those measures tap either a specific approach to identity formation or the endorsement of a specific set of African-based values or ideology, the generalizability of the findings from these measures to other dimensions of racial identity is largely unexamined. For example, Goodwin (1988) demonstrated that the higher their internalization scores, the less favorably African-American college students rated a taped session in which the counselor was culturally insensitive. However, it is unclear whether the same findings would have been obtained if a measure of multicultural experiences or racial attitudes had been used to assess racial identity (e.g., Perceived Racism Scale). Hence, it is important that both the researcher and reader be conscious of the dimension of racial identity that is being measured when discussing the implications of findings about racial identity.

Second, the early measures were almost exclusively measures of racial identity. However, the changing ethnic composition of this nation has created a need for measures appropriate for other ethnic groups as well. Several of the measures included in this chapter are appropriate for assessing either racial or ethnic identity (e.g., MEIM, SEED). A number of additional measures of ethnic identity are available but were not reviewed in this chapter because they are more appropriate for ethnic groups other than African Americans.

Third, a disproportionately high number of the measures were standardized on college samples. This reliance on college samples is evident in much of the existing research on racial identity. Obviously college students may not be representative of the larger community of African Americans. Therefore, more research is needed to determine whether racial identity measures standardized on college samples are appropriate for community samples.

In conclusion, this chapter makes two important contributions to the literature. First, a number of new and established measures are described and reviewed. Second, the development of a new group of measures mandated a revision of the classification system presented in the Burlew & Smith (1993) article. Therefore, a second purpose was to introduce this revised classification system. The revised classification system groups the measures into three categories: measures of Identity Formation, Cultural Connectedness, and Multicultural Experiences. Measures that contain more than one of these three areas are grouped together in a fourth category named Multidimensional Measures.

REFERENCES

Allen, R. L., Dawson, M. C., & Brown, R. E. (1989). A schema-based approach to modeling an African-American racial belief system. *American Political Science Review, 83,* 421–441.

American Psychological Association. (1997). *Visions and transformations.* The final report of the Commission on Ethnic Minority Recruitment, Retention, and Training in Psychology, Washington, DC.

Azibo, D. A. (1996). Black personality questionnaire: A review. In R. L. Jones (Ed.), *Handbook of tests and measures for Black populations* (pp. 241–249). New York: Harper & Row.

Baldwin, J. (1981). Notes on an Africentric theory of Black personality. *The Western Journal of Black Studies, 5,* 172–179.

Baldwin, J., & Bell, Y. (1985). The African self-consciousness scale: An Africentric personality questionnaire. *The Western Journal of Black Studies, 9,* 61–68.

Banks, J. A. (1981). Multiethnic education: *Theory and practice.* Boston, MA: Allyn & Bacon.

Barbarin, O. A. (1996). The IRS: Multi-dimensional measurement of institutional racism. In R. L. Jones (Ed.), *Handbook of tests and measurements for Black populations* (pp. 375–397). New York: Harper & Row.

Barbarin, O. A., & Gilbert, R. (1981). Institutional racism scale: Assessing self and organizational attributes. In O. Barbarin, R. Good, O. Pharr, & J. Siskind (Eds.), *Institutional racism and community competence* (pp. 150–163). (DHHS Publication No. ADM 81-907). Washington, DC: U.S. Government Printing Office.

Bernal, M., & Knight, G. (1993). *Ethnic identity.* New York: State University of New York Press.

Birnbaum, A. (1991). *Measuring level of ethnic identity: A comparison of two new scales.* Unpublished doctoral dissertation, Rutgers University, New Brunswick, New Jersey.

Brookins, C. C. (1994). The relationship between Afrocentric values and racial identity attitudes: Validation of the Belief Systems Analysis Scale on African American college students. *Journal of Black Psychology, 20,* 128–142.

Burlew, A. K., & Smith, L. (1993). Measures of racial identity: An overview and a proposed framework. *Journal of Black Psychology, 17,* 51–69.

Cardo, L. (1994). Development of an instrument measuring valence of ethnicity and perception of discrimination. *Journal of Multicultural Counseling and Development, 22,* 40–59.

Cohen, S., Kamarck, T., & Mermelstein, R. (1983). A global measure of perceived stress. *Journal of Health and Social Behavior, 24,* 385–396.

Cross, W. E. (1971). The Negro-to-Black conversion experience: Toward a psychology of Black liberation. *Black World, 20,* 13–27.

Cross, W. E., Jr. (1978). Models of psychological nigrescence: A literature review. *Journal of Black Psychology, 5,* 13–31.

Crowne, D., & Marlowe, D. (1960). A new scale of social desirability independent of psychopathology. *Journal of Consulting Psychology, 24,* 349–354.

Davis, W. (1979). *Williams' survey questionnaire.* Unpublished manuscript.

Denton, S. E. (1985). A methodological refinement and validational analysis of the DIB-C (Doctoral Dissertation, University of Pittsburgh, 1984). *Dissertation Abstracts International,* DA8617150.

Dohrenwend, B., Krasnoff, L., Askenasy, A., & Dohrenwend, B. (1978). Exemplification of a method for scaling life events: The PERI Life Events scales. *Journal of Health and Social Behavior, 19,* 205–229.

Goodwin, S. (1988). *The influence of Black students' racial identity attitudes on judging a therapist's cultural sensitivity.* Unpublished master's thesis, University of Cincinnati, Ohio.

Grace, C. (1984). *The relationship between racial identity attitudes and choice of typical and atypical occupations among Black college students.* Unpublished doctoral dissertation, Columbia University, New York.

Grills, C., & Longshore, D. (1996). Africentrism: Psychometric analyses of a self report. *Journal of Black Psychology, 22,* 86–106.

Helms, J. E. (1990). *Black and White racial identity: Theory, research, and practice.* Westport, CT: Greenwood.

Helms, J. E., & Parham, T. (1996). The Racial Identity Attitude Scale. In R. Jones (Ed.), *Handbook of tests and measurements for Black population* (pp. 167–174). Hampton, VA: Cobbs & Henry.

Hilliard, A. (1985). *Parameters affecting the African American child.* Paper presented at the Black Psychology Seminar, Duke University, Durham, NC.

Karenga, M. (1980). *Kawaida theory: An introductory outline.* Los Angeles: University of Sankore Press.

Kohatsu, E., & Richardson, T. (1996). Racial and ethnic identity. In L. Suzuki, P. Meller, & J. Ponterotto (Eds.), *Handbook of multicultural assessment: Clinical, psychological, and educational applications* (pp. 611–650). San Francisco: Jossey-Bass.

Landrine, H., & Klonoff, E. (1994). The African American acculturation scale: Development, reliability, and validity. *Journal of Black Psychology, 20,* 104–127.

Landrine, H., & Klonoff, E. (1995). The African American acculturation scale: II. Cross validation and short form. *Journal of Black Psychology, 21,* 124–152.

Landrine, H., & Klonoff, E. (1996). *African American acculturation: Deconstructing race and reviving culture.* Thousand Oaks, CA: Sage.

Longshore, D., Grills, C., Anglin, M. D., & Annon, K. (1998). Treatment motivation among African American drug-using arrestees. *Journal of Black Psychology, 24,* 119–129.

Martinez, D. (1998). The Prejudice Perception Assessment Scale: Measuring stigma vulnerability among African American students at predominantly Euro-American Universities. *Journal of Black Psychology, 24,* 303–319.

McNeilly, M., Anderson, N., Robinson, E., McManus, C., Armstead, C., Clark, R., Pieper, C., Simons, & Saulter, T. (1996). Convergent, discriminant, and concurrent validity of the Perceived Racism Scale: A multidimensional assessment of the experience of racism among African Americans. In R. Jones (Ed.), *Handbook of tests and measurements for Black populations* (Vol. 2, pp. 359–374). Hampton, VA: Cobb & Henry.

Milliones, J. (1980). Construction of a Black consciousness measure: Psychotherapeutic implications. *Psychotherapy: Theory, Research, and Practice, 17,* 175–182.

Mirage, L. (1987). *Valence of ethnicity, perception of discrimination and self esteem in high risk minority college students.* Unpublished doctoral dissertation, Fordham University, New York City, New York.

Montgomery, D., Fine, M., & Myers, L. J. (1990). The development and validation of an instrument to assess an optimal Afrocentric world view. *Journal of Black Psychology, 17,* 37–54.

Myers, L. J. (1988). *An Afrocentric worldview: Introduction to an optimal psychology.* Dubuque, IA: Kendall-Hunt.

Myers, M. A., & Sanders-Thompson, V. (1994). Africentricity: An analysis of two culture specific instruments. *The Western Journal of Black Studies, 18,* 179–184.

Nickerson, K. J., Helms, H. E., & Terrell, F. (1994). Cultural mistrust, opinions about mental illness, and Black students' attitudes toward seeking psychological help from White counselors. *Journal of Counseling Psychology, 41,* 378–385.

Nunnally, J. (1978). *Psychometric theory* (2nd ed.). New York: McGraw-Hill.

Parham, T. A., & Helms, J. E. (1981). The influence of Black students' racial identity attitudes on preferences for counselor's race. *Journal of Counseling Psychology, 28,* 250–257.

Parham, T. A., & Helms, J. E. (1985). Relation of racial identity attitudes to self-actualization and affective states of Black students. *Journal of Counseling Psychology, 32,* 431–440.

Phinney, J. S. (1990). Ethnic identity in adolescents and adults: Review and research. *Psychological Bulletin, 108,* 499–514.

Phinney, J. S. (1992). The multigroup ethnic identity measure: A new scale for use with diverse groups. *Journal of Adolescent Research, 7,* 171–183.

Pomales, J., Claiborne, C. D., & LaFromboise, T. D. (1986). Effects of Black students' racial identity on perceptions of White counselors varying in cultural sensitivity. *Journal of Counseling Psychology, 33,* 57–61.

Ponterotto, J. G., & Wise, S. L. (1987). Construct validity of the Racial Identity Attitude Scale. *Journal of Counseling Psychology, 34,* 218–223.

Rothery, C. R. (1992). *An exploration of ethnic identity and self-esteem in Black females from two college settings.* Unpublished doctoral dissertation, Rutgers University, New Brunswick, New Jersey.

Sabnani, H. B., & Ponterotto, J. G. (1992). Racial/ethnic minority-specific instrumentation in counseling research: A review, critique, and recommendations. *Measurement and Evaluation in Counseling and Development, 24,* 161–187.

Sanders-Thompson, V. (1992). A multifaceted approach to the conceptualization of African American identification. *Journal of Black Studies, 23,* 75–85.

Sellers, R., Rowley, S., Chavous, T., Shelton, J. N., & Smith, M. (1997). Multidimensional inventory of Black identity: A preliminary investigation of reliability and construct validity. *Journal of Personality and Social Psychology, 73,* 805–815.

Speight, S. L., Vera, E. M., & Derrickson, K. B. (1996). Racial self-designation, racial identity, and self-esteem revisited. *Journal of Black Psychology, 22,* 37–52.

Spencer, M. B., & Markstrom-Adams, C. (1990). Identity process among racial and ethnic minority children in America. *Child Development, 61,* 290–310.

Stokes, J., Murray, C. B., Peacock, M. J., & Kaiser, R. (1994). Assessing the reliability, factor structure, and validity of the African self consciousness scale in a general population of African Americans. *Journal of Black Psychology, 20,* 62–74.

Tajfel, H. (1981). *Human groups and social categories.* New York: Cambridge University Press.

Taylor, K. E. (1990). The dilemma of difference: The relationship of the intellectual development, racial identity, and self-esteem of Black and White students to their tolerance for diversity [CD-ROM]. *ProQuest File: Dissertation Abstracts Item:* AAG9028099.

Terrell, F., & Terrell, S. (1981). An inventory to measure cultural mistrust among Blacks. *The Western Journal of Black Studies, 5,* 180–185.

Thomas, C. (1971). *Boys no more: A Black psychologist's view of community.* Beverly Hills, CA: Glencoe.

Whittler, T., Calantone, R., & Young, M. (1991). Strength of ethnic affiliation: Examining Black identification with Black culture. *Journal of Social Psychology, 131,* 461–467.

Williams, R. L. (1981). *The collective Black mind: An Africentric theory of Black personality.* St. Louis, MO: Williams & Associates.

Williams-Flournoy, D., & Anderson, L. (1996). The Acculturative Stress Scale: Preliminary findings. In R. Jones (Ed.), *Handbook of tests and measurements for Black populations* (Vol. 2, pp. 351–358). Hampton, VA: Cobb & Henry.

Wright, B., & Isenstein, V. (1978). *Psychological tests and minorities* (DHEW Publication No. ADM. 78-482). Washington, DC: Government Printing Office.

9

Social Psychological Perspectives on Changing Self-Identification Among American Indians and Alaska Natives

Joseph E. Trimble
Western Washington University

> *The Caterpillar and Alice looked at each other for some time in silence: at last the Caterpillar took the hookah out of its mouth, and addressed her in a languid, sleepy voice. "Who are you?" said the Caterpillar. Alice replied, rather shyly, "I–I hardly know, Sir, just at present-at least I know who I was when I got up this morning, but I think I must have been changed several times since then." "You!" said the Caterpillar contemptuously. "Who are* you?"
>
> —Lewis Carroll (1865)

> *"Why do you call us Indians?" (an unnamed indigenous native from Massachusetts addressing the 17th Century missionary, John Eliot)*
> —quoted by Robert F. Berkhofer, *The White Man's Indian* (1978)

Many youth today call it *claiming* when "a brown-skinned girl with a Mexican father and a white mother 'claims' her Mexican side, while her fair-skinned sister 'claims' white" (Bernstein, 1995, p. 87). Although long recognized as a developmental stage marked as an *identity crisis* (Stevens, 1983), many of today's adolescents, especially those of distinct ethnic heritage, appear to be quite concerned about the hybridization of their backgrounds. "There's also something going on out here (in California)," maintained Bernstein (1995) "that transcends adolescent faddishness and pop culture exoticism" (p. 90). Youth appear to be choosing ethnic groups with which to identify in order to gain entry into cliques, gangs, and segments of their social lives that bolster self-esteem and perceived acceptance.

Claiming is one variant of America's growing preoccupation with ethnic identity. It is an outbreak of what might be called *ethnic fever*, maintained Steinberg (1981). More and more Americans appear to realize that their biological ancestors wittingly and unwittingly influence their lives. To gain some understanding and perhaps to add structure and meaning, many are searching their attics for long lost records describing their social histories, and constructing *symbolic identity* from the discoveries. "If you wish to understand persons—their development and their relations with significant others," maintained Strauss (1959), "you must be prepared to view them as embedded in historical context" (p. 164). In the course of constructing and maintaining the identity, common historical symbols are identified, shared, and passed along to future generations. The symbols also can serve as a public affirmation of one's ethnic claim. Clothing, decals, adornments, flags, food, language, and celebrations often serve as instrumental expressions of ethnic artifacts.

People can *dis-identify* with the way they view themselves and the way they believe others perceive them. As often is the case, an individual may be dissatisfied or disillusioned with their self-image and may, in the course of time, seize the occasion to change or pass by validating other images (see Strauss, 1959). Today, more than ever, Americans are becoming more tolerant and accepting of diverse ethnic and cultural backgrounds. Indeed many are making active choices about who and what they are.

The Caterpillar's query to the woefully perplexed and bewildered Alice fits within any discussion about ethnic identity and self-recognition. To answer the query "Who am I?," one may appeal to a variety of personal and familiar characteristics, social categories including class and ethnicity, current vocation, and geographic residence. In offering a reply, most people prefer to rely on commonly accepted categories. Unless the person is a member of the majority group, the reply usually includes an ethnic identifier. Categories and people, however, are protean. At some point, identity declarations require external validation, and therefore the judgments of others play a key role in the transaction.

Identity is not merely a set of observable categories. The psychoanalyst Erik Erikson (1980), for example, maintained that identity is located in the self or core of the individual and that one's communal culture, self-esteem, and sense of affiliation and belongingness are deeply affected by the identity process. Fitzgerald (1993) pointed out that identity is inextricably linked to self-understanding and can be posited "as the academic metaphor for self-in-context" (p. ix).

People typically construct their identities within the context of their biological backgrounds and the sociopolitical contexts in which they are socialized. Moreover, people often construct autobiographies to place themselves in the social order and seek out settings and situations for confirmation (Harré, 1989). Hence, we find people constructing their identities and self-images to fit sociocultural contexts and constructing the situations and contexts to fit the image (Fitzgerald, 1993). A person may have multiple identities that emerge in different social contexts. For example, within a tribe an American Indian may self-identify as a member of a clan, outside the tribe among other American Indians as a member of a particular tribe, among non-Indians as an Indian, and outside the country as an American. Identity is not static and invariant; society changes, people change, contexts change, and ethnic identities and the sense of self-satisfaction with those identities change accordingly. Without a context, identity formation and self-development cannot be maintained. Alice lost all familiar contexts and could not answer the Caterpillar's query.

America's preoccupation with ethnicity has introduced an opportunistic element into the arena of self-identification. Roosens (1989) called it *ethnogenesis*, or *ethnic consciousness.* "Ethnicity," maintained Daniel Bell (1975), "is a means (now) for disadvantaged groups to claim a set of rights and privileges which the existing power structures have denied them" (p. 174). Faced with the possibility of financial gain, job security, and numerous social and health benefits, individuals whose ethnic identities have been submerged or only remotely salient or whose status has been denigrated in the past are proclaiming their ethnic heritage: "They develop and publicly present a self-conscious ethnicity" (Fitzgerald, 1993, p. 83). However, we cannot assume that interest in ethnic identity is purely for self-gain. Many Americans, especially those of American Indian heritage, maintain their Indian identification in part because they are deeply concerned that the traditional ways are decaying and eroding through influences and changes occurring at a larger societal level (Meyrowitz, 1986). These factors may underlie renewed interest in Americans' identifying with their Indianness. Clifton (1989) noted that between 1950 and 1990 the census count for people identifying themselves as American Indian increased by well over 400%, whereas the general U.S. population count increased by 61% during the same period. Demographers claim that such an increase is almost impossible especially for an indigenous ethnic population. Immigration typically doesn't occur among American Indians; thus the enormous increase must be attributed to the penchant for an increasing number of ethnically marginal Americans to declare their *Indianness.* Clifton (1989) summarized by observing that "every time the value of being Indian increases, the number of persons of marginal or ambiguous ancestry who claim to be Indian increases" (p. 17).

To understand some of the social psychological forces that bear on American Indian self-identification, background information concerning ethnicity, ethnic groups, and the measurement of ethnic identification must be summarized. A summary follows these introductory comments and thoughts. The chapter then proceeds to discuss the provocative problems germane to the second question posed earlier, "Why do you call us Indian?" and to another question, "Why do individuals call themselves American Indian or some other referent indicative of aboriginal status?" Two points must be made clear: (a) Provincial and theoretical attempts to explain and predict ethnic identity are inconclusive and speculative; and (b) people do construct life stories for themselves that often are mutable and the uncertainty of the story can be sufficient motivation for one to seek and find a portion of their ancestral history to lend structure, meaning, and stability to their lives.

ETHNICITY, ETHNIC GROUPS, AND ETHNIC IDENTIFICATION

The term *ethnic* has Latin and Greek origins; *ethnicus* and *ethnikos* mean nation. The term can be and has been used historically to refer to people as heathens. *Ethos*, in Greek, means custom, disposition, or trait. *Ethnikas* and *ethos* taken together therefore can mean a band of people (nation) living together who share common customs. The social and behavioral science literature abounds with ethnic terms that are derived from the lexical roots. Anthropology contains the most references, followed by sociology and history. Within the past decade or so interest in ethnicity and related topics has also slowly eased its way into psychology. In fact, *ethnos* is now a component of many academic disciplines; ethnobotany, ethnoscience, ethnomedicine, ethnopsychiatry, and ethnoculture are examples of scholars' attempts to align their fields with the ethnic concept. Fusing *ethnos* with an orthodox academic discipline is presumably intended to convey the notion that the discipline attends to something cultural.

Ethnicity

Several sociologists, anthropologists, and historians have written extensively on ethnicity (see Steinberg, 1981; Thompson, 1989; van den Berghe, 1981, for reviews). In its broadest form, ethnicity refers to "any differentiation based on nationality, race, religion, or language" (Greeley, 1974, p. 187). Barth (1969) believed that ethnicity is the native's worldview and thus defines relationships, boundaries, lifestyle, and thoughtways. The sociobiological perspective is represented by Pierre van den Berghe (1981), who maintained that "there exists a general predisposition, in our species as in many others, to react favorably toward other organisms to the extent that those organisms are biologically related to the actor" (p. 19). Yinger (1986) pointed out that "ethnicity has come to refer to anything from a sub-societal group that clearly shows a common descent and cultural to persons who share a former citizenship although diverse culturally . . . to pan-cultural groups of persons of widely different cultural and societal backgrounds who can be identified as 'similar' on the basis of language, race or religion mixed with broadly similar statuses" (p. 23).

Ethnic Group

Adding *group* to *ethnic* does not clarify the ethnic contruct; some authors, in fact, have rejected use of the construct. Yinger (1986), for example, preferred to use the term *ethnie* and van den Berghe (1981) preferred *ethny*. For an *ethnie* to exist, Yinger maintained that three conditions must be present: (a) a segment of a larger society must be viewed by others as sharing and demonstrating a distinct language, religious preference, and an ancestral homeland; (b) group members must concur with their designation and shared common characteristics; and (c) members, in general, must participate in the events, ceremonies, and activities embedded in their cultural lifeways and thoughtways.

Smith (1991) proposed a definition in which an *ethnic group* is viewed as a reference group where "people who share a common history and culture may be identifiable because they share similar physical features and values, and who identify themselves as being a member of that group" (p. 181). Identity development and the texture and disposition of groups constitute the core of Smith's definition. Hence, she preferred to use the term *ethnic reference group* and in so doing drew attention to the "individual *in* his or her group and cultural setting and (the) cultural setting relative to its members" (Sherif & Sherif, 1964, pp. 36–37). The reference group serves to set goals and regulate behavior and provides a setting in which individual members gauge their identities and belonging on the basis of responses from like-minded members. American Indians meet this definition of an ethnic group or ethnic reference group, especially those American Indians who live at least part of the time on reservations or in communities that retain traditions, ceremonies, and activities.

In some societies or countries certain groups are numerically in the minority; hence, such groups have been labeled *ethnic minority* groups, adding another element to the definition. Willemsen and van Oudenhoven (1989) defined these groups as those who "differ from the majority of the people in the country or society in which they live. Differences may refer to language, race or religion or a combination of these characteristics" (p. 11). A history of oppressed status, power imbalances, lack of economic opportunities, and basic conflicts of interest often characterize these groups; however, some ethnic groups may be numerically in the minority but lack the wretched history of oppression and prejudice. To refer to an

ethnic group without considering the full range of its influences, characteristics, and history would misrepresent and distort its essence.

Greeley (1974) suggested that identification may not always reflect
one's ethnic origins; thus, the author proposed other questions: "How do
those of mixed ethnic origins determine which identification they are
going to choose? [And] to what extent does such a choice lead to attitudes
and behavior that the chooser defines as being pertinent to the identification he has given himself?" (p. 310).

Ethnic Identity and Ethnic Identification

Ethnic identity is an affiliative construct in which individuals are viewed
by themselves and/or by others as belonging to a group. It tends to be
a classification—a decision as to whether one is a member of a particular
group. Cheung (1993) defined ethnic identity as "the psychological attachment to an ethnic group or heritage" and thus centers the construct
in the domain of self-perception (p. 1216). Saharso (1989) extended the
definition to include social processes that involve one's choice of friends,
selection of a future partner, perception of one's life-chances, and the
reactions of others in one's social environment. Both definitions involve
boundaries that reflect a distinction one makes about "self" and "other."

An individual may strongly identify psychologically with an ethnic
group; however, the strength and authenticity of the identity are contingent on the acceptance and acknowledgment of in-group and outgroup
members. Ethnic identity is contextual and situational because it "is a
product of social transaction insofar as one assumes an ethnic identity by
claiming it and demonstrating the conventional signs of membership. A
claimant is always subject to the response of others who may concur with
or deny the claim" (Casino, n.d., p. 18). Affiliation can be influenced by
racial, natal, symbolic, and cultural factors (Cheung, 1993). Racial factors
involve the use of physiognomic and physical characteristics, and natal
factors refer to homeland (or ancestral home) origins. Symbolic factors
include those factors believed to typify or exemplify an ethnic group (e.g.,
holidays, foods, clothing, artifacts, etc.). Cultural factors refer to the specific lifeways and thoughtways of an ethnic group and are probably the
most difficult to assess and measure (see Cheung, 1993, for more details).

Phinney (1990) eloquently and succinctly summarized the ethnic identity literature. She stated that "there is no widely agreed on definition of
ethnic identity" and that "the definitions that were given reflected quite
different understandings or emphasis regarding what is meant by ethnic
identity" (p. 500). Social and behavioral scientists undoubtedly believe
they have a general sense about the meaning and implications of the
construct. Some are rather firm about their positions (see van den Berghe,

1981; Weinreich, 1988), but about a quarter of the studies reviewed by Phinney were not built on a theoretical framework.

Ethnic labeling involves the use of tags or markers to refer to and categorize groups and their members. For example, Buriel (1987) pointed out that numerous labels exist to refer to the Mexican-descent population in the United States: Mexican, Mexicano, Mexican American, Mestizo, and Chicano make up most of the labels. Over the years, outgroup members have also coined pejorative and offensive labels to refer to those of Mexican descent, most of which are lodged in stereotypical, prejudicial, and racist thoughts.

The terms *American Indian* and *Alaska Native* are *ethnic glosses* (Trimble, 1991, 1995). They refer to the aboriginal populations of North America and are terms imbued with political and sociocultural considerations. In this chapter *American Indian* and *Indian* are typically used for the sake of brevity and are not meant to demean the distinct heterogeneity that exists among the many native tribes and villages and those who prefer to identify with these entities rather than the broad glosses. The terms *race* and *racial* should be avoided where possible because they do not have relevance for American Indians and Alaska Natives. The concepts are *academic anachronisms* and have little scientific and practical value, in part, because of their elusive, unbounded nature (see Yee, Fairchild, Weizmann, & Wyatt, 1993).

For social and behavioral scientists, ethnic labeling has a distinct sociopolitical value and function, especially for census and demographic studies. Where generalizations about distinct cultural orientations are not used, ethnic labels serve a useful function. However, all too often researchers use ethnic labels to wittingly or unwittingly convey a deeper cultural meaning than the labels actually permit. In eliciting ethnic-specific samples for behavioral and social science research, researchers often rely only on ethnic labels to describe and differentiate their respondent groups. In so doing, they assume that the respondents share a common, modal understanding of their ethnic and nationalistic lifeways and thoughtways; it is as if the researcher believes that such groups as American Indians, African Americans, Asian Americans, and others share commonly held culturally unique mannerisms, styles, and states. In fact, researchers who rely solely on an ethnic gloss to describe ethnic groups actually ignore the richness of cultural variations within these groups and the numerous subgroups characterized by distinct lifeways and thoughtways (Trimble, 1992, 1995). Although census and demographic studies and studies aimed at policy may utilize ethnic glosses such as *American Indian* appropriately, use of broad ethnic glosses to describe an ethnic group in a research venture in which personal or cultural characteristics are assumed to apply to members of the group is poor science. Apart from the fact that glosses are gross misrepresentations, their use violates certain tenets concerning external validity and, indeed, fosters stereotyping. Heath (1978) argued that "categories of people such as those compared under the rubric of 'ethnic groups' are often not really meaningful units in any sociocultural sense" (p. 60). He went on to add that "it is little wonder that epidemiological and other data collected under such rubrics (i.e., ethnic minorities and other nationalistic groups) are virtually meaningless" (p. 60).

Although it is not often drawn in the literature, there may be a useful distinction between ethnic identity and ethnic identification. *Ethnic identity* is usually a categorical term. It can consist of an attribution of an ethnic label by an outsider based on some observable characteristic or characteristics or it can be the assumption of an ethnic label by an individual. The term *ethnic identification* should probably be reserved for a more complex concept that does not relate to labeling by an outsider but is the person's own identification with an ethnic group. It should include not only a qualitative assignment marking the person's willingness to assume an ethnic identity, but also a quantitative element that describes the strength of the identification.

Ethnic self-identification is a distinct psychological variable and "refers to the description of oneself in terms of a critical ethnic attribute; that is, an attribute that defines more than merely describes the ethnic group" (Aboud, 1987, p. 33). In most social settings, use of one attribute may be sufficient. However, other settings may require the use of several related attributes to indicate the strength of identity. Vaughn (1987) viewed self-identification as a form of personal identity and differentiated the two from social identity. Personal identity "derives from a sense of self based on interpersonal comparisons" and social identity "from group membership" (Vaughn, 1987, p. 74). Rosenthal (1987) and Phinney (1990) viewed subjective identity as a starting point that eventually leads to the development of a social identity based on ethnic group membership. But Rosenthal added that "ethnic identity arises in interaction and is a function not only of the individual and his or her relation to the ethnic group but of the group's place in the wider social setting" (p. 160).

At an individual level, one may rely on labels to describe ethnic affiliation and subsequently identity. Use of the label is a small part of the identity process, however, because one is likely to expand the labeling to include other identifiers, such as natal background, acculturative status, ego involvement, and attitudes toward own and other groups. In addition, behavioral preferences such as language usage, friendship affiliations, music and food preferences, and participation in cultural and religious activities may be included (Trimble, 1992, 1995). See Fig. 9.1 for a classification of the various interactive factors that make up ethnic self-identification.

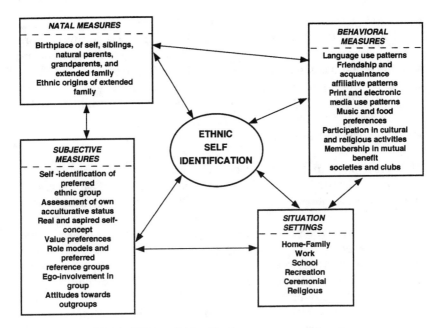

FIG. 9.1. Ethnic self-identification measurement domains.

SOME ATTEMPTS AT DEFINING AMERICAN INDIAN

The query of the Massachusetts native—"Why do you call us Indian?"—was sincere; the term had no meaning for the native. Yet for Eliot, the term was rife with imagery. "In short, character and culture were united into one summary," remarked Robert Berkhofer (1978, p. 25). He pointed out that the use of this gloss persevered, in cases where Euro-Americans are "(a) generalizing from one tribe's society and culture to all Indians, (b) conceiving of Indians in terms of their deficiencies according to white ideals rather than in terms of their own various cultures, and (c) using moral evaluation as description of Indians" (pp. 25–26).

The term *American Indian* is an imposed, invented ethnic category—an ethnic gloss (Trimble, 1992, 1995). It was originally foisted on the Arawak, a now extinct Caribbean-basin tribe. The category continues to be used to the extent that almost all indigenous native peoples of the Western hemisphere are referred to as Indians. Many pejorative historical stereotypical images are incorporated in the meaning when it is used by outgroup members, but contemporary Indians have also found some value in self-identification with this broad gloss. Speaking to this point, Trosper (1981) cogently argued that "American Indians have transformed themselves from a diverse people with little common identity into an ethnic group (and) have done so by mobilizing, with respect to a charter, the shared history of broken treaties" (p. 257). By forging a common ethnic category, America's indigenous population has created a social and political force that has far greater strength and influence than do individual tribal governments; the emergence of the pan-Indian category has created a conventional label with which one can identify (see Hartzberg, 1971).

Tribal-Specific Definitions

Tribal groups had names for themselves and, indeed, linguistic-specific names for other tribal groups. Within their own languages, the names of tribes such as Lakota, Cheyenne, Navajo (Diné), and Hopi mean "human beings" or "the people." Within tribes, bands such as "those with burned thighs" or "those who plant near the water" and moieties such as "Eagle" or "Raven" were given specific names that refer to some idiosyncratic or spiritual characteristic. In addition, tribes such as the Lakota referred to other tribes according to stereotyped physical features and characteristics; the Cheyenne were referred to as *Sihiyena* (people with a shrill voice), the Winnebago as *Hotanke* (loud-voice people), and the Navajo as *Sna-hde-hde-ha* (those with striped blankets). Such distinctions were typically ignored by American colonialists, historians, and novelists, leaving the world with the erroneous impression that American Indians were a distinctive but singular lot. It is apparently more convenient to gloss a group than to deal with the discrete entities within it.

Government Attempts at a Definition

The federal government, through the Bureau of Indian Affairs (BIA), found it necessary to provide a legal definition of an American Indian— the only ethnic group in the United States afforded this distinction. The definition has undergone numerous revisions in the past 100 years or so, but currently the BIA defines an American Indian as a person whose American Indian blood quantum is at least one fourth and who is a registered or enrolled member of the 300 or more federally recognized tribes. The hard-and-fast criteria eliminated many people of American Indian background who affiliated in one form or another with some 60 federally nonrecognized tribes—ones that in many cases never signed formal treaties with the government or that were part of scattered, small groups in the northwest and southwest (see Snipp, 1989, 1996).

Some recognized or *treaty* tribes do not agree with the BIA criteria and have developed their own specifications. Some have lowered the blood quantum criterion to one eighth and even one 128th, and a few have increased it to one half. In the late 1960s, one tribe in Oklahoma opened its rolls to anyone who could prove ancestral ties; specific blood quantum was not viewed as an important criterion. About 7% of the tribes require that one have more than one fourth blood quantum and about 32% have no set blood quantum criteria. Whatever the criteria, one must be able to establish their claim by providing documentation showing that one or more of their relatives or ancestors are on some version of a tribe's role or census (Thornton, 1996).

The U.S. Bureau of Census and the Department of Education (DOE) each developed their own criteria. The Census Bureau allows each citizen to declare his or her ethnic origin on the basis of the group with which he or she most identifies—in a word, the criterion is self-enumerative. After conducting an extensive survey among Indian people throughout the United States, DOE staff generated some 70 distinct definitions of *American Indian*. After a careful review of the results, DOE decided on a definition that closely resembles BIA criteria but provides more latitude for tribal-specific criteria regardless of federal status (United States Department of Education, 1982).

Government definitions are developed largely to determine who is eligible for services provided by treaty arrangements and congressionally mandated programs. The definitions do not include the extent to which an individual follows tribal custom and tradition or the degree to which he or she professes an ethnic identification.

Interaction and Validation Styles

Among many American Indians, merely being federally recognized and fitting the definitional criteria of the BIA and DOE are not sufficient. For many, it is vitally important to glean a sense of the way one lives and subscribes to traditional and readily identifiable lifestyle patterns. As a consequence, when two strangers meet and it is apparent that both possess distinctive physical characteristics—dark, straight hair; dark brown eyes; brown skin; high cheekbones; broad nasal structure; and other distinguishing features—they seek to elicit information from each other to substantiate degree of ethnic affiliation. Using a nesting procedure, one will ask questions—Where are you from? What tribe do you belong to? Who are you related to?—in an effort to generate some commonly shared background. If one or the other does not quite fit the physical stereotype, the conversation may well turn to identifying which parent or grandparent was non-Indian and what the person's blood quantum might be. This is usually a delicate subject, so it is often handled rather carefully. If all of the information appears authentic and genuine, the conversation may lapse into one in which each shares stories about presumed common life experiences. Often the conversation takes on a form of *homeland centrism*, in which the daily, contemporary lifestyle of the individual's origins is emphasized over tribal customs and traditions. Hence, Indians from reservations are likely to discuss socializing influences more indicative of contemporary lifeways back home than to give attention to classic tribal customs. In a subtle way, the conversation is designed to provide evidence not only that the participants are American Indians by definition but that they have the experiences to back that up—experiences that demonstrate the authenticity and strength of the identity with one's ethnic origins.

Ethnic group validation and confirmation dialogues vary considerably from one tribe to another. Among the members of the Navajo (Diné) Nation in the southwest, two individuals who meet for the first time will follow a highly stylized, almost ritualized, dialogue guided by strict protocol. Typically, the first speaker (usually the one who appears to be the elder) will begin by introducing him or herself, by name, in the Navajo language. The introduction is followed by an identification of the speaker's maternal clan, the paternal clan, the maternal grandfather's clan, and then the paternal grandparents' clan. Then the speaker will identify up to four different clans that belong to the maternal side of his or her family; these clans are usually not stated until the maternal clan is identified. The speaker then identifies whether he or she comes from the eastern or western side of the vast Navajo reservation; this is an important distinction because of some distinct and unique linguistic differences between the two sides. Finally, the first speaker will mention something distinctive about a parent or grandparent, such as "My grandfather is known for horses." The second speaker follows the form in the exact order presented to him or her. The two speakers may then continue the introductory dialogue until they have mutually identified their kinship and clan connections with each other. Once this is done, the conversation can then—and only then—lapse into other topics of mutual interest.

Although there are a generalized set of definitions and colloquial efforts to promote further clarification of ethnic origins, American Indians make up an extraordinarily diverse and complicated ethnic group. According to the 1990 U.S. Census, there are close to 2 million American Indians and Alaska Natives in a national population of more than 260 million people. There may be many more because many Indians either refuse to participate in the census or do not want to be identified as Indians for a multitude of personal and social reasons.

Why Do People Identify as American Indian?

Tajfel's (1981) social identity theory proposes that people tend to categorize their social world into groups consisting of similar others and groups that are dissimilar to their preferred group. Membership, however achieved, influences one's self-concept, and the valence of the concept is tied to one's evaluation of other dissimilar groups. Social categorization and social comparisons work collaboratively to help people develop and nurture views of themselves and others in their social environment. One assigns individuals to groups on the basis of known features and characteristics and then the members are compared with other groups. If belonging to one group enhances one's self concept, then the value of the group increases relative to other groups. Within the tenets of social identity theory, Clifton (1989) asserted that "being Indian, therefore, is an aspect of the self, one that affects a person's right and obligations, always in association with others occupying complimentary social positions" (p. 31).

The motives guiding people to identify as American Indians cannot be subsumed under a single social psychological theory, in part, "because objective criteria have never been established for deciding who is and is not an American Indian, and who is and is not a Cherokee; any such criterion is controversial" (Thornton, 1990, p. 203). Yet nearly 2 million people self-identified as American Indian or Alaska Native in the 1990 U.S. Census. Indeed, many if not most know unequivocally that they are American Indians and Alaska Natives, thus, for them an explanatory motive and theory are not salient and the question is irrelevant.

The identity question is most salient and relevant for those "who report their race as Indian but include non-Indian ancestry in their ethnic background" and those "who cite a non-Indian race yet claim Indian ancestry for their ethnic background" (Snipp, 1989, p. 51). Because of their mixed ethnic backgrounds, such individuals presumably have a choice of groups with which to identify. Indeed, many may be enrolled or registered members of a tribe or village corporation, making the choice straightforward. Others are not, yet many choose to identify more with their Indian background than some other part of their ethnic lineage. Then there are those who do not have any Indian or Alaska Native ancestors but nonetheless choose to identify themselves as American Indians. Perhaps the most illustrious of these individuals is Grey Owl, or Archie Belaney, who claimed that he was a descendant of the Jicarilla Apache band on his mother's side. Biographical evidence indicates that he was not, yet he was accepted by some Canadian Indians and non-Indians as an Indian, because of his wilderness lifestyle, knowledge of Ojibwa traditions, and deep, abiding concern about wildlife preservation (Dickson, 1973).

Finally, there are countless Americans who could legitimately claim Indian ancestry but choose not to do so; their motives and reasons are as varied as droplets of snow on a mountain lake. Many choose to pass as Euro-American or Anglo because of the perceived opportunities available to them. Others prefer to identify with some other salient aspect of their ethnic heritage. Because they do not identify themselves as Indian, we may never be able to identify them to explore their rationales.

Some Conventional Explanations

Now more than ever, Americans are keenly interested in their genealogy, ancestral heritage, and the meaning attributed to locating a long-forgotten ancestor. In addition, interest in promoting multicultural awareness is finding its way into the classroom through specialized curricula and by the designation of certain weeks to celebrate diversity and ethnic differences. With this attention to ethnicity, a revival in celebrating and pronouncing traditions has occurred such that many Americans somehow or other believe they must declare an ethnic background or identity so that they may join in the celebration. Self-pride and a sense of belonging may be among the motives for declaring Indian roots.

Another side to the movement is represented by individuals who believe they can receive awards and attention for their ethnic declaration. Clifton (1989) calls it the *Indian windfall syndrome*, in which individuals and "reconstituted Indian communities" stand to gain substantial economic benefits as witnessed by the alleged growing profits of reservation-based Indian casinos. It is likely that many Americans declare their Indian identity in hopes of receiving economic dividends generated by the gaming profits. To lend credence to their declaration, some appeal to the *Cherokee grandmother effect* (Thornton, 1990) and identify as descendants of the widely distributed Cherokee Nation. The 1990 U.S. Census data show that Cherokee is the most frequently mentioned tribe.

Rewards and incentives have driven many Americans to self-identify as Indian to enhance their likelihood for securing jobs, receiving preference for admission to academic institutions and corresponding grants and scholarships, and placing them in a unique position to receive entitlements that otherwise would not be available. Out of this momentum has emerged the "academic Indian" (Clifton, 1989, p. 20), who claims his or her Indian ancestry to gain a foothold in entering and climbing up the rigorous steps of the academy's promotion and tenure ladder. The phenomenon has become so widespread that the Association of American Indian and Alaska Native Professors has undertaken an intensive study of abuses of the declaration process.

Apart from the economic and avaricious motives, many Americans of Indian ancestry choose to identify because it creates a new identity for them. This identity brings with it pride and the desire to learn about tribal customs, traditions, and language. In addition, there are many who, regardless of the degree of their blood quantum, are obligated by family tradition to continue their identities as Indian. Invariably they are descended through matrilineal or patrilineal lines that are part of a highly complex clan or moiety system in which identity and participation serve to preserve and sustain a deeply shared belief system. To sever the tie often brings about banishment from the clan and, hence, the tribe, often casting a shadow of foreboding on the entire extended family.

Relying on extensive interviews with people of mixed ethnic background, Root (1994) identified four basic reasons that multiethnic individuals would choose to identify with particular groups regardless of how others may view the individuals. Specifically, Root maintained that (a) it enhances their sense of security in understanding a distinct part of their ethnic heritage; (b) parental influences stimulated by the encouragement of grandparents promote identity, thereby granting permission to the offspring to make a choice; (c) racism and prejudice associated with certain groups lead to sharing experiences with family, thereby assisting one to develop psychological skills and defenses to protect oneself (the shared experiences help to build self-confidence and create the sense that one can cope with the negative elements often associated with the group); and (d) "gender alignment between parents and children may exert influence on ethnic and racial socialization particularly when they have good relationships and are mutually held in esteem" (p. 15).

There are other provincial explanations that are invidious, inflammatory, insulting, and degrading to the individual. These descriptions are often spawned by envy, insecurity, and fear. To explore the nefarious explanations would only lend credence that is not deserved.

Ego and Ethnic Development

Ethnicity, perceived membership in a cultural group, and ethnic identification, the strength of one's affiliation with a group, develop primarily through interactions with primary socialization sources, the family, the school, and peer clusters (Oetting, Donnermeyer, Trimble, & Beauvais, 1998). The primary socialization process is embedded in the culture or ethnic group, hence culture influences primary socialization even as the primary socialization process transmits that culture. Culture determines who transmits the culture and determines the norms that are transmitted by the socialization process. Ethnicity is an intimate and integral part of primary socialization and influences to varying degrees the extent to which one feels involved in a culture. Ethnic self-identity therefore can be viewed as developmental process and even orthogonal as one can choose the degree to which they want to invest themselves in one or more ethnic groups (Oetting & Beauvais, 1991).

Several theorists have linked ethnic identity to a developmental progression, ego identity, and self-esteem. Writing about 20 years ago, Cross (1971) developed the first of his series of iterations of Nigrescence Theory (literally the process of becoming Black or dark), presenting a developmental sequence of five stages. Phinney (1989) developed an Ethnic Identity Development Measure that assessed four stages in development, and Helms (1990) proposed a five-stage model based on avoidance of prejudicial feelings. In general, these models assume that ethnic identification is a developmental process moving from lack of awareness to acceptance and internalization of the ethnic identity. Figure 9.2 provides a listing of the stages in each of these models, although the alignment across stages is not meant to be precise. Because the models make different assumptions and development follows somewhat different paths, it is not possible to match stages one for one.

The social status of the group influences the process of identification. If an ethnic group has experienced a long, oppressive history of prejudice and discrimination, group members could experience a devalued sense of self (Tajfel, 1981). However, if the self-evaluation of the group is positive, commitment is strong, and contentment is high, there is involvement in ethnic behaviors and activities and one can achieve a strong secure identity with the group (Phinney, 1991). Another model is presented by Rowe, Bennett, and Atkinson (1994), who felt that the key element in the process of identification is the role of dissonance; "dissonance between previously held attitudes and new attitudes and feelings resulting from recent, intense and/or significant life event" (p. 142) can change ethnic identification.

All of the models assume that the process of identification is related to development of the ego and self-esteem, although research relating group identity to self-esteem has produced mixed results (Cross, 1991). Because of these problems, Cross revised his levels to increase complexity, indicating that identification is not salient for everyone, that identification with a group can have varying effects on ego functioning depending on the social situation, and that self-esteem is therefore not necessarily correlated with identity. His revised model shows that ethnic identification can be unimportant for some individuals and highly salient for others. This model may be particularly appropriate for American Indian identity development. For instance, the lack of awareness of Indian identity among younger children can be directly observed. One young girl, for example, when asked what she was afraid of, said "Indians." She had watched old westerns, identified with the heroes, and had no idea that she was Indian. Many young adult American Indians, particularly those who live off reservations, have little concern with Indian identification. However, the stage of immersion–emersion, in which old and new identities create a struggle for the individual, are apparent among many American Indian college students. They are often trying to deal with the conflicting demands and beliefs of their academic professors, families, and culture. As a vivid example, during a final oral examination, a young Diné woman who was training as a practical nurse provided a fully adequate textbook

Ethnic Identity Development Model
Phinney (1989)

Diffused Identity: person shows little or no evidence of having explored her/his ethnicity; there is no understanding of the issues and little interest in the topic.

Foreclosed Identity: person explores ethnicity at a minimal level; her/his ideas are quite clear; parental ideas have been internalized without much question; ethnic ideas may have been a positive or negative valence.

Moratorium Identity: person shows ongoing interest in ethnicity and may be in the middle of an ethnic identity crisis.

Achieved Identity: person's interest in ethnicity is in the past and the identity has been achieved. The habituated identity is effectively integrated into a person's overall self-concept.

Psychological Nigrescence Model
Cross (1991)

Pre-Encounter Stage: person places low salience on ethnicity but has achieved identity in something other than race; person shows signs of having internalized racist notions about own ethnicity, thus has low self-concept and weak ego-development (self-hatred).

Encounter Stage: person concludes that she/he needs to change in direction of greater cultural self-awareness and ethnic self-acceptance.

Immersion-Emersion Stage: marks the transition stage during which the old and emergent identities struggle for dominance.

Internalization Stage: high salience for ethnicity but cluster into divergent camps; some embrace nationalism, others are bicultural or multicultural; positive self-concept and healthy ego-development.

Racial Identity Model
Helms (1989)

Contact Stage: person is not aware of her/his ethnic origins.

Disintegration Stage: person experiences conflict about her/his identity.

Reintegration Stage: anti-ethnic and racial attitudes emerge.

Pseudo-Independence Stage: person accepts, at least intellectually, other ethnic groups.

Autonomy Stage: person achieves full acceptance of her/his identity.

FIG. 9.2. Developmental models of ethnic identity, psychological nigrescence, and racial identity. Data are from Cross (1991), Helms (1990), and Phinney (1989).

description of the causes of cancer. After the exam, she was asked, "What *really* causes cancer?" She immediately answered, "Eating sheep hit by lightning." She was struggling to find a way to function in both cultures, essential to meeting the educational requirements for her certificate and to her functioning as a practical nurse on the reservation. The final stage of internalization commitment can be directly observed in the stability and comfort with their own identity or identities, which is seen in many of the wise and respected tribal elders.

MEASURING ETHNIC IDENTITY AND ETHNIC IDENTIFICATION

The preponderance of theoretical orientations concerning ethnicity, ethnic groups, ethnic identity, and ethnic self-identification mirror the variety of strategies and techniques used to measure the constructs. On this point Phinney (1990) noted that there are "widely discrepant definitions and measures of ethnic identity, which makes generalizations and comparisons across studies difficult and ambiguous" (p. 500). Measurement approaches range from use of a single item (Richman, Gaveria, Flaherty, Birz, & Wintrob, 1987) to scales containing several dimensions (Phinney, 1992; Weinreich, 1986).

Perhaps the most widely used procedure involves the use of a list of ethnic groups. Respondents are merely asked to place a check mark next to the group with whom they most identify, forcing a person with a multiethnic background to choose one group; the list provides no information about intensity of identification. Allowing multiple responses can generate numerous ethnic categories to the point where stratified and subgroup analyses may not be possible. However, use of an item that asks individuals to check or list the group with which they identify can be a starting point; most multi-item identity scales start off with this question. Phinney's (1992) Multigroup Ethnic Identity Measure (MEIM) actually asks respondents to indicate their ethnic affiliation twice in the 23-item scale, assessing self-identification through two dimensions—ethnic identity and other-group orientation. The ethnic identity dimension also taps affirmation, belonging, ethnic identity achievement, ethnic behaviors, and natural parents' ethnicity. The last two items are used only as background information.

Weinreich's (1986) Identity Structure Analysis (ISA) is a complex, highly sophisticated approach to assessing ethnic identity. ISA can be custom designed to measure identity in an idiographic or nomothetic framework through use of bipolar constructs. Indexes can be created to measure such constructs as self-image (past, current, and ideal), values, role models, reference groups, empathetic identification, identification conflicts, evaluation of others, and a few other related identity domains. Weinreich's ISA sets a standard for comprehensiveness and inclusiveness. However, if one is interested in assessing identity within a survey questionnaire format, use of ISA cannot be recommended.

Waters (1990) developed an interview schedule containing over 100 questions designed to explore the nature and meaning of ethnicity. Waters maintained that "one constructs an ethnic identification using knowledge about ancestries in one's background" and that "this information is selectively used in the social construction of ethnic identification within the prevailing historical, structural, and personal constraints" (p. 19). Waters' interview schedule moves through a carefully developed set of domains that assists the respondent in constructing an identity.

Caetano (1986) developed a fourfold measure of ethnic identification to assess drinking problems and patterns among a sample of Hispanic households. The scale contains items that assess: (a) ethnicity of family of origin, (b) own or subjective ethnic identity, (c) country of ancestors, and (d) respondent's country of birth. Caetano concluded that "ethnicity of family of origin seems to be the encompassing definition, followed by national group, and there is a good level of agreement between these rubrics" (p. 341).

Oetting and Beauvais (1991) maintained that ethnic identity is not a binary, either/or choice for people with mixed ethnic backgrounds. They maintain that cultural dimensions are independent of each other and that identification with one ethnic group does require decreasing identification with another. In essence, people may identify with more than one ethnic group at various levels of intensity. Oetting and Beauvais relied on their orthogonal identification theory to account for and predict the phenomenon where individuals are provided the opportunity to independently express identification or lack of it with a list of different ethnic groups. In the expectation that American Indian youth often choose to identify to some degree with other groups, the tenets of orthogonal identification theory were put to a test.

Figure 9.3, a measurement model of the American Indian self-identification scale, shows the seven factor dimensions derived from 14 Likert-type scale items used to measure orthogonality. The confirmatory factor model was constructed from items to conform to the four-part ethnic measurement model, specifically natality, behavioral orientations, and subjective perceptions advocated by Trimble (1991, 1995). The item reliability or alpha for the items was 0.84; initially, the items formed three exploratory factor dimensions through use of a principal components analysis. The scale was administered to 846 self-identified American Indian youth in eight communities located in both reservation and nonreservation settings in the central southwestern region of the United States.

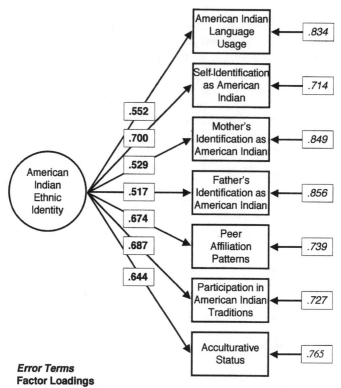

FIG. 9.3. Measurement model of American Indian self-identification scale.
Data are from Bates, Beauvais, and Trimble (1997).

Figure 9.4 shows the percentage of respondents' degree of identification
with American Indian and other ethnic groups. About 71% *all* or *nearly
all* identified with the American Indian group. The results also indicate
that some of the Indian self-identified youth identified to some degree
with other groups (e.g., about 9% indicated that they *mostly* or *nearly all*
identified as Anglo-White and that 7% did so for the Spanish-Mexican
American group). Moreover, 11% indicated that they identified *little* or
not at all as American Indian, yet these respondents self-identified nominally as American Indian.

Perceived ethnic identification of one's parents strongly influences
levels and degrees of identification among offspring. Figures 9.5 and 9.6
show the percentage responses of the youths' perception of their parents'
ethnic identity. The results are not as distinct as those in Fig. 9.4, in part
because the ethnic background of one or both parents varied. Sixty-nine
percent of the youths' mothers were seen as *all or nearly all* Indian as were
58% for their fathers. At the other extreme, some 9% of the mothers' and
13% of the fathers' identity was perceived as *not at all* Indian. An inspec-

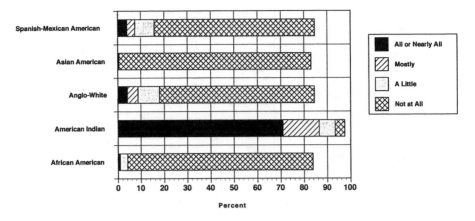

FIG. 9.4. Self-identified American Indian adolescents' degree of identification with own and other ethnic groups ($n = 846$).

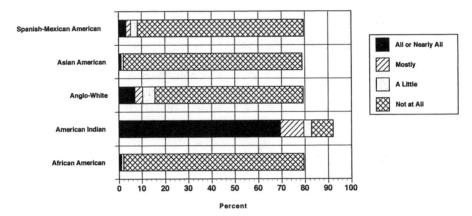

FIG. 9.5. Self-identified American Indian adolescents' perception of mother's degree of ethnic self-identification ($n = 846$).

tion of the middle choice alternatives *most* and *little* show varying degrees of the youths' parents' degree of identity with American Indian and other groups; similar patterns are revealed in Fig. 9.4. Finally, the results reveal that 360 (43%) of the youth who *all or nearly all* identified as Indian indicated that their parents were also seen as identifying at the same level of intensity. Although the results are not presented here, an analysis of responses to the self-identification scale reveal that the youths' degree of identity varied considerably for close to 80% of the respondents.

The measurement of ethnicity and ethnic identification is no small task, especially given the debate surrounding its theoretical foundations. Researchers must consider the "various cultural and structural dimensions

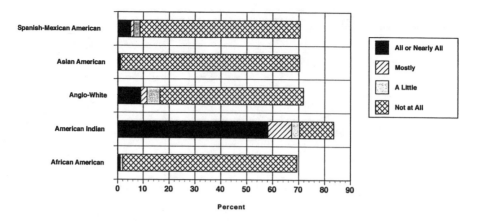

FIG. 9.6. Self-identified American Indian adolescents' perception of father's degree of ethnic self-identification ($n = 846$).

of ethnicity" (Cheung, 1989, p. 72) and "distinguish between general aspects of ethnic identity that apply across groups and specific aspects that distinguish groups" (Phinney, 1990, p. 508). Thus, researchers must move away from viewing ethnic groups as homogeneous entities. In fact, there may be more heterogeneity within certain ethnic minority groups than within the dominant groups in American society (Cheung, 1993; Trimble, 1991, 1995).

SOME CONCLUDING THOUGHTS

The study of ethnicity, ethnic consciousness, ethnic self-identification, and the measurement of the constructs is a complex, intertwined, multidisciplinary process. The complexity is confounded by the increased interest in the constructs across many academic disciplines; the levels of analysis particular to each discipline further complicates matters because the units and methods of inquiry often conflict. In addition, although the definitions of the constructs may resemble one another, the extant theories are at loggerheads with one another both within and between disciplines. Indeed, "the study of 'the invention of ethnicity' is an interdisciplinary field . . . [that gives] ethnic debates such a virulent centrality in the modern world" (Sollors, 1989, p. xx).

Ethnic identity and ethnic self-development theories tend to follow the tenets of Erik Erikson (1990), who maintained that identity is located in the self or core of the individual and that one's communal culture, self-esteem, and sense of affiliation and belongingness are deeply affected by the identity process. Yet there is some evidence to suggest that the relationship between self-esteem and identity is unstable. Research concerning the relationship among American Indians suggests that the degree to which one identifies with being Indian influences responses to items in self-esteem to the extent that the respondents actually are interpreting the self scale items very differently (Trimble & Mahoney, in press). Moreover, we are not certain if ethnic identity follows the developmental progression advocated by Cross (1991), Helms (1990), or Phinney (1989). Further research is recommended on the topic to shed further insight on why and how American Indians and Alaska Natives form identities.

Moynihan (1993), like Erikson, also argued that identity is "a process located in the core of the individual and yet, also, in the case of his communal culture" (p. 64). It is a powerful phenomenon that strongly influences personality, one's sense of belonging, and one's quality of life. The powerful nature of identity can readily be seen in the civil strife and struggles of nations and ethnic groups in Africa and eastern Europe and in the growing preoccupation with ethnic differences in North America, especially in Quebec. At the core of these struggles is the assertion that individuals have an inalienable right to ascribe their identity to a common cultural orientation. On this point Forbes (1990) argues that people have a right to state who and what they are, and hence, we must recognize that there are multiple approaches to achieving and asserting identity. And with this in mind we "must recognize that all ethnic groups and units can change genes, while yet remaining whole and retaining their identity" (p. 48). Adding to this contention, Roosens (1989) argued that one should have a right to his or her own culture without being certain what that is. Do the academy, states, provinces, commonwealths, and governments own the full right to define who one is or is not? There are more intellectual and academic points for conjecture. At a constitutional level, Forbes (1990) correctly maintained that "we must come to recognize that one of the fundamental human rights of individuals and of groups includes the right to self-identification and self-definition, so long as one does not adopt an identity which has the effect of denying the same rights to others" (pp. 48–49).

ACKNOWLEDGMENTS

I want to extend my gratitude to the staff at the Tri-Ethnic Center for Prevention Research at Colorado State University for their assistance and support in writing this chapter. Support was also provided through grants from the National Institute on Drug Abuse (P50 DA07074) and the National Institute on Alcohol Abuse and Alcoholism (AA 08302). I also want to express my sincere gratitude to the following friends and colleagues for their generous and thoughtful assistance in helping me wade through various aspects of the topic: Barbara Means Adams, Alberto Arviso, Scott Bates, Fred Beauvais, Rosemary Christensen, Johanna Clevenger, Bill Demmert, Candace Fleming, Joan LaFrance, Bea Medicine, Bradford Wong Plemons, and Pamela Jumper Thurman. Indeed I want to acknowledge my deep indebtedness to Professor Eugene R. Oetting at Colorado State University, who very thoughtfully and painstakingly pored over each sentence and paragraph of the original manuscript. His careful editing helped shape the final draft. He is a true scholar, superb mentor, and a dear colleague and friend.

REFERENCES

Aboud, F. E. (1987). The development of ethnic self-identification and attitudes. In J. S. Phinney & M. J. Rotheram (Eds.), *Children's ethnic socialization: Pluralism and development* (pp. 32–55). Newbury Park, CA: Sage.

Barth, F. (Ed.). (1969). *Ethnic groups and boundaries*. Boston: Little Brown.

Bates, S. C., Beauvais, F., & Trimble, J. E. (1997). American Indian adolescent alcohol involvement and ethnic identification. *Substance Use & Misuse, 32*(14), 2013–2031.

Bell, D. (1975). Ethnicity and social change. In N. Glazer & D. P. Moynihan (Eds.), *Ethnicity: Theory and practice* (pp. 174n). Cambridge, MA: Harvard University Press.

Berkhofer, R. (1978). *The White Man's Indian: Images of the American Indian from Columbus to present*. New York: Random House.

Bernstein, N. (1995). Teens today "claim" a racial identity. *UTNE Reader, March–April*, 87–99.

Buriel, R. (1987). Ethnic labeling and identity among Mexican Americans. In J. S. Phinney & M. J. Rotheram (Eds.), *Children's ethnic socialization: Pluralism and development* (pp. 134–152). Newbury Park, CA: Sage.

Caetano, R. (1986). Alternative definitions of Hispanics: Consequences in an alcohol survey. *Hispanic Journal of Behavioral Sciences, 12*, 331–334.

Carroll, L. (1865). *Alice's adventures in Wonderland*. London: Macmillan.

Casino, E. (n.d.). *Introduction to ethnicology: Ways of talking about ethnicity*. Unpublished manuscript.

Cheung, Y. W. (1989). Making sense of ethnicity and drug use: A review and suggestions for future research. *Social Pharmacology, 3*(1–2), 55–82.

Cheung, Y. W. (1993). Approaches to ethnicity: Clearing roadblocks in the study of ethnicity and substance abuse. *International Journal of Addictions, 28*(12), 1209–1226.

Clifton, J. (Ed.). (1989). *Being and becoming Indian: Biographical studies of North American frontiers*. Chicago: Dorsey.

Cross, W. (1971). The Negro-to-Black conversion experience. *Black World, 20*, 13–26.

Cross, W. (1991). *Shades of Black: Diversity in African American identify*. Philadelphia: Temple University Press.

Dickson, L. (1973). *Wilderness Man: The strange story of Grey Owl*. New York: Atheneum.

Erikson, E. (1980). *Identity and the life cycle*. New York: Norton.

Fitzgerald, T. K. (1993). *Metaphors of identity: A culture-communication dialogue*. Albany: State University of New York Press.

Forbes, J. D. (1990). The manipulation of race, caste, and identity: Classifying Afroamericans, Native Americans and red-black people. *Journal of Ethnic Studies, 17*(4), 1–51.

Greeley, A. M. (1974). *Ethnicity in the United States*. New York: Wiley.

Harré, R. (1989). Language games and the texts of identity. In J. Shotter & J. J. Gergen (Eds.), *Texts of identity* (pp. 20–35). Newbury Park, CA: Sage.

Hartzberg, H. (1971). *The search for an American Indian identity: Modern Pan-Indian movements.* Syracuse, NY: Syracuse University Press.

Heath, D. B. (1978). Foreword. *Medical Anthropology, 2*(4), 3–8.

Helms, J. (1990). *Black and White racial identity: Theory, research, and practice.* New York: Greenwood Press.

Meyrowitz, J. (1986). *No sense of place: Impact of electronic media on social behavior.* New York: Oxford University Press.

Moynihan, D. P. (1993). *Pandaemonium: Ethnicity in international politics.* New York: Oxford University Press.

Oetting, E. R., & Beauvais, F. (1991). Orthogonal cultural identification theory: The cultural identification of minority adolescents. *International Journal of Addictions, 25*(5A & 6A), 55–685.

Oetting, E. R., Donnermeyer, J. F., Trimble, J. E., & Beauvais, F. (1998). Primary socialization theory: Culture, ethnicity, and cultural identification. The links between culture and substance use: IV. *Substance Use & Misuse, 33*(10), 2075–2107.

Phinney, J. S. (1989). Stages of ethnic identity development in minority group adolescents. *Journal of Early Adolescence, 9*, 34–49.

Phinney, J. S. (1990). Ethnic identity in adolescents and adults: Review of research. *Psychological Bulletin, 108*(3), 499–514.

Phinney, J. S. (1991). Ethnic identity and self-esteem: A review and integration. *Hispanic Journal of Behavioral Sciences, 13*(2), 193–208.

Phinney, J. S. (1992). The multigroup ethnic identity measure: A new scale for use with diverse groups. *Journal of Adolescent Research, 7*(2), 156–176.

Richman, J., Gaveria, M., Flaherty, J., Birz, S., & Wintrob, R. (1987). The process of acculturation: Theoretical perspectives and an empirical investigation in Peru. *Social Science Medicine. 25*(7), 839–847.

Roosens, E. E. (1989). *Creating ethnicity: The process of ethnogenesis.* Newbury Park, CA: Sage.

Root, M. (1994). Reasons racially mixed persons identify as people of color. *Focus: Notes from the Psychological Study of Ethnic Minority Issues, 8*(1), 14–16.

Rosenthal, D. A. (1987). Ethnic identity development in adolescents. In J. S. Phinney & M. J. Rotheram (Eds.), *Children's ethnic socialization: Pluralism and development* (pp. 73–91). Newbury Park, CA: Sage.

Rowe, W., Bennett, S., & Atkinson, D. (1994). White racial identity models: A critique and alternative proposal. *Counseling Psychologist, 22*(1), 129–146.

Saharso, S. (1989). Ethnic identity and the paradox of equality. In J. P. Van Oudenhoven & T. M. Willemsen (Eds.), *Ethnic minorities: Social psychological perspectives* (pp. 97–114). Berwyn, PA: Swets North America.

Sherif, M., & Sherif, C. W. (1964). *Reference groups: Exploration into conformity and deviation of adolescents.* New York: Harper and Row.

Smith, E. J. (1991). Ethnicity identity development: Toward the development of a theory within the context of majority/minority status. *Journal of Counseling and Development, 70*(1), 181–188.

Snipp, C. M. (1989). *American Indians: The first of this land.* New York: Russell Sage Foundation.

Snipp, C. M. (1996). The size and distribution of the American Indian population: Fertility, mortality, residence, and migration. In G. Sandefur, R. Rindfuss, & B. Cohen (Eds.), *Changing numbers, changing needs: American Indian demography and public health* (pp. 17–52). Washington, DC: National Academy Press.

Sollors, W. (Ed.). (1989). *The invention of ethnicity.* New York: Oxford University Press.

Steinberg, S. (1981). *The ethnic myth: Race, ethnicity, and class in America.* New York: Atheneum.

Stevens, R. (1983). *Erik Eriksen: An introduction.* New York: St. Martin's Press.

Strauss, A. L. (1959). *Mirrors and masks: The search for identity.* Glencoe, IL: Free Press.

Tajfel, H. (1981). *Human groups and social categories.* Cambridge: Cambridge University Press.

Thompson, R. H. (1989). *Theories of ethnicity: A critical appraisal.* New York: Greenwood.

Thornton, R. (1990). *The Cherokees: A population history.* Lincoln: University of Nebraska Press.

Thornton, R. (1996). Tribal membership requirements and the demography of "old" and "new" Native Americans. In G. Sandefur, R. Rindfuss, & B. Cohen (Eds.), *Changing numbers, changing needs: American Indian demography and pubic health* (pp. 103–112). Washington, DC: National Academy Press.

Trimble, J. E. (1991). Ethnic specification, validation prospects, and the future of drug use research. *International Journal of the Addictions, 25*(2A), 149–170.

Trimble, J. E. (1992). A cognitive-behavioral approach to drug abuse prevention and intervention with American Indian youth. In L. A. Vargas & J. D. Koss-Chioino (Eds.), *Working with culture: Psychotherapeutic intervention with ethnic minority children and adolescents* (pp. 246–275). San Francisco, CA: Jossey-Bass.

Trimble, J. E. (1995). Toward an understanding of ethnicity and ethnic identity, and their relationship with drug use research. In G. J. Botvin, S. Schinke, & M. A. Orlandi (Eds.), *Drug abuse prevention with multiethnic youth* (pp. 3–27). Thousand Oaks, CA: Sage.

Trimble, J. E., & Mahoney, E. R. (in press). Gender and ethnic differences in adolescent self-esteem in substance use research: A Rasch measurement model analysis. In P. D. Mail & J. Howard (Eds.), *Alcohol and Native North Americans: Multiple perspectives on Native American and Alaska Native alcohol use.* Rockville, MD: National Institute on Alcohol Abuse and Alcoholism Research Monograph Series.

Trosper, R. (1981). American Indian nationalism and frontier expansion. In C. Keyes (Ed.), *Ethnic change* (pp. 247–270). Seattle: University of Washington Press.

United States Department of Education. (1982). *A study of alternative definitions and measures relating to eligibility and service under Part A of the Indian Education Act.* Unpublished report, United States Department of Education, Washington, DC.

van den Berghe, P. L. (1981). *The ethnic phenomenon.* New York: Elsevier North Holland.

Vaughn, G. M. (1987). A social psychological model of ethnic identity development. In J. S. Phinney & M. J. Rotheram (Eds.), *Children's ethnic socialization: Pluralism and development* (pp. 73–91). Newbury Park, CA: Sage.

Waters, M. C. (1990). *Ethnic options: Choosing identities in America.* Los Angeles: University of California Press.

Weinreich, P. (1986). The operationalization of identity theory in racial and ethnic relations. In J. Rex & D. Mason (Eds.), *Theories of race and ethnic relations* (pp. 299–320). Cambridge: Cambridge University Press.

Weinreich, P. (1988). The operationalization of ethnic identity. In J. Berry & R. Annis (Eds.), *Ethnic psychology: Research and practice with immigrants, refugees, Native peoples, ethnic groups and sojourners* (pp. 149–168). Amsterdam: Swets & Zeitlinger.

Willemsen, T. M., & van Oudenhoven, J. P. (1989). Social psychological perspectives on ethnic minorities: An introduction. In J. P. Van Oudenhoven & T. M. Willemsen (Eds.), *Ethnic minorities: Social psychological perspectives* (pp. 11–24). Berwyn, PA: Swets North America.

Yee, A., Fairchild, H., Weizmann, F., & Wyatt, G. (1993). Addressing psychology's problems with race. *American Psychologist, 48*(11), 1132–1140.

Yinger, J. M. (1986). Intersecting strands in the theorization of race and ethnic relations. In J. Rex & D. Mason (Eds.), *Theories of race and ethnicity* (pp. 20–41). Cambridge: Cambridge University Press.

IV

THE MINNESOTA MULTIPHASIC PERSONALITY INVENTORY AND OTHER OBJECTIVE TESTS

The Minnesota Multiphasic Personality Inventory (MMPI) and its derivatives are the most widely used psychopathology personality measures worldwide. Nonetheless, the original MMPI is considered by some psychologists to measure an outdated understanding of psychopathology using relatively unsophisticated psychometrics. These instruments have been particularly vulnerable to criticism for their shortcomings with multicultural populations. Part IV presents cross-cultural and multicultural MMPI issues in chapters 10 and 11. Not only has there been controversy regarding the cross-cultural use of the MMPI external to the MMPI establishment, but there are also degrees of loyalty to the instrument within this establishment. Chapters 10 and 11 clearly portray differences in perceived ease of applications for multicultural applications. The MMPI/MMPI–2 level of cross-cultural/multicultural adequacy may be construed as either half full or half empty depending on the perspective of the psychometrician. Chapter 12 honors the MMPI for past accomplishments as the historic measure of psychopathology and personality as well as a comparative standard for all newer measures in both areas. Nonetheless, readers are encouraged to examine alternative instruments now available for assessment of personality or psychopathology constructed to be more amenable to cross-cultural construct validation.

Chapter 10 begins with detailed background arguments for using the MMPI/MMPI–2. Prediction of specific psychiatric diagnoses in the 1930s was not feasible using an instrument developed to predict eight Kraepelian clinical diagnostic classes, particularly with nonrepresentative norms. Subsequent research was directed instead toward relationships between the scales and clinically relevant behaviors, symptoms, and traits. Empirical correlates and high-frequency combinations of scores or code types soon became the focus for low-inference interpretation. As a consequence, attention was directed away from an obsolete diagnostic system and deficient normative data described as *irrelevant*.

Multicultural applications rested on the premise that this same methodology could be applied in other countries and to ethnic/racial groups in the United States. Chapter 10 examines MMPI and MMPI-2 research with the four major culturally different groups in the United States using mean scale comparisons between matched groups of White and non-White samples. This chapter acknowledges English language proficiency, inept translations, and acculturation status as potential confounds with MMPI psychopathology, also highlighted by Israel Cuéllar's frequently replicated ARSMA research in 1980. Research on empirical correlates could not be addressed in this chapter because no studies have been done. Moreover, the matching of White and non-White samples was always incomplete, and critical moderators as well as moderators of undermined importance were omitted. As a consequence, a residual number of items always remained to compose a non-White scale (e.g., the MEX scale in chap. 11).

The MMPI-2 standardization provided norms that were indeed more representative, characterized in chapter 10 as fulfilling the goal of proportionate representation in 1980 while suggesting that because minorities were included that group comparison differences would now be minimized. Nevertheless, critics have decried an underrepresentation of Hispanics, a social class education skew, and limited numbers of non-White subjects in this standardization. Chapter 10 contends that even a more diverse normative sample could not entirely eliminate group differences. Empirical correlates of scales and code types are argued to be consistent between the MMPI and MMPI-2 because the clinical scales were unchanged notwithstanding significant item changes. MMPI-2 studies from several areas were cited to document profile similarity or mean score differences of less than the five T-score points ostensibly required for clinical significance. In addition, for African Americans, variance was predicted by relevant extratest criteria. Cross-national MMPI-2 applications have not included empirical correlates for the adapted instrument, although cross-national comparisons of factor structures have provided information on problems encountered in adaptation of the instrument. Congruent factor structures suggest that replication of external correlates is feasible. This chapter concludes with recommendations for research and practice.

By contrast, chapter 11 finds potential in the MMPI for "marginalization of other cultures." It clearly documents what this means for practice with non-Euro-American populations by examining existing research studies of linguistic, conceptual, functional, and metric equivalence. Linguistic equivalence has been approached historically by inadequate MMPI translations that were replaced by much better MMPI–2 translations to minimize bias and increase item meaningfulness as a result of using a seven-step strategy. One of these steps—field testing to examine acceptability in the target language—is of critical importance because it is not possible to assume shared semantic and linguistic habits and understandings between bilingual translators and monolingual subjects. Bilingual investigators must interview monolingual informants in field tests to establish the stimulus equivalence of items in original and target languages.

Establishing equivalence of meanings or conceptual equivalence using a multimethod, multitrait approach for construct validity has proved difficult due to the lack of cross-cultural validity for the *Diagnostic and Statistical Manual* (*DSM*) as well as the instruments used as criteria. Although the *DSM* does contain some reliable core symptom patterns (e.g., schizophrenia) in different cultural settings, the narrow inclusion and exclusion criteria homogenize these samples and mask cultural variability. This chapter includes a construct validation example comparing the Diagnostic Interview Schedule (DIS) and a Spanish MMPI–2 version for four diagnostic categories that found only moderate MMPI–2 hit rates. Although there was high sensitivity for schizophrenia and depression, specificity was poor because many persons without these disorders were also included in these diagnostic categories. Proper translation procedures cannot always ensure linguistic equivalence because some items are not translatable from English into other languages. Nor can statistical equivalence guarantee that items generated in the United States will represent the same trait in another country because different symptoms are used to express the same disorder. By use of an etic–emic theoretical model, item equivalence across national/cultural settings can be introduced and evaluated.

Metric equivalence, or similar psychometric properties, was illustrated by item rates of over 25% endorsement in culturally different populations. The MEX MMPI–2 scale provides a powerful example of the possible interpretive consequences by using this methodology for comparison with other MMPI scales. MEX is only one of a long list of moderator variables that affect interpretation of MMPI–2 scale elevations across cultural or national boundaries. The variance accounted for by these moderators and other test-taking attitudes, including individualism collectivism, acculturation status, social class, internal–external control, and threshold for reporting symptoms, needs to be documented. This potential source of uncontrolled variance provides reasonable doubt that the MMPI–2 can provide valid profiles from multicultural clients.

Functional equivalence or "cross-cultural similarity in the function of specific behaviors" can be examined in the translation and data analysis phases. However, functional equivalence has not been forthcoming on the basis of evaluating the translators' knowledge of the linguistic habits of their monolingual populations. This omission calls into question the adequacy of the translation phase. Factor analysis or principal components analysis can suggest the similarity of qualitative relationships, but the same cavils apply as in the assessment of conceptual equivalence. Translation adequacy cannot ensure that tests will occupy comparable positions within the semantic space of original and target languages.

The issues raised by deficiencies in conceptual and functional equivalence have not been resolved, although a recent unpublished meta-analysis reported in chapter 11 suggests that the standard validity and clinical scales do not disadvantage populations of African and Latino Americans. Nonetheless, an artifactual similarity resulting from measurement of overlapping symptoms among cultures, or a lack of representativeness, could account for these meta-analysis findings. The extent to which the code-type approach developed for the MMPI can be applied to MMPI–2 code patterns remains unknown, and these authors suggest some anticipated outcomes for particular diagnostic categories. The modest representation of non-Euro-Americans in the MMPI–2 standardization sample and the skew toward higher educational levels and social class status remain a source of bias. Recommended research includes (a) relationships among item responses, scale scores, and profile patterns with external criteria; (b) examination of group differences on these external criteria; (c) vulnerability of supplemental, content, and subscales with these populations; and (d) the controversial nature of routinely applying the K-correction.

Chapter 12 opens with a balanced discussion of assets and liabilities in the MMPI and MMPI–2. Deficiencies are noted in the absence of empirical derivation from theory, in the standardization sampling, as well as by failure to acknowledge the evolution and fluctuation of the *DSM* criteria for psychopathology across editions. More recent advances in psychometrics include scale construction, empirically based keying methodology, multivariate statistics and computing capabilities, cross-validation, suppression of response styles, and construct validation. These concerns focus on limitations of an empirical strategy in which construct definition is precluded and item-construct linkages to validity cannot be established.

Chapter 12 separates assessment of psychopathology and personality with a detailed description of a sampling of major instruments and mention of others. Used as a criterion measure, the MMPI–2 is contrasted on five salient features with five multiscale psychopathology inventories: the

Personality Assessment Inventory, the Millon Clinical Multiaxial Inventory–III, the Basic Personality Inventory, the Brief Symptom Inventory, and the Holden Psychological Screening Inventory. These features include the number of items, completion time, specific appropriate group, minimum age of respondents, minimum reading level, scale to detect invalid responding, scale intercorrelations, and availability of non-English versions. A table is used to facilitate comparisons. A similar strategy, also tabularized and with the same features, is used for comparisons among personality measures including: the Revised NEO Personality Inventory, the California Psychological Inventory, the Sixteen Personality Factor Questionnaire, the Personality Research Form, and the Multidimensional Personality Questionnaire.

Selecting an instrument requires consideration of the purpose of assessment (or the questions that the data are expected to address), the target group for results, and the consequences of assessment. Choice is further directed and narrowed by overlapping theoretical, psychometric, cultural, practical, and clinical questions. Limitations of the tabularized information and these procedures for selection of a particular measure are emphasized. Similarly, an appropriate and acceptable measure may not be available. Ethical concerns and suggested solutions including the development of new scale(s) are indicated.

Multicultural Assessment With the MMPI-2: Issues for Research and Practice

Richard W. Handel
Yossef S. Ben-Porath
Kent State University

In this chapter, we identify and discuss research and practice issues pertaining to multicultural assessment with the MMPI-2.[1] To place these matters in perspective, we begin by noting that the test's adequacy for multicultural assessment is but one of a number of significant challenges faced by MMPI users almost since the test's initial publication. We believe that it is important to place the challenge of multicultural assessment with the MMPI-2 within this broad framework because resolution of these challenges is based on similar principles. We then review the empirical literature on multicultural assessment with the MMPI/MMPI-2 and conclude with a discussion of future directions for research and practice in this area.

BACKGROUND

The Minnesota Multiphasic Personality Inventory (MMPI; Hathaway & McKinley, 1943) was developed in the 1930s to serve as a tool for differential diagnosis of psychiatric disorders among the medical patient population of the University of Minnesota Hospital. The test's original clinical scales were developed with the aim of predicting membership in one of

---

[1]Throughout this chapter, we refer to the original version of the test as the MMPI and the revised instrument as the MMPI-2.

eight diagnostic classes whose clinical features are no longer viewed from the Kraeplinian perspective, which guided its developers. Norms for the original MMPI were primarily based on a nonrepresentative sampling of visitors to the University of Minnesota Hospital; it consisted of White individuals from a rural background with an average of 8 years of education. Soon after the test was published, its authors discovered that the MMPI did not function effectively as a differential diagnostic instrument. Its ability to predict specific psychiatric diagnoses was limited.

In light of the test developers' dated nosological framework, the exceptionally narrow demographic composition of its original normative sample, and the test's failure to meet its developer's goals, it may seem surprising that the MMPI evolved into the most widely used clinical measure of personality in the United States. It is perhaps even more remarkable that, by way of translation and adaptation, the MMPI came to be used widely in well over 100 other countries varying widely in culture. By examining the test's early history, it is possible to shed light on the MMPI's development into the position of the leading broad-based cross-culturally applied psychometric instrument.

The MMPI was developed at a time and in a place where empiricism was the order of the day. Based initially on their clinical experience, early users of the test observed that, although it was not an effective instrument for differential diagnosis, scores on the MMPI scales were associated with clinically relevant symptoms, traits, and behaviors. This was particularly true of patterns or combinations of scores on the instrument. Guided by the empirical tradition of its developers, subsequent MMPI researchers focused their attention on identifying the empirical correlates of the scales and the more prevalent combinations of scores among them. The latter were labeled *code types*, denoting the practice of referring to MMPI scales by their scale code numbers rather than their defunct diagnostic labels.

Thus, within a decade of the test's original publication, MMPI interpretation was based on the empirically established correlates of the instrument. Once these began to emerge in the research literature, the original diagnostic system and, to a lesser extent, composition of the original normative sample became far less relevant to clinical application of the instrument. The modified empirical foundations of MMPI interpretation were articulated in a series of publications by Meehl (1945, 1954, 1956). Meehl advocated that MMPI interpretation be done in a mechanical manner based on the established empirical correlates of the test that were to be derived through actuarial research. The original diagnostic classes and the original norms of the test were essentially irrelevant to this task.

In response to Meehl's call for empirical research to guide MMPI interpretation, investigators embarked on a series of large-scale studies designed to provide the basis for actuarial application of the test (e.g.,

Gilberstadt & Duker, 1965; Marks & Seeman, 1963). These reference sources provided clinicians with means to follow Meehl's admonition and base their MMPI interpretations on the empirical correlates of the scales and code types identified by their authors. Thus, for example, the validity of Kraeplin's description of *psychasthenia*, Hathaway and McKinley's ability to reliably assign individuals to that particular diagnostic class, and the extent to which the original "Minnesota Normals" had shortcomings as a normative sample were essentially irrelevant to interpreting scores on clinical Scale 7, provided that practitioners based their interpretation of an elevated score on this scale on its empirical correlates rather than on Kraeplin's description of psychasthenics.

Most of the early efforts to identify empirical correlates for MMPI interpretation ignored the issue of multicultural assessment. However, in devising their methodologies, these investigators laid the foundation for subsequent efforts to address matters of multicultural assessment with the MMPI/MMPI-2. As the original diagnostic classes became irrelevant, so too did concerns about the extent to which their underlying nomenclature applied across cultures. As the significance of the original normative sample's narrow population base diminished, so too could worries about the appropriateness of using the test across cultures.

This is not to say that the MMPI's developers and their followers were concerned with multicultural issues or considered these matters in early applications of the test. For several decades after its publication, multicultural issues were largely ignored. Eventually, when MMPI researchers began attending to these issues, they focused initially on normative questions in a manner that was largely inconsistent with the empirical approach to MMPI interpretation. These early writings generated concern about using the test across ethnic groups and cultures. Subsequent research, conducted primarily with the MMPI-2, has begun to address the appropriateness of multicultural assessment with the test from this empirical perspective.

The following sections review the literature on multicultural assessment with the MMPI and MMPI-2. They discuss the implications of this research for current practice with the test and identify research and practice topics for future consideration in multicultural assessment with the MMPI-2.

ORIGINAL MMPI RESEARCH

Use of the MMPI (Hathaway & McKinley, 1943) with various ethnic minority groups has been studied for decades. Because the original MMPI norms were developed based on the responses of White adult "normals" from Minnesota, originally there was some concern about the applicability of the inventory with various ethnic minority groups (Graham, 1993). Comprehensive reviews of this literature have been conducted by a number of authors (e.g., Dahlstrom, Lachar, & Dahlstrom, 1986; Greene, 1987; Pritchard & Rosenblatt, 1980). We review separately the literature on African Americans, Hispanic Americans, Native Americans, and Asian Americans.

African Americans

The most widely studied ethnic minority group has been African Americans (Greene, 1987). Early research (e.g., Ball, 1960; Butcher, Ball, & Ray, 1964; Hokanson & Calden, 1960; McDonald & Gynther, 1962, 1963) focused on normative comparisons and suggested that African Americans typically scored higher than Whites on MMPI Scales L, F, 8, and 9. Gynther (1972) was an early proponent for the construction of new MMPI norms for African Americans based on such research. However, later studies where groups were matched for various demographic characteristics, age, and education suggested that differences between the two groups were small, inconsistent, or not present (Dahlstrom et al., 1986; Penk, Robinowitz, Roberts, Dolan, & Atkins, 1981). In his review of the literature, Greene (1987) concluded that there was no consistent pattern to the differences found between African Americans and Whites on the MMPI. However, other reviewers reported African-American and White mean scale score differences on Scales L, 7 (Pritchard & Rosenblatt, 1980), F, 8, and 9 (Dahlstrom & Gynther, 1986). Greene (1987) suggested that it is important to consider the role of moderator variables in these comparisons and crucial that investigators move beyond group mean comparisons to study whether ethnic groups differ in the validity of their MMPI scores. In other words, rather than examine whether one group scored higher than another on a given scale, the focus should shift to comparing the empirical correlates of MMPI scales across African Americans and Whites.

Pritchard and Rosenblatt (1980) indicated that differences on MMPI scale scores between ethnic minority groups and Whites have questionable relevance to the issue of potential test bias unless subjects are matched for psychopathology and other moderator variables. Pritchard and Rosenblatt suggested that the majority of the research on potential MMPI bias utilized inappropriate strategies for detecting potential bias. They noted that the most commonly used strategy involved testing the significance of mean differences between majority and minority group members on MMPI scales. However, investigating mean scale score differences between majority and minority group members is not particularly relevant to the question of test bias (Graham, 1993). A better strategy involves investigating whether the accuracy of predictions based on the MMPI differs between minority and majority group members (Pritchard & Rosenblatt, 1980).

A number of MMPI studies were conducted that attempted to match participants on moderating variables. Davis (1975) and Cowan, Watkins, and Davis (1975) found that MMPI scores were not significantly different across African Americans and Whites diagnosed with schizophrenia and matched for severity of psychopathology. In another study, Bertelson, Marks, and May (1982) utilized a sample of African-American and White male and female psychiatric patients matched for sex, age, residence, employment, years of education, marital status, socioeconomic status (SES), and hospital status. Bertelson et al. (1982) did not find reliable African-American–White differences and concluded that the MMPI is equally appropriate for African Americans and Whites in a psychiatric setting. Johnson and Brems (1990) matched participants on age, gender, and diagnoses and found no significant differences between African Americans and Whites in an inpatient setting.

To summarize, early MMPI studies focused on mean scale score comparisons across unmatched groups of African Americans and Whites. When investigators began accounting for moderator variables such as SES and severity of psychopathology, what appeared to be substantial normative differences diminished, leading some authors to conclude that they were largely inconsequential. However, few studies focused on comparing empirical correlates of MMPI scales across African Americans and Whites despite that test interpretation was predicated on the empirical correlates of elevated scores and not on normative inferences.

Hispanic Americans

Studies investigating Hispanic and White differences on the MMPI are somewhat difficult to interpret due to the heterogeneity of participants termed *Hispanic* (Graham, 1993) and due to the confound of language proficiency. Greene (1987) noted that Hispanics are often classified so based simply on their surname. Greene investigated 11 empirical studies on Hispanic and White MMPI comparisons and concluded that there was no consistent pattern to the mean scale score differences. However, Velasquez (1992) published a bibliography of 86 MMPI studies involving Hispanics, so it is difficult to ascertain whether Greene's (1987) review is representative of the empirical literature.

In a meta-analysis of 16 studies, Campos (1989) concluded that Hispanics scored about four *T*-score points higher than Whites on the Lie scale. Velasquez and Callahan (1990) matched Hispanic, White, and African-American participants on the diagnosis of schizophrenia and found that Hispanics still scored higher than Whites on Scales F, 1, 7, 8, and 9. However, Velasquez and Callahan did not match participants on any variables other than psychiatric diagnosis. In a later study, Velasquez, Callahan, and Young (1993) matched Hispanics and Whites on age, education, and psychiatric diagnosis and concluded that MMPI differences between Hispanics and Whites are not minimized or eliminated. Velasquez et al. (1993) called for reexamination of the conclusions drawn by Green (1987) and Pritchard and Rosenblatt (1980) based on their findings.

To summarize, research on the use of the original form of the MMPI with Hispanic Americans focused almost exclusively on normative issues. We are aware of no studies that compared the empirical correlates of MMPI scores completed by Hispanic Americans and Whites. Moreover, most early studies did not address the possible confounds of language proficiency and acculturation (Dana, 1996). Many Hispanic Americans are immigrants or were raised in homes where Spanish was the primary spoken language. Although Spanish language translations of the MMPI existed, many were not carefully constructed translations. Moreover, researchers have largely neglected matters of acculturation in multicultural assessment.

Native Americans

There have been few investigations of potential Native-American and White differences on the MMPI. Greene (1987) identified seven studies and concluded that there was no clear pattern of mean scale score differences, although Native Americans scored higher than Whites on some of the clinical scales. Several studies have investigated Native-American and White alcoholics and psychiatric patients.

Kline, Rozynko, Flint, and Roberts (1973) concluded that male Native-American alcoholics' MMPI scores were higher than White alcoholics from the existing literature. Other researchers have concluded that Native-American and White alcoholics' MMPI scores were more similar than different (Page & Bozlee, 1982; Uecker, Boutilier, & Richardson, 1980). Pollack and Shore (1980) investigated different diagnostic groups of Native Americans and found comparability across diagnostic groups. Moreover, in a study of psychiatric inpatients, Butcher, Braswell, and Raney (1983) concluded that MMPI scores of Native Americans were less elevated than those of Whites and African Americans.

Although some investigators attempted to compare samples of Native Americans and Whites who are matched for type and level of psychopathology, we are aware of no original MMPI study that explored the empirical correlates of MMPI scales scores across the two groups. Here, too, matters of language proficiency and acculturation into the dominant Western culture have been left largely uninvestigated.

Asian Americans

Greene (1987) identified only three studies (Marsella, Sanborn, Kameoka, Shizura, & Brennan, 1975; Sue & Sue, 1974; Tsushima & Onorato, 1982) that compared Asian Americans and Whites on the MMPI, and one of these studies (Marsella et al., 1975) only compared Whites and Asian Americans on Scale 2. Marsella et al. (1975) reported higher scores for Asian Americans on Scale 2, which was also reflected in higher scores on the Beck Depression Inventory (BDI). This finding reveals consistency across the two measures in showing higher scores on measures of depression among Asian Americans. Left unanswered, however, is whether such differences would be found in a more carefully matched sample of Asian Americans and Whites and whether these self-report measures of depression are comparably valid across the two groups.

Tsushima and Onorato (1982) found no substantial differences between MMPI scale scores of Whites and Asian Americans when diagnosis was controlled. Sue and Sue (1974) found more differences than the other investigators, but did not report the mean scale scores. These investigators found that male Asian Americans scored higher than their White counterparts on Scales L, F, 1, 2, 4, 6, 7, 8, and 0. In addition, female Asian Americans scored higher than Whites on Scales L, F, and 0.

All MMPI studies of Asian Americans focused strictly on group mean comparisons. We are aware of no investigations that examined empirical correlates across groups. Moreover, as is the case with Hispanic Americans, the label *Asian American* incorporates a broad range of individuals who come from disparate cultural backgrounds. There is no reason to assume, a priori, that findings for one subgroup will generalize to another. In addition, matters of language proficiency and acculturation were largely not addressed in original MMPI studies with Asian Americans.

Summary and Implications of Original MMPI Research

Ethnic group comparisons with the original MMPI focused primarily on normative issues. Initial reports of group mean differences between African Americans and Whites on the MMPI led some to conclude that the test was biased and to recommend establishment of separate norms for minorities. Subsequent research showed that demographic and clinical factors accounted for most of the observed differences. Research with members of other ethnic minority groups suggested an inconsistent pattern of differences. However, the confounding effects of demographics, language, and acculturation were largely unstudied. Critics noted that the test was developed using an exclusively White sample focusing on Eurocentric concepts of psychopathology.

Regrettably, virtually none of the empirical research or commentary focused on addressing the most vital question in MMPI interpretation: Do the empirical correlates of MMPI scales generalize across ethnic groups and cultures? Given the evolution in MMPI interpretation from normatively referenced differential diagnosis to empirically grounded, actuarial description, evaluation of cross-group generalization of the test's empirical correlates is the key to determining its applicability or bias across cultures.

Insofar as multicultural groups within the United States were concerned, this essentially was an unanswered empirical question. Cross-cultural MMPI research offered some direction and reason for anticipating that correlate generalization may indeed be possible. In 1976, Butcher and Pancheri published their *Handbook of Cross-National MMPI Research*. These authors outlined standards for cross-national MMPI adaptations and described results from MMPI research projects conducted in over one dozen countries whose cultures, in some instances, varied dramatically. Although Butcher and Pancheri's (1976) focus was on procedures for cross-national translation and adaptation, research reported in their handbook indicted considerable cross-national generalization of MMPI correlates.

Throughout the 1970s and 1980s, researchers and clinicians in dozens of countries adapted the MMPI for use in their language and culture. Underlying these efforts was an assumption and expectation that the test's correlates would apply across cultures. However, this assumption went largely untested, and it appears that clinicians relied mainly on their experience in determining how to go about using the test in its adopted culture. The widespread popularity of the MMPI across many diverse cultures, and the immediacy with which cross-cultural researchers set about adapting the MMPI–2 after its publication in 1989, suggest that applied experience with the MMPI across cultures was largely positive, and clinicians believed that they were obtaining useful information from the test. Nonetheless, there remained a need for empirical research to verify the generalizability of the test's correlates across cultures.

MMPI–2

The revised version of the MMPI—the MMPI–2—was published in 1989 following a decade-long research project (Butcher, Dahlstrom, Graham, Tellegen, & Kaemmer, 1989). Many factors led the test's publisher, the University of Minnesota Press, to embark on this ambitious project. Among these was recognition that the test's original norms, although appropriate for the originally planned application of the test, had long become inadequate as the test's use expanded far beyond its developers' original intent. Among the concerns leading to the test's revision was the absence of minority group representation in the original normative sample. Thus, one of the goals of the revision project was to collect an up-to-date set of norms for the test based on a sample that proportionally represented the U.S. population. Data reported in the MMPI–2 manual indicate that this goal was largely fulfilled.

To the extent that normative differences existed between Whites and minorities on the original MMPI, these would have been augmented in any comparisons because of the absence of minorities from the original normative sample. Such differences would become diminished with the collection of a more diverse normative sample; however, they would not be eliminated altogether. For such differences to be removed entirely, equal numbers of Whites and ethnic minority participants would be required. Reflecting the demographic makeup of the U.S. population in 1980, roughly 82% of the new normative sample was White. Thus, collecting a more representative normative sample is not sufficient to eliminate cross-group normative differences.

However, as already discussed, MMPI and now MMPI–2 interpretation is based not on normative inferences but on the empirical correlates of the test's scales and code types. Because the clinical scales were essentially unchanged in the revision, their empirical correlates would, in all likelihood, remain nearly identical. Thus, to the extent that the correlates generalized across cultural groups on the original version of the instrument, they would be expected to do so on the MMPI–2 as well. However, as just reviewed, this issue, vital to the test's cross-cultural applicability, went largely unstudied with the original MMPI. The inclusion of a proportional number of ethnic minorities in the MMPI–2 normative sample does not obviate the need for empirical research to address this question. As reviewed next, such efforts have now begun, and their results are promising.

African Americans

Although the original MMPI normative sample included no African Americans, the MMPI–2 (Butcher, Dahlstrom, Graham, Tellegen, & Kaemmer, 1989) normative sample includes African Americans in approximately the same proportion as those indicated in the 1980 census. A number of newer studies have investigated potential African-American differences on the MMPI–2.

Timbrook and Graham (1994) investigated mean scale score differences on the MMPI–2 between African Americans and Whites from the test's new normative sample matched for age, years of education, and total family income. Timbrook and Graham found that African-American men scored significantly higher than White men on Scale 8. For women, statistically significant differences were found on Scales 4, 5, and 9. The mean scale scores for the African-American women were higher than the scores of White women for all three of these scales. However, all of the mean scale score differences for men and women were less than five T-score points. Greene (1987) suggested that scale differences less than five T-score points are not likely to be clinically important.

Recognizing that comparison of MMPI-2 mean scale scores did not address directly the question of test bias, Timbrook and Graham (1994) compared the validity of Scales 2, 4, 7, 9, and 0 across Whites and African Americans using scales developed by Long (1993) as extratest criteria. With the exception of Scale 7 for women, there were no significant differences in the accuracy of prediction of extratest criteria for African Americans versus Whites. Scale 7 underpredicted ratings of anxiety for African-American women.

Ben-Porath, Shondrick, and Stafford (1995) investigated African-American and White MMPI-2 mean scale score differences in a forensic setting that provided pretrial assessment services for criminal court proceedings. Ben-Porath et al. (1995) did not find significant differences between the two groups on any of the validity or clinical scales. However, African Americans scored significantly higher than Whites on the content scales Cynicism and Antisocial Practices. In addition, there were no significant differences between the two groups on the MMPI-2 substance abuse scales. Ben-Porath et al. concluded that the two groups produced highly comparable MMPI-2 profiles although subjects were not matched for SES differences.

In a follow-up study using a much larger sample from the same setting, Gironda (1998) found similar mean scale differences for men and women on the content scales Cynicism and Anti-Social Practices. In addition, Gironda found differences for both genders on the Fears content scale. African-American men scored higher than White men on clinical Scale 9 and on the Revised MacAndrew Alcoholism scale (MAC–R) and African-American women scored higher than White women on clinical Scale 5 and the Addiction Acknowledgment Scale. With the exception of the difference on the MAC–R, all exceeded Greene's (1987) recommended threshold of five T-score points.

In addition to comparing mean group scores, Gironda (1998) contrasted White and African-American defendants using collateral data extracted systematically from their case files. Group differences on these nontest data generally paralleled findings with the MMPI-2 scales. Finally, Gironda compared the validity of MMPI-2 scores across African Americans and Whites by contrasting correlations between MMPI-2 scores and extratest data across the two groups. Forty-seven validity coefficients were compared. Significant differences were found in three instances: The correlation between scores on clinical Scale 8 and collateral indications of psychosis was higher for African Americans than Whites and correlations between scores on the Addiction Potential Scale and collateral indications of substance abuse problems and a history of chemical dependency were higher for Whites than African Americans.

McNulty, Graham, Ben-Porath, and Stein (1997) investigated the comparative validity of MMPI–2 scores for African-American and White community mental health center clients. African-American men scored significantly higher than Whites on the L scale and the Fears content scale. African-American women scored higher than White women on clinical Scale 9, and White women scored higher on the Low Self-Esteem content scale. McNulty et al. (1997) also compared the validity of MMPI–2 scale scores across the two groups by examining correlations between MMPI–2 scores and therapists' ratings of clients' symptoms and personality characteristics. Correlations between MMPI–2 scale scores and extratest criteria were not significantly different between the groups. Based on these findings, McNulty et al. concluded that there was no evidence for MMPI–2 bias against African Americans in their study.

Arbisi, Ben-Porath, and McNulty (1998) compared the validity of MMPI–2 scale scores across African-American and White inpatients. Here, too, although some significant group mean differences emerged from the analyses, there were no significant differences in the ability of MMPI–2 scores to account for variance in extratest data.

In summary, recent investigations of potential bias in the MMPI–2 scores of African Americans addressed the need to go beyond simple comparisons of group mean profiles and focused instead on the empirical of MMPI–2 score across these two ethnic groups. These studies, now conducted with outpatient, inpatient, forensic, and nonclinical samples, show a consistent absence of bias in the ability of MMPI–2 scales to predict variance in relevant extratest criteria in African Americans.

Other Ethnic Minority Groups

Few studies have been published to date examining MMPI–2 scores of Hispanic Americans. Whitworth and McBlaine (1993) compared MMPI and MMPI–2 performance of White and Hispanic university students and concluded that the statistically significant differences they found were less than five T-score points and therefore not clinically meaningful. Whitworth and Unterbrink (1994) compared Hispanic and White MMPI–2 mean scale scores and found that Hispanics scored significantly higher than Whites on two of three validity scales and 4 of the 10 clinical scales. Whites scored higher than Hispanics on the K scale. For the content scales, Hispanics scored higher than Whites on 13 of the 15 scales. However,

Whitworth and Unterbrink concluded that the absolute clinical and content scale score differences were relatively small and that the test should not be considered invalid with Hispanics.

Clearly more research is needed to examine whether bias exists when the MMPI–2 is used with Hispanic Americans. This research is complicated by the heterogeneity of individuals who might be classified as Hispanic Americans, the potential confounds of language fluency, and acculturation. The heterogeneous nature of individuals who might be classified as Hispanic Americans is underscored by the existence of several Spanish-language translations and adaptations of the MMPI–2 (Butcher, 1996). Differences among these translations indicate that there are important differences among these subgroups that must be considered in cross-cultural adaptation of the MMPI–2. Because of the heterogeneous nature of this broad group of cultures, it is in fact not possible to reach any general conclusions about the MMPI–2's appropriateness for use with Hispanic Americans. Issues central to this matter must be addressed separately across subgroups. Central among these is the need to examine the empirical correlates of the MMPI–2 for each of these groups.

To date, we are only aware of one study of the MMPI–2 with Native Americans. Tinius and Ben-Porath (1993) compared the MMPI–2 profiles of Native-American and White patients receiving treatment for substance abuse or psychiatric disorders. Within each disorder type, they found substantial similarity of MMPI–2 profiles. Native Americans receiving treatment for substance abuse resembled their White counterparts far more than they did other Native Americans who were treated for psychiatric disorders.

Sue, Keefe, Enomoto, Durvasula, and Chao (1996) compared the MMPI–2 profiles of Asian-American and White college students. Asian Americans were divided into groups higher and lower in acculturation. The authors reported that low-acculturation Asian-American college students scored significantly higher than Whites on several MMPI–2 scales and that often these differences were clinically significant (i.e., exceeded five T-score points). The authors concluded that their findings may reflect cultural bias in the MMPI–2 scores of Asian Americans, particularly those less acculturated into the predominant Western culture. However, they noted correctly that their data do not address this issue directly. Here, too, the only way to determine whether the test is actually biased or accurately reflects cultural differences is by reference to nontest data and comparison of the test's empirical correlates across groups.

Researchers of the MMPI–2 with Asian Americans face challenges similar to those just noted for Hispanic Americans. The category *Asian Americans* encompasses a broad and heterogeneous array of subgroups that likely should not be aggregated into a uniform whole. Rather, it is important to conduct studies examining the MMPI-2's generalizability across subgroups of Asian Americans who differ substantially among themselves. The possible confounds of language proficiency and acculturation must be incorporated into the appropriate design of studies.

Cross-National Applications of the MMPI-2

Soon after the MMPI-2 was published (and, in some instances, even before formal publication), researchers in well over two dozen countries began adapting the MMPI-2 for use in their language and culture. The initial fruits of many of these efforts are described in Butcher's (1996) edited volume, *International Adaptations of the MMPI-2*. In this handbook, 60 authors from 25 countries describe their efforts to adapt and study the MMPI-2 in their countries and cultures. These studies focus on describing a meticulous process of adapting the instrument to the new culture and initial investigation of its psychometric properties in its adapted format. Most of the studies do not report empirical correlates for the adapted instrument. However, following Ben-Porath's (1990) recommendation, many of the authors report cross-national comparisons of the MMPI-2's factor structure.

Ben-Porath (1990) recommended replicatory factor analysis as a preliminary means of exploring the comparability of cross-cultural adaptations of the MMPI-2. Because the test's internal factor structure in the United states is well established, a comparison of this structure across cultures can provide an initial indication of problems in the adaptation, if they exist. If, in the process of instrument adaptation, the scales' internal structure is no longer maintained, there is little reason to believe that their external correlates could be replicated. However, a finding of congruent factor structures across cultures does not guarantee that the test will maintain its external correlates as well. This must be established through empirical research. With this important caveat in mind, it is encouraging that nearly all of the cross-cultural comparisons reported in Butcher's (1996) handbook reflected substantial congruence.

Implications of MMPI-2 Research and Recommendations for Practice

In the decade since the MMPI-2 was published, substantial progress has been made in examining its effectiveness and potential bias in the clinical assessment of African Americans. A growing body of research indicates that the clinical scales' empirical correlates, which serve as the foundation for MMPI-2 interpretation, generalize to African Americans in outpatient, inpatient, forensic, and nonclinical settings.

Research with other minority groups within the United States has not kept pace with the study of African-American MMPI–2 interpretation. The relatively minor amount of research that has been done has tended to incorporate heterogeneous subgroups of Hispanic or Asian Americans and has largely ignored matters of language proficiency and acculturation. These potential confounds must be considered in future investigations.

The matter of language proficiency can be addressed in a relatively simple and straightforward manner. In MMPI–2 studies of minorities who are immigrants or first-generation born in the United States, language proficiency measures should be incorporated and used to identify participants who do not have the requisite English-language proficiency to complete the MMPI–2. Such research could also quantify the extent to which lack of language proficiency may compromise the MMPI–2 scales' validity.

The issue of acculturation is more complex. The Sue et al. (1996) finding that MMPI–2 scale scores varied as a function of acculturation is not unexpected. To the extent that low acculturation may result in difficulties adapting to life in the United States, these findings may reflect the sequela of these difficulties rather than an inherent bias in the assessment of individuals who are lower in acculturation. Of course both bias and the sequela of lower levels of acculturation could underlie these findings.

Research is needed to extract these two factors. This can be accomplished by research designs similar to those that have established the generalizability of MMPI–2 correlates to African Americans. A prototypical study would involve administration of the MMPI–2, collection of extratest data on participants' functioning, and administration of a validated measure of acculturation to a sample of individuals that includes Whites and, for example, Mexican Americans. Correlations between MMPI–2 measures and extratest clinical data would be compared across the two groups. Should differences emerge, statistical analyses could reveal the extent to which they may be moderated by acculturation.

Correlate comparability studies are also needed in countries that have adapted the MMPI–2. Research reported by the numerous authors included in Butcher's (1996) international handbook indicates that cross-national adaptations of the test have been conducted in a rigorous manner. As a result, any discrepancies in scale correlates are unlikely to be a product of translation or adaptation deficiencies. Many of these authors describe ongoing efforts to produce the kind of research needed to establish the cross-national comparability of the correlates used to interpret the MMPI–2 in the United States.

During the next decade, cross-cultural/national MMPI–2 research should focus on establishing the test's correlates in the cultures and countries where the test is to be used. It is possible that these studies will yield findings similar to those emerging with African Americans, indicating that the empirical correlates of the test generalize broadly across many diverse cultures. It is also possible that, for some groups and some correlates, differences will be found. In such instances, it will be necessary to establish methodically the appropriate empirical correlates for MMPI–2 interpretation for that particular group or application.

Some authors have questioned whether MMPI–2 correlates can be applied broadly across cultures. They point to cross-cultural differences in manifestation and prevalence of psychological disorder, willingness to acknowledge difficulties or perceived shortcomings, important sociopolitical differences, and language nuances as major hurdles in the way of cross-cultural generalizability of the test. These are substantial concerns that must be addressed by empirical research. Should this research indicate that the correlates can be generalized (in a given culture), then practitioners may rely on the incredibly rich existing body of research on MMPI/MMPI–2 correlates. Should discrepancies emerge form this research, it would be important to identify which correlates may still be safely applied and conduct further investigations designed to detect culturally specific correlates. Such an approach to cross-cultural applications of the MMPI–2 falls squarely within the empirical tradition that has guided several decades of the test's users and investigators.

REFERENCES

Arbisi, P. A., Ben-Porath, Y. S., & McNulty, J. L. (1998, August). *Impact of ethnicity on the MMPI–2 in inpatient settings*. Paper presented at the 106th annual meeting of the American Psychological Association, San Francisco, CA.

Ball, J. C. (1960). Comparisons of MMPI profile differences among Negro-White adolescents. *Journal of Clinical Psychology, 16*, 304–307.

Ben-Porath, Y. S. (1990). Cross-cultural assessment of personality: The case for replicatory factor analysis. In J. N. Butcher & C. D. Spielberger (Eds.), *Recent advances in personality assessment* (Vol. 8, pp. 27–48). Hillsdale, NJ: Lawrence Erlbaum Associates.

Ben-Porath, Y. S., Shondrick, D. D., & Stafford, K. P. (1995). MMPI–2 and race in a forensic diagnostic sample. *Criminal Justice and Behavior, 22*, 19–32.

Bertelson, A. D., Marks, P. A., & May, G. D. (1982). MMPI and race: A controlled study. *Journal of Consulting and Clinical Psychology, 50*, 316–318.

Butcher, J. N. (1996). *International adaptations of the MMPI–2*. Minneapolis: University of Minnesota Press.

Butcher, J. N., Ball, B., & Ray, E. (1964). Effects of socioeconomic level on MMPI differences in Negro–White college students. *Journal of Counseling Psychology, 11*, 83–87.

Butcher, J. N., Braswell, L., & Raney, D. (1983). A cross-cultural comparison of American Indian, Black, and White inpatients on the MMPI and presenting symptoms. *Journal of Consulting and Clinical Psychology, 51*, 587–594.

Butcher, J. N., Dahlstrom, W. G., Graham, J. R., Tellegen, A., & Kaemmer, B. (1989). *MMPI–2: Manual for administration and scoring*. Minneapolis: University of Minnesota Press.

Butcher, J. N., & Pancheri, P. (1976). A *handbook of cross-national MMPI research*. Minneapolis: University of Minnesota Press.

Campos, L. P. (1989). Adverse impact, unfairness, and bias in the psychological screening of Hispanic peace officers. *Hispanic Journal of Behavioral Sciences, 11*, 122–135.

Cowan, M. A., Watkins, B. A., & Davis, W. E. (1975). Level of education, diagnosis and race-related differences in MMPI performances. *Journal of Clinical Psychology, 31*, 442–444.

Dahlstrom, W. G., & Gynther, M. D. (1986). Previous MMPI research on Black Americans. In W. G. Dahlstrom, D. Lachar, & L. E. Dahlstrom (Eds.), *MMPI patterns of American minorities* (pp. 24–49). Minneapolis: University of Minnesota Press.

Dahlstrom, W. G., Lachar, D., & Dahlstrom, L. E. (1986). *MMPI patterns of American minorities*. Minneapolis: University of Minnesota Press.

Dana, R. H. (1996). Culturally competent assessment practices in the United States. *Journal of Personality Assessment, 66*, 472–487.

Davis, W. E. (1975). Race and the differential "power" of the MMPI. *Journal of Personality Assessment, 39*, 138–140.

Gilberstadt, H., & Duker, A. (1965). *A handbook for clinical and actuarial MMPI interpretation*. Philadelphia, PA: W. B. Saunders.

Gironda, R. J. (1998). *Comparative validity of MMPI–2 scores of African Americans and Caucasians in a forensic diagnostic sample*. Unpublished doctoral dissertation, Kent State University, Kent, OH.

Graham, J. R. (1993). *MMPI–2: Assessing personality and psychopathology* (2nd ed.). New York: Oxford University Press.

Greene, R. L. (1987). Ethnicity and MMPI performance: A review. *Journal of Consulting and Clinical Psychology, 55*, 497–512.

Gynther, M. D. (1972). White norms and Black MMPIs: A prescription for discrimination. *Psychological Bulletin, 78*, 386–402.

Hathaway, S. R., & McKinley, J. C. (1943). *The Minnesota Multiphasic Personality Inventory*. New York: The Psychological Corporation.

Hokanson, J. E., & Calden, G. (1960). Negro–White differences on the MMPI. *Journal of Clinical Psychology, 16*, 32–33.

Johnson, M. E., & Brems, C. (1990). Psychiatric inpatient MMPI profiles: An exploration for potential racial bias. *Journal of Counseling Psychology, 37*, 213–215.

Kline, J. A., Rozynko, V. V., Flint, G., & Roberts, A. C. (1973). Personality characteristics of male Native-American alcoholic patients. *International Journal of the Addictions, 8*, 729–732.

Long, K. A. (1993). *The relations between socioeconomic status and the MMPI-2 scores of men and women*. Unpublished doctoral dissertation, Kent State University, Kent, OH.

Marks, P. A., & Seeman, W. (1963). *The actuarial description of personality: An atlas for use with the MMPI*. Baltimore, MD: Williams & Wilkins.

Marsella, A. J., Sanborn, K. O., Kameoka, V., Shizura, L., & Brennan, J. (1975). Cross-validation of self-report measures of depression among normal populations of Japanese, Chinese, and Caucasian ancestry. *Journal of Clinical Psychology, 31*, 281–287.

McDonald, R. L., & Gynther, M. D. (1962). MMPI norms for southern adolescent Negros. *Journal of Social Psychology, 58*, 277–282.

McDonald, R. L., & Gynther, M. D. (1963). MMPI differences associated with sex, race and class in two adolescent samples. *Journal of Counseling Psychology, 27*, 112–116.

McNulty, J. L., Graham, J. R., Ben-Porath, Y. S., & Stein, L. A. R. (1997). Comparative validity of MMPI–2 scores of African American and Caucasian mental health center clients. *Psychological Assessment, 9*, 464–470.

Meehl, P. E. (1945). The dynamics of "structured" personality tests. *Journal of Clinical Psychology, 1*, 296–303.

Meehl, P. E. (1954). *Clinical versus statistical prediction: A theoretical analysis and a review of the evidence*. Minneapolis: University of Minnesota Press.

Meehl, P. E. (1956). Wanted: A good cookbook. *American Psychologist, 11,* 263–272.

Page, R. D., & Bozlee, S. (1982). A cross-cultural MMPI comparison of alcoholics. *Psychological Reports, 50,* 639–646.

Penk, W. E., Robinowitz, R., Roberts, W. R., Dolan, M. P., & Atkins, H. G. (1981). MMPI differences of male Hispanic-American, Black and White heroin addicts. *Journal of Consulting and Clinical Psychology, 49,* 488–490.

Pollack, D., & Shore, J. H. (1980). Validity of the MMPI with Native Americans. *American Journal of Psychiatry, 137,* 946–950.

Pritchard, D. A., & Rosenblatt, A. (1980). Racial bias in the MMPI: A methodological review. *Journal of Consulting and Clinical Psychology, 48,* 263–267.

Sue, S., Keefe, K., Enomoto, K., Durvasula, R., & Chao, R. (1996). Asian American and White college students' performance on the MMPI–2. In J. N. Butcher (Ed.), *International adaptations of the MMPI: Research and clinical applications* (pp. 206–220). Minneapolis: University of Minnesota Press.

Sue, S., & Sue, D. W. (1974). MMPI comparisons between Asian-American and non-Asian students utilizing a student health psychiatric clinic. *Journal of Counseling Psychology, 21,* 423–427.

Timbrook, R. E., & Graham, J. R. (1994). Ethnic differences on the MMPI–2? *Psychological Assessment, 6,* 212–217.

Tinius, T., & Ben-Porath, Y. S. (1993, March). *A comparative study of native and Caucasian Americans undergoing substance abuse treatment.* Paper presented at the 28th annual symposium on recent developments in the MMPI–2 and MMPI–A, St. Petersburg Beach, FL.

Tsushima, W. T., & Onorato, V. A. (1982). Comparison of MMPI scores of White and Japanese-American medical patients. *Journal of Consulting and Clinical Psychology, 50,* 150–151.

Uecker, A. E., Boutilier, L. R., & Richardson, E. H. (1980). "Indianism" and MMPI scores of men alcoholics. *Journal of Studies on Alcohol, 41,* 357–362.

Velasquez, R. J. (1992). Hispanic-American MMPI research (1949–1992): A comprehensive bibliography. *Psychological Reports, 70,* 743–754.

Velasquez, R. J., & Callahan, W. J. (1990). MMPIs of Hispanic, Black, and White *DSM–III* schizophrenics. *Psychological Reports, 66,* 819–822.

Velasquez, R. J., Callahan, W. J., & Young, R. (1993). Hispanic-White MMPI comparisons: Does psychiatric diagnosis make a difference? *Journal of Clinical Psychology, 49,* 528–534.

Whitworth, R. H., & McBlaine, D. D. (1993). Comparison of the MMPI and MMPI–2 administered to Anglo- and Hispanic-American university students. *Journal of Personality Assessment, 61,* 19–27.

Whitworth, R. H., & Unterbrink, C. (1994). Comparison of MMPI–2 clinical and content scales administered to Hispanic and Anglo-Americans. *Hispanic Journal of Behavioral Sciences, 16,* 255–264.

11

Issues in the Cross-Cultural Adaptation and Use of the MMPI–2

David S. Nichols
Oregon State Hospital—Portland

Jesus Padilla
Oregon State Hospital—Salem

Emilia Lucio Gomez-Maqueo
National University of Mexico

The Minnesota Multiphasic Personality Inventory (MMPI, MMPI–2, and MMPI–A) is the most widely used and researched psychodiagnostic instrument in the world. Indeed, the MMPI boasts an extensive research base, and the number of research efforts continues to rise. Cultural changes in the U.S. population and acknowledged limitations of the MMPI prompted a restandardization that culminated in the production of the current form—the MMPI–2. Although the restandardization produced valuable changes in the instrument, rendering it more appropriate for use with a more culturally diverse American society, numerous concerns over the cross-cultural application of the MMPI–2 have recently been raised (e.g., Dana, 1993, 1996).

Of primary concern is whether the MMPI–2 is appropriate for use with cultures whose worldviews differ significantly from the Euro-American culture. The answer to this question seems obvious in light of the fact that changes in U.S. culture precipitated a restandardization of the MMPI and that the cultural differences within the United States are ostensibly not as great as they are between American and non-American cultures. Proponents of the intercultural use of the MMPI–2 cite evidence that the scales of the MMPI–2 measure constructs that are universal (etics) and are thus presumably not culture specific. Others contend that, because the MMPI–2 was developed within a specific culture, the constructs measured by the MMPI–2 are necessarily specific (emics) to that culture alone; use of the MMPI–2 across cultures will obscure culture-specific constructs and require awkward and poorly conceived and untested adjustments to the interpretation.

Numerous studies have shown strong cultural variance in the manner in which individuals respond to the MMPI and MMPI–2. The confound between acculturation to the United States and MMPI–2-measured psychopathology has been well documented (cf. Canul & Cross, 1994; Montgomery, Arnold, & Orozco, 1990). Cultural factors attributed to discrepancies in MMPI–2 scores between cultures include intracultural linguistic differences, differences in worldview (e.g., group and individual identity, culture-specific cognitions, values, and beliefs), acculturation, socioeconomic status (SES), education, and reaction to racism. Although some argue that these confounding variables cannot be reconciled, and thus require that norms specific to each culture be established, others contend that such an approach would be tantamount to the creation of a new and different instrument. This would render the plethora of research on the original MMPI unusable in the understanding of data generated by the new instrument.

Even if norms were established for individual cultures, many cross-cultural psychologists contend that instruments developed in one culture cannot be used with other cultures because they introduce destructive cultural biases. For example, Misra (1994) argued that,

> Mapping reality through Western constructs has offered a pseudo understanding of the peoples of alien cultures and has had debilitating effects in terms of misconstruing the special realities of other peoples, and exorcising or disregarding psychologies that are non-Western. Consequently, those from other cultures exposed to Western psychology find their identities placed in question, and their conceptual repertoires rendered obsolete. (p. 3)

To be sure, this proposition assumes an extreme relativist position, particularly with regard to the delineation of categories of psychopathology. It is not impossible, for example, that numerous Western psychiatric categories, such as schizophrenia or bipolar disorder, do reflect universal constructs. However, there are conceivably many Western constructs (such as depression) that do not map well onto constructs of non-Western psychology, and tacit acceptance of all psychiatric categories as universal is a genuine concern for the integrity of non-Western cultures.

A recent study reporting strong differences in numerous scaled scores between the American and Chinese versions of the MMPI–2 exemplifies Misra's concern. Cheung, Leung, Fan, Song, and Xie (1996) asked whether the higher scores produced by the Chinese on the MMPI–2 reflect a more prevalent psychopathology of the Chinese people or whether differences can be explained as a lack of cross-cultural equivalence for some of the constructs measured by the MMPI-2. They concluded that, "Despite some cultural differences, the overall cross-cultural equivalence of the MMPI-2 has been supported." Arguably, acceptance of near equivalence of Western psychological constructs could signal the beginning of the loss of Chinese conceptual repertoires.

The implications of a priori assumptions about the universality of constructs has the potential for marginalization of other cultures that are not given voice in the dominant sphere, to say nothing of the risks such assumptions pose for the suboptimal classification and treatment of persons needing psychiatric and psychological services. In an assessment of the Maori people of New Zealand, Durie (1994) noted that Maori psychiatric admission rates (per use of *DSM* classification schemes) are two or three times those of non-Maori and that there are no simple explanations for this fact. Lawson-Te Aho (1993) pointed out that Western assumptions underlying *DSM* classification are seen by the Maori as representing part of the policing mechanisms of a neocolonial state. Within the United States, racial groups including African Americans, Hispanic/Latinos, American Indians, and Asian Americans have long voiced similar protests.

RESEARCH ISSUES IN CROSS-CULTURAL USE OF THE MMPI-2

The original MMPI was translated into numerous languages, but its transcultural iterations proved to be relatively poor. With the advent of the restandardization and subsequent MMPI-2, a new surge of translations and transcultural research with the instrument ensued. Among other articles, Greene's (1987) literature review on the cross-cultural use of the MMPI suggested that the MMPI's performance was inconsistent and that the construct validity of the instrument for use with cultures different from that within which it was normed remained, in large part, ambiguous.

Explanatory arguments for the MMPI's inconsistency included: problems with language translations, cultural differences, psychometric bias arising from cultural inequivalence, and questionable validity. In a discussion about the legitimate use of an instrument in a separate culture, Lonner (1979) described four kinds of equivalence: linguistic, conceptual, functional, and metric.

Linguistic Equivalence

Criticisms regarding the inadequacy of translations of the MMPI (including one example in which the MMPI was literally translated by undergraduate students and subsequently published and used for many years;

Butcher, 1996) prompted MMPI–2 researchers to adopt specific translation strategies, the goal of which was to retain the meaningfulness of the items and simultaneously minimize bias. Butcher outlined the general translation strategy of the MMPI–2 used by most researchers as including: (a) the use of two or more translators who have a high degree of knowledge of both original and target languages who then independently perform an initial translation followed by a comparison and discussion phase in which translators collaborate on a final translation; (b) a back translation by an independent translator equally versed in both languages; (c) a comparison of the back-translated document with the original English version; and (d) a study of equivalency in which the inventory is field tested to determine the acceptability of the instrument in the target language. Butcher also added three more suggestions in the preparation for MMPI–2 use in other cultures: (a) a comparative study to determine the adequacy of American norms, (b) the development of new norms specific to the target culture, and (c) ongoing research with the translated instrument to assess its validity within the target culture.

Once the translation has been established, the typical approach to research with the MMPI–2 has been to administer the inventory to different cultural groups matched on specific variables and then assess its efficacy by comparing the results with performance by American counterparts. If these comparisons reveal a good correspondence between cultures, the instrument is thought to be credible for use with American norms. Concurrently, local cultural norms may be established and made available for further research on its cross-cultural validity.

Following Butcher's recommendations, modern translations of the MMPI–2 have improved to the point that linguistic equivalence has been generally established across translations. However, language variability is prominent even within cultures, and the issue of linguistic equivalence has arisen within same-language cultures. For example, the Mexican, Chilean, Argentine, and Spanish versions, all in Spanish language, are each generally not considered usable with Spanish-language cultures other than those within which they were produced. The tasks of translation are rendered even more formidable when the substantial intercultural diversity within both the United States and other countries are taken into account.

To take a few obvious examples, among undereducated, impoverished, inner-city African Americans, the language of the MMPI–2 may seem stilted, intrusive, and less than fully accessible, as compared with the natural grammar, idiom, and rhythms of speech in their communities. Moreover, for such respondents, the language of the MMPI–2 may be personologically active in the sense of not merely assessing but actually stimulating traits that constitute, in part, the object of assessment (e.g., passivity, dependency, fatalism, hopelessness, suspiciousness, etc.).

The extreme profiles generated by otherwise normal deaf American college students (Rosen, 1966) suggest a potentially vastly different cultural milieu among the hearing impaired and an experience of the dominant culture of the hearing that is partially at odds with that of those whose hearing is within normal limits. Gynther, Fowler, and Erdberg (1971) found that a socially isolated but otherwise normal African-American sample exhibited extreme profile elevations (and, e.g., a 58% endorsement of the item *Evil spirits possess me at times* as compared with a minuscule endorsement rate by the normative sample).

Although the well-developed translation strategy outlined by Butcher (1996) may be necessary for the creation of cross-culturally viable test forms, the importance of Step 4—field testing—cannot be underestimated. Because the purpose of translation is to extend the instrument for use with monolinguals, it cannot simply be assumed that monolinguals of the target group—the group to which the MMPI–2's interpretive apparatus is to be applied/generalized—will share the same semantic and linguistic habits and understandings as do bilingual personnel involved in the translation, front or back, or who may be recruited as subjects in efforts to establish metric equivalence. That is, an ethnographic component of field testing in which bilingual investigators conduct interviews with a heterogeneous group of monolingual informants may be essential to establish that the stimulus values of the items in the target language are equivalent to those of the same items in the original language.

Conceptual Equivalence

Conceptual equivalence refers to the equivalence of meanings that individuals give to concepts. Of the various equivalencies noted by Lonner, conceptual equivalence is at once the most important and most difficult to verify. Conceptual equivalence is a term related to the concept of construct validity, which is generally established by constructing a nomological network (Cronbach & Meehl, 1955) or by using a multitrait, multimethod matrix approach (Campbell & Fiske, 1959). This requires the formation and analysis of a correlation matrix of variables of interest with measures of other psychological constructs. For the last 40 or so years, this approach to construct validation has been considered the gold standard.

Arguing against this approach, Butcher (1996) pointed out that validating the conceptual equivalence of instruments for cross-cultural use utilizing these methods is overly costly and time-consuming. He stated,

> Suppose one adapts an instrument such as the MMPI into a culture and attempts to establish its conceptual equivalence by correlating each scale with scale scores from the Multidimensional Personality Questionnaire (Tellegen, 1982) or with psychiatric diagnoses (based on the *DSM–IV*). This

would require establishing cross-cultural equivalence for the other two instruments. If there are no well established nomological networks in the source culture, simultaneous development of extensive, fully articulated nomological networks in both cultures is required, which is difficult, perhaps even impossible, in practical terms. (pp. 49–50)

One might add to this realistic catalogue of difficulties the problem of establishing the psychometric credentials of whatever criterion measures are chosen to investigate the validity of the MMPI–2. That is, unless the reliability and validity of extratest measures equal or exceed those of the MMPI–2, the application and generality of the correlates discovered in the course of validity investigations are apt to be limited and unstable.

Although some researchers (Butcher, 1996) express doubt as to the point at which the creation of the nomological network should be initiated, others (Dana, 1997) argue that the first step in the construct validation of instruments that purport to measure psychopathology (particularly as identified by diagnostic manuals such as the *DSM–IV*; American Psychiatric Association, 1994) for cross-cultural use should be in the establishment of nomological networks for culturally relevant psychiatric diagnoses. Instruments measuring psychopathology that are originally partially or wholly validated using the *DSM–IV* may produce misleading results when used in the measurement of psychopathology in other cultures.

Indeed, the authors of the *DSM–IV* recognize the cultural limitations of this system of classification and the potential lack of generalizability of Western psychiatric nosology across cultures:

Aberrant behavior that might be sorted by a diagnostician using *DSM–IV* into several categories may be included in a single folk category, and presentations that might be considered by a diagnostician using *DSM–IV* as belonging to a single category may be sorted into several by an indigenous clinician. Moreover, some conditions and disorders have been conceptualized as culture-bound syndromes specific to industrialized cultures (e.g., Anorexia Nervosa, Dissociative Identity Disorder) given their apparent rarity or absence in other cultures. It should also be noted that all industrialized societies include distinctive subcultures and widely diverse immigrant groups who may present with culture-bound syndromes. (p. 844)

Butcher (1996) also acknowledged the difficulty of approaching the cross-cultural validation of the MMPI–2 with reference to standard diagnostic systems such as the *DSM* because the cross-cultural validity of such systems is in question. For example, in the International Pilot Study of Schizophrenia (World Health Organization, 1973, 1979), psychiatrists from seven Western industrialized and nonindustrialized countries, all rigorously trained in the Present State Examination (PSE), achieved high interrater reliabilities for the core symptoms of schizophrenia both within and across centers. Although the core pattern of schizophrenic symptoms was present at all centers, the majority of patients assessed were excluded for falling outside the narrow inclusion and exclusion criteria for diagnosis. However, it is just these patients who would be expected to show the greatest culturally determined variability (Kleinman, 1988).

Narrow selection criteria lead to a homogenization across samples and suggest that findings of similarity were more an artifact of the methodology than reflective of true similarity. Even within cohorts meeting diagnostic criteria for core schizophrenia, significant differences were found across centers (e.g., catatonia was common in two centers—India and Nigeria—relative to the others, and the course of illness was better for patients assessed in the nonindustrialized study centers than for those from industrialized countries).

Kleinman (1988) stated further that these presumed similarities in psychopathology mistakenly form a base for arguing erroneously for biological explanations in psychiatry. He noted that evolutionary biologists argue just the opposite. He cites Rosenfield (1986):

> There are good biological reasons to question the idea of fixed universal categories. In a broad sense, they run counter to the principles of the Darwinian theory of evolution. Darwin stressed that populations are collections of unique individuals. In the biological world, there is no typical plant. . . . Qualities we associate with human beings and other animals are abstractions invented by us that miss the nature of the biological variation. (p. 22)

There is only one study known to us in which construct validation was performed with a Spanish version of the MMPI–2 in the United States (Fantoni-Salvador & Rogers, 1997). Criterion validation of four diagnostic categories (major depression, schizophrenia, anxiety disorders, and alcohol dependence) was attempted using a Spanish version of the Diagnostic Interview Schedule (DIS) for *DSM* as the external measure. These investigators found only moderate hit rates for the MMPI–2. Sensitivity for depression (.97) and schizophrenia (1.0) was very good, but specificity for these disorders was poor (.49 and .31, respectively). Sensitivity for anxiety disorders was moderate (.78) but also better than specificity (.45). Sensitivity and specificity for alcohol dependence varied widely with scale, but the Addiction Acknowledgment Scale (AAS; Weed, Butcher, McKenna, & Ben-Porath, 1992) appeared to be more promising than either the MacAndrew Alcoholism Scale (MAC; MacAndrew, 1965) or the Addiction Potential Scale (APS; Weed, Butcher, McKenna, & Ben-Porath, 1992). In addition, correlations between selected scales and DIS symptoms varied widely and were in the low to moderate range.

Thus, although the MMPI–2 performed generally well in capturing people with depression and schizophrenia, persons without these disorders were also likely to have clinical elevations. Fantoni-Salvador and Rogers (1997) also correctly cautioned that interviews based on *DSM* categories should not be considered the gold standard because of the inherent cultural limitations of *DSM* classification: "The limitations of codetypes and clinical elevations is that they do not take into account the number of symptoms experienced by Hispanic patients" (pp. 33–34) Cross-cultural findings of elevations on MMPI–2 scales (e.g., Butcher, 1996) congruent with mental disorders originally diagnosed using *DSM* typology merit the same caveat. In Mexico, for example, because of its relative poverty and agrarian economy, the technology of scientific psychiatry is largely imported (e.g., note the extensive use of the Spanish translation of the *DSM–IV*). At least in its urban centers, the indigenous manifestations and categories of mental illness have been assimilated to the *DSM*. In many parts of rural Mexico, however, folk medicine (i.e., *curanderismo*) remains the dominant epistemology for construing and treating the manifestations of mental disorder.

Considering the large (and expensive) undertaking required to establish construct validity using strategies such as the multitrait, multimethod approach, Butcher (1996) recommended that other methods for establishing cross-cultural equivalence be adopted. He cited factor similarity indexes such as the congruence coefficient (i.e., degree of factorial similarity; Tucker, 1951), factor score correlations (i.e., comparability coefficient; Everett & Entrekin, 1980), and confirmatory factor analysis (Joerekog, 1971) as having good potential. He correctly pointed out, however, numerous drawbacks to using the first two (e.g., their overestimations of the degree of similarity) and the third (e.g., although adequate when a single goodness of fit is required, when multiple comparisons are made it cannot be established which factors are similar and which are not). Because no one index is suitable for comparison by itself, it is recommended that two or three such indexes be used in conjunction. Even with these suggestions, out of all of the transcultural studies cited by Butcher (1996), he reported only two that have used these methods (Japanese vs. American MMPI and Japanese vs. American MMPI–2) for establishing degree of similarity between factors.

Despite statistical advances, use of statistical techniques for establishing construct validity appears to be subject to the same criticism as stated earlier. That is, the creation of a test in one culture and validating the translated version of that test in a separate culture by using comparison data from the original test is "largely a bootstrapping operation that builds incrementally on the validity of existing measures" (Fantoni-Salvador & Rogers, 1997, p. 38). One argument (Moreland, 1996) asserted that items of an inventory devised for use in one culture should be developed in such a way as to measure a representative sample of the universe of items pertaining to the specific culturally bound trait. Even if statistical equivalence could be established, there is no way of knowing whether the items selected as representative for a trait in one culture are representative of the universe of items within a similar trait in another culture.

The oft-cited difference in the psychological experience and behavioral manifestation of depression between Americans and Mexicans (also Chinese and other cultures) is a good example. Mexicans reportedly experience a higher degree of somatic symptomatology when suffering with depression than their American counterparts. With regard to depression, although there may be overlapping symptoms between the two cultures, there are differential symptoms extant in the construct of depression in the Mexican culture. These symptoms not only produce a different syndrome, but they also add to and modify the symptoms within the overlapping space. Because instruments such as the MMPI–2, which were developed in one culture reflecting specific culture-relevant diagnostic syndromes, presumably capture only the overlapping symptoms, spurious findings of similarity could occur. It is for this reason also that the first priority of establishing the equivalency of measures between cultures should be the demonstration of the equivalency of psychiatric nosology through detailed research.

That equivalency of psychiatric constructs between cultures will be found remains a research question, however. Results of current research appear to argue for the lack of equivalency of psychiatric constructs in specific and many psychological constructs in general. In cross-cultural studies (Turkish vs. American) of ethnopsychological conceptualizations of mental health, child development, and family, Gulerce (1990, 1992) found evidence for strong differences in traditional moral, religious, and sociocultural values when checked against *DSM–III* typologies, developmental psychology, and contemporary family models. In his pioneering work on conceptual equivalence, Diaz-Guerrero (1994) found significant differences between Mexicans and Americans on a multitude of concepts, including respect and the concept of the self, through the use of a semantic differential technique. Markus and Kitayama (1998) demonstrated that there are palpable differences between Japanese and American students in the construal of the self (collectivistic vs. individualistic) as well.

Citing strong cultural differences as contributing to the limitations of the cross-cultural use of psychological instruments, the Chinese have established a number of culturally relevant measures such as the Ko

Mental Health Questionnaire (KMHQ; Ko, 1977, 1981) and the Chinese Personality Inventory (CPAI; Cheung, 1996; Cheung et al., 1996). The Chinese example is noteworthy in that, although the KMHQ was developed using a similar development strategy as that used in the production of the MMPI–2, the factor structure produced by the KMHQ is radically different from the factors produced by the MMPI–2. This reflects the cultural differences in the construal and experience of Chinese psychopathology. In another study, a higher order factor analysis of the CPAI revealed a dimension beyond the Big Five dimensions labeled Chinese Tradition (Cheung & Leung, 1998), again reflecting clear cultural differences.

Metric Equivalence

Metric equivalence refers to the extent to which an instrument manifests similar psychometric properties (distributions, ranges, etc.) across cultures. Metric equivalence can be established by demonstrating the commonality of metrics across cultures. One way to establish metric equivalence is through the analysis of the rate of item endorsement across samples. If responses to specific items reveal a significant difference in their rate of endorsement for two groups (at or above 25%; Butcher, 1996), the potential cause for such differences could lie with either translation problems or cultural differences.

In the Mexican translation, the item *Dirt frightens or disgusts me* is translated as *La suciedad me molesta o me horroriza.* The concept *la suciedad* refers to something like *dirtiness* and does not include the overlapping notion of dirt as in soil or earth. Likewise, *me molesta* means *it bothers me* rather than *it frightens me*. This item exhibited one of the largest endorsement rate differences between a Mexican college sample of 1,107 females and 814 males (Gomez-Maqueo & Reyes-Lagunes, 1994) and the MMPI–2 restandardization sample of 1,462 females and 1,138 males (Butcher, Dahlstrom, Graham, Tellegen, & Kaemmer, 1989; 58%–68% higher True responses by Mexicans). The difference appears to be the result of both translation and cultural differences. In essence, Mexican subjects appear to be asserting that dirtiness bothers (or horrifies) them. Culturally speaking, people living in conditions in which dirtiness is often equated with diseases or infection should be bothered or even horrified by it.

In another example of culturally driven differences, Waller, Thompson, and Wenk (1998) found that their youthful African-American offenders were more likely than their Euro-American counterparts to endorse the item *When I leave home I do not worry about whether the door is locked and the windows closed*, even when the two groups were matched on a phobias and fears dimension. The reason for this difference is evident in the fact that many of the African-American youths issued from neighborhoods heavily impacted by crime and in which unlocked doors and windows invite burglary and robbery.

Of course, culturally or semantically biased items do not ensure that their parent scale will fail to perform as intended. Differences in group endorsement frequencies spread over many items may cancel each other out, leaving the scale composed of items that, in the aggregate, are bias free. Indeed, using an item response theory (IRT) approach with unidimensional factor scales, Waller et al. (1998) found that differences in the MMPI performance of a large sample of Euro- and African-American youthful offenders could not be ascribed to biased measurement.

To gain some insight into the possible cross-cultural biases on the MMPI–2 for Mexicans, the item responses of the MMPI–2 Mexican college sample (Gomez-Maqueo & Reyes-Lagunes, 1994) were compared with those of the MMPI–2 restandardization sample. Items for which differences in their proportional endorsement rates exceeded 25% for both male and female Mexican college students were gathered into a scale. Product–moment correlations were then computed between the resulting scale of 29 items (*MEX*), keyed for the Mexican student respondents, and a large selection of MMPI–2 scales. Because the individuals comprising the MMPI–2 restandardization sample were considerably older than those of the Mexican sample, the correlational values were statistically controlled for age. However, this control did not significantly alter the magnitude or pattern of results obtained.

The MMPI–2 scale correlates of *MEX* are generally of modest magnitude but are highly patterned. Among the standard validity and clinical scales, Mania correlates positively (*Ma*; .20); Depression (*D*; –.22), Hysteria (*Hy*; –.21), Paranoia (*Pa*; –.23), and Social Introversion (*Si*; –.19) are correlated inversely with *MEX*. The remaining standard scales are all negatively correlated with *MEX*, with *K* at –.10. These trends are clarified among the Harris and Lingoes (1968) and *Si* (Ben-Porath, Hostetler, Butcher, & Graham, 1989) subscales, in which a positive correlation for *Ma1* (.30) is found along with negative correlations for *D1* (–.20), *Hy2* (–.20), *Pa3* (–.28), *Sc2* (–.21), *Sc4* (–.18), and *Si2* (–.27).

These correlates are consistent with a view of *MEX* as reflecting qualities of buoyancy, optimism, cheerfulness, and gregariousness, along with skepticism about the motives of others. This pattern of correlates is largely replicated among the MMPI–2 content and content component (Ben-Porath & Sherwood, 1993) scales, with positive correlations with MEX for Cynicism (*CYN*, .29; *CYN1*, .32), Antisocial Practices (*ASP*, .35; *ASP1*, .39), and Type A Personality (*TPA*, .27; *TPA2*, .26) and a negative correlation with Social Discomfort (*SOD*, –.19; *SOD1*, –.24). These correlates extend the inferences given earlier in the direction of a skeptical and expedient view of rules, regulations, and authority and a capacity for vindictive responses to being wronged.

Correlations between *MEX* and a variety of supplemental scales follow the pattern established previously, with negative values for Welsh's *R* (−.28) and Social Responsibility (Re; −.21) and positive values for *MAC-R* (.18), Hostility (*HO*; .27), Aggression (*AGG*; .32), and Positive Emotionality/Extraversion (*PEE*; .37). These correlates would appear to emphasize a mobilized and largely positive emotionality, social disinhibition, and a relaxed attitude toward duty while reiterating themes of reluctance to take others at face value and a readiness to retaliate for injuries suffered from others.

The interpretive inferences given herein issue from a Euro-American understanding of the correlates of these MMPI scales. The combination of cynicism and gregariousness could lead to the assumption that Mexican individuals live in a constant state of conflict between an openness to social engagement on the one hand and a lack of trust on the other. However, when considered from a Mexican cultural perspective, it may be argued that the attitude (cynical vs. gregarious) depends to some degree on the nature of the relationship between the actor and the other. If the other's existence lies within the person's group (identified, therefore, with the self), the general attitude is that of positive emotionality, social disinhibition, openness, and so on. If the other is in the outgroup (thus not identified with the self), the attitude is one of mistrust.

Notwithstanding conceptual, functional, and psychometric variables, there is some evidence that other cultural variables affect the construct validity of the MMPI–2. That is, in addition to collectivistic versus individualistic views of self, level of acculturation, education, age, and so on, internal versus external control, just world beliefs, conservative versus liberal attitudes, traditionalism versus modernism, and tolerance for deviance, to name a few, also need to be considered. Moreover, cultural groups seem to differ in test-taking attitudes as well. Latinos may have a lower threshold for reporting symptoms on questionnaires than Whites or African Americans (Haberman, 1976; Krause & Carr, 1978; Vernon & Roberts, 1982). Confirmation of this effect with the MMPI–2 would not only implicate another culturally based factor that could affect MMPI–2 validity, but it would also spotlight the perennial questions surrounding the use of the *K* correction (cf. Greene, 1991) and the lack of convincing justification for its use even among White Americans. There can be little doubt that its use among Mexicans and Mexican Americans rests on an especially arbitrary set of assumptions, both cultural and psychometric.

The current findings with the *MEX* data may be further illuminated by Landrine's (1992) distinction between the referential and indexical self. In dominant Western cultures, the self is viewed as separate, egocentric, independent, unique, autonomous, continent, agentic, and operant; the cause, creator, and controller of behavior; the center of a singular mental and emotional universe and the awareness thereof, from which flow thought, feeling, judgment, and action. It is seen as context-free, with its attributes being bounded neither by time nor situation.

In this context, failures to develop and maintain conventional distinctions of self and nonself invite psychopathological attributions such as enmeshment, dependency, pathological (e.g., projective) identifications, loss of ego boundaries, identity diffusion, delusion, *folie a deux*, and so on. Locating the causes of one's behavior outside the self is also to risk attributions like transfer of blame, externalization, rationalization, projection, and delusion. Any experience of the self as alien or nonagentic, as a machine without a ghost, will suggest depersonalization, derealization, dissociation, depression, or delusion. Lapses from a premise of conscious purpose to influence, manage, act on, dominate, master, and control interactions, events, circumstances, and material in the way one acts vis-à-vis the nonself may be ascribed to learned helplessness, amotivation, passivity, or personal deficits. If the self as such, through thought, wish, will, or feeling, is believed to instigate or affect change in the material world (nonself), attributions of magical ideation, thought disorder, delusion, or superstitiousness may be forthcoming. In the same way, any view of the physical world as animate may be considered grounds for attributions of disordered thought, delusion, or magical ideation.

By contrast, Landrine (1992) described the indexical self as context bound, constituted, and renewed in social interactions, relationships, and activities. It persists neither in time nor across the situations in which it finds itself; it has no attributes that persist in isolation from its relationships and contexts. Descriptions of the self are couched in stories that describe characteristic or defining situations or interactions in concrete detail. Thus, the invitation to the non-Westerner to describe him or herself is likely to produce not a Western adumbration of static traits (such as often requested in the MMPI–2), but a potpourri of stories and descriptions of events that Western auditors may regard as evasive, circumstantial, tangential, overproductive, concrete, rationalized, uncooperative, and reflecting a lack of insight and psychological mindedness.

These considerations highlight the issue of how observed differences in item endorsement frequencies and the areas of content that they identify are to be interpretively construed. It can be conceded that the 29 items of *MEX* and their content domains will not bear the weight of firm interpretive implications, however suggestive these may be. It should be borne in mind, however, that the Mexican college students and the restandardization sample may be far more similar to one another than either would be to a representative sample of Mexican nationals.

The concerns about Western-focused interpretations of non-Western styles of communication and self- and worldviews have not gone unnoticed. Witness, for example, the new ethnography of cultural anthropology (Geertz, 1988), social constructionist and narrative theory in psychology (Parker & Shotter, 1990; Sarbin, 1986), and the movement toward qualitative research in family therapy (Gulerce, 1992; Zayas & Solari, 1994).

Functional Equivalence

Functional equivalence refers to the cross-cultural similarity of the function of specific behaviors. For example, in the United States the handshake is functionally equivalent to the head bow with hands held together in India. Thus, although the actual behaviors are topographically distinct, they may serve the same social function. Functional equivalence is generally assessed during the translation phase, where cross-cultural differences and similarities in the functions of behavior form the basis for the translation of specific items and then again during data analysis. Review of numerous cross-cultural adaptations of the MMPI–2 suggests that translators were acutely aware of functional equivalence. Although judgment-based procedures appeared to be adequate in the numerous studies appearing in Butcher (1996), the translators' knowledge of the linguistic habits of monolingual indigenous peoples was not mentioned, rendering questionable the degree of success in the production of functional equivalence during the translation phase.

Functional equivalence might also be evaluated after the data have been gathered through an examination of the internal structure of the inventory via factor analysis or principal components analysis. Comparable factor structures or similarity in patterns of correlation between cross-cultural samples suggests similarity in qualitative relationships among concepts. However, because these are the same procedures used to assess conceptual equivalence, they are subject to the same problems noted previously.

Demonstrations of test–retest stability, internal consistency, factorial or profile congruence, and the like cannot, in principle, attest to the validity in one cultural context of an instrument developed in another. The most scrupulous efforts at translation will not ensure that a given test item will occupy a comparable position within the semantic space of the target language as it enjoys within the language of its origin. Moreover, the fixed item pool of the MMPI–2 may prove a significant obstacle in accessing relevant and representative features of psychopathology in indigenous groups. For example, in a Hopi translation of the NIMH-sponsored Diagnostic Interview Scale (DIS), Manson, Shore, and Bloom (1985) found that an item containing the concepts of guilt, shame, and sinfulness could not be clearly translated without creating three separate questions because each of the terms of the item was found to have a distinctive meaning. Similarly, in the development of a depression scale for Vietnamese clients, Kinzie et al. (1982) found that shame and dishonor rather than guilt formed the core features of depression as experienced by the Vietnamese.

PROGRESS AND DIRECTIONS FOR THE FUTURE

Since the substantial reviews of Greene, (1987), Greene (1991), and Zalewski and Greene (1996), studies in this area continue to be typified by comparisons of one sample identified by its ethnic characteristic (e.g., Hispanic abusive and neglectful parents) with a sample of their nonethnic (i.e., Euro-American) counterparts. A large collection of such studies—published and unpublished—involving U.S. Latinos has recently become available (Velasquez, Ayala, & Mendoza, 1998). Unfortunately, the great majority of such studies have neither incorporated the methodologic refinements identified by Greene (1987) nor the rigor of the requirements outlined by Lonner (1979). As a result, the attribution of group differences to the effects of ethnicity, when such differences are found, remains hazardous.

A recent meta-analysis of comparisons involving African-American males, African-American females, and Latino-American males with their Euro-American counterparts provides a degree of reassurance that scores on the standard validity and clinical scales of the MMPI/MMPI–2 do not systematically disadvantage these groups (Hall, Bansal, & Lopez, 1999). This review covered 31 years, a wide variety of populations (normal college, normal noncollege, psychiatric, forensic, pain, substance abusing, etc.), and 50 reports covering 8,633 subjects, of whom about 65% were Euro-American comparison subjects. Inclusion criteria were relatively loose. Although some consistencies in score differences were found, such as lower scores on Maculinity–Femininity (*Mf*) for Latino males, for none of the variables examined (e.g., ethnicity, sociodemographic factors, research setting, or MMPI vs. MMPI–2) did effect sizes attain or exceed a medium level ($d = .60$). In none were score differences such as would meet a level of clinical significance defined by five *T*-score points. These findings are consistent with those reported by Waller et al. (1998) for unidimensional factor scales, discussed earlier in this chapter. However, these findings are not sufficient to render the issues raised by functional and conceptual equivalence of no concern. As mentioned earlier, the lack of detected differences could easily result from both the lack of representativeness (i.e., similarity may be an artifact resulting from the measurement of overlapping symptoms between the cultures) and the fact that interpretation of symptoms is, in important respects, a culture-driven affair.

Although the outlook for use of the MMPI/MMPI–2 with ethnic groups within the United States appears favorable from the standpoint of measurement bias, the answers to questions regarding the validity of the instrument in such groups remain shrouded in a vast darkness. It has been less than a decade since the publication of the MMPI–2. In the years preceding its release, the dominant code-type approach to clinical interpretation had become established on the basis of empirical correlates of profile patterns referenced to the original MMPI normative sample. At this point, the extent to which the code-type correlates developed within the MMPI environment can be applied to corresponding MMPI–2 code patterns remains uncertain. For most profile patterns, there is no reason to expect large shifts in the suitability of interpretive implications on the basis of the newer norms. Indeed, it appears likely that for some code types (e.g., Psychopathic Deviate/Schizophrenia [Pd-Sc/Sc-Pd]), the older correlates may apply even more reliably. For some code types, however, the MMPI correlates will probably not achieve satisfactory transition to the MMPI–2 environment.

When it is realized that no large-scale studies of MMPI–2 code-type correlates have yet reached publication (although one such study is to be released shortly; Graham, Ben-Porath, & McNulty, 1999), the application of the standard interpretive principles and materials to the test results of ethnic minorities is seen to rest on validity inferences that are at a substantial remove from the actual data supporting them. To be sure, the inclusion of African, Latino, Asian, and Native Americans in the MMPI–2 restandardization sample renders the new norms better suited to U.S. demographic patterns in the 1990s. However, their modest representation in this sample is insufficient to guarantee freedom from ethnic biases, particularly among persons without competence in English.

Hence, there is a continuing, if not urgent, need for MMPI–2 studies that focus on the relationships among item responses, scale scores, profile patterns, and external criteria among both Euro-American and ethnic minority subjects. There is also a need for studies of differences between Euro-American and ethnic minority subjects on such criteria. In the latter regard, the results of the few studies that have been completed are encouraging. For example, in a sample of community mental health center clients, McNulty, Graham, Ben-Porath, and Stein (1997) found that observed differences in the MMPI–2 scores of African Americans and Euro-Americans and therapist ratings were more parsimoniously attributed to genuine differences in the severity of rated symptoms than to the effects of ethnicity. In another study, Arbisi, Ben-Porath, and McNulty (1998) failed to find differences between African-American and Euro-American

VA inpatients in the ability of MMPI–2 scale scores to predict to a variety of extratest criteria gathered from a medical record review form. They found, for example, that *Hs* predicted chronic medical stress and *D* predicted a diagnosis of depression equally well for both groups.

Another pressing need in cross-cultural assessment with the MMPI–2 is for research addressing the vulnerability of supplemental, content, and subscales to ethnic differences. Pending the satisfactory demonstration that interpretive guidelines based on standard validity and clinical scales and their code types are valid for African, Asian, Latino, and Native Americans, interpretive strategies that are based on the relatively unidimensional content and subscales are likely to find greater accord with the minority respondent's own views of the symptoms and problems that bring him or her into contact with the assessment clinician.

A final pressing need is research addressed to the application of the *K* correction. As matters stand currently, the justification for the routine adjustment of scores on five of the eight basic clinical scales using fractions of *K* among Euro-Americans remains controversial. The routine use of the *K* correction among ethnic minorities and in cross-cultural investigations rests on little more than faith. This is not to criticize the *K* correction as such, as its elimination from the MMPI–2 would sever important connections between the MMPI–2 and the literature on profile patterns that has taken decades to accumulate. However, this literature has been overwhelmingly developed on Euro-American samples. The lack of sufficient research documenting the correlates of profile patterns among ethnic minority individuals renders the current code-type literature tenuously applicable to them. Therefore, investigators engaged in cross-cultural research need not and should not feel beholden to the tradition of *K* correction; to do so is to beg precisely those questions about the use of *K* that are most in need of answers. If past research is any guide, future research is likely to show that the *K* correction will attenuate predictor-criterion relationships for most external criteria while possibly strengthening them for a few. However, it is important to know which are which.

There is little doubt that the use of the MMPI–2 among non-Euro-Americans will continue and continue to increase. Among countries of the third world, given the availability of adequate translations and sufficient data to establish the validity of traditional and indigenous constructs and empirical correlates, we see no compelling reasons to deny the MMPI–2 a foundational role in the construction of psychopathological systems. Any empirically based local system is likely to be preferable to any Euro-American import such as the *DSM–IV*. However, the adequacy of the MMPI–2 to this task must be demonstrated—it cannot be assumed.

The current fixed-item pool is one obstacle to progress in the cross-cultural use of the MMPI–2. However, given the current lag in the production of data to establish the empirical correlates of MMPI–2 scales, scores, and profile patterns, even among Euro-Americans, this obstacle is a minor one. Until such data become available, MMPI–2 clinicians serving non-Euro-American patients, whether such patients are within or outside the United States, will be plying a difficult and risky trade in rather dim light. To abandon the MMPI–2 in such contexts is to settle for reduced illumination and increased hazard. Increased illumination will require hard work and there is much of it to do.

REFERENCES

American Psychiatric Association. (1994). *Diagnostic and statistical manual of mental disorders* (4th ed.) Washington, DC: Author.

Arbisi, P. A., Ben-Porath, Y. S., & McNulty, J. L. (1998, August). *The impact of ethnicity on the MMPI–2 in inpatient psychiatric settings.* Paper presented at the annual meeting of the American Psychological Association, San Francisco.

Ben-Porath, Y. S., Hostetler, K., Butcher, J. N., & Graham, J. R. (1989). New subscales for the MMPI–2: Social introversion (*Si*) scale. *Psychological Assessment, 1,* 169–174.

Ben-Porath, Y. S., & Sherwood, N. E. (1993). *The MMPI–2 content component scales* (MMPI–2/MMPI–A Test reports No. 1). Minneapolis: University of Minnesota Press.

Butcher, J. N. (1996). Translation and adaptation of the MMPI–2 for international use. In J. N. Butcher (Ed.), *International adaptations of the MMPI–2* (pp. 3–46). Minneapolis: University of Minnesota Press.

Butcher, J. N., Dahlstrom, W. G., Graham, J. R., Tellegen, A., & Kaemmer, B. (1989). *MMPI–2: Manual for adminstration and scoring.* Minneapolis: University of Minnesota Press.

Campbell, D. T., & Fiske, D. W. (1959). Convergent and discriminant validity by the multitrait-multimethod matrix. *Psychological Bulletin, 56,* 81–105.

Canul, G. D., & Cross, H. J. (1994). The influence of acculturation and racial identity attitudes on Mexican-Americans' MMPI–2 performance. *Journal of Clinical Psychology, 50,* 736–745.

Cheung, F. M. (1996). The assessment of psychopathology in Chinese disorders. In M. H. Bond (Ed.), *The handbook of Chinese psychology* (pp. 393–411). Hong Kong: Oxford University Press.

Cheung, F. M., Leung, K., Fan, R. M., Song, W. Z., & Xie, D. (1996). Development of the Chinese Personality Inventory. *Journal of Cross-Cultural Psychology, 27,* 181–199.

Cheung, F. M., & Leung, K. (1998). Indigenous personality measures. *Journal of Cross-Cultural Psychology, 29,* 233–248.

Cronbach, L. J., & Meehl, P. E. (1955). Construct validity in psychological tests. *Psychological Bulletin, 52,* 281–302.

Dana, R. H. (1993). *Multicultural assessment perspectives for professional psychology.* Needham Heights: Allyn & Bacon.

Dana, R. H. (1996). Culturally competent assessment practice in the United States. *Journal of Personality Assessment, 66,* 472–487.

Dana, R. H. (1997). Multicultural assessment and cultural identity: An assessment-intervention model. *World Psychology, 3,* 121–141.

Diaz-Guerrero, R. (1994). *Psychology of the Mexican: Discovery of ethnopsychology.* Mexico: Trillas.

Durie, M. H. (1994). Maori psychiatric admissions: Patterns, explanations and policy implications. In J. Spicer, A. Trlin, & J. A. Walton (Eds.), *Social dimensions of health and disease: New Zealand perspectives* (pp. 194–203). Palmerson North, New Zealand: Dunmore.

Everett, J. E., & Entrekin, L. V. (1980). Factor comparability and the advantages of multiple group factor analysis. *Multivariate Behavioral Research, 15,* 165–180.

Fantoni-Salvador, P., & Rogers, R. (1997). Spanish versions of the MMPI-2 and PAI: An investigation of concurrent validity with Hispanic patients. *Assessment, 4,* 29–39.

Geertz, C. (1988). *Works and lives: The anthropologist as author.* Stanford, CA: Stanford University Press.

Gomez-Maqueo, E. L., & Reyes-Lagunes, I. (1994). New version of the Minnesota Multiphasic Personality Inventory MMPI-2 for Mexican college students. *Revista Mexicana de Psicologia, 11,* 45–54.

Graham, J. R., Ben-Porath, Y. S., & McNulty, J. L. (1999). *Using the MMPI-2 in outpatient mental health settings.* Minneapolis: University of Minnesota Press.

Greene, R. L. (1987). Ethnicity and MMPI performance: A review. *Journal of Consulting and Clinical Psychology, 55,* 497–512.

Greene, R. L. (1991). *The MMPI-2/MMPI: An interpretive manual.* Boston: Allyn & Bacon.

Gulerce, A. (1990). Public awareness, perceived seriousness, and conceptual definition of psychological maladjustment in Turkey. In N. Bleichrondt & P. J. Drenth (Eds.), *Contemporary issues in cross-cultural psychology* (pp. 285–296). Amsterdam: Swets and Zeitlinger B. V.

Gulerce, A. (1992). *Family structure assessment device: The manual and Turkish norms.* Istambul: Alphagraphics.

Gynther, M. D., Fowler, R. D., & Erdberg, P. (1971). False positives galore: The application of standard MMPI criteria to a rural, isolated, Negro sample. *Journal of Clinical Psychology, 27,* 234–237.

Haberman, P. W. (1976). Ethnic differences in psychiatric symptoms among Puerto Ricans in Puerto Rico and New York City. *Ethnicity, 3,* 133–144.

Hall, G. C. N., Bansal, A., & Lopez, I. R. (1999). Ethnicity and psychopathology: A meta-analytic review of 31 years of comparative MMPI/MMPI-2 research. *Psychological Assessment, 11,* 186–197.

Harris, R. E., & Lingoes, J. C. (1968). *Subscales for the MMPI: An aid to profile interpretation.* Mimeographed materials, Department of Psychiatry, University of California at San Francisco.

Joerekog, K. G. (1971). Simultaneous factor analysis in several populations. *Psychometrika, 36,* 409–426.

Kinzie, J. D., Manson, S. M., Vinh, D. T., Tolan, N. T., Anh, B., & Pho, T. N. (1982). Development and validation of Vietnamese language depression rating scale. *American Journal of Psychiatry, 139,* 1276–1281.

Kleinman, A. (1988). *Rethinking psychiatry: From cultural category to personal experience.* New York: The Free Press.

Ko, Y. H. (1977). *Ko's Mental Health Questionnaire manual.* Taipei: Chinese Behavioral Science Press.

Ko, Y. H. (1981). *Ko's Mental Health Questionnaire: Revised manual.* Taipei: Chinese Behavioral Science Press.

Krause, N., & Carr, L. G. (1978). The effects of response bias in the survey assessment of the mental health of Puerto Rican migrants. *Social Psychiatry, 13,* 167–173.

Landrine, H. (1992). Clinical implications of cultural differences: The referential versus the indexical self. *Clinical Psychology Review, 12,* 401–415.

Lawson-Te Aho, K. (1993). The socially constructed nature of psychology and the abnormalization of Maori. *New Zealand Psychological Society Bulletin, 76,* 25–30.

Lonner, W. J. (1979). Issues in cross-cultural psychology. In A. J. Marsella, R. Tharp, & T. Cibarowski (Eds.), *Perspectives on cross-cultural psychology* (pp. 17–45). New York: Academic Press.

MacAndrew, C. (1965). The differentiation of male alcoholic outpatients from nonalcoholic psychiatric outpatients by means of the MMPI. *Quarterly Journal of Studies on Alcohol, 26,* 238–246.

Manson, S., Shore, J. H., & Bloom, J. D. (1985). The depressive experience in American Indian communities: A challenge for psychiatric theory and diagnosis. In A. Kleinman & B. Good (Eds.), *Culture and depression* (pp. 331–368). Berkeley: University of California Press.

Markus, H. R., & Kitayama, S. (1998). The cultural psychology of personality. *Journal of Cross-Cultural Psychology, 29,* 63–87.

McNulty, J. L., Graham, J. R., Ben-Porath, Y. S., & Stein, L. A. R. (1997). Comparative validity of MMPI–2 scores of African Americans and Caucasian mental health center clients. *Psychological Assessment, 9,* 464–470.

Misra, G. (1994). Psychology of control: Cross-cultural considerations. *Journal of Indian Psychology, 12,* 8–48.

Montgomery, G. T., Arnold, B. R., & Orozco, S. (1990). MMPI supplemental scale performance of Mexican-Americans and level of acculturation. *Journal of Personality Assessment, 54,* 328–342.

Moreland, K. L. (1996). Persistent issues in multicultural assessment of social and emotional functioning. In L. A. Suzuki, P. J. Meller, & J. G. Ponterotto (Eds.), *Handbook of multicultural assessment: Clinical, psychological, and educational applications* (pp. 51–76). San Francisco: Jossey-Bass.

Parker, I., & Shotter, J. (1990). *Deconstructing social psychology.* London: Routledge.

Rosen, A. (1966, September). *MMPI responses of deaf college preparatory students.* Paper presented at the annual meeting of the American Psychological Association, New York.

Rosenfield, I. (1986). Neural Darwinism: A new approach to memory and perception. *New York Review of Books, 33*(15), 21–27.

Sarbin, T. R. (1986). *Narrative psychology: The storied nature of human conduct.* New York: Praeger.

Tellegen, A. (1982). *A brief manual for the Differential Personality Questionnaire.* Minneapolis: University of Minnesota Press.

Tucker, L. R. (1951). *A method for synthesis of factory analysis studies* (Personal Research Section Report No. 984). Washington, DC: Department of the Army.

Velasquez, R. J., Ayala, G. X., & Mendoza, S. A. (1998). *Psychodiagnostic assessment of U.S. Latinos with the MMPI, MMPI–2, and MMPI–A: A comprehensive resource manual.* East Lansing: Michigan State University, Julian Samora Research Institute.

Vernon, S. W., & Roberts, R. E. (1982). Use of the SADS-RDC in a tri-ethnic community survey. *Archives of General Psychiatry, 39,* 47–52.

Waller, N. G., Thompson, J., & Wenk, E. (1998). *Black–White differences on the MMPI: Using IRT to separate measurement bias from true group differences on homogeneous and heterogeneous scales.* Unpublished manuscript.

Weed, N. C., Butcher, J. N., McKenna, T., & Ben-Porath, Y. S. (1992). New measures for assessing alcohol and drug abuse with the MMPI–2: The *APS* and *AAS. Journal of Personality Assessment, 58,* 389–404.

World Health Organization. (1973). *The international pilot study of schizophrenia.* Geneva: Author.

World Health Organization. (1979). *Schizophrenia: An international follow-up study.* Chichester: Wiley.

Zalewski, C., & Greene, R. L. (1996). Multicultural usage of the MMPI–2. In L. A. Suzuki, P. J. Meller, & J. G. Ponterotto (Eds.), *Handbook of multicultural assessment: Clinical, psychological, and educational applications* (pp. 77–114). San Francisco: Jossey-Bass.

Zayas, L. H., & Solari, F. (1994). Early childhood socialization in Hispanic families: Context, culture, and practice implications. *Professional Psychology: Research and Practice, 25,* 200–206.

12

Are There Promising MMPI Substitutes for Assessing Psychopathology and Personality? Review and Prospect

Ronald R. Holden
Queen's University at Kingston

The assessment of individual differences in personality and psychopathology has a long and noble history. Psychological testing putatively has its roots in Ancient China (Dubois, 1970; Jackson & Paunonen, 1980; Wiggins, 1973). However, the modern practice of psychometrics and psychological testing is often traced to the anthropometric laboratory of Sir Francis Galton in the 1880s, which emphasized the careful measurement of numerous physical and behavioral characteristics (Holden, in press). Perhaps the first published paper-and-pencil measure designed to assess psychopathology was the symptom list of Heymans and Wiersma (1906). Subsequently, published inventories emerged where items were scored on scales, beginning with Woodworth's (1917) Personal Data Sheet. The following 23 years then saw the development of numerous psychological tests that assessed various domains of individual differences (Goldberg, 1971). Then, in 1940, Hathaway and McKinley published the Minnesota Multiphasic Personality Inventory (MMPI). The MMPI rapidly gained ascendence over other psychological tests. In fact, the MMPI (or its descendant, the MMPI–2) has been the predominantly used structured test of adult personality or psychopathology (Piotrowski & Keller, 1984, 1989; Piotrowski & Lubin, 1990) for most of the last 60 years.

HISTORY OF THE MMPI

The development of the MMPI (Hathaway & McKinley, 1940) represented a milestone in the modern assessment of personality and psychopathology. One part of the MMPI's success has come from its scope. The rationale for the MMPI's construction was to produce a new personality inventory that would be particularly relevant for medical and psychiatric settings. Consequently, an emphasis was placed on formulating an instrument that (a) spanned a wide variety of psychiatrically relevant behavior, (b) involved relatively simple wording and response requirements, and (c) provided a large pool of items from which a relatively large number of personality descriptions might be garnered.

Items for this new inventory were derived from a variety of sources: clinical experience, psychiatric textbooks, medical and neurological case-taking directions, psychiatric examination forms, and other personality and social attitude inventories. From an initial pool of over 1,000 items, expert editorial review and revision reduced this number down to 504 items. Generally, these items sampled from the following 25 groupings:

1. General Health	14. Sexual Attitudes
2. General Neurologic	15. Religious Attitudes
3. Cranial Nerves	16. Political Attitudes—Law and
4. Motility and Coordination	Order
5. Sensibility	17. Social Attitudes
6. Vasomotor, Trophic,	18. Affect, Depressive
Speech, Secretory	19. Affect, Manic
7. Cardiorespiratory	20. Obsessive–Compulsive
8. Gastrointestinal	21. Delusions, Hallucinations,
9. Genitourinary	Illusions, Ideas of Reference
10. Habits	22. Phobias
11. Family and Marital	23. Sadistic, Masochistic
12. Occupational	24. Morale
13. Educational	25. Lie

This version of the MMPI items was then originally administered as a pack of cards that respondents then sorted into categories of *true*, *false*, and *cannot say*. Over the years, the MMPI has evolved into a different response format involving question booklets and answer sheets. Short forms of the inventory, supplementary scales and norms, and computerized scoring systems for the MMPI have also been developed and used.

Another reason for the MMPI's success came from its empirical focus. Whereas many inventories predating the MMPI were based on rational test-construction strategies, development of normative data and scales for the MMPI was based on the responses of Minnesota normals and how MMPI item responses differentiated between this normative group and appropriate clinical criterion groups (Graham, 1977). The normative group comprised University of Minnesota Hospital patients' family members and friends, students seeking guidance from the University of Minnesota Testing Bureau, local Work Progress Administration workers, and nonpsychiatric patients (almost exclusively White Americans) at the University of Minnesota Hospitals. Clinical criterion groups were composed of psychiatric patients at the University of Minnesota Hospitals and included diagnostic subgroups representing: hypochondriasis, depression, hysteria, psychopathic deviate, paranoia, psychasthenia, schizophrenia, and hypomania. Scale derivation and item keying were implemented using an empirical method of scale construction whereby items became scored on a particular scale based on the items' abilities to differentiate between the normal group and the relevant clinical subgroup (Greene, 1991). This produced eight clinical scales corresponding to the aforementioned clinical subgroups. Subsequently, two additional clinical scales— Masculinity–Femininity and Social Introversion—were added. The end result was a 566-item inventory whose standard profile included 10 clinical and 4 validity scales.

REVISION OF THE MMPI: THE MMPI–2

In 1989, a revision to the MMPI, the MMPI–2 (Hathaway & McKinley, 1989), was published. This revision was motivated by concerns about the representativeness of the original standardization sample of the general population in the late 1930s, historical changes in the nature of the American citizenry over 50 years, outdated and objectionable item content, sexist language, problematic reading level, poor grammar and punctuation, and inadequate content validity (Graham, 1990). In emending the MMPI, changes were made both to the general item set and to specific items. Initial revisions produced an experimental form (Form AX) that, relative to the MMPI, involved the deletion of the 16 repeated items; the rewriting of 82 items regarded as either sexist, outdated, grammatically unclear, or overly complex; and the addition of 154 new items focusing on substance abuse, suicide, eating disorders, Type A behavior, family functioning, job attitudes, and amenability to treatment.

Form AX (704 items) of the MMPI was subsequently normed on a final sample of 2,600 Americans between the ages of 18 and 90 (Hathaway & McKinley, 1989). To ensure the representativeness of this sample, special care was taken to include couples (married or cohabiting for at least a year), Native Americans, and military personnel (Graham, 1990). In general, this restandardization sample appears more similar to the U.S. population than did the original MMPI's normative group; however, discrepancies still exist. For example, relative to the 1980 U.S. Census, the restandardization sample has an underrepresentation of Hispanic and Asian Americans. Further, postcollege-educated persons and upper socioeconomic groups are overrepresented, and there is an underrepresentation of individuals with only high school education or less.

The 567-item MMPI–2 currently in use evolved from the 704 items on Form AX of the MMPI. This development involved striking a balance among the deletion of objectionable item content, a desire for continuity of the old MMPI's standard validity and clinical scales, the inclusion of items to be scored on new scales that were judged to be important, and statistical considerations. The move from the MMPI to the MMPI–2 required deleting 106 items (16 repeated items, 13 items scored on the standard validity and clinical scales, and 77 other items) and adding 107 items (89 items scored on new content scales and 18 other items). In addition to the 14 basic validity and clinical scales associated with the basic scale profile scored on the MMPI, the MMPI–2 now contains further validity scales and an additional 15 content scales: Anxiety, Fears, Obsessiveness, Depression, Health Concerns, Bizarre Mentation, Anger, Cynicism, Antisocial Practices, Type A, Low Self-Esteem, Social Discomfort, Family Problems, Work Interference, and Negative Treatment Indicators.

PSYCHOMETRIC PROPERTIES OF THE MMPI–2

Psychometrically, the MMPI–2 possesses both assets and limitations. The manual (Hathaway & McKinley, 1989) reports internal consistency reliabilities ranging from .34 to .87 for the basic scales and from .68 to .86 for the content scales. One-week test–retest reliabilities vary between .67 and .92 and between .78 and .91 for the basic and content scales, respectively. For validity, much of the assertion of the MMPI–2's validity rests on the generalizability of validity research done on the original MMPI (Greene & Clopton, 1994). However, the MMPI–2 manual provides new data on significant correlations between MMPI–2 scales and relevant scales from other inventories. Further, other validity data (e.g., Ben-Porath, Butcher, & Graham, 1991) are also steadily accumulating. Normative data for the MMPI–2 are extensive, and norms for different populations are emerging on a regular basis. Somewhat distressing are the magnitudes of the MMPI–2 scale intercorrelations (some above .80; Hathaway & McKinley, 1989). These can lead to a questioning of the differential interpretation of different MMPI–2 scales.

NOTABLE FEATURES OF THE MMPI–2

The MMPI–2 has a number of functional characteristics that can make the instrument appealing to a variety of assessment professionals. In particular, the following practical features are to be noted:

1. The MMPI–2 assesses the broad domain of psychological maladjustment.
2. The MMPI–2 has a variety of checks designed to ascertain the validity of an individual's test responses.
3. The inventory may be used with both clinical and nonclinical populations.
4. The MMPI–2 is appropriate for respondents who are at least 18 years old (an adolescent version of the MMPI–2, the MMPI–A, is also available).
5. The MMPI–2 is a self-report.
6. Only an eighth-grade reading level is required to complete the MMPI–2.
7. The inventory takes approximately 90 minutes to complete.
8. Nonclinicians may administer and score the MMPI–2.
9. The MMPI–2 is amenable to group testing.
10. Computerized scoring and interpretation of the MMPI–2 are available.
11. The MMPI–2 is available in a variety of languages.

STRENGTHS AND WEAKNESSES OF THE MMPI–2

Many of the practical features of the MMPI–2 and its forerunner, the MMPI, have served to produce an instrument with widespread, international popularity. Some have gone so far as to say that, "the sun never sets on the MMPI," implying that at any time of the day, somewhere, someone is completing the inventory. In contrast to this dedicated following, however, others (e.g., Helmes & Reddon, 1993) have bemoaned the imperial nature of the MMPI empire. Certainly both the proponents and detractors of the MMPI and MMPI–2 have bases to their relative positions.

Particular strengths for the MMPI–2 include its rich history, popularity, clinical usefulness, and psychometric diversity. First, the staggering wealth of information that has been accumulated concerning the MMPI–2 and its predecessor must be regarded as an asset. Normative data are available for many different populations, supplementary scales have been developed to assess a variety of psychological factors or identify various psychological subtypes, and previously established MMPI code types may be considered for use with the MMPI–2. Notwithstanding issues concerning the appropriateness of this reference material, the plethora of archival data is especially appealing because it can make MMPI–2 interpretation appear to be relatively simple and straightforward. Second, the popularity of the MMPI has led to the development of a number of practically attractive variations and services. This has resulted in a measure that is easily used and readily amenable to many different testing contexts. The MMPI–2 has been translated into numerous languages; is available in different booklet, audiocassette, and computer-administered (e.g., Brunetti, Schlottmann, Scott, & Hollrah, 1998) forms; has a variety of response sheets available for different methods of scoring; may be hand or computer scored; and has many computerized interpretation services available. Third, the MMPI–2 may be used in conjunction with assorted clinical activities. For example, the MMPI–2 can offer important information to researchers and clinicians involved in planning treatment and evaluating treatment outcome and client change (Butcher, 1990; Greene & Clopton, 1994). MMPI–2 scales are also related to *DSM–IV* (American Psychiatric Association, 1994) clinical diagnoses (e.g., Castlebury, Hilsenroth, Handler, & Durham, 1997). Fourth, the number and nature of the MMPI–2's items provide a wealth of psychometric diversity that make the inventory an itemmetrician's paradise. For example, MMPI–2 items range in length from 3 to 32 words, vary in terms of direction of keying and the presence of negations, have a large range of social desirability values, and differ markedly in terms of subtlety. Any researcher in test development would clearly find the size and variability of the MMPI–2's item pool and associated databases to lend themselves readily to investigation.

Despite these strengths, the MMPI–2 also possesses a number of weaknesses that are regarded by many as being serious shortcomings. First, MMPI–2 item keying is largely empirically based, rather than explicitly derived from theory. An implicit theory did underlie the initial selection of particular criterion groups in the original MMPI, however. This implicit theory was based on conceptualizations of psychopathology that may no longer be relevant in current theories (Helmes & Reddon, 1993). Thus, the MMPI–2's clinical domain is entrenched in implicit views of maladjustment from the 1930s. Consequently, there may be merit to the argument that theories of psychopathology have advanced since those times and that the MMPI–2 is now theoretically outdated. Second, modern practice in test construction would not follow the largely empirical strategy taken by the developers of the MMPI. Current methods would likely place considerable emphasis on theoretical definitions, convergent and discriminant validity, response style suppression, cross-validation, and the use of large, representative samples. Further, more recent multivariate techniques implemented through modern computing capabilities would be used to assist in dealing with these concerns. Methods of scale construction have made substantial progress in the last six decades. Third, concerns exist about the stability of the MMPI–2's empirically based keying that was derived from extremely small and dated samples of questionable representativeness. For example, the 48 items scored on the *Pt* (Psychasthenia) scale were selected using a criterion group from the 1940s that comprised only 20 psychasthenia Minnesota hospital inpatients, some of whom appear to have been misdiagnosed (Greene, 1991; McKinley & Hathaway, 1942). Even if the same empirical approach to item selection originally used was to be employed again today, would the same items end up being keyed on a *Pt* scale if a large sample of similarly diagnosed psychasthenic patients of various nationalities comprising different sociodemographic and ethnic backgrounds was used as the criterion group? Fourth, considerable item overlap exists among the standard MMPI–2 clinical scales—a structural problem that compromises the discriminant validity of the scales. Consider that 20 of 32 items on the *Hs* scale are also scored on the *Hy* scale. With such a degree of item redundancy, is it legitimate to interpret *Hs* as distinct from *Hy* or is the former merely a subset or facet of the latter? Fifth, depending on the assessment context, some of the MMPI–2 items may still include potentially objectionable or legally prohibited content. For example, items pertaining to sexual orientation may present a legal difficulty if the MMPI–2 was to be used in an employment hiring situation. In a similar context, the religious content of some items may also be objectionable. In addition to these major concerns, a number of other more minor criticisms of the MMPI–2 and its predecessor have also been offered (see Faschingbauer, 1979; Helmes & Reddon, 1993).

Despite the criticisms of the MMPI–2, the inventory appears to be doing something right. Although conceptualizations of psychopathology have progressed, strategies of test construction have evolved, society has changed since the 1930s, redundancy in the test has been recognized, and legal limitations to the test's uses have developed, the MMPI–2 endures. Is this merely inertia on the part of test users or do the instrument's strengths outweigh its weaknesses? The answer to that question inevitably depends on the particular focus that a practitioner or researcher has in undertaking the assessment of personality or psychopathology. For some circumstances, the MMPI–2 may continue to play an important, relevant role; for other contexts, alternatives to the MMPI–2 may prove to be more psychometrically valid and may demonstrate greater practical utility.

METHODOLOGICAL ADVANCEMENTS IN TEST CONSTRUCTION SINCE THE ORIGINAL MMPI

Clinically, psychometrically, and practically, the conceptualization and development of the MMPI in the 1930s and 1940s by Hathaway and McKinley must be hailed as a landmark accomplishment for its time.

Although other instruments for clinical assessment did exist prior to this time, the MMPI's creation served to firmly establish a particular strategy of test development, the empirical strategy, and its associated reliance on statistical methodology for the selection of items to be scored on particular scales of personality and psychopathology. Other philosophies of test development (e.g., projective, rational) did have their origins earlier in time, but were now being challenged on theoretical and evidential grounds (e.g., Ellis, 1946). Although the empirical approach to test construction did predate the MMPI (Jackson & Paunonen, 1980), Hathaway and McKinley's bold contribution was to implement this empirical approach to derive a self-report inventory of multiple clinical scales. Indeed, this was a marvelous accomplishment for the time.

Nevertheless, the science of the assessment of personality and psychopathology has not stalled since Hathaway and McKinley's pioneering undertaking. Theoretically, the emergence of the construct approach to test construction in the 1950s (Cronbach & Meehl, 1955) and the initial formulation of methods for evaluating convergent and discriminant validity (Campbell & Fiske, 1959) resulted in an enormous influence on both test theory and test construction. In this particular approach, the roles of theory and theoretical definitions of underlying scale dimensions are paramount. Tests are to be tools of psychological theory (Loevinger, 1957) and will be valid "to the extent and only to the extent, that they are derived from an explicitly formulated, theoretically based definition of a trait" (Jackson, 1971, p. 232). In espousing the basic principles for this construct strategy of personality scale development, Jackson (1970) stressed (a) the need for psychological theory, (b) the importance of response style suppression, (c) the merits of scale homogeneity and generalizability, and (d) the benefits of an ongoing concern for convergent and discriminant validity. Practical guidelines for implementing this construct approach to test construction have subsequently been published in a variety of sources (e.g., DeVellis, 1991; Kline, 1986; Rust & Golombok, 1989; Spector, 1992; Streiner & Norman, 1995), and inventories constructed according to this approach have come into widespread use (e.g., the Personality Research Form; Jackson, 1984). Further, the importance of construct validity is explicitly acknowledged and endorsed in the *Standards for Educational and Psychological Testing* put forth by the American Educational Research Association, the American Psychological Association, and the National Council on Measurement in Education (1985). Although some debate concerning the relative merits of various approaches to personality inventory construction exists (Burisch, 1984), research does now seem to indicate that the empirical strategy, as associated with the MMPI, is a suboptimal method of test development (Broughton, 1984; Jackson, 1975). Indeed, construct definition and direct item-construct links are important precursors to validity (Holden, 1989; Holden & Fekken, 1990; Holden & Jackson, 1979, 1985).

Technically, advances in test construction have been driven both by progress in psychometric theory and by a remarkable growth in computing capabilities. Scale development has graduated from simple item selection techniques based on the ability of an item to discriminate between members and nonmembers of a relevant criterion group. More sophisticated multivariate techniques have now come to be routinely included into the development of newer measures (e.g., the NEO Personality Inventory; Costa & McCrae, 1992). Latent variable techniques that encompass both exploratory (e.g., Waring, Holden, & Wesley, 1998) and confirmatory (e.g., Walker, Smith, Garber, & Van Slyke, 1997) factor analytic methods can now be readily incorporated into scale development. Thus, with the common availability of computing power that is capable of processing data for large numbers of test items and virtually infinite numbers of test respondents, psychometric analyses that were logistically impossible in the 1930s are now performed in seconds on desktop machines.

PROMISING GENERAL ALTERNATIVES TO THE MMPI–2: DESCRIPTIONS, ASSETS, AND LIMITATIONS

In considering various alternatives to the MMPI–2 that exist, presentation is restricted to self-report—structured measures that assess multiple constructs and are primarily developed for use with adults. Also, a distinction is drawn between those instruments that are directed toward the assessment of psychopathology and those that focus on the measurement of nonpathological personality. Further, the focus is on the standard version of the instrument that is being discussed. Summaries of some of the major features of each of the discussed inventories are presented in Tables 12.1 and 12.2.

THE ASSESSMENT OF PSYCHOPATHOLOGY

The Personality Assessment Inventory

The Personality Assessment Inventory (PAI; Morey, 1991) is a 344-item, multiscale inventory composed of 22 scales that are relevant for clinical assessment. Responses to each item are made on a four-alternative scale. Clinical scales include Somatic Complaints, Anxiety, Anxiety-Related Dis-

TABLE 12.1
Comparative Features of the MMPI-2 and Other Multiscale Inventories of Psychopathology

Feature	MMPI-2	PAI	MCMI	BPI	BSI	HPSI
Number of items	567	344	175	240	53	36
Completion time	90 minutes	50 minutes	25 minutes	30 minutes	8 minutes	5 minutes
Specific appropriate group	No	No	Patients	No	No	No
Appropriate minimum age of respondents	18 years	18 years	18 years	12 years	13 years	14 years
Minimum required reading level	Grade 8	Grade 4	Grade 8	Grade 7	Grade 6	Grade 7
Scale to detect invalid responding	Yes	Yes	Yes	Yes	No	Yes
Scale intercorrelations	Not minimized	Minimized	Not minimized	Minimized	Not minimized	Minimized
Non-English versions available	Yes	Yes	Yes	Yes	Yes	Yes

TABLE 12.2
Comparative Features of Multiscale Inventories of Personality

Feature	NEO–PI–R	CPI	16PF	PRF	MPQ
Number of items	240	462	185	352	300
Completion time	35 minutes	60 minutes	35 minutes	45 minutes	35 minutes
Specific appropriate group	No	No	No	No	No
Appropriate minimum age of respondents	17 years	12 years	16 years	13 years	18 years
Minimum required reading level	Grade 6	Grade 4	Grade 5	Grade 7	Grade 12
Scale to detect invalid responding	No	Yes	Yes	Yes	Yes
Scale intercorrelations	Minimized	Not minimized	Minimized	Minimized	Minimized
Non-English versions available	Yes	Yes	Yes	Yes	Yes

277

orders, Depression, Mania, Paranoia, Schizophrenia, Borderline Features, Antisocial Features, Alcohol Problems, and Drug Problems. There are also five treatment scales (Aggression, Suicidal Ideation, Stress, Nonsupport, and Treatment Rejection), two interpersonal scales (Dominance and Warmth), and four validity scales (Inconsistency, Infrequency, Negative Impression, and Positive Impression). The PAI is appropriate for individuals ages 18 to adulthood, requires a Grade 4 reading level, has a completion time of approximately 50 minutes, is commercially published in both English and Spanish, and has been translated into a number of other languages.

Strengths of the PAI include its strong psychometric background (Morey & Henry, 1994). In particular, construction of the inventory emphasized the use of rigorous quantitative methods applied to item selection procedures. The end result is impressive. For clinical scales, both internal consistency reliabilities and 3- to 4-week test–retest stabilities average above .80. In terms of validity, the PAI scales demonstrate appropriate patterns of convergent and discriminant validity with other multiscale inventories such as the MMPI–2 and the NEO–PI–R. Norms are available for various populations including general adults, clinical patients, and university students (Morey, 1991). One potentially limiting feature of the PAI is its 50-minute administration length. Nevertheless, as a relatively new inventory whose full clinical and research applications remain to be entirely delineated, the PAI is a promising instrument.

The Millon Clinical Multiaxial Inventory–III

Millon's (1994) Clinical Multiaxial Inventory–III (MCMI–III) is a self-report inventory focusing on the assessment of personality disorders associated with *DSM–IV* and on the measurement of various clinical syndromes related to Millon's theory of personality. Commercially, the MCMI–III is available in English and Spanish. The inventory consists of 175 true–false items, requires approximately 25 minutes to complete, and is appropriate for adults ages 18 years or older with at least a Grade 8 reading ability. Personality disorders are evaluated with Schizoid, Avoidant, Depressive, Dependent, Histrionic, Narcissistic, Antisocial, Aggressive (Sadistic), Compulsive, Passive–Aggressive, Self-Defeating, Schizotypal, Borderline, and Paranoid scales. More extreme clinical conditions are assessed with Anxiety Disorder, Somatoform Disorder, Bipolar: Manic Disorder, Dysthymic Disorder, Alcohol Dependence, Drug Dependence, Posttraumatic Stress Disorder, Thought Disorder, Major Depression, and Delusional Disorder scales. The determination of the validity of a MCMI–III profile is assisted through the presence of four scales: Disclosure, Desirability, Debasement, and Validity.

The MCMI–III has a number of particularly appealing strengths. It is closely aligned with *DSM–IV*, particularly Axis II disorders. This contributes to the instrument's effectiveness for assisting clinicians in providing differential diagnoses of patients. Further, because the focus is on Axis II of *DSM–IV*, the MCMI–III may be regarded as a complement rather than a competitor to other measures that focus on Axis I (Groth-Marnat, 1997). In addition, the MCMI–III is linked closely to Millon's theory of personality. Consequently, elevated scale scores may have rich interpretations that emerge from Millon's theory of personality. Psychometrically, the inventory demonstrates some strong features. Scale internal consistency reliabilities typically exceed .80 and 1- to 2-week test–retest stabilities average about .90. For validity, MCMI–III scales demonstrate appropriate convergence with other tests of corresponding constructs (Millon, 1994). Notwithstanding the assets associated with this inventory, some limitations are to be noted. Although the MCMI–III may be useful for assessing *DSM–IV* Axis I and Axis II disorders, as stated, the focus is on Axis II. Further, the target group for the inventory is a clinical population; the instrument is not designed for nonclinical populations. Psychometrically, the MCMI–III still manifests at least one basic problem with its scales— item overlap. A consequence of this is that MCMI–III scales correlate rather substantially, some in excess of .80 (Millon, 1994), thus attenuating the discriminant validity and differential interpretation of these scales. Overall, however, the MCMI–III is an exciting new instrument that is establishing itself as a valuable clinical and research tool for use with clinical patients.

The Basic Personality Inventory

The Basic Personality Inventory (BPI; Jackson, 1997a) is a multiscale inventory of psychological maladjustment and personal strengths. The inventory consists of 240 true–false items, is appropriate for adolescents and adults, requires a Grade 7 reading level, and can be completed in approximately 35 minutes. The BPI's 12 scales include Hypochondriasis, Depression, Denial (a scale to detect invalid responding), Interpersonal Problems, Alienation, Persecutory Ideas, Anxiety, Thinking Disorder, Impulse Expression, Social Introversion, Self-Depreciation, and Deviation. BPI test booklets are published in English, Spanish, or French, and the test has been translated into other languages.

The BPI incorporates more recent principles of test development (Jackson, 1970, 1971) and modern multivariate techniques into the construction of psychometrically strong and relatively independent scales that measure the factors underlying the MMPI and MMPI–2. Psychometrically, the BPI appears strong (Jackson et al., 1989). Median scale internal consistency reliability is approximately .72, and 1-month test–retest reliabilities average approximately .77. The BPI's item factor structure is well established across general adult, psychiatric, and high school populations. BPI scales show appropriate patterns of convergent and discriminant validity in terms of correlations with scales of other inventories and with criterion ratings provided by clinicians. The test manual presents normative data for general adults, adolescents, college students, and psychiatric patients. Offsetting the positive features of the BPI is the lack of an extensive data and literature base for the inventory. In particular, the availability of more clinical data with links to diagnostic categories would be an asset for this measure. Thus, the BPI represents a psychometrically sound instrument with the potential to make an important contribution to the measurement of the components of psychological adjustment in both clinical and nonclinical populations.

The Brief Symptom Inventory

The Brief Symptom Inventory (BSI; Derogatis, 1993) is a 53-item, self-report instrument constructed to assess the psychological symptom patterns of adolescent and adult respondents. Items are responded to on 5-point scales and focus on the amount of distress caused by particular symptoms in the past 7 days. The inventory is commercially available in both English and Spanish and has been translated into other languages. Completion of the BSI requires between 8 and 10 minutes. The nine primary symptom dimensions scored on the BSI are Somatization, Obsessive–Compulsive, Interpersonal Sensitivity, Depression, Anxiety, Hostility, Phobic Anxiety, Paranoid Ideation, and Psychoticism. In addition, three global indexes are also produced: Global Severity Index, Positive Symptom Total, and Positive Symptom Distress Index.

The BSI possesses a variety of appealing features. In particular, it is brief and focuses on clinically relevant constructs. Further, the BSI is amenable to repeated administration to individuals, and the inventory's scales are sensitive to clinical change. Derived as a short form of the SCL–90–R (Derogatis, 1977), the BSI has a large supporting database. Large sample normative data are available for adult nonpatients, adult psychiatric outpatients, adult psychiatric inpatients, and adolescent nonpatients. Psychometrically (Derogatis, 1993), the BSI possesses strong internal consistency reliability with alpha coefficients ranging between .71 and .85. Test–retest stabilities are reported to vary between .68 and .91 for a 2-week interval. For validity, BSI scales demonstrate significant convergent validities with scales from the MMPI. Some limitations to the BSI are to be noted. The BSI does not possess an index to detect invalid responding. Thus, careless or faked test protocols may be problematic for the inventory. Further, the differential validity of BSI scales has been raised as an issue. In particular, the BSI's item factor structure does not strongly support the inventory's scoring key, and the magnitude of scale intercorrelations suggests that the BSI scales lack discriminant validity (Boulet & Boss, 1991; Piersma, Boes, & Reaume, 1994). Overall, the BSI represents one of the most widely used multiscale, brief screening measures of psychopathology.

The Holden Psychological Screening Inventory

The Holden Psychological Screening Inventory (HPSI; Holden, 1996) is a 36-item, self-report inventory designed to assess the higher order dimensions of the domain of psychopathology as traditionally defined by the MMPI–2 and the BPI. The HPSI requires approximately 5 minutes to complete, is appropriate for both clinical and nonclinical respondents, may be administered to individuals over 14 years of age, and is amenable to multiple testings where there is a desire to evaluate change. HPSI scales include Psychiatric Symptomatology, Social Symptomatology, and Depression.

Assets of the HPSI include its brevity and psychometric strengths (Holden, 1996). For internal consistency reliability, the median scale coefficient alpha is approximately .74. Four-week test–retest stability coefficients vary between .83 and .88. The item factor structure of the scale matches closely the instrument's scoring key. For validity, scale scores show convergent associations with peer and clinical evaluations and with scores on relevant scales from other inventories. Additionally, the HPSI is designed to be capable of indicating treatment effects, and the inventory has been shown to be sensitive in the detection of clinical change in patients. Limitations to the HPSI include its lack of normative data for various populations, and the lack of an extensive literature base for the instrument. Nevertheless, the HPSI represents a new inventory whose scope and application are promising, but not yet fully delineated.

Others

Although not multidimensional in nature, there are many individual scale instruments that are particularly noteworthy for the domain of psychopathology. Based on popularity in research and practice, and/or on strong psychometric properties (Butcher, Fekken, & Taylor, 1998; Maruish, 1994; Piotrowski & Keller, 1984, 1989), these include the Beck Depression Inventory (BDI; Beck, 1978; Beck & Steer, 1993), the Beck Hopelessness Scale

(BHS; Beck, Weissman, Lester, & Trexler, 1974), the State–Trait Anxiety Inventory (STAI; Spielberger, Gorsuch, & Lushene, 1970), and the State–Trait Anger Expression Inventory (STAXI; Spielberger, 1988). All of these instruments represent popular, strong measures that have a more specific focus of assessment than that provided for by the multiphasic inventories.

THE ASSESSMENT OF PERSONALITY

The Revised NEO Personality Inventory

The Revised NEO Personality Inventory (NEO–PI–R; Costa & McCrae, 1992) is a measure consisting of 240 self-report items that focus on the assessment of the dimensions associated with the five-factor model of personality (Digman, 1990). Domain scales include Neuroticism, Extraversion, Openness, Agreeableness, and Conscientiousness. Completion of the NEO–PI–R requires between 30 and 40 minutes. Versions of the inventory are available commercially in English and Spanish, and the instrument has also been translated into a considerable number of other languages. The instrument is appropriate for individuals 17 years of age or older and requires a minimum of a Grade 6 reading ability. A short-form version of the inventory, the NEO–FFI, includes 60 items and requires between 10 and 15 minutes for completion.

The NEO–PI–R and its associated measures (i.e., the NEO–PI, NEO–FFI) have become an ever increasingly popular set of instruments. Underlying this popularity are the combination of the NEO–PI–R's strong psychometric properties and the decades of data that, through factor analyses, have repeatedly yielded the five factors corresponding to the NEO–PI–R's scales. The manual for the inventory supplies normative data for American adults and for a mix of American and Canadian college students. For reliability, domain scale alpha coefficients range between .86 and .92. For test–retest reliability, domain scale stabilities exceed .78, .67, and .62 for retest intervals of 3 months, 3 years, and 7 years, respectively. Structurally, the NEO–PI–R is extremely strong, demonstrating impressive congruences between its item factor structure and the instrument's scoring key. For the validity of the domain scales, correlations all exceed .35 and .33 with corresponding ratings by peers and spouses, respectively. Further, scales demonstrate appropriate patterns of convergent and discriminant validity with scales from other personality inventories. One of the primary shortcomings of the NEO inventories has been their lack of an appropriate index to indicate invalid responding (Ben-Porath & Waller, 1992). For example, faking is a potential problem that is not monitored by the NEO–PI–R. Despite this limitation, however, the NEO–PI–R represents a strong and increasingly popular general inventory of personality.

The California Psychological Inventory

The California Psychological Inventory (CPI; Gough, 1987) consists of 462 true–false items appropriate for individuals between the ages of 12 and 70. A minimum of a Grade 4 reading ability is required to complete the measure, and completion time is approximately 60 minutes. Commercially, the CPI is available in numerous languages. The 20 basic scales of the CPI are Dominance, Capacity for Status, Sociability, Social Presence, Self-Acceptance, Independence, Empathy, Responsibility, Socialization, Self-Control, Good Impression, Communality, Well-Being, Tolerance, Achievement via Conformance, Achievement via Independence, Intellectual Efficiency, Psychological-Mindedness, Flexibility, and Femininity/Masculinity. Three structural scales (i.e., Internality, Norm-Favoring, and Self-Realization) are also routinely scored. However, it should be noted that the emphasis of the CPI is not on the measurement of traits, but on the prediction of behavior.

Part of the CPI's attractiveness is its focus on common personality variables that are relevant across different cultures. Scales are described as *folk concepts*, are intended to have considerable power for predicting behavior, and their names are meant to be easily understood in various cultures. Thus, the instrument strives to be practical, relevant, understandable, and behaviorally predictive. Extensive normative data for the CPI are provided in the manual (Gough, 1987). For reliability, basic and structural scale coefficients alpha vary between .52 and .85 (median of .70). One-year test–retest stabilities range between .43 and .79 (median of .68). In terms of validity, CPI basic and structural scales demonstrate appropriate convergence with corresponding scales from other inventories. Further, a variety of equations using CPI scale scores have been shown to be valid for predicting various behavioral outcomes and performance measures. Detractors of the CPI point to a number of limitations for the inventory. For example, with considerable item overlap, scales tend to correlate substantially (e.g., .81 for scales of Achievement via Independence and Intellectual Efficiency based on 1,000 females; Gough, 1987), calling into question the differential interpretation of the scales or even the need to have separate scales. Further, the validity of the CPI variables or equations for predicting outcomes or performances is generally modest, indicating merit for group but not individual prediction (Domino, 1984). Nevertheless, the CPI represents a popular inventory for assessing the everyday, interpersonal nature of people in general.

The Sixteen Personality Factor Questionnaire

The fifth edition of the Sixteen Personality Factor Questionnaire (16PF; Cattell, Cattell, & Cattell, 1993) is composed of 185 questions using a three-choice response format, requires a Grade 5 reading ability, and takes between 35 and 50 minutes to complete. The test is most appropriate for persons 16 years of age and older and is commercially available in dozens of different languages. Although historically the 16PF basic scales have been labeled with letters, common language names for the scales are: Warmth, Reasoning, Emotional Stability, Dominance, Liveliness, Rule-Consciousness, Social Boldness, Sensitivity, Vigilance, Abstractedness, Privateness, Apprehension, Openness to Change, Self-Reliance, Perfectionism, and Tension. Five higher order factor scales include Extraversion, Anxiety, Tough-Mindedness, Independence, and Self-Control. In addition, three validity scales, Impression Management, Infrequency, and Acquiescence, are present on the inventory.

The 16PF emerged as Raymond B. Cattell's general-purpose measure of the source traits of personality. Development of the fifth edition of the 16PF involved extensive, large sample, factor, and item analytic procedures to select and revise the best items from previous forms of the inventory. The 16PF has a large literature base, and its impressive psychometric properties are provided in two manuals (Conn & Rieke, 1994; Russell & Karol, 1994). The primary normative data are for general U.S. adults. For the 16 scales, the mean coefficient alpha reliability is .74, the mean 2-week test–retest reliability is .80, and the average 2-month test–retest reliability is .70. For validity, 16PF scales demonstrate appropriate correlations with similar scales from other inventories. Practically, the 16PF's major uses have been in career guidance, vocational exploration, and occupational testing. Some limitations with the 16PF pertain to the recency of its revision and the lack of a database that is specific to the new edition. The addition of normative data for populations other than general U.S. adults and the provision of additional validity information would clearly be welcomed. In general, however, the revised 16PF has the potential to be an important tool for the field of personality assessment.

The Personality Research Form

The Personality Research Form (PRF; Jackson, 1984) (Form E) is a 352-item, 22-scale inventory focusing on the assessment of dimensions associated with Murray's (1938) framework for the description of personality. Scales include Abasement, Achievement, Affiliation, Aggression, Autonomy, Change, Cognitive Structure, Defendence, Dominance, Endurance, Exhibition, Harmavoidance, Impulsivity, Nurturance, Order, Play, Sentience,

Social Recognition, Succorance, Understanding, Infrequency, and Desirability. Completion of the PRF requires a Grade 7 reading level, and it takes approximately 45 minutes to complete. The PRF is available commercially in English, Spanish, and French, and has also been translated into various other languages.

The PRF is a model of the application of an extremely rigorous, sequential procedure to the development of a general personality measure. The result is a psychometrically superior inventory that has a large literature and a substantial database. The test manual (Jackson, 1984) provides normative data for adults, college students, school children and adolescents, juvenile offenders, psychiatric patients, military personnel, and a variety of other particular groups. The reported median internal consistency reliability for content scales exceeds .70. For validity, content scales on average correlate .52 with ratings provided by significant others. Further, content scales demonstrate appropriate patterns of both convergent and discriminant validity in their associations with scales from other major inventories. Somewhat disappointing is that, although the PRF professes to be developed out of the personality theory of Henry Murray, the interpretation of individual respondents' PRF scale scores is not closely tied to this theory. Overall, however, the PRF stands as an exemplar of the end result associated with sophisticated methods of test construction.

The Multidimensional Personality Questionnaire

Formerly known as the Differential Personality Questionnaire, the Multidimensional Personality Questionnaire (MPQ; Tellegen, 1982) consists of 300 items each with two response options. Eleven content scales (Well-Being, Social Potency, Achievement, Social Closeness, Stress Reaction, Alienation, Aggression, Control, Harm Avoidance, Traditionalism, and Absorption) and six validity scales may be scored for the inventory. Although not explicitly stated, the MPQ will take an estimated 35 minutes to complete and requires a Grade 12 reading level.

The MPQ represents an exploratory approach to test construction whose development iteratively involved theory and data analysis. The resulting product is a psychometrically strong questionnaire. The preliminary manual for the MPQ (Tellegen, 1982) provides normative data, but primarily for college students. For the 11 content scales, Tellegen and Waller (in press) reported a median internal consistency reliability of .85, a median 1-month test–retest stability of .85, and a median validity of .49 based on using relevant ratings by significant others as criteria. Content scales also demonstrate appropriate convergence with similar scales from other inventories (e.g., DiLalla, Gottesman, Carey, & Vogler, 1993). Two particular limitations to the MPQ are to be noted, however. First, extensive normative data for the measure are not readily available. Second, neither the instrument nor a full manual is yet commercially published. Nevertheless, despite these shortcomings, the impressive psychometric characteristics, to date, of the MPQ make it a viable, alternative personality questionnaire.

Others

Many other multiscale inventories of nonpathological adult personality exist. Either because of past or current popularity, or due to psychometric merit (Butcher, Fekken, & Taylor, 1998; Maruish, 1994; Piotrowski & Keller, 1984, 1989), test users may also wish to consider the following inventories: the Adjective Check List (Gough & Heilbrun, 1983), the Eysenck Personality Questionnaire (Eysenck & Eysenck, 1975), the Jackson Personality Inventory–Revised (Jackson, 1997b), the Myers–Briggs Type Indicator (Myers, 1977), and the Profile of Mood States (McNair, Lorr, & Droppleman, 1971).

ISSUES IN SELECTING AN INVENTORY

Given that a researcher or clinician has decided to undertake some form of assessment, these issues should be considered: (a) the question that is intended to be answered by the assessment, (b) the individuals or groups who are to be assessed, (c) the target group to whom the results of the assessment are directed, and (d) the consequences associated with having undertaken the assessment (Acklin, 1995). At a more specific level, the choice of a particular, structured, self-report measure can be guided by considering overlapping theoretical, psychometric, cultural, practical, and clinical questions:

   1. Theoretically, what is the domain and extent of the domain to be assessed? Is the focus on the normal range of personality or is the measurement of psychopathology important? Does the assessment focus on one or multiple dimensions of individual differences? Do the scales on a particular inventory match closely with the assessor's definitions of the constructs of interest?

   2. At a psychometric level, is the inventory appropriate? Do the inventory's scales have strong internal consistency reliability? If appropriate, do they have adequate test–retest reliability? Does the instrument's item factor structure confirm the inventory's scoring key? Do the scales show validity in terms of predicting appropriate external criteria (e.g., peer ratings, clinician ratings)? Do the scales demonstrate convergent and

discriminant validity with similar scales from other inventories? If desired, is the inventory capable of indicating change? Does the inventory have an adequate amount of relevant normative data?

3. Culturally, is it appropriate to use a particular inventory in the proposed cultural context? Is the domain of interest (e.g., psychopathology) relevant for the particular culture? Do the dimensions of interest exist within that culture? Do the inventory's definitions of these dimensions generalize from its culture of origin to the culture of the participants being assessed? How relevant is the inventory's existing database (e.g., norms) and literature base for that culture? Would the use of an inventory represent an inappropriate imposed etic approach, where use of an emic test (Dana, 1995) would be more meaningful?

4. Practically, what constraints exist for the assessment? How much time is available for respondents to complete the assessment? Less than 15 minutes? More than an hour? Is the inventory's required reading level appropriate for the respondents? What language is required for the assessment material? Is there a concern that some respondents may not be responding in a valid fashion?

5. Are there clinical requirements for the assessment? If so, should the inventory be linked to a diagnostic categorization (e.g., *DSM–IV*)? Is it desirable to use an inventory that can indicate specific treatment interventions? Is it important to use a measure that can monitor clinical change on an ongoing basis?

Consideration of these issues can assist the user in deciding among the many inventories that may be selected. Furthermore, an examination of features listed in Tables 12.1 and 12.2 may also provide a starting point from which to choose an appropriate instrument. At least two cautions, however, warrant comment.

First, the list of inventories discussed in this chapter is by no means exhaustive. It represents a sampling of structured, self-report, multiscale inventories that have been developed for the assessment of personality and psychopathology in English-speaking adults. Unstructured (e.g., projective), nonself-report, single-dimension, or non-English-developed measures have not been included in this review. In many circumstances, such other instruments can merit serious consideration. Also not included in this chapter are domains outside of personality and psychopathology (e.g., cognitive ability, vocational interest, etc.). Measures of other domains can also be relevant foci for the psychological inquiry of individual differences.

Second, an acceptable inventory or scale may not be readily available. Perhaps existing inventories are inappropriate for the cultural context of the assessment. For example, the imposed etic approach (Dana, 1988) of taking an American, English-language inventory, translating it, and administering it to non-American or non-English speaking individuals can result in grossly misleading or uninterpretable results (Brislin, 1986). Alternatively, perhaps an existing, psychometrically strong inventory of appropriate constructs does exist for a particular population (e.g., non-clinical adults), but is inappropriate for the target group (e.g., psychiatric patients) of interest. The use of the inventory with a population for which it was not developed can be completely inappropriate, and any data generated may have the danger of being misinterpreted when they should be regarded as meaningless. Yet another possibility is that no one has currently developed an inventory or scale to assess the construct(s) of interest. Under this or any of the other circumstances, where no strongly acceptable instrument already exists, the use of an existing inventory simply because it is already available is not necessarily advisable and may be highly improper. In such circumstances, it may be more appropriate to develop a new scale or set of scales that are designed for the particular construct(s) and assessment situation of interest. Recommended resources for those wishing to undertake their own scale construction include texts by DeVellis (1991), Kline (1986), Rust and Golombok (1989), Spector (1992), and Streiner and Norman (1995).

COMMENT

On May 6, 1954, Roger Bannister set a new standard of excellence. His breaking of the 4-minute barrier for the mile run was an incredible feat. Over the last 45 years, however, this standard has been bettered numerous times and the current world record is some 15 seconds faster. The science of track and field has evolved to the point where Bannister's standard can now routinely be surpassed. Nevertheless, even today, the running of a 4-minute mile represents a noteworthy feat, and the name and accomplishment of Sir Roger Bannister still rightfully evoke a great amount of respect and admiration.

Sixty years ago, with the MMPI, Starke R. Hathaway and J. Charnley McKinley set a new standard of excellence in psychological testing. At the time, the development and publication of the MMPI was a momentous event. However, like track and field, psychometrics and the science and practice of test construction have also evolved over the decades. Consequently, it is possible to do better than the MMPI or its revision, the MMPI–2. There are particular scales or inventories that, for particular purposes, can readily outperform the MMPI–2. As this chapter attests, promising alternatives to the MMPI–2 exist and are available. This is not to dismiss the relevance or validity of the MMPI–2 in particular circumstances. The MMPI, the MMPI–2, and their authors still warrant considerable regard, appreciation, and gratitude. The MMPI–2 does endure as a standard to be reckoned with. Test users will wisely continue to consider the MMPI–2 when selecting among the meritorious, alternative inventories or assessment options to be used for the measurement of psychopathology and personality.

REFERENCES

Acklin, M. W. (1995). How to select personality tests for a test battery. In J. N. Butcher (Ed.), *Clinical personality assessment: Practical approaches* (pp. 19–27). New York: Oxford University Press.

American Educational Research Association, American Psychological Association, & National Council on Measurement in Education. (1985). *Standards for educational and psychological testing.* Washington, DC: American Psychological Association.

American Psychiatric Association. (1994). *Diagnostic and statistical manual of mental disorders* (4th ed.). Washington, DC: Author.

Beck, A. T. (1978). *BDI.* San Antonio, TX: Psychological Corporation.

Beck, A. T., & Steer, R. A. (1993). *Beck Depression Inventory manual.* San Antonio, TX: Psychological Corporation.

Beck, A. T., Weissman, A., Lester, D., & Trexler, L. (1974). The measurement of pessimism: The Hopelessness Scale. *Journal of Consulting and Clinical Psychology, 42,* 861–865.

Ben-Porath, Y. S., Butcher, J. N., & Graham, J. R. (1991). Contribution of the MMPI–2 content scales to the differential diagnosis of schizophrenia and major depression. *Psychological Assessment, 3,* 634–640.

Ben-Porath, Y. S., & Waller, N. G. (1992). "Normal" personality inventories in clinical assessment: General requirements and the potential for using the NEO Personality Inventory. *Psychological Assessment, 4,* 14–19.

Boulet, J., & Boss, M. W. (1991). Reliability and validity of the Brief Symptom Inventory. *Psychological Assessment, 3,* 433–437.

Brislin, R. W. (1986). The wording and translation of research instruments. In W. J. Lonner & J. W. Berry (Eds.), *Field methods in cross-cultural research* (pp. 137–164). Beverly Hills, CA: Sage.

Broughton, R. (1984). A prototype strategy for construction of personality scales. *Journal of Personality and Social Psychology, 47,* 1334–1346.

Brunetti, D. G., Schlottmann, R. S., Scott, A. B., & Hollrah, J. L. (1998). Instructed faking and MMPI–2 response latencies: The potential for assessing response validity. *Journal of Clinical Psychology, 54,* 143–153.

Burisch, M. (1984). Approaches to personality inventory construction: A comparison of merits. *American Psychologist, 39,* 214–227.

Butcher, J. N. (1990). *MMPI–2 in psychological treatment.* New York: Oxford University Press.

Butcher, J. N., Fekken, G. C., & Taylor, J. (1998). Objective personality assessment with adults. In C. R. Reynolds (Ed.), *Comprehensive clinical psychology: Vol. 4. Assessment* (pp. 403–429). Oxford, England: American Book Co.

Campbell, D. T., & Fiske, D. W. (1959). Convergent and discriminant validation by the multitrait–multimethod matrix. *Psychological Bulletin, 56,* 81–105.

Castlebury, F. D., Hilsenroth, M. J., Handler, L., & Durham, T. W. (1997). Use of the MMPI–2 personality disorder scales in the assessment of *DSM–IV* antisocial, borderline, and narcissistic personality disorders. *Assessment, 4,* 155–168.

Cattell, R. B., Cattell, A. K. S., & Cattell, H. E. P. (1993). *Sixteen Personality Factor Questionnaire* (5th ed.). Champaign, IL: Institute for Personality and Ability Testing.

Conn, S. R., & Rieke, M. L. (1994). *The 16PF fifth edition technical manual.* Champaign, IL: Institute for Personality and Ability Testing.

Costa, P. T., Jr., & McCrae, R. R. (1992). *Revised NEO Personality Inventory (NEO PI–R) and NEO Five–Factor Inventory (NEO–FFI) professional manual.* Odessa, FL: Psychological Assessment Resources.

Cronbach, L. J., & Meehl, P. E. (1955). Construct validity in psychological tests. *Psychological Bulletin, 52,* 281–302.

Dana, R. H. (1988). Culturally diverse groups and MMPI interpretation. *Professional Psychology: Research and Practice, 19,* 490–495.

Dana, R. H. (1995). Culturally competent MMPI assessment of Hispanic populations. *Hispanic Journal of Behavioral Sciences, 17,* 305–319.

Derogatis, L. R. (1977). *SCL–90–R: Administration, scoring and procedures manual for the revised version.* Baltimore: Clinical Psychometric Research.

Derogatis, L. R. (1993). *Brief Symptom Inventory (BSI): Administration, scoring, and procedures manual.* Minneapolis, MN: National Computer Systems.

DeVellis, R. F. (1991). *Scale development: Theory and applications.* Newbury Park, CA: Sage.

Digman, J. M. (1990). Personality structure: Emergence of the five-factor model. *Annual Review of Psychology, 41,* 417–440.

DiLalla, D. L., Gottesman, I. I., Carey, G., & Vogler, G. P. (1993). Joint factor structure of the Multidimensional Personality Questionnaire and the MMPI in a psychiatric and high-risk sample. *Psychological Assessment, 5,* 207–215.

Domino, G. (1984). California Psychological Inventory. In D. J. Keyser & R. C. Sweetland (Eds.), *Test critiques* (Vol. I, pp. 146–157). Kansas City, MO: Test Corporation of America.

Dubois, P. H. (1970). *A history of psychological testing.* Boston: Allyn & Bacon.

Ellis, A. (1946). The validity of personality questionnaires. *Psychological Bulletin, 43,* 385–440.

Eysenck, H. J., & Eysenck, S. B. G. (1975). *Manual: Eysenck Personality Questionnaire.* San Diego: Educational and Industrial Testing Service.

Faschingbauer, T. R. (1979). The future of the MMPI. In C. S. Newmark (Ed.), *MMPI clinical and research trends* (pp. 373–398). New York: Praeger.

Goldberg, L. R. (1971). A historical survey of personality scales and inventories. In P. McReynolds (Ed.), *Advances in psychological assessment* (Vol. 2, pp. 293–336). Palo Alto, CA: Science and Behavior Books.

Gough, H. G. (1987). *California Psychological Inventory: Administrator's guide.* Palo Alto, CA: Consulting Psychologists Press.

Gough, H. G., & Heilbrun, A. B. (1983). *The Adjective Check List manual: 1983 edition.* Palo Alto, CA: Consulting Psychologists Press.

Graham, J. R. (1977). *The MMPI: A practical guide.* New York: Oxford University Press.

Graham, J. R. (1990). *MMPI–2: Assessing personality and psychopathology.* New York: Oxford University Press.

Greene, R. L. (1991). *The MMPI–2/MMPI: An interpretive manual.* Boston: Allyn & Bacon.

Greene, R. L., & Clopton, J. R. (1994). Minnesota Multiphasic Personality Inventory–2. In M. E. Maruish (Ed.), *The use of psychological testing for treatment planning and outcome assessment* (pp. 137–159). Hillsdale, NJ: Lawrence Erlbaum Associates.

Groth-Marnat, G. (1997). *Handbook of psychological assessment.* New York: Wiley.

Hathaway, S. R., & McKinley, J. C. (1940). A multiphasic personality schedule (Minnesota): I. Construction of the schedule. *Journal of Psychology, 10,* 249–254.

Hathaway, S. R., & McKinley, J. C. (1989). *Minnesota Multiphasic Personality Inventory–2.* Minneapolis, MN: The University of Minnesota Press.

Helmes, E., & Reddon, J. R. (1993). A perspective on developments in assessing psychopathology: A critical review of the MMPI and MMPI–2. *Psychological Bulletin, 113,* 453–471.

Heymans, G., & Wiersma, E. (1906). Beitrage zur speziellen psychologie auf grund einer massenuntersuchung [Contributions to a special psychology based on large-scale investigation]. *Zeitschrift fur Psychologie, 43,* 81–127, 158–301.

Holden, R. R. (1989). Disguise and the structured self-report assessment of psychopathology: II. A clinical replication. *Journal of Clinical Psychology, 45,* 583–586.

Holden, R. R. (1996). *Holden Psychological Screening Inventory (HPSI).* North Tonawanda, NY: Multi-Health Systems.

Holden, R. R. (in press). Psychometrics. In A. E. Kazdin (Ed.), *Encyclopedia of psychology.* Washington: American Psychological Association.

Holden, R. R., & Fekken, G. C. (1990). Structured psychopathological test item characteristics and validity. *Psychological Assessment, 2,* 35–40.

Holden, R. R., & Jackson, D. N. (1979). Item subtlety and face validity in personality assessment. *Journal of Consulting and Clinical Psychology, 47,* 459–468.

Holden, R. R., & Jackson, D. N. (1985). Disguise and the structured self-report assessment of psychopathology: I. An analogue investigation. *Journal of Consulting and Clinical Psychology, 53,* 211–222.

Jackson, D. N. (1970). A sequential system for personality scale development. In C. D. Spielberger (Ed.), *Current topics in clinical and community psychology* (Vol. 2, pp. 61–96). New York: Academic Press.

Jackson, D. N. (1971). The dynamics of structured personality tests: 1971. *Psychological Review, 78,* 229–248.

Jackson, D. N. (1975). The relative validity of scales prepared by naive item writers and those based on empirical methods of personality scale construction. *Educational and Psychological Measurement, 35,* 361–370.

Jackson, D. N. (1984). *Personality Research Form manual* (3rd ed.). Port Huron, MI: Research Psychologists Press.

Jackson, D. N. (1997a). *The Basic Personality Inventory.* Port Huron, MI: Sigma Assessment Systems.

Jackson, D. N. (1997b). *Jackson Personality Inventory–revised.* Port Huron, MI: Sigma Assessment Systems.

Jackson, D. N., Helmes, E., Hoffmann, H., Holden, R. R., Jaffe, P., Reddon, J. R., & Smiley, W. C. (1989). *Basic Personality Inventory manual.* Port Huron, MI: Sigma Assessment Systems.

Jackson, D. N., & Paunonen, S. V. (1980). Personality structure and assessment. *Annual Review of Psychology, 31,* 503–551.

Kline, P. (1986). *A handbook of test construction: Introduction to psychometric design.* New York: Methuen.

Loevinger, J. (1957). Objective tests as instruments of psychological theory. *Psychological Reports, 3,* 635–694.

Maruish, M. E. (Ed.). (1994). *The use of psychological testing for treatment planning and outcome assessment.* Hillsdale, NJ: Lawrence Erlbaum Associates.

McKinley, J. C., & Hathaway, S. R. (1942). A multiphasic personality schedule (Minnesota): IV. Psychasthenia. *Journal of Applied Psychology, 26,* 614–624.

McNair, D. M., Lorr, M., & Droppleman, L. F. (1971). *Profile of Mood States.* San Diego: Educational and Industrial Testing Service.

Millon, T. (1994). *Manual for the MCMI–III.* Minneapolis: National Computer Systems.

Morey, L. C. (1991). *Personality Assessment Inventory professional manual.* Odessa, FL: Psychological Assessment Resources.

Morey, L. C., & Henry, W. (1994). Personality Assessment Inventory. In M. E. Maruish (Ed.), *The use of psychological testing for treatment planning and outcome assessment* (pp. 185–216). Hillsdale, NJ: Lawrence Erlbaum Associates.

Murray, H. (1938). *Explorations in personality.* Cambridge, MA: Harvard University Press.

Myers, I. B. (1977). *Supplementary manual: The Myers–Briggs Type Indicator.* Palo Alto, CA: Consulting Psychologists Press.

Piersma, H. L., Boes, J. L., & Reaume, W. M. (1994). Unidimensionality of the Brief Symptom Inventory (BSI) in adult and adolescent inpatients. *Journal of Personality Assessment, 63,* 338–344.

Piotrowski, C., & Keller, J. W. (1984). Psychodiagnostic testing in APA-approved clinical psychology programs. *Professional Psychology: Research and Practice, 15,* 450–456.

Piotrowski, C., & Keller, J. W. (1989). Psychological testing in outpatient mental health facilities: A national study. *Professional Psychology: Research and Practice, 20,* 423–425.

Piotrowski, C., & Lubin, B. (1990). Assessment practices of health psychologists: Survey of APA Division 38 clinicians. *Professional Psychology: Research and Practice, 21,* 99–106.

Russell, M., & Karol, D. (1994). *The 16PF fifth edition administrator's manual.* Champaign, IL: Institute for Personality and Ability Testing.

Rust, J., & Golombok, S. (1989). *Modern psychometrics: The science of psychological assessment.* New York: Routledge.

Spector, P. E. (1992). *Summated rating scale construction: An introduction.* Newbury Park, CA: Sage.

Spielberger, C. D. (1988). *Manual for the State-Trait Anger Expression Inventory (STAXI).* Odessa, FL: Psychological Assessment Resources.

Spielberger, C. D., Gorsuch, R. L., & Lushene, R. D. (1970). *STAI: Manual for the State-Trait Anxiety Inventory.* Palo Alto, CA: Consulting Psychologists Press.

Streiner, D. L., & Norman, G. R. (1995). *Health measurement scales: A practical guide to their development and use* (2nd ed.). New York: Oxford University Press.

Tellegen, A. (1982). *Brief manual for the Multidimensional Personality Questionnaire.* Unpublished manuscript.

Tellegen, A., & Waller, N. G. (in press). Exploring personality through test construction: Development of the Multidimensional Personality Questionnaire. In S. R. Briggs & J. M. Cheek (Eds.), *Personality measures: Development and evaluation* (Vol. 1). Greenwich, CT: JAI Press.

Walker, L. S., Smith, C. A., Garber, J., & Van Slyke, D. A. (1997). Development and validation of the Pain Response Inventory for children. *Psychological Assessment, 9,* 392–405.

Waring, E. M., Holden, R. R., & Wesley, S. (1998). Development of the Marital Self-Disclosure Questionnaire (MSDQ). *Journal of Clinical Psychology, 54,* 817–824.

Wiggins, J. S. (1973). *Personality and prediction: Principles of personality assessment.* Reading, MA: Addison-Wesley.

Woodworth, R. S. (1917). *Personal data sheet.* Chicago: Stoetling.

PROJECTIVE METHODS: THE RORSCHACH COMPREHENSIVE SYSTEM AND HOLTZMAN INKBLOT TEST

This part contains five chapters on the use of inkblots as assessment stimuli. Four of these chapters examine the use of the Rorschach Comprehensive System (RCS), and one chapter presents the Holtzman Ink Blot Test (HIT). Beginning with a theoretical framework for cross-cultural/multicultural RCS research and practice (chap. 13), specific research studies from Northern Europe/Africa (chap. 14) and Iberoamerica (chap. 15) are described and interpreted. The process by which national norms were developed in one country, Portugal, is described in chapter 16. The findings presented in chapter 16 augment interpretations of the meaning of RCS cultural differences suggested in chapters 13 and 15. In chapter 16, the HIT provides a sophisticated psychometric alternative to the RCS; it was designed to be used for cross-cultural personality research and assessment.

Chapter 13 presents an etic–emic approach to the RCS that proceeds from general universal categories to distinct and varied cultural thematic expressions of these categories. The question of whether one should begin with a theoretical structure (etic) or with national norms and data sets (emic) to progress toward an integrated etic–emic approach probably cannot be answered definitively at this time. However, there is consensus on the basis of convincing empirical data that the central focus of Rorschach interpretation, introversion–extraversion (Erlebnistypus), is a universal personality construct (see Dana, 1993, for review). The basic structure and dynamics of personality, elaborated by a variety of scores and ratios, derives from this construct. De Vos's etic–emic distinction, the theoretical rationale for this chapter, specifies that the Rorschach measures intrapsychic adjustment (the universal template) as well as acceptable social adaptation (the culture-specific template). Erlebnistypus, in my thinking, refers to the complex interrelationship of cognitive processes and affect—or how the head and heart commingle to spell out the ingredients of a human circumstance. This human condition is always grounded in culture to determine the nature of the complex interface tapped by Erlebnistypus. Culture-specific social rules for living coded into language and represented as learned cognitive structures and acceptable expressions of affect become external information resources required to interpret personality structure and dynamics and to evaluate the presence of psychopathology as well. Thus, the availability of national norms implies a readiness to consider the emic context for expression of basic human personality. Without this context, and by recourse to RCS norms developed in the United States, the Rorschach becomes a pseudoetic used as an etic that can only provide invidious comparisons across cultures. Invidious comparisons serve to reinforce and solidify ethnocentrism, increase intercultural misunderstandings and conflict, and, at an individual level, foster stereotypy, caricature, and dehumanization. This argument for national norms is presented precisely because the research applications for demonstrating cross-cultural construct equivalence are not credible at the present time. In fact, this handbook clearly presents both the limitations of research methodology and the promise of more adequate methodologies. Until and unless cross-cultural construct validation is demonstrated unequivocally, national norms become a constructive alternative that does not interfere with the development of etic–emic approaches for increasing cross-cultural understanding. In fact, there is a complementarity to the simultaneous development of these norms and an overarching theoretical approach.

Chapter 13 continues with an examination of key issues in culturally relevant research and practice. Beginning with a description of the adult, workplace-recruited RCS normative sample, comparisons were made with more limited national samples using the major Erlebnistypus components and other scores. Simplified information processing, more subjective approaches to cognitive mediation, less human movement in interpersonal perception, and less expressed affect were typical of these national samples. This apparent constriction of basic universal human personality using RCS norms from the United States strongly documents the workings of culture on the Erlebnistypus system; it also indicates the invidious interpretive consequences of using pseudoetic norms for cross-cultural comparisons. Moderator variables, particularly socioeconomic status (SES), educational level, and setting, raise the question of potential confounds with a cultural explanation. Similarly, there is an absence of research on the relationship of score differences to external correlates, both in the United States and in these other countries. RCS external validation has included relationships between test and extratest variables and clusters of variables differentiating clinical and normal groups. Comparable external validation studies in other countries have not been reported.

The important issue of describing the normative behavior evoked by the Rorschach can be illuminated by an examination of response sets or response styles. Different cultures have different responses sets/styles that affect the responsivity to psychological tests. Although there is awareness of acquiescence, evasiveness, under or overreporting of symptoms, loss of face, and so on, there has been insufficient empirical research in this area. An interesting alternative explanation for differences in population norms is that Iberoamericans assimilate the Rorschach stimuli to an internal reality by personalizing the stimuli. This approach clearly differs from an accommodation to the perceptual demands of the inkblots favored in the United States. However, because these styles are culturally determined, their existence only strengthens the argument for cultural influence. However, interpretation should acknowledge response sets/styles by familiarity with available literature as well as by describing the functions served by these behaviors within a particular cultural context.

Construct bias can be examined by empirical and rational endeavors using statistical analysis and extratest cultural group knowledge. Illustrative examples in this chapter affirm the necessity for a depth of cultural understanding that is not ordinarily available without sufficient language skill for extensive reading of emic materials. Acquiring cultural information as a supplement to available cross-cultural construct validation research findings is a task of greater magnitude than learning the mechanics of RCS scoring and interpretation (see Dana, 1998b).

A final issue raised in this chapter concerns the secondary RCS focus on psychopathology formulations using personality concepts and indexes (e.g., depression and schizophrenia). Caution in cross-cultural applications of these indexes is required as well as the development of new indexes to examine somatization and other culture-specific idioms of distress, for examples. Culturally competent assessment practices are described including service delivery style, use of client's first language, cultural orientation assessment, multicultural norms, and contextual interpretation. Adopting an MMPI/MMPI-2 practice of using dual profile comparisons of culture-specific norms with national norms for individual assessees is suggested in addition to the development of acculturation status norms. Contextual interpretation requires the understanding and use of other data from the assessee's social environment—an undertaking requiring considerable familiarity with cultural orientation status as well as cultural and social class origins. The chapter concludes with recommendations that future research identify variables of interest to be less global and more specific in focus. Practitioners would also benefit from an RCS casebook containing difficult cross-cultural diagnostic problems. This suggestion provides a major assessment contribution to recent publications of cultural formulations for *DSM–IV* diagnoses derived primarily from interviews.

Chapter 14 begins with an introduction to the history of clinical psychology in Europe, where it was initially accepted as a clinical method that included the Rorschach and other tests. In Scandinavia, the Netherlands, Belgium, and more recently in Spain, this method recognized and incorporated empirical approaches. However, in Southern Europe the orientation has remained primarily psychoanalytic. Beginning in 1971, a Rorschach Comprehensive System (RCS) introduction was focused on training and the collection of normative data. Moreover, the introduction of the RCS in Europe was initially viewed as a "backward move toward technicality, pedestrian measurements, and low-class psychology."

The findings from normative studies conducted in Belgium and Spain are summarized in this chapter. The implications of these findings for research and practice are discussed particularly for the variables Lambda, Experience Actual (EA), Texture (T), Shading (Y), and average proportion of good form (X+%). These findings, which include only protocols with equivalent numbers of responses, depart substantially from normative data developed in the United States. This chapter suggests that the interpretation of some RCS variables may differ as a function of cultural differences. For example, Lambda decreases with level of education or "intellectual sophistication." It was speculated that these Europeans, in fact, may be very sensitive to shading and color but chose not to belabor the obvious and used a pure form approach instead. The author recalls that Hermann Rorschach posited three sensitivity types: kinesthetic, color, and form. Color occurred with lower frequencies in these samples, but when it does appear, CF typically exceeded FC. This reversal of the expected ratio is due to the fact that spontaneous emotional expression is valued in these European cultures and is viewed as evidence of high-level social skills. Shading in the form of T is infrequently present and generally with either zero or one response in a protocol. Europeans may only express a craving for closeness when confronted with frustrated needs for affection. As a consequence, an absence of RCS T does not necessarily indicate an absence of affection in daily living. High Vista (V) may also represent a "sophisticated cognitive aspect in highly educated persons" linked to positive utilization of introspection in daily life.

Form quality appears very responsive to culture and this may merit the development of form-quality tables for each culture/language. However, an alternative suggestion has been historically embedded in F+ (common and superior form) versus F– (inadequate form). European Rorschachers added a third category (F±) for responses lacking specific form, but there was agreement that form tables were necessary for the common response (F+), whereas in the United States, subcategories for form were developed. The RCS shifted progressively from form accuracy (blot shape vs. accurate assessee recognition of blot shape) to a frequency definition of a specific object or word rather than blot shape. The "conventionality" of vocabulary was thus described as dissimilar from the traditional interpretation of X+%, which measures an assessee's discrepancy from "average American language use and reference world." This semantic and linguistic explanation suggested that form-quality levels reflected linguistic and environmental differences rather than differences in reality testing.

Diminished movement and color responses in these samples resulted in a lowered EA and impacted the positive Coping Deficit Index (CDI) and positive Repression Index (DEPI). As a consequence, these indexes were not recommended for use with Europeans. X+% was low and contributed to an increased presence of positive Schizophrenia Indexes (SCZI). An interpretation of the adequacy of reality contact and conventional thought processes using the RCS ordinarily cannot be accomplished in the absence of form-quality tables. The preparation of such tables becomes controversial if the conventional RCS interpretation is not acceptable. Finally, European Popular (P) responses, defined by presence in one of three protocols, were tabularized to suggest universal and culture-specific modes of perceiving reality. Nine RCS Populars, ostensibly universals, are reported to have appeared consistently.

An unpublished study from the 1970s rescoring children's protocols found differences between the RCS records of French and U.S. children that can be explained either as a consequence of cultural differences or sampling bias. French children were found to have lower numbers of movement responses, higher Sum Shading, and differences in content within a context of greater total numbers of responses. However, the responses were characterized by poor form and positive SCZI (i.e., from low X+% and high X–%). Overall, these 250 French children from 6 to 12 years of age remained closer to the natural world, more inhibited in emotional expression, and less self-centered than children in the United States. However, the selection of the French children by unanimous parental consent included the entire sample as contrasted with very selective voluntary parental consent in the United States that included only 20% of the desired sample.

Chapter 15 provides a perspective and panorama on the Iberoamerican RCS research and normative data briefly referred to in the previous chapter. Iberoamerica is described as a clearly distinguishable cultural unit from Anglo countries including the United States. These differences are described as authoritarian, nonegalitarian social interactions, increased anxiety from uncertainty, and stress defended by established rules and rituals within a collectivist orientation. As contact cultures, both physical contact and spontaneous and uninhibited emotional expression are characteristic within a cultural script emphasizing warmth, shared feelings, and respect toward others designed to facilitate harmony.

An RCS history of importation and development within various countries contained similarities in findings from 10 studies of several variables from limited samples. This history provides background that would not ordinarily be available to readers in the United States. It provides evidence for the cultural differences documented in the preceding paragraph and expressed in the style of research presentations that may also be seen in chapters 19 and 23. The RCS variables described by these studies include national differences in numbers of Popular responses as well as fewer Popular responses than in the United States. Similarly, there were systematic differences on almost every other variable. These variables describe good psychological adjustment within their cultural contexts and unstable adjustment that is close to psychopathology when interpreted by U.S. RCS norms. After an intensive examination of these cross-national data, a tentative explanation for the Erlebnistypus differences from U.S. norms is that fewer resources are required by Iberoamericans to cope with the conditions of their lives probably because of collectivist values. Moreover, situation variables such as Shading may impact more directly by association to variables associated with emotional control. An explanation for their near zero Texture scores may be found in the socialization processes of contact cultures, where the early physical contact continues throughout life. Vinet (chap. 15) notes that the interpretive meaning of Texture remains unchanged, although the obtained scores reflect the cultural context.

The RCS originator, John Exner, recognized that perceptual styles are cultural in origin. Thus, the initial visual input and encoding of the inkblot stimulus are culturally determined, and the potential response repertoire is associated with aspects of daily life. Censorship of some responses and selectivity of responses are provided by implicit norms and values. Language and learned ways of expression also contribute to the articulation of responses. The test situation and the participant roles have a specific cultural meaning. In Iberoamerican countries, the Rorschach test situation is both novel, anxiety inducing, and without specific rules. Authority and power are vested in the examiner, often due to social class differences. As a result, respect, obedience, and conformity in the social context of simpatía may be accompanied by uncooperativeness and distrust. Thus, defensiveness, low affective engagement, and high scores on Shading may link passivity and anxiety with a pervasive inability to respond. A more subjective approach to reality coupled with unconventional behaviors is relevant to perceptions of norms and regulations by ingroup members when society represents the outgroup. This interpretation also applies to the frequent finding of few Populars with low X+% and F+% and more Xu% and X–%. The Form-Quality tables in chapter 15 were developed from U.S. samples and may not be universal in application, although a solution by preparation of local Form-Quality tables remains controversial, as suggested in chapter 14. Chapter 15 concludes with a description of future prospects for the RCS in Iberoamerica. National and cross-national normative studies are recommended as well as research on the response process and testing situation. The scoring of Form-Quality and derived indexes, in addition to the preparation of working tables, requires consensus and collaborative investigations. Finally, research specifying the linkage between specific cultural aspects and interpretation is sorely needed and can have important consequences for Iberoamerican populations in the United States.

National norms for the RCS are required to either confirm or deny the concerns presented in chapters 13 and 15 that the Exner norms developed in the United States have severe limitations for personality study in Iberoamerica. Questions of the adequacy of sample sizes and representativeness vie with the rationality of clinical inferences made across Iberoamerican RCS studies. Chapter 16 describes a continuing process of developing national norms for Portugal. This chapter begins by providing a context of the national history and population demographics. Using the 1991 census, gender, age, education, and six geographic regions were used for a sample of 309 persons who were examined by seven examiners in a large number of settings. This population was White only, and samples from the small Black and gypsy populations will be tested at a later date for separate population norms. Scoring reliability was high, and the obtained scores on RCS variables were not normally distributed.

Chapter 16 describes the sample and procedures in detail. The results from the entire sample were tabularized using descriptive statistics for all scores and structural variables. Coping styles (ambitent, introversive, extraversive) were presented as a function of 41 variables with means, standard deviations, and significance levels for each style. Formal education level was examined separately because of the magnitude of change over time in number of years of formal education. Because the mean number of years of education was 4 years less in Portugal than in the United States, three levels of education were used for comparisons. Next, the Portuguese sample was compared with Exner's normative study, which led to conclusions affirming the important role of culture and new questions calling for continued research.

Without attempting to describe these findings in detail, it is apparent that there were extreme differences in the Portuguese normative data from Exner's norms developed in the United States. For example, there were many response locations on the cards that are not found in the United States—a finding that could have been anticipated from the locations reported by Vaz (1997) for Brazil. These locations were initially scored as *Dd* because they were not contained in Exner's tables, and some of these responses may represent *Ds* for Portugal. Similarly, *S* responses were much higher than in the United States. With few exceptions, the reported scores are lower than in the United States, particularly those scores that compose Erlebnistypus. Moreover, when Erlebnistypus is categorized by coping styles of ambitent, introversive, and extratensive, the differences in percentages differ remarkably between Portugal and the United States. One half of the population is ambitent and only 22% is extratensive as opposed to 20% and 44%, respectively, in the United States. Not only do the Erlebnistypus data document Vinet's conclusions in chapter 15, but the coping style data augment the description of cultural differences. The low form quality reported using Exner's tables is further examined by the development of form-quality tables for Portugal—another concern voiced in chapter 15.

In sharp contrast to the RCS chapters in Part IV discussed thus far, the HIT has a long history of cross-cultural construct validation and usefulness in many different countries. However, the HIT has not been widely used for clinical assessment in the United States despite its psychometric sophistication. In nearly 40 years of Rorschach teaching, only one student asked to learn the HIT; years later he admitted to me that this was a mistake. There are some good reasons that low-inference interpretation was eschewed in favor of high-inference Rorschach interpretation in 1961 when the HIT was published and continuing until a training manual was published in 1972. Early generations of clinical psychologists were trained to use high-inference interpretation typically with psychoanalytic theory as an interpretive frame of reference. Furthermore, clinical psychology graduate student selection during this era favored Beta persons who constructed reality in humanistic terms rather than Alphas who preferred scientific terms (Dana, 1998a). It was not until the Boulder training model was firmly established and the learning theory was applied to behavioral explanations, assessment instruments, and interventions that the training model favored students who preferred low-inference interpretation and considered the Rorschach to be unscientific. By this time, it was too late for the HIT to become widely accepted among assessors due to professional prejudice against any inkblot test by growing numbers of behavioral and cognitive psychologists. The massive research effort by Exner, Weiner, and others to document the psychometric respectability of the

Rorschach in the form of the RCS was sufficiently successful to maintain continued clinical usage as an instrument second only in popularity to the MMPI. The RCS has faltered somewhat in cross-cultural and multicultural applications due to psychometric limitations and equivocal status as a pseudoetic instrument, and chapter 17 was included in the handbook for this reason.

The HIT uses 22 variables that cover the important scoring categories, has two parallel forms of 47 chromatic and achromatic inkblots, and requires only one response per inkblot followed by an inquiry. Each response can be scored for all variables, and total scores for each variable are summed across 45 cards. Short forms and a method for group administration are also available. Computerized scoring has been developed. Chapter 17 presents this scoring system, reports reliabilities and validities for differential diagnosis, and examines an extensive cross-cultural literature. Research has focused both on transcultural universals and differences across nations. Differentiation among 16 Latin American countries using multiple discriminant analysis suggested differences in cultural identities described by the HIT variables with only minimal misclassification. An intensive 6-year longitudinal study compared 800 Mexican and American children and was designed to examine cultural differences in coping styles. An interesting contrast in the perception of the test situation in Mexico and the United States adds consistent information from Mexico to the rationale developed in chapter 15.

Chapter 17 is essentially a review of research literature to acquaint readers with an alternative to the RCS for cross-cultural and multicultural clinical assessment. As a low-inference instrument with a cross-cultural research history, fewer scoring variables than the RCS, and a roughly equivalent administration–scoring–interpretation time, the HIT now offers possibilities for clinical applications to multicultural populations in the United States rather than competition with the RCS in other countries. The HIT literature can become an important resource for understanding RCS scores obtained in other countries and reported in this handbook due to the overlap of scores and availability of a large number of HIT data sets. Holtzman (chap. 17) carefully reiterates the psychometric rationale for one response per inkblot to provide an adequate number of responses, as well as the same number of responses for all assessees. There can be a complementarity between the RCS, a clinical assessment instrument applied to individuals, and the HIT—a research instrument providing information on cross-cultural differences and similarities. Greater emic knowledge provided by an improved psychometric instrument, the HIT, can be used to inform RCS use in each of these emic settings. By the same token, both HIT and RCS results from these varied emic settings constitute resources for understanding RCS differences in obtained scores and their interpretation for multicultural groups in the United States, particularly Latinos.

REFERENCES

Dana, R. H. (1993). *Multicultural assessment perspectives for professional psychology*. Boston: Allyn & Bacon.

Dana, R. H. (1998a). *A humanistic science of personality assessment: History, practice, methodology*. Manuscript submitted for publication.

Dana, R. H. (1998b). Personality and the cultural self: Emic and etic contexts as learning resources. In L. Handler & M. Hilsenroth (Eds.), *Teaching and learning personality assessment* (pp. 325–345). Hillsdale, NJ: Lawrence Erlbaum Associates.

Vaz, C. E. (1997). *O Rorschach Teoria e Desemphenho (Terceira edicao revista e ampliada) [Rorschach theory and practice, 3rd ed.]*. Sao Paulo, Brazil: Editora Manole Ltda.

13

Culturally Relevant Research and Practice With the Rorschach Comprehensive System

David Ephraim
Universidad Central de Venezuela

The current popularity of the Rorschach method for personality assessment in the United States has been explained by the extensive use of the Rorschach Comprehensive System (RCS; Exner, 1991, 1993; Exner & Weiner, 1995), which provides more empirical support to interpretation than was available through earlier Rorschach systems (Butcher & Rouse, 1996). Although the RCS is based on empirical and clinical data from a predominantly middle-class Euro-American population, it is being used with individuals who might be significantly different in terms of their culture. On the one hand, the RCS is applied to persons from a variety of ethnocultural groups within the United States and Canada. On the other hand, it has become increasingly popular worldwide, particularly in Europe and South America. This cross-cultural/multicultural expansion requires consideration of the system's validity and usefulness for personality assessment and clinical diagnosis across different nations as well as with culturally different clients, who in addition might live in radically diverse socioeconomic environments within the United States and other multicultural societies.

Research in this area is insufficient. Lindzey (1961) pointed out a number of methodological flaws in the early Rorschach literature on culture and personality. Regarding current RCS cross-cultural research, only a handful of comparative studies, often methodologically limited, have been recently conducted worldwide. As to the multicultural personality assessment field in the United States, it has been described as "pervaded by more opinion and fewer data than most" (Moreland, 1996, p. 52). Despite these gaps in research, significant advances could be made by attending to helpful words from pioneers in Rorschach cross-cultural research as well as from reflecting on tentative findings reported by the international comparative studies based on the RCS. Also, conceptual and methodological concerns in cross-cultural psychology could clarify the issues involved when using the Rorschach across cultures. Finally, current multicultural awareness in the field of psychological assessment provides a new set of concepts and practical concerns with competence and fairness that need to be addressed.

Drawing on the previously mentioned diverse sources, the main purpose of this chapter is to provide a preliminary framework for the cross-cultural/multicultural use of contemporary Rorschach approaches, particularly the RCS, in basic research and clinical practice. To this end, the chapter reviews the following subjects: (a) pertinent methodological and conceptual themes in cross-cultural psychology, (b) current approaches to Rorschach validity and usefulness across cultures, and (c) a series of key issues and recommendations for culturally relevant research and practice with the RCS and other contemporary Rorschach developments.

CONCEPTUAL AND METHODOLOGICAL
CONCERNS IN CROSS-CULTURAL PSYCHOLOGY

Two fundamental themes in cross-cultural psychology frame the subsequent comments: (a) the distinction between etic and emic approaches, and (b) the notion of equivalence and its various types. The distinction between etic (universal, culture-general) and emic (indigenous, culture-specific) approaches has been applied across a variety of disciplines. The terms *etic* and *emic* were originally coined by Pike (1967) for distinguishing sounds that take place in all languages (phon*etics*) and sounds that are unique to one language (phon*emics*). Cross-cultural psychologists describe themselves as using emics as well as etics because they attempt both to understand behavior in terms that are meaningful to members of a particular culture and compare behaviors in different cultures from an external perspective (Triandis, 1994). The emic–etic distinction highlights the danger of operating with pseudouniversals, called *imposed etics* (Berry, 1969) or *pseudoetics* (Triandis, Malpass, & Davidson, 1973). Berry (1969) presented a combined etic–emic sequence of typical steps in cross-cultural psychology: A comparative research program would start with a question in one's own culture (emic A); the concept or instrument is transported provisionally to study a behavior in another culture (imposed etic); a discovery strategy is then developed within the second culture (emic B).

Finally, emic A and emic B are compared. Comparison is only possible for those features that both cultures have in common (derived etic). Geertz (1984) made a compelling presentation of the etic–emic dilemma in anthropological analysis. For him, the real question with *experience-near* and *experience-distant* concepts is the respective roles they play:

> Or, more exactly, how, in each case, ought one to deploy them so as to produce an interpretation of the way a people lives which is neither imprisoned within their mental horizons, an ethnography of witchcraft as written by a witch, nor systematically deaf to the distinctive tonalities of their existence, an ethnography of witchcraft as written by a geometer. (p. 125)

Meaningful cross-cultural comparisons can only be made if the data from different cultures are comparable. Brislin (1993) outlined three areas of equivalence in cross-cultural psychology: (a) translation equivalence, (b) conceptual equivalence, and (c) metric equivalence. Conceptual or *construct equivalence* implies that the construct's meaning is comparable across particular cultural groups, in which case it can be equivalently operationalized. An often used example of conceptual inequivalence is Wober's (1974) demonstration that the smart-fast component of Western's construct of intelligence is unsatisfactory for the Baganda of Uganda, whose concept of intelligence involves wisdom, slow thoughtfulness, and proper social behavior (Trimble, Lonner, & Boucher, 1983). *Metric equivalence* refers to the assumption that the same numbers on a scale can be used to measure a conceptually equivalent concept across cultures.

CURRENT APPROACHES TO RORSCHACH CROSS-CULTURAL/MULTICULTURAL VALIDITY AND USEFULNESS

Exner recently expressed his confidence in the validity of the RCS norms and interpretations across cultures (Butcher, Nezami, & Exner, 1998; Exner & Weiner, 1995). As to the system's metric equivalence, he sustained that the adult and children norms may have a broad cross-cultural applicability despite being based exclusively on U.S. data (Exner & Weiner, 1995). Exner's opinion was based in the following research findings: (a) a report comparing 30 protocols from the 10-year-old American sample with 30 protocols of children of the same age collected from three Spanish-speaking countries; and (b) data regarding the distribution of scores for subgroups drawn randomly from 293 adult nonpatient protocols collected from 12 different countries (as detailed in Butcher, Nezami, & Exner, 1998). The distribution of scores for each of the structural variables was reported as similar with few exceptions. The following conclusion was reached after reporting some minor differences in Form Quality percentages:

> These findings might lead some to argue that normative data for the test should be established by country, or language, or even by culture. Such a suggestion is probably not very realistic unless very large samples are available. Instead, it seems more reasonable to suggest that the items in the Form Quality Table be reviewed for frequency. . . . This is a very different procedure from that involved in attempting to establish separate normative data. (Exner & Weiner, 1995, p. 50)

Comparative studies conducted in some Southern European and Latin American countries using the RCS consistently opposed this last conclusion, as presented next. Weiner (1997b) called attention to the importance of large-scale normative studies that would permit comparing Rorschach responses of individuals around the world with those of persons who share their cultural background.

Regarding issues of conceptual equivalence, there is consensus among most Rorschach examiners about the universal validity of Rorschach constructs and interpretations. This view was summarized by Weiner (1996b):

> Abundant evidence indicates that wherever people live, whatever their ethnic or national origin, and regardless of their sociocultural background or station in life, their Rorschach responses indicate the type of person they are and the types of conflicts and concerns that influence their behavior. (p. 1)

According to Weiner, extensive cross-cultural research with the Rorschach has established that culture "gives context to personality functioning but it does not determine its basic structure and dynamics" (pp. 1–2). Some immediate questions brought up by the etic approach to Rorschach interpretation are as follows: Even if Rorschach examiners worldwide might find the method useful for personality assessment, it does not necessarily follows that Rorschach findings are interpreted in the same way. In addition, the universal applicability of Rorschach constructs should not be assumed but carefully demonstrated. As Weiner (1996a) stated regarding Rorschach's validity in general, it "works only as well as certain of its indexes serve certain purposes" (p. 212).

Issues of cultural variability has not been taken into consideration by other important contemporary Rorschach approaches, such as the psychoanalytic clinical approach inspired by object relations theory (Blatt, Brenneis, Schimek, & Glick, 1976; Gacono, & Meloy, 1994; Kissen, 1986; Kwawer, Lerner, Lerner, & Sugarman, 1980; Lerner, 1991; Lerner & Lerner, 1988; Mayman, 1967; Meloy, Acklin, Gacono, Murray, & Peterson, 1997).

A series of scales often based in Rorschach thematic imagery were developed within this tradition. Such scales mostly came out of clinical studies conducted in the United States, with samples of severely disturbed persons often located in inpatient and correctional settings. In the absence of normative data and external validation studies, the cross-cultural/multicultural relevance of the Rorschach object-relations scales is still unknown. As illustrated next, there is a significant risk of interpretation bias when using these kinds of scales and concepts across cultures.

A strong endorsement for the etic assumption that common principles of Rorschach interpretation could be applied to protocols of people with any cultural background comes from De Vos' approach to cross-cultural Rorschach research in psychological anthropology. De Vos' most recent publication (De Vos & Boyer, 1989) was described by Draguns (1991) as a solitary but vigorous reassertion of the Rorschach's value for sophisticated cross-cultural research. Based on his own and collaborative studies throughout various decades with three cultural groups—Japanese, Algerian Arab, and Native American—De Vos defended the feasibility and validity of Rorschach testing across cultures, taking issue with the cultural relativism that currently prevails in cultural anthropology. De Vos' (1993) recent personal recollection of his professional life also contained a strong defense of an etic approach to projective assessment:

> I can assure the skeptical that tests work cross-culturally regardless of what one hears to the contrary. On a psychological level people are people regardless of cultural differences. . . . The pan-human psychodynamic processes at work are the same, despite strong cultural emphasis and the special debilitative and rigidifying stresses apparent in one society more than another. (p. 17)

According to De Vos (De Vos & Boyer, 1989), Rorschach cross-cultural comparisons must distinguish between the concepts of intrapsychic *adjustment* (an etic concept referring to universals in personality structure and functioning) and social *adaptation* (an emic concept referring to adequate role behavior as judged by the particular sociocultural group's normative standards). De Vos' etic approach to Rorschach assessment considers the method as a measure of adjustment, which evaluates universals of maturation in intrapsychic psychological structures. Assuming an ideal universal concept of mental health, De Vos used the inkblot method to identify differences among cultural groups in personality features, such as flexibility or rigidity, maturity or primitiveness in thinking, or proneness to resort to particular coping strategies or defense mechanisms. Nevertheless, he cautioned, individual personality adjustments as measured by the Rorschach (e.g., primitiveness in cognitive structures) can be socially adaptive or maladaptive from the perspective of different cultural contexts. Norms will inevitably differ because the tendency would be for some common findings in one group to be deviant in another.

As described by Draguns (1996), researchers and/or practitioners start out with a choice between an etic or emic orientation, neither of which is inherently superior or inferior to the other. From a predominantly etic perspective, as represented by De Vos' approach (De Vos & Boyer, 1989) and Weiner's (1996b) remarks, Rorschach responses reflect universals in personality functioning; culture differences would be mostly regarded as external moderator variables. Conversely, emic approaches would start by assuming that cultural factors constitute a relevant context for all aspects of Rorschach assessment. From an emic perspective, variations across ethnocultural groups might be expected in Rorschach behaviors, structural variables (reflecting culture-specific personality traits and states), and thematic imagery (reflecting culture-specific needs, attitudes, concerns, or conflicts). Emic approaches are not common in contemporary Rorschach literature. An exception would be Dana's (1993) set of recommendations regarding the cross-cultural usage of both picture-story and inkblot techniques:

> First, the stimuli should be culturally relevant. Second, the scoring should reflect variables that are culturally important for psychopathology and/or problems-in-living. Third, normative data should be available for the intended population(s). Fourth, the interpretation of findings should make use of information available within the living context of intended assessees, to amplify and verify the meaning of the scoring variables. Fifth, culturally relevant personality theory should be used to insure that the data provided by scoring variables constitute a sufficient basis for personality study. (p. 147)

When assessment instruments are transported across cultures, researchers and clinicians tend to ignore indigenous perspectives that are intrinsic to the particular sociocultural system (Marsella & Kameoka, 1989). A more balanced approach than the prevailing universalistic orientation in Rorschach assessment would consist of assuming that, as in other areas that have been researched cross-culturally, "there would be both important similarities and *equally* important differences" (Kleinman, 1988, p. 22) when using the Rorschach across cultures.

KEY ISSUES IN CULTURALLY RELEVANT RESEARCH AND PRACTICE WITH THE RCS

A series of issues and recommendations to conceive and advance the cross-cultural/multicultural use of the RCS and other contemporary Rorschach developments emerges from the early cross-cultural Rorschach literature, recent international comparative studies based on the RCS, and current approaches to multicultural assessment in the United States. The following aspects are considered herein: normative data, normative orientations and response sets, constructs' equivalence, assessment of psychopathology and clinical diagnosis, and assessment practices. Rorschach findings from various international and multicultural populations are presented as illustrations. General implications are drawn from examples of our research data involving Latin Americans from Venezuela.

Normative Data Across Cultures

The international applicability of the RCS adult and children norms based in U.S. data has come under scrutiny. Because the international studies cited next have mostly involved adult participants, a brief description of the RCS adult normative sample is necessary (Exner, 1993). It consisted of 700 nonpatient protocols randomly selected from a larger pool of 1,332. The selection was stratified to include equal numbers of females and males and reflect the five U.S. geographic areas. The mean age for the group was 32.26, and the subject's average years of education was 13.25 with a range of 8 to 18 years. The classification for socioeconomic status (SES) included three subdivisions for each of the three following categories: upper (9%), middle (59%), and lower (32%). Exner reported that the sample included 81% Whites, 12% African Americans, 6% Hispanics, and 1% Asians. The administration settings were described as follows: 486 subjects volunteered through their workplaces usually under encouragement by supervisors or union leaders, 172 volunteered through social or interest organizations to which they belonged, and the remaining 52 were recruited with the help of social service agencies.

The issue of special norms for the U.S. multicultural populations are presented in the section on multicultural assessment practices. In this section, comments are made about the results from studies conducted in some Southern European (Portugal, Spain) and Latin American (Chile, Venezuela) countries, which compared RCS local data with Exner's norms (Alvarez et al., 1993; Ephraim, Riquelme, & Occupati, 1996; Miralles Sangro, 1997; Pires, 1993, 1996; Sendín, 1987; Silva, Novo, & Prazeres, 1991; Vinet, Saiz, & San Martín, 1995). With only one exception (Sendín, 1987), these comparative investigations questioned the RCS norms' applicability for their respective societies. Sample sizes for most of the studies were between 200 and 300 subjects, often equally divided by sex. The participants' age, SES, and level of education varied, with most samples stratified for SES to reflect the intended populations. As to the administration setting, more than half used community samples.

The results of the comparisons intended by the international studies must be considered tentative. Most of the studies presented limitations in generalizability because of limited samples and small sample sizes. Also differences in demographics as well as the scores that were analyzed make some comparisons difficult (undetected differences in the scoring criteria might have also occurred). Only some general findings necessary to support our subsequent discussion are presented here (detailed data from the Latin American and Portuguese studies are presented in other chapters of this handbook and in the original sources).

An interesting finding from the international studies that analyzed a broad range of current RCS variables was their shared discrepancies with Exner's norms. Those studies involved the following cities and/or countries: Barcelona, Spain (Alvarez et al., 1993); Caracas, Venezuela (Ephraim, Riquelme, & Occupati, 1996); Chile (Vinet, Saiz, & San Martín, 1995); and Portugal (Pires, 1993, 1996). The shared discrepancies with the RCS norms affected, among others, the following aspects:

1. *Information Processing.* Substantially higher proportions of participants from the Southern European and Latin American countries tended to simplify the inkblot stimulus field, as expressed by the percentage of *Pure F* responses or *Lambda* (for the international studies, *Lambda* means ranged from 1.06 to 1.46 compared with the RCS normative sample mean of 0.58).

2. *Cognitive Mediation.* Participants from the U.S. sample were comparatively more oriented toward giving conventional and perceptually adjusted responses, whereas participants from the international studies seemed to take a more subjective approach to the task. (Huge discrepancies were found in the number of Populars and Form Quality percentages.) For example, the mean values for *X+%* in the international studies ranged from 0.45 to 0.55, compared with the RCS normative sample mean of 0.79.

3. *Affects.* Participants from the RCS original sample were more responsive to chromatic color (*Afr*). Large differences were found on responses of socialized affect (for the international studies, *FC* means ranged from 1.50 to 2.20, compared with the RCS normative sample mean of 4.09).

4. *Interpersonal Perception.* The participants from Barcelona, Portugal, and Venezuela (the Chilean study does not include these data) gave substantially fewer movement responses involving two or more objects in which the interaction was clearly positive or cooperative (*COP* means ranged from 0.24 to 0.88, compared with the RCS normative sample mean of 2.07).

Could the previous discrepancies be safely attributed to shared cultural differences in personality among the nations involved and Exner's predominantly Anglo-American sample? There are some problems with this conclusion, as discussed below. In any case, these findings question the metric equivalence of the RCS norms for the cultural groups involved. To develop special norms seems justified by the consistent pattern of differences. Consequently, using the RCS normative data for interpretation within the nations represented in the previous international studies may create various problems. Concerning biases in interpretation, it would imply giving privilege to an Anglo-American worldview. As regards practice, without quantitative local normative data, clinicians would be unable to draw distinctions between what is adaptive or psychopathological as well as inform about the individuals' within-group particular status.

The previous international studies used a comparative research strategy that entailed some typical methodological problems. As described by Greene (1987) regarding investigations on ethnicity and MMPI, a number of issues must be considered before concluding that the discrepancies in test performance reflect cultural differences. A key issue is the confounding role of moderator variables, such as SES, educational level, and type of setting. For example, if a study compares less educated nationals from one country with more educated U.S. subjects, it is doubtful whether the obtained differences could be interpreted solely on the basis of cultural differences. The role of SES or educational level as a moderator variable was considered in some of the previous cross-cultural studies. Cultural differences in the variables reported earlier were consistent across SES groups in the Venezuelan study (Ephraim, Riquelme, & Occupati, 1996), whereas some of such differences were affected by the educational level in the Portuguese study. Because Rorschach performance is strongly affected by the type of setting, its confounding role remains an unresolved issue—the strategy for recruiting normal participants might reflect significant cultural differences making the data noncomparable. Exner's recruitment procedure mostly through workplaces might have made his adult normative sample more homogeneous and institution-specific than desirable. New RCS nonpatient data have occasionally been reported with small and limited U.S. samples. The results of these partial studies seem to differ substantially from Exner's normative data (Shaffer, Erdberg, Haroian, Van Patten, & Hamel, 1996; Viglione, Gaudiana, & Gowri, 1997).

Another methodological issue in comparisons between ethnic or cultural groups with personality assessment instruments is the lack of investigations that directly evaluate whether differences in scores affect the empirical correlates (Greene, 1987). The RCS external validation proceeded by using two research strategies: examining relationships between individual Rorschach variables and extratest variables, and identifying clusters of Rorschach variables that discriminated between clinical and normal groups (Ganellen, 1996). The cross-cultural and multicultural empirical validity of those variables and clusters should be independently established. Incidentally, local practice and research could eventually lead to the consolidation of the Rorschach as a culture-specific method. Such a process may have taken place in various countries without explicit recognition. An emic approach of this kind does not contribute to Rorschach development as a universal diagnostic framework to be used anywhere if it remains isolated and does not proceed cumulatively. However, it probably enhances the sensitivity of the instrument in specific cultural contexts.

A research program based on replicating the RCS investigations across cultures could be helpful. However, it would not solve all the potential problems of cultural relevance and sensitivity because static group comparisons often miss the emic component (Lonner & Ibrahim, 1996). A related methodological problem for international studies involves difficulties in the interpretation of any differences that are found. The risk here consists of comparing culture or ethnic groups on the basis of emic standards. A frequent pitfall on cross-cultural comparisons consists of wrongly assuming various forms of equivalence (e.g., that the groups being compared approached the task with the same normative expectations or that a particular construct exists or may be defined in the same way in both cultures). These problems are considered in the following sections.

Cultural Normative Orientations and Response Sets

People from around the world or culturally different clients in multicultural societies may differ in their normative behavior when facing the task proposed by the Rorschach. Such differences could make the data noncomparable. In a broad sense, cultural normative orientation corresponds to what Lindzey (1961) described as the significance of taking the test from the perspective of the local culture. In a restricted sense, the term refers to culture-specific response sets or styles (e.g., a response set of *evasiveness* has often been described in cross-cultural Rorschach studies). A popular illustration of the significant impact of response style on clinical assessment was Dohrenwend and Dohrenwend's (1969) series of studies, which consistently found that Puerto Ricans in U.S. cities tended to report a higher number of symptoms in self-report psychiatric measures than other minority groups. The authors demonstrated that the difference in the reported level of psychopathology was better explained by a response set—the symptoms were viewed as less socially undesirable—than by an actual higher rate of psychopathology.

Kaplan (1961) stated that the wide cross-cultural variability found in how the Rorschach works from one culture to another—rich and expressive records from the Hindu, stereotyped and defensive from the Ojibwa, vague and diffuse from the Melanesian, tiny details from the Pilaga—appears to be a matter of the participants' approach to the task. Kaplan's conclusion was reportedly based on the close examination of raw Rorschach and TAT material of 75 culture and personality studies:

> The important point to be emphasized is that the personality study situation is dominated by the prevalent social conceptions of what people are supposed to be like. The subject's production must be understood in relationship to them. The description and analysis of these social conceptions is perhaps the first step to be undertaken in the interpretation of personality materials in all personality studies, cross-cultural or otherwise. (p. 309)

Contrasts in cultural normative orientations to the Rorschach task might contribute to the differences found between Exner's norms and the data from some Southern European and Latin American countries in the RCS variables related to cognitive mediation (Populars and Form Quality). The participants from the latter samples seemed to be comparatively more inclined to personalize the stimulus. In Piagetian terms, they tended to *assimilate* the stimulus to their internal reality rather than *accommodate* their responses to the inkblot perceptual demands. Conversely, Exner's subjects could be described as comparatively more inclined toward an instrumental, problem-solving, consensus-oriented approach to the Rorschach task, as expressed by their tendency to be more realistic and precise in their perceptions.

The following response to Card IX from a female middle-class homemaker illustrates the kind of assimilative approach to the task often found in the Latin-American protocols from Venezuela: "I don't see anything. It looks like mountains (D1). And there (DS8), to infinity, far away, I see God, the crowned God (Dd25)." Interestingly, Card IX has been described as the most often rejected and most difficult Rorschach card because of its unstructured quality (Aronow, Reznikoff, & Moreland, 1994). People who approach the Rorschach task with a matter-of-fact orientation would probably feel more intimidated by the ambiguity of Card IX than the participant who gave the previous response.

Differences in cultural normative orientations to the Rorschach task may lead to biases in interpretation, as exemplified by comparing RCS norms and the Venezuelan data on some Ideation variables (*FABCOM1* > 0: 16% compared with 44%; Critical Special Scores Level 2 > 0: 3% compared with 27%; *M*- > 0: 3% compared with 39%). According to the RCS, the *FABCOM1* responses "reflect the very loose associations that often occur in thinking which is inconsistent, disorganized, and primitive" (Exner, 1993, p. 480), the Critical Special Scores Level 2 reflect from serious to severe cognitive dysfunction, and the presence of even one *M*- response "is sufficient to raise concern about peculiarity in ideation" (Exner, 1993, p. 482). Because these types of response are so common in the Venezuelan records, a change in interpretation is required, which takes into account cultural differences in tolerance for illogical combinatory thinking, when responding to the inkblots and in other contexts. To report incongruous Rorschach percepts ("sea horses drinking shakes" at Card IX; "two women, just the upper part, sitting over butterfly wings" at Card VII) is consistent with Latin American core cultural traditions, such as those expressed in a widespread syncretism or in the so-called *magic realism* literature (e.g., the novels and short stories of Nobel laureate Gabriel García Marquez might be described as relying heavily on the type of combinations the RCS would identify as immature, inappropriate, or even bizarre). This discussion might be relevant for the Rorschach assessment of Latinos in the United States. The confound of culture and psychopathology regarding so-called peculiarities in ideation was exemplified in a pioneer article by Padilla and Ruiz (1975) in the following way: the percept "the evil eye"—probably an *M*-response by the RCS scoring rules—would ordinarily raise questions about paranoid ideation among clinicians. However, as the authors stated, this response may have a more benign connotation for some Mexican Americans who share folk magic beliefs.

Dana (1993) provided an example of interpretive failures in the culture and personality studies that also illustrates well the importance of taking into account the cultural normative orientations to the Rorschach task. On the basis of his Rorschach protocol, a Native-American shaman was diagnosed as suffering from a character disorder with oral and phallic fixations and occasional hysterical dissociations (Klopfer & Boyer, 1961). Conversely, Dana suggested that the published record documented a holistic view that connected everything with everything else, as in the following response to Card I: "The birds of the cloud . . . an enemy in the cloud . . . giant bat . . . he resembles the traveling star" (Klopfer & Boyer, 1961, p. 157). Dana's interpretation of the previous response allows the identification of a culture-specific normative orientation to the Rorschach task: Instead of distancing himself from the blot in the Anglo-American fashion by carefully providing boundaries, the shaman "entered the inkblot stimulus and incorporated both the blot and his perception of it in an overarching cosmology" (Dana, 1993, p. 157).

Cross-Cultural Construct Relevance and Sensitivity

Construct bias occurs when psychological concepts are not identical across cultures. Issues of Rorschach constructs' cross-cultural validity have been overlooked in the early and current Rorschach literature. The early cross-cultural Rorschach studies were criticized for the mechanical application of scoring and interpretive schemes that were uncritically assumed to be culture-free (Lindzey, 1961). As Lindzey concluded: "Actually, if we removed from this literature all interpretive statements dependent upon Klopfer's specific generalizations, we would probably eliminate three quarters of the results we have examined" (p. 300). This finding was contrary to his expectation that projective methods in anthropological research would rely more on complex contextual cues. The current multicultural practice of personality assessment in the United States also tends to disregard issues of cross-cultural construct validity. Moreland (1996) reported his experience as a consultant for a test publisher: He was often asked about special norms for minority populations, but never about issues of functional or conceptual equivalence. Finally, the recent international studies reported earlier focused on whether the RCS norms were cross-culturally applicable. Issues of construct equivalence, such as the system's cultural relevance regarding scoring categories and interpretation strategies, were not a cause of concern.

The RCS scoring rules and interpretation strategies are based on a number of personality constructs, such as stress tolerance, egocentricity, need for closeness, cooperativeness, affect modulation, cognitive complexity, conventionality, problems in judgment, and so on. Despite the system's tendency to rely on low-inference concepts and interpretations, it cannot be taken for granted that its constructs have the same meaning or are equally relevant and/or sensitive for personality assessment across cultures. From an emic perspective, establishing the cultural relevance of the RCS constructs would require the study of what they mean in the new context. The personality characteristics addressed by the interpretation clusters must be understood in each culture's terms before assuming its comparability.

The assessment of construct bias cannot be established by statistical means alone. It must rely on extra-instrument knowledge about the specific cultural groups (Van de Vijver & Leung, 1997). Classical contributions from the early cross-cultural Rorschach literature by Hallowell (1953) and Henry (1961) stated the need for extensive cultural knowledge to avoid construct bias. Based on blind studies made by experienced Rorschach examiners, Hallowell concluded that common principles of Rorschach interpretation could be applied to protocols of people with any cultural background. Nevertheless, he considered those blind studies to be just pioneer experiments. For Hallowell, the serious and systematic characterization of individuals from a particular cultural group through the Rorschach method would rely on both an adequate sample and "knowing everything about their culture" (Hallowell, 1953, p. 516). Henry (1961) considered it unreasonable to presume that a cultural group could be described on the basis of Rorschach data alone:

Certainly, direct field observations, as well as social structure, beliefs and
myths are of utmost relevance, not merely to the understanding of the
culture from the anthropologist's point of view, *but also for the proper interpretation of the test responses themselves.* (p. 590; italics added)

Interestingly, Henry added that the need to integrate the previous types
of cultural data and test analysis was as great within the North American
mainstream culture as when using the method with distant cultures.

The cross-cultural study of Rorschach dependency contents is a good
illustration of potential construct bias. The term *dependency* has negative
connotations of immaturity and incompetence in the United States,
whereas indigenous forms of dependency and/or interdependency are
highly valued in other parts of the world (Marsella & Kameoka, 1989).
Markus and Kitayama (1991), among others, described remarkable differences between the independent view of the self prevailing in North
America and many Western European cultures and the interdependent
views of the self characteristic of Asian, Latin American, and many Southern European cultures. Given these cultural differences, it would not be
appropriate to assess dependency-related personality issues and concerns
across cultures with Rorschach variables and constructs based exclusively
in Anglo-American interpersonal standards.

The Venezuelan sample described previously presented a high percentage of records with responses in the following dependency-related
thematic categories: (a) Thirty-six percent (36%) of the protocols had at
least one response of *body fusion* (Boyer, Dithrich, Harned, Stone, & Walt,
1988)—that is, responses where joining of normally discrete bodies or
body parts occur (e.g., "two bears joined at the knees"). (b) Twenty-six
percent (26%) of the records had at least one response of *symbiotic fusion,
birth* or *separation-division*, which the psychoanalytic Rorschach literature
identifies with primitive object relations and the diagnosis of borderline
psychopathology (Coonerty, 1986; Kwawer, 1980). The following response
to Card X from a highly functioning female Venezuelan journalist illustrates the frequent theme of *merging* in the Venezuelan protocols: "Fantastic animals of cheerful colors. Very much as seen through a child's
mind: birds, sea horses, crabs, small mice. All wrapped up, nebulous.
This is something that connects them and keeps them together. Keeps
them in the space, but not loose, united."

There are no normative data regarding the frequency of the previous
thematic categories in nonpatient U.S. samples. It can be speculated that
this type of Rorschach thematic imagery would not be expected to be
frequent in Anglo-American normal records given the cultural emphasis
in independence from others. In any case, the presence of fusional or
merging responses in the Venezuelan records does not have the extreme
negative consequences associated with them on the basis of clinical studies

with U.S.-selected samples of severely disturbed persons. A modified interpretation would again be called for, which takes into account the culturally specific issues and concerns of individuals who share a comparatively more fluid and sociocentric concept of self (Marsella & White, 1982). Family attachments and support have a greater salience for Latin Americans and Latinos in the United States than for Anglo Americans. In Venezuela in particular, the paramount importance of a life-long relationship with the mother, or *matricentrism*, has often been described by psychologists and social scientists (e.g., Montero, 1982; Moreno, 1993).

The RCS does not have a content scoring category for the response of merging and togetherness reported earlier. It would not qualify as a cooperative response (COP) because the animals are not clearly interacting. To become more culturally inclusive, Rorschach variables and constructs should ideally be based on a broad range of human experience because in another society or for members of an ethnic minority group, other personality characteristics might be equally or more important than the variables currently included in the RCS.

Assessment of Psychopathology and Clinical Diagnosis

Weiner (1997a) identified differential diagnoses among the clinical purposes the Rorschach method is expected to serve in applied practice. However, he warned that the method bears only secondarily on diagnostic status and exclusively in those instances where a psychopathological condition could be clearly formulated in terms of personality concepts and variables. Exner (1997) has been critical of the current trend in the U.S. mental health scene to excessively rely on diagnostic categories for assessment and treatment planning. He associated the relevance of the Rorschach for future tasks of applied psychology and psychiatry to the success of the opposite trend (i.e., a renewed interest in personality differences and in the person as a unique entity). The previous cautions are important because the RCS, which provides indexes for schizophrenia (SCZI) and Depression (DEPI), is more directly involved in clinical differential diagnoses than the earlier U.S. Rorschach systems.

Are the RCS psychopathological indexes cross-culturally useful? The DEPI is used to illustrate the complex issues of metric and conceptual equivalence involved when using the Rorschach for differential diagnosis across cultures. Regarding DEPI's metric equivalence, the RCS international studies reported earlier provide some tentative orientations. Apropos DEPI cutoff scores, Exner suggested that a value of 5 is likely to imply depressive features, whereas a value of 6 or 7 would probably identify a major depressive episode or a chronic disposition to become pathologically depressed (Exner, 1991; Exner & Weiner, 1995). The studies from

Portugal (Pires, 1996) and the cities of Barcelona, Spain (Alvarez et al., 1993) and Caracas, Venezuela (Ephraim, Riquelme, & Occupati, 1996) reported a substantially higher proportion of high-DEPI protocols compared with the RCS adult normative sample (e.g., the Venezuelan study reported 24% DEPI = 5, 6% DEPI = 6, and 2% DEPI = 7 compared with 1% DEPI = 5, 0% DEPI = 6, and 0% DEPI = 7 in the RCS normative sample). Differences in DEPI scores are related to clear discrepancies in some of the individual variables that compose the index, such as $S > 2$ (26% in the Venezuelan sample compared with 10% in the U.S. sample), COP < 2 (98% compared with 61%), *Afr* < .50 (46% compared with 7%), *Blends* < 4 (*M Blends*: 2.90 compared with 5.16). Incidentally, the linkage between a depressive condition in other countries and these variables is not obvious from a conceptual perspective (Weiner, 1986). Studies that directly assess the empirical correlates of the previous cross-cultural differences in DEPI scores would be advantageous. Meanwhile, to apply the cutoff scores proposed by Exner for the clinical diagnosis of depression within the national groups involved seems questionable.

Issues of conceptual equivalence, even if less noticeable, are also involved in evaluating DEPI's cross-cultural usefulness. A close scrutiny of Exner's procedure on developing the current DEPI reveals some consequential decisions. Selected from an original pool of 1,400 subjects diagnosed as affectively disturbed, the index target sample consisted of 471 subjects sorted on the basis of being either emotionally or cognitively depressed. A third sample, defined as socially immature or helpless, was excluded and used for the development of a new index, the Coping Deficit Index (CDI; Exner, 1993). Exner's justification for the previous decision about target samples was that the diagnosis of depression or affective disorder is invariably associated with emotional distraught and/or cognitive pessimism, lethargy, and self-defeating behavior. Exner's decision might seem obvious. However, according to Kleinman (1996), in many societies worldwide the most real depressive manifestations are physical (fatigue, headaches, sleep disturbances, loss of appetite, etc.). Asians in particular have been found to report somatic symptoms rather than strict depressive symptomatology (Sue, 1996). DEPI's cultural bias in favor of the psychological versus the physical components of depression might constitute a problem when assessing culturally different individuals.

Researchers and clinicians interested in the Rorschach assessment of psychopathology across cultures cannot ignore the widespread role of somatization as a culturally meaningful mode of expressing distress. Regarding mood and anxiety disorders, medical anthropologists have identified diverse culture-specific *idioms of distress* that focus on somatic manifestations, such as *heart distress* in Iran (Good, 1977), complaints of *heat in the head* and *crawling sensations of worms and ants* from Nigerian psychiatric patients (Ebigbo, 1982), or *nervios* and *ataques de nervios* in Puerto Ricans and other Hispanic populations (e.g., Guarnaccia, Good, & Kleinman, 1990).

Further attention to Rorschach somatic contents might lead to useful indexes for clinical diagnosis. On the basis of his coding system for Rorschach symbolic contents, De Vos (De Vos & Boyer, 1989) reported that groups going through an acculturation process—immigrant Japanese as well as urbanized Algerians—presented more *body preoccupation* responses with a morbid sadomasochistic quality than comparable samples. Commenting on some early research studies of low-SES African Americans, De Vos suggested that the presence of considerable morbid anatomy responses in their protocols symbolized the chronic social stress of individuals who experience minority group status and perceive the host culture as hostile and deprecatory.

Issues of cultural relativism have a strong impact on the cross-cultural/multicultural assessment of psychopathology. De Vos and Boyer (1989) warned against adopting an extreme relativistic position by reducing psychopathology to culture: "Some emotional and physical states of disorder or 'emotional' problems cause human misery, regardless of the culture in which they occur" (p. 38). Clinicians involved in cross-cultural and multicultural assessment must be aware of the tendency to overpathologize by confounding culture and psychopathology. There is also the risk of underestimating pathology by attributing to culture obvious signs of psychological disturbance (López, 1989).

Culturally Competent Assessment Practices With Multicultural Clients in the United States

Dana's (1993, 1996) comprehensive guidelines for culturally competent assessment services with multicultural populations in the United States are also relevant for Rorschach assessment. Dana's guidelines included the following major components: adjustments in service delivery style, use of client's first language, evaluation of cultural orientation, adjustments in assessment methodology and culturally appropriate feedback. Brief comments about how some of these components apply specifically to Rorschach multicultural assessment are included in this section.

Service Delivery Style. Dana (1996) described that Anglo-American assessors, influenced by the medical model, expect their assessment client to have an impersonal "immediate task-orientation" (p. 475). As illustrated earlier, this might not be the prevalent mental set of culturally different clients when looking at inkblots. Kaplan (1961) criticized the requirement of a standard procedure for Rorschach administration regardless of its results: "This is directly counter to my belief that *good* results—in the sense that they reflect personality adequately—depend upon tailoring the procedures to the characteristics of the subject and its culture" (p. 303).

Use of Client's First Language. Because of the strong impact of language in Rorschach coding and interpretation, Weiner (1998) recommended that both subject and examiner were fluent in the language being used: "Rorschach clinicians faced with the need to evaluate a subject who is not fluent in English are well-advised either to find an examiner fluent in the person's first language or to omit the Rorschach from their battery" (1998, p. 51).

Assessment of Cultural Orientation. It is necessary to collect information regarding cultural orientation or acculturation status when using the RCS with culturally different clients. Interpreting their Rorschach records on the sole basis of the RCS norms, interpretive strategies, and personality theory might be irrelevant and even detrimental. Research and clinical data in this area are badly needed, particularly regarding differences in Rorschach responses associated with acculturation status. As suggested by Dana (1998), acculturation measures used as moderator variables can provide adjustments for traditional, bicultural, and marginal cultural orientations. Consistent differences in Rorschach response patterns associated with acculturation status might be used by clinicians as an indirect measure of cultural orientation, together with the self-report and interview measures of acculturation currently in use.

Multicultural Norms. There is disagreement about the utility of special norms for testing minority members in the United States. Jones and Thorne (1987) cautioned about the difficulty of developing special norms given the minorities' extreme within-group heterogeneity and the continually changing sociocultural context. However, Dana (1998) suggested that acculturation status norms for particular minority populations are now possible by using contrasting cultural orientation status groups.

Greene's (1987) recommendations regarding MMPI and ethnicity are also relevant in collecting Rorschach normative data for minority members. A clear definition of group membership is needed, contrary to the frequent practice of describing participants as African Americans, Asian Americans, Hispanic Americans, or Native Americans without assessing first whether the individuals actually identify with their ethnic group. Another pertinent recommendation for multicultural Rorschach research and clinical practice consists of considering the within-group cultural variability, particularly the role of educational level and SES as moderator variables (see also Frank, 1992, 1993). The established RCS data might be more valid for highly acculturated people who have typically been more exposed to the U.S. educational system and achieved middle-class status. However, many highly acculturated individuals in the United States remain grounded simultaneously in their original culture. Given the lack of research in this area, this is still an unsettled question.

The investigation of extratest correlates for RCS variables across minority groups would help to establish whether certain scores have different psychological consequences, in which case a change in interpretation is required. If separate norms are developed, the use of a dual profile might be useful for particular clients, as suggested by Dahlstrom (1986) regarding multicultural assessment with the MMPI. The dual profile method, as applied to the Rorschach, would consist of comparing two profiles from the client—one plotted on Anglo-American norms (which might reflect how the individual is viewed from the perspective of the dominant culture) and another against the minority-based norms (which would provide a within-group perspective).

Contextual Interpretation. De Vos and Boyer (1989) emphasized that Rorschach results must be interpreted in the context of other data regarding the social environment. Dana (1993) recommended that projective interpretations across cultures should be contextually grounded. To follow these guidelines requires extensive experience with both normative and clinical populations from the client's cultural or ethnic group. Developing a collaborative assessment relationship (Fischer, 1985) would be particularly important when working with multicultural clients. However, according to Dana (1993), good intentions do not compensate for the extensive training and experience required to provide culturally competent services. A particular danger to be avoided would be the tendency to stereotype entire cultural groups. The otherwise laudable efforts to identify culture-specific features could rapidly lead to increased stigmatization (Good, 1996b).

CLOSING COMMENTS AND FURTHER
SUGGESTIONS FOR FUTURE RESEARCH
AND PRACTICE

There is consensus that both etic and emic approaches have their respective place in personality assessment (Dana, 1993; Draguns, 1996). Regarding the Rorschach method, etic approaches have been more popular because Rorschach examiners tend to agree that common principles of Rorschach interpretation could be applied to protocols of people from any cultural background. However, there is still a need to establish, conceptually as well as empirically, which those common principles are. As raised in previous sections, RCS and other contemporary Rorschach variables and constructs should not be assumed as culturally relevant and/or sensitive for personality assessment and clinical diagnosis regardless of culture without further inquiry. Nevertheless, not much progress has been made in the development of systematic indigenous approaches to Rorschach assessment despite the "enormous global need for a psychology of practical significance" (Gergen, Gulerce, Lock, & Misra, 1996).

The inclusion of culturally different individuals enriches the science of psychology by broadening the range of human behavior to be examined and understood (Okazaki & Sue, 1995). The combination of etic and emic Rorschach perspectives can significantly enrich our understanding of the method. As underlined by Berry (1990), etic and emic perspectives did not form a dichotomy in Pike's original proposal. As with stereographic glasses, each perspective gives a different image; taken together, their "added perception is startling indeed" (Pike, 1967, p. 41). Pike's kind of three-dimensional understanding represents the ideal to be pursued in research and practice with the Rorschach method across cultures:

> Through the etic "lens" the analyst views the data in tacit reference to a perspective oriented to all comparable events . . . of all people, of all parts of the earth; through the other lens, the emic one, he views the same events at the same time, in the same context, in reference to a perspective oriented to the particular function of these particular events in that particular culture, as it and it alone is structured. (p. 41)

Finally, some recommendations taken from neighboring disciplines can be useful to improve research and practice across cultures with the RCS and other contemporary Rorschach approaches. Regarding research, Henry (1961) examined the issue of whether we have been asking questions that are too broad for meaningful answers and suggested research studies that utilize only specific and limited aspects of the records to test specific hypotheses. De Vos and Boyer (1989) also proposed that comparative Rorschach studies should avoid using the method in a diffuse and global fashion, addressing instead specific and relevant problems in particular sociocultural contexts. These recommendations coincide with the current agreement in cross-cultural psychology that culture, as a global concept, must be *unpackaged*. Van de Vijver and Leung (1997) suggested to identify in advance those variables that may likely account for the expected cultural differences; they defended the use of a systematic sampling approach in which cultures are selected in a theory-guided fashion.

The second recommendation involves Rorschach cross-cultural/multicultural practice. Regarding *DSM* diagnosis and culture, Good (1996a) proposed the creation of a task force to develop a case book of prototypical cases reflecting the difficult diagnostic problems that grow out of the cultural diversity in the American society. A similar effort might be valuable to advance the field of cross-cultural/multicultural Rorschach practice worldwide as well as within particular multicultural societies.

ACKNOWLEDGMENTS

I thank Richard Dana, George A. De Vos, and Irving B. Weiner for their valuable comments, Juan J. Riquelme for his collaborative work in the Venezuelan normative studies, and Frances McQueen and Cristina Santaella for their thoughtful editing. Appreciation is expressed to the Universidad Central de Venezuela for granting a leave of absence that made possible the preparation of this chapter, and to James Marcia and Simon Fraser University for their continued support.

REFERENCES

Alvarez, M., Baeza, A., Campo, V., García, J. M., Montlleó, T., De Jesús, A., Jirón, P., Mateos, M. L., Minobis, J., Navarro, J., Perez, V., Pouso, R., Prófumo, L., Torras, C., Zayas, M., & Guardia, J. (1993). Primera aproximación a un estudio normativo de la ciudad de Barcelona y su entorno [Exploratory study of Rorschach norms for the city of Barcelona and its surroundings]. *Revista de la Sociedad Española del Rorschach y Métodos Proyectivos, 6*, 6–17.

Aronow, E., Reznikoff, M., & Moreland, K. (1994). *The Rorschach technique: Perceptual basics, content interpretation, and applications.* Boston: Allyn & Bacon.

Berry, J. W. (1969). On cross-cultural comparability. *International Journal of Psychology, 4*, 119–128.

Berry, J. W. (1990). Imposed etics, emics, and derived etics: Their conceptual and operational status in cross-cultural psychology. In J. N. Headland, K. L. Pike, & M. Harris (Eds.), *Emics and etics: The insider–outsider debate* (pp. 84–97). Newbury Park, CA: Sage.

Blatt, S. J., Brenneis, C. B., Schimek, J., & Glick, M. (1976). Normal development and the psychopathological impairment of the concept of the object on the Rorschach. *Journal of Abnormal Psychology, 85*, 264–273.

Boyer, L. B., Dithrich, C. W., Harned, H., Stone, J. S., & Walt, A. (1988). *A Rorschach handbook for the Affective Inferences Scoring System–Revised.* Berkeley: Boyer Research Institute.

Brislin, R. (1993). *Understanding culture's influence on behavior.* New York: Harcourt, Brace.

Butcher J. N., Nezami, E., & Exner, J. E. (1998). Psychological assessment of people in diverse cultures. In S. S. Kazarian & D. R. Evans (Eds.), *Cultural clinical psychology* (pp. 61–105). New York: Oxford University Press.

Butcher, J. N., & Rouse, S. V. (1996). Personality: Individual differences and clinical assessment. *Annual Review of Psychology, 47*, 87–11.

Coonerty, S. (1986). An exploration of separation-individuation themes in the borderline personality disorder. *Journal of Personality Assessment, 50*, 501–511.

Dahlstrom, L. E. (1986). MMPI findings on other minority groups. In W. G. Dahlstrom, D. Lachar, & L. E. Dahlstrom (Eds.), *MMPI patterns of American minorities* (pp. 50–86). Minneapolis: University of Minnesota Press.

Dana, R. H. (1993). *Multicultural assessment perspectives for professional psychology.* Boston: Allyn & Bacon.

Dana, R. H. (1996). Culturally competent assessment practice in the United States. *Journal of Personality Assessment, 66*(3), 472–487.

Dana, R. H. (1998). Cultural identity assessment of culturally diverse groups: 1997. *Journal of Personality Assessment, 70*(1), 1–16.

De Vos, G. A. (1993). A personal odyssey. In L. B. Boyer, R. M. Boyer, & H. Stein (Eds.), *The psychoanalytic study of society* (Vol. 18, pp. 5–22). Hillsdale, NJ: The Analytic Press.

De Vos, G. A., & Boyer, L. B. (1989). *Symbolic analysis cross-culturally: The Rorschach test.* Berkeley: University of California Press.

Dohrenwend, B. P., & Dohrenwend, B. S. (1969). *Social status and psychological disorder: A causal inquiry.* New York: Wiley.

Draguns, J. G. (1991). Inkblots across cultural lines. *Contemporary Psychology, 36*(5), 432.

Draguns, J. G. (1996). Multicultural and cross-cultural assessment: Dilemmas and decisions. In G. R. Sodowsky & J. C. Impara (Eds.), *Multicultural assessment in counseling and clinical psychology* (pp. 37–83). Lincoln, NE: Buros Institute of Mental Measurements.

Ebigbo, P. (1982). Development of a culture-specific (Nigeria) screening scale of somatic complaints. *Culture, Medicine and Psychiatry, 6,* 29–44.

Ephraim, D., Riquelme, J. J., & Occupati, R. (1996). Características psicológicas de habitantes de Caracas según el Sistema Comprehensivo del Rorschach. Datos normativos y comparación transcultural [Psychological characteristics of Caracas inhabitants through the Comprehensive Rorschach System. Normative data and cross-cultural comparison]. In D. Ephraim (Ed.), *El método Rorschach en la actualidad* (pp. 45–66). Caracas: Monte Avila Editores.

Exner, J. E., Jr. (1991). *The Rorschach: A comprehensive system: Vol. 2. Interpretation* (2nd ed.). New York: Wiley.

Exner, J. E., Jr. (1993). *The Rorschach: A comprehensive system: Vol. 1. Basic foundations* (3rd ed.). New York: Wiley.

Exner, J. E., Jr. (1997). The future of Rorschach in personality assessment. *Journal of Personality Assessment, 68*(1), 37–46.

Exner, J. E., Jr., & Weiner, I. B. (1995). *The Rorschach: A comprehensive system: Vol. 3. Assessment of children and adolescents* (2nd ed.). New York: Wiley.

Fischer, C. T. (1985). *Individualizing psychological assessment.* Monterey, CA: Brooks-Cole.

Frank, G. (1992). The response of African Americans to the Rorschach: A review of the research. *Journal of Personality Assessment, 59*(2), 317–325.

Frank, G. (1993). The use of the Rorschach with Hispanic Americans. *Psychological Reports, 72,* 276–278.

Gacono, C. B., & Meloy, J. R. (1994). *The Rorschach assessment of aggressive and psychopathic personalities.* Hillsdale, NJ: Lawrence Erlbaum Associates.

Ganellen, R. J. (1996). *Integrating the Rorschach and the MMPI–2 in personality assessment.* Mahwah, NJ: Lawrence Erlbaum Associates.

Geertz, C. (1984). From the native's point of view. On the nature of anthropological understanding. In R. A. Shweder & R. A. LeVine (Eds.), *Culture theory: Essays on mind, self and emotion* (pp. 123–136). New York: Cambridge University Press.

Gergen, K. J., Gulerce, A., Lock, A., & Misra, G. (1996). Psychological science in cultural context. *American Psychologist, 51*(5), 496–503.

Good, B. J. (1977). The heart of what's the matter: The semantics of illness in Iran. *Culture, Medicine and Psychiatry, 1,* 25–38.

Good, B. J. (1996a). Cultural comments on mood and anxiety disorders: II. In J. E. Mezzich, A. Kleinman, H. Fabrega, & D. L. Parron (Eds.), *Culture and psychiatric diagnosis: A DSM–IV perspective* (pp. 123–129). Washington, DC: American Psychiatric Press.

Good, B. J. (1996b). Knowledge, power and diagnosis. In J. E. Mezzich, A. Kleinman, H. Fabrega, & D. L. Parron (Eds.), *Culture and psychiatric diagnosis: A DSM–IV perspective* (pp. 347–351). Washington, DC: American Psychiatric Press.

Greene, R. L. (1987). Ethnicity and MMPI performance: A review. *Journal of Consulting and Clinical Psychology, 55*(4), 497–512.

Guarnaccia, P. J., Good, B. J., & Kleinman, A. (1990). A critical review of epidemiological studies of Puerto Rican mental health. *American Journal of Psychiatry, 147*(11), 1449–1456.

Hallowell, A. I. (1953). The Rorschach technique in personality and cultural studies. In B. Klopfer, M. D. Ainsworth, W. G. Klopfer, & R. R. Holt (Eds.), *Developments in the Rorschach technique* (Vol. 2, pp. 458–544). New York: Harcourt, Brace.

Henry, W. E. (1961). Projective tests in cross-cultural research. In B. Kaplan (Ed.), *Studying personality cross-culturally* (pp. 587–596). New York: Harper & Row.

Jones, E. E., & Thorne, A. (1987). Rediscovery of the subject: Intercultural approaches to clinical assessment. *Journal of Consulting and Clinical Psychology, 55*, 488–495.

Kaplan, B. (1961). Personality study and culture. In B. Kaplan (Ed.), *Studying personality cross-culturally* (pp. 301–311). New York: Harper & Row.

Kissen, M. (Ed.). (1986). *Assessing object relations phenomena*. New York: International Universities Press.

Kleinman, A. (1988). *Rethinking psychiatry: From cultural category to personal experience*. New York: The Free Press.

Kleinman, A. (1996). How is culture important for *DSM–IV*? In J. E. Mezzich, A. Kleinman, H. Fabrega, & D. L. Parron (Eds.), *Culture and psychiatric diagnosis: A DSM–IV perspective* (pp. 15–25). Washington, DC: American Psychiatric Press.

Klopfer, B., & Boyer, L. B. (1961). Notes on the personality structure of a North American Indian shaman: Rorschach interpretation. *Journal of Projective Techniques and Personality Assessment, 25*, 170–178.

Kwawer, J. S. (1980). Primitive interpersonal modes, borderline phenomena and Rorschach content. In J. S. Kwawer, H. D. Lerner, P. M. Lerner, & A. Sugarman (Eds.), *Borderline phenomena and the Rorschach Test* (pp. 89–105). New York: International Universities Press.

Kwawer, J. S., Lerner, H. D., Lerner, P. M., & Sugarman, A. (Eds.). (1980). *Borderline phenomena and the Rorschach Test*. New York: International Universities Press.

Lerner, P. (1991). *Psychoanalytic theory and the Rorschach*. Hillsdale, NJ: Analytic Press.

Lerner, H., & Lerner, P. (Eds.). (1988). *Primitive mental states and the Rorschach*. New York: International Universities Press.

Lindzey, G. (1961). *Projective techniques and cross-cultural research*. New York: Appleton-Century-Crafts.

Lonner, W. J., & Ibrahim, F. A. (1996). Appraisal and assessment in cross-cultural counseling. In P. B. Pedersen, J. G. Draguns, W. J. Lonner, & J. E. Trimble (Eds.), *Counseling across cultures* (4th ed., pp. 293–322). Newbury Park, CA: Sage.

López, S. R. (1989). Patient variable biases in clinical judgment. Conceptual overview and methodological considerations. *Psychological Bulletin, 106*, 184–204.

Markus, H. R., & Kitayama, S. (1991). Culture and the self: Implications for cognition, emotion and motivation. *Psychological Review, 98*(2), 224–253.

Marsella, A. J., & Kameoka, V. A. (1989). Ethnocultural issues in the assessment of psychopathology. In S. Wetzler (Ed.), *Measuring mental illness: Psychiatric assessment for clinicians* (pp. 231–256). Washington, DC: American Psychiatric Association.

Marsella, A. J., & White, G. M. (1982). Introduction: Cultural conceptions in mental health research and practice. In A. J. Marsella & G. M. White (Eds.), *Cultural conceptions of mental health and therapy* (pp. 3–38). Boston, MA: Reidel.

Mayman, M. (1967). Object-representations and object-relationships in Rorschach responses. *Journal of Projective Techniques, 31,* 17–35.

Meloy, J. R., Acklin, M. W., Gacono, C. B., Murray, J. F., & Peterson, C. A. (Eds.). (1997). *Contemporary Rorschach interpretation.* Mahwah NJ: Lawrence Erlbaum Associates.

Miralles Sangro, F. (1997). Location tables, form quality, and popular responses in a Spanish sample of 470 subjects. *Rorschachiana, 22,* 38–62.

Montero, M. (1982). *La estructura familiar y su influencia en la formación de estereotipos sexuales* [Family structure and sexual stereotypes]. Unpublished manuscript.

Moreland, K. L. (1996). Persistent issues in multicultural assessment of social and emotional functioning. In L. A. Suzuki, P. J. Meller, & J. G. Ponterotto (Eds.), *Handbook of multicultural assessment: Clinical, psychological, and educational applications* (pp. 51–73). San Francisco: Jossey-Bass.

Moreno, A. (1993). *El aro y la trama. Episteme, modernidad y pueblo* [The ring and the plot. Episteme, modernity and people]. Valencia: CIP–Universidad de Carabobo.

Okazaki, S., & Sue, S. (1995). Methodological issues in assessment research with ethnic minorities. *Psychological Assessment, 7*(3), 367–375.

Padilla, A. M., & Ruiz, R. A. (1975). Personality assessment and test interpretation of Mexican Americans: A critique. *Journal of Personality Assessment, 39*(2), 103–109.

Pike, K. L. (1967). *Language in relation to a unified theory of the structure of human behavior.* The Hague: Mouton.

Pires, A. (1993, July). *O estudo normativo do teste de Rorschach na população portuguesa: resultados parciais* [Rorschach norms for the Portuguese population. Preliminary results]. Paper presented at the XIV International Congress of Rorschach and Projective Methods, Lisboa, Portugal.

Pires, A. (1996, July). *The Rorschach normative study in Portugal: Cross-cultural comparison with the U.S. normative data.* Paper presented at the XV International Congress of Rorschach and Projective Techniques, Boston, MA.

Sendín, M. C. (1987). *Datos normativos en sujetos españoles* [Normative data from Spain]. Unpublished manuscript.

Shaffer, T. W., Erdberg, P., Haroian, J., Van Patten, K., & Hamel, M. (1996, August). *Rorschach norms for the '90s.* Poster presented at the XV International Congress of Rorschach and Projective Techniques, Boston, MA.

Silva, D. R., Novo, R., & Prazeres, N. (1991). Serão os dados normativos do Rorschach apresentados por Exner válidos para a população europeia? Ensaio com uma amostra portuguesa [Are Exner's Rorschach normative data valid for an European population? Exploratory study with a Portuguese sample]. *Separata do Revista Portuguesa de Psicologia,* No. 27.

Sue, S. (1996). Measurement, testing and ethnic bias: Can solutions be found? In G. R. Sodowsky & J. C. Impara (Eds.), *Multicultural assessment in counseling and clinical psychology* (pp. 7–37). Lincoln, NE: Buros Institute of Mental Measurements.

Triandis, H. C. (1994). *Culture and social behavior.* New York: McGraw-Hill.

Triandis, H. C., Malpass, R. S., & Davidson, A. R. (1973). Psychology and culture. *Annual Review of Psychology, 24,* 355–378.

Van de Vijver, F. J. R., & Leung, K. (1997). Methods and data analysis of comparative research. In J. W Berry, Y. H. Poortinga, & J. Pandey (Eds.), *Handbook of cross-cultural psychology: Vol. 1. Theory and method* (2nd ed., pp. 257–300). Boston: Allyn & Bacon.

Viglione, D. J., Gaudiana, S., & Gowri, A. (1997, March). *Two questions about Rorschach norms: Cultural issues and divergence?* Paper presented at the midwinter meeting of the Society for Personality Assessment, San Diego, CA.

Vinet, E., Saiz, J. L., & San Martín, C. (1995). Necesidad de normas nacionales en el Sistema Comprensivo del Psicodiagnóstico de Rorschach: el caso de Chile [The necessity of national norms for the Rorschach Comprehensive System: The Chilean case]. *Revista Iberoamericana de diagnóstico y evaluación psicológica, 1,* 189–201.

Weiner, I. B. (1986). Conceptual and empirical perspectives on the Rorschach assessment of psychopathology. *Journal of Personality Assessment, 50*(3), 472–479.

Weiner, I. B. (1996a). Some observations on the validity of the Rorschach Inkblot Method. *Psychological Assessment, 8*(2), 206–213.

Weiner, I. B. (1996b). Speaking Rorschach: A test for all seasons. *Rorschachiana, 21,* 1–2.

Weiner, I. B. (1997a). Current status of the Rorschach Inkblot Method. *Journal of Personality Assessment, 68*(1), 5–19.

Weiner I. B. (1997b). Editor's comment. *Rorschachiana, 22,* 64–66.

Weiner, I. B. (1998). *Principles of Rorschach interpretation.* Mahwah, NJ: Lawrence Erlbaum Associates.

Wober, M. (1974). Towards an understanding of the Kiganda concept of intelligence. In J. W. Berry & P. R. Dasen (Eds.), *Culture and cognition* (pp. 261–280). London: Methuen.

14

Use of the Rorschach Comprehensive System in Europe: State of the Art

Anne Andronikof-Sanglade
Université Paris X

In Europe, the Rorschach Comprehensive System (RCS) was introduced in the early 1980s and is currently still progressing at a somewhat slow but steady pace. To facilitate the scientific exchange between countries, a European Rorschach Association (ERA) was founded in 1989, which today groups researchers and practitioners from 14 countries[1] and holds a European Congress every 2 years.

Although it has enormously expanded throughout Europe and even recently reached Tunisia in Northern Africa, use of the RCS remains, as it were, somewhat confidential in many countries. Researchers and clinicians who use it are still to be considered as pioneers and are not always looked on kindly by the projective technique establishment.

HISTORY OF THE RCS IN EUROPE

Interest for the RCS arose in Europe almost as soon as it was published in the United States (see, e.g., a presentation of the system in France by Miljkovitch, 1979) and some English-speaking researchers started to try it out along with the traditional systems they were familiar with. Following the 1979 congress of the International Rorschach Society in Freiburg (Switzerland), John Exner was invited to lecture in Barcelona, where the RCS

---

[1]Austria, Belgium, Denmark, Italy, Finland, France, Norway, The Netherlands, Portugal, Spain, Sweden, Switzerland, Tunisia, Yugoslavia.

started to be taught. In 1982, an RCS training school opened in Madrid (Spain) as a satellite to Rorschach Workshops[2] and another in Milan (Italy).[3] In the other countries, persons interested in the RCS individually attended workshops in the United States for acquiring their training until the ERA was founded and started organizing workshops throughout Europe.

EUROPEAN TRADITIONS IN CLINICAL PSYCHOLOGY

In Europe, clinical psychology—both as an academic matter and as a practice—is borne out of a complex cradle composed of (a) a strong philosophical tradition dominated by Greek and German philosophers such as Plato, Aristotle, Kant, Hegel, and Husserl (i.e., a speculative, abstract-oriented approach of the world) as opposed to authors as Hume, Locke, and other champions of empiricism; (b) a positivistic ideology in medicine that claims that the human mind (and body) is nothing other than cells, neurons, and chemicals that can be visualized and measured, that its dysfunctioning is due to the lesion of an organ and can be mended or destroyed by chemical or surgical means; and (c) Freudian psychoanalytic theory.

While experimental psychology, as it was called, was fully recognized as a science in itself and taught at universities, clinical psychology was still fighting its way up and entered the university as late as the 1960s. The situation in France is somewhat exemplar of the process. At that time, clinical psychology was equated to testing (i.e., it consisted of mechanically applying measuring tools and techniques produced by scientists). Paralleling that technical field, psychiatrists, philosophers, and anthropologists plunged into psychoanalysis, which was divided into various schools. Psychologists who worked in the clinical field, in want of recognition, heavily relied on the specificity of the psychoanalytic theory and its approach of mental disturbances to fight against the label *psychotechnician*, which plagued them, and to ascertain their identity. So powerful was this position that clinical psychologists united under the psychoanalytic banner and finally obtained recognition and respect. The drawback today is that, in many countries, and especially in the southern ones of Latin tradition, clinical psychology has become a synonym of psychoanalytic psychology.

---

[2]J. E. Exner, Asheville, NC.
[3]Scuola Lombarda Rorschach, Zanchi, B.

For many in Europe, the term *clinical* defines neither a field of practice nor a concern and care for the mentally disturbed or psychologically suffering persons. Rather, it designates a specific approach of the human being based on the individual and unique relationship between two unconsciouses. The *clinical method*, as it is called, stands opposite—and in opposition—to all other approaches, such as the experimental, cognitive, and behaviorist.

It is in that context that the Rorschach developed in Europe to become a privileged and unique tool for clinical psychologists who found in it an ideal way to probe the psychic functioning of individuals in terms of drives, anxiety levels, fantasies, and defense mechanisms. Introduction of the RCS was seen as a backward move toward technicality, pedestrian measurements, and low-class psychology. Still there is a difference to be made among European countries: The Scandinavian countries and The Netherlands, traditionally much more open to empirical approaches and the American influence, seem to offer less resistance to the concepts and modes of understanding on which the RCS is based. Contrasting with the rest of Latin Europe, Spain and Belgium recently adopted the empirical point of view. France appears to be a particularly resistant country partly because of the clinical tradition described earlier, but mainly because it has developed a sophisticated system for interpreting the Rorschach, which is taught at the University of Paris V and more or less considered as the official Rorschach method.

DEVELOPMENT OF THE COMPREHENSIVE SYSTEM

Nevertheless, the RCS is spreading, even in France. Its development is being stimulated by clinical psychologists who work in mental health hospitals where psychiatrists are confronted with an ever-growing reference to it in the international literature, as well as by researchers in universities who seek reliable tools to approach psychological functioning (Andronikof-Sanglade, 1998).

In all the European countries, training in the RCS is mostly performed on a private basis outside of the official university education system—either through workshops sponsored by the ERA or, quite frequently, in an autodidactic manner by reading Exner's workbook and/or Volume I, whatever edition is available. The workbook has been translated into various languages, but Volumes I and II are still available only in French (Exner, 1995) and Spanish (Exner, 1994).

Having dealt with the epistemological and/or ideological context and with some practical issues, we can now turn to more fundamental considerations and research findings.

NORMATIVE ISSUES

Researchers throughout Europe have started collecting normative data for the RCS, and findings were presented at each of the ERA's congresses held since 1990—in Paris (France), Oslo (Norway), Lisbon (Portugal), Liège (Belgium), and Madrid (Spain). These were tentative studies of relatively small samples of subjects (up to 260) yielding rather disquieting results—results strangely similar, in some aspects, to those obtained in South American countries. We say they were disquieting because some of the core features of Rorschach data, such as Lambda, EA, Texture shading, and X+%, came out far from American norms, whereas the average number of responses is the same.

Two major normative studies were performed: one in Madrid by Dr. Concepcion Sendin (1993) and the other in Belgium by Dr. Christian Mormont (1998). Table 14.1 presents some of the main results in Sendin's, Mormont's, and Exner's samples (Exner, 1993).

Lambda and EA

In all nonpatient groups, high Lambdas are extremely common (35% in Mormont's sample). Consequently, EA is lower, averaging approximately 6 (as opposed to 8 in Exner's norms), and so is the number of blends. EA is low because both M and color responses are less expressed (see means for M and FC+CF+C in Table 14.1). This constant feature of poor articulation of determinants in European data is difficult to interpret and demands more refined analysis of the data and the demographic variables of samples.

As of now, these data have to be considered seriously because high Lambda and low EA have an impact on other important variables, such as the Coping Deficit Index (CDI). In Mormont's sample, 40% of the subjects present a positive CDI (see Table 14.1) against 3% in Exner's sample. Similarly, 30% of Mormont's subjects have a positive DEPI (vs. 3% in Exner's sample), and 10% of those have a DEPI > 5 (vs. 0% in Exner's sample). This huge amount of positive DEPI is probably explained by the variable overlap with the CDI.

The major lesson to be learned here is that neither the CDI nor the DEPI are suited for European subjects. A clinical confirmation of that statement was given as early as 1990 in a study by Mormont, Andronikof-

TABLE 14.1
A Selection of Normative Data in Europe Compared With Exner's Data

	Sendin's Sample	Mormont's Sample	Exner's Sample
Lambda	1.6	1.05	0.58
L >.99	—	35%	5%
EA	—	6.57	8.82
M	2.3	3.61	4.30
FC+CF+C	3.4	3.99	6.54
SumC'	0.3	2.32	1.53
SumT	0.9	0.48	1.03
T=0	—	68%	11%
Blends	4.6	3.94	5.16
Ego	0.38	0.36	0.39
Ego< .33	—	43%	16%
X+%	0.73	0.51	0.79

Sanglade, Vermeylen-Titron, and Pardoen, who used the RCS in a comparison of unipolar and bipolar depressive patients (*DSM–III* criteria). They found that none of these patients had a positive DEPI in their Rorschach.

Texture Response

One common feature of protocols in Europe is the absence of Texture, all results presented zero texture as being the rule (T = 0 varies between 60% and 80% of nonpatient subjects in various samples). Of course, this has important bearings on the interpretation of Texture as well as the frequency of the Hypervigilance Index (HVI).

X+%

Perhaps the most constant difference, and the most disquieting, is the average proportion of good form responses obtained in European nonpatient samples. In Mormont's sample (see Table 14.1), X+% has a mean of .51, whereas other studies display values around .65. Moreover, the average X–% is higher than in Exner's norms (.21 in Mormont's sample vs. .07 in Exner's), indicating that the low X+% is not only due to an abundance of unusual responses. This raises a fundamental question: How cultural is a good form?

The first consequence of the low X+% is a dramatic increase of positive schizophrenia indexes (SCZI), with 10% to 20% of all nonpatient protocols (and in some samples even more) presenting a SCZI = 4 positive index (12% in Mormont's sample). Indeed, four of the six conditions can be true on the sole basis of form quality. This of course has a direct bearing on the validity of the SCZI index in Europe and/or needs a shift of threshold from 4 to 5 to be considered positive. In the case of a positive SCZI index at 4, a close review of the positive items is adamant, rendering this index unusable in research.

Because of the uncertainty on what the average of good form should be in nonpatients, interpretation of form in terms of contact with reality and/or conventional thought is hazardous to say the least. It leads many clinicians to either conclude pathology where there is none or discard the importance of form quality, reverting instead to indiscriminate content interpretation. To give a trivial example, the response "A monster" will not have the same interpretive value when seen in a good form, as on Card IV, or in some DD99 arbitrary location. In the first instance, the response is based on a recognition of reality and conventional images (it's a good blending of cognitive and affective elements), whereas the second response is a projective mechanism with a failing grip on reality. The issue of X+% is a crucial problem and might be the most important to deal with for cross-cultural purposes.

CROSS-CULTURAL ISSUES

This section discusses the trends in European normative data presented earlier in terms of their bearing on cross-cultural issues. First we have to discuss a critical aspect—the upstream validity of the nonpatient samples used for normative data. How have these persons been selected, are they representative of a country population in terms of their socioeconomic status (SES) and level of education, and, an aspect not to be neglected, how skilled in the RCS were the psychologists who tested the subjects? Unfortunately, this kind of information is not readily available and sheds suspicions on the reliability of the data obtained. Nevertheless, some of the trends are so congruent across samples that they seem compelling and merit to be discussed.

The Issue of Determinants

Why are the variety and number of determinants usually found in a European Rorschach protocol so often restricted to a minimum, with pure F the most preferred approach to the task? Let us discard for a moment the hypothesis of bad administration of the test and poor inquiry.

In the RCS, scoring of a determinant relies exclusively on the subject's articulation of the objective features of the blot, which are recognized as having influenced the choice of content. This recognition is based on (a) a willingness and capacity to analyze one's perception, and (b) an acceptance of being challenged or simply having to explain or justify oneself. Both these conditions seem to be less developed in the average European folk. It is not that these people are less sensitive to the shading or color aspects of the blot. Rather, they either are not aware of this influence or find it so obvious that it is not even worth mentioning. One of the data supporting this hypothesis is that, in many instances, EA increases and Lambda diminishes with the education level or intellectual sophistication of the subjects.

Yet in some highly educated persons, the pure form approach remains dominant, which is strangely reminiscent of Hermann Rorschach's (1967) statement that there seems to be three types of sensitivities to the world (*Weltandschauung*): the kinesthetic, the color, and the form.

Would it mean that a high Lambda person (and what is the threshold for high Lambda?) is not necessarily an oversimplifying and impoverished type, but might function in a highly sophisticated manner? More reliable data have to be gathered before this question can be answered.

The color determinant, as mentioned earlier, also appears with a lower frequency than in the American samples. Often the distribution of FC versus CF and C is different: CF+C is often greater than FC in various samples (14% in Mormont's sample vs. 4% in Exner's, as seen on Table 14.1), especially in the Southern countries. This aspect, if confirmed in further normative studies, could have a straightforward cultural explanation. Latin cultures greatly value spontaneous expression of emotional states and their exaggeration. To burst out laughing or crying and to be effectively aroused are markings of higher level social skills. Psychologists tend to interpret a higher level of FCs (as opposed to CF and C) as indicating a defensive attitude toward the processing of affect (the cold fish syndrome). This popular and professional attitude toward little re-strained emotional display also has a theoretical root in some of the dominant models of structural development in France, which consider the hysterical structure as the higher stage of development.

Shading determinants are also distributed differently. Texture is sel-dom found; whenever it is, there is usually more than one present in the protocol. If interpreted in accordance with the RCS as a need for closeness, it appears that Europeans express it only when it reaches a proper need level, a craving for closeness, thus indicating a sense of frustration of this natural and therefore not to be mentioned aspect of one's life. Common sense does not permit us to interpret the absence of T as indicating a lack of experiences in closeness or a need to keep others at a distance, especially in the Latin countries where touching, cuddling, and kissing are common and conventional means of interaction. We might say that Southern Euro-peans express *behaviorally* what they do not express *verbally* through the texture response.

Special mention of the Vista response is required here, although there are not enough data yet to offer valid comments. Based on small samples of highly educated persons working in the literary and artistic fields (unpublished work) and on clinical experience, we have found a high frequency of Vista responses without any particular notion of self-disgust or guilt feelings. On the contrary, many of these people feel and display good self-esteem if not straightforward overglorification of self. The Vista response appears to have a sophisticated cognitive aspect that might predominate the affective aspect in highly educated persons, which is also linked to a high capacity for and familiarity with, introspection, but not in the systematic negative sense that Exner gives it.

THE ISSUE OF FORM QUALITY

Form Quality certainly is one of the key variables of the Rorschach test. It shares with the Popular variable the unique characteristic of being dependent on the content of the response, as opposed to structural variables such as location and determinant. By *content* we mean the words used to designate an object or shape. In that sense, content is a product of language, and we know that language is the making of culture. We are born in a culture, and we encounter the world through a language. Language is the utmost expression of a culture, its identity mark, both its core experience and symbol.

Therefore, it is legitimate to consider the content of the response as the variable most influenced by the culture of the subject. What are the consequences of such a statement on the notion of Form Quality? The most obvious approach would be to have as many Form-Quality tables as they are cultures or languages. Would not that decision question the celebrated universality of the Rorschach and preclude any form of cross-cultural comparisons? We think that there might be another approach, but that approach requires a careful reconsideration of the concept of Form Quality.

Questions of Definition

Rorschach thought of Form Quality as indicating the extent to which the shape of the object chosen by the subject in his response resembled the shape of the blot (or area of the blot used). This implies that he was aware that the blots did present specific form demands and he was interested in evaluating the form adequacy (to the blot) of the response. Most of his followers adopted the same definition but differed on the way to determine good form responses.

Rorschach's scoring of Form Quality was an either–or proposition: Either the response was adequate (F+) or inadequate (F–). He distinguished two types of good form responses: the common and the superior. Common good form corresponds to the responses frequently given to a blot or a certain part of it. Superior good form corresponds to rare contents (appearing once in 100 protocols) or even unique responses in which form has a perfect fitting with the blot. Rorschach had a special score of "Orig +" to mark these responses. It is important to note that both these types of responses were scored as good form (i.e., F+). It is even more important to remember that Rorschach considered the common responses as just tolerably adequate, quite evident, and easily seen, whereas the more accurate ones are far less frequent.

In Europe, all the systematizers applied Rorschach's rule (Beizmann, 1966; Loosli-Usteri, 1965; Rausch de Traubenberg, 1990), adding a third category (F±) for the responses in which the object lacks specific form demands (islands, leafs, maps, etc.).

All these systems acknowledge the necessity of establishing frequency tables for determining the *goodness of fit* of the common responses, but none is willing to deny the status of good form to infrequent responses if judged adequate.

The Underlying Concept

For Rorschach and most of his followers, the question of Form Quality refers to the resemblance of two shapes: the objective shape of the blot and the objective shape of the object identified by the subject. This manner of conceptualizing Form Quality legitimates the interpretation of X+% in terms of reality testing.

North American authors also stuck to Rorschach's concept of Form Quality but devised qualitative subcategories to make room for the *not so good* and *not so bad* use of form (Klopfer & Kelly, 1942; Mayman, 1970; Rapaport, Gill, & Schafer, 1946). Klopfer introduced the notion of *conventionality* of concepts (Klopfer & Kelly, 1942), only to state that unconventional must never be equated with inaccurate and that a careful investigation of the response is required in the inquiry phase before the response is judged adequate or inadequate. For all these authors, the core point is to determine whether the subject has taken into account the form requirements of the blot or disregarded/distorted them, however unconventional (personal) the response would appear.

In the RCS, there seems to be a two-step conceptual shift from form accuracy to conventionality and then from conventionality of shape to conventionality of vocabulary. *Good form* is solely defined by the frequency of occurrence of a specific object as designed by a word, as opposed to a frequent occurrence of a specific shape identifying a certain class of objects meeting the form requirements of the blot.[4]

We could agree with that definition if the RCS clearly departed from the traditional interpretation of X+% (reality testing) and announced that it only measures the distance of the subject to the average American language use and reference world. Although the interpretation of conventionality is put forward by Exner (1993), there still remains some confusion about the concept, this author seeming to endorse the notion that it also expresses the attitude toward reality.

Form Quality and Culture

By now the reader understands that discrepancies in Form-Quality levels throughout the world are due to the basically cultural (and even maybe subcultural) RCS definition of *good form*. It is truly natural to find different common objects in different cultures, and even more natural to find semantic differences in designating the same object among languages. In contrast, it would be totally unnatural to find perceptual differences among cultures (e.g., a circle being perceived as a rectangle).

Thus, the constant finding of low mean for X+% in Europe, when Form Quality is scored according to the RCS tables, can only be interpreted as evidence of language and environmental differences across cultures. Until proper lists of frequent responses are established for the European countries, no interpretation in terms of socially acceptable behaviors, individualistic orientation, or reality testing would be legitimate.

POPULAR RESPONSES IN EUROPE

Studies on Popular responses in Europe have yielded interesting results because they both confirm a universal mode of perceiving reality and a cultural specificity in doing so. Table 14.2 presents the list of Popular responses in a French sample of 4,274 responses of 204 nonpatients and outpatients (psychotic and schizophrenic patients excluded). The *Popular response* is defined as content appearing in at least one protocol out of three.

Nine out of the 13 Popular responses listed in the RCS are also Popular in France. The four that are missing are the bat on Card I (26%), the spider (16%) and the crab in D1 on Card X, and the humanlike figures in D3 on Card IX.

---

[4]In pure contradiction with this rule is the extrapolation principle, which captures the traditional concept of good form but leads to the alogical fact that a content so unique as to be absent from the list of unusual objects can be scored *ordinary*.

TABLE 14.2
Popular Responses in France

Card	Location	Content	%
I	W	Butterfly	39%
II	D1	Animal (dog, elephant, bear)	50%
III	D1/9	Human	76%
IV	W/D7	Human/Humanlike	36%
V	W	Butterfly	48%
	W	Bat	46%
VI	W/D1	Animal skin	46%
VII	D1/9	Human head (usually part of whole human figures in W or D2)	46%
VIII	D1	Animal (4-legged)	93%

These nine responses seem to be the core universal perceptive aspects of the Rorschach and were found in all previous studies throughout the world. Differences appear in the exact wording of the object, with the most familiar type of image corresponding to a general class of objects. For instance, the humanlike figure on Card IV is often given as a *troll* by people from Scandinavia and as an *ogre* by French subjects. Animals on Card VIII (D1) include all the usual types, but in France a chameleon (listed *unusual* in the Comprehensive System Form Quality Table) is seen as often as a beaver or cat.

If we lower the threshold for Populars to 20%, we obtain a list quite similar to that of the RCS, except for Cards IX and X. We also catch three other frequent contents: a winged insect on Card I (W), two humans on Card II (W), and a butterfly or bow-tie[5] on Card III (D3).

COMPARISON OF FRENCH AND AMERICAN DATA FOR CHILDREN: CULTURAL DIFFERENCES OR SAMPLING BIAS?

In the 1970s, three schools were selected as representative of French children from 6 to 12 years of age on demographic and educational criteria; these 250 children constituted the population for standardization of many tests in psychological assessment. Four experienced psychologists collected all the material, including a Rorschach test administered in a rigorous manner with a thorough inquiry and detailed location sheet. These protocols were rescored recently using the RCS by two trained psychologists.

---

[5]In French, a bow-tie is called a "butterfly-tie."

Table 14.3 presents a selection of indexes and variables for children ages 6 and 7 that present some striking differences with the data published by Exner and Weiner (1995).

An analysis of Table 14.3 indicates that children in the French sample give much more responses than their American peers, but that a great number of these responses are restricted to form. Positive SCZI indexes are exclusively caused by a low X+% (.40) and high X–% (.28)—a fact that can be confirmed by a low percentage of the Six Critical Special Scores. This result is similar to those found in adult samples and confirms the Form-Quality problem discussed earlier.

The overwhelming majority of high Lambdas might explain many of the other results, such as CDI, absence of Texture, and positive DEPI, by suggesting that French children would be less prone to articulate determinants in general. However, a close analysis of the determinants contradict this easy explanation, as is seen in Table 14.4.

Two features define the French group in striking difference with the American sample: (a) the means and frequencies of movement responses (both M and FM) are incredibly low, and (b) Sum Shading is astonishingly high. At 7 years of age, the mean for human movement in the American sample demonstrates an important leap up and reaches a mean of .40 at 11. In the French sample, the mean progresses steadily but slowly and reaches only .30 at 12. The low mean for M is to be referred to a low production of human contents (see Tables 14.3 and 14.4). However, the low mean for FM has no explanation and seems to indicate that the expression of needs is inhibited in this sample.

As for the shading responses, the high number of C′, the quasiabsence of T, and the presence of V make an interesting pattern that stands in

TABLE 14.3
A Selection of Ratios, Percentages, and
Special Indexes for Ages 6 and 7 Combined

	French sample (N = 61)		American sample (N = 200)	
Ratios . . .	Freq	%	Freq	%
SCZI > 3	10	16	0	0
DEPI > 4	19	31	0	0
CDI > 3	38	62	28	14
Lambda > .99	38	62	23	12
Sum T = 0	51	84	21	11
Ego < .33	49	80	4	2
Pop < 4	44	72	11	6
Sum 6 Sp. Sc. > 6	4	7	44	22
Pure H = 0	16	26	0	0

Note. Protocols with R > 13 | Mean R = 26 (French) & 20 (American)

TABLE 14.4
Determinants for Ages 6 and 7

Determinants	6 years old		7 years old	
	Mean	%	Mean	%
M	**1.12**	56	1.53	61
	1.96	*100*	*3.02*	*100*
FM	**1.64**	72	1.39	58
	4.52	*100*	*5.92*	*100*
Sum Color	**4.08**	100	4.42	97
	5.56	*100*	*6.15*	*100*
Sum Shading	**3.28**	88	3.94	88
	1.95	*95*	*2.48*	*100*
Sum C'	**2.04**	68	2.25	75
	0.58	*57*	*1.25*	*72*
Sum T	**0.24**	12	0.31	19
	0.83	*86*	*0.93*	*91*
Sum V	**0.20**	8	0.22	16
	0.00	*0*	*0.00*	*0*
Sum Y	**0.80**	52	1.17	52
	0.54	*46*	*0.23*	*30*

Note. **Bold: French sample.** *Italics: American sample.*

contrast with the American one, in which T is the main shading determinant, with very little C' and no V. The high Sum Shading goes with a lowering of Chromatic Color responses—a finding strangely reminiscent of previous results published both in the United States by Ames Bates, Learned, Métraux, and Walker (1952) and in Switzerland by Loosli-Usteri (1929, 1965). These authors found that perception of chromatic color came developmentally later than perception of achromatic color.

Another point of interest is given by the low mean Egocentricity Index (EGO) in the French sample, where 80% of the children have less than .33.

Contents

Following the previously stated hypothesis that culture specificity best expresses itself in the actual contents of Rorschach protocols, which also have the advantage of escaping administration and/or scoring biases, we can look at the kind of contents given by the French children of the sample considered and compare them to Exner's sample. Table 14.5 displays a selection of contents that show some important differences in the referential world of the children.

The main features are as follows: Compared with their American peers, French children give many more Animal, Nature, and Botany responses

TABLE 14.5
A Selection of Contents for Ages 6 and 7

Contents	6 years old		7 years old	
	Mean	%	Mean	%
All H	**2.96**	92	2.86	83
	4.28	*100*	*4.63*	*100*
H	**1.52**	68	1.78	77
	2.63	*100*	*1.87*	*100*
(H)	**0.28**	20	0.39	30
	0.78	*82*	*1.64*	*77*
Hd	**1.12**	52	0.69	36
	0.64	*56*	*0.38*	*37*
A	**11.96**	100	9.89	100
	8.24	*100*	*9.26*	*100*
Fd	**0.32**	32	0.17	14
	0.58	*57*	*0.20*	*20*
Na	**1.32**	60	2.03	69
	0.81	*61*	*0.96*	*68*
Bt	**2.76**	80	2.06	75
	1.52	*95*	*2.11*	*100*
Ls	**1.08**	48	0.94	38
	1.27	*100*	*1.21*	*76*
Id	**0.80**	48	0.83	47
	0.15	*15*	*0.53*	*47*

Note. **Bold: French sample.** *Italics: American sample.*

and far fewer Human. They also give less Food responses. At 6 and 7 years of age, American children give much more (H) than do French children, and every one of them gives at least one pure H, whereas some French children (almost 20% at 7) do not give any human content.

Cultural Differences Versus Sampling Biases

In terms of cultural differences, it appears that French children of 6 and 7 years of age do not identify themselves with adult human beings and monsters as American children do. They are closer to the animal and natural worlds and are more inhibited in the expression of emotions and needs when confronted with a new and bizarre school task, as no doubt the Rorschach was perceived. Finally, they are much less self-centered than their American peers.

The French sample was constituted of all the children in a classroom, provided the parents (who had been informed by mail) had not objected to the procedure. All parents gave their consent. Children who presented known learning difficulties were then discarded from the sample. In contrast, the American sample was constituted by asking parents to volunteer for their children. That difference in selection procedure might account for the important differences in results. In some of the districts, as few as 20% of the children were volunteered (J. Exner, personal communication, 1993).

One might say that the French sample, although reduced in number, truly represents the average nonpatient schoolchild, whereas the American one might be biased by the unknown motivations of parents when volunteering or not for their child.

Whatever the reason for these differences, they are too important to be altogether discarded; they point to the evident fact that so-called *normative data* cannot be exported from one continent to another and that further collecting of nonpatient protocols is needed on both sides of the Atlantic.

CONCLUSION

This chapter presented an overview of the development of the RCS in Europe and of the available data. The latter point to the fact that exportation of the RCS to non-American cultures requires some adjustment and cannot be directly made by transferring normative data.

The RCS is both a standardized conceptual tool and an empirical body of data. The empirical part has to be validated in every culture: How does the average Dane, Italian, or Swiss respond to the inkblots? What constellation of variables reflect a major affective disturbance? At what age do children reach the adult distribution of variables? At what pace do they develop? Because the RCS is a powerful means of investigating psychological processes, it will no doubt develop enormously in Europe and be instrumental in reshaping both clinical practice and research models.

REFERENCES

Ames Bates, L., Learned, J., Métraux, R. W., & Walker, R. N. (1952). *Child Rorschach responses.* New York: Brunner/Mazel.

Andronikof-Sanglade, A. (1998). Le Rorschach en Système Intégré dans l'évaluation psychologique: Une nouvelle technique, un nouveau regard clinique [The Rorschach Comprehensive System in psychological assessment: A new technique and clinical approach]. *Revue Française de Psychiatrie et de Psychologie Médicale, 18,* 135–138.

Beizmann, C. (1966). *Livret de cotation des formes dans le Rorschach* [Form Quality tables for the Rorschach]. Paris: ECPA.

Exner, J. E. (1993). *The Rorschach: A comprehensive system: Vol. 1. Basic foundations* (3rd ed.). New York: Wiley.

Exner, J. E. (1994). *El Rorschach: Un sistema comprehensivo* [The Rorschach: A comprehensive system]. (M. Esbert, Trans.). Madrid: Psimática.

Exner, J. E. (1995). *Le Rorschach: Un système intégré* [The Rorschach: A comprehensive system]. (A. Andronikof-Sanglade, Trans.). Paris: Frison-Roche.

Exner, J. E., & Weiner, I. B. (1995). *The Rorschach: A comprehensive system: Vol. 3. Assessment of children and adolescents* (2nd ed.). New York: Wiley.

Klopfer, B., & Kelly, D. M. (1942). *The Rorschach technique.* New York: World Book Company.

Loosli-Usteri, M. (1929). Le test de Rorschach appliqué à différents groupes d'enfants [The Rorschach test applied to various samples of children]. *Archives de Psychologie, 22,* 85.

Loosli-Usteri, M. (1965). *Manuel pratique du Test de Rorschach* [Workbook for the Rorschach test]. Paris: Hermann.

Mayman, M. (1970). Reality contact, defense effectiveness, and psychopathology in Rorschach form-level scores. In B. Klopfer, M. Meyer, & F. Brawer (Eds.), *Developments in the Rorschach technique.* New York: Harcourt Brace Jovanovich.

Miljkovitch, M. (1979). Le système inclusif de cotation du Rorschach par Exner [Exner's comprehensive scoring system for the Rorschach]. *Revue de Psychologie Appliquée, 29*(3), 267–292.

Mormont, C. (1998, August). Données normatives en Belgique pour le Rorschach en Système Intégré [Normative data for Rorschach comprehensive system in Belgium]. Paper presented at the 5th ERA Congress, Madrid.

Mormont, C., Andronikof-Sanglade, A., Vermeylen-Titron, N., & Pardoen, D. (1990). Comparaison de déprimés unipolaires et bipolaires au moyen du Rorschach [Comparison of unipolar and bipolar major depressive disorders with the Rorschach test]. *Revue de Psychologie Appliquée, 40,* 207–224.

Rapaport, D., Gill, M., & Schafer, R. (1946). *Diagnostic psychological testing* (Vol. 2). Chicago: Yearbook Publisher.

Rausch de Traubenberg, N. (1967). *La pratique du Rorschach* [Using the Rorschach] (3rd ed.). Paris: PUF.

Rorschach, H. (1967). *Psychodiagnostic* (4th ed.) (A. Ombredane & A. Landau, Trans.). Paris: P.U.F. (Original work published 1921)

Sendin, C. (1993, July). Rorschach comprehensive system normative data in Spain. Paper presented at the International Congress of the Rorschach and Projective Techniques, Lisbon.

15

The Rorschach Comprehensive System in Iberoamerica

Eugenia V. Vinet
Universidad de La Frontera, Temuco, Chile

This chapter describes the status of the Rorschach Comprehensive System (RCS) in the Iberoamerican countries. First, it assumes a cultural unity between two European countries (Spain and Portugal) and the American countries that received the historical, political, and cultural influence from these two countries. Second, it describes the introduction, development, and present situation of the RCS in some Iberoamerican countries. Finally, it analyzes research studies from these countries on the topic of cultural relevance of the RCS providing a cross-cultural context to be considered in the interpretation process.

IBEROAMERICA AS A CULTURAL UNIT

Iberoamerica includes Spain and Portugal, the two European countries located on the Iberian peninsula, and all the American countries that received the Iberian influence through more than 300 years of direct dominance and colonization (since the discovery of America in 1492 until the independence wars of the early 19th century). After their political independence, American nations established a privileged relationship with their former settlers. This had an important role in the general development of these nations and their peoples; this special relationship has lasted until the present time.

Nevertheless, Iberoamerica is not a homogeneous culture. Spain and Portugal faced the loss of their colonies and have dealt with all the

European political crises during the present century. American countries had to integrate the heritage of their indigenous societies in their specific cultures and, in some cases, the influence of African groups who came as slaves. Later on, they received immigrants from other European and Asian countries, shaping a complex Latin-American culture whose main characteristics began to be studied by psychologists only a few decades ago.

Despite these facts, and because of the shared historical roots and a long period of close interaction among Iberian and Latin-American countries, which included the transmission and assimilation of language (Spanish and Portuguese), traditions, religion, values, a way of living, and so on, Iberoamerica can now be considered a cultural unit that shares important characteristics related to psychological features of its people.

Some of these common features have been identified by Hofstede (1980). In Hofstede's study of work-related values in 40 countries, the Iberoamerican countries were grouped in a large cluster that included Belgium and Greece and some Asian countries. This group is distant from the Anglo-American cluster that included the United States, Australia, Canada, Great Britain, Ireland, and New Zealand. Iberoamerican countries obtained similar scores on three of the four cultural dimensions analyzed. Iberoamericans scored in the upper third on the dimensions of Power Distance (PD) and Uncertainty Avoidance (UA); they also scored low in Individualism (IDV), with the exception that Spain scored in the middle. Specifically, people from these countries tend to hold more authoritarian values, showing respect for higher class positions and nonegalitarian social interactions (PD). They also tend to experience a higher anxiety level associated with uncertainty and stress, and they defend themselves through well-established rules and rituals (UA). They have a collectivist orientation (IND); they pay attention to the needs, goals, values, and points of view of others to a greater extent than they do to their own. These others form an ingroup that gives protection, demands loyalty, and creates emotional dependence.

Common cultural characteristics have also been noted by Triandis (1981) in studies linking ecology and culture with social behavior. In these studies, Iberoamerica would belong to the contact cultures, which were initially located around the Mediterranean. They are characterized by physical contact on social interactions and open expression of emotions. People from these countries stand close to each other, touch each other frequently, and make eye contact during their social interactions. They also express emotions like joy, sadness, and anger, laughing and crying openly with little inhibition.

Another cultural characteristic of Iberoamericans has been conceptualized by Triandis, Marín, Lisansky, and Betancourt (1984) as the cultural script of *Simpatía*, which is one of the components of the more general pattern of collectivism. An individual who is *simpático* shows "certain levels of conformity and an ability to share in other's feelings, behaves with dignity and respect toward others, and seems to strive for harmony in interpersonal relations" (Triandis et al., 1984, p. 1363).

As is shown later, some of the characteristics mentioned earlier have an expression in the testing situation and in the responses to the Rorschach Test; they may be responsible for several common differences encountered in the Rorschach data of Iberoamerican countries when contrasted with U.S. data.

THE COMPREHENSIVE SYSTEM IN IBEROAMERICA

The RCS entered Iberian countries through Spain, spreading quickly to Portugal and more slowly into the American countries. As a peculiarity and reinforcing the Iberoamerican cultural unit hypothesis, it is interesting to note that the RCS entered the American countries via Spain and Spanish-speaking psychologists, not through the United States, although the geographic distance between the United States and the other American countries is much shorter than the distance between Europe and these countries. The introduction, development, and current status of the RCS in some of the Iberoamerican countries are reviewed as follows.

Iberian Countries

Spain. In 1974, when Exner published the first edition of *The Rorschach: A Comprehensive System*, Spanish psychologists worked mainly with Bohm's (1979) and Klopfer's (Klopfer & Kelly, 1974) systems using a psychoanalytic approach. It took only 3 years for the RCS to take a place in the Spanish Rorschach psychology. In 1977, after the Ninth International Congress of Rorschach held in Fribourg, Switzerland, Exner was invited to Madrid and Barcelona to give two seminars under the auspices of the *Sociedad Española del Rorschach y Métodos Proyectivos* (SERYMP) and the *Sociedad Catalana del Rorschach y Métodos Proyectivos*. In both cities, Exner found professionals who clearly perceived the advantages of the RCS over the previous systems in terms of its conceptual clarity, empirical bases, and teachability. After these seminars, Exner often traveled to Spain to present new developments of the RCS and provide the opportunity for Spanish psychologists to delve into its study.

After being trained in the United States at the Rorschach Research Foundation, C. Sendín started the Spanish branch of the Foundation in Madrid in 1982, offering regular postgraduate courses on the RCS. This branch of the Rorschach Research Foundation also has organized Rorschach Workshops, on a regular basis, with visits from J. E. Exner every 2 years (C. Sendín, personal communication, December 9, 1997). In Barcelona, V. Campo, using a descriptive and dynamic model, integrated the RCS propositions with a psychoanalytic approach to achieve a broad view of personality (Ortiz & Campo, 1993). Under Campo's direction, the *Sociedad Catalana de Rorschach* integrated in their regular courses Exner's propositions, and their teachers traveled repeatedly to Valencia, Murcia, Madrid, and the Basque country "spreading the RCS gospel" (V. Campo, personal communication, December 1, 1997).

The introduction of the RCS to the Spanish universities has been slow but progressive, especially considering the small role that projective techniques play in regular university programs. Despite this, the RCS is now the most firmly established and academically accepted Rorschach method in Spanish universities, and there are master's and doctoral programs in clinical psychology where the RCS is taught, making possible research and many publications. In this area, Ortiz and Campo (1993) reported that a bibliographic search of the available databases on Spanish publications for the 1984 to 1991 period found that 35 of the 66 articles on Rorschach (53%) used the RCS scoring system. The other articles used unspecified systems (29%) or mainly Bohm's (1979) system (11%).

A diversity of topics is being studied using the RCS in Spain. They include descriptive studies for different pathologies, examination of different Exner's indexes, and studies related to the cultural pertinence of RCS normative data to assess Spanish subjects (Ortiz & Campo, 1993). These studies began with a report about Popular responses found among 220 nonpatient adults from Madrid (Sendín, 1981). The principal findings included only 10 Popular responses instead of the 13 reported by Exner (1974), two independent Popular responses on Card IV (giant or monster, 38%, and animal skin, 33%), and the failure to obtain a Popular response on Card IX. Later, in a similar study done with nonpatient subjects from Barcelona, Larraz and Valero (1988) obtained only eight Popular responses, one by each card with failures on Cards II and IX. These authors also reported a Popular responses mean ($M = 5.02$, $SD = 1.3$) as significantly different from Exner's 1986 data ($z = 13.81$; Larraz & Valero, 1988).

Soon after this, two preliminary studies to compare Spanish data with the normative data presented by Exner (1991) were done. Sendín (1993) compared the data obtained by 294 nonpatients from Madrid on 42 basic variables of the Rorschach Test with the normative data from the U.S. population. She found statistically significant differences on four variables: Lambda, Afr, P, and X+%. Alvarez et al. (1993) compared the data obtained by 250 volunteer subjects from Barcelona on all the variables computed by the RCS norms and found, with only a few exceptions, that the basic statistics were significantly different from Exner's normative data and clinically similar to the reported by Silva, Novo, and Prazeres (1991) in Portugal.

Portugal. The RCS was introduced to Portugal in 1985 by Silva and Pires, who adopted it to replace the French method. This change was possible thanks to the workshops conducted by Exner, the support of Weiner, and the seminars organized by Sendín in Spain (Silva & Marques, 1994). The first article about the RCS published in Portugal was by Silva (1986), who concentrated on introducing and describing the RCS. Afterward, results on the temporal consistency of Rorschach variables in Portuguese children (Silva, 1988) presented at the 12th International Congress of Rorschach held in São Paulo, Brazil, in 1987 led Silva to start a research project comparing data obtained from different samples of school-age children with normative data presented by Exner and Weiner (1982) for U.S. children (Silva, 1991; Silva, Novo, & Prazeres, 1996).

The results were surprising because systematic differences in variables as important as X+%, X–%, Lambda, W:D ratio, Shading responses, and Egocentricity Index were obtained. The analysis of those studies demonstrated developmental changes occurring over time on certain Rorschach variables, as well as the importance of recognizing possible differences from the Exner–Weiner normative data in Portuguese children. Taken one step further, Silva and his associates started a normative study with Portuguese children and presented preliminary results from a sample of 117 six- to ten-year-old children (Silva & Prazeres, 1995). Data from 20 variables, when compared with the Exner–Weiner norms for each age group, showed developmental changes in the Portuguese children, which are, in most instances, different from those found in U.S. children.

Another study of the same issue, using an adult sample ($n = 100$), was presented in Paris, France, at the 13th International Congress of Rorschach in 1990 (Silva et al., 1991). These results follow the same trend observed in the samples of children. The authors questioned the adequacy of the Exner normative data used with Portuguese and other European subjects. This provided the basis for a normative study of the Portuguese adult population and an impetus to normative studies in different countries and cultures to sustain the need for culturally pertinent norms for the Rorschach Test.

Latin-American Countries

The status of the Rorschach Test and the RCS in Latin-American countries is reflected by its presence in the recent Interamerican Congress of Psychology held in 1997 in São Paulo, Brazil. This is a traditional meeting organized every 3 years by the Interamerican Society of Psychology (SIP). It presents the principal trends and developments of psychology in the different American countries. Although there were no conferences about the Rorschach Test, there was a symposium with five presentations about Rorschach in different contexts; these presentations included two reports that used the RCS as their scoring method. In addition, there was a round table on culture and psychological assessment in Iberoamerica that included one report about the RCS. Finally, of the 54 presentations held in the open sessions about psychological assessment, there were only 2 that dealt with the Rorschach Test, and 1 of those was about the RCS (Interamerican Society of Psychology, 1997).

Specific information about the RCS in the Latin-American countries is meager, and the sources have different degrees of accuracy. Only a few studies have been published in books or journals. Most of the information comes from oral presentations in national and international congresses, but they are difficult to access because there may be no written reports of these presentations. Besides these sources, there are only personal communications, most of which were obtained for the preparation of this chapter. This section covers the situation of the RCS in 8 of the 17 Latin-American countries on the basis of these sources, noting that it was not possible to obtain information about Mexico, Central American countries, Bolivia, and Paraguay.

Beginning with the countries where the RCS is less known, it is useful to point out that in Colombia and Uruguay there are plans to give introductory workshops about the RCS in the near future. These courses will be offered in Spanish by Latin-American psychologists who are trained on the system and have personal contacts with local psychologists. In the same vein, the first workshop about the RCS held in Ecuador was conducted by A. Tapia, an Ecuadorian-Spanish psychologist, and myself at the Ninth *Congreso Latinoamericano de Rorschach* held in Quito in 1995. In Peru, the RCS was introduced in 1990 by M. Ráez; currently it is taught in five of the nine universities of Lima (M. Ráez, personal communication, November 3, 1997). Finally, it is possible to trace a short history about the RCS in Venezuela, Chile, Brazil, and Argentina. In these countries, there are systematic studies about either the application of the method to different clinical groups or the cultural relevance of normative data from the United States in these countries.

Venezuela. The visits of I. B. Weiner in 1985 and 1986 to the Universidad Central de Venezuela (UCV) and the creation of the Instituto Rorschach de Venezuela in the early 1990s, which adopted the RCS as its basic language, were key factors for the introduction of the RCS. Currently, professionals from the Intituto teach at the UCV and lead different research projects in Rorschach using the RCS (D. Ephraim, personal communication, November 9, 1997).

Two studies on the topic of Rorschach and cultural pertinence are part of Venezuelan research work. The first one (Ephraim, Acevedo, Alvarez, & Rueda, 1993) studied the popular and common responses in a sample of 216 nonpatient adults from Caracas. They found only eight Popular responses using the RCS criteria and lesser frequencies in the appearance of several common responses reported by Exner (1986). They did not offer an interpretation of these differences, but demonstrated statistically that the differences in frequency could not be attributed to the lower socioeconomic level of the Venezuelan subjects. Furthermore, they reported that specific contents for the Popular responses given by males and females are different from those reported by Exner (1986). The second study (Ephraim, Riquelme, & Occupati, 1996) is a normative study done with the same sample. It presents descriptive statistics and analyses differences found with respect to Exner's normative data, concluding with the need to develop local norms to work with the RCS.

Chile. The RCS was introduced to this country by myself. Prior to this, from 1981 to 1982, I took a two-level course on the RCS offered in Madrid by C. Sendín; and in 1982, I took a workshop conducted by J. E. Exner at the Universidad Complutense de Madrid. In 1983, I began to teach Rorschach according to the RCS at Universidad de La Frontera (UFRO), being also a thesis adviser in the regular professional psychology program. This work made it possible for every psychology student from UFRO to receive basic training in Rorschach according to the RCS, and some of them had the opportunity to explore different topics in Rorschach research using the RCS. To spread the RCS out of UFRO has been a difficult task because of the strength of the psychoanalytic and phenomenological approaches in university settings and the reticence of Chilean psychologists to work with a quantitative method. Nevertheless, UFRO's alumni have established a strong national presence for the RCS through their own work with the method. Currently the RCS is taught in several universities in the country and is well known in the national Rorschach community.

It is important to point out three studies related to the applicability of the RCS data to Chilean subjects. The first one (Hernández, Rey, San Martín, & Vinet, 1989) is an exploratory study that compared normative data presented by Exner (1978) with the data obtained by 60 adults from southern Chile with no psychological disturbance. Significant differences were found in 21 of 28 variables. The second one (Vinet, Ascencio, Cea, & Oyarce, 1991) deals with the Popular responses presented by Exner in 1974. In a sample of 120 nonpatients adults, the authors found a mean of

4.2 (SD = 1.4) against the mean of 6.7 (SD = 1.8) reported by Exner and confirmed only 5 of the 13 Popular responses proposed by Exner in his first listing. The authors developed their own listing, which included eight Popular responses that are close to those presented by Exner in 1986. Chilean responses included one response by each card, with failures in Cards IV, VI, and IX, and two independent responses in Card V (bat, 39.2%, and butterfly, 34.2%).

The third study (Vinet, Saiz, & San Martín, 1995) analyzed the necessity of developing Chilean norms according to the new criteria used in the RCS. The sample consisted of 102 nonpatient adults selected according to the 1992 census in the variables of sex, age, educational level, and urban or rural origin. The results show significant differences on 54 (85.7%) variables out of 63 parametric variables reported by Exner (1991). It was concluded that U.S. norms are not applicable to Chilean subjects, and therefore national norms are needed.

Brazil. The 12th International Congress of Rorschach held in Brazil in 1987 played an important role in the introduction of the RCS to this country. Brazilian psychologists realized that many reports presented at the congress used the RCS scoring method, and thus they decided to study it. With the cooperation of Exner and Weiner, they contacted Ephraim from Venezuela who went, in 1990, to the Universidade Federal de São Paulo to teach the bases of the RCS. Later on, the RCS was introduced to other Brazilian universities and to the Sociedade Brasileira de Rorschach. Since then, most of the doctoral theses that include the Rorschach Test use the RCS. Different studies have been presented in national and international congresses in the last 2 years documenting that, despite the strong influence of a Brazilian scoring method and the dynamic approach, the RCS has a place in Brazilian personality assessment (N. L. Semer and R. S. G. F. do Nascimento, personal communication, November 13, 1997; H. C. P. Morana, personal communication, November 30, 1997).

There are two relevant studies on the topic of culturally relevant norms. These studies are based on previous information about the poor psychological assessment results obtained for populations with economic and cultural deficits and the great differences from Exner's normative data obtained by Brazilian psychologists using the RCS with adult patients. The first study (Guntert & Nascimento, 1996) presented preliminary data obtained in a sample (n = 20) of children from low-income families. Comparisons were made with data obtained from other Brazilian studies, with no control for socioeconomic level, as well as with the Exner normative data. They reported significant differences in 16 Rorschach variables related to the cognitive process and the capacity for control. The other report (Nascimento & Guntert, 1997) examined results obtained by

15 nonpatients adults, with no psychological claims in six cognitive Rorschach variables (P, X+%, F+%, Xu%, X-%, and S+%). They found significant differences in each of the six variables. It is important to note that the direction of the differences was similar to those reported in other Iberoamerican studies.

Argentina. According to I. Sanz (personal communication, November 26, 1997), the RCS was not welcomed to Argentina until 1995 to 1996. Although Exner was in Argentina in 1980, attending the Fourth Congreso Latinoamericano de Rorschach held in Rosario, the strong psychoanalytic rooting and a theoretical approach to Rorschach interpretation based on Klopfer's system impeded acceptance of the RCS. Exner was able to interest only a few psychologists at that time. One of them, E. Noceti, started working with the RCS by herself and is now an expert and recognized consultant. After the congress, A. Pascala conducted a workshop communicating Exner's concepts to the Asociación Argentina de Rorschach. However, she soon created her own Rorschach school, which is one of the best-known Argentinean Rorschach developments of the last decade and incorporates only a few Exner's concepts. During this long period, Argentinean psychologists learned about the RCS through the attendance at scientific meetings outside the country, sporadic visits of the Argentinean–Catalan psychologist V. Campo, and the Spanish translation of Exner's textbooks. These facts created a renewed interest in the RCS since 1995, and a few training activities have been organized with the support of some visits from Spain.

In this context, research activity has been sparse. Despite this, the studies done by Noceti (1995, 1996) on specific clusters of variables to get a better understanding of the psychological functioning and disturbances through the RCS are noteworthy. Contributions of Sanz (1997a, 1997b) on organizational activity include a proposed new variable—organizational quality (ZQ)—that is important in the cognitive process of psychotic patients.

RORSCHACH RESEARCH ON CULTURAL PERTINENCE OF THE RCS IN IBEROAMERICAN COUNTRIES

In the last section, 10 studies reporting data about several Rorschach variables in samples from five Iberoamerican countries (Spain, Portugal, Brazil, Chile, and Venezuela) are presented. These samples were all composed of nonpatient volunteers, with the exception of 33 males from Portugal who took the test in a job-selection process. Nevertheless, these samples are not strictly comparable because they differ on important variables such as age range, education, and socioeconomic level. However, it is useful to understand the similarities found among these Iberoamerican studies, especially when these data are compared with U.S. data.

The Data

Tables 15.1 and 15.2 present data about Popular responses. As shown in Table 15.1, all means are lower than the U.S. mean by aproximately two points. In addition, the total number of Populars found in these countries ($M = 8$) is lower than the 13 U.S. Populars. The list of the contents of Popular responses shown in Table 15.2 roughly coincides with Exner's 1986 list. These countries share six Popular responses (located on Cards I, III, V, VII, VIII, and X) and the failure to obtain a Popular on Card IX. All of them have a Popular (bat or butterfly) on Card I, but in most cases these two contents are considered together as in Exner's list of 1974. The same situation occurs on Cards V (butterfly and bat) and X (spider and crab). Popular responses to Cards II, VII, and VIII are present in every study and are very similar to Exner's Populars. Differences from Exner's list include the absence of Populars on Cards II, IV, and VI in some studies and the presence of two new Populars, Card IV,"animal skin" on W, specific for the Madrid sample (Spain 3), and Card X, "animal forms" on

TABLE 15.1
Popular Responses in Nonpatient Samples
From the United States and Iberoamerican Countries

Country	n	M	SD	Total Number
United States				
Exner (1991)	700	6.89	1.39	13
Brazil				
Nascimento & Guntert (1997)	15	4.80	1.57	—
Chile				
Vinet et al. (1991)	120	3.99	1.42	8
Vinet et al. (1995)	102	4.66	1.80	—
Portugal				
Silva et al. (1991)	90	4.31	1.29	8
Spain				
Alvarez et al. (1993)	250	5.75	1.50	6
Larraz & Valero (1988)	200	5.02	1.39	8
Sendín (1981)	220	—	—	10
Sendín (1993)	294	5.10	1.50	—
Venezuela				
Ephraim et al. (1993)	216	—	—	8
Ephraim et al. (1996)	218	4.83	1.57	—

Note. Dashes indicate that data were not reported.

TABLE 15.2

Contents and Percentages of Popular Responses Found in the United States and in Six Studies From Iberoamerican Countries

Card	Location	Content	United States	Chile	Portugal	Spain–1	Spain–2	Spain–3	Venezuela
I	W	Bat	48	—	38	—	—	—	41
I	W	Butterfly	40	—	40	—	—	—	—
I	W	Bat or butterfly[a]	—	47	—	—	53	52	—
II	D1	Animal forms	34	48	—	—	—	39	—
III	D1 or D9	Two human figures or representations thereof	89	66	75	62	90	87	80
IV	W or D7	Human or humanlike figure	53	—	—	51	40	38	39
IV	W	Animal skin or rug	—	—	—	—	—	33	—
V	W	Butterfly	46	34	35	36	—	—	39
V	W	Bat	36	39	45	51	—	—	57
V	W	Butterfly or bat[a]	—	—	—	—	87	94	—
VI	W or D1	Animal skin, hide, rug, or pelt	87	—	—	38	61	54	—
VII	D1 or D9	Human head or face	59	35	58	—	42	43	53
VIII	D1	Whole animal figure	94	87	84	84	94	97	65
IX	D3	Human or humanlike figures	54	—	—	—	—	—	—
X	D1	Spider	42	—	—	—	—	—	—
X	D1	Crab	37	—	—	—	—	—	—
X	D1	Spider or crab[a]	—	48	—	—	35	43	35
X	D8	Animal forms	—	—	33	—	—	—	—

Note. Data from United States are taken from Exner (1986). Data from Chile are taken from Vinet et al. (1991). Data from Portugal are taken from Silva et al. (1991). Data on Spain–1, Spain–2, and Spain–3 are from Alvarez et al. (1993), Larraz and Valero (1988), and Sendín (1981), respectively. Data from Venezuela are taken from Ephraim et al. (1996). Dashes indicate that those contents were not reported as Populars on the corresponding listings.
[a]These contents categories include the two contents originally considered in the 1974 listing.

355

D8, specific for the Portuguese sample. These findings give credibility to the universality of the RCS listing of Populars, but also support Piotrowski's (1957) hypothesis about cultural variations. Similarities on these listings support the idea of considering Iberoamerican countries as a unit that shares an important cultural background. There are fewer Populars than in the United States. Differences between particular lists and the U.S. list suggest some differences among specific national cultures.

To provide an integrated view, the data reported in four studies with adult samples (two European and two Latin American) in 22 Rorschach variables have been organized in Table 15.3. A comparison with Exner data shows systematic differences on almost every variable. The most meaningful are the values of Lambda (Iberoamerican $M = 1.26$ vs. U.S. $M = 0.58$); the differences in Populars already presented; the systematic differences in the four cognitive mediation variables (low X+%, low F+%,

TABLE 15.3
Descriptive Statistics for 22 Rorschach Variables in the
United States and Four Iberoamerican Countries

	USA		Chile		Portugal		Spain		Venezuela	
Variables	M	SD	M	SD	M	SD	M	SD	M	SD
R	22.67	4.23	20.86	7.04	23.36	12.64	24.53	8.21	20.80	6.98
L	0.58	0.26	1.46	1.53	1.07	0.82	1.06	0.89	1.43	2.53
Zf	11.81	2.59	9.15	4.62	13.57	5.73	12.38	4.86	10.84	5.05
Zd	0.72	3.06	−1.33	3.78	−1.15	4.97	−0.52	4.36	−0.42	4.30
P	6.89	1.39	4.66	1.80	4.31	1.29	5.75	1.94	4.83	1.87
X+%	0.79	0.08	0.52	0.18	0.53	0.13	0.55	0.13	0.45	0.14
F+%	0.71	0.17	0.51	0.23	0.53	0.21	0.50	0.19	0.44	0.22
X−%	0.07	0.05	0.15	0.12	0.13	0.08	0.19	0.10	0.18	0.11
Xu%	0.14	0.07	0.30	0.13	—	—	0.25	0.10	0.36	0.14
Afr	0.69	0.16	0.49	0.16	0.61	0.29	0.56	0.22	0.52	0.21
M	4.31	1.92	2.19	1.67	3.46	2.90	4.24	2.94	3.41	2.71
WSumC	4.52	1.79	2.34	2.08	3.52	2.37	2.66	2.03	2.14	1.74
EA	8.83	2.18	4.50	2.91	6.98	4.07	6.90	3.85	5.55	3.42
es	8.20	2.98	6.91	4.35	10.12	6.16	8.92	5.11	7.63	4.61
FM	3.70	1.19	2.85	1.98	3.37	2.81	3.67	2.35	3.27	2.25
m	1.12	0.85	1.46	1.89	1.50	1.58	1.21	1.35	0.90	1.25
SumSh	3.39	2.15	2.63	2.26	5.25	3.74	4.04	3.21	3.44	2.88
SumC'	1.53	1.25	0.95[a]	1.25[a]	2.08	2.01	1.40	1.46	1.08	1.41
SumT	1.03	0.58	0.37[a]	0.70[a]	0.53	0.74	0.57	0.93	0.73	1.03
SumV	0.26	0.58	0.24[a]	0.53[a]	0.90	1.32	0.66	1.02	0.64	1.01
SumY	0.57	1.00	1.09[a]	1.26[a]	1.74	1.64	1.40	1.54	1.00	1.54
EA−es	0.63		−2.46		−3.14		−2.02		−2.08	

Note. The data of the different countries are taken from the following sources: United States: Exner (1991), Chile: Vinet et al. (1995), Portugal: Silva et al. (1991), Spain: Alvarez et al. (1993), Venezuela: Ephraim et al. (1996).
[a]These data come from Vinet, San Martín, and Saiz (1994).

high X–%, and high Xu%), which are also found in the studies from Brazil (Nascimento & Guntert, 1997) and Valencia, Spain (Fúster, Sifre, Barriuso, Lobato, & Martínez, 1997) not reported in Table 15.3; the dismished amount of organized resources given by EA including its two components, M and WsumC; the lower value of SumT (Iberoamerican $M = 0.55$ vs. U.S. $M = 1.03$); and the higher value of SumY (Iberoamerican $M = 1.31$ vs. U.S. $M = 0.57$).

Interpretation Hypotheses

Most of the authors have been careful in their interpretation of these findings by restricting themselves to reporting only the most impressive differences from the U.S. norms and advocating development of national or local norms. Proceeding one step further, Vinet et al. (1995) pointed out that the values obtained in Rorschach variables reflect a good psychological adjustment within the own sociocultural context, even if they describe a vulnerable and unstable psychological adjustment close to psychopathology when interpreted according to U.S. normative criteria.

In an interpretation exercise done with 1995 data, Vinet (1997) created a group structural summary and interpreted it according to the RCS using a strategy for interpretation of clusters based on two key variables: D < AjdD and Lambda > .99 (Exner, 1991). The Lambda value (1.46) commanded the whole interpretation process, although there were a few signals of situation-related stress associated to limited coping resources (low EA). The high-Lambda style included simplification of the significant elements of the field, low interest to process emotional stimuli, and directly influenced cognitive mediation and affect processing. Interpretation resulted in a peculiar style of psychological functioning characterized by apparent low involvement with reality in its cognitive, affective, and interpersonal aspects. Vinet emphasized the nonpatient condition of the subjects and the similarity of these results to Hernández et al. (1989), where high-Lambda scores were interpreted as a decreased effort for information processing that should be understood considering the cultural characteristics of Latino-American society.

Cross-cultural comparisons have been made using the RCS norms and interpretation criteria in groups and profile descriptions. In these descriptions (Alvarez et al., 1993; Ephraim et al., 1996), and partially in Sendín (1993), Iberoamerican subjects are characterized as being less conventional, with a lower orientation to reality, a higher commitment to individuality than U.S. subjects (values on P, X+%, F+%, X–%, and Xu%), and more defensive in the testing situation because of a more simplistic coping style and less responsivity to emotional stimulation (values in L, Afr, and C responses).

Data from Table 15.3 also allow an interpretative hypothesis for the negative Zd value and for the variables grouped in the EA–es difference. Negative Zd could be related to both groups of variables already interpreted. If a subject has motives to be defensive in the testing situation or has an oversimplified coping style, he or she would be more reluctant to engage in effective organizational activity, especially if there is an individualistic perception of reality. The EA–es difference is a raw appreciation of the D score, which "provides information concerning the relationship among resources that are available for use and stimulus demands that are being made on the individual" (Exner, 1986, p. 315). The four studies presented here have a negative EA–es difference (M = −2.43) that comes from low resources and high demands. In contrast, the U.S. difference is positive (+0.63). The analysis of the demand variables (FM, m, SumC', SumT, SumV, SumY) shows that, although there are specific variations by nationalities, values for the situation variables are higher in these studies (m $M = 1.29$ and SumY $M = 1.31$) when compared with U.S. values (m $M = 1.12$ and SumY $M = 0.57$). On the one hand, it is suggested that people from Iberoamerican countries need fewer resources than people in the United States to deal with most living circumstances (systematic lower M and C values). On the other hand, the testing situation, expressed through the situation variables, seems to have a stronger impact on psychological functioning being associated with distress experiences characterized by a loss of the capability for control.

Finally, Iberian researchers have attended to the much lower Texture (T) response values than the U.S. norms. According to Exner (1991), most nonpatients give one T response, which means the individual experiences needs for closeness and emotional contact in a way similar to most other people. If the value for T is zero, it suggests that the subject is distant and conservative in interpersonal situations, overly concerned with personal space, and very cautious about creating and maintaining close emotional ties. Because T values in Iberoamerican countries are close to zero, this interpretative hypothesis should be applied. Nevertheless, Fúster (1993) suggested that the large number of records with no T found in nonpatients may be the result of differences in the socialization process of countries defined as *contact cultures*. In most cultures, physical contact is a frequent behavior in infancy; children are held on an adult's lap—they are touched, hugged, and kissed. They learn an interpersonal interaction pattern from this that includes natural and spontaneous physical contact linked to emotional closeness. The difference in the socialization process arises when children are older (4 to 5 years old). At this age, U.S. children would learn to restrain their natural need for physical and emotional contact to become adapted to a noncontact culture, and they would experience the need for closeness expressed in T responses (T = 1) during adulthood. In contrast, Iberoamerican children would maintain in adulthood the pattern of natural physical contact learned in early infancy, not experiencing any special need for closeness (T = 0) because this need has been satisfied throughout their development in a contact culture (Fúster, 1993). Texture responses keep their interpretative meaning, but their values should be treated differently depending on the characteristic of the cultural context in which the individual experiences the socialization process.

A Cultural Context to the Interpretation Hypothesis

Fúster's hypothesis is an example of a cross-cultural interpretation that includes special features of the subject's cultural context. To clearly understand the meaning of the differences presented in the prior data, it is important to remember the link among culture, perception, and personality. This link was recognized early in cultural studies with the Rorschach Test. Hallowell (1953) stated that the processes that are responsible for the acquisition, transmission, and maintenance of the culture patterns of a people are, at the same time, essential for the acquisition of a personality structure by an individual. The socialization process patterns and motivates the individual's interpersonal relations with other members of the society and allows him or her to be an integral part of the ongoing sociocultural group.

Within this line of reasoning, culture is present in the Rorschach responses as it is present in every other social behavior. Although the inkblots may be considered unstructured, culture-free stimuli, the subject's answers are never culture-free because they are cast in their particular form by the culture to which the individual belongs. When Exner (1978) first examined the response process, he implicitly postulated a specific role for culture in this process. Culture would have its first influence during the initial visual input and encoding of the stimulus because this process operates through the perceptual styles learned by individuals within their specific cultural context. The creation of potential responses is also related to culture because the subject will emphasize those aspects that are typical in the everyday cultural context. In addition, the internalized and socioculturally accepted norms and values will play a role in discarding potential responses through censorship. Finally, culture would also be present in the final articulation of responses, which is made through culturally learned language and expressive modes.

Culture is present in the response process and in the meaning of the testing situation. This fact seems to be important in the cultural context of Iberoamerican countries. The testing situation is a normed social interaction, where both participants—the examiner and client or patient—have specific roles that are in some way culturally determined. In Iberoamerican countries, this situation may be understood in terms of Hofstede's (1980) cultural dimensions as a social interaction characterized by high Uncertainty Avoidance and high Power Distance in a collectivist context. The testing situation is usually a new and unexpected situation for the examinee; it provokes a large amount of anxiety and stress, and there are no structured rules to cope with it. The examiner is perceived as a person with authority and power over the subject who belongs to an outgroup. In this context, the individual will probably behave in a *secure* way, which is characterized by respect, obedience, and conformity, but also by low cooperativeness and low interpersonal trust. Under these circumstances, it is easy to understand a Rorschach record with high Lambda values as a sign of defensiveness, low values in Afr and C responses meaning low affective involvement, and high values in the situation variables, especially in the Shading responses (Y), linking passivity and anxiety as disphoric feelings related to the inability to respond. Furthermore, the subject will not show distressing feelings openly because the situation demands correctness and *Simpatía* (Triandis et al., 1984). The subject will be attentive to the examiner's needs by trying to avoid a difficult situation for the assessor.

The testing situation may also partially explain the EA–es difference noted earlier. Higher demands should be related to the perception of this situation. Nevertheless, nothing has been said about the lesser amount of resources found in Iberoamerican samples. Why do Iberoamericans seem to need fewer resources to deal with most living circumstances than U.S. people? One possible explanation links the development of personal resources to the dimension of individualism-collectivism (Hofstede, 1980; Triandis, 1994). In Iberoamerican countries, the collectivist pole prevails, therefore cooperation with ingroup members, communal exchanges, and help from others are expected behaviors. In this cultural context, an individual will learn that it is possible to rely on ingroup resources to solve everyday problems, personal responsibilities may be shared with the ingroup, success depends on others' help, and personal effort is secondary. As a result, the development of individual resources to cope with everyday living will not be as important as it is in more individualist societies like the United States. This fact would account for the smaller amount of personal resources expressed by lower values in the EA variables.

Finally, issues of unconventionality, low perceptual accuracy, and a subjective approach to reality related to the values of the cognitive mediation variables can only partially be understood through direct cultural characteristics of Iberoamerican countries. The low conventionality and subjective approach apparently contradict a collectivist orientation. Nevertheless, it is useful to emphasize that in collectivist societies there is a sharp distinction between ingroup and outgroup that includes a dual perception of norms and regulations (Hofstede, 1980; Triandis, 1994). Collectivist subjects are conventional and show conformity and respect toward norms and rules originated by the ingroup, but they are prepared to ignore the general society rules with the approval of ingroup members if these rules are perceived as outgroup regulations. In this manner, they may break traffic regulations, arrive late to fixed appointments, and have other unconventional actions. It is suggested that the small number of Populars and the lower values in X+% and F+% with the increment of Xu% and X–% could be partially related to this dual perception about conventions and rules.

To complete this picture, Rorschach users must take into account that conventionality and the other cognitive variables are measured through the Form Quality of the responses scored using tables developed from U.S. samples. These tables do not appear to be universal because they are influenced by perceptual habits derived from the sample's culture. Research on this topic (Alvarez et al., 1993) shows that many responses classified as *ordinary* in a sample of 250 protocols from Barcelona (Spain) using the statistical criteria established in the RCS (2% of the records if the location area is W or D) did not appear or were classified as *unusual* in the RCS working tables. Furthermore, when the authors computed the Form Quality for a smaller group of records ($n = 94$) using their own Form-Quality tables, they obtained higher values in X+% and F+% and lower values for the other two variables. These new figures were still significantly different from the U.S. values, but were also significantly different from the initial values obtained using the RCS tables.

At this point, it is relevant to consider the best way to do Form-Quality scoring. Should Iberoamerican psychologists prepare their own Form-Quality tables as in Barcelona or should they use the RCS tables defining the low and high values according to their own data? The answer is not clear yet. Furthermore, this question evokes other related questions about other tables based on U.S. samples: Location tables, Popular listings, and Z scores tables. Although some Iberoamerican researchers (e.g., Miralles, 1996) have developed Location and/or Form-Quality tables, a definitive answer has not been formulated yet. Miralles' work showed that it is possible to make thorough working tables to give an appropriate framework to specific groups (in this case, Spanish outpatients). However, it also showed that those tables cannot be used properly with other groups of patients or with the nonpatient population. These projects are difficult to implement under the research conditions in most Iberoamerican countries because large samples are required, together with well-trained examiners and research teams prepared to work for a long period of time.

Future Development of the RCS in Iberoamerica

At the end of this chapter, several aspects emerge as significant:

1. There is enough evidence to postulate systematic differences between normative data from the United States and Iberoamerica.
2. Some of these differences can be better understood if common cultural characteristics of Iberoamerican countries are taken in account.
3. National and cross-national normative studies are needed to properly assess Iberoamerican individuals.
4. Research examples are scarce, local, and isolated.
5. There is a need for transnational research teams to develop culturally pertinent use of the RCS in Iberoamerican countries.

Empirical research on the response process and testing situation is required to clearly determine the role of cultural variables on them. In addition, a common and rationale approach to different aspects of the RCS working tables is needed, especially a thoughtful decision on Form-Quality scoring and the indexes derived from it. Furthermore, more intuitive and theoretical contributions (e.g., Fúster, 1993) are needed to illuminate the link between specific cultural aspects and interpretation theory. Later on, linking hypothesis should be tested. It would be of particular interest to continue the research on child development begun in Portugal. If Silva's results are replicated, empirical data about the way culture affects developmental changes occurring in Rorschach variables would be available as new bases to document relevant hypotheses concerning the differences observed in adult populations.

Any step toward these goals will first benefit Iberoamerican individuals by providing Rorschach assessment for them that considers their own cultural context. Second, minority groups in the United States such as Latinos and Hispanics, who share some cultural characteristics with Iberoamericans, will also be benefited. The culturally competent assessment advocated by Dana (1995) would be enriched if the RCS provides a framework including cultural variables in assessment with the Rorschach Test. Third, these studies will increase an understanding of the links between culture and individual psychological functioning. Finally, the theoretical and empirical bases of the RCS will be enriched if the role of culture is integrated in the response process, testing situation, and some individual stylistic variables.

ACKNOWLEDGMENTS

Chilean studies had the support of the Dirección de Investigación y Desarrollo de la Universidad de La Frontera (DIDUFRO; research project 9307). I thank the following Iberoamerican psychologists who kindly collaborated with me by providing written material and information about the RCS in their countries: Vera Campo, Fátima Miralles, and Concepción Sendín from Spain; Danilo Silva from Portugal; Isidro Sanz and Elida Noceti from Argentina; Regina G. do Nascimento, Norma L. Semer, and Hilda Morana from Brazil; Matilde Ráez from Peru; Alicia Muniz from Uruguay; and David Ephraim from Venezuela. I also thank Dr. Richard Dana for his careful revisions of previous manuscripts of this chapter and his suggestions to improve English readability.

REFERENCES

Alvarez, M., Baeza, A., Campo, V., García, J. M., Guardia, T., Montlleó, A., Jirón, P., Mateos, M. L., Minobis, J., Navarro, J., Pérez, V., Pouso, R., Prófumo, L., Torras, C., & Zayas, M. (1993). Primera aproximación a un estudio normativo de la ciudad de Barcelona y su entorno [First approach to a normative study in Barcelona and surroundings]. *Revista de la Sociedad Española del Rorschach y Métodos Proyectivos, 6*, 6–20.

Bohm, E. (1979). *Manual del Psicodiagnóstico de Rorschach* (7ª edición) [Manual of Rorschach Psychodiagnosis (7th ed.)]. Madrid: Morata.

Dana, R. H. (1995). Orientaciones para la evaluación de hispanos en los Estados Unidos de Norteamérica utilizando la prueba de Rorschach y el Test de Apercepción Temática [Guidelines for assessment of Hispanics in the United States using the Rorschach and Thematic Apperception Tests]. *Revista de la Sociedad Española del Rorschach y Métodos Proyectivos, 8*, 176–187.

Ephraim, D., Acevedo, E., Alvarez, C., & Rueda, S. (1993). Diferencias nacionales en la frecuencia de respuestas populares y comunes al Rorschach. Un estudio de sujetos venezolanos [National differences in the frequency of popular and common responses to the Rorschach: An study with Venezuelan subjects]. *Revista de la Sociedad Española del Rorschach y Métodos Proyectivos, 6*, 28–35.

Ephraim, D., Riquelme, J., & Occupati, R. (1996). Características psicológicas de habitantes de Caracas según el Sistema Comprensivo del Rorschach. Datos normativos y comparación trancultural [Psychological characteristics of people from Caracas according to the Comprehensive System. Normative data and cross-cultural comparison]. In D. Ephraim (Ed.), *El método Rorschach en la actualidad* (pp. 45–66). Caracas, Venezuela: Monte Avila Editores Latinoamericana.

Exner, J. E. (1974). *The Rorschach: A comprehensive system* (Vol. 1). New York: Wiley.

Exner, J. E. (1978). *Sistema Comprensivo del Rorschach. Tomo III* [Rorschach Comprehensive System. Vol. 3]. Madrid, Spain: Pablo del Río.

Exner, J. E. (1986). *The Rorschach: A comprehensive system: Vol. 1. Basic foundations* (2nd ed.). New York: Wiley.

Exner, J. E. (1991). *The Rorschach: A comprehensive system: Vol. 2. Interpretation* (2nd ed.). New York: Wiley.

Exner, J. E., & Weiner, I. B. (1982). *The Rorschach: A comprehensive system: Vol. 3. Assessment of children and adolescents.* New York: Wiley.

Fúster, J. (1993). ¿Por qué T o no T en el Rorschach? [Why T or not T in Rorschach?]. *Revista de la Sociedad Española del Rorschach y Métodos Proyectivos, 6,* 39–44.

Fúster, J., Sifre, S., Barriusi, I., Lobato, E., & Martínez, M. (1997). Comparación de una muestra de población normal valenciana con la muestra barcelonasa [Comparison of a sample of normal population from Valencia with the sample from Barcelona]. *Revista de la Sociedad Española del Rorschach y Métodos Proyectivos, 10,* 58–65.

Guntert, A. E. V. A., & Nascimento, R. S. G. F. (1996, October). *Rorschach: Estudo preliminar comparativo entre resultados obtidos em criancas de periferia de São Paulo e dados normativos* [A preliminary study comparing results of peripheral children from São Paulo with normative data]. Paper presented at the 2nd Encontro da Sociedade Brasileira do Rorschach, Ribeirao Preto, Brazil.

Hallowell, A. (1953). The Rorschach technique in personality and cultural studies. In B. Klopfer (Ed.), *Developments in the Rorschach technique* (pp. 459–543). New York: Hartcourt, Brace.

Hernández, P., Rey, R., San Martín, C., & Vinet, E. (1989). Diferencias entre las culturas angloamericana y latinoamericana en las respuestas dadas al Psicodiagnóstico de Rorschach [Differences between Anglo-American and Latin-American cultures in the answers given to the Rorschach Test]. *Terapia Psicológica, 11,* 62–66.

Hofstede, G. (1980). *Culture's consequences. International differences in work-related values* (abridged ed.). Newbury Park, CA: Sage.

Interamerican Society of Psychology. (1997). *XXVI Interamerican Congress of Psychology, Abstracts.* São Paulo, Brazil: Author.

Klopfer, B., & Kelly, D. (1974). *Técnica del Psicodiagnóstico de Rorschach* (3ª edición) [Rorschach Technique (3th ed.)]. Buenos Aires: Paidos.

Larraz, L., & Valero, A. (1988). Respuestas populares al Test de Rorschach en población española. Muestra de Barcelona [Popular responses to the Rorschach Test in Spanish population. Sample of Barcelona]. *Revista de la Sociedad Española del Rorschach y Métodos Proyectivos, 1,* 47–54.

Miralles, F. (1996). *Rorschach: Tablas de localización y calidad formal en una muestra española de 470 sujetos* [Rorschach: Location and form quality tables in a Spanish sample of 470 subjects]. Madrid, Spain: Universidad Pontificia Comillas.

Nascimento, R. S. G. F., & Guntert, A. E. V. A. (1997, July). *Um estudo piloto das medias de qualidades formal em um grupo de sujeitos nao-pacientes de São Paulo, conforme o Sistema Integrado de Exner* [A pilot study about means of form quality in a non-patient group from São Paulo according to Exner's Comprehensive System]. Paper presented at the 1st Congresso da Sociedade Brasileira de Rorschach e outros Métodos Projetivos, Ribeirao Preto, Brazil.

Noceti, E. (1995, November). *Las personas desvalidas: CDI+* [The helplessness persons: CDI+]. Paper presented at the 9th Jornadas Nacionales de Psicodiagnóstico, Buenos Aires, Argentina.

Noceti, E. (1996, July). *Analysis of characteristics studied in 48 patients in diagnostic process according to the Comprehensive System.* Paper presented at the 15th International Congress of Rorschach and Projective Techniques, Boston, MA.

Ortiz, P., & Campo, V. (1993). The present status of the Rorschach Test in Spain. *Rorschachiana, 18,* 26–44.

Piotrowski, Z. (1957). *Perceptanalysis.* New York: Macmillan.

Sanz, I. (1997a, July). *Nuevas propuestas de evaluación de alteraciones cognitivas en el Test de Rorschach. Su aplicación en una muestra de pacientes psicóticos internados* [New propositions for the assessment of cognitive disturbances with the Rorschach Test. Application in a sample of psychotic in-patients]. Paper presented at the 1st Congreso Iberoamericano de Evaluación Psicológica, Porto Alegre, Brazil.

Sanz, I. (1997b, July). *Aportes a la exploración de funciones cognitivas en el Test de Rorschach* [Contributions to the exploration of cognitive functions with the Rorschach Test]. Paper presented at the 26th Interamerican Congress of Psychology, São Paulo, Brazil.

Sendín, C. (1981, July). *Identification of Popular Responses among Spanish adults.* Paper presented at the 10th International Congress of Rorschach and Projective Techniques, Washington, DC.

Sendín, C. (1993, July). *Non-patient transcultural comparison.* Paper presented at the 14th International Congress of Rorschach and Projective Techniques, Lisbon, Portugal.

Silva, D. R. (1986). Exner e a reposicao do teste de Rorschach [Exner and the revival of the Rorschach Test]. *Revista Portuguesa de Pedagogia, 20,* 135–168.

Silva, D. R. (1988). Um estudo da consistencia temporal no Rorschach [A study about the temporal consistency in Rorschach]. *Revista Portuguesa de Psicologia, 24,* 159–170.

Silva, D. R. (1991). Analise do Rorschach de tres grupos de criancas Portuguesas no termo do 1º ano de escolaridade [Rorschach analyses in three groups of Portuguese children at the end of the first school year]. *Revista Portuguesa de Psicologia, 27,* 61–73.

Silva, D. R., & Marques, M. E. (1994). The Rorschach and other projective methods in Portugal. *Rorschachiana, 19,* 24–46.

Silva, D. R., Novo, R., & Prazeres, N. (1991). Serao os dados normativos do Rorschach apresentados por Exner validos para a populacao europeia? Ensaio com uma amostra Portuguesa [Are Exner's normative data valid for the European population? Study with a Portuguese sample]. *Revista Portuguesa de Psicologia, 27,* 13–27.

Silva, D. R., Novo, R., & Prazeres, N. (1996). The evolution of some Rorschach variables in Portuguese children. *European Journal of Psychological Assessment, 12,* 53–58.

Silva, D. R., & Prazeres, N. (1995). Sobre dados de alguns estudos normativos do sistema integrativo do Rorschach (SIR) de Exner fora dos E.U [Data from normative studies on the Exner's Comprehensive System of Rorschach outside USA]. *Revista Iberoamericana de Diagnóstico y Evaluación Psicológica, 1*(2), 161–187.

Triandis, H. C. (1981). Influencias culturales en el comportamiento social [Cultural influences in social behavior]. *Interamerican Journal of Psychology, 15,* 1–28.

Triandis, H. C. (1994). Theoretical and methodological approaches to the study of collectivism and individualism. In U. Kim, H. C. Triandis, C. Kagitcibasi, A. Choi, & G. Yoon (Eds.), *Individualism and collectivism: Theory, method and applications* (pp. 41–51). Thousand Oaks, CA: Sage.

Triandis, H. C., Marín, G., Lisansky, J., & Betancourt, H. (1984). *Simpatía* as a cultural script of Hispanics. *Journal of Personality and Social Psychology, 47,* 1363–1375.

Vinet, E. (1997, July). *Qué es lo "propio" en la evaluación con el Sistema Comprehensivo del Rorschach? Un estudio con sujetos chilenos* [What is the "one's own" in the assessment with the Rorschach Comprehensive System? A study with Chilean subjects]. Paper presented at the 26th Interamerican Congress of Psychology, São Paulo, Brazil.

Vinet, E., Ascencio, M., Cea, S., & Oyarce, E. (1991, August). *Test de Rorschach: Aplicabilidad en Chile del listado de respuestas populares de Exner (1974)* [Rorschach Test: Application in Chile of Exner's Popular responses listing from 1974]. Paper presented at the 4th Congreso Nacional de Psicólogos, Santiago, Chile.

Vinet, E., Saiz, J. L., & San Martín, C. (1995). Necesidad de normas nacionales en el Sistema Comprehensivo del Psicodiagnóstico de Rorschach: El caso de Chile [Need for national norms in the Comprehensive System of Rorschach Test: The Chilean case]. *Revista Iberoamericana de Diagnóstico y Evaluación Psicológica, 2,* 189–201.

Vinet, E., San Martín, C., & Saiz, J. L. (1994). *Chilean data of nonparametric variables for the Comprehensive System.* Unpublished raw data.

16

National Norms for the Rorschach Normative Study in Portugal

António Abel Pires
Universidade do Porto, Portugal

This chapter presents the methodology and discussion of some results from the total sample. Results are presented by styles (ambitent, introversive, extratensive) and high and low Lambdas. It also presents the results by formal education levels. Finally, a comparison is made among 40 variables in our results and those of Exner's.

THE NORMATIVE STUDY

The idea of the Rorschach Test Normative Study on the Portuguese Population came up with the interest of the usage of this tool in psychological research. The Normative Study carried out in the 1970s by John Exner on the U.S. population was the only one that existed, and the question raised then dealt with the possibility of using Exner's normative results on populations within a different cultural background from the North American's.

This question led us to our study hypothesis connected to the influence of culture on personality. To what extent might culture (seen on a broader context as encompassing language, history, psychoeducational practices, the sociocultural context, socioeconomic organization, and the organization of the institutions) have an important influence on the psychological development and structuring of the individual's personality? The hypothesis of the influence of culture on personality has been the subject of various research studies in the cross-cultural field. Lindzey (1961) was one of the first authors to write on the role of projective techniques in cross-cultural research. In his book and concerning the Rorschach, he concluded in a pessimistic vein due to methodological limitations in the late 1950s. Other works in this same field deserving reference are Levine's (1973) study on culture, behavior, and personality, and Abel's (1973) analysis of the utilization of several psychological assessment tools within different cultural contexts, devoting a large piece of his study to Rorschach. More recently, Dana's (1993) study concerned the multicultural evaluation in the United States and the need to supply services that are adapted to the cultural diversity of the individuals in the assessment and psychological intervention areas, and Matsumoto's (1996) study looked at the influence of culture in the psychological functioning.

One of the goals of the current work was to conduct a study of the Rorschach Test on the Portuguese population so that this tool might be used in a reliable manner both in clinical work and research. The stimulus material comprising the 10 cards set up over 75 years ago by Hermann Rorschach in Switzerland has been used unchanged the world over, and it is not our purpose to modify this material. All research efforts will fall on the normative data, giving us information for the correct use of this tool. By carrying out this study, we will also have access to interesting information on the Portuguese population. To correctly evaluate its specificity, we are most interested in comparing the results of our population with those of other populations—namely, the United States.

Following Exner's (1993) Rorschach Normative Study, several normative studies were undertaken in several countries; partial results from these studies were presented on the last International Congresses of Rorschach and Projective Methods. Among them we count Portugal (Pires, 1990, 1993, 1994, 1996; Pires & Borges, 1990; Silva, 1993, 1996; Silva & Prazeres, 1990), Spain (Miralles Sangro, 1996; Sendin, 1993; Silva, 1996), Finland (Mattlar et al., 1993), Venezuela (Ephraim, Riquelme, & Occupati, 1992; Riquelme & Ruos, 1996), and China (Harada, 1996).

METHODOLOGY

Population and History

Portugal is a European country with a population of approximately 10 million. It is one of Europe's oldest nations and has the most stable borders. From the beginning of the 15th century to the 17th century, Portugal played a major role in the discoveries. It was one of the first countries to abolish the death penalty in the 19th century. In the 20th century, the country was ruled by a single-party dictatorship (from 1926 to 1974), which actively supported Franco during the Spanish Civil War; it was benevolently neutral toward Hitler during World War II.

It was a 500-year colonial empire, covering, in the 1960s, five African countries (Cabo Verde, Guiné-Bissau, S. Tomé and Príncipe, Angola, and Mozambique) and one Asian country (East Timor, which is presently occupied by Indonesia). A liberation war against Portuguese colonialism was started in the early 1960s in Guiné-Bissau, Angola, and Mozambique and lasted until 1974. The lack of alternatives to the colonial war and the saturation of the guerrilla warfare fighting led to the politicizing of a relatively important number of armed forces officials and brought them to carry out a military coup on April 25, 1974. Its objective was to promote democratization of the country, ensure freedom of the press, and guarantee freedom of association with the creation of political parties. It was the liberation of a gagged country.

There was a large flow of emigration in the 1960s, mainly for economic reasons. This gave rise to important communities in France, Brazil, the United States, Canada, South Africa, the United Kingdom, Spain, and Germany. The total of the Portuguese emigrant population and its descendants is currently about 4 million.

Democracy has been reaching consistency and stability since 1974. Nowadays, Portugal has a stable democratic regime like the Western democracies. Strong economic and social development have also been noted since that date, and especially since 1987, when it joined the European Economic Community (EEC). The last 24 years have seen profound changes in this country concerning development, with many significant changes in lifestyle regarding economic, technological, social, and cultural aspects. The working population was well distributed by sectors in 1974: primary (34.3%), secondary (33%), and tertiary (32.7%). In 20 years, these distributions have been radically changed: 11.8%, 32.6%, and 55.6%, respectively.

Schooling is relatively low among the adult population when compared with Western countries. The exception is the 18- to 25-year-old age group, which is quickly closing in on the European average.

Sample

The sample constitutes nonpatient adults and was layered according to gender, age group, schooling, and the region in function of the 1991 Population Census. An equal number of men and women was sought despite the Census indicating a slightly higher number for female gender (males = 48.2%, females = 51.8%). Six age groups were considered: from 18 to 65 (Table 16.1). The sample distribution by age does not correspond

TABLE 16.1
Demography Variables for 309 Adult Nonpatients

Variables	Number	%
Marital status		
Single	84	27
Lives w/S.O.	2	1
Married	201	65
Separated	6	2
Divorced	10	3
Widowed	6	2
Unlisted	0	0
Sex		
Male	155	50
Female	154	50
Age		
18–25	74	24
26–35	81	26
36–45	71	23
46–55	46	15
56–65	28	9
Over 65	9	3
Race		
White	308	100
Black	0	0
Hispanic	0	0
Asian	0	0
Other	1	0
Unlisted	0	0
Education		
Under 7	102	33
7–9 years	69	22
10–12 years	77	25
13+ years	61	20
Unlisted	0	0

exactly to the population; the older age groups are less represented because it was here that the largest number of protocols were discarded. According to the 1991 Census data, the Portuguese population distribution by age is as follows: 18–24 = 14.9%, 25–34 = 19.3%, 35–44 = 17.6%, 45–54 = 15.3%, 55–64 = 14.8%, 65–74 = 11.0%, and 75+ = 7.2%.

Schooling was divided into three levels: primary (0–6 years), secondary (7–12 years), and superior (13 years +). Primary level corresponds to the compulsory schooling being 6 years for the over 30-year-old group and 9 years for the under 30s. The 1991 Census shows that the distribution of the adult population according levels of schooling is as follows: 0–6 years = 73%, 7–12 years = 18.5%, and 13+ years = 8.5%. Nevertheless, for the 18 to 25 age group, this distribution is somewhat different: 0–6 years = 47.2%, 7–12 years = 39.8%, and 13+ years = 13.1%. As we can see, the majority of individuals of this second group have more than 8 years of schooling, and this age group has been increasing its schooling every year. 1997/1998 data for the 18 to 25 age group show figures close to 0–9 years = 50%, 10–12 years = 30%, and 13+ years = 20%. The female population has become more and more numerous in university and presently constitutes the majority in almost all courses.

Bearing in mind the minimum representativeness of each of these groups, we decided that the primary level would represent 50% of the sample, secondary level 30%, and superior level 20%. The collected protocols are: primary = 44%, secondary = 36%, and superior = 20%. Six regions were chosen throughout the large regions of the north, center, and south. Each of these large regions was divided into one coastal and one inland subregion, totaling six regions. We considered the population living in urban areas and rural areas for all regions.

Because the majority of the Portuguese population is White, with only two small minorities of Black and Gypsy, we opted at this stage to choose only White subjects, except for one subject who is of mixed extraction (Black mother and White father, born in Angola). We are planning representative samples for each of the two minority ethnic groups, whose protocols will be collected at a later date.

The initial sample calculation predicted 501 subjects. After discarding the nonvalid protocols or those that raised serious doubts as to the way in which the psychologist carried out the contact, errors in the collection, or if it was found that the subject was under any kind of psychological or psychiatric treatment when the protocol was collected, we ended up with 309 protocols that were correctly collected and whose validity is certain.

The average age for the total sample is 37.25 (SD = 13.29, median = 35, mode = 26), with a range of 18 to 76 years. The subjects have an average of 9.33 years of education with a range of 1 to 18 years. The other demographic variables are shown in Table 16.1.

Procedure

The protocols were collected by seven psychologists, but more than 60% were collected by the author due to the difficulty in finding properly trained technicians with enough availability to carry out this study. The protocols were collected and scored according to the Rorschach Integrating System (Exner, 1991, 1993). All subjects were volunteers and were contacted in various sites within each region through local institutions such as schools, parishes, City Halls, churches, cooperative sites, and psychologists. The contacts were informal. After an explanation of the study's goal, protection by professional secrecy, and the promise that the results would be conveyed to each subject, the subject decided to accept or refuse the Rorschach Test. Generally, the protocols were not collected at the institution, but contacts were made there that allowed finding subjects among friends, neighbors, and acquaintances. The protocols were presented to the subjects in the conditions defined in the sample, such as nonpatient, age, gender, and schooling level. Each institution or initial contact allowed us to find one to seven subjects.

Data were processed using RIAP 3.0 for coding, structural summary, and file exportation for statistical analysis. Descriptive statistics were calculated by SPSS 3.0 for DOS. The normality tests (Kolmogorov-Smirnov) were calculated by SPSS 8.0 for Windows. This statistical package was also used to calculate the significant differences among the results of the different subgroups. The normality tests showed that the majority of the variables did not have a normal distribution; as a consequence, nonparametric tests were used: the Kruskal–Wallis test and the Mann–Whitney U test. The interscorer agreement is 86%, with maximum percentage being 98% in location and minimum 72% in the special scores.

RESULTS

Total Sample

All the protocols were scored according to the Rorschach Comprehensive System (RCS). Because we have not yet processed all the data to set up location, Form Quality, and Popular answers tables, we used Exner's (1993) tools. As a consequence, the D, Dd, X+%, F+%, Xu%, X–%, and P results do not bear the desired reliability because they correspond to the results of a population of different culture. Only after having set up these lists for the Portuguese population protocols can we rescore, and only then can we evaluate the impact due to culture in locations, Form Quality, and Popular answers.

Our sample descriptive statistics are listed in Table 16.2. We highlight the variables with high and low values in relation to the interpretation rules as set out by Exner's works (Exner, 1991; Exner & Sendin, 1995). In a later analysis, we compare our sample results with Exner's (1993). The Dd value in the locations is high ($M = 5.27$, $SD = 4.37$, median = 4.00, mode = 3.00), and this is explained by a high number of partial locations that are not part of Exner's tables. Only after setting up the Portuguese location lists can we see if this value remains high (e.g., there may be a cultural influence) or if some of these locations become classified as D in

TABLE 16.2
Descriptive Statistics for 309 Adult Nonpatients

Variable	M	SD	MIN	MAX	FREQ	MEDIAN	MODE	SK	KU
AGE	37.25	13.29	18.00	76.00	309	35.00	26.00	0.57	-0.51
YRSEDUC	9.33	4.23	1.00	18.00	309	9.00	4.00	0.22	-0.94
R	22.07	7.88	14.00	61.00	309	20.00	16.00	1.74	4.13
W	7.02	4.20	0.00	28.00	303	6.00	5.00	0.97	1.93
D	9.78	5.60	0.00	32.00	307	9.00	8.00	1.10	1.50
Dd	5.27	4.37	0.00	28.00	300	4.00	3.00	1.98	5.61
SPACE	2.26	2.22	0.00	14.00	249	2.00	2.00	1.88	5.04
DQ+	5.15	3.39	0.00	19.00	297	5.00	3.00	0.93	1.23
DQO	15.90	6.58	4.00	46.00	309	15.00	12.00	1.33	3.14
DQV	0.89	1.35	0.00	8.00	137	0.00	0.00	1.94	4.31
DQv/+	0.13	0.38	0.00	2.00	35	0.00	0.00	3.06	9.24
FQX+	0.23	0.84	0.00	11.00	43	0.00	0.00	8.05	91.06
FQXO	10.51	3.82	2.00	28.00	309	10.00	10.00	0.77	1.35
FQXU	8.37	4.64	1.00	30.00	309	7.00	6.00	1.63	4.18
FQX-	2.72	1.95	0.00	11.00	279	2.00	2.00	1.14	2.15
FQXNONE	0.25	0.58	0.00	3.00	60	0.00	0.00	2.82	8.83
MQ+	0.10	0.41	0.00	3.00	23	0.00	0.00	4.60	23.35
MQO	1.61	1.42	0.00	7.00	231	1.00	1.00	0.87	0.49
MQU	0.79	1.23	0.00	8.00	135	0.00	0.00	2.53	9.40
MQ-	0.29	0.73	0.00	4.00	55	0.00	0.00	2.80	7.85
MQNONE	0.04	0.27	0.00	3.00	10	0.00	0.00	7.32	60.95
SQual-	0.54	0.92	0.00	8.00	116	0.00	0.00	3.29	17.94
M	2.84	2.60	0.00	15.00	258	2.00	1.00	1.38	2.19
FM	3.62	2.87	0.00	19.00	284	3.00	2.00	1.94	6.64
m	1.34	1.51	0.00	7.00	192	1.00	0.00	1.26	1.07

(Continued)

TABLE 16.2
(Continued)

Variable	M	SD	MIN	MAX	FREQ	MEDIAN	MODE	SK	KU
FC	1.25	1.52	0.00	10.00	188	1.00	0.00	1.80	4.48
CF	1.80	1.80	0.00	10.00	224	1.00	0.00	1.24	1.55
C	0.26	0.57	0.00	3.00	61	0.00	0.00	2.34	5.27
CN	0.02	0.19	0.00	3.00	3	0.00	0.00	13.94	210.70
FCCFCCN	3.32	2.76	0.00	15.00	271	3.00	2.00	1.20	1.52
WSUMC	2.81	2.45	0.00	13.00	271	2.00	0.00	1.22	1.46
SUMC'	1.32	1.53	0.00	7.00	180	1.00	0.00	1.24	1.22
SUMT	0.68	0.80	0.00	4.00	154	0.00	0.00	1.06	0.74
SUMV	0.59	1.03	0.00	6.00	109	0.00	0.00	2.49	7.60
SUMY	1.20	1.54	0.00	8.00	169	1.00	0.00	1.58	2.49
SUMSHD	3.78	3.33	0.00	16.00	265	3.00	4.00	1.26	1.64
FR+RF	0.35	0.91	0.00	5.00	55	0.00	0.00	3.02	9.41
FD	1.46	1.48	0.00	9.00	222	1.00	1.00	1.69	4.39
F	9.62	4.58	1.00	28.00	309	9.00	7.00	0.87	1.12
PAIR	7.73	4.82	0.00	32.00	303	7.00	7.00	1.50	4.34
EGO	0.39	0.18	0.00	1.14	307	0.39	0.33	0.51	1.00
LAMBDA	1.21	1.71	0.06	19.00	309	0.75	0.50	6.11	51.99
FM+m	4.96	3.54	0.00	24.00	297	4.00	3.00	1.75	5.28
EA	5.65	4.20	0.00	24.50	296	4.50	4.50	1.38	2.39
ES	8.74	5.42	0.00	32.00	307	8.00	8.00	1.27	2.21
DTOTAL	-0.89	1.46	-7.00	3.00	171	0.00	0.00	-1.07	1.54
ADJD	-0.43	1.21	-7.00	4.00	151	0.00	0.00	-0.82	3.88
a(ACTIVE)	5.06	3.69	0.00	22.00	297	4.00	2.00	1.47	3.14
p(PASSIVE)	2.79	2.51	0.00	19.00	265	2.00	2.00	1.97	7.29
Ma	1.78	1.85	0.00	9.00	224	1.00	0.00	1.44	2.17
Mp	1.09	1.35	0.00	7.00	169	1.00	0.00	1.46	2.29
INTELLCT	2.24	2.58	0.00	15.00	217	2.00	0.00	1.89	4.52
ZF	10.56	4.82	1.00	34.00	309	10.00	10.00	0.84	1.92

Variable									
ZD	-1.13	4.47	-13.50	16.00	297	-1.00	-0.50	-0.13	0.84
BLENDS	3.53	3.00	0.00	15.00	274	3.00	1.00	1.19	1.39
BLNDS/R	0.16	0.12	0.00	0.67	274	0.14	0.00	0.97	1.04
Col-Shd Bld	0.66	1.05	0.00	7.00	122	0.00	0.00	2.18	6.72
AFR	0.56	0.23	0.19	1.63	309	0.53	0.50	1.02	1.67
POPS	4.93	1.82	0.00	11.00	308	5.00	5.00	0.19	0.04
X+%	0.50	0.13	0.19	0.88	309	0.50	0.50	0.10	-0.19
F+%	0.49	0.19	0.00	1.00	305	0.50	0.50	0.15	0.20
X-%	0.12	0.07	0.00	0.31	279	0.12	0.00	0.29	-0.41
Xu%	0.37	0.12	0.06	0.74	309	0.36	0.33	0.31	0.24
S-%	0.20	0.31	0.00	1.00	116	0.00	0.00	1.51	1.16
Isolate/R	0.22	0.17	0.00	0.94	276	0.19	0.00	0.83	0.65
H	1.90	1.83	0.00	10.00	248	1.00	1.00	1.63	3.29
(H)	0.79	0.97	0.00	5.00	161	1.00	0.00	1.47	2.44
HD	1.25	1.70	0.00	14.00	189	1.00	0.00	3.12	15.69
(Hd)	0.31	0.69	0.00	5.00	70	0.00	0.00	2.96	11.39
HX	0.24	0.72	0.00	6.00	43	0.00	0.00	4.04	20.16
All H Cont	4.26	3.45	0.00	22.00	290	4.00	3.00	1.98	5.88
A	8.59	3.70	2.00	29.00	309	8.00	6.00	1.06	2.50
(A)	0.21	0.49	0.00	3.00	53	0.00	0.00	2.54	6.60
AD	2.67	2.32	0.00	21.00	275	2.00	1.00	2.60	14.04
(Ad)	0.07	0.29	0.00	2.00	21	0.00	0.00	4.06	17.33
AN	1.38	1.68	0.00	11.00	195	1.00	0.00	1.96	5.38
ART	1.53	1.65	0.00	9.00	204	1.00	0.00	1.44	2.83
AY	0.25	0.61	0.00	4.00	56	0.00	0.00	2.95	9.94
BL	0.25	0.53	0.00	3.00	62	0.00	0.00	2.23	4.71
BT	1.50	1.61	0.00	10.00	212	1.00	0.00	1.74	4.76
CG	1.24	1.47	0.00	9.00	184	1.00	0.00	1.57	3.53
CL	0.26	0.57	0.00	3.00	61	0.00	0.00	2.20	4.19
EX	0.18	0.53	0.00	3.00	41	0.00	0.00	3.32	11.73
FI	0.45	0.82	0.00	6.00	95	0.00	0.00	2.48	8.58

(Continued)

TABLE 16.2
(Continued)

Variable	M	SD	MIN	MAX	FREQ	MEDIAN	MODE	SK	KU
FOOD	0.24	0.50	0.00	3.00	63	0.00	0.00	2.21	5.02
GEOG	0.29	0.78	0.00	7.00	59	0.00	0.00	4.27	24.87
HH	0.65	0.94	0.00	5.00	132	0.00	0.00	1.80	3.77
LS	0.81	1.12	0.00	7.00	144	0.00	0.00	1.79	4.09
NA	0.85	1.18	0.00	6.00	141	0.00	0.00	1.47	1.78
SC	0.67	1.17	0.00	6.00	114	0.00	0.00	2.22	5.05
SX	0.43	0.93	0.00	6.00	79	0.00	0.00	2.88	9.62
XY	0.22	0.66	0.00	6.00	47	0.00	0.00	4.55	27.08
IDIO	0.61	0.92	0.00	6.00	124	0.00	0.00	1.86	4.61
DV	0.31	0.58	0.00	3.00	77	0.00	0.00	1.84	2.79
INCOM	0.31	0.67	0.00	5.00	72	0.00	0.00	2.80	10.61
DR	0.14	0.47	0.00	4.00	33	0.00	0.00	4.25	22.52
FABCOM	0.27	0.53	0.00	3.00	74	0.00	0.00	2.07	4.81
DV2	0.00	0.06	0.00	1.00	1	0.00	0.00	17.58	309.00
INC2	0.00	0.06	0.00	1.00	1	0.00	0.00	17.58	309.00
DR2	0.00	0.00	0.00	0.00	0	0.00	0.00	—	—
FAB2	0.01	0.08	0.00	1.00	2	0.00	0.00	12.37	151.97
ALOG	0.07	0.26	0.00	1.00	22	0.00	0.00	3.35	9.29
CONTAM	0.00	0.00	0.00	0.00	0	0.00	0.00	—	—
SUM6	1.12	1.19	0.00	6.00	200	1.00	1.00	1.37	2.26
LVL2	0.01	0.14	0.00	2.00	3	0.00	0.00	11.89	152.20
WSUM6	2.88	3.37	0.00	20.00	200	2.00	0.00	1.66	3.57
AB	0.23	0.64	0.00	5.00	49	0.00	0.00	3.91	19.11
AG	0.59	0.95	0.00	7.00	122	0.00	0.00	2.57	9.64
CFB	0.00	0.06	0.00	1.00	1	0.00	0.00	17.58	309.00
COP	0.91	1.02	0.00	6.00	179	1.00	0.00	1.43	3.02
CP	0.04	0.22	0.00	2.00	10	0.00	0.00	6.40	44.36
MOR	1.25	1.33	0.00	7.00	202	1.00	0.00	1.39	2.23
PER	1.11	1.30	0.00	7.00	183	1.00	0.00	1.45	2.26
PSV	0.14	0.36	0.00	2.00	42	0.00	0.00	2.31	4.11

the Portuguese population. The S value (Space) is also relatively high (M = 2.26, SD = 2.22, median = 2.00, mode = 2.00), but this first reading of the results does not allow us to conclude that the Portuguese population has accentuated opposing characteristics in relation to the environment.

The variables that constitute EA are relatively low. There mean values are: M = 2.84 (SD = 2.60, median = 2.00, mode = 1.00) and WsumC = 2.81 (SD = 2.45, median = 2.00, mode = 0.00). Taking SumC, CF (M = 1.80) is higher than FC (M = 1.25). In this sample, 34% of the subjects have a higher CF+C value than FC. Sum T is relatively low (M = 0.68), with 50% of the subjects having Sum T = 0 and 15% with Sum T > 1. Sum Y (M = 1.20) and Sum V (M = 0.59) are relatively high. The Lambda value (M = 1.21, SD = 1.71, median = 0.75, mode = 0.50) is high in relation to the limit values of 0.99, with 111 subjects (i.e., 36% of the sample) having a Lambda greater than 0.99. EA (M = 5.65, SD = 4.20) is relatively low and can be explained by the higher Lambda values and lower average values for M and Wsum C. The Popular answers (P) have a mean of 4.93 (SD = 1.82), which is a relatively low value. We also note that 68 subjects (22%) have Populars less than 4, and only 7% (22 subjects) have a Popular value greater than 7. The work accomplished to set up the Popular answers table already allows us to state that, for Card IX, we are not going to get any answer with enough frequency to be considered a Popular response.

The variables related to Form Quality have very low values. However, because the scoring was done according to the American tables (Exner, 1993), we only come to a conclusion after the Form Quality table has been finished for the Portuguese population. In the contents area, Pure H value is low (M = 1.90, SD = 1.83, median = 1.0, mode = 1.0). We also note that 160 subjects (52%) have Pure H values less than 2, and 20% of the sample actually have Pure H = 0. The COP values (M = 0.91, SD = 1.02) and AG (M = 0.59, SD = 0.95) are also low. The MOR value (M = 1.25, SD = 1.33) is relatively high.

As seen in Table 16.3, we wish to note that 50% of the sample (n = 155) has an ambitent EB, with 28% being introversive (n = 85) and 22% being extratensive (n = 69). Another surprising result was the positive CDI value seen in 48% of the sample (n = 148), with CDI = 4 in 29% of the sample and CDI = 5 in 19%. Another interesting result is DEPI index, which is positive according to Exner's data in 32% of the sample (n = 100), (DEPI = 5: 19%, DEPI = 6: 12%, DEPI = 7: 1%).

In what respects sex differences, they are not very frequent. Differences only come up in six variables: with the level of significance $p < .05$, we have D, (2), Sum T, and Afr; with $p < .01$, we have two contents—Ay and Ex. By this comparison, we can state that the differences in results by gender are not relevant. After having highlighted some interesting results in the total sample and before we elaborate on the interpretations of these

TABLE 16.3
Frequencies and Percentages for 33 Structural
Variables for 309 Adult Nonpatients

Variable	Frequency	%
EB Style		
Introversive	85	28
Superintroversive	50	16
Ambitent	155	50
Extratensive	69	22
Superextratensive	44	14
EA–es Differences: D-scores		
D Score > 0	23	7
D Score = 0	138	45
D Score < 0	148	48
D Score < –1	82	27
Adj D Score > 0	38	12
Adj D Score = 0	158	51
Adj D Score < 0	113	37
Adj D Score < –1	50	16
Zd > +3.0 (Overincorp)	47	15
Zd < –3.0 (Underincorp)	91	29
Form Quality deviations		
X+% > .89	0	0
X+% < .70	287	93
X+% < .61	246	80
X+% < .50	146	47
F+% < .70	276	89
Xu% > .20	284	92
X–% > .15	96	31
X–% > .20	42	14
X–% > .30	2	1
FC:CF+C ratio		
FC > (CF+C) + 2	15	5
FC > (CF+C) + 1	36	12
(CF+C) > FC+1	104	34
(CF+C) > FC+2	65	21
S-Constellation Positive	20	6
HVI Positive	9	3
OBS Positive	3	1
SCZI = 6	0	0
SCZI = 5	0	0
SCZI = 4	1	0
DEPI = 7	2	1
DEPI = 6	38	12
DEPI = 5	60	19
CDI = 5	58	19
CDI = 4	90	29
Miscellaneous variables		
Lambda > .99	111	36
Dd > 3	180	58

(Continued)

TABLE 16.3
(Continued)

Variable	Frequency	%
DQv + DQv/+ > 2	40	13
S > 2	100	32
Sum T = 0	155	50
Sum T > 1	47	15
3r+(2)/R < .33	107	35
3r+(2)/R > .44	108	35
Fr + rF > 0	55	18
PureC > 0	61	20
PureC > 1	16	5
Afr < .40	79	26
Afr < .50	128	41
(FM+m) < Sum Shading	99	32
(2AB+Art+Ay) > 5	66	21
Populars < 4	68	22
Populars > 7	22	7
COP = 0	130	42
COP > 2	19	6
AG = 0	187	61
AG > 2	12	4
MOR > 2	44	14
Level 2 Sp.Sc. > 0	3	1
Sum 6 Sp. Sc. > 6	0	0
Pure H < 2	160	52
Pure H = 0	61	20
p > a+1	31	10
Mp > Ma	69	22

values, we try to find out how these results distribute personality styles and formal education as frames of reference.

RESULTS BY COPING STYLE

We compare the results of 41 variables by coping styles: ambitent, introversive, and extratensive. Then we compare the results considering high Lambda (>.99) and low Lambda (<1.0). These 41 variables were chosen because they are considered extremely important for the interpretation of the results. Table 16.4 contains results of 41 variables (M and SD) and five ratios or proportions (CF+C > FC, DEPI > 4, DEPI > 5, T = 0, and CDI > 3) and respective intergroup comparison.

TABLE 16.4
Comparison Among Coping Style for 41 Variables

Variable	Ambitent (n = 155)		Introversive (n = 85)		Extratensive (n = 69)	
	M	SD	M	SD	M	SD
Years Educ	8.48	4.09	10.39	4.45	9.94	3.89
R *	20.73	6.61	24.20	10.22	22.46	6.58
W *	6.47	3.70	6.91	4.65	8.38	4.44
Dd	4.84	3.28	6.48	6.18	4.77	3.53
S	2.04	2.25	2.53	2.33	2.41	1.98
M **	2.11	2.10	5.21	2.57	1.58	1.64
FC	1.15	1.39	1.09	1.35	1.67	1.91
CF **	1.41	1.43	1.12	1.39	3.49	1.96
C	0.17	0.44	0.11	0.38	0.64	0.80
WSUM C **	2.24	1.97	1.82	1.95	5.28	2.35
CF+C>FC	27%		15%		71%	
FM+m *	4.60	3.32	6.05	4.28	4.42	2.69
SUM T	0.64	0.82	0.63	0.80	0.83	0.77
SUM C' *	1.15	1.41	1.18	1.47	1.85	1.76
SUM V	0.48	0.91	0.67	1.12	0.72	1.17
SUM Y **	0.88	1.25	1.28	1.58	1.81	1.88
Lambda **	1.62	2.26	0.82	0.72	0.76	0.46
EA **	4.35	3.97	7.03	4.30	6.86	3.68
ES *	7.75	4.96	9.81	6.19	9.64	5.07
Fr+rF	0.27	0.78	0.42	0.96	0.45	1.08
EGO **	0.38	0.16	0.48	0.18	0.34	0.17
FD *	1.26	1.25	2.00	1.89	1.25	1.19
ACTIVE **	4.48	3.45	7.08	3.99	3.88	2.80
PASSIVE **	2.27	2.01	4.26	3.24	2.14	1.64
AFR	0.54	0.20	0.58	0.25	0.59	0.26
BLENDS **	2.88	2.82	4.14	3.26	4.23	2.77
ColShblends **	0.53	0.95	0.47	0.81	1.19	1.32
P *	4.78	1.73	5.49	1.86	4.58	1.84
X+%	0.51	0.13	0.50	0.13	0.46	0.13
X-%	0.13	0.07	0.12	0.07	0.11	0.07
XU% *	0.35	0.12	0.37	0.13	0.40	0.12
H **	1.47	1.48	3.39	2.04	1.04	1.03
All H CONT **	3.50	2.85	6.89	3.94	2.71	2.01
A *	8.61	3.76	9.19	3.43	7.81	3.80
Bl *	0.21	0.49	0.14	0.35	0.46	0.72
Ex	0.16	0.43	0.14	0.49	0.29	0.73
Fi *	0.37	0.71	0.38	0.64	0.72	1.15
Food	0.20	0.45	0.21	0.44	0.35	0.66
AB	0.21	0.70	0.29	0.59	0.20	0.56
COP **	0.70	0.81	1.53	1.20	0.61	0.88
AG *	0.54	0.89	0.86	1.19	0.35	0.64
MOR	1.19	1.33	1.32	1.44	1.29	1.21
DEPI>4	28%		33%		42%	
DEPI>5	11%		11%		20%	
T=0	54%		54%		38%	
CDI>3	60%		23%		49%	

*$p < .05$. **$p < .001$.

The Portuguese sample results surprised us with the coping styles proportion. The ambient group constitutes the majority or 50% ($n = 155$) of the total sample, with the introversive being 28% ($n = 85$) and the extratensive being 22% ($n = 69$). If we compare the proportion of the coping styles distribution with studies carried out in other countries, we find relatively similar results in the Riquelme and Ruos (1996) study. This study done in Venezuela with a 218-subject sample, in which 54% were ambient, 32% introversive, and only 10% are extratensive. In comparison with the Exner (1991) results, the difference is huge: In the American sample, 20% are ambient, 36% are introversive, and 44% are extratensive. Grounded on this comparison, we could conclude that the differences of coping styles distribution might be explained in a cross-cultural perspective.

Let it be said that the ambient frequency is related to formal education. By consulting Table 16.8 (p. 389), we see that higher formal education equates to a lower ambient percentage, a higher introversive percentage, and relatively stable extratensive value. According to the three levels of formal education, the ambient represent 58%, 48%, and 36%, the introversive 21%, 29%, and 39%, and the extratensive 20%, 23%, and 25%, respectively. Despite this variation according to the formal education level, we still see a significant difference in relation to the North American sample. Here we can look to cross-cultural factors to explain this difference.

As is seen in Table 16.4 (the comparison among ambients, introversives, and extratensives), there are 12 variables in which there is a significant difference with level of significance at $p < 0.5$: R, W, FM+m, Sum C', es, FD, P, Xu%, A, Bl, Fi, and AG; with $p < .001$, there are 14 variables: M, CF, WSUM C, Sum Y, Lambda, EA, Ego index, a (total active), p (total passive), Blends, Color shading blends, Pure H, All H contents, and COP.

Ambitents

In these 26 variables with significant differences, the ambients have the lowest values for R ($M = 20.73$), W ($M = 6.47$), Sum C' ($M = 1.15$), Sum Y ($M = 0.88$), EA ($M = 4.35$), es ($M = 7.75$), Blends ($M = 2.88$), Xu% ($M = 0.35$), and Fi ($M = 0.37$), and they are the ones with the lowest percentage for DEPI > 4 (28%). The variables for which the ambient have the highest results are Lambda ($M = 1.62$), and it is the group with the highest percentage of subjects with T = 0 (54%) and CDI > 3 (60%). We confirm that the ambient results are poor—namely, with the lowest results for R, W, EA, and Blends and the highest Lambda result. The ambients weight in relation to the high Lambda is enormous because it is the only coping style with Lambda greater than 0.99; the introversives having a mean Lambda of 0.82 and the extratensives have a mean of 0.76. It may be emphasized that this ambient high Lambda value is responsible for the high mean normative value ($M = 1.21$). Because the ambient have lower

R, EA, and Blends results and a higher Lambda, we see that this coping style is caused by the high Lambda in detriment of the variables that constitute EA (M and Sum C). This enables us to classify the group of subjects with this coping style as the avoidant group by excellence.

Introversives

This group of subjects has the lowest results for CF ($M = 1.12$), Wsum C ($M = 1.82$), Color shading blends ($M = 0.47$), and Bl ($M = 0.14$) and the lowest percentages for CF + C > FC (15%) and CDI > 3 (23%). Out of the three coping styles, the introversives have the highest results for 15 variables: R ($M = 24.20$), M ($M = 5.21$), FM + m ($M = 6.05$), EA ($M = 7.03$), es ($M = 9.81$), Ego index ($M = 0.48$), FD ($M = 2.00$), a – total active ($M = 7.08$), p – total passive ($M = 4.26$), Popular ($M = 5.49$), Pure H ($M = 3.39$), All H contents ($M = 6.89$), A ($M = 9.19$), COP ($M = 1.53$), and AG ($M = 0.86$). Together with the ambitent, they have the highest percentage for T = 0 (54%). These results are most interesting because, in most variables with significant differences in which the introversive are on one end, be it high or low, the extratensive have results for the same variables on the opposite end, which is in accordance with the Rorschach conceptualization.

For the four variables (CF, Wsum C, Color shading blends, and Bl) and two ratios (CF + C > FC, CDI > 3) in which the introversives get the lowest results for the three coping styles, the extratensives get the highest results except for CDI > 3. Out of the 15 variables (R, M, FM+m, EA, es, Ego index, FD, a-total active, p-total passive, Popular, Pure H, All H contents, A, COP, and AG) and one ratio (T = 0), the extratensives get the lowest results for 13 variables in the three coping styles except for R, EA, es, in which the ambitents have the lowest results. Therefore, the introversives have the lowest results in the variables concerned with affect features and the highest results in the variables concerned with ideation, as well as in the relational variables concerned with COP and AG.

Extratensives

The extratensive group has the lowest results for 13 variables: M ($M = 1.58$), FM + m ($M = 4.42$), Ego index ($M = 0.34$), FD ($M = 1.25$), a-total active ($M = 3.88$), p-total passive ($M = 2.14$), Popular ($M = 4.58$), Pure H ($M = 1.04$), All H contents ($M = 2.71$), A ($M = 7.81$), COP ($M = 0.61$), AG ($M = 0.35$), and Lambda ($M = 0.76$), and T = 0 (38%). The variables with significant differences in which the extratensives had the highest results were W ($M = 8.38$), CF ($M = 3.49$), Wsum C ($M = 5.28$), Sum C' ($M = 1.85$), Sum Y ($M = 1.81$), Blends ($M = 4.23$), Color shading blends ($M = 1.19$), Xu% ($M = 0.40$), Bl ($M = 0.46$), and Fi ($M = 0.72$), as well as ratios CF + C > FC (71%) and DEPI > 4 (42%).

As mentioned in the result analysis for the introversive coping style, the extratensives have the highest results in the variables concerned with affect features and are on the opposite end of the variable results in relation to the introversives. Besides seeing the lowest Lambda result and high results for Wsum C and Blends, we also see that they have very high results for Sum C', Sum Y, Color shading blends, and DEPI > 4. It is worth noting that 71% of the extratensive subjects have a value of CF + C > FC, which seems to show a lack of affect modulation. In this case, we need research on the lack of affect modulation and on the high level of positive depression index (42%).

Lambda

As is seen in Table 16.5, the comparison between subjects with Lambda < 1.0 (n = 198; 64% of the sample) and with high Lambda > 0.99 (n = 111; 36% of the sample), for the 41 variables, 32 variables have significant differences. We have six variables with level of significance of $p < .05$: R, Pure C, Fr+rF, Popular, X+%, and AB. With $p < .001$ we have 26 variables: W, Space, M, FC, CF, Wsum C, FM+m, Sum T, Sum C', Sum V, Sum Y, EA, es, FD, a-total active, p-total passive, Blends, Color shading blends, Pure H, All H contents, Bl, Ex, Fi, COP, AG, and MOR. In all of these variables, we see that the subjects with high Lambda have lower results except for X+%, and for the ratios of T = 0, CDI > 3. It is also worth noting that the positive depression index comes up in the low-Lambda group (41% vs. 18%). This index increases in the low-Lambda subgroups, and the coping deficit index (CDI) increases in the high-Lambda subgroups, showing a negative correlation between these two results.

Formal Education Level

In the history of Portugal's development, we see that the formal education level measured in years of education had great importance to evaluate the intracultural dimension. We see that reading habits (newspapers and books), access to information, command of computing, access to the Internet, and the most important administration jobs are directly connected with the highest schooling level and with holding a university degree. We see that secondary level schooling (7–12 years) corresponds to the intermediate jobs in the secondary and tertiary sectors. The lower schooling (0–6 years) corresponds to primary sector jobs and secondary and tertiary on the lower level. There are exceptions, as is the case with a significant number of entrepreneurs, maybe the majority, who have the lower level schooling (0–6 years). The last 20 years in Portugal have seen a great social mobility directly linked to the significant increase in schooling. There are many thousands of middle and top executives whose parents are illiterate or have but minimum schooling (0–4 years).

TABLE 16.5
Comparison Between Low- and High-Lambda Protocols for 41 Variables

Variable	Low Lambda (n = 198)		High Lambda (n = 111)	
	M	SD	M	SD
Years Educ	10.33	4.27	7.55	3.52
R *	23.09	8.64	20.26	5.92
W **	8.04	4.32	5.19	3.28
Dd	5.25	4.67	5.32	3.80
S **	2.71	2.39	1.45	1.60
M **	3.67	2.76	1.37	1.38
FC **	1.49	1.68	0.83	1.07
CF **	2.28	1.92	0.93	1.13
C *	0.33	0.64	0.12	0.37
WSUM C **	3.53	2.53	1.52	1.65
CF+C>FC	43%		16%	
FM+m **	6.08	3.73	2.95	1.99
SUM T **	0.82	0.87	0.43	0.60
SUM C' **	1.77	1.62	0.50	0.91
SUM V **	0.80	1.19	0.21	0.49
SUM Y **	1.50	1.69	0.66	1.02
Lambda (**)	0.54	0.22	2.39	2.42
EA **	7.20	4.26	2.89	2.20
ES **	10.97	5.27	4.76	2.77
Fr+rF *	0.47	1.05	0.13	0.49
EGO	0.40	0.17	0.38	0.18
FD **	1.81	1.55	0.83	1.07
ACTIVE **	6.38	3.86	2.72	1.70
PASSIVE **	3.44	2.69	1.63	1.62
AFR	0.55	0.21	0.58	0.25
BLENDS **	4.68	3.05	1.48	1.37
ColShblends **	0.86	1.18	0.31	0.63
P *	5.18	1.79	4.49	1.80
X+%*	0.49	0.13	0.52	0.14
X–%	0.12	0.07	0.12	0.07
XU%	0.38	0.12	0.35	0.12
H **	2.29	1.98	1.21	1.26
All H CONT **	4.96	3.72	2.99	2.47
A	8.34	3.58	9.04	3.89
Bl **	0.33	0.59	0.10	0.36
Ex **	0.26	0.62	0.04	0.25
Fi **	0.60	0.94	0.18	0.45
Food	0.26	0.52	0.20	0.46
AB *	0.31	0.72	0.09	0.44
COP **	1.12	1.08	0.53	0.77
AG **	0.77	1.09	0.26	0.50
MOR **	1.51	1.41	0.77	1.03
DEPI>4	41%		18%	
DEPI>5	17%		6%	
T=0	43%		62%	
CDI>3	37%		67%	

*p < .05. **p < .001.

For the reasons mentioned, we feel that it would be important to analyze the results by comparison among the formal education levels, shown in Table 16.6, to control the importance of intracultural aspects. In Table 16.6, Level 1 corresponds to the primary education level (0–6 years or 0–9 for the under 30s), Level 2 corresponds to the secondary level (7–12 years or 10–12 years for the under 30s). Level 3 is the superior level (13+ years), which in most cases corresponds to holding a university degree. Primary level has n = 137 (44% of the sample), secondary level has n = 111 (36%), and the superior level has n = 61 (20%). Out of the 41 variables analyzed on Table 16.6, there are significant differences in 5 variables having level of significance of $p < .05$: FM+m, Fr+rF, Ex, Fi, and AG and 25 with $p < .001$: R, W, Space, M, FC, CF, Wsum C, Sum T, Sum C', Sum V, Sum Y, Lambda, EA, es, FD, a-total active, p-total passive, Blends, Color shading blends, Popular, Pure H, All H contents, AB, COP, and MOR.

In these variables with significant differences, the primary level only has the highest result for the Lambda variable ($M = 1.73$), for which the secondary level has a mean of 0.90 and the superior level has a mean of 0.58. It also has the highest results for $T = 0$ (61%) and CDI > 3 (67%). For all the other variables, secondary schooling always has intermediate results, with the higher results belonging to the superior education level. Therefore, Level 3 has R ($M = 25.57$), W ($M = 9.39$), Space ($M = 3.28$), M ($M = 5.07$), FC ($M = 2.13$), CF ($M = 2.87$), Wsum C ($M = 4.55$), FM+m ($M = 5.82$), Sum T ($M = 1.02$), Sum C' ($M = 2.08$), Sum V ($M = 1.16$), Sum Y ($M = 1.79$), EA ($M = 9.61$), es ($M = 11.87$), Fr+rF ($M = 0.49$), FD ($M = 1.90$), a-total active ($M = 7.20$), p-total passive ($M = 3.75$), Blends ($M = 6.13$), Color shading blends ($M = 1.28$), Popular ($M = 5.66$), Pure H ($M = 2.98$), All H contents ($M = 6.64$), Ex ($M = 0.26$), Fi ($M = 0.64$), AB ($M = 0.67$), COP ($M = 1.46$), AG ($M = 1.02$), and MOR ($M = 1.70$), and values for DEPI > 4 (48%) and CF + C > FC (41%).

We need to point out that the Level 3 results (13+ years of formal education) are the most interesting, highlighting a Lambda with a mean of 0.58; all the other variables are concerned with affect, with ideation and relational having high results in this subject group, although the positive DEPI has a high frequency (almost half the subjects in this group). As with the earlier analyses, the positive CDI index increases with a high Lambda and the positive DEPI index behaves inversely, increasing when Lambda is lower.

COMPARISON OF THE PORTUGUESE SAMPLE RESULTS WITH EXNER'S NORMATIVE STUDY

Through a superficial comparison of the Portuguese population results and those of the American population (Exner, 1991), laid out in Table 16.7 with the means and standard deviations of 41 variables, we note that

TABLE 16.6
Comparison Among Levels of Education for 41 Variables

Variable	Educ. Level 1 (n = 137)		Educ. Level 2 (n = 111)		Educ. Level 3 (n = 61)	
	M	SD	M	SD	M	SD
Years Educ	5.52	2.02	10.49	1.27	15.80	1.11
R **	20.32	6.68	22.31	7.55	25.57	9.67
W **	5.86	3.50	7.13	4.05	9.39	4.88
Dd	5.36	4.32	5.00	4.02	5.57	5.09
S **	1.74	1.81	2.32	2.09	3.28	2.87
M **	1.80	1.76	2.92	2.51	5.07	2.95
FC **	0.90	1.33	1.20	1.41	2.13	1.78
CF **	1.22	1.36	1.92	1.80	2.87	2.13
C	0.16	0.46	0.29	0.56	0.41	0.74
WSUM C **	1.91	1.72	2.95	2.35	4.55	3.00
CF+C>FC	28%		36%		41%	
FM+m *	4.40	3.32	5.17	3.07	5.82	4.54
SUM T **	0.47	0.65	0.76	0.81	1.02	0.96
SUM C' **	0.82	1.17	1.50	1.56	2.08	1.81
SUM V **	0.34	0.78	0.58	1.01	1.16	1.32
SUM Y **	0.78	1.28	1.40	1.73	1.79	1.48
Lambda **	1.73	2.33	0.90	0.86	0.58	0.39
EA **	3.71	2.53	5.87	4.02	9.61	4.65
ES **	6.81	4.42	9.40	4.98	11.87	6.48
Fr+rF *	0.24	0.77	0.41	0.95	0.49	1.07
EGO	0.39	0.18	0.39	0.19	0.40	0.16
FD **	1.12	1.32	1.64	1.67	1.90	1.26
ACTIVE **	4.01	2.75	5.20	3.60	7.20	4.67
PASSIVE **	2.23	2.34	2.95	2.08	3.75	3.20
AFR	0.54	0.21	0.59	0.25	0.57	0.22
BLENDS **	2.15	1.91	3.81	2.84	6.13	3.42
ColShblends **	0.32	0.64	0.75	0.98	1.28	1.52
P **	4.39	1.72	5.21	1.67	5.66	1.94
X+%	0.49	0.13	0.52	0.13	0.49	0.13
X–%	0.13	0.08	0.12	0.07	0.11	0.07
XU%	0.37	0.12	0.35	0.12	0.39	0.12
H **	1.26	1.36	2.10	1.85	2.98	2.12
All H CONT **	3.11	2.53	4.36	3.00	6.64	4.62
A	8.46	3.72	8.83	3.63	8.44	3.83
Bl	0.23	0.54	0.20	0.42	0.38	0.66
Ex *	0.11	0.43	0.23	0.59	0.26	0.60
Fi *	0.30	0.78	0.53	0.74	0.64	1.00
Food	0.20	0.46	0.22	0.45	0.34	0.65
AB **	0.07	0.28	0.19	0.61	0.67	0.99
COP **	0.62	0.84	0.96	1.03	1.46	1.13
AG *	0.46	0.82	0.50	0.84	1.02	1.26
MOR **	0.93	1.21	1.40	1.27	1.70	1.53
DEPI>4	22%		37%		48%	
DEPI>5	9%		14%		22%	
T=0	61%		45%		34%	
CDI>3	67%		41%		19%	

*p < .05. **p < .001.

TABLE 16.7
Descriptive Statistics for 41 Variables

Variable	Portugal (n = 309)		United States[a] (n = 700)	
	M	SD	M	SD
AGE	37.25	13.29	32.36	11.93
YRSEDUC	9.33	4.23	13.25	1.60
R	22.07	7.88	22.67	4.23
W	7.02	4.20	8.55	1.94
Dd	5.27	4.37	1.23	1.70
SPACE	2.26	2.22	1.47	1.21
M	2.84	2.60	4.30	1.92
FC	1.25	1.52	4.09	1.88
CF	1.80	1.80	2.36	1.27
C	0.26	0.57	0.08	0.28
WGSUM C	2.81	2.45	4.52	1.79
FM+m	4.96	3.54	4.82	1.52
SUM C'	1.32	1.53	1.53	1.25
SUM T	0.68	0.80	1.03	0.58
SUM V	0.59	1.03	0.26	0.58
SUM Y	1.20	1.54	0.57	1.00
FR+RF	0.35	0.91	0.08	0.35
FD	1.46	1.48	1.16	0.87
EGO	0.39	0.18	0.39	0.07
LAMBDA	1.21	1.71	0.58	0.26
EA	5.65	4.20	8.82	2.18
ES	8.74	5.42	8.21	3.00
a (active)	5.06	3.69	6.48	2.14
p (passive)	2.79	2.51	2.69	1.52
Afr	0.56	0.23	0.69	0.16
BLENDS	3.53	3.00	5.16	1.93
POPULAR	4.93	1.82	6.89	1.38
X+%	0.50	0.13	0.79	0.08
F+%	0.49	0.19	0.71	0.17
X–%	0.12	0.07	0.07	0.05
XU%	0.37	0.12	0.14	0.07
H	1.90	1.83	3.40	1.80
All H Cont	4.26	3.45	5.42	1.63
A	8.59	3.70	8.18	2.04
Bl	0.25	0.53	0.15	0.40
Ex	0.18	0.53	0.13	0.34
Fi	0.45	0.82	0.42	0.67
Food	0.24	0.50	0.23	0.50
AB	0.23	0.64	0.15	0.40
COP	0.91	1.02	2.07	1.52
AG	0.59	0.95	1.18	1.18
MOR	1.25	1.33	0.70	0.82

[a]Data from Exner, 1991.

standard deviations have a greater amplitude in the Portuguese population. This denotes lesser population homogeneity and a greater intragroup variability. We note three groups of variables: a small group whose results are close in both populations, another in which the variables have higher mean results in the Portuguese population, and the last group of variables whose results are higher in the American population.

Therefore, R, FM+m Ego index, es, a-total active, p-total passive, All H contents, Ex, Fi, and Food have relatively similar results in both populations. The American population shows higher results for W, M, FC, CF, WsumC, Sum C', Sum T, EA, Afr, Blends, Popular, X+%, F+%, Pure H, COP, and AG. The Portuguese population shows higher results for the variables of Dd, Space, Pure C, Sum V, Sum Y, Fr+rF, FD, Lambda, X–%, Xu%, AB, and MOR, as well as for DEPI > 4, CDI > 3, T = 0, and CF + C > FC.

There are important differences here—namely, for Lambda, M, Wsum C, Sum T, EA, Blends, X+%, COP, and AG. Before trying a cross-cultural explanation, we are going to verify if these differences hold after an analysis in an intracultural perspective. Table 16.8 shows the results of the Portuguese sample (*M* and *SD*) on each of the formal education levels and finally the Exner (1991) results. The more significant differences— namely, the mean value of W, Lambda, EA, M, Wsum C, Sum T, Blends, Pure H, and AG—stand out across the education level; when the latter increases, the results become similar to those of the American population, the difference being accounted for in an intracultural perspective.

However, some variables keep stable in all groups of the Portuguese population and different from the American population results. Therefore, Dd, Space, Pure C, CF + C > FC, Sum V, Sum Y, Fr+rF, Afr, P, X+%, X–%, Xu%, DEPI > 4, and COP are variables whose differences with the American population have to be accounted for in a cross-cultural perspective. We can only come to a conclusion for the Dd, X+%, X–%, Xu%, and P variables once we have set out the tables of locations, Form Quality, and Popular answers.

CONCLUSION

This study of Rorschach norms in Portugal gave us access to interesting information on this assessment tool and the personality of Portuguese people. However, these same results raise important issues whose solutions call for new research. These results of the Portuguese population show that there are significant differences by style. It is more and more important to analyze the results by coping style for the ambient, introversive, and extratensive with a high Lambda and a low Lambda.

TABLE 16.8
Comparison Among Total Portuguese Sample, Its Subgroups by Levels of Education, and Exner's Study in United States

Variable	Portugal, 98 (n = 309) M	SD	Portugal L1 (n = 137) M	SD	Portugal L2 (n = 111) M	SD	Portugal L3 (n = 61) M	SD	Exner, 90 (n = 700) M	SD
Years Educ	9.33	4.23	5.52	2.02	10.49	1.27	15.80	1.11	13.25	1.60
R	22.07	7.88	20.32	6.68	22.31	7.55	25.57	9.67	22.67	4.23
W	7.02	4.20	5.86	3.50	7.13	4.05	9.39	4.88	8.55	1.94
Dd	5.27	4.37	5.36	4.32	5.00	4.02	5.57	5.09	1.23	1.70
S	2.26	2.22	1.74	1.81	2.32	2.09	3.28	2.87	1.47	1.21
M	2.84	2.60	1.80	1.76	2.92	2.51	5.07	2.95	4.30	1.92
FC	1.25	1.52	0.90	1.33	1.20	1.41	2.13	1.78	4.09	1.88
CF	1.80	1.80	1.22	1.36	1.92	1.80	2.87	2.13	2.36	1.27
C	0.26	0.57	0.16	0.46	0.29	0.56	0.41	0.74	0.08	0.28
WSUM C	2.81	2.45	1.91	1.72	2.95	2.35	4.55	3.00	4.52	1.79
CF+C>FC	34%	—	28%	—	36%	—	41%	—	4%	—
FM+m	4.96	3.54	4.40	3.32	5.17	3.07	5.82	4.54	4.82	1.52
SUM T	0.68	0.80	0.47	0.65	0.76	0.81	1.02	0.96	1.03	0.58
SUM C'	1.32	1.53	0.82	1.17	1.50	1.56	2.08	1.81	1.53	1.25
SUM V	0.59	1.03	0.34	0.78	0.58	1.01	1.16	1.32	0.26	0.58
SUM Y	1.20	1.54	0.78	1.28	1.40	1.73	1.79	1.48	0.57	1.00
Lambda	1.21	1.71	1.73	2.33	0.90	0.86	0.58	0.39	0.58	0.26
EA	5.65	4.20	3.71	2.53	5.87	4.02	9.61	4.65	8.82	2.18
ES	8.74	5.42	6.81	4.42	9.40	4.98	11.87	6.48	8.21	3.00
Fr+rF	0.35	0.91	0.24	0.77	0.41	0.95	0.49	1.07	0.08	0.35
EGO	0.39	0.18	0.39	0.18	0.39	0.19	0.40	0.16	0.39	0.07
FD	1.46	1.48	1.12	1.32	1.64	1.67	1.90	1.26	1.16	0.87
ACTIVE	5.06	3.69	4.01	2.75	5.20	3.60	7.20	4.67	6.48	2.14

(Continued)

TABLE 16.8
(Continued)

Variable	Portugal, 98 (n = 309)		Portugal L1 (n = 137)		Portugal L2 (n = 111)		Portugal L3 (n = 61)		Exner, 90 (n = 700)	
	M	SD	M	SD	M	SD	M	SD	M	SD
PASSIVE	2.79	2.51	2.23	2.34	2.95	2.08	3.75	3.20	2.69	1.52
AFR	0.56	0.23	0.54	0.21	0.59	0.25	0.57	0.22	0.69	0.16
BLENDS	3.53	3.00	2.15	1.91	3.81	2.84	6.13	3.42	5.16	1.93
P	4.93	1.82	4.39	1.72	5.21	1.67	5.66	1.94	6.89	1.38
X+%	0.50	0.13	0.49	0.13	0.52	0.13	0.49	0.13	0.79	0.08
X-%	0.12	0.07	0.13	0.08	0.12	0.07	0.11	0.07	0.07	0.05
XU%	0.37	0.12	0.37	0.12	0.35	0.12	0.39	0.12	0.14	0.07
H	1.90	1.83	1.26	1.36	2.10	1.85	2.98	2.12	3.39	1.80
All H CONT	4.26	3.45	3.11	2.53	4.36	3.00	6.64	4.62	5.43	1.63
A	8.59	3.70	8.46	3.72	8.83	3.63	8.44	3.83	8.16	2.04
BI	0.25	0.53	0.23	0.54	0.20	0.42	0.38	0.66	0.15	0.40
Ex	0.18	0.53	0.11	0.43	0.23	0.59	0.26	0.60	0.13	0.34
Fi	0.45	0.82	0.30	0.78	0.53	0.74	0.64	1.00	0.42	0.67
Food	0.24	0.50	0.20	0.46	0.22	0.45	0.34	0.65	0.23	0.50
AB	0.23	0.64	0.07	0.28	0.19	0.61	0.67	0.99	0.15	0.40
COP	0.91	1.02	0.62	0.84	0.96	1.03	1.46	1.13	2.07	1.52
AG	0.59	0.95	0.46	0.82	0.50	0.84	1.02	1.26	1.18	1.18
MOR	1.25	1.33	0.93	1.21	1.40	1.27	1.70	1.53	0.70	0.82
DEPI>4	32%	—	22%	—	37%	—	48%	—	3%	—
DEPI>5	13%	—	9%	—	14%	—	22%	—	0%	—
Ambitent	50%	—	58%	—	48%	—	36%	—	20%	—
Introversive	28%	—	21%	—	29%	—	39%	—	36%	—
Extratensive	22%	—	20%	—	23%	—	25%	—	44%	—

Nevertheless, the most important aspect of this study is the salience of the intracultural aspect. In this case, it expresses through the levels of formal education, which are decisive in explaining the results of our study. This allows us to identify the variables whose differences can be accounted for by cross-cultural aspects and variables whose differences can be explained in an intracultural perspective.

Although it may be recognized that the existence of larger differences are accounted for by intracultural aspects, this fact cannot make us overlook the importance of cross-cultural differences. It is a fact that results from the representative sample of the Portuguese population, which are different in many variables when compared with the results of the American sample. Similarly both global and group results in the Portuguese sample present much higher dispersion and variability than the American ones. This might be explained by a lesser homogeneity of our population.

Because the populations are not homogeneous, it is more and more necessary to carry out increasingly finer analyses within each cultural space, forcing us to elaborate norms not only on the total population and by coping styles, as referred to earlier, but also by socioeconomic, regional, or other subgroups. Carrying out normative studies with Rorschach in different areas or cultural groups is still an exciting area that allows us to better understand this test and understand the influence of culture or cultures on the psychological functioning of individuals and groups.

REFERENCES

Abel, T. (1973). *Psychological testing in cultural contexts.* New Haven, CT: College and University Press.

Dana, R. (1993). *Multicultural assessment perspectives for professional psychology.* Boston: Allyn & Bacon.

Ephraim, D., Riquelme, J., & Occupati, R. (1992). Características psicológicas d' habitants de Caracas según el sistema comprehensivo del Rorschach [Psychological features in the inhabitants of Caracas according to the Rorschach comprehensive system]. *Boletin de la AVEPSO, 15*(1–3), 98–108.

Exner, J., & Sendin, C. (1995). *Manual de interpretación del Rorschach para el sistema comprehensivo* [Interpretation manual for the Rorschach Comprehensive System]. Madrid, Spain: Psimática.

Exner, J. (1991). *The Rorschach: A comprehensive system: Vol. 2. Interpretation* (2nd ed.). New York: Wiley.

Exner, J. (1993). *The Rorschach: A comprehensive system: Vol. 1. Basic foundations* (3rd ed.). New York: Wiley.

Harada, N. (1996, July). *Normative data of Chinese women.* Paper presented at the 15th International Congress of Rorschach and Projective Methods. Boston, MA.

Levine, R. (1973). *Culture, behavior and personality.* Chicago: Aldine.

Lindzey, G. (1961). *Projective techniques and cross-cultural research.* New York: Appleton-Century-Crofts.

Matsumoto, D. (1996). *Culture and psychology.* Pacific Grove: Brooks/Cole.

Mattlar, C., Carlsson, A., Forsander, C., Norrlund, L., Oist, A. S., Maki, J., & Alanen, E. (1993, July). *Rorschach features characteristic of adult Finns in cross-cultural comparison.* Paper presented at the 14th International Congress of Rorschach and Projective Methods. Lisboa, Portugal.

Miralles Sangro, F. (1996). *Rorschach: tablas de localización y calidad formal en una muestra Española de 470 sujetos* [The Rorschach: location and form quality tables with a Spanish sample of 470 subjects]. Madrid, Spain: Universidad Pontificia Comillas.

Pires, A. (1987). *O teste de Rorschach na avaliação psicológica: fundamentação, validade e estudo normativo na população portuguesa* [The Rorschach test in psychological assessment: basis, validity and normative study in the Portuguese population]. Porto, Portugal: FPCE-UP.

Pires, A. (1990, July). *L'étude normative du test de Rorschach au Portugal: Étude préliminaire dans la région de Porto* [The Rorschach normative study in Portugal: preliminary study in the Porto area]. Paper presented at the 13th International Congress of Rorschach and Projective Methods. Paris, France.

Pires, A. (1993, July). *O estudo normativo do teste de Rorschach na população portuguesa: Resultados parciais* [The Rorschach normative study in the Portuguese population: partial results]. Paper presented at the 13th International Congress of Rorschach and Projective Methods. Lisboa, Portugal.

Pires, A. (1994, July). *The Rorschach normative study in Portugal: First results and comparison with the Exner normative study in the U.S.A.* Paper presented at the 5th Annual Convention of the International Council of Psychologists. Lisboa, Portugal.

Pires, A. (1996, July). *The Rorschach normative study in Portugal: Cross-cultural comparison with the U.S.A. normative data.* Paper presented at the 15th International Congress of Rorschach and Projective Methods. Boston, MA.

Pires, A., & Borges, M. I. (1990). O estudo normativo do teste de Rorschach na população Portuguesa: A região do grande Porto [The Rorschach normative study in the Portuguese population: The Porto metro area]. *Jornal de Psicologia, 9*(2), 12–16.

Riquelme, J., & Ruos, M. (1996, July). *Intra-cultural Rorschach interpretation beyond cross-cultural research.* Paper presented at the 15th International Congress of Rorschach and Projective Methods. Boston, MA.

Sendin, M. (1993, July). *Non patient transcultural comparison.* Paper presented at the 14th International Congress of Rorschach and Projective Methods. Lisboa, Portugal.

Silva, D. (1993, July). *Dados para um estudo de normas do Rorschach em crianças portuguesas dos 6 aos 10 anos* [Data for a Rorschach study of norms with Portuguese children from 6 to 10 years old]. Paper presented at the 14th International Congress of Rorschach and Projective Methods. Lisboa, Portugal.

Silva, D. (1996, July). *Cultural differences between Rorschach responses of Portuguese and American children.* Paper presented at the 15th International Congress of Rorschach and Projective Methods. Boston, MA.

Silva, D., & Prazeres, N. (1990, July). *Les données normatives du Rorschach presentées par Exner sont-elles valables in extenso pour la population européene? Essai avec un échantillon portugais* [The Rorschach normative data presented by Exner are they valid in extenso for the European population? essay with a Portuguese sample]. Paper presented at the 13th International Congress of Rorschach and Projective Methods. Paris, France.

Application of the Holtzman Inkblot Technique in Different Cultures

Wayne H. Holtzman
The University of Texas at Austin

Almost universal in its applications, the Holtzman Inkblot Technique (HIT), like the Rorschach, has proved useful in a number of different cultures ranging from primitive original societies to highly industrialized countries. During the 40 years since its development, the HIT has been the primary object of study or the featured assessment method in over 800 publications, most of which have been briefly abstracted and compiled in an annotated bibliography (Swartz, Reinehr, & Holtzman, 1999). Before reviewing applications of the standard HIT and its variations in different cultures, it would be helpful to recall the background and essential features of the technique and how it differs in stimuli and method from the Rorschach.

Over 100 years ago, Alfred Binet experimented with the use of inkblots as a test of imagination in his studies of intelligence. Two decades later, Hermann Rorschach began his experiments with mental patients. Unfortunately, he died in 1922 shortly after publishing his now-famous 10 inkblots and system for analysis. His original work was actually based on 35 inkblots, but he only had funds sufficient to publish 10 now known as the Rorschach. In the ensuing years, a number of competing systems for administration, scoring, and interpretation of the Rorschach have been proposed, the most recent and successful of them being the Rorschach Comprehensive System (RCS; Exner, 1993). Although these systems differ markedly, they are all based on the same 10 inkblots with unlimited response to each card.

The mainstream of academic psychology has always looked askance at the Rorschach movement, criticizing it for appearing cultist in character and lacking rigorous scientific discipline. This criticism reached a peak in the 1950s with the publication of a growing number of studies that usually, although not always, yielded essentially negative results. Despite these negative findings and inherent weaknesses in the preferred method of using only 10 inkblots with an uncontrolled number of responses to each, the fundamental ideas underlying the technique continue to be intuitively attractive especially in the hands of a skilled clinician.

One way of overcoming serious flaws in the Rorschach while continuing to exploit the rich, projective qualities of the inkblot technique would be to design a completely new set of inkblots with parallel forms and a sufficient number of different inkblots to ensure satisfactory reliability for the most important perceptual and content measures. Studies by Blake and Wilson (1950) and by Zubin and Eron (1953) clearly demonstrated that the first response to an inkblot was the most important, and that a simple inquiry could follow each response without adversely affecting subsequent responses. Exploratory research confirmed these ideas; with the help of a professional artist, many hundreds of new inkblots were produced and tested in a series of preliminary studies. Only 1 in 50 inkblots survived the rigorous screening that occurred before the 92 inkblots comprising Forms A and B of the HIT were selected.

The initial development and standardization of the HIT took place from 1956 to 1961. Although its basic development was carried out by a small group of psychologists at Texas, a large number of American clinicians participated in its subsequent refinement and standardization; they did so by collecting samples from well-defined populations of individuals ranging in age from 5 years old to adult and including schizophrenic patients, depressed individuals, and mentally retarded persons. More recently, normative reference groups have been published for delinquents, neurotics, and alcoholics. Psychometric studies of interrater scoring agreement, internal consistency reliability, parallel-forms test–retest stability over time, factor analysis, and differential diagnosis were carried out on 22 scoring variables for protocols from nearly 2,000 individuals. The details of this early developmental research are presented in a monograph by Holtzman, Thorpe, Swartz, and Herron (1961) and are summarized in a number of shorter articles (Holtzman, 1963, 1965, 1968, 1975, 1976, 1986, 1988).

ESSENTIAL FEATURES OF THE STANDARDIZED TECHNIQUE

The 22 variables that are scored were drawn largely from early work on the Rorschach by Beck (1937), Hertz (1936), Klopfer and Kelley (1942), Rapaport, Schafer, and Gill (1946), Schafer (1954), and Zubin and Eron

(1953), as well as from the specific Rorschach content studies of anxiety and hostility by Elizur (1949) and of barrier and penetration by Fisher and Cleveland (1958). The HIT differs from the Rorschach in several important ways:

1. The HIT consists of two parallel forms each containing 47 original inkblots, only the first two of which are identical in both Forms A and B, as compared with only 10 inkblots in the Rorschach. Many of the blots are multicolored, some are achromatic, most but not all are symmetrical, and some are quite different from the Rorschach cards.
2. The subject is asked to give only one response to each inkblot rather than an unlimited number of responses.
3. A brief inquiry follows each response rather than waiting until all inkblots are viewed.
4. All 22 variables within the standardized system can be scored on each of the responses.
5. The number of inkblots (items) rejected by the subject becomes a meaningful score when rejections occur.

The 22 basic variables scored for the standard HIT cover nearly all of the important scoring categories and dimensions in the five major Rorschach systems extant at the time of the test development. A brief definition of each variable follows:

Reaction Time (RT)—the time, in seconds, from presentation of the inkblot to the beginning of the primary response.

Rejection (R)—score 1 when the subject returns the inkblot to the examiner without giving a scorable response.

Location (L)—tendency to break down the inkblot into smaller fragments; score 0 for use of the whole blot, 1 for use of a large area of the blot, and 2 for use of smaller areas of the blot.

Space (S)—score 1 for response involving a figure–ground reversal where white space constitutes the figure and the inkblot is the ground.

Form Definiteness (FD)—a five-point scale ranging from a score of 0 for a concept having a completely indefinite form (*squashed bug*) to a score of 4 for highly specific form (*man on horse*).

Form Appropriateness (FA)—goodness of fit of the form of the concept to the form of the inkblot; score 0 for poor, 1 for fair, and 2 for good form.

Color (C)—importance of both chromatic and achromatic color as a determinant; score 0 when not used, 1 when used only in a secondary manner (like FC in the Rorschach), 2 when the color is a a primary determinant but some indefinite form is present or implied (as in Rorschach CF), and 3 when color is primary and no form is present (like C in the Rorschach).

Shading (Sh)—importance of shading or texture as a determinant; score 0 when not used, 1 when used only in a secondary manner, and 2 when shading is a primary determinant.

Movement (M)—a five-point scale for measuring the degree of movement, tension, or dynamic energy projected into the percept by the subject regardless of content; score 0 for none, 1 for static potential (sitting, looking, resting), 2 for casual movement (walking, talking), 3 for dynamic movement (dancing, weeping), and 4 for violent movement (whirling, exploding).

Pathognomic Verbalization (V)—a five-point scale ranging from 0 (no pathology present) to 4 (very bizarre verbalizations) for measuring the degree of disordered thinking represented by fabulations, fabulized combinations, queer responses, incoherence, autistic logic, contaminations, self-references, deteriorated color responses, and absurd responses.

Integration (I)—score 1 when two or more adequately perceived blot elements are organized into a larger whole.

Human (H)—score 0 for no human content present; 1 for parts of human beings, featureless wholes, or cartoon characters; and 2 for differentiated human beings or the human face if elaborated.

Animal (A)—score 0 for no animal content, 1 for animal parts, and 2 for whole animals.

Anatomy (At)—score 0 for no penetration of the body wall; 1 for X-rays, medical drawings, or bone structures; and 2 for viscera or internal organs.

Sex (Sx)—score 0 for absence of any sex references, 1 for socially accepted sexual activity and expressions (buttocks, nude figures), and 2 for blatant sex responses (penis, vagina).

Abstract (Ab)—score 0 if no abstract concept is present, 1 if abstract elements are secondary, and 2 if the response is wholly abstract (*reminds me of happiness*).

Anxiety (Ax)—a three-point scale for rating the degree of anxiety apparent in the content of the response as reflected in feelings or attitudes (*frightening animal*), expressive behavior (*girl escaping*), symbolic responses (*dead person*), or cultural stereotypes of fear (*witch*); score 1 when debatable or indirect, and 2 when clearly evident.

Hostility (Hs)—a four-point scale for rating degree of hostility apparent in the content of the response, with increasing score as hostility moves from vague or symbolic expressions to more directly violent ones in which human beings are involved.

Barrier (Br)—score 1 for reference to any protective covering, membrane, shell, or skin that might be symbolically related to the perception of body image boundaries.

Penetration (Pn)—score 1 for concepts symbolic of body penetration.

Balance (B)—score 1 where the subject expresses concern for the symmetry–asymmetry dimension of the inkblot.

Popular (P)—score 1 if a popular response is given, with popular responses being defined statistically for specific areas of the inkblots in earlier normative studies of the HIT.

The total score for each of the 22 variables is obtained by summing across the 45 cards. In addition to total scores, it is a simple matter to derive a number of other special scores from the basic elements coded for each blot. For example, the number of W, D, or Dd responses in Rorschach terms can be determined by counting the number of cards coded 0, 1, or 2, respectively, on Location. The number of FD, CF, or pure C scores is easily obtained by counting the number of responses in a protocol coded C1, C2, or C3, respectively. For those who wish to derive a Human Movement score from the basic HIT variables, it is a simple matter to combine the H and M coding for each response, thereby deriving the familiar Human Movement score well known in various Rorschach systems. Such configural scoring is easy to do directly from the summary sheet or after computer entry of the basic codes. This kind of derived scoring opens up a large number of special-purpose scores, some of which are entirely new and others that are highly similar to scores in the several Rorschach systems.[1]

The existence of truly parallel forms provides a unique opportunity— one that is unavailable in the Rorschach—for undertaking test–retest studies to determine stability over time or to examine the effects of experimental interventions on selected aspects of personality, cognition, and perception. Test–retest stability over periods of time—ranging from 1 week to 1 year—varies from a low of .36 for Popular to a high of .81 for Location, regardless of the age or culture of the subjects tested. Interscorer

---

[1]Published by the Psychological Corporation, the HIT materials consist of Forms A and B, Record Forms with schematic outlines of blots and spaces for recording responses, Summary Sheets for scoring, and the Guide to Administration and Scoring, which contains detailed instructions and many examples to facilitate accurate coding and scoring.

agreement is exceptionally high; only Penetration and Integration fall below correlations of .95; in many cases, the interscorer agreement approaches 1.00. Split-half reliabilities are also moderately high, median values for 50 different samples falling generally in the .70s and .80s. Only Anxiety, Penetration, and Popular fell below this level in the initial standardization, whereas Reaction Time, Rejection, and Location had average reliability coefficients above .90. These results for reliability have been repeatedly confirmed in other studies, both in the United States and elsewhere, and are similar to reliability coefficients frequently obtained for subtest scores that measure mental abilities. For most HIT scores, as well as patterns of scores, the reliability of measurement and stability across time are sufficiently high to justify clinical use in the assessment of individuals.

As in the case of the Rorschach and other personality assessment devices, validity of the HIT is a much more complex matter because one must always state the question in terms of validity for what purpose and for what population. A technique may prove to be valid for a specific purpose, such as the differential diagnosis of mental illness in adults, and worthless for some other equally important assessment purpose or population. Major differences in HIT score distributions across well-defined populations comprising the initial standardization studies are strong evidence supporting validity claims for differential diagnosis among schizophrenic, psychotically depressed, or mentally retarded patients. However, they say little about other forms of differential diagnosis with distinctly different populations. In each case, additional empirical research is essential to define the validity and limitations of individual scores or patterns of scores.

Use of the HIT for differential diagnosis of mental disorders has been reported by several other investigators in a variety of settings. Barnes (1963) was able to discriminate between brain-damaged individuals and normal controls with about 80% accuracy. Using HIT factor scores, Connors (1965) found highly significant differences between emotionally disturbed children seen in an outpatient clinic and normal controls of the same age and background. Cleveland and Fisher (1960) differentiated sharply between arthritic patients and those with ulcers, using only the HIT Barrier score. Cleveland and Sikes (1966) discriminated between alcoholics and nonalcoholics using HIT Penetration and two new inkblot variables developed specifically for their research. Hartung and Skorke (1980) found psychedelic drug users scored significantly higher on C, M, H, Ab, V, Hs, and Sx than nondrug users matched for age, sex, and amount of education. Shukla (1976) has been successful in the differential diagnosis of organics, schizophrenics, neurotics, and normals in India, finding that 21 of 22 standard HIT variables significantly differentiated among the four groups.

A short-cut procedure to validation that can be very powerful while also carrying high risk of error in specific instances is to ground the empirical results of validity studies in emerging theory, thereby developing a deeper understanding of the psychological meaning of scores from which inferences can be generalized to untested situations. Fortunately, there is an extensive scientific literature, largely from the Rorschach, that provides a theoretical grounding for the 22 variables of the HIT, as well as for certain patterns of scores. Much of the earlier work pertaining to validity and clinical use of the HIT has been compiled in a useful handbook by Hill (1972). Only a few highlights of findings can be presented here.

Movement, Integration, and Human repeatedly define a factor indicative of well-organized ideational activity, good imaginative capacity, and well-differentiated ego boundaries. Form Definiteness, Popular, and Barrier also frequently load highly on this factor, tending to vary somewhat from one population to the next. As one would expect from theory as well as other empirical research, these variables show marked developmental correlates with age in normal children, as well as striking differences across different populations of mental patients. Each of the variables has other correlates from independent studies that make them interesting in their own right. For example, dream deprivation results in higher Movement scores (Feldstein, 1973), and Movement is correlated with the discharge or inhibition of cognitive energy (Covan, 1976).

Pathognomic Verbalization (V), based on Rapaport's original work, has been shown to be the best single indicator of psychopathology in different populations. The bizarre perception and autistic logic underlying high scores on this variable are characteristic either of schizophrenic thinking or extreme artistic license in responding to inkblots. Nine different kinds of Pathognomic Verbalization have been defined: Fabulation, Fabulized Combination, Queer Response, Incoherence, Autistic Logic, Contamination, Self-Reference, Deterioration Color, and Absurd Response. Normal individuals tend to give fabulations with notable affectivity (scored a low V1), mildly fabulized combinations of otherwise acceptable percepts (scored V2), or even occasional queer responses that are often described in a playful manner. Schizophrenics manifest a severe loss of distance between themselves and the inkblots, often giving severely fabulized combinations (V3 or V4), contaminations (V3 or V4), queer responses (V3), special kinds of autistic logic (V3 or V4) that show faulty, fantastic reasoning as a justification for the response, or Self-Reference (V3 or V4), in which a personal reference is fused pathologically with the response. Incoherence (V4) and Deterioration Color (V4) are clearly signs of mental deterioration and confusion. Absurd responses (V3) are also generally indicative of mental deterioration or retardation.

Signs of anxiety or hostility in the fantasy content form the basis for the Anxiety (Ax) or Hostility (Hs) scores. Moderate-level scores on both of these symbolic content scales are normal, particularly in young children, but very high scores should be interpreted as having likely clinical significance. The most important evidence comes from experimental studies. Individuals with high Ax are less tolerant of pain (Nichols & Tursky, 1967) and more rapidly acquire the conditioned eyelid response (Herron, 1965). Individuals who show a marked increase in Hs score after a frustrating situation are those who also have a predisposition to hostility.

A high Color (C) score has been found to be related to impulsivity and is predictive of poor performance under stressful field conditions (Holtzman et al., 1966). Based on the results of her research on the clinical use of the HIT, Hill (1972) recommended paying attention to the quality of C, particularly those given to inkblots having a high stimulus strength for Color, in making interpretations about the lability of affect.

Three variables—Location (L), Form Definiteness (FD), and Form Appropriateness (FA)—are interesting to consider together because of the dynamic tension that is created within an individual who is confronted with the task of organizing various percepts into a single response. For example, the high-achievement-oriented perceptual style characteristic of many Americans is to use the entire inkblot (W scored as L 0) with percepts that are fairly form definite (FD 3 or 4) and form appropriate (FA 2)—a task that is difficult on the more amorphous, asymmetrical inkblots. Does the individual resolve this difficulty by focusing down on a smaller portion of the blot (L 1 or 2) while ignoring the rest? By choosing a vaguer percept (FD 1 or 2)? By ignoring the lack of high form approriateness? By playfully using a mildly fabulized combination (V 2)? Or by some combination of the first three coping strategies? Calling for a single response to each inkblot, rather than allowing the subject to give an unlimited number of responses, accentuates this dynamic tension in many individuals.

Sex (Sx), Anatomy (At), and Penetration (Pn) are three content scores dealing primarily with bodily preoccupation. Blatant sex responses (Sx2) are relatively rare but significant when they do appear. High At has been found to be closely associated with a high degree of somatic preoccupation (Endicott & Jortner, 1967). Together with Barrier, Pn is identical to the original body image concepts developed by Fisher and Cleveland (1958).

VARIATIONS OF THE STANDARD HIT

The standardized, 45-card version of the HIT is the preferred method for clinical applications and for most research studies involving the assessment of important personality characteristics that are not readily measured by interpersonal ratings or personality questionnaires. The existence of parallel forms with highly reliable scores makes possible accurate assessments before and after a treatment intervention or experimental procedure. Yet there are numerous occasions when a variation of the standard technique would be highly desirable. The most popular variations are of two kinds: (a) the use of a group method for administration, and (b) the use of a shorter form than 45 inkblots.

Unlike the Rorschach, the HIT is particularly well suited for group administration because the format involves only one response per inkblot, with each response being followed immediately by a simplified, standardized inquiry. In addition, of course, a group method is more economical because large numbers of individuals can be tested at one time. In small, well-monitored groups, individual sets of inkblots can be given face down in the proper order to each individual, together with a special group form for the individual to use in recording the location and writing the response. The more common procedure is to use colored slides projected on a screen in front of the group, large or small, allowing one minute for the subject to jot down a response before moving on to the next inkblot. A number of studies have demonstrated that the group method can be substituted for the individual method in cases dealing with individuals who are competent to write their own responses, although Reaction Time, Balance, and some of the qualitative richness are lost. Details concerning the standardized method of group administration are given by Swartz and Holtzman (1963).

Split-half reliability and test–retest stability using parallel forms with a 1-week interval are generally as high for the group method as for the individual, at least when administrated to college students. Using a latin-square design involving Forms A and B given to large numbers of students by both the individual and group methods 1 week apart, Holtzman et al. (1963) made a systematic comparison of the group and individual methods of administration. Only 5 of the 18 inkblot scores studied showed any significant mean differences attributable to method of administration. Location, Space, and Color scores were higher for the group method, and Barrier and Popular scores were higher for the individual method. Standard deviations of scores were the same for all variables except Anxiety, which had a higher variance in the group method. Comparing the cross-method correlations in a multitrait-multimethod matrix revealed a striking degree of similarity across the two methods. The more economical group method, using colored slides and the standard Record Form, can be safely substituted for the individual method when one is dealing with subjects who can write out their own responses to the inkblots.

The discussed studies show the equivalence of the individual and group forms for most of the HIT scores when used with literate, cooperative subjects. This encouraged Moseley, Gorham, and Hill (1963; see also Gorham, 1964; Gorham, 1967) to develop a method of scoring 17 HIT variables by computer. A dictionary-building program was written that alphabetizes words and counts their frequency of occurrence for any sample of protocols, where the responses have first been properly entered into the computer. An empirically derived dictionary containing about 7,000 words was then compiled in several languages to facilitate cross-cultural studies. Each word in the dictionary was assigned multiple scoring weights by an individual experienced in scoring HIT variables. These weights were checked and refined by independent expert review. When stored in a computer as a large table of scoring weights, the dictionary provides an automatic scoring system in any language for which words and weights have been compiled.

The amount of agreement between hand scoring by an expert and computer scoring the same protocols with the dictionary is surprisingly high despite that syntax is taken into account by the computer program in only a rudimentary way. Intercorrelations between the two methods of scoring are moderately high—above .80 for seven variables: Rejection, Location, Movement, Human, Color, Form Definiteness, and Animal. Cross-method correlations for Hostility, Popular, Anxiety, Anatomy, Shading, Penetration, Abstract, Sex, and Integration range from .62 to .75. The lowest correlation for the 17 variables studied was .50 for Barrier. These results were achieved in a cross-validation of the scoring method by applying it to 101 Form A protocols obtained from college students tested earlier by Swartz and Holtzman (1963). Cross-validation on 84 Form B protocols yielded equally high correlations between computer and hand scoring of the same records.

An extension of the computer-scored HIT for computer-based personality interpretation was developed by Holtzman (1975). More recently, further automation of the HIT was successfully demonstrated by Vincent (1982, 1987), who developed an experimental system for administration, scoring, and interpretation by computer. High-fidelity, colored images of the inkblots are presented serially on a screen, and the subject enters his or her responses using the computer keyboard. Unfortunately, none of these interesting ideas has been followed up, leaving unfinished a promising area for further development that might eventually have important clinical applications.

A second major variation in the standard, 45-card HIT is to shorten the test by reducing the number of inkblots. Some clinicians who are accustomed to only 10 inkblots in the Rorschach complain that 45 inkblots in one series is too many. Indeed it is if the examiner allows unlimited responses to each card or encourages extensive elaborations by the inquiry. A shortened form based on the first 25 or 30 cards, instead of all

45, is a reasonable compromise that would also be less expensive to produce and market. Because Cards 1A and 1B and subsequent identically numbered cards through 30A and 30B consist of pairs of inkblots with similar stimulus characteristics, a shortened version of the HIT would be most useful if based on some combination of these first 30 pairs of Form A and Form B cards. Moreover, if the number of responses was still limited to one per inkblot, the time for administration could be shortened from the current average of 50 minutes to about 35 minutes. Unfortunately, as Herron (1963) found in experimenting with a 30-card form allowing only one response per card, reliability of measurement falls sufficiently to limit the value of the results.

The most promising short form is HIT 25—an experimental version consisting of the first 25 inkblots in each form (Holtzman, 1988). The subject is encouraged to give two responses to each card, yielding a maximum total of 50 responses per protocol—a sufficient number to yield reliable scores. In one study, HIT 25 protocols were individually collected from 30 hospitalized patients diagnosed as schizophrenic and 30 normal, undergraduate college students. Separate analyses were made of the first and second responses to each inkblot to determine the difference, if any, that could be attributed to the new instructions calling for two responses per card rather than the usual one response. Only Popular and Rejection showed any significant differences between first and second responses. As one would expect, if a Popular response occurs at all, it tends to appear in the first response rather than the second. Rejection proved to be almost nonexistent among the normals and was surprisingly low among the first responses for schizophrenics. These results indicate that the first and second responses are sufficiently independent to sum across all responses to obtain total scores on each of the major variables.

Comparison of score distributions for HIT 25 with the published reference norms of schizophrenics and college students on the standard HIT yields interesting results. When encouraged to give two responses per card, the subject reacts more quickly than when forced to organize his or her percept into a single response. The faster Reaction Time for HIT 25 suggests that many subjects find it easier to organize their percepts and accompanying associations into two separate responses rather than combining them into a single response. Other highly significant differences consisted of higher Location scores (fewer wholes) on HIT 25 and lower scores on Color, Shading, Pathognomic Verbalization, Integration, and Penetration. Encouraging the subject to give two responses per card provides the freedom to focus on smaller detail for one of the responses while choosing the whole inkblot for the other. Coping with the task is easier because the whole and its parts can be given in separate responses. Unsuccessful attempts by the subject to integrate components into a whole

response in the standard HIT also contribute to a higher score on Pathognomic Verbalization, especially where fabulized combinations or confabu-
lations arise.

As expected, striking differences between the 30 normals and 30 schizophrenics were found for 11 of the 22 variables. Among schizophrenics,
Rejection was far more prevalent. The three determinants—Color, Shading, and Movement—show differences between schizophrenics and normals for HIT 25 similar to those obtained for the standard 45-card HIT.
When Color is broken into its individual components, most of the differences appeared to be due to less C1 (identical to Rorschach FC) among
schizophrenics. Pathognomic Verbalization was also highly significant,
largely due to more pathological responses (V scored 3 or 4) among the
schizophrenics. Popular, Animal, and most of the symbolic content scores
also proved highly significant. When all of these differences are translated
into a simple set of clinical rules or signs with decision criteria and then
cross-validated on new samples from the same populations, only 1 of 30
normals and 1 of 30 schizophrenics were falsely identified (Holtzman,
1989).

It is still too early to say whether the shortened HIT 25 version will
prove as useful as the standard 45-card HIT. Little additional developmental work has been done on the use of fewer than 45 cards for practical
applications, especially in clinical settings. These preliminary studies indicate that at least some of the resulting scores in a 25-card version with
two responses per card are of sufficient interest to justify continued
research and development.

CROSS-CULTURAL STUDIES

The HIT is ideally suited for cross-cultural studies ranging from industrialized societies to primitive, nonliterate tribes. The nonverbal, meaningless
nature of inkblots and the standard, simple instructions to give only one
response per card are easily understood in many cultures from the age of
5 upward. Although the most extensive studies have been done in Mexico,
cross-cultural research involving many countries throughout the world
have been published. Among the earliest is a series of studies by Gorham
and his colleagues using the group form of the HIT with indigeneous,
well-trained psychologists giving the test in their native language to
beginning college students (Gorham, Moseley, & Holtzman, 1968).

Over 2,200 protocols were collected in 16 countries and scored for 17
variables by the computer-based method described earlier. In one study,
Moseley (1967) developed a formula using multiple discriminant analysis

for differentiating seven Spanish and English-language cultures in North, Central, and South America: Argentina, Mexico, Panama, Venezuela, the United States, and two subcultures of Colombia—Bogota and Cartegena. He then applied his formula to 714 new cases, about 100 from each culture, and compared the actual cultural identity with that predicted solely from inkblot responses. Although the psychological meaning of his results is uncertain, the outcome is nevertheless quite interesting.

Not a single student from Argentina, Colombia, or Venezuela (the three South American countries) was misclassified as a Mexican, Panamanian, or North American, nor were any of the Mexicans or Panamanians mis-classified as Argentines. Only two Mexicans and five Panamanians were misclassified as Colombians, and only one Mexican and no Panamanians were misclassified as Venezuelans. It is interesting to note which countries seem closest to others in their patterns of responses. Among the six Latin-American cultures, only Mexico appeared close to the United States; 21% of the Americans were misclassified as Mexicans, compared with less than 1% of Americans misclassified in any other culture. Of the Mexicans, 17% were misclassified as Americans, their neighbor to the north, whereas 24% were misclassified as Panamanians, their neighbor to the south. Likewise, Cartegena was closer to Panama than was Bogota. The degree of cultural exchange and diffusion between two countries is strikingly parallel to the degree of similarity in personality patterns as measured by inkblot scores.

The group-administered HIT has also been used in a search for transcul-tural universals rather than differences. Knudsen, Gorham, and Moseley (1966) derived popular concepts using the same statistical methods and criteria employed in the derivation of Popular for the standard HIT. The majority of Populars appeared universally in all five countries studied: Denmark, Germany, Hong Kong, Mexico, and the United States. Although interesting idiosyncracies were noted in each culture, only 1 of the 25 original Populars in Form A failed to appear in at least two samples.

The most extensive cross-cultural study that has ever been undertaken involving the HIT is the longitudinal study of personality, cognitive, and perceptual development in 800 school-age children in Austin, Texas, and Mexico City (Holtzman, Diaz-Guerrero, & Swartz, 1975).[2] As illustrated in Table 17.1, an overlapping, longitudinal design was used in both cultures with annual testing for 6 years, beginning with approximately 150 children in the first, fourth, and seventh grades. This kind of design provides both cross-sectional and longitudinal measures on every age

---

[2]Because the book describing this study is out of print, a summary of the most salient results involving the HIT is presented here.

TABLE 17.1
Overlapping Longitudinal Design for 6 Years of Repeated Testing

Group	Initial Age*	Number of Cases		School Grades Covered
		United States	Mexico	
I	6.7	133	150	1 2 3 4 5 6
II	9.7	142	143	4 5 6 7 8 9
III	12.7	142	150	7 8 9 10 11 12

*The starting ages of 6.7, 9.7, and 12.7 years were chosen because most children in the public schools of Texas reach these exact ages at some time during the school year, September 15 to May 15. Actual time of testing took place within 30 days of the age as specified in the table.

from 6 to 18 in both cultures, resulting in nearly 10,000 measures on each variable for analysis even after minor attrition due to mobility of families.

Clear and uniform differences were found across the two cultures for many psychological dimensions and test scores regardless of sex, age, or socioeconomic status (SES) of the child. All the cognitive measures, almost all of the cognitive-perceptual style variables, most of the personality and attitudinal measures, and most of the items obtained from interviews with mothers yielded significant cross-cultural differences. On the HIT, every score revealed main effects or higher order interactions that involved cross-cultural differences. Space permits only a few of these to be presented here.

Significant mean differences between Mexican and American children matched for age, sex, and SES were obtained for seven of the HIT variables. Mexican children had slower response times (RT), less pathology in fantasy (V), more small detail areas (W), less movement in fantasy (M), lower integration of parts into whole (I), and less anxiety (Ax) or hostility (Hs) in fantasy. When taken together with the cross-cultural outcomes for many other variables, these results strongly suggest that a primary difference between the American and Mexican children is their coping style.

As Diaz-Guerrero (1965) pointed out, most Mexicans, particularly women, believe that life is to be endured rather than enjoyed, that it is better to be safe than sorry, and that it is better to proceed slowly rather than fast. In general, when faced with a testing situation, Mexican children are willing to cooperate, although seldom taking the initiative; instead, they tend to be cautious and please the adult examiner. Mexican children are more passively obedient and adapt to stresses in the environment rather than trying to change them.

By contrast, American children see the testing situation as a challenge to be mastered—an opportunity to show how much they can do. In attempting to deal with all aspects of the inkblots by using larger portions of the inkblot, giving responses with definite form while maintaining good form appropriateness, and incorporating other stimulus properties of the inkblots, American children try to deal with the testing situation in a much more active fashion than the Mexicans, even when unable to do so successfully.

In addition to the HIT with alternating Forms A and B in a counterbalanced fashion, the tests repeated every year for all children consisted of the Vocabulary and Block Design subtests from the Wechsler Intelligence Scale for Children (WISC) and the Human Figure Drawing Test (Harris–Goodenough developmental score and Masculinity–Femininity ratings). The complete WISC was obtained in both cultures the first year, and Arithmetic and Picture Completion were obtained for all 6 years in the Mexican samples. Analysis of repeated intercorrelations among these variables showed a clustering of Movement, Integration, Human, and Barrier from the HIT with Vocabulary in both cultures and for all ages. Movement was especially consistent in this regard, with a mean of .23 for the 36 correlations, indicating that a low but significant portion of Movement measures cognitive ability in both cultures. The correlations between Movement and either Block Design or the Harris–Goodenough score were substantially lower; only 7 of the 36 correlations for Block Design and 9 for Human Figure Drawing were statistically significant in a positive direction.

Several self-report inventories of personality were given to all children at least once during the 6 years of testing. Sarason's Test Anxiety Scale for Children (Sarason et al., 1960) was administered in all years but the first. Jackson's (1967) Personality Research Form and Diaz-Guerrero's (1972) Occupational Values Inventory were only given in the last year of the study. Parental attitudes toward childrearing, family lifestyle, social class, and environmental measures were obtained by an extensive parental interview in the home of every child halfway through the 6-year study. Social class, high or low, was used together with child's sex and age for precise matching across the two cultures in the cross-cultural comparisons. Although a number of these measures yielded major cross-cultural differences of great interest in understanding the two societies, few proved to be significantly correlated with HIT variables. Test anxiety proved to be unrelated to the HIT, but several of the personality scales for teenagers were quite significant.

Of special interest are correlations between the HIT given in the early years of the longitudinal study and the PRF scales in the last year of the study. High scores on Color were associated 5 years later with high scores on Exhibition, Impulsivity, and Nurturance in two or more of the six samples. The traditional interpretation of Color as indicative of affective response to one's interpersonal environment and sensitivity to the emotions of others is consistent with these findings.

Integration was positively correlated with later Understanding for all the American children, but only for the oldest group among the Mexicans—a finding consistent with the cognitive loadings of Integration reported earlier. As one might expect, Pathognomic Verbalization correlates positively with later Impulsivity for both Mexican and American children.

Still another study of HIT precursors of later personality was undertaken by Currie, Holtzman, and Swartz (1974), who obtained additional data on 46 children from the youngest American group 4 years after completion of the main longitudinal project. Ratings of personal adjustment on a four-point scale were obtained from teachers and counselors who knew the children well. Four HIT variables proved to be significant predictors of good adjustment 9 years later: Pathognomic Verbalization ($r = -.38$), Anxiety ($r = -.37$), Hostility ($r = -.39$), and Form Appropriateness ($r = .28$). With the exception of Form Appropriateness, all of these inkblot scores are marker variables for Factor 3, which deals with psychopathology in repeated factor analyses of the HIT variables. In the case of Form Appropriateness, the direction of the relationship indicates that children with poor form level in the HIT are more likely to be maladjusted in later life. These results strengthen substantially some of the earlier interpretations of the meaning of variables in the HIT.

A closely related study by Tamm (1967) involved Mexican and American children in the bilingual American School in Mexico City. Thirty children in the first, fourth, and seventh grades were given the HIT and WISC in their native language, providing a precise parallel to the larger longitudinal, cross-cultural project. One half of the children were native Mexicans from upper-class families whose parents had a strong desire for their children to obtain an American-style education. The other half were Americans whose parents wanted them to develop bilingual skills and attitudes. The American school curriculum was taught half in English and half in Spanish. In addition to the usual developmental differences with age in both groups, marked differences were found between the Mexican and American children—differences that in every respect were essentially the same as the major differences found for the HIT in the larger cross-cultural study. On the WISC, only Digit Span proved significant across the two cultures, with the Mexicans doing slightly better than the Americans; the reverse was found for the WISC in the larger cross-cultural study. The sociocultural premises underlying American and Mexican societies and the basically different styles of coping with the challenges of life in the two cultures provide a key to the interpretation of these results.

APPLICATIONS IN OTHER SOCIETIES

Although the HIT is used for a variety of purposes in many societies, the most productive countries in terms of recently published research are Germany, Argentina, Japan, India, France, Italy, Brazil, Romania, and French-speaking Quebec. During the past 10 years, over three times as many articles have been published in foreign journals as in those of North America. A sampling of these articles reveals that many of them deal in one way or another with the issues of psychodiagnosis, particularly differential diagnosis of schizophrenia, depression, neurosis, and borderline personality disorders.

A series of studies by Leichsenring and his colleagues at the University of Gottingen focused on the linguistic and qualitative aspects of HIT records, particularly deviant verbalizations, to differentiate among normals, neurotics, both acute and chronic schizophrenics, and individuals diagnosed as having borderline personality disorders (Leichsenring, 1989, 1990, 1991a, 1991b, 1991c, 1991d; Leichsenring & Meyer, 1992, 1994; Leichsenring, Roth, & Meyer, 1992). Group differences among normals, borderline patients, and mixed neurotic disorders were reported for indicators in the HIT of primitive defense mechanisms such as splitting, projective identification, devaluation, idealization, denial, and projection. Primary process thinking in borderline patients appeared to be closely connected with high levels of anxiety and hostility, projection, primitive denial, and sadomasochistic object relationships. Significant differentiation of all five groups was achieved by comparisons of deviant verbalizations.

Leichsenring also found significant cognitive style differences among these five groups, analyzing HIT responses for avoidance of ambiguity using Ertel's Dogmatism Text Analysis and for reduced level of abstraction using Gunther and Groeben's Abstractness Suffix Procedure. Correlations between this type of cognitive style and Anxiety and Hostility were also analyzed. In a related study, Leichsenring and Hager (1992) compared the HIT and Rorschach by having university students rate the inkblots for degree of stimulus ambiguity. The higher ambiguity ratings for the HIT formed the basis for concluding that the greater amount of deviant verbalizations in the HIT was due to the increased average ambiguity of the HIT inkblots. In other German studies, Hiller and Duhm (1989) reported on the validity of HIT scores for diagnosing depression, and Tameling and Sachsse (1996) studied body image scores on the HIT and their correlations with other symptoms and presence of trauma in psychiatric inpatients with self-injurious behavior.

Significant psychodiagnosis of psychiatric patients by the HIT has been reported recently in other cultures as well. Pokhriyal and Ahmad (1988) differentiated among acute schizophrenics, endogeneous depressives, and normal subjects in India. Impairment from head injuries among Indian patients was identified in 80% of the cases by the HIT when used together with the WAIS and the Bender Gestalt Test (Kishore & Dutt, 1988). A more intensive study of focal cerebral lesions with a modification of the HIT among Finnish adults by Vilkki (1987) showed that left-hemisphere-damaged patients had poor ideational productivity, whereas right-hemisphere-damaged patients had a perceptual disturbance as indicated by a high number of diffuse color responses to whole blots. Patients with anterior lesions were inferior to those with posterior lesions in perceptual integration and memory for inkblots.

Quite different applications of the HIT are those reported in France, Romania, and Italy. Gaudriault (1986–1987) assessed the psychodynamics of a request for psychotherapy by 110 French adults. The subjects consisted of three groups—those who were stable in requesting therapy, those who were unstable, and those who did not request therapy. The hypothesized correlations between HIT results and the quality of the request for psychotherapy were validated. A related French study by Gaudriault (1988) reported that the illusion of recurrence often found in the HIT and the Rorschach is manifested particularly by individuals placed in the dependent position of therapy seekers.

In Romania, Pitariu, Landy, and Becker (1986) reported that nine of the standard HIT variables were useful in predicting the success of 110 long-distance, professional truck drivers who had to drive under highly stressful conditions through dangerous territories in the Middle East and Asia. In Italy, Pierri (1992) found the HIT highly useful in family therapy and with couples when used like a consensual Rorschach. In a first session, each member of the couple independently responds to 80 inkblots from both forms of the HIT that are projected four at a time on a screen, having only 20 seconds to make a choice as to which they like best among the four. In a second session, each individual is shown inkblots chosen by the partner. In a third sesson, a concordant choice is requested from the two partners together on the whole set of 90 inkblots. A new series of studies by Pierri and his colleagues of both normal and pathological family interactions has been completed, forming the basis for a novel approach to marital and family therapy (G. Pierri, personal communication, January 29, 1998).

Investigators in many different cultures have applied the HIT to the study of normal children and adults often using the group method. A series of studies has been reported by Sacchi and Richaud de Minzi in Argentina (1988, 1989, 1990). Typical of their work is a report of personality characteristics in children associated with different levels of social integration ranging from shanty town residents to high-income families (1988) and studies of 633 children (1989) and 736 teenagers (1990) for whom normative tables were compiled to use as reference groups in other applications. Ethiopian adolescents were found by Jacobsson and Johansson (1985) to be significantly higher on Anatomy and lower on Integration, Abstract, Anxiety, Hostility, and Popular than Swedish adolescents of comparable education in a cross-cultural study. Ohki (1990) found HIT scores related to Type A behavior as measured by the Jenkins Activity Survey for Health Prediction among college students in Japan.

FUTURE POSSIBILITIES

In many respects, the standard 45-card HIT given individually by a trained clinician has proved sufficiently useful to justify its continued use in many different cultures and settings. Most clinical research to date has focused on the improvement of differential diagnosis to ascertain the value of the HIT for use in a battery of techniques for definitive psychodiagnosis. Unlike the Rorschach, the HIT has acceptable psychometric characteristics while also lending itself to more valid, replicable variations of the standard method of administration. The variation that has been most widely used in research involving literate individuals capable of writing out their responses is the group method with the 47 inkblots of either Form A or Form B projected on a screen. This approach is severely limited in its clinical application for psychodiagnosis. Nevertheless, the group method continues to be highly attractive because of its objectivity, low cost per subject, and demonstrated equivalence, at least for some of the more important scores, to the individual method of administration.

Complete scoring of an individual protocol by hand takes 20 to 25 minutes for a well-trained scorer who can be a technician rather than an experienced clinician. As demonstrated by Gorham et al. (1969), computer-based scoring represents a promising approach that deserves much more research and development. For the moment, however, hand scoring is the only reliable method of fully capturing the major characteristics of individual differences in inkblot perception that are relevant to personality assessment and psychodiagnosis.

The 22 scores in the standard HIT bear critical examination and possible revision. Although some variables have proved highly reliable and valid for certain purposes, others have only rarely been of sufficient interest to retain in the future. Among the more stable scores of continuing interest are those defining Factor 1 in repeated analyses (Integration, Movement, and Human), Factor 2 (Color, Shading, Form Definiteness reversed), Factor 3 (Pathognomic Verbalization, Anxiety, and Hostility), Factor 4 (Location and Form Appropriateness), and Factor 5 (Reaction Time, Animal,

Rejection reversed). In addition, Popular, Barrier, Penetration, and Anatomy have proved useful in a number of studies.

Sex, Balance, Abstract, and Space are rarely of great interest, although they are still worth noting in those unusual cases where high scores occur. One way in which these four variables might be more reliably measured would be to develop special smaller subsets of inkblots designed to maximize the pulling power concerning one or more of the variables. For example, the card-by-card statistics for the 90 inkblots from the original standardization samples listed in Appendix E by Holtzman et al. (1961) can be thought of as item parameters for selecting the best inkblots for special subsets. If one were interested in a subset to maximize figure-ground reversals scored 1 for Space, Cards 7, 16, 22, 29, 35, 36, 37, and 40 from Form A and Cards 1, 7, 18, 22, 3, 31, 35, and 44 from Form B could be selected as a special set of 16 cards with pulling power for figure-ground reversals. With only 16 cards, the subject could be asked to give two responses per inkblot, like HIT 25, resulting in 32 responses with higher likelihood of reliable Space scores worthy of further study.

Of special interest for future development are various forms of configural scoring that combine the basic elements of the 22 standard scores into patterns with associated decision rules. The efficacy of such scores has been demonstrated in a study using normative tables of HIT scores for 205 U.S. Navy enlistees to define 60 configural patterns (Holtzman, 1975). An interpretative statement was prepared for each configuration by a panel of experienced clinicians and entered into a computer program together with its accompanying configural score. This experimental, computer-based scoring and interpretation program was applied to an independent sample of 58 normals, 78 neurotics, and 100 depressed patients with significant results. Two configurations clearly differentiated 10% of the normals while yielding no false positives among the neurotics or depressed patients; 14 pattern scores identified significantly higher percentages of neurotics than either normals or depressed patients; and 5 configural patterns differentiated 3% to 7% of the depressed patients with no false positives among the normals or neurotics. In most instances, the statements and configural scores associated with neurotic, depressed, or normal individuals are those one would hypothesize in advance. Despite promising results, no further work along these lines has been done.

Such configural scoring is not unlike what Exner and his colleagues (Exner, 1993) have done in developing and refining their RCS for the Rorschach, as described elsewhere in this book. Many of the configural scoring patterns or constellations and associated decision rules that have been developed by Exner for the Rorschach could easily be adapted to the HIT because the inkblots have similar stimulus characteristics. Of course, there would have to be a whole new series of empirical studies to accomplish such an adaptation in a scientifically appropriate manner. A number of Exner's score constellations have proved clinically useful primarily when the subject gives a sufficiently large number of responses to yield stable results. The psychometric advantages of the HIT with its two parallel forms—its proved reliability and the promising validity that has been obtained—make it a highly attractive alternative to the Rorschach for future clinical applications of the more significant score patterns in Exner's system. This is especially so because the 10 inkblots in the Rorschach have become too well known by the general public and have outlived their protection under copyright law.

A major flaw inherent in the Rorschach method, from a psychometric point of view, is the uncontrolled number of responses (R). With only 10 inkblots and limited variation in stimulus qualities, the only way to obtain an adequate number of responses for reliable analysis of the Rorschach is to encourage the subject to report as many percepts as desired. Uncontrolled R is highly correlated with most formal Rorschach scores—a serious problem for which the Rorschach has been repeatedly criticized. There is no truly adequate statistical solution because most of the correlations are not even linear. Recently, for example, Meyer (1993) reported that R was significantly associated with 26 of the 29 configural scores or constellations that are based on raw numbers and significantly correlated with total scores on each of the constellations in Exner's RCS. The problem of uncontrolled R has been resolved in the HIT by using 45 inkblots, with one response per card instead of only 10 inkblots with an unlimited number of responses per card.

Another future direction in which applied research with the HIT could be fruitful is just the opposite of the psychometric approach taken thus far. Except for the major book by Aronow and Reznikoff (1976) on Rorschach content interpretation, little has been done on intensive qualitative analysis of inkblot responses since Schafer's (1954) early work on the psychoanalytic interpretation of the Rorschach. HIT 25 is sufficiently short, therefore its administration could easily be followed by a more in-depth, free-style, inquiry session that would produce rich associative material for such qualitative analysis without impairing the psychometric validity of responses given in the initial testing.

Still another way of looking at the HIT is to consider the 90 inkblots as a series of rich stimuli or items on each of which a great deal is now known concerning its stimulus and response characteristics. Several of the studies cited in this chapter have used the HIT inkblots in novel, experimental ways that are promising and should encourage others to experiment with the materials. The number of publications using the Rorschach has decreased considerably. This is evidenced by the fact that, in the leading journal for such publications, the *Journal of Personality Assessment*, an actual count of the number of Rorschach articles per year has dropped in the past 10 years. It is time for a renaissance in new ideas and empirically based studies involving inkblot perception and personality—a field that still holds a fascination for many psychologists and other clinicians.

REFERENCES

Aronow, E., & Reznikoff, M. (1976). *Rorschach content interpretation*. New York: Grune & Stratton.

Barnes, C. (1963). *Prediction of brain damage using the Holtzman Inkblot Technique and other selected variables*. Unpublished doctoral dissertation, University of Iowa.

Beck, S. J. (1937). Introduction to the Rorschach method: A manual of personality study. *American Orthospychiatric Association Monographs, 1*, 1–278.

Blake, R. R., & Wilson, G. P. (1950). Perceptual selectivity in Rorschach determinants as a function of depressive tendencies. *Journal of Abnormal & Social Psychology, 45*, 459–472.

Cleveland, S. E., & Fisher, S. (1960). A comparison of psychological characteristics and physiological reactivity in ulcer and rheumatoid arthritis groups. *Psychosomatic Medicine, 12*, 283–293.

Cleveland, S. E., & Sikes, M. P. (1966). Body image in chronic alcoholics and non-alcoholic psychiatric patients. *Journal of Projective Techniques & Personality Assessment, 30*, 265–269.

Connors, C. K. (1965, August). *Effects of brief psychotherapy, drugs, and type of disturbance on Holtzman Inkblot scores in children*. Proceedings of the 73rd annual convention of the American Psychological Association, Washington, DC.

Covan, F. L. (1976). *The perception of movement in inkblots following cognitive inhibition*. Unpublished doctoral dissertation, Yeshiva University, New York.

Currie, S. F., Holtzman, W. H., & Swartz, J. D. (1974). Early indicators of personality traits viewed retrospectively. *Journal of School Psychology, 12*, 51–59.

Diaz-Guerrero, R. (1965). Sociocultural and psychodynamic processes in adolescent transition and mental health. In M. Sherif & C. W. Sherif (Eds.), *Problems of Youth* (pp. 129–152). Chicago: Aldine.

Diaz-Guerrero, R. (1972). Occupational values of Mexican school children. *Totus Homo, 4*, 18–26.

Elizur, A. (1949). Content analysis of the Rorschach with regard to anxiety and hostility. *Rorschach Research Exchange, 13*, 247–284.

Endicott, N. A., & Jortner, S. (1967). Correlates of somatic concern derived from psychological tests. *Journal of Nervous and Mental Disease, 144*, 133–138.

Exner, J. (1993). *The Rorschach: A comprehensive system: Vol. 1. Basic foundations* (3rd ed.). New York: Wiley.

Feldstein, (1973). REM deprivation: The effects of inkblot perception and fantasy processes (Doctoral dissertation, The City University of New York, 1972). *Dissertation Abstracts International, 33*, 3934B–3935B.

Fisher, S., & Cleveland, S. E. (1958). *Body image and personality*. Princeton, NJ: Van Nostrand.

Gaudriault, P. (1986–1987). Examen de la demande de psychotherapie au moyen de tests de taches d'encre [Assessing the request for psychotherapy by means of inkblot perception]. *Bulletin de Psychologie, 40*(18), 857–862.

Gaudriault, P. (1988). Illusion of recurrence dans des tests de tache d'encre et demande de traitement psychologique [Recurrence illusion in inkblot tests and among patients seeking psychotherapy]. *Revue de Psychologie Appliquee, 38*(3), 239–252.

Gorham, D. R. (1964, December). *Development of a computer scoring system for inkblot responses.* Proceedings of the Ninth Congress of the Interamerican Society of Psychology, Miami, FL.

Gorham, D. R. (1967). Validity and reliability studies of a computer-based scoring system for inkblot responses. *Journal of Consulting Psychology, 31,* 67–70.

Gorham, D. R., Moseley, E. C., & Holtzman, W. H. (1968). Norms for the computer-scored Holtzman Inkblot Technique. *Perceptual and Motor Skills Monograph Supplement, 26,* 1279–1305.

Hartung, J. R., & Skorke, D. (1980). The HIT clinical profile of psychodelic drug users. *Journal of Personality Assessment, 44,* 237–245.

Herron, E. W. (1963). Psychometric characteristics of a thirty-item version of the group method of the Holtzman Inkblot Technique. *Journal of Clinical Psychology, 19,* 450–453.

Herron, E. W. (1965). Personality factors associated with the acquisition of the conditioned eyelid response. *Journal of Personality and Social Psychology, 2,* 775–777.

Hertz, M. R. (1936). The method of administration of the Rorschach ink-blot test. *Child Development, 7,* 237–254.

Hill, E. F. (1972). *The Holtzman Inkblot Technique: A handbook for clinical application.* San Francisco: Jossey-Bass.

Hiller, W., & Duhm, E. (1989). Zur Konstruktvaliditat der Holtzman Inkblot Technik (HIT) bei depressiven neurotischen Storungen [On the construct validity of the Holtzman Inkblot Technique in depressive, neurotic disorders]. *Zeitschrift fur Differentielle und Diagnostische Psychologie, 10*(2), 77–89.

Holtzman, W. H. (1963). Inkblot perception and personality: The meaning of inkblot variables. *Bulletin of the Menninger Clinic, 27,* 84–95.

Holtzman, W. H. (1965). A brief description of the Holtzman Inkblot Test. In B. I. Murstein (Ed.), *Handbook of projective techniques* (pp. 417–421). New York: Basic Books.

Holtzman, W. H. (1968). The Holtzman Inkblot technique. In A. I. Rabin (Ed.), *Introduction to modern projective techniques* (pp. 136–170). New York: Springer.

Holtzman, W. H. (1975). New developments in Holtzman Inkblot Technique. In P. McReynolds (Ed.), *Advances in psychological assessment* (Vol. 3, pp. 243–274). San Francisco: Jossey-Bass.

Holtzman, W. H. (1976). Inkblots through the looking glass. In M. H. Siegel & H. P. Zeigler (Eds.), *Psychological research: The inside story* (pp. 306–321). New York: Harper & Row.

Holtzman, W. H. (1986). The Holtzman Inkblot Technique with children and adolescents. In A. I. Rabin (Ed.), *Projective techniques for adolescents and children* (pp. 168–192). New York: Springer.

Holtzman, W. H. (1988). Beyond the Rorschach. *Journal of Personality Assessment, 52*(4), 578–609.

Holtzman, W. H. (1989). Personality assessment through inkblot perception. In P. F. Lovibond & P. Wilson (Eds.), *Clinical and abnormal psychology* (Proceedings of the XXIV International Congress of Psychology, Vol. 9, pp. 301–310). Amsterdam: Elsevier Science Publishers.

Holtzman, W. H., Diaz-Guerrero, R., & Swartz, J. D. (1975). *Personality development in two cultures.* Austin: University of Texas Press.

Holtzman, W. H., Moseley, E. C., Reinehr, R. C., & Abbott, E. (1963). Comparison of the group method and the standard individual version of the Holtzman Inkblot Technique. *Journal of Clinical Psychology, 19,* 441–449.

Holtzman, W. H., Santos, J. F., Bouquet, S., & Barth, P. (1966). *The Peace Corps in Brazil.* Austin: University of Texas International Office.

Holtzman, W. H., Thorpe, J. S., Swartz, J. D., & Herron, E. W. (1961). *Inkblot perception and personality.* Austin: University of Texas Press.

Jackson, D. N. (1967). *Manual for the Personality Research Form*. New York: Research Psychologists Press.

Jacobsson, L., & Johansson, S. (1985). Aspects of personality structure in Ethiopian and Swedish adolescents: A transcultural study of the Holtzman Inkblot Technique. *Acta Psychiatrica Scandinavica, 72*(3), 291–295.

Kishore, R., & Dutt, K. (1988). Psychometric assessment of head injury cases. *Indian Journal of Clinical Psychology, 15*(1), 34–57.

Klopfer, B., & Kelley, D. M. (1942). *The Rorschach technique*. Yonkers-on-Hudson, NY: World Book Company.

Knudsen, A. K., Gorham, D. R., & Moseley, E. D. (1966). Universal popular responses to inkblots in five cultures: Denmark, Germany, Hong Kong, Mexico, and United States. *Journal of Projective Techniques and Personality Assessment, 30*, 135–142.

Leichsenring, F. (1989). Aspekt von Objektbeziehungen bei Borderline und neurotischen Patienten: Eine empirische Untersuchung mit der Holtzman Inklot Technik [Aspects of object relations in borderline and neurotic patients]. *Psychotherapie Psychosomatik Medizinische Psychologie, 39*(12), 463–470.

Leichsenring, R. (1990). Discriminating borderline from neurotic patients. A study with the Holtzman Inkblot Technique. *Psychopathology, 23*(1), 21–26.

Leichsenring, F. (1991a). Primary process thinking, primitive defensive operations and object relationships in borderline and neurotic patients. *Psychopathology, 24*(1), 39–44.

Leichsenring, F. (1991b). "Fruhe" Abwehrmechanismen bei Borderline und neurotischen Patienten [Primitive defense mechanism in borderline and neurotic patients]. *Zeitschrift fur Klinische Psychologie Forschung und Praxis, 20*(1), 75–91.

Leichsenring, F. (1991c). Auffalligkeiten des Denkens und der Affekte bei Borderline und neurotischen Patienten [Disturbances of thinking and affects in borderline and neurotic patients]. *Zeitschrift fur Differentielle und Diagnostische Psychologie, 12*(2), 107–123.

Leichsenring, F. (1991d). Discriminating schizophrenics from borderline patients: Study with the Holtzman inkblot Technique. *Psychopathology, 24*(4), 225–231.

Leichsenring, F., & Hager, W. (1992). Reizambiguitat beim Rorschach Test und bei der Holtzman Inkblot Technik [Stimulus ambiguity in the Rorschach Test and the Holtzman Inkblot Technique]. *Zeitschrift fur Differentielle und Diagnostische Psychologie, 13*(2), 91–96.

Leichsenring, F., & Meyer, H. A. (1992). Kognitiver Stil bei Schizophrenen: Ambiguitats-Vermeidung und verminderte Abstraktheit [Cognitive style in schizophrenics: Avoidance of ambiguity and reduced level of abstraction]. *Zeitschrift fur Klinische Psychologie, Psychopathologie und Psychotherapie, 40*(2), 136–147.

Leichsenring, F., & Meyer, H. A. (1994). Reduzierung von Ambiguitat: sprachstatistische Untersuchungen an "Normalen," Neurotikern, Borderline Patienten und Schizophrenen [Reduction of ambiguity: Linguistic statistics from normal persons amd patients with neuroses, borderline disorders, or schizophrenia]. *Zeitschrift fur Klinische Psychologie, Psychopathologie und Psychotherapie, 42*(4), 355–372.

Leichsenring, F., Roth, T., & Meyer, H. A. (1992). Kognitiver Stil bei Borderline—im Vergleich zu neurotischen Patienten: Ambiguitats-Vermeidung und verminderte Abstracktheit [Cognitive style of borderline patients as compared with neurotic patients: Avoidance of ambiguity and abstraction]. *Diagnostica, 38*(1), 52–65.

Meyer, G. J. (1993). The impact of response frequency on the Rorschach constellation indices and on their validity with diagnostic and MMPI-2 criteria. *Journal of Personality Assessment, 60*(1), 153–180.

Moseley, E. C. (1967). Multivariate comparison of seven cultures: Argentina, Colombia (Bogota), Colombia (Cartegena), Mexico, Panama, United States, and Venezuela. In C. F. Hereford & L. Natalicio (Eds.), *Aportaciones de la psicologia a la investigacion transcultural* (pp. 291–304). Mexico City, Mexico: Trillas.

Moseley, E. C., Gorham, D. R., & Hill, E. (1963). Computer scoring of inkblot perceptions. *Perceptual and Motor Skills, 17,* 498.

Nichols, D. C., & Tursky, B. (1967). Body image, anxiety, and tolerance for experimental pain. *Psychosomatic Medicine, 29,* 130–110.

Ohki, M. (1990). Type A behavior and personality examined using the Holtzman Inkblot Technique. *Japanese Journal of Health Psychology, 3*(2), 14–21.

Pierri, G. (1992). Methods for evaluating normal and pathological couples and families according to the elementary pragmatic model. *Annali dell'Istituto Superiore di Sanita, 28*(2), 177–184.

Pitariu, H., Landy, F. J., & Becker, W. (1986). Utilizarea testului Holtzman in examenul psihologic al conducatorilor auto [The use of the Holtzman test in the psychological examination of truck drivers]. *Revista de Psihologic, 32*(2), 96–103.

Pokhriyal, R., & Ahmad, H. (1988). Response pattern of acute schizophrenics and endogeneous depressives on Holtzman Inkblot technique. *Journal of Personality and Clinical Studies, 4*(2), 205–207.

Rapaport, D., Schafer, R., & Gill, M. (1946). *Diagnostic psychological testing: Vol. II.* Chicago: Year Book Publishers.

Sacchi, C. J., & Richaud de Minzi, M. C. (1988). Relacion entre integracion social y personalidad [Studying the relationship between social integration and personality]. *Acta Psiquiatrica y psicologica de America Latina, 34*(2), 135–141.

Sacchi, C. J., & Richaud de Minzi, M. C. (1989). The Holtzman Inkblot Technique in pre-adolescent personality. *British Journal of Projective Psychology, 34*(2), 2–11.

Sacchi, C. J., & Richaud de Minzi, M. C. (1990). Normas para adolescentes argentinos de la tecnica de las manchas de tinta de Holtzman [Holtzman Inkblot Technique norms for Argentinian adolescents]. *Interdisciplinaria, 9*(2), 91–115.

Sarason, S. B., Davidson, K. S., Lighthall, F. F., Waite, R. R., & Ruebush, B. K. (1960). *Anxiety in elementary school children.* New York: Wiley.

Schafer, R. (1954). *Psychoanalytic interpretation in Rorschach testing.* New York: Grune & Stratton.

Shukla, T. R. (1976). Pathological verbalization on inkblots and psychodiagnosis. *Indian Journal of Clinical Psychology, 3,* 17–21.

Swartz, J. D., & Holtzman, W. H. (1963). Group method of administration for the Holtzman Inkblot technique. *Journal of Clinical Psychology, 19,* 433–441.

Swartz, J. D., Reinehr, R., & Holtzman, W. H. (1999). *Holtzman Inkblot Technique: Research guide and bibliography.* Austin, TX: Hogg Foundation for Mental Health.

Tameling, A., & Sachsse, U. (1996). Symptomkomplex, Traumapravalenz und Korperbild von psychisch Kranken mit selbstverletzendem Verhalten (SVV) [Symptom complex, prevalence of trauma, and body image in patients with self-injurious behavior (SIB)]. *Psychotherapie Psychosomatik Medizinische Psychologie, 46*(2), 61–67.

Tamm, M. (1967). Resultados preliminares de un estudio transcultural y desarrollo de la personalidad de ninos Mexicanos y Norteamericanos [Preliminary results of a cross cultural study of personality development in Mexican and American children]. In C. F. Hereford & L. Natalicio (Eds.), *Aportaciones de la psicologia a la investigacion transcultural* (pp. 159–164). Mexico City, Mexico: Trillas.

Vilkki, J. (1987). Ideation and memory in the inkblot technique after focal cerebral lesions. *Journal of Clinical and Experimental Neuropsycholoigy, 9*(6), 699–710.

Vincent, K. R. (1982). The fully automated Holtzman interpretation. In K. Herman & R. M. Samuels (Eds.), *Computer: An extension of the clinician mind, a reference book* (pp. 123–125). Norwood, NJ: Ablex.

Vincent, K. R. (1987). *The full battery cookbook: A handbook of psychological test interpretation for clinical, counseling, rehabilitation, and school psychology.* Norwood, NJ: Ablex.

Zubin, J., & Eron, L. (1953). *Experimental abnormal psychology* (preliminary ed.). New York: New York State Psychiatric Institute.

VI

PROJECTIVE METHODS: THE THEMATIC APPERCEPTION TEST AND OTHER PICTURE-STORY TESTS

Part VI contains three chapters on the Murray Thematic Apperception Test (TAT) and two chapters using other picture-story stimuli. Historically, the TAT was a peer of the Rorschach but has declined in usage in the United States because there has been no consensual scoring system that could have led to the development of norms for low-inference interpretation and a clinical research literature. To be sure, there were many early scoring systems, including Murray's need press system that generated a respectable research literature on several needs. These early systems could have been consolidated into a unified system, as Exner did with Rorschach scoring systems to create the Rorschach Comprehensive System (RCS), and six of these systems were still taught to graduate students as recently as 1981. Since that time, training in graduate programs has diminished the TAT to a *projective interview*.

The chapters in Part VI offer some resolution to the problematic history of the TAT in the United States. Chapter 18 offers potential remediation using a research-based TAT scoring system. Chapter 19 demonstrates that the TAT is alive and prospering in multicultural Brazil using high-inference interpretation. Chapter 20 provides a scoring system, based primarily on scores developed in the United States, that has extensive normative data for low-inference TAT interpretation in Spain. Chapter 21 describes a culture-specific thematic test primarily for adolescents with entirely new pictures developed from a clear rationale and provided with low-inference interpretation based on objective scoring. Chapter 21 presents a picture-story test developed in Portugal for children; it combines low- and high-inference interpretation. As these chapters indicate, the exportation of projective assessment instruments can now be accompanied by importation of new instruments and a scoring system for the TAT.

Chapter 18 describes a psychocultural scoring system for content analysis of TAT stories developed by De Vos. Exemplar stories from Card 1 are used to illustrate the workings of the system with Anglo-Americans, Korean Americans, Japanese, Japanese Americans, Latin Americans, and Mexican Americans. Applications of this system for cross-cultural/multicultural personality assessment are included. This system is distinctive in representing an etic–emic approach to psychological assessment using general themes (etic) that are reproduced in a variety of cultural settings (emic). This system has origins in Murray needs and the Parsons–Bales research on small-group interactions.

At the risk of oversimplifying a complex approach, a few general comments are included to suggest the multiple dimensions and procedure. The etic framework contains 10 basic thematic concerns in human relations expressed as instrumental and expressive themes. The system includes vertical and horizontal scoring categories to reflect equal or unequal status, and outcomes are also coded. Analysis proceeds from the identification of general thematic issues to specific subcategories. Rereading the stories many times for increased understanding and subsequent elaboration of scoring fosters a search for objectivity and leads to a systematic use of quantitative comparisons.

The psychocultural approach can potentially meet many of the requirements for cross-cultural assessment. The scoring categories are culturally appropriate, interpretations are contextually grounded, culturally relevant personality theory can be applied, and the development of normative data is feasible. However, the Murray pictures are dated and may not be recognized or addressed in the same way in different cultural settings. The crucial issue is whether the original Murray cards are suitable for use in all cultural settings or whether the cards need to be redrawn for ethnic/racial differences in the figures and/or altered to depict culturally recognizable settings and décor; this issue has not been resolved by research. One advantage in retaining the original pictures, as chapter 20 strongly indicates, is that a known and respected research history can be applied directly. By contrast, however, this research history can also be applied to the development of new pictures with cultural/ethnic figures and relevant backgrounds and new scoring categories (see chap. 21). The psychocultural approach can also provide acculturation status information useful for describing the cultural self perhaps in a more direct manner than high-inference interpretation permits. For example, I count the number of stories containing cultural themes and then calculate the percentage of all stories containing these themes as a rough indication of cultural orientation status. A secondary analysis of the contents of these themes provides details concerning the cultural self that can be used in cultural formulations for *DSM–IV*. Using the psychocultural approach in assessment training provides a formal, structured context for sensitizing students to the complexity of the TAT and would promote the use of repeated readings to attend to a large number of interactive variables simultaneously. This approach to training as a teaching device may be compared with Silvan Tomkins' (1947) systematic and logical analysis of TAT structure and content. A training manual addressing scoring issues and interpretation would be helpful for students.

Chapter 19 reviews Brazilian TAT literature for contrast and comparison with studies in the United States. The frequency of TAT use varies considerably in different states and cities of Brazil. Normative data are needed for regions or states rather than national norms due to the extreme differences in cultural and demographic variables. Some normative data on common themes were reported during the 1950s in Rio de Janeiro, but there has been no substantial updating. Work during the 1980s is cited to illustrate both similarities and differences in common themes between the United States and Brazil. Although differences in thematic content may be attributed to social class, cultural differences were also apparent. Noteworthy are responses that would be considered distortions and pathological in the United States—a finding reminiscent of interpretations of RCS scores using norms developed in the United States (see chaps. 13 and 15). The use of foreign normative data is rejected as pathologizing in favor of local or regional Brazilian normative data. Recommendations include developing these norms for each card on more objective apperceptive parameters and then, for thematic aspects, including story plots with antecedents and outcomes.

A variety of cultural groups have been studied, including Afro-Brazilians, Tukuna Indians, Germans, Israelis, Italians, Japanese, and Portuguese, as well as immigrants from nine different countries. This research differs somewhat in choice of populations, including various immigrants from Europe. Brazilian populations from diverse countries maintain their separate ethnic/cultural distinctiveness and are simultaneously self-identified and accepted as Brazilians. In the United States, a homogenization of European origin populations or Anglo-Americans may be contrasted with minority populations of African Americans, American Indians/Alaska Natives, Asian Americans, and Hispanic Americans. Many studies with diverse objectives are also described, providing an overview of the applied interests of researchers in Brazil. Examples include maternity and depression, job selection and recruiting, creativity, learning difficulties, prison inmates, institutionalized children, and social class responses to education.

U.S. research includes concern for normative data, minimal social class effect on norms, and studies of different cultural groups.

TAT researchers' points of view in both countries are similar. The history of TAT research has remained salient in recent studies involving cultural groups within a context of willingness to update normative studies and develop new approaches for interpretation. Modifications of the TAT, although appropriate and necessary, have been difficult to develop and apply. With respect to norms, this chapter finds an increase in research on interpretation coupled with a lack of normative data. Many studies underutilize available normative data perhaps because these norms require review and updating. Short-term recommendations include small-scale normative studies of nonclinical and normal protocols as a basis for interpreting protocols collected in clinical settings. Practitioners in Brazil often discount empirical research studies presented in exclusively statistical terms. There is a preference for "linking of objective statistical studies with clinical judgment and intuition."

Chapter 20 provides a strong argument for continuing to use the Murray TAT cards. These cards have been used with a number of scoring variables developed in the United States, as well as Spain to provide a objective scoring system that was standardized on a normal Spanish population. TAT research and practice in Spain has flourished as a result of low-inference interpretation contained in a published manual used for training clinical psychologists. Chapter 20 describes this scoring system and the standardization in detail. By way of introduction, certain key features of this scoring system are described. First, 12 cards were selected in separate sets for men and women. These cards include the basic cards recommended for use in the United States by a number of separate and independent sources. These cards are highly structured and consequently of the medium ambiguity repeatedly associated with stories containing relevant personality information. Second, the directions include the seven parts I have used both in research and practice as a basis for inferring psychopathology from story structure and content. Third, a structured inquiry is included to standardize the test situation by uniform supporting questions from the examiner and use of nonintrusive verbal comments/answers. Fourth, an Integrative Analysis System with procedural steps leading to a narrative TAT report is introduced. These steps include (a) transcribing/coding verbal and nonverbal responses, (b) computing formal variables to moderate the thematic analysis, and (c) intrasubject quantitative/qualitative analysis or estimations of five specific Needs, Thematic Contents, Emotional Tone, Interpersonal Relations Content, Experiential-Integrative Content, and decoding of speech organization processes. Fifth, comparisons are made with inter- and intrasubject normative data. Sixth, a formal analysis of traditional variables, including vocabulary, is used. Seventh, a TAT psychogram is prepared containing all indexes, raw data, profiles, and base rates that can be added to the narrative TAT report.

Several new scores were introduced, including an Expression Speed Index, which describes the cognitive ability to produce narratives moderated by defenses, and an Expression Rapidity Index of the cognitive ability to perform the TAT task. The normative data were basically similar to norms developed in the United States and France with additional cultural and situational elements. This finding suggests that the TAT and the Rorschach may tap universal dimensions of personality. Avila-Espada has joined Shneidman in presenting empirical information concerning what the TAT can measure, but also has suggested a potential for cross-cultural TAT application as a genuine etic measure that is in accord with the psychocultural approach in chapter 18.

Chapter 21 presents the Tell-Me-A-Story Test (TEMAS)—an alternative solution to the continued use of the Murray TAT cards that combines new cards with a parallel form designed for Anglo-American, Latin-American, African-American, and Asian-American populations in the United States. Many modified or redrawn card sets, as well as newly designed card sets for various cultural/racial groups, are reviewed historically in this chapter to develop the rationale for TEMAS. Test bias is recognized in intelligence tests and by implication in personality testing and diagnostic evaluation. By acknowledging the role of cultural elements in test stimuli designed to elicit personality characteristics, this source of bias can be reduced. This conviction recognizes that standard tests were developed as Anglo-American emics and subsequently used as pseudoetics with culturally different populations. Furthermore, the logic in applying these standard tests has been the presumption of no bias, whereas the raison d'etre for TEMAS is the presumption of bias in standard picture-story tests. If this sounds like a familiar theme, chapter 3 renders this argument in statistical terms by calling for a reversal of the null hypothesis, whereas chapter 1 depicts an assessment–intervention model as an example of the consequences of reversing the null hypothesis. TEMAS embodies a projective test example of this reasoning.

TEMAS can be described as a psychometrically sophisticated picture-story test developed for children and adolescents within a dynamic-cognitive theoretical orientation. It is a unique representative of a culture-specific personality test because this test went further than merely modifying the Murray TAT cards. Acknowledging that personality develops within a sociocultural system, the chromatic TEMAS cards are of low ambiguity and highly structured to expose the everyday conflicts of persons recognizable as similar to the assessee in race or ethnicity. TEMAS has an objective scoring system for structure and content, including cognitive, personality, and affective functions. Normative data are available for multicultural groups. The standardization sample represents four ethnic/racial groups in three age-range groups. A 23-card long form and a 9-card short form are available. Internal consistency, test–retest, and interrater reliabilities have proved satisfactory. Content validity, relationships to other measures, and predictive validity have been investigated. There has been a systematic program of multicultural and cross-cultural validity studies reported in detail. These cross-cultural studies have been conducted with Puerto Ricans in Puerto Rico and New York, as well as in Argentina and Peru. These studies provide suggestions of national and acculturation differences. Thus, TEMAS meets the requirements for bona fide cross-cultural assessment. The accumulating research provides data for redesigning some pictures, refining psychometric properties, and contributing to knowledge of multicultural populations in the United States, as well as to increased understanding of differences among national groups in Latin America.

Storytelling to pictures antedates projective techniques and tests as an avenue for play, self-expression, communication, instruction, and relationship. Storytelling tests have been called *projective techniques* because they have essential elements of stimuli, responses, and interpretations. Chapter 22 presents the Once-Upon-A-Time test, which differs from earlier storytelling techniques/tests in several ways that make it a promising substitute for all predecessors. First, there is an expectation for active, goal-directed play. By presenting three cartoon pictures providing a partial story to be completed by the child using other pictures, the child enters a playlike setting that is being observed and recorded by the examiner. The task is intrinsically of interest and requires active involvement in choosing pictures, making decisions, imagining outcomes, and putting the entire process into words. Historically, only the Make-A-Picture-Story Test required child-selected figures to place against examiner-selected cards with backgrounds. However, when children also select their own backgrounds, their stories have a dramatically increased potential for interpretation.

Second, the Once-Upon-A-Time Test objectifies dynamic ideas about play as a transition space between fantasy and reality by using an explicit and carefully designed scoring system that has high scorer agreement. The pictures were selected to represent anxiety, fantasy, and reality solutions permitting elaboration of pleasurable and anxiety-producing everyday scenes. The scoring details the anxiety, fantasy, and reality scenes chosen for sequences used to complete the stories and provides linkages between the stories and contents of associated verbalizations. The scoring procedures permit a focus on the child's feelings, constructions of experience, problems in living, and sense of an emerging self as a basis for subsequent interventions. As a consequence, this test only provides psychopathology information indirectly, in contrast with current practice with storytelling tests in the United States where psychiatric diagnosis is their primary purpose. Nonetheless, diagnostic inferences can be made from the child's behavior, verbalizations during testing, how the stories are told and organized, and particularly from the normative data.

Third, as an instrument for planning subsequent psychological interventions, this test pinpoints situations and behaviors that may be either setting-specific or generalized across settings and that are potentially upsetting for the child and disruptive for parents, teachers, and other children. This test does not dictate the choice of particular psychological interventions, but orchestrates data to permit dynamic, behavioral, or cognitive approaches to be applied.

The use of separate sets of pictures for boys and girls permits examination of gender-specific developmental sequences that would be anticipated to differ in time of occurrence and elaboration across cultures and by social class/caste and other variables within one society. The availability of norms by gender and age permits development of expectations for good functioning and poor functioning at home, in the school, and with peers at play. Moreover, the norms also encourage use of this test in health settings, where it is mandatory to acknowledge and understand the emotional consequences for children of illness, chronic disease, surgical trauma, and physical handicaps. Information on the self may be gathered using this test as a new avenue to augment understanding of cultural/racial identity. Storytelling using picture-story tests provides access to the life story or personal identity that encompasses ethnicity, culture, race, and class. This is a model storytelling test for these purposes because the scenes are etic in nature, at least in modern and postmodern societies, and the norms are demonstrably emic. Although reference norms would be required for each country in which this test is applied, such data would foster international comparisons of child development by gender and provide data on the effectiveness of standard etic psychological interventions for dysfunctions in various countries.

REFERENCE

Tomkins, S. (1947). *The Thematic Apperception Test.* New York: Grune & Stratton.

18

A Psychocultural Approach to TAT Scoring and Interpretation

David Ephraim
Universidad Central de Venezuela

Picture-story methods intended for cross-cultural assessment should meet some of the following requirements according to Dana (1993): culturally relevant stimuli, scoring categories that reflect culturally important variables, availability of normative data, contextual grounding of interpretations, and culturally relevant personality theory. Only the first requirement of culturally relevant stimuli has historically had an impact in the TAT literature by the creation of culture-specific sets of cards (incidentally, according to Teglasi, 1993, research findings have revealed that these adaptations do not necessarily elicit richer stories than the traditional TAT cards). Regarding the other requirements, a lack of consensus on any TAT scoring system (Dana, 1993; Vane 1981) remains the major difficulty for using picture-story methods cross-culturally in a systematic and cumulative way.

George A. De Vos, a psychologist and anthropologist, has developed throughout many years a combined etic–emic approach for scoring TAT narratives across cultures. De Vos' approach intended both to identify TAT thought patterns from the culture-specific emic perspective of particular ethnocultural groups and to compare those thought patterns from a culture-general etic perspective. De Vos' system has been used to analyze TAT stories from different ethnocultural groups in various societies around the world (De Vos, 1983; De Vos & Caudill, 1973; De Vos & Kim, 1993; De Vos & Vaughn, 1992; Ephraim, Söchting, & Marcia, 1997; Scheper-Hughes, 1979; Suárez-Orozco, 1989; Suárez-Orozco & Suárez-Orozco,

1995). The TAT research studies based on De Vos' system have repeatedly found both general themes elicited regardless of the sociocultural setting and clear differences in normative responses when comparing one group with another.

Although most of the TAT comparative research based on the psychocultural approach was not specifically directed to clinical assessment of individuals, De Vos' system has been described as highly relevant for cross-cultural/multicultural personality assessment. According to Dana (1998b), "at present the system is invaluable for detailed personality study and as an exemplar of etic-emic methodology in which the study of the cultural self can be addressed" (p. 13).

The objective of this chapter is to introduce the TAT psychocultural scoring system to researchers and practitioners in the field of cross-cultural/multicultural personality assessment. The first section of the chapter describes the system. The second section illustrates how the system works by analyzing examples of stories to TAT Card 1 from various ethnocultural groups. The third section includes some closing comments about the application of the TAT psychocultural system to cross-cultural/multicultural personality assessment.

DESCRIPTION OF THE TAT PSYCHOCULTURAL SCORING SYSTEM

The psychocultural scoring system analyzes TAT narratives according to a framework of 10 basic thematic concerns in human relations (see De Vos & Vaughn, 1992, for a recent presentation of the system including a tabular format). The proposed framework may also be used to analyze interviews and other cultural material, such as dreams, folklore, ritual, or literary productions (De Vos often used his TAT framework as a leading thread in systematizing ethnographic data of various kinds; e.g., De Vos, 1992). The *instrumental* themes or concerns included in the psychocultural system are *achievement, control, cooperation–competition, competence,* and *responsibility*. The *expressive* themes or concerns are *pleasure, nurturance, affiliation, appreciation,* and *harmony.* Separate from the previous interpersonal themes, the system also codes themes or concerns with *inanimate* objects and *impersonal* topics, such as destiny or fate.

Some of the themes coded by the psychocultural scoring system were part of Murray's (1943) original list of needs, which De Vos considered too extensive and without a unifying framework. McClelland, Atkinson, and associates consecutively researched themes of achievement, power, affiliation, and intimacy (see Smith, Atkinson, McClelland, & Veroff, 1992, for a comprehensive presentation of this approach). Although also interested in developing an objective scoring procedure, De Vos was not satisfied with McClelland and Atkinson's atomistic approach, which proceeds by isolating a few motives. Conversely, the TAT psychocultural approach aims to identify the relative saliency of those motives or themes, as well as any others, by classifying all the story material in a complex fashion (De Vos & Kim, 1993). The categories of the psychocultural system were described by De Vos as universals or culture-general elements that appear in every social group. However, he added: "Cultures differ as to how these concerns are relatively emphasized, interrelated, or blended with one another in molecular patterns that may be quite culture-specific" (De Vos & Suárez-Orozco, 1990, p. 35).

De Vos' distinction between instrumental and expressive concerns follows the research work in small-group interactions by Parsons and Bales (1955), who proposed to differentiate between the task leader and the emotional-social leader. The instrumental–expressive dichotomy would parallel McAdams' (1993) distinction between agency and communion themes, but De Vos' approach is more psychosocial than strictly psychological. For example, *achievement* is defined by the psychocultural system as a concern with accomplishment that guides behavior according to the value system of a particular society. Its opposite is not *failure*—the negative of a concern with competence—but *alienation*, which occurs when "there is a loss of a need to attain some success within established value patterns viewed positively by the society" (De Vos & Vaughn, 1992, p. 128).

A distinction is made by the psychocultural system between vertical and horizontal scoring categories. The expressive concern with nurturance and the instrumental concern with control operate in human relationships of unequal status. Affiliation and cooperation–competition are, respectively, the expressive and instrumental categories for human relations of equal status. Thematic concerns are also coded as *positive*, *unresolved*, or *negative* regarding their outcome. The latter codes are assigned from the narrator's perspective.

The coding routine proceeds by identifying thematic issues as they unfold in the stories. Each narrative is typified by one or more dominant concerns and often contains additional subthemes depending on the story's length and complexity. De Vos proposed to code the stories as *active* or *passive*. Over the years, he also divided the main categories into numerous subcategories. In their current formulation, both features add unnecessarily to the system's complexity. However, it is important to keep in mind that assigning a general, more abstract code, such as *negative control* or *positive harmony*, may not capture the substance of a specific concern. The culture-general categories proposed by De Vos initially inform the analysis by allowing the identification of plot structures. However, those general categories often need to be further specified or sub-categorized according to the particular experiential thought patterns in an open-ended inductive process. Such a process shares the openly dialogical nature of the hermeneutic inquiry (Packer, 1985), as the scorer returns repeatedly to the story, searching each time for an increased understanding that would allow for a more complete interpretation. The advantages of picture-story over self-report methods for exploratory research of this kind were often described in the early TAT literature. For example, according to Neugarten and Guttman (1958), "the richness and unstructured nature of projective data enable the investigator to follow an inductive process; he can follow up clues as they appear in the data rather than check dimensions and hypotheses defined in advance" (p. 58). The subjective nature of the data does not preclude a search for objectivity. The system intends to be as objective as possible to allow quantitative comparisons in a systematic way.

"THE BOY WITH THE VIOLIN" ACROSS CULTURES

TAT stories of individuals from different ethnocultural backgrounds are analyzed in this section to illustrate how the psychocultural system works. To provide enough context for the examples, some information is included about the different research projects from which the examples were selected. Given the complexity of the scoring procedure, only stories to TAT Card 1 are presented. This card depicts a young boy contemplating a violin that rests on a table in front of him (Murray, 1943).

Holt's (1978) normative guide to the use of TAT cards has been considered as a most comprehensive discussion of TAT's common themes (Cramer, 1996). According to Holt's description of normative responses to TAT Card 1, "a boy is confronted by a violin, in our culture, for either of two main reasons—because his parents think he should study it or because he has some more self-generated interest" (Holt, 1978, p. 81). Holt's characterization of TAT Card 1 stimulus pull can be considerably enriched by using the psychocultural scoring system across cultures.

Achievement and Competence Themes in the Early Comparative Research of Japanese Immigrants to the United States, Japanese Americans and White Americans. De Vos' interest in the TAT started in the early 1950s as part of a collaborative research on the Japanese achievement motivation (Caudill & De Vos, 1956; De Vos & Caudill, 1973). As described by De Vos (1983), the focus of this early research was to explain the successful postwar adaptation of Japanese immigrants (Issei) and their children born in the United States (Nissei), despite severe discrimination that culminated in internment during World War II. Based on observations

and psychological testing, the researchers concluded that the Issei's remarkable resiliency was related to motivation and social attitude patterns
pertaining to their cultural heritage. The previous conclusion was partly
based on a comparison of TAT data from small community samples collected by Caudill; such comparison involved male and female records
from 30 Japanese immigrants (median age was approximately 50), 40
Japanese Americans (median age was approximately 28), and 60 White
Americans (40 from a lower middle-class and 20 from an upper lower
class background, matched for age with the Nissei). The Japanese immigrants' TAT Card 1 narratives were the highest in positive self-initiated
achievement. They also often expressed a concern with competence or
adequacy. For example:

> (Female, age 44) What is this? A violin? He has a violin and he's thinking,
> "How shall I do it?" It looks very difficult and so he rests his face on his
> hand and worries [concern with *competence*]. He thinks, "I can't play it yet,
> but if I study hard, someday maybe I will be a good musician." In the end
> because he holds steady, he becomes a good player [concern with *achieve-
> ment*]. He'll grow up to be a fine persevering young man. (De Vos & Caudill,
> 1973, p. 231)

Competence is scored in the previous story because the boy is worried
about his ability to perform ("*Can* I do the task?"). The key element for
scoring achievement is his concern with a long-range goal ("*Will* I become
a violinist?"). Because the boy is described as successful, the story is scored
positive. To explain this kind of story, Caudill referred to the Japanese
strong determination to succeed by realistic work devoid of any fantasy
or magical thinking: "Even if one is tired and puzzled, and if the outer
world conditions are such as to defeat one, one must nevertheless keep
on and never give up" (Caudill, 1952, p. 47).

The prevailing concern with competence–failure themes in the TAT
stories from Japanese samples serves to illustrate the importance of contextual grounding of interpretations and culturally relevant personality
theory in cross-cultural/multicultural personality assessment (Dana,
1993). As described by De Vos and Vaughn (1992), the Japanese are
concerned with incompetence or failure as a necessary step toward achieving greater mastery, whereas failure themes in an American TAT protocol
would probably imply feelings of unworthiness or low self-esteem at the
individual level.

A distinctive feature of some Japanese-American TAT narratives, when
compared with those from the Japanese immigrants, was their reference
to control issues ("I *must* do the task!") in narratives of parental pressure.
For example:

(Female, age 26) Is he supposed to be sleeping? Probably practicing. I guess the mother must of—something the mother is forcing on him. He's a little bored and disgusted, but he can't go against his mother's wishes. He's probably just sitting there daydreaming about the things he'd like to do rather than practicing. Something that was forced upon him. He'll probably be just a mediocre player. (De Vos & Caudill, 1973, p. 232)

Negative control stories of the previous kind were additionally sub-categorized as *negativistic compliance and self-defeat*. As suggested by the comparative data presented next, the shift from achievement and adequacy to control themes seems related to changes in acculturation. Another specific subtheme regarding control issues of parental pressure was identified by Caudill and De Vos in the stories of the 20 upper lower class White Americans. The boy's reaction was often seen as either one of open refusal or doing only what was required and then quitting. For example:

(Female, age 32) Doesn't want to play his violin. Hates his music lessons. His mother wants him to be a musician but he's thinking about breaking the violin. (De Vos & Caudill, 1973, p. 232)

Culture-Specific Thematic Concerns With Autonomy or Nurturance in Achievement Stories From High School Students in Japan and the United States. Vaughn used the psychocultural scoring system to compare TAT Card 1 stories of 17- and 18-year-old youths at two Japanese public high schools in Tokio and Takasaki and at a U.S. high school rated among the top 10 in the California school system (De Vos & Vaughn, 1992; Vaughn, 1983). When comparing 85 stories from each country, achievement and competence issues were dominant in the Japanese narratives, whereas control issues of parental pressure were dominant in the U.S. stories. The following story of parental pressure from an American youth illustrates a typical control theme together with an expressive concern that is unusual for this particular card:

(Male) "I hate school. It's so boring," thought the boy. Another music lesson. "Why does Mommy make me take violin lessons? I can't play as well as the teacher wants me to." . . . He couldn't stand the long, cold halls of the school. The unfriendly teachers always berating him for this or that. But Mommy wouldn't listen to his pleas, so he returned each day. (De Vos & Vaughn, 1992, p. 134)

The previous narrative portrays concerns with control and competence as well as negative affiliation or negative nurturance in its reference to *cold* halls and *unfriendly* teachers. De Vos and Vaughn presented a series of narratives to illustrate typical achievement concerns representative of either an American or Japanese achievement orientation. For our purpose of illustrating TAT Card 1 alternative stories, an interesting finding from their study was the identification of a culture-specific concern with autonomy in the TAT stories of some elite U.S. youths. Opposition to parental pressure was typically depicted in positive terms. For example:

> (Female, age 17–18) There is only one thing in the whole world that Arthur hates, and that's the violin.... Every time he had to practice he would think of ways to avoid it. "There had to be a way out of playing the violin for good," he thought.... What Arthur liked best and was best at was the drums. "The drums!!!" Arthur's mother exclaimed when he came home that day. Arthur told her that he played this instrument the best and that he should let him play what *he* wanted, and not what *she* wants. So Arthur's mother gave in and thanked Arthur for teaching her a lesson. He taught her that all persons are individuals and should be treated that way. If they want to dress strange with blue hair then that is their choice. Just like Arthur wanted to play the drums and not the violin. (De Vos & Vaughn, 1992, p. 136)

The previous story is scored as *positive control (autonomy)* ("Do I *want* to play?"). It illustrates another distinctive feature identified by De Vos and Vaughn in the U.S. youths' narratives: They tended not to emphasize effort and hard work, but ability as the reason for success. In strong contrast with the U.S. stories, where positive achievement was associated with independence from the family, Japanese youths' TAT stories typically combined themes of achievement and family nurturance. De Vos and Vaughn (1992) quoted a series of narratives where the boy was described as dependent on his mother for advice, deeply attached to his father, feeling grateful toward a teacher, or inspired by a parent or ancestor. In terms of the scoring system, these narratives are double-scored as *positive achievement* and *positive nurturance*. For example:

> (Male, 17–18) He's looking at the violin which is a memento from his grandfather. He's thinking about his grandfather, and talking to his spirit. He will practice and will succeed greatly as a violinist. (p. 133)

> (Female, 17–18) The boy is said to be a musical genius. He has been practicing late and has a headache. He's massaging his temple. His headache has not disappeared. Recalling his mother's advice not to work too hard, he will take some medication and go to bed. (pp. 132–133)

Achievement Versus Alienation Themes in Stories From Korean Minorities in the United States and Japan. Cross-cultural/multicultural assessors often deal with the psychological consequences for individuals experiencing exploitation and/or racism in the current situation or across previous generations (Dana, 1997; Draguns, 1996). As described by Good (1996), cross-cultural and subcultural misunderstandings are a real problem when caring for many of the most disadvantaged U.S. populations, such as patients who are recent immigrants, members of minority groups, or persons who are poor or living on the fringe of society.

In a recent recollection of his professional career, De Vos (1993) stated that his abiding theoretical interest has been to understand "the effects of minority status, whether caste, class, or ethnic in nature, upon the psychological development of the individual in the primary family and social group" (p. 31). A piece of De Vos' research dealing with such issues through the TAT psychocultural scoring system contrasted narratives from Korean youths in Japan and Korean adult immigrants to the United States (De Vos & Kim, 1993). According to the authors, the present generation of Korean youths in Japan experience varied symptoms of social alienation, such as a high delinquency rate, in response to the disparagement and degradation suffered since the arrival of their parents or grandparents. In contrast, Korean immigrants to the United States were characterized by De Vos and Kim as remarkably successful in establishing themselves, as reflected by their rapid upward educational and socioeconomic mobility.

The TAT Card 1 stories from the sample of 50 Korean adult immigrants tested in Los Angeles were described by De Vos as remarkably similar to the Japanese narratives reported earlier in terms of their positive self-initiated achievement themes (De Vos, 1983). In contrast, the TAT narratives from the 31 Korean-Japanese youths tested in the Kyoto–Osaka area revealed a lack of incentive to positively resolve achievement themes. Fifty percent of the stories collected in Los Angeles ended up successfully, compared with only 6% of those collected in Kyoto and Osaka (De Vos & Kim, 1993). Some TAT Card 1 narratives from Korean-Japanese youths illustrate alienation themes—or negative achievement themes—in their lack of any positive future orientation. For example:

(Male, age 25) He was bought and given a violin. But he does not know how to play the violin, so he's watching the instrument. He's worrying if he will become a violinist. I wonder if he has a toothache. That's all. (De Vos & Kim, 1993, pp. 223–224)

(Male, age 18) Well, he's practicing the violin, and it seems that he's tired of playing the violin. And now he sighs, looking at the violin. He's completely fed up with it.... And after all, when he is asked if he wants to quit the violin, he cannot decide. I don't know. (De Vos & Kim, 1993, p. 224)

Issues of Class, Privilege, and Opportunity in Latin-American Stories From Venezuela. The Importance of Feedback for Interpretation. The TAT method has been described by McAdams (1994) as exceptionally sensitive to variable factors and influences in the person as well as the situation; TAT motives would be expected to change more than personality traits both over time and under the influence of all kinds of situational variables. The TAT sensitivity to sociohistorical factors has been less emphasized in the literature. A major, and still unexplored, strength of the TAT method for cross-cultural/multicultural assessment would be its sensitivity to what Shweder (1991) called "the historically variable and cross-culturally diverse" (p. 87). Some TAT comparative data of Venezuelan youths from various socioeconomic backgrounds illustrate issues of class, privilege, and opportunity, as reflected in TAT data, and the crucial importance of feedback for interpretation. The study included TAT stories from three groups (24 participants each) of high school youths collected in the capital city of Caracas, where extremes of poverty and wealth coexist side by side.

A first sample was collected at a private high school located in an affluent suburban area. The youths' families belonged to a Venezuelan small privileged sector of at least high middle-class status. A high proportion of these families experienced a rapid economic success under a speculative economy and a corrupt political system. At the TAT Card 1, only one student from this elite group—who happened to be a misplaced middle-class participant—made a successful self-initiated achievement story. The rest of the TAT narratives from this group concerning achievement and competence themes were unresolved or negative. An interesting nuance in some narratives was the devaluation of a self-initiated achievement goal. In the following two examples, achievement efforts do not pay enough or in a timely fashion:

(Male, age 18) The boy wants to study music. . . . The story ends with him beginning to handle the violin and learning to play. (Inquiry) He graduates, but works in something totally different to what he studied, nothing to do with music. . . . Because he doesn't make enough money.

(Male, age 16) 1 think he's studying. Well, he was given a violin as a present [*nurturance*] and he was looking at it for the first time. I don't know what to say [*adequacy*]. Now that the boy has the violin, I suppose he will like it [*pleasure*]. . . . He learned to play the violin very well. He gave a concert and was considered a child genius [*achievement*]. Well, later, what else, just when you need it, imagination doesn't come [*adequacy*]. He gets married [*affiliation*]. He dies of old age, just after he became famous, just after he had made all that progress.

Regarding other TAT themes, five stories displayed parental pressure with negativistic compliance—this theme was almost absent in other

Venezuelan urban and rural samples of lower SES—and another five narratives referred to negative affects unrelated to the instrumental task. Qualified informants were interviewed regarding the results at the various research settings to help with the interpretations. To the investigators' surprise, the informants invariably found the results consistent with their expectations. Regarding this particular group, an experienced and highly committed program coordinator confessed with dismay: "There is nothing more difficult than educating kids whose parents have the money to buy them all they want."

A second small sample of Venezuelan youths involved students from a working class neighborhood attending a demanding public high school run by a religious group. Unresolved or negative achievement or competence themes were dominant for this group. The difficulty of the task was often emphasized. For example:

> (Male, age 17) A boy with a violin. He performed in public. He just finished his performance and he's sad now because he made many mistakes. He thinks he played much worse before and has improved now. But he also knows that if he works harder he will be able to play much better.

> (Male, 16) A boy looking at a violin. He dreams of playing it, of being able to handle it. He's thinking that some day he could be a great piano performer. He's full of dreams. That's his only goal. He particularly likes to listen to classical music. He will stay there and will attempt to play the violin once again.

The first story is coded as *unresolved* given the lack of a definite positive outcome. Unresolved achievement is also the main concern in the second narrative, which depicts a highly valued achievement goal. When interviewed, staff and teachers talked about the institution's prestige and high standards: "Compared with those from other schools that serve the same population, our students are very well prepared. But they never know how good they are until after they graduate. Not even the best ones are ever confident about their performance." Staff and teachers came across as particularly devoted to their work. At the feedback session, they found the results entirely consistent with their educational philosophy and everyday observations. Incidentally, a lively and valuable discussion based on the TAT research findings took place at the feedback session; essential issues were examined at that session, such as the advantages and drawbacks of the school's extremely high standards for students who have to compete in a harsh environment of limited opportunities.

In sharp contrast with the previous groups, where different kinds of TAT incompetence themes were dominant, students from another public high school in Caracas told a remarkably high proportion of positive self-initiated achievement stories. Meeting with the staff and teachers was again necessary to understand the TAT findings. This public high school, located in a middle-class neighborhood, previously served the local community. Local middle-class families now send their children to private schools elsewhere because the school's quality has declined over the years due to a lack of funding for public education. Interestingly, the students that currently attend the school and were tested by the research team came from families of a lower SES who live nearby in poorer and deteriorated neighborhoods. According to the teachers and staff, these families are tenacious and make every effort to give their children the best education possible, which means sending them to this particular school despite the distance and other difficulties they face by doing so. The high frequency of positive self-initiated achievement stories told by the students of this sample probably reflects not only the students' motivation but their parents' commitment to higher achievement standards.

The previous comparison illustrates the TAT's sensitivity to a multiplicity of sociohistorical and current ecological/contextual factors, such as, in this particular case, issues of class, privilege, and opportunity as well as differences in the educational philosophy and environment. Although "one does not need large numbers of informants to learn the dominant stories of any culture" (Howard, 1991, p. 191), it is not an easy task to sort out how a variety of factors influence TAT data in a particular study. An unavoidable consequence of using a contextually sensitive assessment approach is that, as described by Geertz (1995) regarding ethnography, "everything is a matter of one thing leading to another, that to a third, and that to one hardly knows what" (p. 20). As illustrated by the previous examples, institutional feedback about the research findings is paramount for contextually grounded interpretations. Regarding cross-cultural/multicultural assessment, some authors have emphasized community involvement and consultation as essential elements for verifying the interpretations and relating the research or clinical data to goals valued by the community (Dana, 1993; Suzuki, Meller, & Ponterotto, 1996).

Combined Achievement and Nurturance-Deprivation Themes in Stories of Youths From Central-American and Venezuelan Rural Areas. Suárez-Orozco (1989) used the psychocultural system to analyze TAT stories of 50 Central-American recent immigrant youths at two U.S. inner-city schools. The stories often displayed positive achievement themes. According to Suárez-Orozco, the most striking feature of Card 1 narratives from this sample was the high number of stories in which an older figure was invoked as a source of nurturance. Combined TAT achievement–nurturance themes were also frequent in a Venezuelan mountain rural sample of 16 students attending high school at a small village in Los Andes. For example:

(Male, age 18) Once upon a time there was a boy that wanted to learn to play the violin, but it was too difficult for him. One day someone moved close to where he lived. That person knew how to play the violin. As the boy insisted so much, he gave him a violin as a present. The boy was saddened when he learned that the violin was so difficult to play, but he was very ambitious. He tried and tried hard until he was able to play it. He was so excited that he felt he was the happiest person in the world. He became one of the best violin players.

As illustrated by the previous narrative, a distinctive subtheme often found in the Latin-American TAT Card 1 achievement stories was task-related pleasure ("He was so excited that he felt he was the happiest person in the world"). Regarding other typical achievement-nurturance themes, the following Venezuelan story includes concern with deprivation, the negative of a concern with nurturance, which is solved positively:

(Female, age 17) This boy is very sad [negative of *pleasure*] because his parents do not have the money to pay for his violin lessons [*deprivation*]. He solved the problem by himself [*competence* and *autonomy*]. He worked and got some money for his violin lessons. After some years he became famous, and, together with his parents, fulfilled the dream of his life [*achievement-affiliation*].

The previous achievement story does not involve the kind of individualistic self-advancement identified by McClelland, Atkinson, Clark, and Lowell (1953) in their classic studies of achievement motivation. According to Suárez-Orozco and Suárez-Orozco (1995), Latinos' achievement needs "flourish in an atmosphere of affiliation and interdependence" (p. 183).

Deprivation themes are common in TAT narratives of Latin Americans from poor rural areas. These stories refer to material or financial deprivation or the absence of an adult figure to help the child with the instrument. The following Venezuelan story from the Andean area involved no reference to instrumental themes of achievement or capacity, but expressive issues of affective deprivation: "Well, it looks like a sad boy, a lonely and abandoned boy. And ... he has been abused, without a family, without anyone to guide him."

A second Venezuelan rural sample of 16 high school students was collected at the more poverty-stricken coastal region of Barlovento. The African influence is predominant in this part of the country, where slaves were brought during the 18th century to supply labor for a short-lived cacao boom. A different economic system took place in this area compared with the Andean region. Slaves worked for the plantations located along the coast, whereas the mountains were settled by Spanish homesteaders who owned their land. The heritage of exploitation and the current indigence experienced by the Barlovento inhabitants is reflected in their TAT stories. Although there were narratives of positive self-initiated achievement, a distinctive feature in some stories was the lack of a long-term goal, even in narratives with a positive outcome. For example:

(Male, age 18) Once there was a boy who thought about something that worried him. He longed to find a solution to a problem he had. He had failed an exam. He reached a conclusion: to study more for the next exam in order to obtain a better grade.

Interestingly, six participants from this group did not identify the violin in their narratives, as in the previous story. Nevertheless, they were equally attracted by the card's instrumental stimulus pull. Achievement was combined with deprivation and reciprocal nurturance in the following story, which also shows a concern with appreciation or esteem, unusual in this card:

(Male, age 20) He feels sad [negative of *pleasure*]. He wants to continue studying but he doesn't have any help from his parents or a relative [*deprivation*]. He wants to be somebody in the future to prove that he is useful for something [*appreciation*], and help someone else who might need his help [*nurturance*].

TAT themes of being helped (or not being helped) and helping others, as in the previous story, are frequent in poor areas. Such themes correspond to the description by social scientists of the wheel of reciprocity turning around in societies of scarce resources. The following sad achievement story from Barlovento illustrates a concern with fate—another unusual theme at the TAT Card 1:

(Male, age 17) Luis was a self-made musician. Since he was a little boy he knew how to make good music. He continued practicing and when he was older he became one of the most popular musicians in the area.... He became a great musician and people talked a lot about him, particularly in Venezuela. But Luis fell and hurt his arms which were the most important part of his body to play the violin and advance on his career. He felt downhearted for a long time and people didn't talk much about him anymore.

Themes of deprivation and sadness at the TAT Card 1 have been reported by anthropologists who collected stories from people living in conditions of extreme poverty and/or social disintegration in different parts of the world. In his study of an impoverished village in Southern Italy, Banfield (1958) reported many TAT Card 1 stories of deprivation.

In some of them, a nurturant figure rescues the boy from poverty and abandonment. For example:

> (Female, age 41) A little boy, left an orphan, lived by begging, charity, and by playing his guitar. One day his one possession, that is the guitar, broke and the child cried because he no longer knew what to do. Then a gentleman saw him and gave him a new guitar. (p. 176)

Differences in socialization between the sexes were identified by Scheper-Hughes (1979) in her study of a disintegrating small village in western Ireland. A high proportion of the village boys and male psychiatric patients who participated in the study told stories of negative achievement to TAT Card 1, in which the main character withdrew from the task and felt bored, sleepy, or otherwise uninterested (e.g., "This one is either bored at his work, or he doesn't understand the lesson he has gotten, or he might be giving himself a little rest," p. 173). According to Scheper-Hughes, the male stories reflected how the young boys from the village, most of them condemned to work the family farm, were socialized into feelings of personal inadequacy and hostile dependency on their parents. Conversely, a high proportion of both the village girls—most of whom were contemplating emigration—and hospitalized young women told positive achievement stories.

TAT narratives take an almost obsessive quality under conditions of extreme deprivation, as described by Scheper-Hughes (1992) regarding hunger themes in the stories of people from Alto do Cruzeiro, an impoverished shantytown in northeast Brazil. Their narratives at different cards seemed all alike. For example:

> (Card 1) This boy is thinking about his life. . . . He wants to be able to give things to his children when he grows up. He is going to see to it that they always have something to eat.

> (Card 3BM) (kneeling figure next to a small object) The boy is crying. . . . He is all alone in the world and he's hungry. (p. 168)

Issues of Acculturation and Minority Status in Achievement Stories From Mexican-American Youths. Suárez-Orozco and Suárez-Orozco (1995) compared TAT stories from small samples of Mexican middle-class, Mexican immigrant lower class, lower class second-generation Mexican-American, and middle-class White American youths. Their study involved 189 adolescents of both sexes attending public middle and high school. The authors reported that the Mexican and immigrant Mexican samples displayed self-motivated achievement themes more often in their TAT Card 1 stories than either the White American or Mexican-American samples. A distinctive feature of the Mexican-American narratives, when compared with the other samples, was the prevalence of failure themes (28% of their stories would be scored as *negative competence* or *negative achievement*, compared with 2% among Mexican and immigrant Mexicans and 4% among White Americans). For example:

> The child was very interested in playing the violin in the beginning. Now he doesn't know what to do without any help. Now he is going through stages where he puts in too much effort and nothing is happening. So he is feeling depressed. He loses his interest in music and now has a mental block. He can't solve other problems. He gives up all interest in music and has a mental block. He loses confidence in solving problems. (Suárez-Orozco & Suárez-Orozco, 1995, p. 179)

Based on the previous findings, the researchers questioned the assumption made by a number of authors that their cultural background is responsible for the relatively high levels of school failure experienced by Latinos in the U.S. school system. The elevated school dropout among Mexican-American youths would be explained instead by other factors such as minority status, discrimination, alienating schools, and economic hardship. Regarding acculturation issues in Card 1 narratives of Mexican-American youths, some of their stories included themes of parental pressure similar to the ones of White American youths, whereas other narratives overlapped with the nurturance and reciprocal nurturance themes of the Mexican and immigrant Mexican samples.

CLOSING COMMENTS ON CROSS-CULTURAL/MULTICULTURAL ASSESSMENT WITH THE TAT PSYCHOCULTURAL SCORING SYSTEM

There are not many assessment tools available that are as sensitive to history, culture, ecology, or context as the TAT methods. The psychological discipline as a whole has mostly taken the opposite direction. As stated by Shweder (1991), the main force in psychology has been the notion of a central processor that is context and content independent. This is also true regarding research and practice with picture-story methods. Past and current significant developments in the field have mostly involved the study of the structural features in TAT narratives for personality description and the diagnosis of psychopathology. Such is the case in the United States with the ego-psychological approach (e.g., Holt, 1958; Schafer, 1958), as well as with the more recent development of clinical scales for assessing defense mechanisms (Cramer, 1996) or object relations (Westen,

1991). Conversely, the psychocultural approach to the TAT is based on the narratives' content, not in their structural features; it intends to address issues regarding the experiential self not the personality traits or weaknesses.

The psychocultural approach to the TAT offers concrete advantages for a culturally informed psychological practice. As illustrated earlier, the system's sensitivity to multiple influences facilitates the attainment of essential requirements for cross-cultural/multicultural assessment, such as contextually grounded interpretations and utilization of culturally relevant personality theory (Dana, 1993). The requirement of ethnocultural or acculturation status norms (Dana, 1998a) can also be met through the psychocultural scoring system, which allows the development of normative data without sacrificing the stories' complexity (Ephraim, Söchting, & Marcia, 1997). Practitioners may easily develop local norms to be used within their particular setting regarding the specific issues involved in their work.

On the basis of appropriate comparative data from minority groups and the mainstream culture, TAT narratives could provide indirect information about acculturation status in multicultural societies. Supplementing the interview or self-report acculturation measures, TAT narratives would furnish subjective, spontaneously generated data about cultural orientation regarding concrete instrumental and expressive issues. Another advantage of De Vos' system involves clinical training. Sets of TAT stories could be used to encourage awareness of the cultural self (Dana, 1997). By revealing differences between groups as well as within-group variations, TAT narratives help students avoid stereotyped images of culturally different persons.

Dana (1998b) mentioned some limitations of the psychocultural system for its routine use by practitioners, such as its limited research basis and the unavailability of simplified training procedures. The psychocultural system's research basis exhibits the typical problems identified by the literature in assessment research with ethnic minorities (Greene, 1987; Okasaki & Sue, 1995). Most of the research studies quoted earlier were methodologically deficient in the following areas: complete information on basic subject parameters, adequate sample size, translation procedures, report of interscorer agreement level by examiners, role of moderator variables, and contextual considerations regarding community or high school samples.

Clinical training with the TAT psychocultural system might appear difficult due to the system's intricacy. However, as illustrated by this chapter, which focused on TAT Card 1, and a previous article focused on TAT Card 6BM (Ephraim, Söchting, & Marcia, 1997), the narratives' complexity may become more manageable once the alternative possibilities of a particular card have been explored across cultures. Practitioners and students trained to use the psychocultural system by way of a 1-day workshop reported the system accessible as well as directly applicable in their practice. In any case, simplified training procedures should be available, such as a training manual on practical issues of scoring and interpretation.

The psychocultural scoring system combines quantitative and qualitative features. Both aspects could be improved for a more extensive use by practitioners. As a standardized quantitative coding procedure, studies of interrater agreement would help to establish the extent to which the categories can be reliably scored. As a qualitative interpretive procedure for content analysis, categories and subcategories could be enhanced on the basis of data collected from a broad range of cultural groups and subgroups. A limited set of TAT cards can be researched extensively to reach saturation through collaborative efforts by researchers and practitioners worldwide as well as within multicultural societies.

ACKNOWLEDGMENTS

I thank George A. De Vos, José Miguel Salazar, and Richard Dana for their valuable comments, Darling Campos, Verushka Anato, and Isabel Diaz for their assistance collecting Venezuelan data, and Frances McQueen and Cristina Santaella for their thoughtful editing. Appreciation is expressed to the Universidad Central de Venezuela for granting a leave of absence that made possible the preparation of this chapter, and to James Marcia and Simon Fraser University for their continued support. Portions of this chapter were presented at the midwinter meeting of the Society for Personality Assessment, San Diego, CA, March 1997.

REFERENCES

Banfield, E. C. (1958). *The moral basis of a backward society*. New York: The Free Press.

Caudill, W. G. (1952). Japanese-American personality and acculturation. *Genetic Psychology Monographs, 45*, 3–102.

Caudill, W. G., & De Vos, G. A. (1956). Achievement, culture and personality: The case of Japanese Americans. *American Anthropologist, 58*(6), 1102–1126.

Cramer, P. (1996). *Storytelling, narrative and the Thematic Apperception Test*. New York: Guilford.

Dana, R. H. (1993). *Multicultural assessment perspectives for professional psychology*. Boston: Allyn & Bacon.

Dana, R. H. (1997). Personality assessment and the cultural self: Emic and etic contexts as learning resources. In L. Handler & M. Hilsenroth (Eds.), *Teaching and learning personality assessment* (pp. 325–346). Thousand Oaks, CA: Sage.

Dana, R. H. (1998a). Multicultural assessment of personality and psychopathology in the United States: Still art, not yet science, and controversial. *European Journal of Psychological Assessment, 14*(1), 62–70.

Dana, R. H. (1998b, March). *Using the TAT in cross-cultural/multicultural assessment.* Paper presented at the midwinter meeting of the Society for Personality Assessment, Boston, MA.

De Vos, G. A. (1983). Achievement motivation and intra-family attitudes in immigrant Koreans. *Journal of Psychoanalytic Anthropology, 6*(1), 25–71.

De Vos, G. A. (1992). *Social cohesion and alienation: Minorities in the United States and Japan.* Boulder, CO: Westview.

De Vos, G. A. (1993). Psychological anthropology: A professional odyssey. In L. B. Boyer, R. M. Boyer, & H. Stein (Eds.), *The psychoanalytic study of society: Vol. 18* (pp. 23–88). Hillsdale, NJ: The Analytic Press.

De Vos, G. A., & Caudill, W. G. (1973). Achievement, culture and personality. In G. A. De Vos (Ed.), *Socialization for achievement: Essays on the cultural psychology of the Japanese* (pp. 220–247). Berkeley: University of California Press.

De Vos, G. A., & Kim, E.-Y. (1993). Koreans in Japan and the United States: Attitudes toward achievement and authority. In I. Light & P. Bhachu (Eds.), *Immigration and entrepreneurship: Culture, capital and ethnic networks* (pp. 205–241). New Brunswick: Transaction Publishers.

De Vos, G. A., & Suárez-Orozco, M. (1990). *Status inequality: The self in culture.* Newbury Park, CA: Sage.

De Vos, G. A., & Vaughn, C. A. (1992). The interpersonal self: A level of psychocultural analysis. In L. B. Boyer & R. M. Boyer (Eds.), *The psychoanalytic study of society: Vol. 17* (pp. 95–142). Hillsdale, NJ: The Analytic Press.

Draguns, J. G. (1996). Multicultural and cross-cultural assessment: Dilemmas and decisions. In G. R. Sodowsky & J. C. Impara (Eds.), *Multicultural assessment in counseling and clinical psychology* (pp. 37–83). Lincoln, NE: Buros Institute of Mental Measurements.

Ephraim, D., Söchting, I., & Marcia, J. (1997). Cultural norms for TAT narratives in psychological practice and research: Illustrative studies. *Rorschachiana, 22,* 13–37.

Geertz, C. (1995). *After the fact: Two countries, four decades, one anthropologist.* Cambridge, MA: Harvard University Press.

Good, B. J. (1996). Knowledge, power and diagnosis. In J. E. Mezzich, A. Kleinman, H. Fabrega, & D. L. Parron (Eds.), *Culture and psychiatric diagnosis. A DSM-IV perspective* (pp. 347–351). Washington, DC: American Psychiatric Press.

Greene, R. L. (1987). Ethnicity and MMPI performance: A review. *Journal of Consulting and Clinical Psychology, 55*(4), 497–512.

Holt, R. R. (1958). Formal aspects of the TAT—A neglected resource. *Journal of Projective Techniques, 22,* 163–172.

Holt, R. R. (1978). *Methods in clinical psychology: Vol. 1. Projective techniques.* New York: Plenum.

Howard, G. S. (1991). Culture tales: A narrative approach to thinking, cross-cultural psychology and psychotherapy. *American Psychologist, 46*(3), 187–197.

McAdams, D. P. (1993). *Stories we live by. Personal myths and the making of the self.* New York: Morrow.

McAdams, D. P. (1994). *The person: An introduction to personality psychology.* Fort Worth, TX: Harcourt, Brace.

McClelland, D. J., Atkinson, J. W., Clark, R. H., & Lowell, E. L. (1953). *The achievement motive.* New York: Appleton-Century-Crofts.

Murray, H. A. (1943). *Thematic Apperception Test manual.* Cambridge, MA: Harvard University Press.

Neugarten, B. L., & Guttman, D. L. (1958). Age-sex roles and personality in middle age: A thematic apperception study. In B. L. Neugarten (Ed.), *Middle age and aging: A reader in social psychology* (pp. 58–71). Chicago: The University of Chicago Press.

Okasaki, S., & Sue, S. (1995). Methodological issues in assessment research with ethnic minorities. *Psychological Assessment, 7*(3), 367–375.

Packer, M. J. (1985). Hermeneutic inquiry in the study of human conduct. *American Psychologist, 40*(10), 1081–1093.

Parsons, T., & Bales, R. (1955). *Family socialization and interaction process.* Glencoe, IL: The Free Press.

Schafer, R. (1958). How was this story told? *Journal of Projective Techniques, 22,* 181–210.

Scheper-Hughes, N. (1979). *Saints, scholars and schizophrenics.* Berkeley: University of California Press.

Scheper-Hughes, N. (1992). *Death without weeping. The violence of everyday life in Brazil.* Berkeley: University of California Press.

Shweder, R. A. (1991). *Thinking through cultures.* Cambridge, MA: Harvard University Press.

Smith, C. P., Atkinson, J. W., McClelland, D. C., & Veroff, J. (Eds.). (1992). *Motivation and personality: Handbook of thematic content analysis.* New York: Cambridge University Press.

Suárez-Orozco, M. (1989). *Central-American refugees and U.S. high-schools. A psychosocial study of motivations and achievement.* Stanford, CA: Stanford University Press.

Suárez-Orozco, C., & Suárez-Orozco, M. (1995). *Transformations: Immigration, family life and achievement motivation among Latino adolescents.* Stanford, CA: Stanford University Press.

Suzuki, L. A., Meller, P. J., & Ponterotto, J. G. (1996). Multicultural assessment: Present trends and future directions. In L. A. Suzuki, P. J. Meller, & J. G. Ponterotto (Eds.), *Handbook of multicultural assessment: clinical, psychological, and educational applications* (pp. 633–684). San Francisco: Jossey-Bass.

Teglasi, H. (1993). *Clinical use of story telling. Emphasizing the TAT with children and adolescents.* Boston: Allyn & Bacon.

Vane, J. R. (1981). The Thematic Apperception Test: A review. *Clinical Psychology Review, 1,* 319–336.

Vaughn, C. A. (1983). *Cognitive independence, social independence and achievement orientation: A comparison of Japanese and U.S. students.* Unpublished doctoral dissertation, University of California at Berkeley.

Westen, D. (1991). Clinical assessment of object relations using the TAT. *Journal of Personality Assessment, 56,* 56–74.

19

Use of TAT in Multicultural Societies: Brazil and the United States

Eliana Herzberg
University of São Paulo

A review of Brazilian Thematic Apperception Test (TAT) literature followed by some work published in the Unites States is presented first with special emphasis on normative studies. The chapter concludes with a general commentary on the present status and usefulness of the TAT in both countries.

TAT IN BRAZIL

Azevedo, Almeida, Pasquali, and Veiga (1996) sought a long-term goal of researching the tests used most by Brazilian psychologists. Preliminary data from the city of Brasilia (capital of Brazil), gathered from 40 different psychologists, showed that the tests most utilized were the House-Tree-Person (22%) and the Raven (22%). The TAT was not included as one of the top 10 tests. However, the TAT is frequently used in clinical psychology practice in the greater São Paulo area on the basis of the author's personal teaching experience and professional contacts, supported by research involving professors, supervisors, and other members of the Department of Clinical Psychology at the University of São Paulo (Herzberg, Erdman, & Becker, 1995). This study, using 24 (83% of the total) professionals who administered psychological tests, concluded that the TAT was the most frequently used technique (92%). Although there is still insufficient national data to support this conclusion, regional differences certainly are present.

447

Importance of Normative Data

França e Silva, the first psychologist concerned with establishing normative data, authored a book (França e Silva, Ebert, & Miller, 1984) involving the application and interpretation of the TAT within Brazilian culture. Although three Brazilian TAT protocols are analyzed and interpreted in the book, it is França e Silva's early studies (França, 1953; França e Silva 1954, 1957, 1958), referred to later, that show the importance and scope of early normative data in Brazil. França (1953) daringly asserted (at that time) in the introduction of the study: "The principal aim of this study is to have the vision necessary to understand the cultural influences on frequent themes and to understand where and why diversions occur" (p. 7).

Adrados (1995), Andriola (1995), Cunha (1993), Herzberg (1995), and Lourenção van Kolck et al. (1991) recently warned about a lack of systematic studies regarding tests that would permit more adequate and realistic applications in Brazilian society. They made reference to the need for establishing normative data with individuals who represented various regions of Brazil and the necessity for specialized courses in psychological evaluation and guidelines for professional training and continuing education.

Recounting her experience at the Federal University of Rio de Janeiro, with reference to children's Rorschach protocols gathered from the region, Adrados (1995) stated:

> . . . we did not count on the data from the Brazilian norms to support us in establishing conclusive parameters for children's protocols we analyzed in the study groups. Due to this my students resorted to publications by Anzieu, Beizman and Bates. Besides our children were so absurdly different, even worse, they could have been considered at the least, maladjusted. . . . (p. 51)

Adrados positioned herself against the exclusive use of foreign normative data for the interpretation of tests. She concluded her work with the following words:

> Finally, we consider that cultural factors have a great influence on emotional dynamics. This is one of the reasons I had always doubted the universality of normative data gathered from the Projective Techniques. In my point of view, the ideal would be to do periodic studies. This because the personality structural data seems to differ not only country to country, but within the same country and from state to state. Besides, the time and era with it's drastic and dramatic changes change the cultural standards. This acts like a vicious and unending cycle that also changes the emotional reactions of man towards these changes. (Adrados, 1995, p. 53)

Regarding other works dedicated strictly to the TAT, the work of Dias (1983) discussed its theoretical foundation. Jacquemin (1984) and Vilhena M. Silva (1983, 1989) also performed studies relevant to the application, analysis, and interpretation of the test. Adaptation of the original TAT was the theme of works by Meyer-Ginsberg (1966/1967) and Jacquemin (1982). They raised many questions regarding the advantages and disadvantages of adaptations of Murray's original cards. Some researchers like Cunha, Freitas, and Raymundo (1993); Eirado Silva (1981); Lourenção van Kolck (1981); and Montagna (1989) devoted special attention to thematic projective techniques including TAT.

Normative Studies

França e Silva presented the common themes (card by card) to 250 (França, 1953) and 500 (França e Silva, 1954) adults between the ages of 20 and 35. In 1957, fantasies elicited in the protocols of 200 children (ages 7–11) were determined; in 1958, the same study was performed on 100 adolescent protocols. All data were gathered from ISOP (a job and career orientation service) in Rio de Janeiro. Unfortunately, some specific characteristics of the participants were not included in the study (e.g., social level and motives for choosing their professions). These norms are included in the Argentinean manual translation of Murray (1970), which is frequently used as a reference by Brazilian psychologists. The works of França e Silva and the research that branched out from them are renowned for their historical value. Since the publication of her studies, little has been done (excluding a small number of studies) to update TAT norms. This is a cause of constant professional concern.

In Recife, located in northeast Brazil, Guerra and Lopes (1979) studied the personality characteristics of 100 lower class individuals with interpersonal relationship problems. In Rio de Janeiro, Augras (1966, 1976) presented various studies, which paid particular attention to comparisons with "normal groups." For example, borderline or pathological sense of time in stories was studied with the purpose of establishing signs of normalcy based on 50 protocols previously classified as normal.

MORE RECENT NORMATIVE STUDIES

Vilhena M. Silva (1983, 1989) discussed (among other subjects) how the characteristics of the stimuli, cultural diversity, and application situation should all be considered when using TAT as a projective tool for personality investigation.Vilhena M. Silva (1983) studied a group of 30 female São Paulo university students. She studied the influence of some physical characteristics of the stimuli on the responses to the TAT. Because the cards were created in 1936, she wanted to track any changes in areas affected by the stimulus. Cards from the female series were used, and some modified cards were included when the originals were considered old by the majority of the group (e.g., Card 7GF).

In reference to the results she said, "regarding common themes elicited by the different cards, it was observed that this group agreed with the original norms and with Eron's" (p. 61). She concluded her research by defending the validity of the current TAT cards despite their temporally remote situations. Use of modified cards is suggested only for more specific purposes. Despite her concern with the establishment of norms, she concluded by referring the reader to the test manual with no additional comments.

The study of pregnant and postpartum women at an obstetric unit of a São Paulo hospital (Herzberg, 1986) led to normative research with TAT (Herzberg, 1993). The first study (Herzberg, 1986) consisted of a follow-up study of eight pregnant women under prenatal care from the last quarter of pregnancy to immediate postpartum days. Its main purpose was to explore the most efficient way to supply psychological assistance to lower class pregnant women at São Paulo's public hospitals. A difference from the original test manual in the description of the stimulus value of the cards used (1, 2, 3BM, 4, 6GF, 7GF, 8GF, 10, 11, 12F, 13MF, and 16) was noted. This was particularly evident in Cards 1, 2, 7GF, 10, and 12F. When exposed to Card 7GF, for example, only two (33%) of the six pregnant women tested told stories about a doll (or baby); three told stories about a dog, rabbit, cat, or pet, and one overlooked the percept. Vilhena M. Silva (1989) was the only Brazilian researcher (of all those reviewed) to mention perception of a cat instead of a doll in Card 7GF.

Consulting the normative data from França e Silva, as well as several other classic resources, one does not find these types of percepts mentioned. The group (Herzberg, 1986) was composed of nonclinical women who all had a stable relationship with their partners, no previous severe psychological problems, never undergone an abortion, and were experiencing a normal pregnancy with no unusual complications. The question of how to explain the responses was then explored. Had they occurred by chance or as a result of biased participants? Could the responses be typical only during pregnancy or could they also be common in protocols of women in various social levels disregarding pregnancy?

Herzberg (1993) expanded the groups (34 pregnant and 32 nonpregnant) and continued the investigation. The doll in the girl's lap in Card 7GF was no longer interpreted by the majority of the pregnant women as an animal or pet. The majority interpreted it as a doll or baby. Although not occurring in the majority of the interpretations, as in previous research, nor differing statistically between pregnant and nonpregnant women, there was a surprising occurrence of 26% considering the total of the group (66). If the research had not been continued, interpretations related to the distortions that occurred in the first study (Herzberg, 1986) would have been linked to pregnancy and to the state of being pregnant. It would have been feasible to conclude that pregnant women whose stories include dog, cat, rabbit, or pet (where a doll or baby is usually seen) would be making a significant distortion.

Utilizing these data with a new hypothesis (Herzberg, 1993), the distorted interpretations could have been a result of social class, but intriguing questions remained: Why was there a percent rate of 26% in the group of 66 women? Distorted apperceptions of the violin in Card 1 were made by 33% of the women. Of these women, 15% interpreted it as a stringed instrument (viola or guitar). The remaining interpretations varied among a toy, medical instrument, book, piano, purse, ship, and basin. Half of the pregnant women that misinterpreted violin considered it a medical instrument. A possible explanation for this misinterpretation could be that the TAT was administered during prenatal care in a hospital setting. Even if misinterpretation of the violin (Card 1) could be ascribed to the cultural fact that this group had not been exposed to the violin on a day-to-day basis, how could distortions to Card 7GF be explained? It is feasible to assume that the women evaluated have been exposed or are frequently exposed to a doll or baby.

If a comparison is made between the data collected by Rosenzweig (as cited in Murray, 1970) and Herzberg (1993) in relationship to Cards 2 and 12F, it is confirmed that the older woman in Card 2 was perceived as pregnant by 20% and 42%, respectively. In Card 12F, normative data by Rosenzweig and França e Silva, 100% frequency of perception of a young woman occurred. By contrast, what can be said about the occurrence of only 64% in Herzberg? Of the women who produced a perceptual distortion (36%), nearly 73% attributed the percept to a masculine figure, an elderly man, a boy, or a man. Rosenzweig (as cited in Murray, 1970) included in his universal card perception reference tables only the responses that reached or exceeded the 20% level. According to the results obtained by Herzberg (1993), various responses not included in the tables would have to be included (e.g., those cited previously for Cards 2, 7GF, and 12F).

Murstein (1972) had different results than those originally obtained by Murray. He said, "It is noteworthy also that, on occasions the stories depart radically from the description of the cards given by Murray ..." (p. 145). Murstein's explanation seems logical. He attributed these stories to the differences found in the changing standards of fashion. He also mentioned the differences in percept judgment standards due to experience, test instructions, and participants' age and education level. The author concluded that there would always be a place for descriptions of typical patterns of responses for diverse people. In this way, we can question the distortions on Card 12F, where the expected answer of woman was man. This could signal changes in the visual standards of current fashion.

According to Herzberg (1993), greater attention should be paid to perceptual distortions in the TAT. Instead of connoting pathology, which is generally attributed to these distortions, more concern should be placed on the participants to whom the test was administered, and a more evident priority is the need for Brazilian normative studies. Regarding Card 7MF, for instance, according to Holt (1978):

> The commonest perceptual distortion, interpreting the doll as a real baby, occurred in 4% of this normal sample and in 8% of Eron's subjects, but only uneducated, immature, or psychotic patients have ever told me that it is the girl's own baby. (p. 93)

The psychologist should exercise extreme care in interpretation of the protocols especially when classic manuals are used as a base in clinical work due to a lack of updated normative data. It is recommended that parameters for the more objective aspects be established first (e.g., the apperception in the TAT). After that, with acquired confidence in the availability of these objective parameters, other aspects should also be studied—for instance, the thematic. In other words, determining the percept and its location (apperceptive norms), as is done with the Rorschach, seems to add an important contribution to thematic norms (story plots with antecedents and outcomes). To tell a story about a dog or pet animal (Herzberg, 1986, 1993) on Card 7MF, for instance, means that, instead of the doll percept, a dog or pet animal was really seen? Which factors could have led to this response? Was the usual doll percept actually seen but interpreted as a pet animal due to influence of a cultural factor of that particular group? To the other cards cited (1, 2, 10, and 12F; Herzberg, 1993), where differences regarding usual apperceptive responses occurred, to what should those differences be attributed? To divide normative investigation into two set of components, apperceptions and themes, card by card, seems to be helpful for analysis purposes. The mentioned division regarding TAT could contribute to the better understanding of groups' and subgroups' differences. Establishing usual apperception responses is a necessary requirement for the establishment of thematic norms (Herzberg, 1993).

The Study of Different Cultural Groups

Concern with establishing common themes for each card is evident in Meyer-Ginsberg's (1963) research. She did not utilize Murray's original cards. Instead she used seven specially prepared cards. The study sought to discover personality dynamics, main motivations, and ambitions of 63 immigrants from nine different nationalities in the process of adapting to Brazil. The cards were designed by the Brazilian painter Antonio Gomide. According to Meyer-Ginsberg, the cards reflected the common problems encountered by immigrants in their adaptation to a new environment. The author did an analysis of the responses obtained on the basis of expected frequencies of responses for each card. The feasibility of using a modified TAT to distinguish trends in the degree of adaptation of immigrants to a new native country was demonstrated.

A comparative study of anxiety, hostility, and cultural development between Tukuna Indians and White non-Tukuna was conducted by Vaz (1990). He also completed comparative studies with different ethnic groups (Afro-Brazilians, Germans, Israelis, and Italians) on productivity and performance (Vaz, 1993) using the Rorschach and the TAT in both studies. TAT was analyzed using the De Vos (1989) System of Expressive Categories. Although Vaz (1990) made it clear that he was going to present the TAT results at another time, he anticipated that the stories of both groups would be marked by the preoccupation with diseases, feelings of abandonment, and sadness. Disbelief in politicians and the public powers could be noted specifically in the Tukuna. Unfortunately, in 1993, Vaz presented only results obtained with the Rorschach.

Using mainly Card 1, De Vos (1996) conducted comparative cultural studies of stories told by Japanese living in Japan, the United States, and Brazil. A common factor among the three groups was an internal preoccupation with conquest achieved by self-motivation as opposed to conquest achieved from motivation provided by an external authority. Included in this work is a partial analysis of Card 1 data collected by Vaz (1993) from three different Brazilian ethnic groups (Portuguese, Afro-Brazilians, and Italians) from which he concluded that there were notable differences among these groups in the stories told. In De Vos (1997), besides Card 1, analysis of Cards 2, 3BM, 7BM, 16, and 17BM are also included. Referring to a scoring system created by him, De Vos (1989) also emphasized how differences in the subtleties of stories from different ethnic groups in Brazil can be clarified using objective scoring of the manifest content of the stories. Inspired by De Vos' studies, Jacquemin, Benzoni, Martinez, and Salinas (1993) also conducted studies of Portuguese and Japanese descendants in Brazil.

Research Using the TAT for Diverse Objectives

In the state of Rio Grande do Sul in the extreme south of Brazil, several master's dissertations on aspects of maternity used the TAT to relate maternity and depression with the birth of full-term or premature babies

(Eizirik, 1982; Jung, 1985), the type of newborn feeding (Knijnik, 1985), and mania and depression scores in pregnant and nonpregnant women (Felippe, 1980). Eizirik and Felippe utilized the Welch, Schafer, and Dember (1961) scale of mania and depression. This same scale was used by N. K. Freitas (1982), also a researcher from the state of Rio Grande do Sul, who focused on the denial of mania and depression in the mothers of terminally ill cancer patients. Knijnik used Pine's (1960) aggressive indicators in a study of newborn feeding (natural or artificial). Among this group of researchers, Jung was the only one to use results relying on clinical interpretation of qualitative TAT analysis for an in-depth dynamic comprehension of each case. Describing the methodology used in his study, Felippe was concerned about stating the norms used as reference, including, among other authors, Brazilians França e Silva.

The use of the TAT is seen in the works of E. Freitas, Adrados, França e Silva, and Mira (1968) and Beltrame (1985) concerning job selection and orientation. Using as a source a professional selection and orientation agency, E. Freitas et al. explained in detail how various cards were used according to thematic norms from França e Silva to determine the level of aspiration in individuals undergoing professional adjustment. In an exploratory investigation, Beltrame used 40 young men between the ages of 17 and 20 to analyze the elements involved in job selection.

TAT was used to measure the creativity of 182 young adults between the ages of 20 and 25 (Lopes, 1986). The majority of these young adults were from lower classes and resided in the city of Rio de Janeiro. Lopes' objective was to verify early entry into the workforce (before 18 years) as an adverse influence on young adult creativity. Comparison between early and late-entry groups led Lopes to conclude that the early entrance of young adults into the workforce does have an injurious effect on creativity.

The studies of Nunes (1990) and Tiosso (1989) on learning difficulties both cited Murray. Nunes used the TAT to detect depressive traits in groups of 60 children between the ages of 8 and 12. She compared children who repeated grades and those who did not. Tiosso used the TAT in an interdisciplinary study of 19 children between the ages of 9 and 13 dealing with reading and writing difficulties.

Using Murray's framework with a few modifications of her own, Meyer-Ginsberg (1956) presented a psychological study of 31 men in prison for robbery who had all been previously incarcerated. Using data collected from the TAT, including number of references to crime and punishment and quality of interpersonal relationship with parental figures and other significant persons, Meyer-Ginsberg tracked the tendencies that emerged in the group as whole. Great sadness and concern with illness, as well as a high level of aggression, were some of the predominant tendencies. Along the same lines, Lages (1984) proposed rates of TAT regression in a study comparing 30 adolescents with and 30 without violent tendencies. The violence-prone adolescents had higher rates of regression.

Campos (1981) used the TAT to unveil personality characteristics, attitudes, aspirations, and problems of institutionalized children. This study examined problems of reintegration into society using Eirado Silva (1981) as a reference. The TAT is considered an efficient test in Brazil for the diagnosis of male sexual dysfunction (Rodrigues, 1990); this is because it produces important data for diagnosis at a low cost and Brazil generally has meager resources in the health area. Brauer (1974) did an analysis of homosexuality signs in the TAT. Castro (1990) studied six women with endometriosis using TAT interpretations based on psychoanalytic theory to elucidate the meaning underlying the story. Martins (1986) utilized the TAT and Rosenzweig PF Test in a comparative study of two groups with the purpose of detecting psychodynamic aspects associated with obesity. Maturana (1991) used a TAT adaptation by De Vos (1988) to evaluate affiliation under conditions of social confinement for 28 sailors on a Brazilian ship on a journey between Brazil and France.

Card modifications and adaptations of Murray's original TAT administration and scoring system were examined by Araujo and Araujo (1986), Angelini (1955), and Meyer-Ginsberg (1963). Araujo and Araujo used Murray as a reference (without the cards) in an analysis of story narratives from students of different social classes. This study sought to better the education system in regard to children beginning to learn reading and writing. Angelini was interested in evaluating human motivation with his Projective Method of Evaluation of Human Motivation—a method similar to the TAT but with only one original card (8BM) and four cards each for men and women.

TAT IN THE UNITED STATES

Some American studies concerning the use of TAT as a psychological tool indicate that TAT is commonplace in test batteries as a projective technique for personality assessment (Archer, Maruish, Imhof, & Piotrowski, 1991; Ball, Archer, & Imhof, 1994; Rossini & Moretti, 1997). In a survey of directors of clinical psychology programs in the United States, Rossini and Moretti (1997) cited authors opposing the technique to document a decline in use among academic clinical psychologists. The results of this study indicate a lack of adequate TAT development and training in these doctorate programs. They made recommendations concerning the training and use of the TAT and suggested references considered essential to achieve this goal. Among the various recommendations is this blunt suggestion: ". . . the TAT should never be called the Thematic Apperception Test unless a quantified scoring system is used and appropriate normative data are publicly available . . ." (p. 395).

More Recent Normative Studies

A concern for establishment of normative data was the highlight of some studies (Ehrenreich, 1990a, 1990b; Holt, 1978; Murstein & Mathes, 1996). In an effort to locate and use published and unpublished normative studies, Holt (1978) presented norms for each specific picture of the whole TAT set. Besides emphasizing the clinical usefulness of the norms, Holt pointed out the difficulties one faces when attempting to compare various studies. Among these difficulties is the fact that most of them go "back to the decade immediately following the publication of the cards . . ." (p. 77) and that "all studies have sampled whites, relatively few outside the middle class" (p. 77). Murstein and Mathes (1996) maintained that analysis of the amount of a response that can be attributed to stimuli, the test situation, and the personality of the participant are all essential factors for adequate use of a projective technique. In the case of the TAT, this requires knowledge of normative data. According to these authors, unfortunately this is not observed in practice and could be one factor responsible for the decline in the popularity of TAT as well as projective techniques in general.

Ehrenreich (1990a) discussed what influence the participants' social class had on normative responses to the cards. His results were based on a group of 70 nonclinical women—35 from the middle class and 35 from the working class. He concluded that factors linked to the social class did not have enough influence on the normative responses and should not be considered in systematic interpretation. However, he did warn that the fact that differences appeared is sufficient to say that they should be considered in the interpretation of protocols. He also quoted other studies by different researchers with the same outcome. He concluded that cultural factors appeared to be important in the interpretation of the protocols taking into consideration the origin of the participant. In another quantitative preliminary normative study, Ehrenreich (1990b) explored the regressive effect of various cards related to intrapsychic functions. He encountered differences in the levels of regression elicited by the cards and emphasized the importance of these findings in the interpretation of regressed responses from maladjusted persons.

The Study of Different Cultural Groups

Dana (1972) reviewed more then 100 studies concerning the TAT. He made reference to the diverse aspects that interfere and should be considered for adequate and efficient use of the technique. Two of these aspects, among others, were the sex of the examiner and the social class of the participant. One question always stood out among the continuous and constant TAT and other tests studies Dana conducted over the years. This was the necessary adaptation of the psychological evaluation for ethnic minorities within and outside the United States. Dana (1995a, 1995b, 1996a, 1996b, 1996c, 1999) highlighted the importance of the increasing cultural diversity in the country. He proposed solutions aimed at minimizing or at least avoiding improper use of the tests. Therefore, he concluded that a competent cultural assessment should include (among others): The use of the participant's native language, a rapport related to the social norms of the participant, an acculturation evaluation, and the establishment of group norms. These recommendations have as an objective the acknowledgment and acceptance of differences among groups. Dana (1999) criticized the existence of equivalent evaluation systems for everybody, stating that ". . . In the United States, a cultural formulation is now a mandatory assessment accompaniment of any DSM diagnosis with multicultural populations" (p. 183). Nevertheless, he believed the arsenal of Murray's normative data from the original TAT can be implemented and enriched to a form more adequate for the evaluation of minority ethnic groups within and outside the United States. He also affirmed that the TEMAS test of Costantino, Malgady, and Rogler (1988), created especially for the evaluation of Hispanics and African Americans within the United States, would be a suitable alternative for this group in particular.

Following this same direction, French (1993), referring to assessment of neglected or maltreated Hispanic and American Indian children, focused on the need to adapt the traditional projective techniques to culturally diverse populations. He included a description of the differences between these groups justifying modification and adaptation of the stimuli. An integration of the Human Figure Drawing technique with the TAT, with a goal of obtaining more data in the evaluation of these groups, was included.

FINAL COMMENTS

Various American and Brazilian researchers, among them Dana, De Vos, Ehrenreich, Herzberg, Jacquemin, Murstein/Mathes, and Vilhena M. Silva, seem to share a similar point of view. The TAT can still be considered a useful and particularly important technique for studies involving cultural differences and subgroups if caution and judgment are exercised. They also believe that you can not simply disregard the volumes of research on the original TAT. This would imply, however, an enormous dedication on the part of researchers to continually update normative data and include expanding and developing references (each time more adequate) for the analysis and interpretation of protocols. In many cases, creating or modifying a technique appears to be the most adequate solution. More troublesome, however, is the task of researching and gathering experience on which to base the modified technique.

Given the diverse cultural differences that exist in Brazil and the United States, we can deduce a fact about the Brazilian and American norms. To think of norms as ample and unrestricted could be totally debatable. Through a review of the Brazilian studies concerning TAT and contact with various American studies, two facts have become evident. There has been an increase in the numbers of references on analysis and interpretation that have been used for the test and a lack of normative data. A concentrated effort to fill these lacunae would undoubtedly contribute to systematization and unified comparisons of data compiled with this useful technique.

Many of the studies examined (excluding the more theoretical about the test itself) utilized normative data with less frequency than desirable. When these data were applied, they veered from the assumption that the classics continue to be valid without further investigation, as suggested by Murstein and Mathes (1996). Various researchers mentioned the norms of França e Silva (Augras, 1962; Felippe, 1980; Herzberg, 1993), disregarding their age and dire need for review and updating. For example, Herzberg (1993) denoted various differences in relationship to classic references that cannot be ignored, taking into account the fact that the apperception study was conducted with a small sample of 66 nonclinical women.

Although widespread updating of normative data in various regions of Brazil has not been accomplished, there are short-term remediations, as Adrados (1995) already mentioned, that can be implemented. Small-scale normative studies could be conducted at research locations and/or at the psychologists' work areas. Such studies should consist of collection of nonclinical and normal protocols. These studies should seek to contribute to the referent for the interpretation of clinical cases groups or other situations that will be investigated.

It is a common tendency among clinical psychologists in Brazil to not consider the worthiness or to completely discard statistical studies that involve sample studies and comparison of groups. Many times intensely involved in their work, they do not recognize an analysis gone astray. This can be provoked by daily contact with disturbance and the pathological or nonfamiliarity with differences between groups and cultures. The linking of objective statistical studies with clinical judgment and intuition would surely make a large contribution to more competent professional practice.

Regarding TAT, specifically in Brazil, it appears it would be worthwhile to invest in normative studies that would improve practice with the technique. Among the many reasons for this is that, contrary to the graphic techniques, the TAT can act as a way to smooth the contact between examiner and examinee. It would also break down communication barriers, especially in the cases of cultural differences between the two (Herzberg, 1986, 1993; Jung, 1985). The graphic techniques frequently cause embarrassment and inhibition in lower social classes because they are infrequently exposed to pencil-and-paper tasks. Consequently, the TAT can provide more knowledge about the way of life, the beliefs, and the customs of the different groups that live in Brazil. The use of the TAT would also be more practical and less costly especially when compared with the Rorschach (Herzberg, 1986; Rodrigues, 1990).

In the United States as well as in Brazil, some researchers are aware of differences between groups and cultures. These researchers are continuously conscious of the care required for application and interpretation of the TAT. In the same way, there are researchers in both countries who are concerned about the quality of TAT teaching and training as well as the investment in research, particularly normative studies.

REFERENCES

Adrados, I. (1995). Fatores culturais e dinâmica emocional na America Latina—critérios normativos das provas projetivas [Cultural factors and emotional dynamics in Latin America—normative criteria of the projective techniques]. *Boletim da Sociedade Rorschach de São Paulo, 8*(1), 50–53.

Andriola, W. B. (1995). Os testes psicológicos no Brasil: problemas pesquisas e perspectivas para o futuro [Psychological tests in Brazil: Problems, research and prospects for the future]. *Avaliação Psicológica: formas e contextos, 3*, 77–82.

Angelini, A. L. (1955). Um novo método para avaliar a motivação humana [A new method for evaluating human motivation]. *Psicologia Educacional, 207*(6), 1–251.

Araujo, M. G. de, & Araujo, P. G. G. de (1986). A função da narrativa na elaboração dos conflitos infantis: Estudo comparativo de dois grupos de diferentes condições sócio-econômicas [The narrative function in the elaboration of the infantile conflicts: Comparative study of two groups with social and economical different conditions]. *Arquivos Brasileiros de Psicologia, 38*(2), 140–157.

Archer, R. P., Maruish, M., Imhof, E. A., & Piotrowski, C. (1991). Psychological test usage with adolescents clients: 1990 survey findings. *Professional Psychology: Research and Practice, 22*(3), 247–252.

Augras, M. (1962). Notas sobre o simbolismo na prancha XI no TAT [Notes concerning the symbolism of Card 11 of the TAT]. *Arquivos Brasileiros de Psicotécnica, 14*(3), 5–14.

Augras, M (1966). Investigação da vivência temporal através do "Thematic Apperception Test" [Investigation of perception of passing time using "Thematic Apperception Test"]. *Arquivos Brasileiros de Psicotécnica, 2*, 27–43.

Augras, M. (1976). Um modelo para objetivação dos testes de relatos [A model for the objectiveness of the narration tests]. *Arquivos Brasileiros de Psicologia, 28*(2), 3–27.

Azevedo, M. M., Almeida, L. S., Pasquali, L., & Veiga, H. M. S. (1996). Utilização dos testes psicológicos no Brasil: Dados de estudo preliminar em Brasília [Utilization of projective techniques in Brazil: Data from a preliminary study in Brasilia]. *Avaliação Psicológica: Formas e Contextos, 4*, 213–220.

Ball, D. J., Archer, R. P., & Imhof, E. A. (1994). Time requirements of psychological testing: A survey of practitioners. *Journal of Personality Assessment, 63*(2), 239–249.

Beltrame, R. B. L. (1985). *Escolha vocacional: Um estudo exploratório sobre elementos envolvidos nesse processo utilizando-se o TAT* [Vocational choice: An exploratory study on the elements involved in this process by utilizing the TAT]. Unpublished doctoral dissertation, University of São Paulo, São Paulo, Brazil.

Brauer, J. (1974). Análise de pesquisas que propõem a encontrar sinais de homossexualismo no TAT [Analysis of research that proposes to encounter signs of homosexualism in the TAT]. *Boletim de Psiquiatria, 25*, 35–39.

Campos, A. V. D. S. (1981). *Menor institucionalizado: Um desafio para a sociedade (atitudes, aspirações e problemas para sua reintegração à sociedade)* [Minors institutionalization: A challenge for society (attitudes, aspirations and problems for their reintegration into society]. Unpublished doctoral dissertation, University of São Paulo, Brazil.

Castro, C. C. (1990). *Uma interpretação psicodinâmica da observação de mulheres com endometriose* [A psychodinamic interpretation of the observation of infertile women with endometriosis]. Unpublished master's thesis, University of São Paulo, Brazil.

Costantino, G., Malgady, R. G., & Rogler, L. H. (1988). *TEMAS (Tell-Me-Story) manual*. Los Angeles: Western Psychological Services.

Cunha, J. A. (1993). Aspectos culturais dos testes psicológicos [Cultural aspects of psychological tests]. *Psico, 24*(1), 69–74.

Cunha, J. A., Freitas, N. K., & Raymundo, M. G. B. (1993). *Psicodiagnóstico–R* [Psychological assessment–R] (Rev. 4a.ed). Porto Alegre: Artes Médicas.

Dana, R. H. (1972). Thematic Apperception Test. In O. Buros (Ed.), *The seventh mental measurements yearbook* (pp. 457–460). Highland Park, NJ: Gryphon.

Dana, R. H. (1995a). Conferencia de clausura del congreso. Orientaciones para la evaluación de hispanos en los Estados Unidos de Norteamérica utilizando la prueba de Rorschach y el Test de Apercepción Temática [Guidelines for assessment of hispanics in the United States using the Rorschach and Themathic Apperception Tests]. *Revista de la Sociedad Española del Rorschach y Métodos Proyectivos, 8*, 176–187.

Dana, R. H. (1995b). Impact of the use of standard psychological assessment on the diagnosis and treatment of ethnic minorities. In J. F. Aponte, R. Y. Rivers, & J. Wohl (Eds.), *Psychological interventions and cultural diversity* (pp. 57–73). Boston: Allyn & Bacon.

Dana, R. H. (1996a). Assessment of acculturation in Hispanic populations. *Hispanic Journal of Behavioral Sciences, 18*(3), 317–328.

Dana, R. H. (1996b). Culturally competent assessment practice in the United States. *Journal of Personality Assessment, 66*(3), 472–487.

Dana, R. H. (1996c). The Thematic Apperception Test. In C. S. Newmark (Ed.), *Major psychological assessment instruments* (2nd ed., pp. 166–205). Boston: Allyn & Bacon.

Dana, R. H. (1999). Cross-cultural/multicultural use of the Thematic Apperception Test. In M. L. Geiser & M. Stein (Eds.), *Evocative images: The Thematic Apperception Test and the art of projection* (pp. 177–190). Washington, DC: American Psychological Association.

De Vos, G. A. (1988). *Manual for scoring vectoral concerns on the Thematic Apperception Test*. Unpublished manuscript, University of California, Berkeley.

De Vos, G. A. (1989). *TAT scoring manual: Basic interpersonal concerns*. Berkeley: Department of Anthropology, University of California at Berkeley.

De Vos, G. A. (1996). Internalized achievement or external authority: Some cultural comparisons of responses to TAT Card 1. *Rorschachiana, 21*, 91–126.

De Vos, G. A. (1997). Heritage of exploitation: A brief TAT report on south Brazilian youth. *Political Psychology, 18*(2), 439–481.

Dias, S. (1983). *Reflexões sobre os fundamentos teóricos do Teste de Apercepção Temática* [Reflections on the theoretical foundations of the TAT]. Unpublished master's thesis, Pontifícia Universidade Católica of São Paulo (PUC/SP), Brazil.

Ehrenreich, J. H. (1990a). Effect of social class of subjects on normative responses to TAT card. *Journal of Clinical Psychology, 46*(4), 467–471.

Ehrenreich, J. H. (1990b). Quantitative studies of responses elicited by selected TAT cards. *Psychological Reports, 67,* 15–18.

Eirado Silva, M. L. (1981). *Interpretação de testes projetivos: Projeção e representação* [Interpretation of the projective techniques: Projection and representation]. Rio de Janeiro: Editora Campus.

Eizirik, L. S. (1982). *Depressão puerperal—efeitos de prematuridade e risco de vida do recém-nascido no estado emocional da puérpera* [Post-partum depression—the effects of prematurity and the risk of life in the emotional state of postpartum women]. Unpublished master's thesis, Pontifícia Universidade Católica of Rio Grande do Sul (PUC/RS), Porto Alegre, Brazil.

Felippe, Y. M. L. (1980). *Gravidez e depressão. Um estudo comparativo entre gestantes primíparas e não-gestantes* [Pregnancy and depression: a comparative study of first time pregnant women and non-pregnant women]. Unpublished master's thesis, Pontifícia Universidade Católica of Rio Grande do Sul (PUC/RS), Porto Alegre, Brazil.

França, E. (1953). "Thematic Apperception Test": Algumas situações que o teste apresenta dentro da população que frequenta o ISOP [Thematic Apperception Test: Some special situations that occur in the test applied to frequenters of the ISOP]. *Arquivos Brasileiros de Psicotécnica, 5*(1), 7–19.

França e Silva, E. (1954). "Thematic Apperception Test": Algumas situações típicas dentro da amostra de adultos examinados no ISOP [Thematic Apperception Test: some typical situations in a sample of adults tested at ISOP]. *Arquivos Brasileiros de Psicotécnica, 6*(4), 7–36.

França e Silva, E. (1957). Alguns problemas das crianças vistos através de suas fantasias no "Thematic Apperception Test" [Some problems in children as seen trough their fantasies in the Thematic Apperception Test]. *Arquivos Brasileiros de Psicotécnica, 9*(1–2–3), 85–91.

França e Silva, E. (1958). O adolescente, suas fantasias e seus problemas [The adolescent: Their fantasies and problems]. *Arquivos Brasileiros de Psicotécnica, 10*(1–2), 5–26.

França e Silva, E. (Ed.), Ebert, T. de N. H., & Miller, L. M. (1984). *O Teste de Apercepção Temática de Murray (TAT) na cultura brasileira* [The Thematic Apperception Test (TAT) in Brazilian Culture: Application and interpretation manual]. Rio de Janeiro: Editora da Fundação Getúlio Vargas/ISOP.

Freitas, E., Adrados, I., França e Silva, E., & Mira, A. G. de (1968). O nível de aspiração no ajustamento profissional: Aspectos metodológicos da entrevista, do Rorschach, do TAT e do PMK para a identificação dos componentes do nível de aspiração [The aspiration level in professional adjustment: Methodological aspects of the interview, Rorschach, TAT and PMK for the identification of the components of the level of aspiration]. *Boletim de Psicologia, 15*(55/56), 103–110.

Freitas, N. K (1982). Um estudo sobre a negação maníaca e a depressão nas mães de pacientes cancerosos terminais [Maniac denial and depression in mothers of terminal cancer patients as manifested in the Thematic Apperception Test]. *Psico, 5*(2), 94–131.

French, L. A. (1993). Adapting projective tests for minority children. *Psychological Reports, 72,* 15–18.

Guerra, A. G., & Lopes, G. M. S. (1979). Algumas características de componentes da estrutura da personalidade de indivíduos de baixa renda com dificuldade de relacionamento [Some characteristics of personality structure components in low-income individuals with relationship difficulties]. *Arquivos brasileiros de Psicologia, 31*(3), 103–119.

Herzberg, E. (1986). *Aspectos psicológicos da gravidez e suas relacões com a assistência hospitalar* [Psychological aspects of pregnancy and its relation to hospital care]. Unpublished master's thesis, University of São Paulo, São Paulo, Brazil.

Herzberg, E. (1993). *Estudos normativos do Desenho da Figura Humana (DFH) e do Teste de Apercepção Temática (TAT) em mulheres: Implicações para o atendimento a gestantes* [Normative studies of the Human Figure Drawing (HFD) and of the Thematic Apperception Test (TAT) in women: Implications for the assistance to pregnant women]. Unpublished doctoral dissertation, University of São Paulo, São Paulo, Brazil.

Herzberg, E. (1995). Normas em técnicas projetivas: Necessidade urgente [Norms in projective techniques: Urgent need]. *Revista de la Asociación Latino Americana de Rorschach, 3*(4), 65–69.

Herzberg, E., Erdman, E. P., & Becker, E. (1995). Técnicas de Exame Psicológico utilizadas no Departamento de Psicologia Clínica do Instituto de Psicologia da Universidade de São Paulo: Levantamento realizado em 1994 [Psychological examination techniques used in the Department of Clinical Psychology at the University of São Paulo's Institute of Psychology: Poll from 1994]. *Boletim de Psicologia, 45*(102), 85–96.

Holt, R. R. (1978). *Methods in clinical psychology: Vol. 1. Projective assessment* (pp. 77–122). New York: Plenum.

Jacquemin, A. (1982). Les variantes du ""Thematic apperception test"" pour l'étude des groupes cultureles [The variation of the "Thematic Apperception Test" for the study of various cultural groups]. *Revue belge de Psychologie et de Pédagogie, 44*(180), 135–144.

Jacquemin, A. (1984). Papel do Estímulo nas Técnicas Aperceptivo-Temáticas—Análise Crítica em função de modelos teóricos diferentes [The role of stimuli in the Thematic Apperception Techniques—a critical analysis based on different theory models]. *Arquivos Brasileiros de Psicologia, 36*(2), 108–117.

Jacquemin, A., Benzoni, P. E., & Martinez, P. A. S. (1993). As preocupações interpessoais básicas no TAT em descendentes de portugueses e japoneses [The basic interpersonal preoccupations in the TAT in descendants of Portuguese and Japanese]. *Resumos e Comunicações Científicas da XXIII Reunião Anual da Sociedade de Psicologia de Ribeirão Preto, 23*, 416.

Jung, M. E. (1985). *Maternidade e prematuridade. um estudo sobre a relação entre o desenvolvimento de prematuros e o desempenho da maternagem* [Maternity and prematurity: A study concerning the relationship between the development of prematures and the maternity performance]. Unpublished master's thesis, Pontifícia Universidade Católica of Rio Grande do Sul (PUC/RS), Porto Alegre, Brazil.

Knijnik, J. (1985). *Amamentação natural ou artificial—estudo de indicadores de libido e da agressão* [Natural or artificial newborn feeding—a study of the indicators of libido and agression]. Unpublished master's thesis, Pontifícia Universidade Católica of Rio Grande do Sul (PUC/RS), Porto Alegre, Brazil.

Lages, S. R. R. (1984). Um estudo sobre a regressão em adolescentes delinqüentes com periculosidade comprovada e sem periculosidade, através do TAT [A study of regression in juvenile delinquents proven and nonproven violence, using TAT]. *Psico, 8*(1), 38–62.

Lopes, V. L. S. (1986). Adolescência e criatividade: o trabalho precoce e suas relações com a personalidade [Adolescence and creativity: The precocious work and its relation to personality]. *Arquivos Brasileiros de Psicologia, 38*(4), 95–114.

Lourenção van Kolck, O. (1981). *Técnicas de exame psicológico e suas aplicacões no Brasil* (2.ed., Vol. 2.) [Psychological examination techniques and their application in Brazil]. Petropolis: Vozes.

Lourenção van Kolck, O. (Ed.), Mejias, N. P., Silvares, E. F. M., Jacquemin, A., Yazigi, L., Carelli, A., Rosa, T. J., & Hutz, C. S. (1991). Relatório do Grupo de Trabalho: Perspectivas de avaliação e diagnóstico em psicologia [Group work report: Evaluation prospects and diagnostics in psychology]. *Anais do Simpósio Brasileiro se Pesquisa e Intercambio Científico*, 3, 269–272.

Martins, D. F. G. (1986). *Aspectos Psicodinâmicos associados à obesidade: Um estudo comparativo de dois grupos com o TAT e o Rosenzweig* [Psychodynamic aspects associated with obesity: A comparative study of two groups using TAT and Rosenzweig]. Unpublished master's thesis, Instituto Metodista de Ensino Superior, São Bernardo do Campo, Brazil.

Maturana, R. A. G. (1991). *Estudo dos estados emocionais de ansiedade, depressão e afiliação sob a variável confinamento social* [A study of the emotion, anxiety, deprivation and affiliation states under the influence of a social confinement]. Unpublished master's thesis, Pontifícia Universidade Católica of Rio Grande do Sul (PUC/RS), Porto Alegre, Brazil.

Meyer-Ginsberg, A. (1956). Contribuição para o estudo psicológico sobre ladrões habituais (2a. parte) [Contribution to psychological studies of habitual thieves (2nd part]. *Revista de Psicologia Normal e Patológica*, 2(1), 3–22.

Meyer-Ginsberg, A. (1963). Os resultados de um TAT especial aplicado em um grupo de imigrantes estrangeiros no Brasil [The results of a modified TAT in a group of foreign immigrants in Brazil]. *Boletim de Psicologia*, 15(45/56), 19–26.

Meyer-Ginsberg, A. (1966/1967). O uso do TAT nas pesquisas de psicologia social [The use of the TAT in social psychology research]. *Boletim de Psicologia*, 18–19(51/54), 37–42.

Montagna, M. E. (1989). *Análise e interpretação do CAT: Teste de Apercepção Infantil* [Analysis and interpretation of the CAT: Children's Apperception Test]. São Paulo: Editora Pedagógica e Universitária Ltda.

Murray, H. A. (1970). *Test de Apercepción Temática (TAT)* (5a.ed) [Thematic Apperception Test (TAT)]. Buenos Aires: Editorial Paidós.

Murstein, B. I. (1972). Normative written TAT responses for a college sample. *Journal of Personality Assessment* 36(2), 109–147.

Murstein, B. I., & Mathes, S. (1996). Projection on projective techniques = pathology: The problem that is not being addressed. *Journal of Personality Assessment*, 66(2), 337–349.

Nunes, A. N. A. (1990). Fracasso escolar e desamparo adquirido [School failure and learned helplessness]. *Psicologia -Teoria-e-Pesquisa*, 6(2), 139–154.

Pine, F. (1960). A manual for rating drive content in the Thematic Apperception Test. *Journal of Projective Techniques*, 24(1), 32–45.

Rodrigues, O. M., Jr. (1990). Abordagem psicológica do homem sexualmente disfuncional— um modelo [Psychological approach to sexually dysfunctional men: A model]. *Arquivos Brasileiros de Psicologia*, 42(2), 57–62.

Rossini, E. D., & Moretti, R. J. (1997). Thematic Apperception Test (TAT) interpretation: Practice recommendations from a survey of clinical doctoral programs accredited by the American Psychological Association. *Professional Psychology: Research and Practice*, 28(4), 393–398.

Tiosso, L. H. (1989). *Dificuldades na aprendizagem da leitura e escrita: uma visão multidisciplinar* [Difficulties on the learning of reading and writing: A multidisciplinary view point]. Unpublished doctoral dissertation, University of São Paulo, Brazil.

Vaz, C. E. (1990). Ansiedade, hostilidade e aculturação: Estudo comparativo entre índios Tükuna e brancos Não-Tükuna [Anxiety, hostility and acculturation: A comparison of Tukuna Indians and settlers]. *Psico*, 19(1), 9–22.

Vaz, C. E. (1993). Produtividade, cultura e etnia em adolescentes de origem portuguesa, afro-brasileira, alemã, israelita e italiana [Productivity, culture, and ethnicity in Portuguese, African-Brazilian, German, Israeli, and Italian adolescents]. *Psico*, 24(2), 41–52.

Vilhena M. Silva, M. C. (1983). *Características de Época dos Estímulos e sua Influência nas Respostas ao TAT* [The characteristics of stimuli era and their influence in the TAT's responses]. Unpublished master's thesis, Pontifícia Universidade Católica of São Paulo (PUC/SP), Brazil.

Vilhena M. Silva, M. C. (1989). *TAT: Aplicação e interpretação do Teste de Apercepção Temática* [TAT: The application and interpretation of the Thematic Apperception Test]. São Paulo: Editora Pedagógica e Universitária Ltda.

Welch, B., Schafer, R., & Dember, C. (1961). TAT stories of hipomanic and depressed patients. *Journal of Projective Techniques, 25*(2), 221–232.

20

Objective Scoring for the TAT

Alejandro Ávila-Espada
Universidad de Salamanca, Spain

More than 60 years after the first public presentation of the Thematic Apperception Test (TAT; Morgan & Murray, 1935) and the Four Picture Test (FPT; Van Lennep & Houwink, 1930), thematic techniques still hold a distinguished place in psychological assessment, mainly in clinical settings, all over the world. However, although thematic procedures ensure utility to clinical psychologists that use them (Geiser & Stein, 1998), they remain far off the research advancements reached during last decades on standardization and objective analyses by other projective techniques like Rorschach. TAT research achieved its main features during the 1950s and 1960s (Eron, 1950; Murstein, 1963), but its further impact on the practice was inconsistent, lacking in further developments or refinements. In Europe in general, and specifically in Spain, TAT has had a lesser diffusion partly due to the absence of investigations. In the Spanish context, few authors (Ávila-Espada, 1976; Castilla del Pino, 1966; Fernández-Ballesteros, 1973; Siguan, 1953, 1954) could be cited until the late 1970s, when only some qualitative advancements for thematic analyses developed by V. Shentoub in France introduced new research lines. Her work is well known by clinicians with a psychoanalytic frame of reference (Shentoub et al., 1990).

Despite this historic lack of research, the last two decades have produced new European developments that have culminated with the appearance of an empirical and conceptual review (Ávila-Espada, 1983, 1990) and the edition of a new *Operative Manual* (Ávila-Espada, 1985a).

This new manual presents a revised set of instructions and cards and collects the normative, thematic, formal, and stimulus value data for Murray's TAT. This chapter briefly describes the principles and characteristics of the innovative research conducted up through the present time in Spain with TAT. This includes: (a) normative research with normal Spanish population, (b) principal standards of the stimulus value of the TAT, (c) proposal of a new set of instructions and cards for TAT administration, and (d) principal directions that form an *Integrative Analysis System* for the TAT recently presented (Ávila-Espada, 1996; Ávila-Espada, Biezma, & Rodríguez, 1998), including a variety of quantitative and qualitative strategies. All of these improvements favor more accuracy of the TAT use, reducing an unnecessary high level of inference during TAT interpretation, and facilitating some new quantitative indexes to enrich more objective TAT reports.

NORMATIVE RESEARCH

Subjects and Procedure

The fact that, in general, the TAT is being used as a projective interview without taking into account its administration and scoring, its research history is a matter of concern both for clinicians and psychological assessment researchers. Moreover, the implications of normative studies for scientific TAT analysis and test protocol interpretation (see Eron, 1950; Murstein, 1963) and the absence of normative data for the TAT in the general Spanish Population are the basis of renewed interest and efforts oriented to continued normative research. After reviewing prior normative data with normal and psychiatric samples (Eron, 1950, 1953; Murstein, 1972; Rosenzweig & Fleming, 1949; Shentoub & Shentoub, 1961; Zubi, Eron, & Schumer, 1965), a study has been designed with a stratified and randomized sample of 100 subjects (49 males, 51 females) collected in the late 1970s with an average age of 25,84 and 25,69, respectively. Subjects' ages ranged from 14 to 53 years; all were from a middle socioeconomic class, from all geographic regions of Spain, with different occupational levels, and free from psychiatric illness or history. The obtained sample was reasonably representative of the normal Spanish Population, offering the possibility to study a wide collection of 2,000 TAT card stories (Ávila-Espada, 1985b).

In this normative research, the complete set of Murray's TAT (cards and instructions) was administered to a whole sample, controlling adequately the administration bias (examiner's effects). The scoring system used was a special form derived from the first Rosenzweig's norms chosen by Murray as a reference frame for normative interpretation in their TAT complete manual, thus achieving satisfactory values for interjudge reliability on coding protocols (93%–98% of interjudge agreement). Through thorough statistical analyses, we have evaluated the principal indicators of the formal variables (Reaction Time, Total Time, and Word Count), thematic analysis variables (themes and outcomes), as well as the stimulus value variable following Murstein's (1963) recommendations.

Spanish Normative Research Main Findings:
New Formal Indexes

The classical variables of Reaction Time, Total Time, and Word Count showed highly consistent patterns for the description of subjects' response style and for the stimulus–subject interface. However, their interpretation with clinical purposes is problematic, and no clear criteria appear consistently. To improve the utility of these classical formal variables, which are derived from our empirical data, we propose two new quantitative indexes: The *Expression Speed Index* (ESI) and the *Elaboration Rapidity Index* (ERI). The ESI is calculated (card by card) from the following formula:

$$ESI = \text{Words Count} / [\text{Total Time } minus \text{ Reaction Time}]$$

It also allowed for the calculus of a mean ESI score for all TAT cards. ESI focuses on cognitive ability to produce narratives mediated by defenses. Significant changes in intrasubject ESI pattern allow detection of shock related to stimulus content and defensive processes. ESI scores over Q75 and below Q25 in the intrasubject ESI profile across all TAT cards are good predictors of whose cards must be the main focus of qualitative analyses. This is because potential main changes in thematic content could be observed varying from normative narratives.

In a second step, the ERI percentage is expressed as:

$$ERI = 100 \times [\text{card Reaction Time} / \text{card Total Time}]$$

ERI provides a quantitative estimation of subjects' cognitive ability to resolve the TAT task by producing narratives facing stimulus impact of the cards. As with ESI, ERI intrasubject profile peaks (over Q75 and below Q25) allow detection of changes in processing narratives that can be related to structural variables (e.g., amount of effect evoked by cards). ESI and ERI values can also be compared with normative data to explore specific styles relevant to clinical predictions.

TABLE 20.1
ESI and ERI Values for TAT Cards in Spanish Subjects

| | ESI Values | | | | ERI Values | | | |
| | Males | | Females | | Males | | Females | |
Cards	M	SD	M	SD	M	SD	M	SD
1	1.05	0.62	1.00	0.55	9.39	8.16	11.43	10.41
2	1.11	0.66	1.12	0.64	7.49	6.81	11.93	11.57
3BM/GF	1.07	0.72	1.14	0.64	11.89	12.17	12.95	11.19
4	1.27	0.83	1.25	0.80	8.34	9.20	11.90	11.09
5	1.23	0.88	1.29	0.65	11.72	12.65	13.69	14.44
6BM/GF	1.21	0.81	1.22	0.74	9.68	7.14	14.16	12.21
7BM/GF	1.15	0.67	1.24	0.75	11.42	9.20	9.76	8.83
8BM/GF	1.13	0.72	1.15	0.67	10.24	7.76	11.59	11.06
9BM/GF	1.18	0.75	1.15	0.67	11.02	8.43	12.43	9.34
10	1.09	0.77	1.11	0.70	10.19	8.89	11.70	11.12
11	1.04	0.70	0.95	0.57	10.88	10.73	12.53	12.65
14	1.14	0.70	1.12	0.67	10.65	9.78	11.44	8.69
15	1.13	0.69	1.09	0.59	11.82	11.46	11.11	10.46
16	1.18	1.10	0.96	0.59	6.90	6.78	9.86	9.81
17BM/GF	1.19	0.76	1.20	0.82	10.75	9.93	12.80	10.90
18BM/GF	1.32	0.99	1.18	0.77	11.47	9.12	12.13	9.83
19	1.09	0.72	1.13	0.77	11.42	9.69	13.57	14.04
20	1.20	0.78	1.09	0.60	11.01	10.33	10.41	8.59

Together these two indexes are better predictors of the level of significance, shock effects, and protocol productivity than the classical formal variables previously used. Table 20.1 shows the card ESI and ERI values for the Spanish normal population. A relevant conclusion derived from the thematic normative data is that Spanish norms are not at all different from several U.S. or French norms, despite some specific cultural and situational elements. Such changes in the norms more likely reflect cultural cues in each country than objective stimulus properties.

A Review of the Stimulus Value of the TAT

From the large number of TAT variables that could be studied, five were selected to test the stimulus value of the TAT in the Spanish population. These are:

1. The *number of themes produced* (the absolute number of theme subjects and the number of different themes, comparing our data with Eron, 1950, 1953; Irvin & Woude, 1971; Newmark & Flouranzano, 1973).

2. The *verbal productivity* (comparing our data with Rosenzweig & Fleming, 1949; Newbigging, 1955; Ullman, 1957; Friedman, 1972).

3. *Preferences and card rejections* (similar to those proposed in Lebo, 1955; Fisher & Shotwell, 1961).

4. The *turns and peculiar positions* of the cards produced by the subjects.

5. Predominant thematic content areas in the stories produced.

Again our data do not show relevant discrepancies from previous research findings. Table 20.2 shows the ranks obtained by the different TAT cards combined with the first three variables. The turns and characteristic positions are only significant for Cards 11, 16, and 19. This variable clearly depends on the properties of the respective stimuli more than the characteristics of the studied sample.

With respect to the thematic content areas predominately evoked by the set of TAT cards in the Spanish population, Table 20.3 shows the main thematic groups with their respective gender comparisons.

TABLE 20.2
Stimulus Value of the TAT Cards in Spanish Subjects
(Rank Order values)

| | Number of Themes | | | | | |
| | Absolute | | Distincts | | Verbal Productivity | |
Cards	Males	Females	Males	Females	Males	Females
13MF	1	1	1	1	7	6
1	2	3	6.5	12	18	20
2	16	14	4	5	1	4
10	5	6	2	2	10	13.5
14	8.5	5	4	3.5	20	17
20	8.5	16	4	3.5	15	7.5
4	11	8	8.5	8.5	5	12
15	17	11	11.5	15	14	9
11	18.5	14	10	8.5	9	7.5
19	18.5	18	14	15	2	10.5
5	14.5	19	14	19	13	13.5
16	20	20	11.5	8.5	4	18
12M/F	3	7	14	11	11	5
8BM/GF	4	17	6.5	20	6	19
3BM/GF	6.5	10	18.5	8.5	19	10.5
6BM/GF	6.5	12	8.5	18	3	15
18BM/GF	10	4	18.5	15	8	16
7BM/GF	12	2	16.5	6	12	2
9BM/GF	13	14	16.5	15	16	3
17BM/GF	14.5	9	20	15	17	1

TABLE 20.3
Main Themes Elicited by the Complete
Set of TAT Cards in Spanish Subjects

	Males			Females			Gender Comparison
Thematic Area	Mean	Median	V.C.	Mean	Median	V.C.	p (t)
Aggression– hostility	7.08	7.56	0.40	5.49	5.10	0.47	.001
Job–study	5.94	5.28	0.43	4.88	4.42	0.50	.025
Descriptive	5.29	3.47	2.02	4.22	3.80	0.65	—
Parents–children	3.94	3.66	0.63	4.35	3.91	0.59	—
Depression	3.92	3.62	0.71	3.74	3.29	0.85	—
Marriage–love	3.49	3.26	0.49	4.88	4.89	0.51	.005
Sexual content/ relationships	1.47	1.32	0.74	1.27	0.85	1.47	—

A NEW SET OF CARDS AND INSTRUCTIONS FOR THE TAT ADMINISTRATION

From the analysis of the stimulus value of TAT cards, derived from the indexes previously described, a new abbreviated normative set of cards is proposed. This set have been considered empirically equivalent to the complete TAT set with respect to its stimulus value (in terms of the number and classification of themes produced), yet notably reduces the gender-role bias between the male and female series of the TAT.

The new set consists of 12 cards to which others cards from the original set could eventually be added. The male set (adolescents and adults) is composed of Cards 1, 2, 3BM, 4, 6BM, 7BM, 8BM, 10, 13MF, 15, 18BM, and 14. The female set (adolescents and adults) is composed of Cards 1, 2, 3GF, 4, 6GF, 7GF, 9GF, 10, 13MF, 17GF, 18GF, and 8GF. Table 20.4 shows these two sets in perspective, including Murray's card codes.

The administration instructions, now thoroughly translated into Spanish, are disposed according to a standardized pattern that eliminates suggestion or induction of Murray's themes without limiting verbal productivity. The new proposal provides alternatives for individual or collective administration, including options to use a strategy that allows use of test instructions with or without time pressure for the elaboration of the stories as a particular set of TAT administration. An additional protocol facilitates to the examiner adequate recording of the formal and nonverbal manifestations, which are later used as modulating variables in the content analysis.

An extended version of the procedure is completely described in Ávila-Espada (1985a), Ávila-Espada and Biezma-López (1989), and Ávila-Es-

TABLE 20.4
TAT Cards to Be Used: Suggested Sequence of Administration

Integrative System Rank Order of TAT Card Administration	Murray's TAT Card Codes	
	Males	Females
1	1	1
2	2	2
3	3BM	3GF
4	4	4
5	6BM	6GF
6	7BM	7GF
7	8BM	9GF
8	10	10
9	13MF	13MF
10	15	17GF
11	18BM	18GF
12	14	8GF
13 (optionally)	16	16

pada, Biezma, and Rodríguez (1998), but summarized in the following instruction cards, which are now adapted for Spanish-speaking populations. This new set of TAT instructions offers a clear procedure to standardize TAT administration, reducing examiner bias and focusing ambiguity only on the card's content.

TAT Verbal Instructions for TAT Administration

(Standardized English version)	(Standardized Spanish version)
a) Now I am going to show you some pictures that illustrate different scenes or situations.	a) "A continuación le (te)[1] voy a presentar algunas láminas en las que aparecen diversas escenas o situaciones.
b) I would like you to tell me a story about each one	b) Para cada una de ellas tiene (tienes) que relatar una historia,
c) including the past, the background of each scene,	c) que incluya el pasado de la escena -lo que sucedió antes-,
d) the present, that is, the situation as you see it, as well as the thoughts, feelings, and actions of the persons involved,	d) El presente -la situación y las acciones, pensamientos y sentimientos de los personajes-,

---

[1]Between parentheses ( ) are included as alternative terms so that examiners may choose a more informal language expression if needed.

e) and the future—in other words, what you think will happen later on or how the story ends.

f) There's no time limit for telling me each story.

f') You have 5 minutes for telling me each story.

g) I am going to take verbatim notes of your answers, so I would like you to speak slowly if possible, but without omitting any of your thoughts for this reason.

g') To make things easy, I am going to record your answers (on this tape recorder).

h) Have you understood? (Is all of this clear?) [Can be repeated in the same terms if Subject asks it]

i) Right, let's get started with the first picture; you can begin your story as soon as you wish.

e) y el futuro o lo que sucederá después, cómo terminará la historia.

f) No tiene (tienes) límite de tiempo para narrar las historias.

f') Tiene (tienes) un máximo de cinco minutos para narrar cada historia.

g) Tomaré nota literal de sus (tus) respuestas. Si le (te) es posible no hable (hables) muy deprisa, pero no omita (omitas) por eso todo lo que se le (te) ocurra.

g') Sus (tus) respuestas, para una mayor facilidad, las grabaré en este magnetófono.

h) ¿Ha (has) comprendido?. [Can be repeated in the same terms if Subject asks it]

i) Bien. Aquí tiene (tienes) la primera lámina. Puede (puedes) comenzar el relato.

Now the first TAT card (Code 1) is placed on the table in front of the subject, close to his or her hands.

Supporting Questions (only to be included as support phrases during the first and second card)

j) What happened before (that)?

j') What led (him/her/them) to this situation?

k) What's happening to (him/her/them) now?

l) Whats going to happen later?

j) ¿Qué ocurría antes?

j') ¿Qué le (les) ha llevado a esta situación?.

k) ¿Qué le (les) ocurre ahora?.

l) ¿Qué ocurrirá después?

Unintrusive Verbal Comments/Answers That Can Be Given by the Examiner During the Test Administration

m) Any way you want (it to be).

n) Say whatever comes to your mind.

o) Go on.

p) Have you finished?

m) Puede ser lo que usted (tú) quiera (quieras).

n) Diga (dí) lo que le (te) parezca.

o) Continúe (continúa).

p) ¿Ha (has) terminado?.

q) You can end it whenever you want.   *q) Termine (termina) cuando le (te) parezca.*

RECENT DEVELOPMENTS: AN *INTEGRATIVE ANALYSIS SYSTEM* FOR THE SCORING AND INTERPRETATION OF THE TAT

The evolution of TAT scoring and interpretation systems have been marked with confusion because no clear guidelines and proposals for scoring and interpretation emerged from a prolix landscape. At the beginning, following Murray's recommendations, TAT use developed an unsatisfactory qualitative analysis. This detected in the narratives produced to TAT cards needs and environmental pressures of the figure labeled or attributed as *hero*. Extremely dependent on manifest content of the TAT narratives, Murray's system—despite their theoretical value—lacks refinement; they are neither quantitative nor qualitative directions of scoring and interpretation. During the 1950s and 1960s, two main strategies emerged that tried to solve this essential weakness of the TAT method. The first one was the *holistic qualitative way* (Bellak, 1993; Shentoub et al., 1990), which uses TAT like a projective interview with an unsystematic categorial system deeply anchored in theoretical principles whose confirmation are searched in the TAT narrative content. This has evoked strong criticisms (see Rossini & Moretti, 1997) because it makes TAT extremely dependent on clinical expertise. It also reduces its utility to a small collection of sentences drawn from the manifest content of narratives taken as thought samples or some inferences related to defenses, conflictive areas, interpersonal dynamics, and problem-solving strategies.

The second one was the rough *quantitative scoring systems* developed by Eron (1950), Zubin, Eron, and Schumer (1965), and Murstein (1963, 1972). Some refinements were added later, implying a hard and time-expensive scoring procedure without clear connections with clinical interpretation. After Vane's (1981) review, no clear refinements or advancements have been added to the TAT arena. In addition, TAT research lacks in the training programs of psychological assessment students, reducing the interest paid to this relevant method of personality assessment (Moretti & Rossini, 1997). We are both witnesses and conductors of two decades of stimulus value research, potentially leading to many objective scores (see Cramer, 1996), but for a long time lacking of adequate integration within a coherent interpretative system for clinical use and report. The usual richness of TAT narratives produced by clinical subjects needs ways to take the advantage offered. Dana (1998) recently summarized the wide array of potential information about psychological functioning that

TAT offers, comparing Shneidman's (1951) analysis with his own suggestions (Dana, 1986) and the cluster of potential scoring variables proposed by Teglasi (1993).

From those origins, in the last decade, our research efforts have been directed to develop an Integrative Analysis System based on a critical review and collection of several research reports (Dana, 1956, 1959, 1982; Eron, 1950; Fine, 1955; McClelland et al., 1953; Zubin, Eron, & Schumer, 1965). Our aim is to achieve a reliable procedure for TAT scoring and interpretation of psychometric nature, which could reduce the cost of analysis and reach an optimal predictive and diagnostic value without wasting the main features of the qualitative approach.

The procedure of the Integrative Analysis System includes the following phases:

1. The protocol preparation for the analysis includes a thoroughly developed procedure for transcription and coding of verbal and nonverbal responses produced by the set of instructions previously presented.

2. Computation of the formal variables that modulate the thematic content analysis. Some formal indexes are usually computed (e.g., the new ESI and ERI, plus the classical Word Count, Reaction Time, and Total Time values) to detect shock patterns and other differential indexes between cards showed in an intrasubject profile.

3. Intrasubject content analysis (quantitative, qualitative, or both) includes different strategies, with all of them used if possible:

(a) Quantitative analysis of thematic content through a modified version of Eron system (Eron, 1950, 1953; Zubin, Eron, & Schumer, 1965; an introductory example of the normative Spanish data can be viewed in Table 20.5)

(b) Quantitative estimations of Emotional Tone (under the concept and method formulated by Eron in Zubin, Eron, & Schumer, 1965). A descriptive cadre of the normative Spanish data can be viewed in Table 20.6.

(c) Quantitative estimations of specific needs (under the definitions and procedures for coding established by McClelland et al., 1953). The main needs included in our analysis are: Achievement, Aggression, Power, Sex, and Affiliation.

(d) Quantitative estimations of Interpersonal Relations Content (under the coding system developed by Fine, 1955).

(e) Experiential-integrative analysis of content (adapted from Dana, 1982), the more qualitative phase of the analysis, complemented with an adaptation of Kernberg's criteria for personality structural organization that allows a distinction between Normal-Neurotic, Borderline, and Psychotic Structural Organization.

TABLE 20.5

TAT Integrative System Main Themes Elicited by Card 1
Spanish Normative Sample
(Spanish labels and criteria)

Var.	Ref.	Variable Name	Description and Criteria	Both sexes (% = n)	Males % (n)	Females % (n)	T (p)
T100		I. Disequilibrium (Tension)					
T101		A) Interpersonal					
T110		1. Parent or parent figure					
T111	a)	Pressure	Parent or parent figures are prohibitive, compelling, censuring, punishing, disapproving, interfering, checking up, disagreeing with, quarreling with, restraining, or unduly influencing child.	14	14.3 (7)	13.7 (7)	—
T102		B) Intrapersonal					
T251	1	Aspiration	Dreaming of future, hoping for future, determination	30	28.6 (14)	31.4 (16)	—
T263	12	Occupational concern	Deciding between jobs, considering vocations, dissatisfied with present employment or present pastime, worried about job, emphasis on decision that must be made in choosing occupation. (*Not scored in T253 or both.*)	21	20.4 (10)	21.6 (11)	—
T266	15	Reminiscence, sad	Individual is unhappy in his/her memories of the past or contemplation of the future, hopelessness.	18	16.3 (8)	19.6 (10)	—
T283	30	Bored	Central character is bored, has nothing to do.	13	16.3 (8)	9.80 (5)	.001
T287	34	Grief	Central character is very sad; not inconsequential (*not scored in T266*).	20	22.4 (11)	17.6 (9)	.05

475

TABLE 20.6
Card 1—TAT Emotional Tone
Spanish Data
Subjects Percent by Each Emotional Category

Emotion Categories	TAT Story					Outcome						
	0	1	2	3	4	0	1	2	3	4	?	X
Males	2	34	32	20	12	0	16	32	32	14	6	0
Females	0	60	18	20	2	0	28	8	30	22	8	5

(f) Decoding the speech organization processes through Shentoub's series (A: Control; B: Lability; C: Conflict Withdrawal; E: Primary Process emergence; adapted from the method proposed by Shentoub et al., 1990). This allows detection of defense processes and structural levels of organization that could be a validation of the inferences extracted from the Kernberg's criteria.

4. Now comparisons with the intra- and intersubject normative data are performed. Despite that subjects' TAT stories were codified, idiosyncratic responses could be compared with normative ones (see e.g., Table 20.5). Thematic content that are out of normative patterns can be detected and could be introduced as part of the narrative report. Those idiosyncratic phrases or terms could be chosen as foci for new qualitative assessment strategies.

5. Lately we can complete the analysis with a specific formal analysis; some traditional variables drawn from formal analysis procedures are performed. One of our main directions of research is the vocabulary analyses, computing base rates for all terms used in the stories across subjects. This procedure allows normative comparisons across cards within and across subjects within each specific card.

6. After we have collected all the indexes, raw data, profiles, and base rates, we can display the data in a TAT psychogram in a readable style.

7. Now a discussion of the inferences derived directly from the psychogram data could be added to the essential narrative TAT report.

8. Finally the main interpretative estimations close the extended narrative report. A computer-aided system to facilitate the TAT report of the IAS is now in preparation.

As a brief presentation of the reference frame for normative interpretation, the Spanish normative results for the TAT Card 1 (boy with a violin), displayed under Eron's modified criteria for quantitative scoring of content analysis, are presented in Table 20.5, complemented with emotional tone indicators (see Table 20.6). A more extended case record completely reported under this IAS procedure is now in preparation (Ávila-Espada & Rodríguez, in press).

An extended description of a preliminary version of this system can be also found in Ávila-Espada (1985a, 1991), and a more complete one is found in Ávila-Espada, Biezma, and Rodríguez (1998). Further research data (Ávila-Espada, 1990; Ávila-Espada & Rubí-Cid, 1990; Ávila-Espada, Biezma, & Rodríguez, 1998) from this analysis system show how effectively it provides an improved procedure in the use of thematic techniques. The major advantage of this new Integrative Analysis System is that it includes quantitative scoring strategies based on a revision of well-known previous approaches (Eron, 1950; Murstein, 1963), thus integrating qualitative procedures oriented to content analysis derived from recent psychoanalytic developments contributed by French TAT school (Brelet, 1986; Shentoub et al., 1990). Using this method, TAT reports are more complete and useful for the clinician and the researcher. They offer a more secure basis for interpretation and are more sensitive with respect to cultural differences (Ephraim, Sochting, & Marcia, 1997).

ACKNOWLEDGMENTS

Parts of this chapter have been drawn from a previous paper presented to the XV International Congress of Rorschach & Projective Methods (Boston, July 8–12, 1996) within the symposium: "European perspectives on the Rorschach and Picture-Story Tests," chaired by Richard H. Dana.

REFERENCES

Ávila-Espada, A. (1976). Análisis e interpretación del T.A.T. en base a un modelo temático-formal de variables estadísticas [TAT intepretation and analysis under a formal-thematic statistical model]. *Revista de Psicología General y Aplicada, 31,* 141–142, 977–979.

Ávila-Espada, A. (1983). *El Test de Apercepción Temática de H. A. Murray en la población española: Estudio normativo y análisis para una adaptación* [The Thematic Apperception Test of H. A. Murray with Spanish population: Normative study and adaptation analysis]. Unpublished doctoral dissertation, Editorial de la Universidad Complutense de Madrid, Madrid.

Ávila-Espada, A. (1985a). *Manual Operativo para el Test de Apercepción Temática* [Operative Manual for the TAT]. Madrid: Editorial Pirámide.

Ávila-Espada, A. (1985b). Investigación normativa con el T.A.T. de Murray en la población española [Normative Spanish research with Murray's TAT]. *Revista de Psicología General y Aplicada, 40*(2), 277–316.

Ávila-Espada, A. (1990). *Fundamentos empíricos del Test de Apercepción Temática* [Empirical foundations of the Thematic Apperception Test]. Madrid: Facultad de Psicología, U.C.M.

Ávila-Espada, A. (1991). Un Sistema Integrado de base empírica para el Test de Apercepción Temática: Nuevas propuestas para su aplicación y valoración [An empirically based Integrated System for the Thematic Apperception Test: New proposals for use and analysis]. *Revista de la Sociedad Española del Rorschach y Métodos Proyectivos, 4,* 9–17.

Ávila-Espada, A. (1996, July). Quantitative and qualitative strategies for Thematic Apperception Test interpretation. In R. Dana (Chair), *European perspectives on the Rorschach and Picture-Story Tests Symposium conducted at the XV International Congress of Rorschach & Projective Methods* (Boston, MA).

Ávila-Espada, A., & Biezma-López, J. (1989). *Guía para la utilización del TAT en la evaluación psicológica y en la investigación* [A guide for the use of TAT in psychological assessment and research]. Madrid: Facultad de Psicología, U.C.M.

Ávila-Espada, A., Biezma, J. M., & Rodríguez, S. (1998). *Sistema Integrado para la utilización clínica del Test de Apercepción Temática (T.A.T.)* [Integrated system for clinical use of the TAT]. Salamanca: Monografías de la Unidad de Investigación en Psicología Clínica y Psicoterapia—Universidad de Salamanca.

Ávila-Espada, A., & Rodríguez, S. (in press). *A case example for the integrative analysis system for the T.A.T.* Salamanca: Monografías de la Unidad de Investigación en Psicología Clínica y Psicoterapia—Universidad de Salamanca.

Ávila-Espada, A., & Rubí-Cid, M. L. (1990). *Révision de l'étude normative espagnol pour le TAT, dans son utilisation avec le système intégratif du TAT.* Poster presented at the 13th International Congress on Rorschach and Projective Methods, Paris.

Bellak, L. (1993). *The Thematic Apperception Test, the Children's Apperception Test, and Senior Apperception Test in clinical use* (5th ed.). Boston: Allyn & Bacon.

Brelet, F. (1986). *Le T.A.T. Fantasme et situation projective.* Paris: Dunod.

Castilla del Pino, C. (1966). *Un estudio sobre la Depresión.* Barcelona: Editorial Península.

Cramer, P. (1996). *Storytelling, narrative, and the Thematic Apperception Test.* New York: Guilford.

Dana, R. H. (1956). Selection of abbreviated TAT sets. *Journal of Clinical Psychology, 12,* 36–40.

Dana, R. H. (1959). Proposal for objective scoring of the TAT. *Perceptual and Motor Skills* (Monograph), *9,* 27–43.

Dana, R. H. (1982). *A human science model for personality assessment with projective techniques.* Springfield, IL: Charles C. Thomas.

Dana, R. H. (1986). Thematic Apperception Test used with adolescents. In A. I. Rabin (Ed.), *Projective techniques for adolescents and children* (pp. 14–36). New York: Springer.

Dana, R. H. (1998, March). *Using the TAT in cross-cultural/multicultural assessment.* Paper presented at the midwinter meeting of the Society for Personality Assessment, Boston.

Ephraim, D., Sochting, I., & Marcia, J. E. (1997). Cultural norms for TAT narratives in psychological practice and research: Illustrative studies. *Rorschachiana, 22,* 13–37.

Eron, L. D. (1950). A normative study of the Thematic Apperception Test. *Psychological Monographs, 64*(9).

Eron, L. D. (1953). Responses of women to the Thematic Apperception Test. *Journal of Consulting Psychology, 17,* 269–282.

Fernández-Ballesteros, R. (1973). Ensayo de sistematización de los resultados del TAT. *Revista de Psicología General y Aplicada,* 123–125, 1017–1023.

Fine, R. (1955). A scoring scheme for the TAT and other verbal projective techniques. *Journal of Projective Techniques, 19,* 306–309.

Fisher, G. M., & Shotwell, A. M. (1961). Preference rankings of the Thematic Apperception Test cards by adolescents normals, delinquents and mental retardates. *Journal of Projective Techniques, 25,* 41–43.

Friedman, R. J. (1972). TAT story length in children. *Psychology in the Schools, 9*(4), 411–412.

Geiser, M. L., & Stein, M. (Eds.). (1998). *Celebrating the Thematic Apperception Test.* Washington, DC: American Psychological Association.

Irvin, F. S., & Woude, K. (1971). Empirical support for a basic TAT set. *Journal of Clinical Psychology, 27,* 514–516.

Lebo, D. (1955). Immediate affective reaction to TAT cards. *Journal of Clinical Psychology, 11,* 297–299.

McClelland, D. C. (Ed.). (1953). *The achievement motive.* New York: Irvington.

Morgan, Ch. D., & Murray, H. A. (1935). A method for investigating fantasies: The Thematic Apperception Test. *Archives of Neurology and Psychiatry, 34,* 289–306.

Murstein, B. I. (1963). *Theory and research in projective techniques (emphasizing the TAT).* New York: Wiley.

Murstein, B. I. (1972). Normative written TAT responses for a college sample. *Journal of Personality Assessment, 36*(2), 109–147.

Newbigging, P. L. (1955). Influence of a stimulus variable on stories told to certain TAT pictures. *Canadian Journal of Psychology, 9,* 195–206.

Newmark, Ch. S., & Flouranzano, R. (1973). Replication of an empirically derived TAT set with hospitalized psychiatric patients. *Journal of Personality Assessment, 37*(4), 340–341.

Rosenzweig, S. H., & Fleming, E. (1949). Apperceptive norms for the Thematic Apperception Test (II). An empirical investigation. *Journal of Personality, 17,* 483–503.

Rossini, E. D., & Moretti, R. J. (1997). Thematic Apperception Test (T.A.T.) Interpretation: Practice recommendations from a survey of clinical psychology doctoral programs accredited by the American Psychological Association. *Professional Psychology: Research and Practice, 28,* 393–398.

Shentoub, V. (Ed.). (1990). *Manuel d'utilisation du T.A.T. (Approche psychanalytique).* Paris: Dunod.

Shentoub, V., & Shentoub, S. A. (1961). Recherche expérimentale et clinique du theme banal dans le TAT. *Psychiatrie de l'enfant,* III, 2, Paris: PUF.

Shneidman, E. S. (1951). *Thematic Apperception Test Analysis.* New York: Grune & Stratton.

Siguan, M. (1953). Para la interpretación del TAT. *Revista de Psicología General y Aplicada,* VIII, (27), 431–478.

Siguan, M. (1954). Formulario para la interpretación y registro de los datos del TAT. *Revista de Psicología General y Aplicada,* IX, (30–31), 305–312.

Teglasi, H. (1993). *Clinical use of story telling emphasizing the T.A.T. with children and adolescents.* Boston: Allyn & Bacon.

Van Lennep, A. J., & Houwink, R. H. (1930). Utrecht: *Four Picture Test.*

Vane, J. R. (1981). The Thematic Apperception tests: A review. *Clinical Psychology Review, 1,* 319–336.

Zubin, J., Eron, L. D., & Schumer, F. (1965). *An experimental approach to projective techniques.* New York: Wiley.

Multicultural and Cross-Cultural Utility of the TEMAS (Tell-Me-A-Story) Test

Giuseppe Costantino
Lutheran Medical Center and
Fordham University

Robert G. Malgady
New York University

> *All Human beings must be alike, because no human being is ever mistaken for anything else; but they must be different because no human being is ever mistaken for another human being.*
>
> —Montaigne

Understanding the personality functioning of individuals of different cultures has been facilitated by psychological assessment and anthropological observation. Historically, the most widely used instruments have been the TAT and Rorschach (Goh & Fuller, 1983; Henry, 1947; Hutton, Dubes, & Muir, 1992; Kennedy, Faust, Willis, & Piotrowski, 1994; Murstein, 1963, 1972). The Rorschach inkblots have been used without modification in cross-cultural research, whereas Murray's (1943) TAT pictures were modified because the TAT cards "... were representative of a culture that was not sufficiently familiar to the subjects to permit ready identification with the content of the pictures" (Henry, 1947, p. 263). Consequently, a series of TAT pictures with Native-American characters and themes of their cultures were developed in 1942 to undertake the first cross-cultural study of approximately 1,000 children ages 6 to 18 years from Papago, Zuni, Zia, Hopi, Navaho, and Sioux tribes (Henry, 1947). Culturally relevant TAT pictures were also developed to study southwest Africans in Africa by Boris Inflund and South Pacific Micronesians by Francis Mahoney and William Lessa (Henry, 1947). However, the recent work of Monopoli (1984; cited in Dana, 1986) reported that culture-relevant stimuli were necessary for the personality assessment of unacculturated Hopi and Zuni Indians, but the Murray (1943) TAT was somewhat useful with individuals accultured within the Euro-American culture. Similarly, Avila-Espada (1986) showed that the traditional TAT pictures, coupled with newly developed objective scoring and norms, are clinically useful for the personality assessment of European Spaniards because they can readily identify with the White characters in the pictures.

The first African-American TAT was developed by Thompson (1949) based on the assumption that similarity and congruence between the projective stimuli and examinees facilitates identification with the characters in the pictures and promotes greater verbal fluency and self-disclosure. The original study using 26 African-American college student veterans showed the superiority of Thompson TAT (T–TAT) over the Murray TAT (M–TAT) with respect to verbal fluency. However, subsequent studies (e.g., Cook, 1953; Light, 1955; Schwartz, Reiss, & Cottingham, 1951) found that Thompson's results did not apply to all African Americans of various cultures. Consequently, the use of the T–TAT has declined over the years. Nonetheless, later research by Dana (1986) and Murstein (1963) indicated that the early criticism of the T–TAT may have been associated with failure to control for certain methodological factors, that the socioacademic climate of the 1950s was prejudiced against African Americans, and African Americans in the 1950s did not fully identify with African-American-oriented stimuli because of the racial social mores of the times.

Following the civil rights movement of the early 1960s, more systematic efforts to develop a culturally sensitive TAT were undertaken. Cowan and Goldberg (1967) assessed achievement need (n-Ach) in African-American females by using the M–TAT and a modification of the T–TAT; they found that African-American females wrote lengthier stories in response to African-American projective stimuli than to White stimuli and attributed n-Ach more to male figures than female figures. Subsequently, Bailey and Green (1977) compared the M–TAT, the T–TAT, and an Experimental TAT (E–TAT) developed by the authors with characters who reflected African-American racial characteristics and expressed African-American themes. The results show that both the E–TAT and T–TAT produced lengthier stories than the M–TAT. Following Thompson's cultural hypothesis, Williams (1972) developed the Themes Concerning Blacks Test (TCB), which is composed of 20 African-American and White cards, 19 depicting African-American characters engaged in psychosocial activities and reflecting African-American themes, and one picture showing white dots on a black background. Preliminary research based on a sample of 64 African-American school-age children and several case studies indicate that TCB pulls for more positive thematic responses than the TAT and that the TCB is preferred over the TAT. The Themes Concerning

Blacks (TCB) has some potential as a culturally sensitive test for African Americans, but more research regarding its validity and reliability is needed. At present, the test, which is published by the author, is not commercially distributed (Dana, 1993; Ness, 1985).

CULTURALLY SENSITIVE AND COMPETENT INSTRUMENTS

French philosopher Montaigne said that all human beings are alike because they share the same condition that makes them human. However, all individuals are different because they have their own particular characteristics that make them distinct. When applied to individuals from different cultural groups, this statement embodies both the emic and etic perspectives in anthropology.

> An emic perspective can provide an approach to more veridical and enriched assessment conceptualization of other persons by an emphasis on understanding individuals in their cultural contexts. (Dana, 1993, p. 142)

Conversely, an etic perspective emphasizes the universal condition of the human personality. Consequently, culturally diverse individuals living in the United States tend to exhibit on a continuous acculturation process both their culturally specific personality functions and general personality functions specific to the Anglo-European American culture.

Traditionally, psychological tests, both intelligence and personality instruments, have been developed in a biased manner because they have been constructed and normed based on the Anglo-European American majority group and then applied to culturally diverse minority groups such as Latinos and African Americans. An emic-sensitive instrument takes into consideration those elements that are indigenous to a given cultural group with respect to personality characteristics, and thus reduces test bias.

The propriety of administering psychological tests standardized on nonminority, middle-class, and English-speaking populations to examinees who are linguistically, culturally, and/or ethnically diverse has been a controversial issue for over five decades (Costantino & Malgady, 1996; Dana, 1993; Malgady, 1997; Olmedo, 1981; Padilla, 1979; Padilla & Medina, 1996). This controversy originally focused on intelligence testing of African Americans. However, similar allegations of bias toward Latinos have been made with respect to personality testing and diagnostic evaluation.

In the absence of empirical evidence to the contrary, the prevailing view is that standard psychological assessment procedures are considered unbiased (e.g., López, 1988). Conversely, others have argued that clients' variations in English language proficiency, cultural background, or ethnic profile pose potential sources of bias for standard assessment and diagnostic practices (e.g., Dana, 1993; Malgady, 1996; Malgady, Rogler, & Costantino, 1987, 1988). Moreover, Dana (1993, 1996) emphasized that most personality tests are assumed to be genuine etic or culture general and universal in their assessment.

Consequently, the use of an etic orientation with multicultural groups has erroneously minimized cultural differences and hence has generated inappropriate inferences using Anglo-European personality constructs. This has created unfavorable psychological test results and unfair clinical dispositions (Costantino, 1992; Dana, 1993; Malgady, 1996). Dana (1993) further emphasized that a correct etic orientation needs to be used to demonstrate multicultural construct validity. In the same vein, even in the absence of compelling empirical evidence, assessment procedures should not be routinely generalized to different cultural groups, and multicultural tests and assessments with both emic and etic constructs should be developed and used. The T–TAT (Thompson, 1949) and TCB test (Williams, 1972) both embody the emic and etic constructs and thus can be labeled culturally sensitive instruments.

DEVELOPMENT OF TEMAS
AS A MULTICULTURAL/CROSS-CULTURAL
PROJECTIVE INSTRUMENT

In the same tradition, the Tell-Me-A-Story (TEMAS) test was developed to revive the TAT technique for culturally and linguistically diverse children and adolescents. Because of its unique contribution to ethnic minority assessment, the TEMAS test has been evaluated as a valid multicultural projective instrument, a revivor of the dormant TAT technique, and ". . . a landmark event for multicultural assessment because it provides a picture-story test that has psychometric credibility" (Dana, 1993, p. 10). Ritzler (1993) wrote: "It also represents the first time a thematic apperception assessment technique has been published in the United States with initial, expressed purpose of providing valid personality assessment of minority subjects" (p. 4). Prior to the TEMAS, a few apperception techniques (e.g., McArthur & Roberts, 1982; Thompson, 1949) were modified to give the people in the stimulus pictures minority (i.e., African American) physical characteristics, but the TEMAS goes well beyond simple alteration of the physical characteristics.

Ritzler (1996) favorably compared TEMAS with the Rorschach Comprehensive System (RCS) as a valid and reliable multicultural projective test and has encouraged research comparing the two tests (Elliot, 1998). Notwithstanding some weak psychometric properties and the need to improve the reliability of some scored functions (Bernal, 1991; Flanagan & DiGiuseppe, 1999; Ritzler, 1993, 1996),

> ... its degree of empirical validity appears superior to that of other thematic apperception measures (e.g. RATC, TAT). Therefore, it appears to be a better choice than the other instruments in the diagnosis of social-emotional problems for those school psychologists wishing to use a projective test. The TEMAS may prove useful in the differentiation of special education from regular education if used as apart of a comprehensive assessment paradigm.... (Flanagan & DiGiuseppe, 1999, p. 28)

Based on these considerations, the TEMAS test (which in English is an acronym for Tell-Me-A-Story, and in Spanish means themes) was developed as a multicultural thematic apperception test for use with Puerto Rican, other Hispanic, African-American, and White children. The TEMAS represents a number of improvements over previous thematic apperception tests: (a) the test was specifically developed for use with children and adolescents, (b) it comprises two parallel sets of stimulus cards—minority and nonminority versions, (c) adequate normative data are available for multicultural groups, and (d) an objective scoring system was developed for both thematic content and structure.

The TEMAS pictures embody the following features: structured stimuli and diminished ambiguity to pull for specific personality functions; chromatically attractive, ethnically, and racially relevant and contemporary stimuli to elicit diagnostically meaningful protocols; and representation of both negative and positive intra- and interpersonal functions in the form of conflicts that require a solution (or problem solving).

The TEMAS test was developed to address a need for a psychometrically sound and multicultural thematic apperception test designed specifically for use with both minority and nonminority children and adolescents. Normatively, the test can be used with children and adolescents ages 5 to 13 and clinically with children and adolescents up to 18 years old. The TEMAS test was constructed within the dynamic-cognitive theoretical framework, which posits that personality development occurs within a sociocultural system. Within this system, individuals internalize cultural values, attitudes, and beliefs of the family and society (Bandura & Walters, 1959, 1967; Sullivan, 1953). Personality functions are initially learned through modeling (Bandura, 1977) and are then developed through verbal and imaginal processes (Piaget & Inhelder, 1971; Paivio, 1971). Those personality functions are governed by motives, which, as learned and internalized dispositions, interact with environmental stimuli to determine overt behavior in specific situations. Because these dispositions are not directly observable in clinical evaluation, projective techniques prove to be useful instruments in probing beneath the overt structure or phenotype of the personality, thereby arousing the latent motives imbedded in the personality genotype. Hence, projective tests assess relatively stable individual differences in the strength of underlying motives that are expressed in narration or storytelling (Atkinson, 1981). Atkinson emphasized that analysis of narration (thematic content) has a more solid theoretical foundation than ever before and

> remains the most important and virtually untapped resource we have for developing our understanding of the behavior of an animal distinguished by its unique competence in language and use of symbols. (Atkinson, 1981, p. 127)

The Stimulus Cards

The settings, characters, and themes were created by Costantino (1978), and the artwork was rendered by Phil Jacobs, who recently completed the Asian-American TEMAS pictures. The 23 standardized cards were selected from 50 pictures. There are two parallel versions of TEMAS pictures: The minority version consists of pictures depicting predominantly Latinos and African-American characters in urban settings, and the nonminority version consists of corresponding pictures showing predominantly White characters in urban settings. A third set, the Asian-American version of TEMAS, which depicts Asian-American characters, is presently undergoing preliminary validation (Costantino, Tsui, Lee, Flanagan, & Malgady, 1998).

Both the minority and nonminority versions have a short form composed of nine cards, four of which are administered to both genders and five of which are gender-specific. Of the 23 long form cards, 12 are for both genders, 11 are gender-specific, and 1 is age-specific. Furthermore, there are four cards with multicultural characters that can be used interchangeably for both the minority and nonminority versions.

The TEMAS Measures

There are 17 cognitive functions that can be scored for each TEMAS protocol: Reaction Time, Total Time Fluency, Total Omissions, Main Character Omissions, Secondary Character Omissions, Event Omissions, Setting Omissions, Total Transformations, Main Character Transformations, Secondary Character Transformations, Event Transformations, Setting Transformations, Inquiries, Relationships, Imagination, Sequencing, and Conflict.

The nine personality functions are assessed within the dynamic-cognitive theoretical framework. Each stimulus card pulls for one to four of the following personality functions: Interpersonal Relations, Aggression, Anxiety/Depression, Achievement Motivation, Delay of Gratification, Self-Concept, Sexual Identity, Moral Judgment, and Reality Testing.

In addition, the TEMAS scoring system evaluates seven affective functions: Happy, Sad, Angry, Fearful, Neutral, Ambivalent, and Inappropriate Affect.

Examiner Qualifications

To eliminate assessment bias when testing culturally, linguistically, and ethnically/racially diverse children, examiners should (a) be fluent in the language in which the examinee is dominant, (b) understand the effect of culture and ethnicity on the personality development of ethnic minorities, (c) be familiar with the cultural and ethnic/racial heritage of the child being tested, and (d) recognize cultural, linguistic, and cultural diversity (American Psychological Association, 1993; Costantino, 1992; Costantino, Malgady, & Rogler, 1988; Dana, 1993; Fuchs, 1986; Malgady, Rogler, & Costantino, 1987; Padilla & Medina, 1996).

Administration

The administration of TEMAS was derived from both the TAT and RCS administrations. The TEMAS standard administration is conducted individually. Recently, group administration in classroom settings have been carried out (Flanagan, Anderson, Ferri-Siegel, & Costantino, 1999). After developing a rapport with the examinee, the examiner says:

> I would like you to tell me a story. I have a lot of (several, or a few) interesting pictures that I'm going to show you. Please look carefully at the people and the places in the pictures and then tell me a complete story about each picture; a story that has a beginning and an end.

Two types of instructions are used by the examiner: instructions of temporal sequencing and structured inquiries. During the instructions of temporal sequencing, the examiner, while showing the back of the first picture to the examinee, says:

> Please tell me a complete story about this picture and all the other pictures I will show you. The story should answer three questions: 1. What is happening in the picture now? 2. What happened before? 3. What will happen in the future?

Following these instructions, the examinee tells spontaneous stories, during which the examiner may ask clarifying questions that are not part of the structured inquiries. These questions are recorded as question marks in the narrative. Once the child has ended his or her spontaneous storytelling, the examiner asks any of the following structured inquiries that are missing from the story: 1a. Who are these people? or 1b. Do they know each other? 2a. Where are these people? 2b. Where is this person? 3a. What are these people doing and saying? 3b. What is this person doing and saying? 4a. What were these people doing before? 4b. What was this person doing before? 5a. What will these people do next? 5b. What will this person do next? 6a. What is this person (main character) thinking? 6b. What is this person (main character) feeling?

Recording Time

Examiner should record reaction time (RT) and total time (TT; the time the examinee has taken to complete the story, including the time taken by the examiner to ask the structured inquiries). It is useful to record spontaneous time, which is the time during which the examinee has told the story spontaneously just before the structured inquiries.

Scoring

TEMAS protocols are scored on a record booklet; each story is scored separately for cognitive, affective, interpersonal, and intrapersonal functions. The 18 Cognitive Functions are scored as following: *Reaction Time* is scored in seconds; *Total Times* in minutes and seconds; *Fluency* in number of words per story; *Conflict* is scored 1 if it not recognized, blank if it is recognized and resolved, and 1 if it is only recognized but not resolved; *Sequencing* is scored 1 or 2 or 3 if all three sequences "now, before, and after" are omitted and blank if they are all recognized; *Imagination* is scored 1 if the narrative is stimulus-bound (i.e., stories are purely descriptive) and blank if it abstracts beyond the stimulus; *Relationships* are scored 1 if they are recognized and blank if they are not recognized; *Inquiries* are scored 1 through 10 if they are unanswered and blank if they are all answered; *Omissions* and *Transformations* are scored in accordance with the number of omissions and transformations of Main Character, Secondary Character, Event, and Setting.

All *Affective functions* such as Happy, Sad, Angry, and Fearful are scored 1 if they are present in the story and left blank if they are not mentioned. It is important to score the affective function given as a response to Inquiry 6b following the resolution of the conflict at the end of each story. *Personality functions* (*Interpersonal Relations* [Control of], *Aggression* [Coping with], *Anxiety/Depression, Achievement Motivation, Delayed Gratification, Self-Concept, Sexual Identity, Moral Judgment,* and *Reality Testing*) are scored on a 4-point Likert-type scale, with 1 representing the most maladaptive resolution of the conflict and 4 the most adaptive.

Personality function pulls for each card were established psychometrically (Costantino, Malgady, & Rogler, 1988). A personality function is scored as "N" when the particular function is not pulled. The "N" value represents the defense mechanism of the examinee in accordance with the Sullivanian construct of *selective inattention*. This scale, together with the *Omission* and *Transformation* scales, have been found to discriminate between clinical and nonclinical children (Costantino, Malgady, Rogler, & Tsui, 1988; Costantino, Malgady, Colon-Malgady, & Bailey, 1992). A score of 1 for any personality function indicates a highly maladaptive resolution for a particular card.

For example, themes of murder, rape, and assault are scored 1 for interpersonal relations, aggression, and moral judgment. A suicidal theme earns a 1 under the anxiety/depression function or the lingering belief that the monster in the dream could be under the bed. The decision to drop out of school or steal rather than work results in a 1 for achievement motivation and delay of gratification. The anticipation of complete failure and concomitant refusal to attempt a given task results in a 1 for self-concept of competence. A character who changes or rejects his or her gender earns a 1 in sexual identity. Scores of 1 in moral judgment reflect a total lack of regard for the consequences of antisocial behavior. Severely impaired reality testing would be scored only for the most bizarre and impossible resolutions (e.g., inanimate objects come alive and kill, a child causes harmful events to occur by a strange power of the mind).

A score of 2 for any personality function reflects a moderately maladaptive resolution. For example, children cheat and/or steal and get away with it (*Moral Judgment*); a conflict is resolved by fighting (*Aggression*); money is used to satisfy immediate gratification rather than saved to satisfy delayed gratification (*Delayed Gratification*); homework is avoided in favor of play (*Achievement Motivation*); a child fails to carry out a parental command or runs away from home and never returns (*Interpersonal Relations* with parental figures); the monster in a dream causes so much anxiety that the examinee does not readily recover from the dream (*Anxiety/Depression*).

A score of 3 represents a moderately adaptive resolution. For example, examinees decide not to cheat because if they do so they are caught and punished (*Moral Judgment*); examinees decide not to resort to fighting because they can get hurt and/or punished by authorities (*Aggression*); homework is completed only for fear of punishment of external pressure (*Achievement Motivation*); a child grudgingly decides to obey the parent.

A score of 4 represents a highly adaptive resolution. The examinee must perceive the intended conflict and solve the problem in a mature, age-appropriate manner. Implicit in a score of 4 is a striving for the greater good, a sense of responsibility, and an intrinsic motivation. For example, an examinee rejects the notion of cheating as contrary to learning and morally wrong (*Moral Judgment*), and conflicts are discussed and an optimal compromise is reached. To obtain a score of 4 in *Delayed Gratification*, the character in the story must forgo immediate gratification and decide to save the money to buy a larger reward at a later date while working or doing chores to save additional money; homework is completed because good grades are valued and the child wishes to go to college or practice hard with his or her teammates to win a soccer game (*Achievement Motivation*); dreams are never real and cause only temporary anxiety that the child learns to master as the conflict is solved (*Anxiety/Depression* and *Reality Testing*); a child decides to obey his or her parent(s) for the good of everyone concerned (*Interpersonal Relations* with parents); or a child resolves the conflict with his or her younger sibling in an amicable manner (*Interpersonal Relations* with siblings) or peers (*Interpersonal Relations* with peers).

It needs to be clarified that, to analyze the complexity of the *Interpersonal Relation* Function, it has become necessary to score the various IRs with a given story (i.e., IR toward parents, IR toward peers, IR toward siblings). All three scores if necessary are entered in the triangle of the scoring booklet and then averaged out before they are carried out as sums (Costantino & Malgady, 1997).

Standardization: Standardization Sample

The TEMAS was standardized on a sample of 642 children (281 males and 361 females) from public schools in the New York City area. These children ranged in age from 5 to 13 years and had a mean of 8.9 years ($SD = 1.9$). The total sample represents four ethnic/racial groups: African Americans, Puerto Ricans, other Hispanics, and Whites. Combined samples were created so the clinicians could have greater flexibility in selecting the normative group that best fits a given child's ethnic/racial background. The participating students were from predominantly lower and middle-income families.

Stratification of the Standardization Sample

In the standardization sample, significant correlations of low magnitude were found between age and many of the TEMAS functions. Correlations ranged from .01 to .52 (see Table 21.1). Although these correlations are

TABLE 21.1
Correlations of TEMAS Indexes With Age

Function	Hispanic	African American
Cognitive		
Reaction Time	.00	.22
Total Time	.11	.01
Fluency	.18	.20
Total Omissions	−.23	−.11
Total Transformations	−.17	−.52*
Inquiries	−.13	−.25
Main Character Omissions	−.17	−.19
Main Character Transformations	−.14	−.35*
Secondary Character Omissions	−.01	−.24
Secondary Character Transformations	−.12	−.40*
Event Omissions	−.13	−.11
Event Transformations	−.05	—
Setting Omissions	−.31*	.00
Setting Transformations	−.19	−.37*
Conflict	−.21	−.18
Sequencing	−.11	−.38*
Imagination	−.14	−.31*
Relationships	−.20	−.39*
Personality		
Interpersonal Relations	−.21	.17
Aggression	−.26*	.02
Anxiety/Depression	−.18	.34*
Achievement Motivation	.02	.23
Delayed Gratification	.07	.20
Self-Concept	−.05	.10
Sexual Identity	−.34*	.29
Moral Judgment	.05	.12
Reality Testing	−.10	.18
Affective		
Happy	.16	−.12
Sad	−.28*	.08
Angry	.08	.13
Fearful	.12	.04
Neutral	.00	−.29
Ambivalent	.00	.12
Inappropriate Affect	−.09	.05

Note. $N = 115$ (73 Hispanics, 42 African Americans). Father SES, $n = 54$ Hispanics, 27 African Americans. Mother SES, $n = 69$ Hispanics, 39 African Americans.
*$p < .05$.

small, it is believed that they reflect real developmental trends in children's cognitive, affective, and personality functioning. Thus, to accommodate the effects of these trends while retaining respectable sample sizes, age was collapsed into three age-range groups: 5- to 7-year-olds, 8- to 10-year-olds, and 11- to 13-year-olds.

There were no significant differences due to gender for any of the TEMAS scoring indexes. This is consistent with results of other studies that have investigated the effects of gender on TEMAS functions.

The correlations between the 23-card long form of the TEMAS and the 9-card short form for each function were computed separately for the total sample and for each ethnic/racial group (see Tables 21.2–21.6). The correlation between the long and short forms was uniformly high across samples. The median correlation between forms was .81 for the Total Sample, .82 for Whites, .80 for African Americans, .80 for Puerto Ricans, and .81 for other Hispanics.

Reliability

Internal Consistency

Long Form. Internal consistency reliabilities of the TEMAS functions were derived using a sample of 73 Hispanic and 42 African-American children (see Table 21.3). The internal consistency reliability coefficients for the Hispanic sample ranged from .41 for Ambivalent to .98 for Fluency, and with a median value of .73. For the African-American sample, coefficients ranged from .31 for Setting Transformations to .97 for Fluency, with a median of .62.

Reaction Time, Fluency, and Total Time demonstrated high levels of internal consistency in both the Hispanic and African-American samples. However, in general, Omissions and Transformations of perceptual details (Main Character, Secondary Character, Event, and Setting) had lower magnitudes of internal consistency than other TEMAS functions in both samples. This may be attributable to the fact that these two functions, being clinical scales, tend to occur less frequently in nonclinical children (Costantino, Colon-Malgady, Malgady, & Perez, 1991). The internal consistency reliabilities for Omissions and Transformations were uniformly lower for African Americans than for Hispanics.

Conflict, Imagination, and Relationships demonstrated moderate to high internal consistency reliability in both ethnic/racial groups. The alpha coefficient for sequencing was moderately high in the Hispanic sample but low in the African-American sample. With respect to affective functions, reliability estimates in the Hispanic sample were highest for Happy, Sad, Angry, and Fearful, whereas in the African-American sample, the highest reliabilities were evident for Sad, Angry, Neutral, and Ambivalent.

TABLE 21.2
Correction Between TEMAS Long and Short Forms

Function	White Sample		Puerto Rican Sample		Other Hispanic Sample		African-American Sample	
	N	r	N	r	N	r	N	r
Quantitative Scale								
Reaction Total	87	.95	117	.95	84	.94	113	.96
Total Time	124	.97	122	.98	84	.97	114	.99
Fluency	123	.98	125	.97	86	.97	113	.97
Total Omissions	172	.72	164	.70	93	.81	206	.74
Interpersonal Relations	143	.95	164	.87	45	.99	206	.91
Aggression	136	.92	164	.96	38	.99	206	.95
Anxiety/Depression	171	.90	151	.84	100	.83	206	.89
Achievement Motivation	172	.79	163	.79	100	.81	203	.88
Delayed Gratification	163	.89	161	.87	84	.82	203	.96
Self-Concept	166	.82	155	.70	98	.77	193	.82
Sexual Identity	145	.69	76	.86	86	.80	127	.90
Moral Judgment	158	.81	163	.78	90	.64	197	.73
Reality Testing	171	.75	125	.84	100	.66	206	.83
Happy	172	.87	163	.81	94	.96	206	.71
Sad	172	.82	163	.79	94	.94	206	.72
Angry	172	.77	163	.84	94	.87	206	.77
Fearful	171	.88	163	.83	94	.88	206	.80
Qualitative Indicator								
Neutral	171	.86	163	.86	94	.86	206	.91
Ambivalent	171	.72	163	.61	94	.79	206	.94
Inappropriate Affect	171	.77	163	.39	94	.86	206	.74
Conflict	172	.77	163	.80	100	.82	206	.91
Sequencing	172	.82	163	.57	100	.79	206	.57
Imagination	172	.82	163	.97	96	.84	206	.65
Relationships	172	.62	163	.76	94	.75	206	.59
Total Transformation	172	.76	164	.80	96	.72	206	.71
Inquiries	172	.87	162	.04	98	.66	206	.72
Main Character Omissions	172	.64	164	.82	95	.79	206	.95
Secondary Character Omissions	172	.78	164	.75	98	.78	206	.80
Setting Omissions	172	.69	164	.65	100	.60	206	.64
Event Omissions	172	.68	164	.66	100	.87	206	.63
Main Character Transformations	172	.47	164	.57	96	.63	206	.55
Secondary Character Transformations	172	.60	164	.68	100	.65	206	.34
Setting Transformations	172	.66	164	.94	100	.76	206	.61
Event Transformations	172	.83	164	.73	100	.72	206	.70

TABLE 21.3
Internal Consistency (Alpha) Reliability and
Test–Retest (r) Reliability Over 18-Week Interval

Function	Hispanic	Black	N	r
Cognitive				
Reaction Time	.95	.92	50	.17
Total Time	.98	.97	50	.06
Fluency	.98	.97	50	.45
Total Omissions	.80	.75	50	.13
Total Transformation	.64	.45	51	.05
Inquiries	.82	.51	51	.27
Main Character Omissions	.76	.59	51	.04
Main Character Transformations	.52	—	51	−.05
Secondary Character Omissions	.65	.56	51	−.06
Secondary Character Transformations	.77	.36	51	−.07
Event Omissions	.74	.72	51	.27
Event Transformation	.48	—	51	.46
Setting Omissions	.75	.60	51	.15
Setting Transformation	.55	.31	51	−.08
Conflict	.69	.83	51	.53
Sequencing	.82	.46	51	−.01
Imagination	.98	.75	51	.11
Relationships	.75	.68	51	.39
Personality*				
Interpersonal Relations (16)	.92	.62	50	.24
Aggression (8)	.84	.78	50	.16
Anxiety/Depression	.50	.49	50	.45
Achievement Motivation	.65	.52	48	.11
Delayed Gratification (4)	.45	.45	50	.17
Self-Concept (4)	.59	.45	45	−.07
Sexual Identity (3)	.58	.63	33	.38
Moral Judgment	.72	.70	49	.07
Reality Testing	.56	.44	49	.21
Affective				
Happy	.86	.67	51	.35
Sad	.89	.79	51	.15
Angry	.76	.77	51	−.04
Fearful	.82	.50	51	.25
Neutral	.50	.84	51	−.03
Ambivalent	.41	.77	51	.45
Inappropriate Affect	—	—	—	

*The number of pictures pulling each function is indicated in parentheses.

With respect to personality functions, pictures pulling for Interpersonal Relations, Aggression, and Moral Judgment showed the highest levels of internal consistency in the Hispanic sample, whereas Anxiety/Depression, Achievement Motivation, Delayed Gratification, Self-Concept, Sexual Identity, and Reality Testing had low to moderate reliability. For

TABLE 21.4
Interrater Reliabilities for Hispanics and African-American
Samples (N = 27) Across 23 TEMAS Cards

Function	Hispanic Sample		African-American Sample	
	Range r	Median r	Range r	Median r
Cognitive				
Omissions	.54–1.00	.82	.33–1.00	.87
Transformations	.32–.95	.69	.37–1.00	.80
Congruence	.47–1.00	.80	.42–1.00	.69
Affective				
Happy	.70–1.00	.87	.79–1.00	.92
Sad	.70–1.00	.85	.65–1.00	.85
Angry	.55–1.00	.85	.46–1.00	.85
Fearful	.61–1.00	1.00	.40–1.00	.78
Neutral	.30–1.00	.84	.40–1.00	.75
Ambivalent	.55–1.00	.75	.68–1.00	.78
Personality				
Interpersonal Relations	.27–.80	.63	.40–.88	.62
Aggression	.35–.81	.50	.54–.87	.73
Anxiety/Depression	.43–.73	.52	.33–.85	.58
Achievement Motivation	.20–.65	.51	.41–.80	.59
Delayed Gratification	.53–.58	.56	.40–.87	.54
Self-Concept	.59–.84	.65	.38–.73	.59
Sexual Identity	.32–.36	.34	.66–.87	.76
Moral Judgment	.44–1.00	.80	.31–1.00	.69
Reality Testing	.32–.60	.39	.74–.83	.75

African Americans, alphas were again uniformly lower than for Hispanics, with the highest reliabilities associated with Aggression and Moral Judgment. Low reliabilities for the personality functions may be due partially to the fact that personality function scores are based on relatively few TEMAS cards.

The internal consistency reliabilities for the standardization sample differentiated by ethnic/racial group membership for the long form were, for the most part, in the moderate range, with a median coefficient alpha of .83 for the total sample. On these functions, the median reliability ranged from .80 for African-American children to .69 with other Hispanic children. On the short form, internal consistency reliability was generally lower, with a median reliability of .68 for the total sample on the quantitative scales. Reliability coefficients for ethnic/racial groups on these functions ranged from a median coefficient of .65 for the White sample to .54 for the African-American sample. Reliability coefficients on the qualitative indicators were lower due, in large part, to the nonmetric nature of the scoring system used with these scales.

TABLE 21.5
TEMAS Means and Standard Deviations in Six Hispanic Groups

Index	PR Public (n = 140) M	SD	PR Private (n = 140) M	SD	PR Clinic (n = 50) M	SD	NY Public (n = 167) M	SD	NY Clinic (n = 67) M	SD	ARG Public (n = 59) M	SD
Inquiries	.36	.59	.20	.53	.58	.76	.02	.08	.06	.15	.06	.14
Fluency	85.97	27.75	101.64	36.02	68.35	20.72	111.48	40.59	107.22	33.48	181.00	8.43
Time	3.63	1.09	3.41	1.05	1.14	.33	3.78	1.04	3.16	1.32	3.52	1.53
Omissions	1.62	.77	1.60	.59	2.97	.96	.82	.50	1.61	.76	.74	.71
Trans	.17	.18	.11	.01	.21	.73	.12	.11	.18	.19	.17	.19
Conflict	.21	.19	.12	.14	.19	.19	.09	.10	.07	.06	.17	.16
Happy	.40	.20	.43	.22	.40	.21	.47	.21	.33	.22	.32	.18
Sad	.28	.15	.28	.15	.39	.18	.38	.22	.29	.20	.32	.20
Angry	.09	.10	.08	.09	.11	.13	.17	.13	.11	.12	.10	.11
Fearful	.08	.10	.10	.11	.07	.07	.07	.10	.09	.09	.10	.09
Neutral	.13	.25	.10	.19	.17	.26	.05	.08	.06	.16	.01	.13
Ambivalent	.01	.04	.01	.03	.02	.05	.01	.02	.01	.04	.08	.10
Congruence	.06	.09	.03	.06	.07	.11	.02	.03	.05	.12	.03	.10
Person Relat.	2.52	.22	2.67	.29	2.45	.20	2.87	.21	2.49	.33	2.77	.43
Aggression	2.06	.22	2.31	.39	2.14	.25	2.78	.20	2.44	.38	2.66	.42
Anx./Depress.	2.27	.29	2.48	.37	2.16	.22	2.90	.18	2.33	.35	2.58	.37
Ach. Motiv.	2.80	.29	2.92	.30	2.80	.28	3.03	.25	2.79	.35	3.17	.49
Delay Gratif	2.66	.40	2.76	.44	2.55	.37	2.79	.23	2.62	.52	3.14	.61
Self-Concept	2.70	.47	2.89	.50	2.63	.46	3.00	.46	2.73	.33	3.19	.68
Sex. Identity	2.80	.42	2.83	.55	2.64	.48	3.40	.51	2.50	.52	2.76	.88
Moral Judgment	2.32	.31	2.56	.39	2.29	.30	2.91	.36	2.52	.34	2.74	.68
Reality Testing	2.45	.54	2.77	.50	2.47	.37	2.73	.65	2.62	.62	2.77	.71

TABLE 21.6
ANOVA and Scheffé Results Comparing Groups on TEMAS Indices

Index	F(5, 617)	Significant* Scheffé Contrasts
Inquiries	20.65*	3–2, 4, 5, 6; 4–1
Fluency	115.25*	6–1, 2, 3, 4, 5; 3–2, 4, 5; 4–1
Time	70.23*	3–1, 2, 4, 5, 6
Omissions	117.74*	3–1, 2, 4, 5, 6; 4–1, 2, 5; 6–1, 2, 5
Transformations	1.96	none warranted
Conflict	12.09*	1–4, 5; 3–5
Happy	8.87*	4–5, 6
Sad	5.62*	none significant
Angry	6.48*	4–1, 2
Fearful	1.86	none warranted
Neutral	8.15*	3–6
Ambivalent	33.20*	6–1, 2, 3, 4, 5
Congruence	5.19*	none significant
Person Relations	32.96*	3–2, 4, 6; 4–1, 2, 5; 6–1, 5
Aggression	71.70*	1–2, 4, 5, 6; 4–2, 3, 5; 5–3 6–2, 3
Anxiety/Depression	68.93*	4–1, 2, 3, 5, 6; 6–1, 3, 5; 2–3
Achievement Motiv.	20.15*	6–1, 2, 3, 5; 4–1, 3, 5
Delay Gratif.	21.24*	6–1, 2, 3, 4, 5
Self-Concept	15.79*	6–1, 3, 5; 4–3
Sexual Identity	29.30*	6–1, 3, 5; 4–3
Moral Judgment	31.44*	4–1, 2, 3, 5; 6–1, 3
Reality Testing	5.32*	none significant

Note. Group 1 = PR Public, 2 = PR Private, 3 = PR Clinical, 4 = NY Public, 5 = NY Clinical, 6 = ARG Public.

*$p < .001$ (family-wise significance level, $p = .022$).

Test–Retest Reliability (Short Form)

Test–retest stability of the TEMAS functions was computed for the short form by correlating the results of two administrations separated by an 18-week interval. The sample used in this study consisted of 51 subjects chosen at random from the 210 Puerto Rican students screened for behavior problems. Results indicate that TEMAS functions exhibit low to moderate stability over an 18-week period (see Table 21.3). The eight TEMAS functions with significant test–retest correlations are Fluency, Event Transformations, Conflict, Relationships, Happy, Neutral, Anxiety/Depression, and Sexual Identity. Several explanations for the generally low level of test–retest reliability have been proposed. First, it is possible that subjects are inconsistent during this developmental period. Second, test–retest correlations may be lower bound estimates of reliability in this case because different raters were employed at pre- and posttesting. Therefore, they include error variance due to interrater reliability. Third, the indicators from this instrument have limited range, hence the correlation is attenuated. Finally, children who exhibit behavior problems may prove to have less stable scores than children who do not manifest such problems.

Interrater Reliability

The original interrater reliability with the minority version was conducted in 1986; protocols of 27 Hispanic and 26 African-American children were drawn at random from the sample of 73 Hispanics and 42 African Americans described previously in the section on internal consistency of the long form. Each protocol was scored independently by two raters. These scores were then correlated to estimate the degree to which the two raters agreed in their scoring of a particular picture for a given TEMAS personality function.

Interrater reliabilities in scoring Total Omissions and Transformations are generally moderate to high for both the Hispanic and African-American protocols (see Table 21.4). Little difference is evident as a function of ethnic/racial group. Raters generally showed greater agreement in scoring Omissions than Transformations. Although illogical synthesis and integration of ideas regarding resolution of Conflict, Sequencing, Imagination, and Relationships rarely occurred in both samples, available estimates of correlations are suggestive of moderate to high interrater agreement.

For the affective functions, the pattern of correlation between raters is generally high, with no substantive differences between Hispanic and African-American samples. With respect to the personality functions, correlations are low to moderate for Reality Testing and Sexual Identity in the Hispanic sample and substantially higher for the remaining functions. Contrary to the pattern of internal consistency reliability estimates, the interrater reliabilities obtained for the Hispanic are generally higher than for the African-American sample.

Interrater reliability was also established in a recent study of the non-minority version of the TEMAS Short Form (Costantino, Malgady, Casullo, & Castillo, 1991). Two experienced clinical psychologists (one with extensive training scoring TEMAS and the other a newly trained scorer) independently rated 20 protocols. The results of this study indicate that there is a high interrater agreement in scoring protocols for personality functions ranging from 75% to 95%. The mean level of interrater agreement was 81%, and in no cases were the two independent ratings different than one rating scale point.

It is important to clarify that whereas the interrater agreement for personality functions in the first interrater reliability study ranged from 31% to 100%, in the recent study, the interrater agreement ranged from 75% to 95%. The explanation for this discrepancy is that, during the first study, which was conducted in 1986, the TEMAS scoring system was still undergoing changes; in the second study, which was conducted in 1990, the scoring system and instructions were completely formulated.

Content Validity

TEMAS pictures were designed to pull for specific personality functions based on the nature of the psychological conflict represented in each picture. As previously described in the scoring section, all TEMAS pictures are scored for at least two personality functions. A study was conducted to assess the concordance among a sample of practicing school ($N = 8$) and clinical ($N = 6$) psychologists regarding the pulls of each TEMAS picture for specific personality functions. With respect to ethnicity, seven were White, one was African American, and six were Hispanic. The clinical orientations of the psychologists in this sample included eclectic, psychoanalytic, cognitive, and ego psychology. Those psychologists were presented the TEMAS pictures in random order and were asked individually to indicate which, if any, of the nine functions were pulled by each picture. The percentage of agreement among the 14 clinicians reveals high agreement (71%–100%) across the pictures, thus confirming the pulls scored for specific personality functions.

Relationship to Other Measures

A group of 210 Puerto Rican children screened for behavior problems were administered a number of measures along with the TEMAS; their adaptive behavior in experimental role-playing situations was observed and rated by psychological examiners. The measures administered included: the Sentence Completion Test of Ego Development (SCT; Loevinger & Wessler, 1970) or its Spanish version (Brenes-Jette, 1987); the Trait Anxiety Scale of the State–Trait Anxiety Inventory for Children (STAIC; Spielberger, Edwards, Lushene, Montuori, & Platzek, 1973) or its Spanish version, *Inventario de Ansiedad Rasgo-Estago Para Ninos* (Villamil, 1973); the Teacher Behavior Rating scale (TBR; Costantino, 1980, described in subject screening); and the parallel Mother Behavior Rating Scale (MBR; Costantino, 1980) in both English and Spanish. Finally, the children participated in four experimental role-playing situations designed to elicit adaptive behavior.

Results of the regression analyses indicate that TEMAS profiles significantly ($p < .05$) predicted ego development (SCT), $R = .39$; teachers' behavior ratings (TBR), $R = .49$; delayed gratification (DG), $R = .32$; self-concept of competence (SCC), $R = .50$; disruptive behavior (DIS), $R = .51$; and aggressive behavior (AGG), $R = .32$. However, the multiple correlation for predicting trait anxiety was not significant. TEMAS functions accounted for between 10% (for DG and AGG) and 26% (for DIS) of the variability in scores on the criterion measures.

Predictive validity was established using hierarchical multiple regression analysis to assess the utility of TEMAS profiles for predicting post-therapy scores ($N = 123$) on the criterion measures independent of pre-therapy scores. Results of these analyses show that pretherapy TEMAS profiles significantly predicted all therapeutic outcomes, ranging from 6% to 22% variance increments, except for observation of self-concept of competence. Overcome measures were the sentence-completion test of ego development (14%) Trait Anxiety Inventory for children (22%), Conners Behavior Rating Scale (6%), and observational tasks measuring delayed gratification (20%), disruptive behavior (17%), and aggression (14%).

Multicultural Validity Studies

A systematic program of TEMAS research has been carried out at the Hispanic Research Center, Fordham University, and the Sunset Park Mental Health Center of Lutheran Medical Center. Herein we summarize a few of the studies. Costantino, Malgady, and Vazquez (1981) conducted a study with 72 Hispanic children (mostly Dominican and Puerto Rican) in fourth and fifth grades attending public schools in New York City. The study assessed the responsiveness of the Hispanic children to the TEMAS compared with the TAT (Murray, 1943). Results indicate that the participants were more verbally fluent to TEMAS pictures than TAT pictures. Furthermore, results indicate that bilingual participants were more likely to respond in Spanish to the TEMAS and switch from English on the TAT to Spanish on the TEMAS.

The results on the language of choice in telling stories on the TEMAS and TAT give support to Thompson's (1949) assumption that similarity between the projective characters' physical features and the examinees' increase the identification of examinees with the characters and produce more fluent stories. They also give support to the face validity of TEMAS by showing that the projective characters looked Hispanic and the themes and settings were culturally familiar to them, hence the examinees felt compelled to tell the stories in Spanish. In contrast, they perceived the TAT characters as *gringo*, hence they were motivated to tell the stories in English.

The results also show the relationship between culturally relevant stimuli and language. The latter hypothesis has been widely confirmed in cross-cultural studies using the Fruit Tree Drawing Test. South African and Australian children who spoke both English and their indigenous dialects were instructed in English in a research situation to draw a fruit tree; they drew a tree (e.g., apple, cherry) that grows in English-speaking countries or around the houses of English settlers. Conversely, when instructed in their native dialects, they drew a banana bush tree, which grows in their own environment (Adler, 1982).

Another study conducted by Bernal (1991) in Los Angeles assessed the emic validity of TEMAS versus the Roberts Apperception Test for children (RATC). Examinees were 40 (24 female and 16 males) 12-year-old Mexican-American and Anglo-American children. The Vineland Adaptive Behavior Scales Survey Form or Classroom Edition were utilized to define participants' adjustment, and the System of Multicultural Pluralistic Assessment (SOMPA) Urban Acculturation Scale was utilized to define acculturation level. Results indicate that both the RATC and TEMAS were valid instruments for assessing personality functioning among Anglo-American children. However, the TEMAS was a more culturally sensitive projective test to assess personality functioning among Mexican-American children, as indicated by the mean scores on the TEMAS cognitive, personality, and affective scales, which were not significantly different across acculturation groups. These findings were not true for both the RATC Adaptive Scales and Clinical Scales mean scores.

Hence, the TEMAS test appears to be a culturally sensitive and appropriate assessment instrument for assessing personality functioning among Mexican- and Anglo-American children. This study is important in many ways. First, it shows that the TEMAS test, which was standardized in New York City area primarily with Puerto Ricans and other Caribbean Hispanics, is appropriate with west coast Hispanics and Mexican Americans. Second, it shows more emic validity with the Mexican students, both nonaccultured and accultured ones, than the RATC. Third, studies assessing the appropriateness of projective tests with ethnic minority populations are scarce, and traditionally such research has overlooked acculturation issues.

In another study, Costantino and Malgady (1983) administered the minority and nonminority versions of TEMAS and TAT to 72 Hispanics, 41 African-American, and 43 White examinees in Grades K to 6 in a fully integrated elementary public school in New York City. Results indicate that Hispanics and African Americans were more verbally fluent on both TEMAS tests compared with the TAT. Hispanics and African Americans were more verbally fluent on the minority TEMAS than the nonmimority TEMAS.

Encouraged by these results, the following two studies investigated the clinical utility of TEMAS with African-American, Hispanic, and White children. Costantino, Malgady, Rogler, and Tsui (1988) investigated the clinical utility of TEMAS discriminating public school and clinical Hispanic and African-American children. The participants were 100 outpatients at mental health centers and 373 public school students from low socioeconomic status (SES) urban families. All examinees were tested individually by examiners of the same ethnicity. Results indicate that TEMAS profiles significantly ($p < .001$) discriminated the two groups and explained 21% of the variance independent of ethnicity, age, and SES. Classification accuracy, based on the discriminate function, was 89%. The TEMAS profiles interacted with ethnicity; better discrimination was evident for Hispanics than African Americans.

Costantino, Malgady, Colon-Malgady, and Bailey (1992) investigated the validity of the nonminority version by discriminating 49 public school and 36 outpatient White examinees of low to middle SES households. Results indicate that TEMAS profiles significantly ($p < .001$) discriminated between the normal functioning and clinical groups, with 86% classification accuracy. These last two studies are important because they establish the differential clinical utility of the minority and nonminority with the three major normative groups—African Americans, Hispanics, and non-Hispanic Whites.

Cross-Cultural Validity Studies

The cross-cultural validity of TEMAS was investigated in New York City, San Juan, Puerto Rico, and Buenos Aires, Argentina, (Costantino, Malgady, Casullo, & Castillo, 1991). This research compared the normative profiles, reliability, and criterion-related validity of TEMAS with school and clinical children from the three different Hispanic cultures.

The native Puerto Rican children were public and private school students ($n = 280$) and psychiatric outpatients ($n = 50$) from San Juan, Puerto Rico. The school sample consisted of 140 public and 140 private school students nearly equally distributed with respect to gender in kindergarten through sixth grade.

The New York Puerto Rican examinees consisted of 167 first to sixth graders in public schools and 67 outpatients from a community mental health center, both groups nearly equally distributed with respect to gender. The public school students' mean age was 9.26, whereas the outpatient children were slightly older ($M = 10.15$ years). All New York examinees were from low to lower middle SES families (Hollingshead SES $M = 4.64$). The clinical and public school samples were also comparable in terms of household composition: The father was present in only 31% of the households. About half of the clinical children were diagnosed as having adjustment disorders. The next most common diagnosis was conduct disorder (22%), followed by developmental disorder (14%). The remaining cases were diagnosed as anxiety disorders.

The South American examinees were 59 public school children from Grades 2 to 7 in Buenos Aires, Argentina, once again nearly equally divided by gender, with a mean age of 9.67. These children were largely from middle-class families in which fathers were primarily employed in managerial or professional occupations and mothers were either house-wives or employed in skilled occupations. To assess concurrent validity of TEMAS, the children were also administered the Trait scale of Spiel-berger's State–Trait Anxiety Inventory (*Inventario de Ansiedad Estado Y Rasgo para Ninos*), the Piers–Harris Self-Concept scale (Spanish transla-tion), and the NIMH Center for Epidemiological Studies–Depression scale (CES–D; Spanish translation). Validity estimation for New York Puerto Ricans has been reported elsewhere (see Costantino et al., 1988). Officials in the Argentina public schools permitted only the Piers–Harris scale to be administered.

Results show that the groups differed significantly on all major cogni-tive indexes except transformations, all affective functions except fearful-ness, and on all personality functions. Comparisons among Puerto Rican samples (see Tables 21.5 and 21.6) revealed that the clinical children required more inquiries or prompts to complete a story and told shorter stories than the private school children; they also spoke for less time and more often omitted details (characters, settings, events) than both the public and private school samples. Affectively, there were no significant differences between these three groups. With regard to personality func-tioning, private school children had themes expressing more adaptive person relations and greater control of anxiety and depressive feelings than the clinical children; they also had better control of aggressive im-pulses than public school children.

The Puerto Rican children in New York public schools differed cogni-tively from their clinical counterparts in a tendency to commit fewer omissions, and affectively in expressing happier themes. The public school children also related themes expressing more adaptive person relations, control of aggression, control of anxiety/depression, achievement moti-vation, sexual identity, and moral judgment.

Among public school children, native Puerto Ricans required more inquiries, were less fluent, and demonstrated less recognition of conflict than New York Puerto Ricans; they made more omissions than both New York and Argentinean children. Argentinean children were more verbally fluent than New York children. Affectively, New York children expressed happier themes than Argentineans, but paradoxically angrier themes than native Puerto Ricans. Conversely, Argentinean children's stories were more ambivalent than the other two subcultures.

In terms of personality functioning, the New York Puerto Rican and Argentinean children expressed themes with more adaptive person rela-tions, control of aggression, achievement motivation, and moral judgment than native Puerto Rican children. New York children's stories also revealed more adaptive control of anxious/depressive feelings and sexual identity than did Argentinean or Puerto Rican children's stories. However, Argentinean children expressed the most ability to delay gratification and also expressed more positive self-concept than Puerto Rican children.

The comparisons between the native and New York Puerto Rican clinical groups revealed consistently higher cognitive functioning in the latter sample. New York Puerto Ricans required fewer prompts to complete stories, had lengthier stories, spent more time telling stories, omitted fewer details, and more often recognized the conflict depicted in the TEMAS pictures. In general, the results of the present study lend support to the use of TEMAS with examinees in Puerto Rico and Argentina.

The Argentinean children who were administered the nonminority short form showed significantly higher means on six of the nine personality functions (i.e., more adaptive profiles) than native Puerto Ricans, but largely on par with the New York group. This difference in normative profile may be attributable to several factors, such as the different number of TEMAS pictures, differential training of examiners, and psychosocial or sociopolitical conditions. Further analyses indicate the need to revise the characteristics of some of the individual pictures because the characters, setting, and events of some pictures were not appropriate for the Argentinean and Puerto Rican cultures. New TEMAS cards were redesigned as results of these findings, as discussed later.

In another cross-cultural study, Costantino, Malgady, Gomez-Dupertuis, and Faiola's (1997) examinees were 46 nonclinical Argentinean (25 males and 21 females) elementary school children from Buenos Aires and 44 Peruvian (25 males and 19 females) elementary school children from Lima. The groups were relatively homogeneous in age; the Argentinean students had a mean age of 9.33 years and the Peruvians had a mean age of 9.50 years. The Peruvian sample was composed of children whose parents generally had high school, normal school, or university educations. The 23-card version of TEMAS was administered in Spanish to the Argentinean and Peruvian children. The Argentinean children were administered the nonminority form because all children were of European descent. The Peruvian children were administered the minority version of TEMAS because all examinees were of native South American descent. The TEMAS protocols for both groups were scored according to the standardization procedures.

The means and standard deviations of the main TEMAS scoring indexes for the Argentinean and Peruvian samples are presented in Table 21.7. The reported scores represent averages across pictures. The mean scores of the two groups were compared by independent t tests for each TEMAS index. The between-group variances were compared using the Levene Test, which indicated that in no case were they significantly different.

TABLE 21.7
Means, Standard Deviations, and *t* tests Comparing Argentinean
and Peruvian Children on TEMAS Indices (*N* = 90)

Index	Argentina (*n* = 46)		Peru (*n* = 44)		
	M	SD	M	SD	t
Inquiries	.02	.09	.009	.04	1.04
Fluency	87.77	25.49	61.87	43.18	3.48*
Time	2.45	.91	3.08	1.09	2.62
Omissions	.16	.12	.74	.42	8.88*
Omission/Event	.08	.09	.37	.23	7.88*
Omission/Setting	.03	.05	.18	.16	−5.85*
Omission/Secondary Character	.05	.06	.14	.12	−4.44*
Omission/Main Character	.004	.01	.02	.04	−3.08
Transformations	.26	.22	.14	.24	2.57
Transformation/Secondary Character	.09	.09	.02	.05	4.33*
Conflict	.26	.24	.13	.19	2.95
Happy	.38	.20	.22	.13	4.51*
Sad	.23	.14	.13	.19	2.95
Angry	.20	.11	.13	.12	
Fearful	.18	.14	.17	.12	.24
Neutral	.08	.15	.08	.13	.04
Ambivalent	.12	.12	.04	.01	3.63*
Congruence	.02	.06	.01	.04	1.53
Person Relations	2.64	.16	2.57	.24	1.58
Aggression	2.52	.23	2.53	.36	−.19
Anxiety/Depression	2.48	.23	2.52	.37	−.70
Achievement Motivation	2.74	.22	2.71	.56	.58
Delayed Gratification	2.68	.32	2.64	.30	.66
Self-Concept	2.83	.20	2.72	.29	2.21
Sexual Identity	2.78	.33	2.83	.26	−.78
Moral Judgment	2.47	.30	2.48	.33	−.15
Reality Testing	2.61	.26	2.60	.36	.13

*$p < .001$ (family-wise significance level, $p = .027$).

Because of the large number of univariate comparisons being made, the
Bonferroni test was applied with a level of .001, giving a family-wise
significance level of .027. An analysis of variance (ANOVA) was also
performed to test for the effects of country and gender of subjects. No
significant interactions were found, and there were no main effects for
gender.

Significant differences between the two groups were found in the area
of cognitive functioning. The results indicate that the Argentinean children
had significantly higher verbal fluency scores than the Peruvian children,
with an effect size of .6 *SD* units. The most notable differences between
the two groups were in the area of omissions. The Peruvian children had

significantly more than the Argentineans, with an effect size of 4.8 SD units. Of the different types of omissions (i.e., inattention to essential aspects of the stimulus pictures, which include omissions of event, omissions of primary character, omissions of secondary character, and omissions of settings), omissions of event contributed the greatest amount of variance. Omissions of setting and secondary character were also significant. Coupled with the significant difference between the two groups on omissions, there was also a significant difference on the conflict score. The latter indicates that the Peruvian children produced stories that did not acknowledge or resolve the pulled-for interpersonal conflict embodied by the story to a greater extent than the Argentinean children. Although there was no significant difference between the two groups in the total number of transformations for each picture, the Argentinean children scored significantly higher on transformations of secondary character than the Peruvian children.

The two groups also differed in terms of affective functions. The Argentineans expressed significantly more happy affect in their themes than did the Peruvians, with an effect size of 1.23 SD units. The two groups did not differ significantly in the expression of other affects. However, in terms of percentage of total affective responses given, the Peruvian children expressed sad affect in 31.41% of their affect responses, compared with 23.14% for the Argentinean children.

The Argentinean and Peruvian children did not show significant differences on any of the nine personality functions pulled for on the stimulus cards. The major difference between the two groups was seen in the high number of N responses scored by the Peruvians. N scores are related to omissions scores. The Peruvian students' high Ns accentuated that they frequently responded with stories that did not incorporate the pulled-for personality functions.

This study presents some interesting results with respect to the cross-cultural and multicultural sensitivity of TEMAS as applied to the two diverse Hispanic cultures tested. Cultural similarities and differences of the two groups are highlighted, as well as the effects of sociopolitical variables on cognitive styles and functioning. A previous study that compared cognitive, affective, and personality functions of children from Argentina and Puerto Rico with New York children of Puerto Rican descent indicated that there were significant differences in areas of cognitive, affective, and personality functioning as measured by TEMAS functions (Costantino, Malgady, Casullo, & Castillo, 1991).

That such differences were demonstrated, along with the support for the concurrent validity provided by other assessment instruments, supports the utility of TEMAS for personality assessment with the Argentinean and Puerto Rican children as well as the New York children of Puerto Rican descent, which represents one of the major cultural groups for whom TEMAS was originally standardized. The Argentinean and Peruvian children under present investigation did not manifest differences in personality functions, perhaps indicating the relative degree of cultural similarity between the two groups.

At the same time, the significant cognitive differences between the Argentinean and Peruvian responses must be acknowledged. To some extent, the differences may be explained as a consequence of sociopolitical and psychosocial variables in the two countries at the time the data for this study were collected. The year 1989 was a time of considerable social turmoil and demographic change in Peru. As a result of insurgent activity by the Sentero Luminoso, a considerable portion of the rural population of the country relocated. Of the Peruvian children tested, a number had fathers who were in the military, some of whom were deceased. The Omissions scale of TEMAS serves as a clinical indicator of repression or selective inattention (Costantino, Malgady, Colon-Malgady, & Bailey, 1992; Costantino, Malgady, & Rogler, 1988). The relatively higher score on Omissions by the Peruvian children may be reflective of psychological distress caused by stimuli presenting potentially violent situations and a relative cognitive inability to make sense of them. Because all potentially mediating variables were not controlled for in the collection of the data for the present study, the sources of variability can only be speculated at present. Further investigation, with greater control of variables, is indicated for a future study. An important difference between Peru and Argentina relates to the ethnic composition of the populations. The population of Lima is largely mestizo and indigenous, whereas Buenos Aires is predominantly European. The more open expression of happy affect by the Argentinean subjects and the relatively higher percentage of expression of sadness by the Peruvians may reflect ethnocultural differences in expression of affectivity. Indigenous populations in the Americas tend to internalize emotions to a large degree. The combined effect of traditional culture, sociopolitical marginalization, and exploitation contribute to a sense of helplessness and passivity. The difference in happy response of Argentinean and Peruvian children may be associated with ethnocultural and psychosocial factors in expression of happy emotions.

This study is a preliminary investigation for a more thorough cross-cultural TEMAS standardization. Although the relative similarity of scores of the Argentinean and Peruvian groups on personality functions indicates that TEMAS is appropriate for both groups, differences in cognitive scores, such as omissions and conflict, must be investigated with greater control of mediating variables.

DISCUSSION

The development of projective instruments with both emic and etic validity and the collection of multicultural and cross-cultural norms is an
arduous process that has spanned more than half a century (Costantino,
Malgady, & Rogler, 1988; Dana, 1986, 1993; Exner & Weiner, 1994; Henry,
1945; Murray, 1943; Thompson, 1949; Williams, 1972). The standardization
of TEMAS on Hispanic, African-American, and White children in the
United States and our gathering of comparative normative data on native
Puerto Rican, Argentinean, and Peruvian children is a systematic attempt
to create a projective test that has multicultural and cross-cultural validity
(Dana, 1993, 1996; Ritzler, 1993, 1996). In addition, the cross-cultural
research with postwar adjustment of Salvadoran children showed that
the two TEMAS cards and two WISC-RM subtests with other observed
cognitive functions were the two most valid measures in assessing the
psychosocial functioning of 54 Salvadoran children exposed to the war.
More recently, the authors also reported that the TEMAS stories of well-
adjusted Salvadoran children showed themes with an "optimistic vision
of the future" (Walton, Nuttall, & Vazquez-Nuttall, 1997, 1998).
    In a way, TEMAS research is similar to the early attempts to use the
TAT in cross-cultural studies (Henry, 1947). It is also like Avila-Espada's
(1986) development of a comprehensive scoring system for the TAT and
norms for European Hispanics to assess, among other variables, interpersonal functioning, aggression, depression, and achievement motivation.
In another way, our research has followed Anastasi's (1988) suggestion
and followed the TAT as a valuable model to develop a more valid and
culturally sensitive projective instrument (Dana, 1993, 1996; Elliot, 1998;
Flanagan & DiGiuseppe, 1999).
    The minority version of the TEMAS apperception test was originally
developed as a clinical tool to present ethnically/racially familiar characters
in urban and fantasy settings to facilitate minority children's identification
with the stimuli and thereby enhance verbal fluency and self-disclosure.
Earlier studies with New York City examinees indicated that Hispanic and
African-American children were indeed more verbally fluent in telling
stories about TEMAS pictures in comparison with TAT pictures (Costantino & Malgady, 1983; Costantino, Malgady, & Vasquez, 1981).
    Other studies established the reliability of TEMAS and gave some
evidence of concurrent validity and clinical utility in detecting psychotherapeutic outcomes (Costantino et al., 1988; Malgady et al., 1984). Additional studies have shown the predictive validity of the TEMAS achievement motivation with multicultural youths in the United States (Cardalda,
1995; Cardalda, Costantino, Malgady, & Maron, 1998; Torres, 1996) and
children in El Salvador (Walton, Nuttall, & Vazquez-Nuttall, 1997, 1998).

The results of the two cross-cultural studies lend support to the use of TEMAS with children and adolescents in Puerto Rico, Argentina, and Peru. However, further analyses in this study suggested that the characters, settings, and themes of some pictures were not appropriate in Argentinean and Puerto Rican cultures. Hence, several cards were redesigned to depict more culturally relevant settings and events for those countries. For example, when responding to Card 1, which shows a typical New York City urban setting with Brownstones, the Puerto Rican and Argentinean children often remarked, "why all these houses have outside stairs" because houses and buildings in these two Latin countries have stairs inside the main entrances. New pictures, which are used in research, have been redesigned to depict European architecture styles that are prevalent in the Hispanic Caribbean countries and South America. In addition, one picture (Card 15) was redrawn to show children playing soccer instead of basketball; in the same picture, a policeman rewarding a baseball team was redrawn to depict a coach rewarding a soccer team. Similarly, a picture showing report card grades of "A" and "F" was changed to the Argentinean school systems of "10" and "1," respectively.

It was interesting to note that the majority of these children scored lowest in moral judgment and reality testing because they perceived the P.A.L. policeman/coach (in Card 15) as a punitive agent. These results were related to sociopolitical events, as Argentina was emerging from a military regime in which the police were perceived as punitive authority in 1984 to 1985 when the study was completed. These redesigned TEMAS cards were used in subsequent studies in Argentina and Peru.

A new set of TEMAS pictures has been created for Asian-American children and adolescents in the United States. Preliminary results of a pilot study indicate that Asian-American examinees exhibit higher verbal fluency and more adaptive themes when responding to the Asian-American version than to the nonminority version of TEMAS (Costantino, Tsui, Lee, Flanagan, & Malgady, 1998).

The TEMAS research demonstrates that the standardization of a thematic apperception test in both multicultural and cross-cultural settings must take into serious account variations in the stimuli necessitated by many aspects of cultural and ethnic diversity. The multicultural and cross-cultural validity of this projective test depends on a continuing program of research to refine its psychometric properties (Dana, 1993; Flanagan & DiGiuseppe, in press; Ritzler, 1996).

ACKNOWLEDGMENTS

Parts of this chapter were published in the following publications: Costantino, G., Malgady, R. G., & Rogler, L. H. (1988). *TEMAS (Tell-Me-A-Story) Manual*, Western Psychological Services, Los Angeles, CA; Costantino, G.,

Malgady, R. G., Casullo, M. M. and Castillo, A. (1991). Cross-cultural standardization of TEMAS in three Hispanic subcultures. *Hispanic Journal of Behavioral Sciences, 13,* 48–62; Costantino, G., Malgady, R. G., Gomez-Dupertuis, D., & Faiola, T. (1997, July). Cross-cultural standardization of TEMAS with Argentinean and Peruvian children. ICP Cross-Cultural Conference, Padua, Italy. The authors would like to thank Drs. Joan Riley Walton, Ronald L. Nuttal, Ena Vazquez Nuttall, Elsa Cardalda, Tresa Elliot, and Gloria Torres for their contributions to the multi- and cross-cultural TEMAS research and to Drs. Richard Dana, Barry Ritzler, Rosemary Flanagan, and Raymond DiGiuseppe for their constructive reviews.

Material from the *TEMAS (Tell-Me-A-Story) Manual,* copyright © 1988 by Western Psychological Services, was reprinted by permission of the publisher, Western Psychological Services, Wilshire Boulevard, Los Angeles, California, 90025, USA. This material should not be reprinted in whole or in part for any additional purpose without the expressed, written permission of the publisher. All rights reserved.

REFERENCES

Adler, L. L. (1982). Children's drawings as an indicator of individual preferences reflecting group values: A programmatic study. In L. Loeb Adler (Ed.), *Cross-cultural research at issue* (pp. 71–97). New York: Academic Press.

American Psychological Association. (1993). Guidelines for providers of psychological services to ethnic, linguistic and culturally diverse populations. *American Psychologist, 4,* 45–48.

Anastasi, A. (1988). *Psychological testing* (6th ed.). New York: Macmillan.

Atkinson, H. W. (1981). Studying personality in the context of advanced motivational psychology. *American Psychologist, 36,* 117–128.

Avila-Espada, A. (1986). *Manual operativo para el Test de Apercepcion Tematica.* Madrid: Ediciones Piramide, South America.

Bailey, B. E., & Green, J. I. (1977). Black thematic apperception test stimulus material. *Journal of Personality Assessment, 41*(1), 25–30.

Bandura, A. (1977). *Social learning theory.* Englewood Cliffs, NJ: Prentice-Hall.

Bandura, A., & Walters, R. H. (1959). *Adolescent aggression.* New York: Ronald.

Bandura, A., & Walters, R. H. (1967). *Social learning and personality development.* New York: W. W. Norton.

Bernal, I. (1991). *The relationship between level of acculturation, the Robert's Apperception Test for Children, and the TEMAS (Tell-Me-A-Story).* Unpublished doctoral dissertation, California School of Professional Psychology, Los Angeles.

Brenes-Jette, C. (1987). *Mother's contribution to an early intervention program for Hispanic children.* Unpublished doctoral dissertation, New York University.

Cardalda, E. (1995). *Socio-cognitive correlates to school achievement using the TEMAS (Tell-Me-A-Story) culturally sensitive test with 6th, 7th, and 8th grade Puerto Rican students.* Unpublished doctoral dissertation, New School for Social Research, New York.

Cardalda, E., Costantino, G., Malgady, R. G., & Maron, N. (1998, August). *Multicultural achievement motivation as assessed by TEMAS.* Poster presented at the 106th annual APA Convention, San Francisco, CA.

Cook, R. A. (1953). Identification and ego defensive in thematic apperception. *Journal of Projective Techniques, 17*, 312–315.

Costantino, G. (1978, November). *TEMAS, a new thematic apperception test to measure ego functions and development in urban Black and Hispanic children*. Paper presented at the 2nd annual conference on Fantasy and Imaging Process, Chicago, IL.

Costantino, G. (1980). Development of the Teacher Behavior Rating Scale and of the Mother Behavior Rating Scale. New York: Fordham University.

Costantino, G. (1992). Overcoming bias in educational assessment of Hispanic students. In K. F. Geisinger (Ed.), *Psychological testing of Hispanics* (pp. 89–98). Washington, DC: American Psychological Association.

Costantino, G., Colon-Malgady, G., Malgady, R. G., & Perez, A. (1991). Assessment of attention deficit disorder using a thematic apperception test. *Journal of Personality Assessment, 57*, 87–95.

Costantino, G., & Malgady, R. G. (1983). Verbal fluency of Hispanic, Black and White children on TAT and TEMAS, a new thematic apperception test. *Hispanic Journal of Behavioral Sciences, 5*, 199–206.

Costantino, G., & Malgady, R. G. (1996). Development of TEMAS, a multicultural thematic apperception test: Psychometric properties and clinical utility. In G. R. Sodowsky & J. C. Impara (Eds.), *Multicultural assessment in counseling and clinical psychology* (pp. 85–136). Lincoln, NE: Buros Institute of Mental Measurements, University of Nebraska–Lincoln.

Costantino, G., & Malgady, G. R. (1997). Modification of the TEMAS (Tell-Me-A-Story) Test Scoring. Brooklyn, NY: Sunset Park Mental Health Center of Lutheran Medical Center.

Costantino, G., Malgady, R., Casullo, M. M., & Castillo, A. (1991). Cross-cultural standardization of TEMAS in three Hispanic subcultures. *Hispanic Journal of Behavioral Sciences, 13*, 48–62.

Costantino, G., Malgady, R. G., Colon-Malgady, G., & Bailey, J. (1992). Clinical utility of the TEMAS with non-minority children. *Journal of Personality Assessment, 59*, 433–438.

Costantino, G., Malgady, R. G., Gomez-Dupertuis, & Faiola, T. (1997, July). *Cross-cultural standardization of TEMAS with Argentinean and Peruvian children*. Paper presented at the ICP Cross-Cultural conference, Padua, Italy.

Costantino, G., Malgady, R., & Rogler, L. (1988). *TEMAS (Tell-Me-A-Story) manual* (chaps. 1–7). Los Angeles, CA: Western Psychological Services.

Costantino, G., Malgady, R. G., Rogler, L. H., & Tsui, E. (1988). Discriminant analysis of clinical outpatients and public school children by TEMAS: A thematic apperception test for Hispanics and Blacks. *Journal of Personality Assessment, 52*, 670–678.

Costantino, G., Malgady, R. G., & Vaszquez, C. (1981). A comparison of the Murray TAT and a new thematic apperception test for urban Hispanic children. *Hispanic Journal of Behavioral Sciences, 3*, 291–300.

Costantino, G., Tsui, E., Lee, J., Flanagan, R., & Malgady, R. G. (1998). *Validation of the Asian-American version of TEMAS: Case studies*. New York: St. John's University.

Cowan, G., & Goldberg, E. (1967). Need achievement as a function of the race and sex of figures in selected TAT cards. *Journal of Personality and Social Psychology, 5*, 245–249.

Dana, R. H. (1986). Personality assessment practice in native americans. *Journal of Personality Assessment, 50*, 480–500.

Dana, R. H. (1993). *Multicultural assessment perceptive for professional psychology*. Boston, MA: Allyn & Bacon.

Dana, R. H. (1996). Culturally competent assessment practice in the United States. *Journal of Personality Assessment, 66*, 472–487.

Elliot, T. L. (1998). *Differential validation of the TEMAS (Tell-Me-A-Story) with Rorschach as criterion: A comparison of projective methods*. Unpublished doctoral dissertation, Long Island University, New York.

Exner, J. E., & Weiner, I. B. (1994). *The Rorschach: A comprehensive system: Vol. 3. Assessment of children and adolescents* (2nd ed.). New York: Wiley.

Flanagan, R., Anderson, T., Ferri-Siegel, V., & Costantino, G. (1999, Nov.). The use of rational-emotive education to promote growth in children's coping as assessed by the TEMAS: A Work in Progress. Poster Proposal accepted for the Annual Convention of the Association for Advancement of Behavior Therapy, Toronto.

Flanagan, R., & DiGiuseppe, R. (1999). A critical review of the TEMAS: A step within the Development of Thematic Apperception Instruments. *Psychology in the schools.*

Fuchs, D. (1986, August). *You can take a test out of a situation, but you cannot take the situation out of a test: Bias in minority assessment.* Paper presented at the 94th annual American Psychological Association Convention, Washington, DC.

Goh, D., & Fuller, G. B. (1983). Current practices in the assessment of personality by school psychologists. *School Psychology Review, 12,* 240–243.

Henry, W. E. (1947). The thematic apperception technique in the study of culture–personality relations. *Genetic Psychology Monograph, 35,* 3–135.

Hutton, J. B., Dubes, R., & Muir, F. (1992). Assessment practices of school psychologists, 10 years later. *School Psychology Review, 21,* 271–284.

Kennedy, M. L., Faust, D., Willis, W. G., & Piotrowski, C. (1994). Socio-emotional assessment practices in school psychology. *Journal of Psychoeducational Assessment, 12,* 228–240.

Light, B. H. (1955). A further test of the Thompson TAT rationale. *Journal of Abnormal Social Psychology, 51,* 148–150.

Loevinger, J., & Wessler, R. (1970). *Measuring ego development 1: Construction and use of a sentence completion test.* San Francisco: Jossey-Bass.

Lopez, S. R. (1988). Empirical basis of ethnocultural and linguistic bias in mental health evaluations of Hispanics. *American Psychologist, 24,* 120–126.

Malgady, R. G. (1996). The question of cultural bias in assessment and diagnosis of ethnic minority clients: Let's reject the null hypothesis. *Professional Psychology: Research and Practice, 27,* 1–5.

Malgady, R. G., Costantino, G., & Rogler, L. H. (1984). Development of a thematic apperception test (TEMAS) for urban Hispanic children. *Journal of Consulting and Clinical Psychology, 52,* 986–996.

Malgady, R. G., Rogler, L. H., & Costantino, G. (1987). Ethnocultural and linguistic bias in mental health evaluation of Hispanics. *American Psychologist, 42,* 228–234.

Malgady, R. G., Rogler, L. H., & Costantino, G. (1988). Reply to the empirical basis for ethnocultural and linguistic bias in mental health evaluations of Hispanics. *American Psychologist, 43,* 1097.

McArthur, D. S., & Roberts, G. E. (1982). *Technical manual: The Roberts Apperception Test for Children.* Los Angeles: Western Psychological Services.

Murray, H. A. (1943). *Thematic Apperception Test Manual.* Cambridge: Harvard University Press.

Murstein, B. L. (1963). *Theory and research in projective techniques.* New York: Wiley.

Murstein, B. L. (1972). Normative written responses for a college sample. *Journal of Personality Assessment, 41,* 194–247.

Ness, M. K. (1985). *Review of themes concerning Blacks.* In J. V. Mitchell, Jr. (Ed.), *The ninth mental measurements yearbook* (p. 1618). Lincoln, NE: The University of Nebraska Press.

Olmedo, E. L. (1981). Testing linguistic minorities. *American Psychologist, 36,* 1078–1085.

Padilla, A. M. (1979). Critical factors in the testing of Hispanic Americans: A review and some suggestions for the future. In R. Tyler & S. White (Eds.), *Testing, teaching, and learning: Report conference on testing* (pp. 219–243). Washington, DC: National Institute of Education.

Padilla, A. M., & Medina, (1996). Using tests in culturally appropriate ways. In L. A. Suzuki, P. J. Meller, & J. G. Ponterotto (Eds.), *Handbook of multicultural assessment: Clinical, psychological, and educational applications* (pp. 3–28). San Francisco: Jossey-Bass.

Paivio, A. (1971). *Imagery and verbal processes.* New York: Holt, Rinehart & Winston.

Piaget, J., & Inhelder, B. (1971). *Mental imagery in the child.* New York: Basic Books.

Ritzler, B. (1993). A new slant on an old theme. *Journal of Psychoeducational Assessment, 11,* 381–389.

Ritzler, B. (1996). Projective methods for multicultural personality assessment: Rorschach TEMAS, and the Early Memories Procedures. In L. A. Suzuki, P. J. Meller, & J. G. Ponterotto (Eds.), *Handbook of multicultural assessment: Clinical, psychological, and educational applications* (pp. 115–135). San Francisco: Jossey-Bass.

Schwartz, E., Reiss, B., & Cottingham, A. (1951). Further critical evaluation of the Negro version of the TAT. *Journal of Projective Techniques, 15,* 394–400.

Spielberger, C. D., Edwards, C. D., Lushene, R. E., Montuori, J., & Platzek, D. (1973). *Preliminary test manual for the State-Trait Anxiety Inventory for Children.* Palo Alto, CA: Consulting Psychologist Press.

Sullivan, H. S. (1953). *The interpersonal theory of psychiatry.* New York: W. W. Norton.

Thompson, C. E. (1949). The Thompson modification of the thematic apperception test. *Journal of Projective Techniques, 17,* 469–478.

Torres, G. (1996). *The relationship of bilingualism and school achievement to self-concept and trait anxiety in 4th, 5th, and 6th grade Puerto Rican children.* Unpublished doctoral dissertation, Centro Caribeno de Estudio Postgraduados, San Juan, Puerto Rico.

Villamil, B. (1973). *Desarrollo del Inventario de Ansiedad Estado Y Rasgo para ninos* [Development of the State-Trait Anxiety Inventory for children]. Unpublished master's thesis, University of Puerto Rico.

Walton, J. R., Nuttall, R. L., & Vazquez-Nuttall, E. (1997). The impact of war on the mental health of children: A Salvadoran study. *Child Abuse & Neglect, 21,* 737–749.

Walton, J. R., Nuttall, R. L., & Vazquez-Nuttall, E. (1998, August). Effects of war on children's motivation reflected in TEMAS stories. In G. Costantino (Chair), *Multicultural/cross-cultural motivation as assessed by TAT and TEMAS.* Symposium presented at the 106th annual APA convention, San Francisco, CA.

Williams, R. L. (1972). *Themes concerning Blacks.* St. Louis, MO: Williams & Associates.

22

The Once-Upon-A-Time Test

Teresa Fagulha
University of Lisbon

"Once upon a time . . ." is a storytelling projective technique for children. The stimuli are presented as pictures in a cartoon format, and the task is to complete the story. To do so, the children must choose some drawn scenes, organize them in sequence, and then *tell* the story they have organized. The purpose of this technique is to describe the way children deal with their emotions—namely, anxiety and pleasure—in a transitional space (Winnicott, 1971) between reality and fantasy. In psychodynamic theories, emotions are considered creators and organizers of all mental processes (Leal, 1975); they are present since birth and affect the way children understand the surrounding world and build their inner interactions. This technique is used with children from 5 to 11 years old and requires between 20 and 30 minutes for administration.

This chapter describes the theoretical and conceptual background used to develop this technique, and the technique is subsequently placed in the context of storytelling. The stimuli are described and interpretation using the Answer Analysis Chart is discussed. The research history, including availability of norms, exploratory studies on specific populations, and validation research, are included. Finally, a case example is used to illustrate administration procedures and the child's selection of scenes and development of stories. Interpretative procedures and a card-by-card narrative are presented.

DEVELOPMENT OF THE "ONCE UPON A TIME..." TECHNIQUE

Various schools of psychology generally accept that play and the world of stories are a child's natural way of expression. Children give substance to their own experiences in the transitional space of illusion to take them beyond the confines of everyday life—into the past, future, and might be. The psychologist can access their internal organization using both play and story techniques.

Play is an alternative method of communication familiar to children and particularly adapted to the characteristics of psychological development— namely, the evolution of thought—from nonreasoning to logical reasoning (Piaget & Inhelder, 1966/1989), as well as from primary to secondary process of the mind's functioning (Freud, 1911/1978) and the acquisition of language and its use in communicating experiences and emotions.

As first described by Freud (1908/1978), play is an integral part of human activity, and the capacity to play exists throughout life. Freud linked play to the creative function because, in play, children are the creators of their world, enacting indirectly the pleasures and conflicts of their unconscious life. Freud (1908/1978) established a parallel between artistic creation and children's play in "Creative Writers and Day Dreaming." In this conception, play and artistic creation are rooted in the world of unconscious fantasies, basically dominated by the pleasure principle and, simultaneously, establishing a link between fantasy and reality because it is an external and symbolic expression of the inner world. Play is an early strategy to deal with reality frustrations; through this activity, children are able to fulfill their unconscious wishes without missing the contact with reality.

Later on, Freud (1920/1978) stressed the relationship between play and the compulsion to repeat. He used his grandson's symbolic activity with the "da-fort" game as an example. The child allowed his mother to go away without protesting because he was not only able to re-create but repeat the situation of being abandoned by playing with an object he made disappear and return. Through the process of repetition, the child passed from a position of passivity to an active one by handling the disagreeable experiences and discovering new strategies to deal with and assimilate them. Play also gives the illusion, through his mastery over objects, that the child controls the situation.

Ego psychology is interested in play as revealing the degree of the ego's adaptation to reality, focusing on strategies that children use to solve their problems. This perspective demonstrates an interest in the healthy part of the ego in the functions of play, from both therapeutic and development dimensions, related to the possibility that this activity provides an opportunity to reenact unintegrated experiences and master unpleasant and traumatic situations. Play is "the royal road to the understanding of the infantile ego's effort at synthesis" (Erikson, 1950).

Winnicott (1971) introduced a new perspective by stressing the function of the activity of play. He enlarged the concept, mainly regarded as an attitude toward life, to cover the transitional phenomenon. This particular attitude toward life is neither an activity with a purely external purpose nor an internal one. It is developed in a potential space—a metaphoric zone of psychological experience, an intermediate area between reality and fantasy, the location of symbolic thought, play, and cultural experience.

Storytelling is also a fundamental way to express ourselves and our world to others (McAdams, 1993). Each time children make up a story about something that might have happened to them or others, they expand their world by constructing parts of their past, adding to their sense of who they are, and sharing that sense with others (e.g., the psychologist assessor). By telling stories, children develop a personal voice to communicate their unique experiences and worldview.

In recent years, there has been a renewed emphasis in storytelling and story listening as ways of reflecting the values, meanings, and ideas of the narrator and the listener. Edelson (1992) stated that both the patient as analysand and the psychoanalyst tell stories. These concepts facilitate rapprochement between psychoanalysis and neighboring disciplines, allowing closeness between different approaches and enrichment to clarify some issues of psychoanalytic theory. Psychologists use storytelling and story completion, in addition to play and drawings, to understand children and share with them their own feelings, wishes, and fantasies. These activities can convey the "infinite subtleties that are to be found in play by those who seek" (Winnicott, 1971, p. 39).

The "Once upon a time ..." technique was designed to contemplate the creative, constructive, and expressive aspects of the playing and storytelling world. As such, it can be considered a standardization of the "playing interview" that is stimulating and easy to use in terms of application and interpretation (Fagulha, 1992, 1993, 1994, 1995).

Arnold (1962) stated that storytelling techniques do not add any particular information that an experienced clinician could not obtain through a long intimate relationship. Nevertheless, because the task is organized to respect the characteristics of projective techniques, including the essential elements of stimuli, responses, and interpretations, access to that information can be gained in a much shorter time.

THE "ONCE UPON A TIME ..." TECHNIQUE
IN THE CONTEXT OF PROJECTIVE STORYTELLING

Cramer (1996) described the history of the Thematic Apperception Test (TAT) and referred to several precedents in the use of storytelling as a means of understanding personality. Morgan and Murray (1935) used stories generated by subjects to a standard set of relatively ambiguous pictures to discover patients' fantasies. Subjects project their private world of needs, motives, expectancies, and anxieties into the stories, being largely unaware of personality revelations and the significance of material attributed to the characters in their stories (Murray, 1938).

The TAT has been used with adults as well as adolescents and children. However, projective storytelling using cards more suitable for the use with children were soon developed in the United States as well as in Europe. The Children's Apperception Test (CAT), designed by Bellak and Bellak in 1948 (Bellak, 1993) as an extension of the TAT, used pictures of animal characters and focusing problems, situations, and roles especially relevant to children. An alternative form, the CAT–H, contains human figures. In France, Corman (1961/1981) created the Black Leg (*Patte Noir*) using a little pig experiencing different family situations that are representative of the developmental conflicts according to psychoanalytic theory. Corman adopted some ideas presented by Blum (1950) two decades ago in the Blacky Pictures, including the use of the same characters throughout the test. The Make-A-Picture Story (MAPS; Shneidman, 1952, 1966) presented cards with typical life and fantasy situations. The MAPS was designed to permit more active participation by assessees by encouraging greater choice among the background cards and the characters to place against these backgrounds.

Full-story responses to projective storytelling techniques are sometimes difficult to obtain from some children (e.g., inhibited or hyperactive children, children with language difficulties). Story-completion methods, in which a brief story or scene is presented and the children are asked to complete the story or respond to a question at the end of the story, make the task easier (e.g., Düss, 1950/1971; Koppitz, 1982).

The "Once upon a time . . ." technique has some completion storytelling characteristics (Fagulha & Dana, 1997). The task is to complete a story; three cartoon pictures provide a partial story to be completed by the child using other pictures; the child then tells the story. The task requires active involvement in choosing the pictures, making decisions, imagining outcomes, and putting the entire process into words. The technique was designed to include an expectation for active, goal-oriented play. By choosing the drawn scenes, the child enters a playlike setting. "To control what is inside one has to *do* things, not simply to think or to wish. Playing is doing" (Winnicott, 1971, p. 41).

The responses, over and above the constructive aspect of building a story based on an episode of a character's life (presented on each card), reveal the appearance of manipulation and choice. For example, in the MAPS or in "Play Techniques," the children are offered a set of toys to promote expression of feelings, wishes, and fantasies as revealed in the objects chosen and in what is done with them. As in Black Leg or the Blacky Pictures, the same character is presented in all the different cards. Because the character is a child, the technique has a masculine version for males and a feminine version for females to ensure equality of identification. The stimuli cards present the character experiencing common events in the life of any child. These events are referred not only to anxious situations, but also to pleasant events. The purpose is to describe the way children deal with anxiety and pleasure, whose adaptive functions (Klein, 1932) are relevant to the psychological development and shape the quality of object relations.

FEATURES OF THE STIMULI—GENERAL STRUCTURE

The technique consists of seven stimulus cards (identified by Numbers I–VII and the theme), one card for training and one smaller card for finishing the test. Among the seven stimulus cards, five are designed to elicit anxious events and two are designed to elicit pleasurable events (Fagulha, 1997a).

There are 10 scenes drawn for each card. Nine of these scenes are given to the child; he or she is to choose three from which to build the story. Scene 10 represents an actual resolution of the event suggested in the card. This resolution is placed and described by the psychologist after the child has organized the scenes in sequence and told the story.

The test situation is structured as an equivalent to a dialogue, in which both the psychologist and child participate. The purpose is to encourage the practice of mutual relationship (Leal, 1975, 1993). After the psychologist shows and describes the card using standardized directions, the child is asked to choose three scenes to complete the story. The initial description is then repeated by the psychologist, and the child is subsequently given an opportunity to tell the story. The 10th scene is then presented and described to conclude the card administration process. This procedure is repeated with each of the cards.

This structure alternates interventions by the psychologist and child to allow the child to be an active participant, as well as experience a situation that is highly expressive; this occurs because the storytelling is achieved by choosing the scenes and verbalizing the stories organized around those scenes.

The relative complexity of the task—to structure the story in sequence—makes use of a sample card for training purposes essential. The task is then explained: "I have a story; it is told with drawn scenes, in a cartoon format, but it is not complete. I would love you to help me finish it. Do you want to see the story?" The training card represents a Halloween scene: The character is looking at a storefront with Halloween toys, buys some toys, and plays with them.

The five cards presenting anxiety-producing events (Cards I, II, IV, VI, and VII) are described. Card I shows a situation in which the character, while walking with the mother, gets lost and is alone. The anxiety of separation at birth is repeated during the course of life. We are born by separation, breaking the unique intimacy of life in the womb; we die by separation from the world we have known. Between these two important events, we are constantly confronted with situations that make us feel the pain or threat of loss, whether material or otherwise (i.e., people we love, fantasies and expectations, etc). Children deal "here and now" with those experiences in the test. Fear of abandonment and/or the reassurance of a mother's consistent presence as the solid inner security provider shapes the manner in which each child deals with the test situation.

Card II shows a situation in which the character is sick and taken to the doctor's office by the mother. When sick, children are confronted with anxieties caused by the fear of losing physical integrity or even death, as well as the fear of pain and separation in the form of confinement. Klein (1932) emphasized the role of anxiety and guilt arising from aggressive sexual impulses—not only in the way children deal with sickness, but also by triggering the sickness itself, which then would have neurotic roots. The experience of being looked after, often associated with the parents' presence and subsequent loving care, usually attenuates the feelings of pain.

Card IV shows a situation in which the sleeping character wakes up with a nightmare. The fear of darkness and nightmares are often anxiety-producing events during childhood. Beginning at birth, mother and child experience, with different levels of anxiety, a fear of abandonment when they go to sleep in separate beds. Later on, feelings of jealousy toward the parents as a couple may occur, triggering behaviors that intrude into their evening together (Daws, 1991).

Card VI shows a family meal, during which the parents fight in the presence of the child/character. In the daily life of a couple, some conflict situations are almost inevitable, and children are often passive or active witnesses. This type of experience produces anxiety, caused by conflict between fear and desire for the parents' separation. The child may then expose the true relationship with the parents: by distance or closeness to one or both of them or assuming his/her own autonomy and identity.

Card VII shows a classroom situation; the teacher asks a question to which all students except the character knows the answer. In a classroom situation, most children experience some level of difficulty. The fact that their peers are witnesses to that difficulty can damage their self-esteem. Often the request for a psychological evaluation is the result of problems due to difficulties in school. In psychological tests, some children reveal capabilities well above their school performances. Their performances may be affected by emotional reactions that need to be understood to plan adequate help.

The two cards that present happy life events (Cards III and V) are described. Card III shows a character walking on the beach with the parents, where a group of children are playing. This situation allows an evaluation of each child's reaction to social interaction with peers. In this stage of life, social interaction plays an important role in development by making it more or less difficult to discover a unique identity. For most children, the opportunity for interaction comes as natural and pleasant. Inhibition, or fear of rejection, can make interaction threatening for some children, who deal with their insecurities by emphasizing *having* objects that attract others rather than on *being*.

Card V shows a birthday party for the character. Parents and friends say "happy birthday" and there is a birthday cake. Birthdays represent a landmark in life: to grow up and be closer to imagined privileges of the adult world. According to Klein (1932), this particular day gives children a chance for renewal and beginning again. Gifts mean to them all the love they had wished for and not received as they had expected. Not receiving gifts may be felt unconsciously as punishment. This is sometimes clearly conveyed in family dynamics such as: "If you do not behave, your wishes will not come true" or "Behave well and you will receive gifts."

When children feel excessive guilt due to their aggressive impulses, fear of disappointment may lead to total suppression of their wishes. When that happens, receiving gifts and affection may not give them pleasure. The expression of desire and pleasure or the anticipation of frustration due to expectations may provide relevant information for a diagnosis.

The card used to complete and finish the test only shows the character (boy or girl). When looking at this card, the psychologist asks the child to name the character, choose a most favorite and least favorite card, and justify those choices. The suggestion to invent another story about what might have happened to that boy/girl is made, thereby allowing the respondent to express other themes freely.

The nine scenes that allow the sequence of the story to progress are codified in three categories: reality, fantasy, and anxiety. There are three scenes for each of these categories. The three reality scenes show events portraying several modes of acceptance or strategic resolution to the reality presented by the card. These scenes have specific characteristics according to themes—either pleasant or unpleasant—portrayed on the cards. The three fantasy scenes only show fantasies of happy events, viable or ubiquitous, that constitute either compensatory or evasive forms of escape from anxiety or fantasies of pleasant events. The three anxiety scenes show events that reflect different levels of this emotion. Obviously the choice of scenes showing happy events on both cards III and V now has a special meaning.

All of the scenes are clearly structured. Generally, some degree of ambiguity is allowed in the drawings of thematic tests, as a channel to allow space for personal interpretation (Rabin, 1981). Clear representation of situations and emotions was chosen in drawing all the characters. The specific features of the scenes and their chain of events in sequence are believed to reveal a personal ability.

In a preliminary study (Fagulha, 1992), descriptions of each scene by children between the ages of 5 and 9 ($N = 163$) concurred with what was intended to be represented in the drawings. Some of these children chose scenes emotionally charged with either anxiety or ubiquitous fantasies. While describing those scenes, some children simply said: "he/she turned this way" or did not mention the scenes at all. The scenes chosen by children can allow for exposure of their fears, fantasies, and desires without having to verbalize them. Verbalization may be threatening, due to *magical thinking*, in which the distinction between talk and action is not completely established.

INTERPRETATION

Interpretation does not aim at a score, but focuses on the child's feelings, construction of experience, and special areas of problems in life. There is an Answer Analysis Chart of 87 items in three blocks (Fagulha, 1997a): (a) attitude, (b) features of the chosen scenes and their sequential structure, and (c) features of the final story, as verbalized, and its interaction with the sequential scenes.

Analysis of the answers proceeds in two phases. Initially, the items pertaining to each card are recorded for an understanding of how each child deals with each situation represented in the scenes. In the second phase, the analysis is global by identifying common relations or pointing out any particular reaction to a certain theme. For example, some children who experience difficulty in dealing with the card representing the parental fight may react adequately to other cards showing specific problems in that area and its conflicts. Other children may show difficulties, or only moderate comfort, in all areas represented by the stimuli.

Attitude—Items 1 to 6

Items related to attitude deal with behavior, including the attitude toward the task. For example, Item 1 refers a special identification with the story's character. This item is signed when the child says "I" instead of "he/she" when telling the story or makes personal comments like "this also happened to me." This item is also signed when the child gives his or her name to the story's character in the last card. Item 3 is signed when the child needs encouragement to pursuit the task. Item 6 refers to the child's hesitation when faced with choice of scenes.

Features of the Chosen Scenes
and Their Sequential Structure—Items 7 to 27

The analysis of the chosen scenes, according to each category (fantasy, reality, anxiety) and its placement in the chain of sequential events, has correspondence in clear answers. A study of these answers was done by age groups.

Items 7 to 21 refer to the category of scene in each position of the sequence. Fantasy scenes are subdivided into *magical* and *viable* fantasy. Anxiety scenes are subdivided into *anxiety* and *strong anxiety*. Items 22 to 25 refer to a systematic category of choice (e.g., all the scenes chosen are fantasy scenes). Items 26 and 27 refer to a special feature of choice: A magical fantasy scene precedes a strong anxiety scene or vice versa. This kind of choice permits the hypothesis of a special difficulty in dealing with anxiety. If it happens in most of the cards, it may reveal primitive mechanisms of dealing with intense anxiety, like splitting (into good and bad objects), omnipotence, and denial, which refer to the paranoid-schizoid position functioning (Klein, 1952).

Projecting themselves in the here and now of the situation presented in each stimulus, children reveal through the choice of scenes and the way they organize the sequences how their emotions are digested. This process of association allows us to describe the mechanisms that regulate emotional life.

The first scene shows the immediate reaction to the situation shown—pleasant or unpleasant. When facing an unpleasant one, some children may internally identify the painful aspect and associate it with the choice of a scene showing anxiety with different levels of intensity. Choosing a reality scene may reveal the capacity to live with it or find strategies to deal with emotional aspect of it. If their choice is fantasy, viable or magic, it reveals the need to escape the conflict and deny pain. In those cards that show pleasant scenes, the choice of anxiety scenes, especially if in the first position, can reveal negative expectations concerning the good things in life.

The second scene they choose gains particular meaning in relation to the first and third scenes. If the children initially hide behind fantasy by choosing an intense anxiety scene for second place, they expose a weak defense mechanism. This in turn causes more anxiety and affects the choice of the third scene. That choice can provide significant information on the degree of capability or difficulty in finding an adequate emotional adjustment. These mechanisms may be efficient for recognizing initial anxiety and providing an opportunity to convert it into fantasy or find strategies to deal with conflict.

The third scene, ending the story, helps in finding a personal resolution to the critical situation presented. Is it possible to find a realistically adequate ending? Does the story end in a way that may be more or less anxious than the one presented in the stimulus? Does the closing represent a scene of viable fantasy, revealing hope in the fact that happy events may help overcome pain caused by unhappy ones? On the contrary, does the story end with a scene of magical fantasy, revealing omnipotence as a way to deal with pain?

Features of the Final Story as Verbalized and Its Interaction With the Sequential Scenes— Items 28 to 87

In Items 28 to 41, the story is analyzed through the three categories— anxiety, fantasy, and reality—postulated to the scenes. Items 42 to 87 refer to formal aspects and story content related to the extent of elaboration of various scenes, as well as to the feelings expressed and verbalized during the test.

Although storytelling frequently involves a description with levels of elaboration (Items 42–45), some children reaccess the situation during this moment of actually telling/verbalizing. They may do this by altering the meaning of the drawn scenes (Items 47 and 48), adding features not present in them (Items 51 and 53), omitting critical features (Item 49), or altering their sequence (i.e., if the initial scene of the story is one of reality and ends with one of anxiety, but the child starts telling it from right to left, that same story will have a happy ending—Item 54).

Another aspect to consider in stories is the relationship between the character and others—children and adults—represented in the scenes and the way those relationships are portrayed. They give us access to the way children relate to their internal or external objects. Some children systematically choose scenes representing an isolated character, whereas others choose the ones where closeness in groups between children and adults is evident. This may show their capability or difficulty in accepting support or gratification from others, or it may expose a feeling of rejection or indifference by others. Items 56 to 74 signal the different kinds of relationship with others—adults and peers—as revealed in the connection of the drawn scenes and the verbalizations associated with them.

Analysis of the individual records requires more meaning when based on the interaction between all aspects of a child's life, including the family situation, history of development, and motives that triggered the request for psychological evaluation.

PRIOR STUDIES

Norms

The percentages of choices from each of the nine scenes in the seven stimulus cards were examined (Fagulha, 1992). The scenes were analyzed to find the most and least popular scenes regardless of anxiety, fantasy, or reality categories. A study of the rules pertaining to these categories in each of the three structured sequences used samples of 245 children between the ages of 6 and 8 years (Fagulha, 1992) and subsequently used samples of 70 five-year-old kindergarten children, 70 fourth-grade children (9 years old), and 70 sixth graders between the ages of 10 and 11 (Fagulha, 1996, 1997a). The tests were administered in both public and private schools in the Lisbon area. This specific aspect of the answers for the first study of rules was chosen because it was an objective and easy to codify element corresponding to a previously established criterion. Tables 22.1 to 22.4 present the percentages of responses organized by different sample groups on each of the seven test cards.

The pattern of answers reflects difference in ages, confirming that as children mature they are able to deal with their difficulties in a more hopeful and active manner, mastering anxiety more completely and showing greater capacity in attending to reality demands (Klein, 1932). Generally, the choices of the children between the ages of 9 to 11 show a

TABLE 22.1
Percent of Choice for Each Category of Scene (A: Anxiety; F: Fantasy;
R: Reality) in the First (1), Second (2), and Third (3) Place
of the Sequence of the Story

Scene	Card I	Card II	Card III	Card IV	Card V	Card VI	Card VII
1A	47.4	48.2	17.9	74.7	18.8	22.8	35.7
1F	21.2	20.0	34.7	10.2	29.8	32.2	20.4
1R	31.4	32.8	47.4	15.1	51.4	45.0	43.9
2A	42.5	38.8	24.1	42.0	25.3	42.2	39.3
2F	28.6	24.9	33.5	34.7	40.8	32.0	27.1
2R	28.9	36.3	42.4	23.3	33.9	25.8	33.6
3A	28.9	37.9	29.8	33.1	23.3	29.9	35.7
3F	31.1	41.2	40.0	42.5	40.0	48.0	36.5
3R	40.0	20.9	30.2	24.4	36.7	22.1	27.8

Note. $N = 246$; age = 6–8 years; mean age = 7.3; $SD = 4.2$.

TABLE 22.2
Percent of Choice for Each Category of Scene (A: Anxiety; F: Fantasy;
R: Reality) in the First (1), Second (2), and Third (3) Place
of the Sequence of the Story

Scene	Card I	Card II	Card III	Card IV	Card V	Card VI	Card VII
1A	57.2	42.9	21.4	81.4	12.9	25.7	51.4
1F	8.6	14.3	18.6	8.6	25.7	8.6	1.4
1R	34.2	42.8	60.0	10.0	61.4	65.7	47.2
2A	44.4	54.3	21.4	57.1	14.3	62.8	34.3
2F	12.8	10.0	35.8	28.6	37.1	17.2	15.7
2R	42.8	35.7	42.8	14.3	48.6	20.0	50.0
3A	14.3	40.0	25.7	15.7	11.5	54.3	32.8
3F	27.1	45.7	27.1	50.0	34.2	38.6	17.2
3R	58.6	14.3	47.2	34.3	54.3	7.1	50.0

Note. $N = 70$; mean age = 9.6; $SD = 3.3$.

TABLE 22.3
Percent of Choice for Each Category of Scene (A: Anxiety; F: Fantasy;
R: Reality) in the First (1), Second (2), and Third (3) Place
of the Sequence of the Story

Scene	Card I	Card II	Card III	Card IV	Card V	Card VI	Card VII
1A	73.1	36.6	12.1	78.1	4.8	26.9	29.3
1F	2.4	2.4	24.5	12.2	24.4	2.4	2.4
1R	24.5	61.0	63.4	9.7	70.8	70.7	68.3
2A	41.5	17.1	19.4	36.6	9.8	68.3	19.4
2F	14.6	24.3	29.3	34.2	36.5	9.7	4.9
2R	43.9	58.6	51.3	29.2	53.7	22.0	75.7
3A	12.2	24.4	9.7	9.7	12.2	36.6	19.5
3F	12.2	56.1	29.3	31.7	36.5	56.2	12.2
3R	75.6	19.5	61.0	58.6	51.3	7.2	68.3

Note. $N = 41$; mean age = 10.7; $SD = 5.09$.

more even pattern. The development of the capacity to diffuse anxiety and more flexibly face reality translates into a tendency to respond to anxious situations by choosing scenes showing anxiety in the first position of the sequence (Cards I and IV) or scenes of reality (Cards II, VI, and VII). In these cases, a lower percentage chooses fantasy scenes in the first position of the sequence. There is also a progressive decrease in choice of anxiety scenes for story endings corresponding to an increase in the choice of reality or fantasy scenes. As children mature, a higher percentage choose reality and fantasy scenes and a lower percentage choose the anxiety ones in the two cards that show pleasant situations. A higher degree of emotional stability allows children to deal with situations in a more mature and well-balanced way.

TABLE 22.4
Percent of Choice for Each Category of Scene (A: Anxiety; F: Fantasy;
R: Reality) in the First (1), Second (2), and Third (3) Place
of the Sequence of the Story

Scene	Card I	Card II	Card III	Card IV	Card V	Card VI	Card VII
1A	35.7	49.9	21.5	52.8	30.0	24.3	28.5
1F	34.3	20.2	37.1	21.4	27.1	38.6	34.3
1R	30.0	29.9	41.4	25.8	42.9	37.1	37.2
2A	30.0	34.3	31.4	42.9	27.2	37.1	45.7
2F	30.0	28.5	30.0	34.3	41.4	37.1	30.0
2R	40.0	37.2	38.6	22.8	31.4	25.8	24.3
3A	21.5	35.8	22.9	35.8	25.7	18.5	27.1
3F	40.0	31.4	58.5	44.2	35.7	55.7	40.0
3R	38.5	32.8	18.6	20.0	38.6	25.8	32.9

Note. $N = 70$; mean age = 5.6; $SD = 3.1$.

Norms for Belgian children ages 6 to 8 years old ($N = 180$) have been developed (Vrebos, 1998). Comparison with Portuguese norms reveals a higher percentage of choice of reality scenes and a smaller percentage of fantasy scenes in the cards presenting anxious themes.

Exploratory Studies in Specific Populations

The fact that responses were not targeted at verbalization led us to explore emotional difficulties in children with oral communication problems: children with cerebral paralysis (Fagulha, 1994) and deaf children (Fagulha, Andersen, & Gama, 1994). In both cases, good acceptance by children and interest expressed by the psychologists who applied the test were the norm. Other studies were done applying this test in pediatric psychology, permitting identification of the psychological mechanisms of children with the HIV virus function (Simões, 1998) and with seriously burned children during the first 2 years of their lives (Partidário, 1996). Use of this test with mentally retarded young adults (Fagulha, 1997b) was considered to contrast with the thematic techniques currently used because this technique helps them express their emotional experiences. A cross-cultural study of African, White, and Hindu children is in progress.

VALIDATION

Based on the results of the Rutter Questionnaire for Teachers (Rutter, 1967), four groups were formed, including children with anxious and aggressive behaviors, children isolated from their peers, and emotionally healthy children. Cluster analysis and canonical discrimination were used for comparisons among groups (Fagulha, 1992).

Using responses from the healthy group as a criterion, scenes were established that could identify the different responses by group statistically. The responses from children with aggressive behavior represented reality solutions and magical fantasy and fewer choices of expressed anxiety scenes. However, scenes revealing persecutory anxiety, infrequently chosen in other samples, were chosen. The isolated children preferred scenes of an isolated character.

Validity studies are currently in progress. Different sequences of the nine available scenes corresponding to the 81 possible sequences for each card are classified according to clinical criteria for the development of norms to describe those sequences analogous to the norms for the chosen scenes.

CASE STUDY

Tom is 8 years old. His mother, a drug addict and prostitute, abandoned him when he was 6 months old. His father, also drug addicted, died 3 years ago. Tom was starving, looking for food in garbage cans, and only entering school after being admitted to a shelter. He is ostracized by his peers, who call him *the pig*, because he suffers from enuresis and occasional encopresis. His stories and interpretation follow.

Card I

Then the little boy put on the wings and began flying through the heaven; he was looking for his mother. And then he found a policeman and asked like this: "Mister policeman, do you know where my mother went?" He said that he did not know.

Then the policeman has gone, a Fairy appeared and the child asked: "Who are you?" "I am the godmother Fairy".

Tom did not choose any anxiety scene. His choice of fantasy scenes, in the first and third positions, put him close to the patterned choices of 5-year-old children. The initial scene represents omnipotent fantasy, revealing his desire to use magical powers to find his mother. It is important that this scene is one of the least often chosen by children of Tom's age (Fagulha, 1992). Children who choose this scene generally refer to someone (often the fairy) who gave them wings. Tom exposes the need for support from his own omnipotence—he gave himself wings and is looking for the imaginary mother in heaven (just like when father died, his culture tells him "he is in heaven"). He then looks for a male adult figure (reality scene) whose help is not good, and he once again takes refuge in an omnipotent fantasy that allows him to contact a mother figure. Tom can neither recognize the painful feelings nor find a realistic solution to his situation.

Card II

He went to the hospital and he was dreaming that he was transformed into a Superman and afterward father came and gave him a gift: it was a toy car.

Tom chooses the three fantasy scenes available in this card, but does not select any anxiety or reality scene, which represents unpleasant feelings associated with sickness. In any of the cards, the systematic choice of this type of scene, especially in those showing anxious themes, is extremely rare (Fagulha, 1992). As in Card I, Tom's first choice is a scene of omnipotent fantasy: He immediately invokes Superman's magical powers. He associates this scene with the idea that his father may give him a gift of the sympathy he needs to permit him to be a child who plays and grows up. Within the available scenes, there is one showing the character being taken by ambulance. By not choosing it, Tom tells the story by saying the character is in the hospital. Children normally associate this situation with separation and fear. In contrast, Tom refers to it in a matter-of-fact form, which in this context may essentially represent a place where he will be looked after—perhaps an equivalent to the shelter that took him in.

Card III

The little boy asked to the father, "May I go and play with those children?" "You can go, but stay close by and you are not allowed out of my eyesight." Then he built a castle after he caught a fish in the sea. The children were furious because the little boy caught the fish. Afterward two little girls were looking at him because he was so beautiful and was lying down in a plastic bed.

If it is true that scenes of anxiety are the least chosen in situations as pleasant as the one described, then the peer rejection Tom lives with daily cannot be ignored. However, although camouflaged, there are signs of this situation. None of the chosen scenes represents shared intimacy; instead, the isolated character (first and third scenes) or confrontation with others (second scene) predominates.

Tom initiates his story by referring to father in a protective role. He did not choose a scene representing the character with parents, but includes them in the story by describing their proximity and desired support. Comforted by these thoughts, he may play close to them and be brave enough to catch a fish. He then proceeds to exhibit the fish, upsetting the others, in a clear projection of aggression. Then the narcissistic desire of evaluation appears: He sees himself beautiful in the eyes of girls who admire him. Like Narcissus, he looks for his image in an echo confirming the idealization and negates the reality of being "the pig" from whom others run away.

Card IV

After he went to call his parents. The parents dressed up, and he went and picked his pistol, that was a real one, and killed the monster and afterward he went to call his parents, who were sleeping, and after he went to bed and dreamt of the black monster again.

Tom chooses a fantasy scene in the first position, which corresponds to the least chosen category in this position. In fact, the pattern choice to close a story for children of this age, and for children between 5 and 9 years old, is of a fantasy scene. The initial fantasy unleashes anxiety motion that makes him look for parental help. Because he cannot find help, anxiety is accentuated in the final scene, in which the character stays alone battling a fear of inner ghosts.

In the narrated story, Tom starts by repeatedly referring to the need for parental support, but to no avail. The character calls them but they do not answer; they go and get dressed. Facing abandonment, he rescues himself by calling for omnipotence, translated by the assertion that he has a real pistol—an assertion never found in children's verbalizations. Once again he evokes the parental help, but they are sleeping. The character stays alone with terrorizing inner ghosts. If it is true that ghosts have multiple representations, it is possible to assume an important role in the fear of death, in which the ghost becomes some kind of "transitional mortal object" (Ferrari, 1985) in the imaginary life of a child. This would simultaneously represent a life experience and knowledge of death and its irreversible nature in returning from death to life. The dead father cannot answer and abandons Tom to the ghost of death.

Card V

And after the friends gave him an airplane; he was thinking he was inside the airplane and after the friends gave him the watch. He said: "What is the watch for?" "It's to look at the time." "Ah! So many gifts! Maybe they are for me!"

Tom chooses scenes of fantasy and reality, which is common when facing an especially pleasant situation. The first scene represents the fantasy of being able to play and grow up with the help of friends who give him the airplane. Immediately after that, they give him another gift representing reality in the present time, as opposed to the imaginary time of infancy. He describes the second scene (usually described in a factual way: "He was given a gift or a watch" or "He was showing his friends the watch") with amazement and difficulty in understanding the need to cope with actual time. When he says "What is the watch for?", it is to count the hours of his difficult days. He then desires and wants sympathy, saying, "So many gifts!" and doubting that the gifts may be for him. He wonders if it is possible to sustain the hope of having what one needs. Tom would like to believe, but feels insecure.

Card VI

After he was thinking that he had a car and he was riding in a car, at night, and then he started crying and the mother was talking to the father, and after the little boy was with mother. "Son, don't be so sad!" Father: "I'm leaving this house. I don't care anymore about you and my son."

Here we find a pattern of choice similar to other 5-year-old children. As in previous cards, Tom initially chooses a magical fantasy scene. The character is grown, can drive a car, and faces the dark night. Right after that, he chooses an anxiety scene in which he cries (it must be noted that, although the character cries in several scenes during the test, Tom chooses tears to communicate his sadness only in the presence of this theme). He cries alone, with his mother's back turned to him. Then he expresses a desire to be comforted by mother, but there is no way to keep the family together. As in his real life, father abandons them and accusation appears concerning father's death, which is perceived as abandonment because he did not want to look after his son and his wife.

Card VII

He started making funny faces at the teacher. Then started thinking of the numbers. "But I cannot do this one, but I shall do everything in the exercise book." He put the book down, didn't do anymore work and went home.

Tom chooses the three available fantasy scenes—a rare sequence. The first scene shows aggression toward the teacher, the second shows the omnipotence of knowledge, and the last reveals the desire to evade. However, while verbalizing, he recognizes difficulty—"but I cannot do this one"—soon followed by the omnipotent and magical solution: "But I shall do everything in the exercise book." The final resolution is dismissal. He puts the book down, giving up. He rejects the academic world that presents challenges for which he fears he is not equipped. He returns home to a family world and his infancy.

Final Story

One day he became an adult, had children, and never abandoned them.

The story has to be re-created in the ideal world where parents look after their children and never abandon them. Due to the present difficulties and hardships of the past, only the future may bring hope.

Tom's stories reveal a lack of trust in his personal resources to deal with life situations. The need to appeal to parental figures is strong, but they do not respond to that need. The tendency to use escape mechanisms through omnipotence appears, accompanied by a systematic denial of painful feelings and losses. Depression only appears in the theme of a fighting family. Grieving for the parents' death or abandonment did not take place, bringing on him a desire to meet them in heaven (Card I) and the return of the protecting and gratifying parental figure (Cards II and III), followed by the frightening nightmare (Card IV) and the feeling of abandonment and rejection (Card VI). Aggression is projected and the narcissistic slip is evident (Card III). The last card exposes dismissal when faced with the demands of real life. The need to recover house and family is projected into the future. A need for adequate support for this child is evident so that Tom can learn to grieve his losses and experience the love and care necessary to acquire confidence in life and himself.

REFERENCES

Arnold, M. B. (1962). *Story sequence analysis: A new method for measuring motivation and predicting achievement.* New York: Columbia University Press.

Bellak, L. (1993). *The T.A.T., C.A.T. and S.A.T. in clinical use* (5th ed.). Boston: Allyn & Bacon.

Blum, G. S. (1950). *The Blacky pictures: Manual of instructions.* New York: Psychological Corporation.

Corman, L. (1981). *Le test PN. Manuel* [The Black Leg test. Manual]. Paris: Presses Universitaires de France. (Original work published 1961)

Cramer, P. (1996). *Storytelling, narrative and the Thematic Apperception Test.* New York: Guilford.

Daws, D. (1991). Infant's sleep problems. In R. Szur & S. Miller (Eds.), *Extending horizons: Psychoanalytic psychotherapy with childrens, adolescents and families* (pp. 107–119). London: Karnac Books.

Düss, L. (1971). *La méthode des fables en psychanalyse infantile* [Fable technique in child psychoanalysis]. Paris: L'Arche. (Original work published 1950)

Edelson, M. (1992). Telling and enacting stories in psychoanalysis. In J. W. Barron, M. N. Eagle, & D. L. Wolitzky (Eds.), *Interfaces of psychoanalysis and psychology* (pp. 99–123). Washington, DC: American Psychological Association.

Erikson, E. (1950). *Childhood and society.* New York: Norton.

Fagulha, T. (1992). *A prova "Era uma vez . . .": Uma prova projectiva para crianças* ["Once upon a time . . ." A projective technique for children]. Unpublished doctoral dissertation, University of Lisbon.

Fagulha, T. (1993). *"Once upon a time . . . ."* Workshop conducted in the 14th International Congress of Rorschach and Projective Techniques, Lisbon.

Fagulha, T. (1994). A prova "Era uma vez . . . ." Uma nova prova projectiva para crianças ["Once upon a time . . ." A new projective technique for children]. *Análise Psicológica,* 4(12), 511–528.

Fagulha, T. (1995). "Era uma vez . . . ." Uma prova projectiva para crianças ["Once upon a time . . ." A projective technique for children]. In L. Almeida, M. Simões, & M. Gonçalves (Eds.), *Provas psicológicas em Portugal* (pp. 223–237). Braga: APPORT.

Fagulha, T. (1996). *"Once upon a time . . .": A portuguese projective technique for children.* Unpublished communication in the 15th International Congress of Rorschach and Projective Methods, Boston.

Fagulha, T. (1997a). *A prova "Era uma vez. . .". Manual e Material* (2nd ed.) [The "Once upon a time . . ." technique. Manual and Material]. Lisbon: CEGOC/TEA.

Fagulha, T. (1997b). *Using the "Once upon a time. . ." technique with mentally retarded young adults. A pilot study.* Unpublished communication in the Fifth European Congress of Psychology, Dublin.

Fagulha, T., Andersen, F., & Gama, O. (1994). *Contributions for the use of the "Once upon a time . . ." projective technique with deaf children.* Unpublished comunication in the 52nd annual convention of the International Council of Psychologists, Lisbon.

Fagulha, T., & Dana, R. (1997). Professional psychology in Portugal, *Psychological Reports,* 81, 1211–1222.

Fagulha, T., & Pires, R. (1997). Mecanismos de defesa avaliados através da prova "Era uma vez . . . ." [An approach to the use of the "Once upon a time . . ." technique to assess defense mechanisms in children]. In L. Almeida, S. Araújo, M. Gonçalves, C. Machado, & M. Simões (Eds.), *Avaliação Psicológica: Formas e Contextos* (Vol. 5, pp. 45–52). Braga: APPORT.

Ferrari, P. (1985). L'enfant atteint de maladies mortelles [The child with terminal disease]. In S. Lebovici, R. Diatkine, & M. Soulé (Eds.), *Traité de Psychiatrie de l'enfant et de l'adolescent: Tome II* (pp. 539–600). Paris: PUF.

Freud, S. (1978). Creative writers and day-dreaming. In *The standard edition of the complete psychological works of Sygmund Freud* (Vol. 9, pp. 141–153). London: Hogarth Press and Institute of Psycho-Analysis. (Original work published 1908)

Freud, S. (1978). Beyond the pleasure principle. In *The standard edition of the complete psychological works of Sigmund Freud* (Vol. 18, pp. 243–476). London: Hogarth Press and Institute of Psycho-Analysis. (Original work published 1920)

Freud, S. (1978). Formulation on the two principles of mental functioning. In *The standard edition of the complete psychological works of Sygmund Freud* (Vol. 12, pp. 213–226). London: Hogarth Press and Institute of Psycho-Analysis. (Original work published 1911)

Klein, M. (1932). *The psycho-analysis of children.* London: Hogarth Press and Institute of Psycho-Analysis.

Klein, M. (1952). Notes on some schizoid mechanism. In J. Riviere (Ed.), *Developments of psycho-analysis* (pp. 292–320). London: Hogarth Press and Institute of Psycho-Analysis.

Koppitz, E. M. (1982). Personality assessment in the schools. In C. Reynolds & T. Gutkin (Eds.), *The handbook of school psychology* (pp. 273–295). New York: Wiley.

Leal, M. R. (1975). *An inquiry into socialization processes in the young child*. Unpublished doctoral dissertation, University of London.

Leal, M. R. (1993). Reciprocal and alternating intercourse. In M. R. Leal (Ed.), *Psychotherapy as mutually contingent intercourse* (pp. 43–61). Braga: APPORT.

McAdams, D. P. (1993). *The stories we live by: Personal myths and the making of the self*. New York: Guilford.

Morgan, C. D., & Murray, H. A. (1935). A method for investigating phantasies: The Thematic Apperception Test. *Archives of Neurology and Psychiatry, 34,* 289–306.

Murray, H. A. (1938). *Explorations in personality*. New York: Oxford University.

Partidário, A. (1996). *Sequelas psicológicas em crianças vítimas de queimaduras* [Assessing psychological problems in severely burned children]. Unpublished dissertation. Lisboa: ISPA.

Piaget, J., & Inhelder, B. (1989). *La psychologie de l'enfant* [Child psychology]. Paris: PUF. (Original work published 1966)

Rabin, A. I. (1981). *Assessment with projective techniques: A concise introduction*. New York: Springer.

Rutter, M. (1967). A children's behaviour questionnaire for completion by teachers: Preliminary findings. *Journal of Child Psychology and Psychiatry, 8,* 1–11.

Shneidman, E. S. (1952). *Manual for the Make-A-Picture Story method*. Projective Techniques Monographs, No. 2. The Society for Projective Techniques and Rorschach Institute.

Shneidman, E. S. (1966). El MAPS aplicado a niños. In A. I. Rabin & M. Haworth (Eds.), *Técnicas proyectivas para niños* (pp. 136–149). Buenos Aires: Paidós.

Simões, A. C. (1998). *Ideias de morte em crianças entre os cinco e os nove anos infectadas pelo vírus da Sida: Estudo exploratório através da prova projectiva "Era uma vez . . ."* [An approach to the study of death fantasies in AIDS children between five and nine years old, using the "Once upon a time . . ." technique]. Unpublished master's thesis. Lisboa: Universidade Lusófona de Humanidades e Tecnologias.

Vrebos, D. (1998). Étude d'une nouvelle épreuve thématique pour enfants: "Il était une fois . . ." [Study of a new thematic test for children: "Once upon a time . . ."]. Unpublished master's thesis, University of Liége, Belgium.

Winnicott, D. W. (1971). *Playing and reality*. London: Tavistock.

VII

SPECIAL ISSUES
IN PRACTICE

Part VII has six chapters that present major issues in assessment practice with multicultural populations in the United States. Two chapters focus on services to Hispanics. In chapter 23, the special role of a bilingual/bicultural psychologist assessor is emphasized using illustrations of client dilemmas as a result of cultural incompetence in a state service delivery system. Chapter 24 unites the Africentric perspective described in chapter 2 with responsible assessment practices for African Americans. Chapter 25 describes the process of describing cultural identity and the preparation of *DSM–IV* cultural formulations for Hispanics. Chapter 26 provides examples of cultural formulations for American Indians/Alaska Natives with an emphasis on depression. Chapter 27 describes the heterogeneity of the Jewish population in the United States and how assessment is affected by diversity. Finally, chapter 28 addresses unresolved issues of how to teach students cultural competence in assessment practice.

Chapter 23, which describes a 13-year assessment practice with Hispanics in Minnesota, is written with passion, commitment, and clinical wisdom from the perspective of a practitioner with the necessary fortitude to help her clients negotiate the bureaucratic labyrinth. Following a description of the state Hispanic population, the impact on clients of the limited mental health services available in Minnesota is described. Similar descriptive materials are required for each multicultural population in every state for an understanding of the needs of these populations and the services and service delivery systems currently available to them. A national composite of this information is needed to plan for culturally competent services as well as to evaluate the adequacy of available services for multicultural populations.

The history and continued daily presence of discrimination and persecution of this population has contributed to a generalized fear of authority and the state bureaucracy, which includes the mental health service delivery system. In addition, the assertiveness levels of Hispanic clients are often minimal. An apparent accommodation to inadequate services may occur on the basis of respect and/or deference to service providers often in the absence of compliance. A majority of these clients, particularly persons who are recent immigrants, use English as a second language, have limited education, and experience economic marginality and instability. These persons may have genuine difficulty receiving services from Anglo-American providers, especially psychologist assessors, because these clients direct all their help-seeking toward a designated provider for a variety of problems that may extend far beyond the referral for assessment services. Psychologist assessors must be able to augment their narrow specialist role by a willingness to respond immediately to client requests for help with problems-in-living and effective communication with the mental health or managed care bureaucracy. As a consequence, the roles of providers—whether as assessors or therapists—are often complex and multifaceted. The meaning of adequate and competent services, even from an assessment specialist, differs for this population. The bottom line in providing competent services to this population is that, because clients are needy in many ways and have little faith in providers, more time is needed for each client. By the same token, knowledge of the client's particular cultural origins, recognition of the diversity of these cultural roots, and sufficient skill in the Spanish language assume equal importance with the technical skills required for assessment.

This chapter provides examples of inadequacies in Rorschach Comprehensive System (RCS) administration, scoring, and interpretation for clients who have limited or second language English skills, as well as those persons who remain traditional in cultural orientation. Fluency in Spanish is considered to be the most important ingredient of cultural competence in assessment. Languages shape social reality perceptions, provide a medium for negotiating social interactions, and transmit cultural values and norms. Fluency in Spanish is often required to administer the RCS, and translators who do not have assessment training are unsatisfactory. When the RCS is administered and scored properly, the norms may indicate psychopathology even when psychological functioning is appropriate and within normal limits by cultural standards (see chap. 15). Local normative data can alleviate some of these problems, but linkage of research done in Latin America and the United States is an even more important avenue for reducing bias in interpretation.

Many problems in using the MMPI/MMPI–2 are not sufficiently addressed by published cultural competence MMPI standards. For examples, an informal evaluation of reading and writing skills should be done prior to administration of a Spanish version due to frequent misrepresentation of educational level and translations problems with 15 to 30 items depending on the translation. Both Spanish and English versions often need to be used with the same client because the items can be answered differently in the Spanish and English versions. Spanish is less precise than English, and the discussion in this chapter of what this difference can mean in behavioral terms with individual clients gets at the heart of how different cultural perspectives are mediated by language. In addition to language issues, culture can influence validity scale responding to the extent that Hispanic clients often appear to have invalid profiles. For example, they may endorse items that suggest perceptual distortions when, in fact, traditional beliefs, superstitions, magical thinking, and even extraordinary life circumstances can be responsible for these answers rather than psychopathology.

Chapter 24 applies the Africentric perspective described in chapter 2 to responsible assessment practice with standard instruments and procedures. This perspective is humanistic in orientation and articulates an African-American construction of reality. Historically, cultural incompetence among assessors, barriers to accessing services, and economic constraints were related to underutilization. In addition, the application of a Eurocentric perspective to African Americans meant that these persons were subjected to invidious comparisons and insufficiently understood using standard pseudoetic assessment instruments. The application of assessment instruments in this chapter begins with a comparison of Eurocentricism and Africentricism; this is followed by a listing of factors preventing self-disclosing and task-orientation with White assessors. There are communication difficulties, race-based transference, race-based prejudice, use of inappropriate racial labels, color blindness, limited understanding of familial roles and boundaries, as well as what behaviors are considered normal in African American communities. The Africentric perspective demands assessor preparation for African-American clients by understanding their common history of discrimination and racism, cultural interconnectedness (e.g., as measured with the African-American Acculturation Scale), and heterogeneity of worldviews. An assessor should be willing to adopt a variety of roles with client, discuss racial differences, use a problem-solving approach focusing on client strengths including the church, and recognize that the cultural context is a primary source of diagnostic information. The assessment process requires an evaluation of acculturation level and stage of racial identity. Finally, assessment should result in a synthesized integration of presenting problems, life history in a cultural context, and racial identity development, leading to a clinical diagnosis, if necessary, and recommendations for culture-general or culture-specific interventions.

Cultural competence is described from an Africentric perspective using the categories of beliefs/attitudes, knowledge, and skills with culture-specific suggestions. Cultural competence also entails overcoming biases of ethnocentrism and stereotyping and developing awareness of the consequences of countertransference in the assessor. The assessor must also recognize client perception of a bad fit with the assessment process or examiner, poor test-taking skills, and client thought processes not congruent with assessment demands. A list of questions concerning the cross-cultural psychometric status of standard instruments is included for clinicians to consider prior to using standard assessment instruments. Because the answers to these questions indicate the deficiencies of standard tests, recommendations for corrections are made in this chapter. First, pluralistic norms should be established. Second, in applying both interviews and tests, opportunities should be offered to clients to provide additional information on cultural experiences by open-ended questions or testing the limits. Third, existing culture-specific tests should be used, and a complete listing of available measures is provided. Fourth, the suggestion is made that two available models—Helms' Racial Identity Development Stages and the assessment–intervention model in chapter 1—should be combined into a hybrid model. The elements of these models are summarized and a composite model is presented in this chapter. Diagnostic considerations and recommendations within the African-American cultural context are included. By way of summary, this chapter recognizes that a comprehensive psychosocial interview, cultural identity evaluation, psychological evaluation, and feedback sessions are essential to culturally competent assessment.

Chapter 25 is a scholarly approach to the history, origins, and composition of cultural identity. An ecological transactional model of human behavior that includes culture provides a theoretical context that traces the history and composition of the cultural self. The cultural self emerges from this systemic approach as a relational construct with a variety of components. The cultural self has boundaries that vary in permeability and rigidity and contents that are infused and given order and prominence by the history of a cultural group identity. Cultural identity is distinguished from ethnic identity. Although containing many cultural aspects, ethnic identity also includes degrees of cultural orientation and/or identification with an ethnic group. Ethnic identity is composed of ethnic behaviors, a sense of affirmation/belonging, and ethnic identity achievement. A sense of ethnic identity is poorly developed for Euro-Americans, whereas Hispanics strongly endorse all three components. Euro-Americans also share an individualistic or self-contained self that contrasts sharply with the collectivist valuing of an extended self, which incorporates and emphasizes the primacy of other persons. Cultural identity descriptions begin with cultural orientation status adaptations of traditional, bicultural, marginal, and assimilated. High and low variants of bicultural orientation have been identified for Hispanics.

Cultural orientation status description is an avenue toward the development of cultural formulations for *DSM–IV*, which can provide a better understanding of cultural identity. Cultural formulations are necessary when clinicians and clients do not share the same cultural identities. The *DSM–IV* includes five components of cultural formulations: individual cultural identity, cultural explanations of illness, cultural factors related to psychosocial environment and levels of functioning, cultural elements in the relationship between client and clinician, and an overall assessment for diagnosis and care.

Chapter 25 describes each component of a cultural formulation in detail, with particular emphasis on Hispanic clients because this information has been omitted from *DSM–IV*. During warmup and screening, psychiatric history, and follow-up, information relevant to a client's cultural identity is obtained using a modified traditional clinical interview following the eight-step outline developed by Kleinman. Assessment of ethnic identity can be evaluated informally by specific questions or measured with available instruments during these first three interview phases. Measurement of ethnicity can occur using the Multigroup Ethnic Identity Measure, and acculturation status can be determined with the ARSMA–II. An understanding of health/illness beliefs is critical in understanding the cultural origins of illness. For example, *nervios*, a culturally interpreted and culturally acceptable symptom among Hispanics, exposes psychosocial distress. *Nervios* follows a stressor after which social roles are temporarily eschewed in favor of impulsivity, dissociation, and perceptual disturbance. This condition may only be understood in the context of the client's cultural history. *Nervios, susto*, and other culture-bound syndromes are not considered to be as serious as *DSM–IV* diagnoses that could be applied to the same symptoms. These symptoms would ordinarily be treated successfully by local *curanderos*. A Folk Belief Subscale may be used to assess reliance on traditional folk illness ideologies in Mexican-American clients. Interview questions may also be used to elicit information on folk belief ideologies. Cultural factors related to the psychosocial environment and level of functioning can be elicited during the interview by examining the client's interpretations of social stressors, evaluating the composition and functioning of the available social support system, and understanding the extent of perceived disability. Cultural elements in the client–clinician relationship often present problems for diagnosis and treatment. The clinician must exercise care in evaluation of this relationship, recognizing limitations in cultural knowledge and always remaining open to the possibility of referral. The overall assessment for diagnosis and care requires an appraisal of the reliability of the entire process in information gathering and data processing of cultural information.

Chapter 26 is concerned with the assessment of depression. Depression was selected for inclusion in the handbook because the description of the concept and phenomenology of depression differs remarkably as a function of culture. Characteristic core and peripheral symptoms, as well as their clustering, intensity, duration, and relative acceptability of affective, behavioral, cognitive, and somatic expressions also differ across ethnic, racial, and national boundaries. For American Indians/Alaska Natives, depression has had various labels, often tribe-specific, to describe remnants of historic syndromes emerging from health/illness beliefs emphasizing harmony–disharmony and an enlarged self with community, spiritual, and natural phenomena as components.

Chapter 26 provides a fusion of the cultural issues surrounding depression with a review of available instruments and their contribution to the preparation of cultural formulations for *DSM–IV*. After a discussion of overarching issues of etic and/or emic conceptualizations and the distinctive composition of the Indian self, four screening instruments, the MMPI, and clinical interviews are introduced, and their research literature is briefly presented in three separate tables. The literature for four screening instruments and the MMPI presents subjects and results, and the structured and semistructured clinical interviews, subjects, designs, and results of studies are noted.

The most widely used instrument for examining depression—the Center for Epidemiological Studies Depression Scale (CES–D)—has a different factor structure for American Indians/Alaska Natives than for other groups. A general factor suggestive of conceptual overlap between somatic and depressed affect item clusters implies linkage with functional abilities and physical illness described by other research. Depression then becomes a more generalized syndrome affecting a large number of persons. An augmented opportunity to focus on this population has been provided by a culture-specific instrument, the Inventory for Diagnosing Depression (IDD). The high percentage of false positives using the CES–D has resulted in the use of other instruments, including the MMPI and structured/semistructured interviews. The frequent use of the MMPI has been controversial due to pathologization and lack of differentiation across diagnostic categories (e.g., depression and schizophrenia). Unfortunately, there are too few relevant MMPI–2 studies at present for clarification of these issues. Although MMPI pathologization of American Indians/Alaska Natives can be partially ameliorated by use of moderator variables (e.g., acculturation) or statistical controls (see chap. 5), the use of these corrections remains controversial, and they have not been incorporated into routine practice with the MMPI/MMPI–2. Interview research has suggested that the loss of cultural support is sufficiently stressful to precipitate depression and attempted suicide with important consequences for interventions. Nonetheless, these interviews also fail to recognize the importance of using moderator variables.

Cultural case formulations provide a potential avenue for reduction of some of the most egregious misdiagnoses using *DSM–IV*. This chapter reviews the history and purposes of cultural formulations as a means to acknowledge the role of culture in the development and expression of psychopathology. Following a description of cultural identity, a cultural explanation for illness and recognition of cultural elements in professional relationships with clinicians leads to an overall cultural assessment for diagnosis and care. Four brief case examples of cultural formulations taken from published literature provide a unique opportunity to examine the process and content of cultural formulations.

Why is chapter 27 in this handbook? First, this chapter provides a wealth of information not generally available to professional psychologists about an ethnic group that is often identified as Euro-American. Second, despite this misidentification, Jews in the United States have shared discrimination, stereotypy, and pathologization with other non-Anglo-American groups. Third, Jewish diversity is comparable in magnitude to other cultural/racial groups described in this handbook.

The diversity of Jews in ethnicity, religious orthodoxy–nonorthodoxy, and race has reflected the countries in which they resided to compose a multitude of Jewish cultures. For examples, Ashkenazic Jews from central and eastern Europe speak Yiddish, a Germanic language written in the Hebrew alphabet, whereas Sephardic Jews from Spain and Portugal spoke a form of Spanish also written in the Hebrew alphabet. Mizrachim Jews were originally from North Africa and the Middle East. Recent Jewish immigrants to the United States do not speak English as a first language. Orthodox/Hasidic Jews differ remarkably from Reform, Reconstructionist, Conservative, and unaffiliated Jews, who are generally acculturated in the United States and speak English as a first language.

Jewish attitudes toward suffering and help-seeking are culturally distinctive. Jews are open and express personal concerns freely, responding immediately not only to physical distress but also to emotional pain. Religious Jews, however, eschew psychological treatment, and Russian Jews deny psychological distress and distrust mental health professionals because mental health problems were equated with political nonconformity and responded to harshly in Russia. Jewish identity is often fractured by an internalized anti-Semitism and fears of visibility, although research findings in this area are equivocal. Many providers display ethnic bias in the form of stereotypy and anti-Semitism. Standard assessment instruments can also provide bias. For example, Orthodox Jewish students have elevated MMPI scores on at least seven clinical scales and respond differently to religious items, but nonreligious Jews also respond differently on the clinical and validity scales. Although religiosity should not be equated with psychopathology, there are distinctions between healthy and unhealthy religiosity that can only be made by clinicians with knowledge of religious practice and lifestyle. Assessment of religious Jews is complicated by the commandment to honor parents, the prohibition against speech that dishonors someone's good name, and modesty in speaking of all areas of life, including being alone in a closed room with a person of the opposite sex. There are also cultural differences in frequencies of particular diagnoses of psychopathology, depressive symptomatology, and responses to symptoms of schizophrenia in various Jewish populations.

Chapter 28 is about teaching students a process—a way of knowing about culture as dynamic and constantly undergoing change. Multiple perspectives or lenses are required to integrate findings from interviews, observations, and tests. The principles that guide the teaching process include tying cultural issues to mainstream conceptual tools, active and critical participation by students using illustrations and laboratory exercises, as well as applications of the tools to cases. These conceptual tools include construct validation, mediators versus moderators, and clinical versus statistical inference. Even the politicized nature of culture, race, and ethnicity can be examined using these tools. This chapter reflects the cultural competency outcomes of three professors engaged in teaching a course that includes intelligence tests, the clinical interview, and the MMPI–2 using different perspectives applied to the same content to demonstrate how culture, race, and ethnicity are basic assessment issues.

Case materials are incorporated to provide examples of how to think about cultural issues. What are the kinds of questions that may be asked of case materials? These materials can be used to develop and test alternative hypotheses by shifting cultural lenses—a movement between lay and professional meaning systems or between client and clinician sets of cultural meanings. Metaphors and exercises to present key ideas are described in the chapter as a supplement to readings and discussion. The focus is on training students to make informed judgments about their culturally different clients. The case materials emphasize the caution and carefulness required in culturally competent assessment. For example, the assessment of bilinguals is introduced by a mock interview involving the use of different languages by client and clinician. Students are allowed to shift their roles during these interviews to experience differences in how and what they communicate in primary and secondary languages. Students are instructed how to identify the primary language by a systematic evaluation and to anticipate differences in cognitive-intellectual and social functioning conveyed by the language chosen for use during the assessment process. As a result, evaluation in both languages may sometimes be necessary. Readers should note that similar recommendations for language assessment are also made in chapter 23 from a practitioner's perspective.

The lack of evidence for racial bias on the MMPI does not mean that a culturally competent assessor assumes that bias cannot exist for a particular client. This potential bias can be examined by going over items contributing to significant scale elevations with clients for misunderstood items as a result of level of reading skill or carelessness and to detect cultural factors that determine how particular items are answered. In addition, a detailed exploration of life circumstances is required whenever there is an extremely deviant profile. Moreover, a single-instrument method using self-report such as the MMPI/MMPI–2 may have to be supplemented by the Rorschach or a structured clinical interview to provide another perspective on the presence of possible psychopathology.

This chapter is a powerful resource for those of us who teach assessment. First, the primary antidote for bias is proper use of scientific training using a method for testing hypotheses and conceptual tools to clarify a critical and active thought process that includes stepwise approach to clinical case materials from multicultural clients. Second, it is vital to develop an ethnorelativistic attitude of respect and interest in cultural materials, including language. Active involvement as a clinician with an examined personal cultural perspective and a continuously expanding overlay of specific and detailed information concerning a client's culture is of equal importance with the technology of personality assessment. Third, a desirable outcome of accumulating cross-cultural experiences and understanding of cultural differences is a personal willingness to expend the additional time and effort to address questions directly to clients and their assessment data. These issues indicate awareness that group similarities rather than group differences have been overemphasized in training and research methodology. It is important to ask questions concerning possible cultural influences at every step during an assessment process; this can increase the reliability of subsequent diagnoses and the validity of cultural formulations to provide the necessary information for an informed choice among available interventions.

23

An Assessment Practice
With Hispanics in Minnesota

Sonia I. Carbonell
California School of Professional Psychology, San Diego

This chapter documents the mental health needs of Hispanics in Minnesota as seen by a clinician in private practice; it identifies differences in assessment practices with Hispanics and Anglo populations in North America. The goal is to increase awareness of the need for culturally competent mental health services. The need to go beyond the acquired fund of theoretical knowledge and clinical skills in the field of psychology is emphasized. These observations do not include a review of the literature and research in the field of assessment of multicultural populations. From this point of view, the observations are intrinsic to clinical experiences and the personal process of being in this country, which means embracing or advocating for a flexible clinical practice with multicultural populations. A flexible practice uses interventions from various systems or schools of thought with an understanding of how those interventions translate into the particular school of thought that guides the overall clinical work.

The use of the word *Hispanics* refers to all individuals in this population regardless of country of origin and length of time in this country. Many people who trace their descent to Mexico or Latin America prefer the terms *Chicano* or *Latino* instead of *Hispanic*. The word *Hispanic* tends to trace a connection to Spain and the Spanish conquerors. Another term often used is *La Raza*, which translates as *the race*. The term was coined in Mexico to reflect the fact that the people of Latin America are a mixture of many of the world's races, cultures, and religions such as European, African, and indigenous Indians, Arabs, and Jews. This mixture of the cultures of the old and new world needs to be considered in psychological assessments of Chicanos/Latinos because it reflects the combination of integrated aspects of different views of reality, cultural practices, and historical process. An assessor must be able to understand the different variables of cultural identity of a Chicano/Latino individual in addition to educational level, class values, and the identity related to skin color.

MINNESOTA'S HISPANIC POPULATION

Like many places in the United States, the Hispanic population in Minnesota is composed primarily of Mexicans and Mexican Americans, including migrant farm workers. There are also Puerto Ricans, Cubans, and immigrants from the Caribbean and Central/South American countries. Census data reported in "Al Dia," a Minnesota Chicano/Latino Newsletter (Chicano Latino Affairs Council, 1998), indicate that Hispanics are the third largest population in the United States. In 1996, 28.3 million Hispanics were estimated, which is 10.7% of the U.S. population. This figure is projected to reach 36.1 million, the largest U.S. minority group, as early as 2005 and one fourth (24.5%) of the total U.S. population by 2050. In 1994, the Hispanic population on the U.S. mainland included the following groups: Mexican American (64.1%), Puerto Rican (10.4%), Cuban (4.2%), and Central and South American (14.0%). The Hispanic population was estimated to be 91.2% White and 5.6% African American in 1996.

The Office of Ombudsperson (1995) reported that the U.S. Census Bureau projection for the Hispanic population in Minnesota was 73,000 persons in 1995, approximately 2% of the state population. However, during the last 10 years, most Hispanic community agencies have calculated that the Hispanic population of the state is greater than 100,000. Mexican and Mexican-American populations are the largest group—an estimated 80% to 90% of the state Hispanic population. Hennepin County, where Minneapolis is located, is the exception, with a total Hispanic population of 13,978 in 1990. Mexicans were estimated to be 50% of this population, followed by 9% Puerto Ricans and 5% Cubans. The other 36% came from other Spanish-speaking countries. An explanation for the concentration of recent Latinos immigrants in Minneapolis historically was perceived as a function of better access to social services. The population concentration of Chicanos and Mexicans in Minnesota's rural areas was due to the availability of jobs in meat processing factories and agriculture. Providers of services estimated that, in September 1998, 35% of school children in the rural areas are Hispanic. There is a growing concern with the inability of the school systems to provide adequate assessment of mental health and educational needs, with provider estimates that 40% to 50% of Chicanos/Latinos receiving social and mental health services are illegal immigrants. This has relevance for the assessment process as well as the delivery of services.

Although Cubans constitute only 5% of the Hispanic population in Minnesota, they are the most challenging group and most in need of culturally competent services. Many chronically mentally ill Cubans came to this country between 1979 and 1980 from psychiatric hospitals, leaving their families in Cuba. They do not speak English and they will probably never learn it. This population cannot function socially or perform routine daily activities without the assistance of others. They cannot adapt or understand the dominant culture and often cannot access services. They are victims of irresponsible political practices. Their pain is invisible to those in power; nobody claims responsibility for their quality of life and living conditions. In Cuba, they were vulnerable adults and they remain so. They are condemned to mental suffering and, in most cases, extreme poverty. The number of chronically mentally ill, homeless Cubans is increasing. New governmental policies or changes restricting and cutting services for legal and illegal immigrants suggest that the few persons receiving services will lose them in the near future. The Cuban mentally disabled individual will be punished for the crime of having been weak or sick when politicians were playing games among themselves. They also will be punished by the mental health and social services system's incompetence in providing services that are culturally appropriate. There were promises and hopes for a better life that did not come through for the mentally ill.

MENTAL HEALTH SERVICES FOR HISPANICS AND THEIR FAMILIES

Mental health services including assessment for Hispanics and their families are extremely limited in Minnesota. There are two nonprofit mental health agencies in the entire state providing counseling in Spanish. Between full- and part-time positions, these two agencies have nine licensed social workers and three licensed psychologists. Psychological testing is provided on a limited basis. There are four psychologists in private practice who speak Spanish, and only one emphasizes culturally competent services and provides testing and psychological evaluations. There are approximately four more bilingual psychologists in administrative positions who do not provide direct services to clients. It is estimated that in the whole state there are six bilingual psychiatrists. The number of bilingual social workers, most of whom work for nonprofit agencies and government Human Services Departments, is larger but insufficient to meet the needs of the population. This information was confirmed by calling each of the agencies serving Hispanics. The Minnesota State Boards of Psychology, Psychiatry, and Social Work do not have statistics on the number of licensed providers who serve multicultural populations or who specifically provide services in Spanish. Lack of statistics is a common problem, although the counties began to include the Hispanic population in their statistics by the late 1980s.

Services in the nonmetropolitan areas of Minnesota are even more limited than in the Twin Cities, and social services are usually provided by paraprofessionals. Six agencies serving Hispanics were identified around the state. The Office of Minority Health (1997) estimated that the Hispanic population has been growing more rapidly in Greater Minnesota, or rural regions outside of the Twin Cities metropolitan area, than any other group. Greater Minnesota not only has experienced a rapid growth of the Hispanic population, but racial hate and discriminatory practices against Chicano/Latino individuals is also increasing.

In the Minneapolis/St. Paul metropolitan area, agencies providing social services, including Child Protection services, typically have one or two social workers who are fluent in Spanish. State agencies and programs providing mental health case management services usually have one or two bilingual social workers. There are no day treatment programs that specialize in providing services to Hispanics. For chronically mentally ill and cognitively disabled individuals needing intensive services, there is not a single program in Minnesota with culturally competent services. There are four chemical dependency programs with services for Hispanics and three additional agencies providing only assessments needed to authorize treatment. Inpatient or outpatient treatment programs specializing in services for Hispanic adolescents do not exist and are inadequate for all cultural groups. There is only one women's shelter providing bilingual services and addressing the domestic abuse needs of the Hispanic population. There is also an agency in the metropolitan area specializing in services for victims of torture coming from a variety of countries, and Hispanics meeting criteria can receive services. Spanish-speaking foster homes for Hispanic children and adolescents are also few in numbers. Family-based inhome therapy to prevent out-of-home placement or facilitate reunification of families is provided by the community agencies offering counseling and other social services.

Many observations about the Hispanic population may be true for other multicultural groups, including the Anglo American, because the existing mental health and social services are insufficient and unsatisfactory for all populations. However, it is necessary to identify the context and limitations of the mental health and educational resources for assessment of Hispanics in Minnesota. There are laws making the delivery of culturally competent mental health services mandatory—the Minnesota Statutes Adult Mental Health Act and the Children's Mental Health Act. However, mechanisms to make agencies and government accountable for delivery of services that respond to the cultural needs of all populations are lacking. These legislative acts do not have provisions to penalize agencies for noncompliance with the law.

The movement over the last 15 years toward understanding cultural diversity did not produce enough changes in the interactions among multicultural populations and the system. Once trends for demographic changes were predicted, the private and public sectors attempted to fix the problem without understanding the complexity of the task. Cultural diversity and cultural sensitivity training became popular and, in some cases, mandatory. Hasty training provided awareness of the existence of culturally diverse populations, but failed to accomplish the goal of improving services or reducing institutionalized prejudice and racism. The experience and information collected indicates that the delivery of culturally competent services has to be mandatory. Pain and the damage to the quality of life due to racism, ethnic discrimination, and intolerance of sexual preference must stop. Changes are imperative if the right to life, liberty, and pursuit of happiness continues to be one of the founding principles of this country. A commitment to address these issues needs to be adequately established through legislation.

Assessment of Hispanic children must take into account socioeconomic status (SES) because children of color are much likely to be poor than are White children. Poverty rates for children of color in Minnesota ranged from 31% for Hispanic to 55% for American Indian (Office of Ombudsperson, 1995). The need for bilingual psychological assessments including testing is overwhelming. Hispanic children with language developmental disorders and other learning disabilities are often not diagnosed for several years. The roots of their problems are initially considered a lack of educational experience and difficulties encountered in the process of learning a second language. Valuable time will be lost until academic performance and rate of knowledge acquisition become the points of reference used by teachers to determine who needs an assessment. The needs for special educational services of a White child can be detected in 2 or 3 months, whereas the Hispanic child's needs are addressed 2 or 3 years later. The delay in the implementation of appropriate, individualized, educational plans and remedial services has a devastating impact on the child's future. Children often become discouraged and frustrated, leading to truancy and a high dropout rate. Providers of mental and social services find that the average age of a dropout in the Hispanic population is between 13 and 15, whereas in the larger culture it is approximately 16. Many Hispanic children enter the workforce at ages 14 and 15 at the expense of their education and future. The Office of Ombudsman (1995) indicated that in the 1993 to 1994 school year, an estimated 3.4% of the state's 7th- to 12th-grade students dropped out of school, a small decrease since 1992 to 1993, although this decrease may be attributable to a change in the definition of dropouts. The state dropout rate for students of color was 10.8% for the 1993 to 1994 school year, whereas White children had a dropout rate in the same year of 3.4%. The dropout rate of 5.4% for Asian children was the smallest of these groups of children of color, whereas children of African Americans had the highest dropout rate (14%), followed by American Indian (13%) and Hispanic children (12.3%).

Leaders in the Hispanic community express concerns with the over-representation of Hispanic children in special education programs in the rural areas of Greater Minnesota. Again the root of this problem is the lack of resources in the school system to provide culturally competent services. The Minneapolis and Saint Paul school districts are presently making strong efforts to address the needs of multicultural populations, but the school system does not have Spanish-speaking psychologists. School psychologists indicated that the use of professional translators began in 1990. As far as I could find out, there are only two school psychologists that provide services for Hispanic children in the metro-politan area of Minneapolis and St. Paul.

The shortage of bilingual, culturally competent providers in all fields, especially in the helping professions, is a consequence of the benign neglect of Minnesota's educational system historically. The school systems in Minnesota have historically failed to value the education and future quality of life for Hispanic children. Often we hear the argument that there are no bilingual school psychologists who can do testing. Although this is true, there is no evidence of a successful undertaking to correct this problem. Recruitment efforts are often limited to administrative and other types of positions that are not linked to direct services for the Hispanic population. Further, there is no future plan to meet the needs of this population.

THE IMPACT OF LIMITED RESOURCES ON THE DELIVERY OF SERVICES

The limited mental health resources for Hispanics has forced those few available clinicians into a position similar to that of a family physician with a general medical practice who works sometimes with all type of problems and with several or all family members. This is usually accepted and even preferred in the Spanish-speaking community. However, in Minnesota, simultaneous assessment and treatment of several family members is not the norm.

Social Service Agencies

County agencies and the Department of Human Services often request psychological assessments for parents and children. Culturally competent assessment is crucial to the implementation of a social service plan. Cognitive limitations and mental illnesses are often unidentified. In only 5% of these cases in which the future of Hispanic children is decided is a culturally appropriate assessment included. Child Protection cases include a request for evaluating the child–parent relationship and the caregivers' parenting skills. The clinician doing the assessment must understand the childraising practices of the particular Hispanic subgroup in which the family functions because each culture has the potential to promote unsafe practices in the care of children. These unsafe practices are usually corrected with information and are not considered pathological. However, when a Hispanic caregiver uses an unsafe practice, the behavior is usually identified as pathological or neglectful.

An example is an infant lying down with a bottle that is supported by pillows and blankets. The problematic behavior is that the baby can choke. However, this is a common practice when Hispanic parents work in the fields or do housekeeping. The Hispanic parent using this practice keeps an eye on the child. Poor judgment could be determined, but the behavior has a cultural and historical context that also must be identified. Information can be provided and even a request that pillows and blanket not be used to feed a baby, but the assessment of the parent's intellectual and psychological functioning is crucial in determining how to address the problematic behavior. Simple routines in the care of children are rooted in socialization practices. We tend to take care of the physical and emotional needs of children according to our personal histories and cultural values. Another example is our attitudes toward food. Hispanic parents generally do not promote or allow children to play with food. A Hispanic teenager mother's refusal to allow her baby to play with food was assessed in a residential treatment facility as evidence of resistance to treatment and lack of nuturance.

Once it has been determined on the basis of physical evidence that abuse occurred, few Hispanic children and their families have access to psychological culturally competent evaluations and treatment. Reunification in cases of sexual abuse is rare. In cases of allegations of physical abuse, Hispanic parents are frequently charged with "malicious punishment of a child." Hispanic families tend to suffer more than benefit from social and protective services.

Forensic Cases

Forensic cases referred by the county attorney and public defenders office illustrate the limitations in services. The requested services include psychological evaluations to obtain general information—"Reference Study of Delinquency Matters," "Competency to Proceed Evaluations," "Medical Examination of Defendant Upon Defense of Mental Deficiency or Mental Illness," "Custody Assessments for Family Court," and "Parenting Assessments" for Juvenile Court in proceedings of termination of parental rights—and evaluations for civil court in sexual harassment cases and worker compensation. Additionally, forensic evaluations' requests presently include two emerging areas related to immigration and worker compensation laws.

A psychological assessment is requested in cases of political asylum to determine the individual's participation in war activities, as in the case of Central American children forced to participate in civil war. Their participation in crimes against humanity is what is being evaluated, as well as their potential to function in mainstream culture. Individuals and families applying for "Suspension of Deportation" are generally under unbearable emotional stress. Psychological evaluations are often requested by lawyers. The role of the psychologist is to assess the emotional hardship individuals and their families would suffer if forced to leave their homes in the United States and return to their countries of origin. Findings in psychological evaluations are used as arguments to prove that deportation would cause extreme hardship to family members. In the case of Hispanic families, this often includes the effects on children that are U.S. citizens. These children often speak Spanish poorly and, if deported, will not have access to education, medical care, and the life-enriching experiences to which they are accustomed. Many children are receiving special education or have medical conditions requiring ongoing treatment. This is an interesting and painful field full of contradictions. Findings of adult mental illness or cognitive impairment are often disqualifying conditions for obtaining permanent lawful residence in the United States.

One of the most painful experiences of Hispanics in this country is their dealings with immigration; this is one area that is often neglected in assessment. Two factors contribute to this neglect—the fact that assessors who are not Chicano/Latino do not have an understanding of the emotional implications of living in fear in their country and that most Chicano/Latinos will not disclose this information unless they are referred by their lawyers. As a mental health provider of Chicano/Latinos, I became aware of this silent, yet powerful contributor of emotional pain by observing how clients are sometimes forced to explain why their name in their place of employment is different than when they are called at home. Even when asked directly, Chicano/Latinos are reluctant to clarify their immigration status. As a rule, you do not disclose this information even to friends because you do not know when it will be used against you. Sometimes an angry neighbor, spouse, boyfriend, supervisor, or coworker will call the Immigration and Naturalization Service (INS) in retaliation for interpersonal conflicts. The changes and new immigration laws are promoting abuses on a major scale, making anyone who looks different vulnerable.

In the Hispanic community at large, there is a growing sentiment that, as a group, they are being singled out for discrimination and persecution. The 1996 November raids of workplaces in the Twin Cities are examples of events that contribute to this generalized fear. There is also an increase in raids of public places such as park and recreation areas where there is a concentration of Chicanos/Latinos. Teenagers are becoming vulnerable to police harassment because they are often stopped with excuses of being suspected of braking the law, and they are later asked to provide documentation regarding their legal immigration status. Many individuals in the Hispanic community perceive that illegal detention or police contact has more frequently occurred since the Illegal Immigration Reform and Immigrant Responsibility Act of 1996 (IIRAIRA). The absence of proper documentation can lead to being taken into custody even if later individuals are not charged with any other crime than not being able to prove legal status in the United States.

Hispanics with illegal immigration status often have one or two unskilled jobs and pay medical insurance premiums, but they cannot use their mental health benefits for psychological services requested by their immigration lawyers. Any testing or assessment with the purpose of assisting in their immigration case is considered a forensic matter. This is more relevant when the family has limited economical resources and earns a minimum wage. Families requesting *suspension of deportation* cannot receive mental health services through nonprofit social services agencies. An assessment for immigration requires a family study and testing for each family member. This type of evaluation usually consumes an average of 30 to 40 hours for an average family of five members, including the parents. Every family member has to be evaluated to determine the possible psychological hardship in case of deportation. The estimate of five million undocumented aliens, as reported by Greg Gordon in the *Star Tribune Washington Bureau Correspondent* on May 6, 1997, can be realistic, but the estimate of 7,200 in Minnesota is not. There are many unskilled jobs performed by Hispanics. Some companies in Minnesota with up to 800 unskilled workers have 90% Hispanic workers. Unskilled Hispanic workers estimate that 80% of them are undocumented. The law permits issuance of only 4,000 hardship waivers per fiscal year; according to the *Star Tribune Washington Bureau Correspondent*, they were already allocated in May 1997.

Social Security Disability Determination Services

Individuals referred by Social Security Disability Determination Services provide another example of limited resources. Non-Spanish Speaking Consultants for Social Security do not like to hear that their assessments with the help of translators are potentially unethical. The role of the consultant for Social Security Disability Determination Services has clear boundaries, with typically only 1 hour of direct contact to collect information about daily functioning and form an opinion about the claimant's mental capabilities to work. No direct feedback or recommendations for treatment are given to the client. Psychological testing for evaluation of memory and cognitive abilities is requested in cases where mental retardation or learning disabilities are considered as part of claimant's impairments in obtaining or retaining employment. Personality testing is requested in special or appeal cases and when Malingering and Somatoform Disorder are suspected. In many cases, the consultative evaluation is the only information obtained about the claimant. It is a difficult and creative process to maintain the boundaries as a consultant for Social Security Disability Determination Services while responding to the needs of the human being in front of you.

Culturally competent assessment of Chicanos/Latinos is a rare event due to limited access to bilingual Social Security Disability consultants and because evaluations are usually conducted with the help of translators. In the past, family members or friends acted as interpreters to assist in the process and professional translators have been used only recently. The 1-hour time period allowed for the assessment sets the stage for an incompetent evaluation. However, there are two other major obstacles: the clinical skill of the translator who cannot provide clinical information based on observations, especially in parts of mental status examinations, and consultants' lack of awareness of cultural differences. Consequently, individuals who are eligible for services often lose access to services because the psychological evaluation fails to properly identify their problems. Consultants often cannot understand the contradictions found in the claimant's presentation of daily functioning and description of psychological problems. These consultants are inclined to diagnose Malingering or disregard information presented as obstacles to retain and maintain employment.

THE IMPACT OF MANAGED CARE IN THE DELIVERY OF MENTAL HEALTH SERVICES TO HISPANICS

Some managed care organizations have added valuable services that are positive and responsive to the needs of various populations seeking mental health services, such as making translators and transportation available. However, managed care has not improved the quality of mental health services. Rather, it has made it impossible to provide adequate assessment services for those who receive public assistance or have low-paying jobs. Children in foster care and individuals receiving Social Security Disability benefits are exceptions who presently use the old medical assistance plan that is less restrictive. However, new 1999 pilot projects to serve individuals with disabilities through managed care will soon end the limited access to culturally competent assessment.

Psychological testing for Hispanic clients has always been a challenge for any clinician serving this population in the United States. Insurance companies and managed care organizations have become added burdens because they tend to perceive testing as an expensive service that is not cost-effective. The prior authorization for testing services is often denied. In the rare cases when testing is approved, some managed care organizations authorize 2 or 3 hours, including the report of findings. This authorization practice is used with all populations; for Hispanic clients, however, it becomes an extremely difficult task to accomplish with such time restrictions. Often insurance companies want a statement to demonstrate the medical necessity of testing. The argument is that testing is an expensive service, and there is no research suggesting that is helpful.

In many cases, time constraints begin with the authorization of two sessions for diagnostic interviews. This is followed by a request for a report that needs to contain specific information that varies according to the policies and rules of each company. Most reports for prior authorization of mental health services require a description of chief complaint, diagnostic impressions, treatment plans, and an objective measure of goals to be accomplished. Most of the time, a non-Hispanic client can be assessed in 1 hour. During the second hour, the client is given feedback regarding the clinician's understanding of the chief complaint, diagnosis, and treatment goals identified during the intake interview.

Hispanic clients often make the first contact after several attempts to leave messages when a voice mail or answering service is being used. When clients begin to complain about the difficulties of communicating on the phone, it is important to respond to the concern and understand how big an obstacle and how stressful something as simple as leaving a phone message can be. Clinicians, insurance, or managed care staff who have never traveled and who have no experience with foreign languages and different cultures might not be able to understand how a simple act such as leaving a phone message needs to be considered in the assessment. Hispanics with an average intellectual level tend to feel mentally retarded when they cannot accomplish simple tasks to perform routine daily activities. Additionally, there must be special attention to the feelings of being powerless and in a dependent position for individuals who have been previously well functioning. To be in a foreign culture brings about a recapitulation of developmental psychological stages. The individual level of regression is closely tied to developmental arrests that the person might have been able to overcome with the help of environmental factors in his or her own culture. However, in the context of a new social system with a different culture and language, accurate assessment and respectful assistance may be necessary.

Prior to the first clinical interview with the Hispanic client, several steps take place. The first is to obtain information about the client's mental health benefits. The second is to obtain authorization for the 2 hours of intake. Even if the client has transportation, directions may be required. Phone calls to the bus company are necessary to help the client identify the correct bus line for transportation to the office. At other times, phone calls are necessary to insurance companies to authorize transportation services. In this case, the client needs to be certified as being eligible for transportation services, which requires an explanation of why the service is needed, and information such as the client's policy numbers, date of birth, dates of service, and so on must be given to the insurance company. In the easiest instances, this process takes 1 hour to complete. Non-Hispanic clients can usually accomplish these tasks with relatively little assistance. They usually can fill out intake forms that help in the process of diagnosis and identification of treatment goals and plans. In contrast, Hispanic clients need assistance filling out all the forms that are necessary for insurance billing purposes, intake, description of symptoms and problems, and so on, lengthening the intake process to 4 to 6 hours.

What is possible to accomplish in two 50-minute sessions with a non-Hispanic client will take at least 4 to 6 hours with a Hispanic client. In addition, services should foster independence because this is a strong value in the Anglo-American culture. Consequently, the Hispanic client needs to be provided with information that could increase the possibilities of self-reliant interactions with the system. An argument can be made that these activities—calling the insurance, verifying coverage, making transportation arrangements, and so on—are not expected professional activities of a psychologist. However, they are clinical interventions that form part of the initial assessment of the client's level of functioning in the main culture. They allow the clinician to have a behavioral sample of the level of adaptation or the client's current place on the bilingual-bicultural continuum of social functioning. Furthermore, it allows the clinician to explore the feelings of competence and inadequacy often found in individuals with a different cultural background than the mainstream society. Thus, assessment of Hispanics is more time consuming because the clinician often begins to intervene or treat during the assessment process. Culturally competent assessment services become a brief therapeutic intervention.

DISCUSSION OF ASSESSMENT PRACTICES

Psychology graduate programs usually offer clinical training for professional work with all types of populations, treatment modalities, psychiatric disorders, psychological issues, and so on. Although this training addresses the needs of individuals from the dominant culture, clinicians are poorly prepared to provide mental health services for multicultural populations including Hispanics. Chicano/Latino clinicians have advantages when providing services to their own ethnic group. Although they would probably be more effective than non-Spanish-speaking providers, they also need to acquire specific clinical experience to become culturally competent. Chicano/Latino and other bilingual mental health providers need to become clinical translators of languages and cultures in the context of providing services. Bilingual and Chicano/Latino clinicians must provide services according to general standards for clinical practice while translating the clinical experience and information into two sets of realities or cultures. They must understand the mainstream culture and the differences in values, norms, beliefs, history, and socialization processes. Chicano/Latino clinicians born in this country or arriving before or about age 10 could have the advantage of speaking English well, but they do not always speak Spanish fluently. They must share and check out their clinical observations and keep updated on research with Hispanics. Chicano/Latino clinicians could struggle more with *Marielitos*—the group that emigrated from Cuba in the late 1970s and early 1980s—than with other Hispanic groups. This is not solely because Cubans exhibit more pathology or behavioral problems, but because other Hispanics do not share the same historical and political process, socioeconomic system, or social reality.

I routinely use the following tests in psychological assessment of Hispanics: Wechsler Memory Scale–Revised; Wechsler Children Intelligence Scale–Third Edition (WISC–III); Wechsler Adult Intelligence Scale (WAIS); The Test of Non-Verbal Intelligence (TONI–2) Form A and B; The Bender Visual Motor Gestalt Test; The Rorschach Inkblot Method; projective drawings including tree, person, and house; projective stories; The Minnesota Multiphasic Personality Inventory–2 (MMPI–2); sentence completions; Bacteria Woodcock Psico-Educativa En Español; the Thematic Apperception Test (TAT); and the Children Apperception Test (CAT).

In the assessment of cognitive skills, the administration of the Wechsler Spanish Version for Adults (EWIA) is no longer used because the norms are out of date (published in 1947, 1955, 1964, and 1968). The test results usually do not correspond to clinical observations. This was particularly true in cases where the individual had exceptional cognitive resources and mental retardation was suspected. There is a version of the Wechsler for children standardized in Spain and, with the exception of some problem items, the test results are usually accurate.

The Wechsler verbal subtests are administrated mainly to obtain clinical observations and an estimate of the individual cognitive processes mediated through language. For example, the Similarities subtest provides valuable information regarding the individual's capacity to form concep-

tual units from verbal material and express these concepts in words. It
also provides direct observations in cases where there is a tendency for
concrete thinking. A common mistake of school psychologists is to administer only the Performance subtests. I often find that developmental
language disabilities are not identified in a timely fashion because the
children's difficulties with academic achievement are attributed to the
process of learning English. However, once a child with language developmental disabilities is identified and educational special services such
as speech therapy are provided, a new problem needs to be considered.
These children do not receive the same training in their first language,
therefore they do not overcome their problems in Spanish. They begin to
communicate primarily in English, and if their parents speak only Spanish
this creates emotional isolation and problems in adequate parenting.

Information and Comprehension subtests leave room for cultural biases
related to alternate cultural background, educational opportunities, as
well as cultural knowledge and expectations. The clinician's cultural competence is decisive in the differential observation of cultural factors and/or
weakness in social judgment. Picture Arrangement is helpful in the determination of a possible deficit in this area. Clinical experience with
middle-class, well-educated, bilingual, acculturated Hispanics suggests
that the administration of the WAIS–R (English version) is appropriate.
However, the administration of the Wechsler scales differs for individuals
from extremely poor economic and educational backgrounds, especially
when they do not speak English. It is important not to take for granted
reports from individuals that they can read and write. A short dictation
of a paragraph or requesting a short essay of the client's description of
problems will usually provide evidence of writing skills and maturity of
handwriting. It is important to be able to determine on what grade level
the individual is functioning. Reading Comprehension is another routine
short test. The individual's math skills should also be determined in
assessments of daily functioning and parenting skills. Child protection
case plans often include a requirement for improving budgeting skill and
money management. Social workers cannot usually identify whether the
root of the problem is a math developmental disability or a maladaptive
pattern rooted in psychological problems. Subtests like Arithmetic allow
the clinician to form an opinion concerning the individual's basic math
skills. To complement, the assessment of verbal arithmetic skills with a
written math test to observe addition, subtraction, multiplication, and
division skills is also useful. Observations indicate that the test results of
the Arithmetic subtest can be misleading when the individual has a high
level of performance anxiety.

The Wechsler Memory Scale is one of the tests I most frequently use,
especially subtests such as Mental Control, Digit Span, and Logical Memory,

which routinely complement intake evaluations and mental status examinations. This test is primarily used to determine brain injury and changes in memory functioning in worker compensation cases, personal injury, and Social Security evaluations. I have translated subtests such as Logical Memory, Verbal Pair Association, and so on, as well as the instructions. As far as I am aware, no Spanish version is available. The Logical Memory subtest is helpful to observe memory and thought process; on occasion, it can even point out a tendency for confabulation, which is often found in clients with brain injury and deterioration of memory functioning.

When it is necessary to rule out malingering, one of the most helpful methods is the Rorschach. Although the Rorschach primarily provides descriptions of personality functioning, it has also been useful for differential diagnosis of psychiatric patients suspected of having an organic brain disorder. Rorschach sign systems for identifying brain impairments have also been used in my clinical observations to determine malingering. Individuals pretending mental illness and mental retardation can often manipulate tests such as the MMPI, intelligence tests, and so on. However, even when they try to give bizarre Rorschach responses, the complexity of the responses usually gives an indication of the individual cognitive resources and allows identification of the possibility of malingering.

In personality assessments, the most useful test is the Rorschach Comprehensive System (RCS). However, clinicians who are not fluent in Spanish should not use the Rorschach with Chicanos/Latinos with limited fluency in English because they have to use translators. The translator must have training in the administration and scoring of the Rorschach to ensure the integrity of responses. During the inquiry phase, the interaction of the assessor and translator will alter the administration process. The identification of Special Scores contained in the responses to Rorschach cards also will be vulnerable to omissions or errors during translation. Translations will have an impact on the identification of unusual verbalization and inadequate combinations. Individuals who are exposed to a second language have transitional losses in the integrity of their conceptual precision. There is an interference of the second language in the use of vocabulary and fluency. The translator must be able to identify and convey information regarding the individual placement in a bilingual continue scale process and other aspects of clinical evaluations such as quality of speech and thought process. Familiarity with cultural differences between Hispanic subgroups is also relevant. Individuals with limited education who come from rural areas of Latin American countries overuse some content categories and do not use others (e.g., less H and more A, more m, etc.). Cultural differences must be especially considered when the individual's quality of object relationships is being identified. An available Spanish version of the Rorschach has incorporated the list of popular responses in Spanish obtained through research (Sendin, 1981) that examined the differential aspects of the original list found in the English version.

The most controversial test for assessment of Hispanics is the MMPI–2. The research in Spanish-speaking countries (Spain, Mexico, Puerto Rico, Nicaragua, Chile, Argentina, and now Colombia and Venezuela) concludes that the MMPI–2 Spanish version discriminates between normal and abnormal populations. U.S. research suggests that the MMPI–2 is appropriate for use with bilingual Latinos in the southwestern United States or that these individuals do not respond differently on the MMPI–2 as a function of language. However, a valid profile is a rare event in evaluation of Hispanics, and only 5% to 10% of the MMPI–2 Spanish version profiles in my experience have provided useful and interpretative clinical data.

The most common finding is profile invalidity due to the MMPI infrequency scale (F), which indicates unusual responses to the item pool by claiming excessive numbers of unlikely symptoms. Culturally, Hispanics can be perceived as having the tendency to exaggerate and dramatize. Even if a Spanish language version is used, the culture does not emphasize the same level of precision in the use of the language and allows for embellishment. The hypotheses for elevated F scores are confusion, reading problems, random responding, severe psychopathology, possible symptom exaggeration, faking psychological problems, and malingering. The elevation in F is often influenced by the membership in a particular cultural group. Forensic cases involving questions of competence to stand trial, work compensation, personal injury, and malingering often produce invalid profiles due to high F scale elevations for Hispanics. In assessment of parenting skills, Chicanos/Latinos produced invalid profiles due to elevations of the L scale. The reasons typically considered for elevations on L include unwillingness to admit even minor flaws, unrealistic proclamation of virtue, claims near of perfect adherence to high moral standards, naive self-views, outright efforts to deceive others about motives or adjustment, and personality adjustment problems (Pope, Butcher, & Seelen, 1993).

In Minnesota, one of the states in which the MMPI is most widely used in forensic cases, there is often a direct request to include the MMPI–2 in the assessment battery. Lawyers seem to love the MMPI. Clinicians tend to overuse the validity scales to determine defensiveness and malingering. The most popular use is the interpretation of *faking bad* and *faking good*. Without mentioning the need for greater cross-cultural construct validity, my most basic and simple observation is that, in most cases where the MMPI–2 Spanish version is used, the clinician does not have the skills to determine the client's reading comprehension level. Further research on the MMPI–2 use with Hispanics in the United States is needed, although by 1995, 115 studies documented their performances of the Hispanics on the MMPI/MMPI-2 and MMPI-A. Sixty-six percent of the research was done using the English versions (Butcher, 1996).

The MMPI-2 could have been designed to eliminate cultural bias inherent in the norms used in the past because the datedness of the original MMPI norms was the main reason for revision (Butcher, Dahlstrom, Graham, Tellegen, & Kaemmer, 1989), but the use of this test with Hispanics continues to be questionable in the United States, even after following their "recommendations for Culturally Competent MMPI-2/ MMPI-A Assessment of Hispanics": (a) to keep in mind the purpose of the assessment, to determine the motivation or mind set of the client and how this is expressed on MMPI-2/MMPI-A profile (i.e., validity scales); (b) to consider the setting in which the evaluation is conducted; and (c) to determine the primary language of the Hispanic client, the educational level and where the education took place, and the language used by the client to express affect or emotion. Clinical experience indicates that bilingual Hispanic individuals taking the MMPI often need both versions— Spanish and English—in addition to dictionaries in both languages. On the average, 15 to 30 items continue to present problems in the translation; (d) to determine the client's ethnic identity for differences in motivation that could affect the test performance; (e) to determine the acculturation level of Hispanic clients; (f) to administer the MMPI-2/MMPI-A in a standard manner; and (g) to always administer the complete MMPI-2. The additional scales are considered the most useful in working with Hispanics; if reading level is in doubt, an audio form of the English or Spanish MMPI-2 should be employed. The interpretation of Hispanics' MMPI-2/MMPI-A performance should always occur in a systematic hypothesis-testing mode, blending with the Hispanic client's sociocultural context. Additional recommendations include the development of a local database (i.e., base rates) by psychologists who specialize in the assessment or treatment of particular Hispanic target groups and the use of peer supervision and consultation with culturally competent experts in MMPI-2/MMPI-A evaluation of Hispanics.

Despite these recommendations, the MMPI-2/MMPI-A continues to have great potential for clinical misuse, promoting incompetent cultural assessments with Hispanics. More adequate MMPI-2 use depends on clarification of cross-cultural differences between Hispanics and other ethnic groups, interpretation of differences and similarities among Hispanics groups, understanding the role of acculturation and the efficacy of the new MMPI-2/MMPI-A indexes including content and supplementary scales, understanding the relationship between MMPI-2 assessment and cultural-bound syndromes, and understanding the linking of research on Hispanics in the United States and Latin America. Butcher and colleagues (1996) are presently developing norms for the Spanish versions of the MMPI-2/MMPI-A as well as an interpretative manual.

One of the most difficult areas in assessing a Hispanic individual is educational background. Basically the client needs an informal reading and writing skills evaluation. In mental status examinations, I often ask the individual to read a paragraph in Spanish to determine reading comprehension. Hispanic clients often say that they have 6 or 9 years of educational experience when their actual skills are at first- or second-grade level. This type of misrepresentation is not considered lying unless you are very close to the family and the individual as a friend or perceived as a helper in an authority position. Psychological assessments done without a clear understanding of the client's basic reading and writing skills have catastrophic consequences in their conclusions. For example, after taking care of four children for 7 years, a Hispanic foster mother went through the process of being evaluated for adoption. She filled out forms and answered questions regarding the children's behavior; after being evaluated by four different mental health providers, the adoption was rejected. The children were perceived to have special needs, and the foster parent was not seen as being able to meet those needs. Nonetheless, the foster placement was continued; when a culturally competent opinion was obtained, it was discovered that because the client did not know how to read or write in English or Spanish all information mediated by reading skills was invalid.

Culturally competent psychological assessment of Chicanos/Latinos must take into consideration the individual's socialization process and the relationship between culture and language. We learn our first language and our values, attitudes, assumptions, and norms through a process of socialization, without conscious awareness of how this process is taking place. Many of our behaviors are learned through socializing and being part of a particular culture and a specific family group. The clinician providing services to multicultural populations must first understand the behaviors, customs, and values of the individual's culture, prior to making assumptions of underlying pathology or identifying personality traits. We tend to see different behaviors as signs of abnormal or pathological conditions; when working with multicultural populations, we need extra caution. While providing services through a Child Protection inhome family-based therapy program, teachers and social workers from a private school described a 7-year-old Mexican American child as having poor social skills. I requested a description of the behavioral indicators for this problem. The child's behaviors during lunch were the only clear example offered: "He eats with his hands, he makes a mess with his bread and tries to use it to pick up his food; he grosses out his peers." I was doing home visits and made arrangements to go to the child's home during dinner. I did not see any problem with the child's manners at the table. Later I realized that the family used tortillas to pick up their food from the plate, which involves a greater use of hands. I also realized that the child was showing an ability to adapt—he was transferring his skills, in a flexible manner, to the new context. I was not sufficiently familiar with the Chicano culture at that time to immediately identify this cultural behavior.

The clinician providing assessments to Hispanics must keep in mind the differences in levels of assertiveness. The Hispanic culture, by and large, does not emphasize being direct in the same way when one suspects that true feelings and thoughts would hurt the clinician's feelings or be disrespectful. Hispanics are taught to respect authority and be considerate of others. Thus, many times they are not perceived as being assertive. The clinician assessing a Chicano/Latino individual must reach that level of trust in which the client can go beyond the polite answer. For example, Hispanics will tell you that they will accommodate your schedule for an appointment when they really cannot make it. If attention is not paid to these details, the client will fail to come to the appointment. Extra time needs to be given to determine if there is an expected obstacle that could interfere with the appointment. This is particularly relevant in cases of Child Protection, where the cooperation of the parents with the assessment will determinate out-of-home placement or termination of parental rights. Clients could appear to have more resistance to treatment or pathological behaviors than they have in reality.

Lack of awareness of issues related to assertiveness and relationships to authority figures could have a devastating impact on the life of the individuals and their families. One of my favorite examples also comes from experience as a social worker for Child Protection, specializing in work with Hispanics. The family of a 7-year-old Hispanic child had been referred to Child Protection by the school after the child's father had burned the child's hand as punishment for stealing. The family assessment indicated the possibility that this was an isolated event stemming from the father's frustration over trying to correct a problem. He had warned the child several times that this was the punishment for stealing. I advocate for stopping all physical means of discipline and always make a contract with parents to report all incidents. One of the goals of parenting skills assessment for Child Protection cases is to identify physical maltreatment. However, during assessments, it is important to understand and identify the root of particular behaviors. I have found that not all physical maltreatment is rooted only in psychological problems. This is particularly true for individuals coming from social systems based on slavery types of relationships, and some Indian groups in South and Central America historically punished stealing through hand burning and other similar types of discipline.

In the previously mentioned case, I was amazed by the strength of the child's family structure. I was concerned with the possibility of overlooking the child's needs and so requested a psychological assessment for the child. He was referred to the best psychologist specializing in child abuse. The father took the day off without pay to take the child to his appointment. When they arrived, the psychologist apologized for canceling the appointment. She had called the house and found out that they were already on their way. The father was angry but accepted a second appointment for 3 weeks later. When they arrived, the psychologist stated that they were not on the schedule. Again the father was angry for taking another day off; he explained that he had a card with the date and was not wrong about the date. The father stated that he was not coming back. The psychologist called and reported the incident. She expressed concern about the father's anger and her fear for ongoing family violence. I visited the family and helped them trace their steps until they were able to find the appointment card. I went to the psychologist, showed her the card, and asked: "Is this your handwriting?" She immediately recognized the card and remembered giving the father the appointment. She apologized and later called the mother offering an assessment at no cost to the parents. The mother stated, "I am sorry, my husband said that he will not bring the child to you again." The psychologist called me and expressed her fear of domestic abuse and recommended obtaining a court order to have the child assessed and placed in temporary shelter while the risk of physical violence was determined. She perceived the mother as completely terrified of the father's authority and questioned the possibility of obtaining accurate information unless the child was in foster care. I went to see the mother and found her statements to be exactly the same as the psychologist reported. After a long pause, I looked her in the eye and said: "*Ahora mi senora, digame usted que piensa de todo esto?*" (Now ma'am tell me, what do you think of all this?). The mother stated: "If my husband changes his mind, I will not allow my child to go to that assessment." I asked "Why?" and she stated: "We cannot trust her. She made us look like liars, and she was not respectful of our family." When I asked why she did not tell this to the psychologist, she stated: "Poor thing, the psychologist was feeling bad about my husband's decision. I did not want her to feel worse knowing that I agreed with his decision." Incidentally, through the years, I have remained in contact with the family because they have a business in the community. The child is now a young adult who works with his father and the assessment of family strengths has proved to be accurate.

Speaking Spanish is the most important and basic requirement for providing culturally competent assessment for Chicanos/Latinos. The clinician must understand how the language shapes the perceptions of social reality, how emotional interactions are negotiated through the language, and how the structure of the language transmits the values and norms of the culture. For example, the use of English calls for precision, and there is a subject responsible for the action. Spanish language does not necessarily promote irresponsibility. Rather, it is less blaming and punitive. It also allows us to use expressions that exaggerate and minimize, and these expressions are usually understood by the members of the culture without misunderstanding. I often use the example of the teacher who reacts to children's statements such as "the homework got lost" with great concern because of the risk that Hispanic children will develop an irresponsible attitude. This type of interaction often is not identified by either individual engaged in the communication. Affect is the most silent and powerful component of communication. Although the teacher emphasizes that the homework did not get lost by itself, the Hispanic child feels the teacher's disapproval and cannot see the point. In the child's world, things happen and nobody has to say "I did it!" The rice gets burned, the keys get lost, and so on. The passive tendency expressed through the use of Spanish is not necessarily pathological. The acceptance of faith and destiny are ingrained and expressed through the use of the Spanish language structure. It has, among other functions, an adaptive quality that allows individuals to deal with their political and socioeconomic realities. The belief that human beings are responsible for and in charge of their destinies is transmitted through the English linguistic structure.

The emotional impact or psychological implications of constantly ne-gotiating two different realities also needs to be well understood. Bilingual Hispanics often switch languages when talking about different subjects. Spanish is used more when the individual is dealing with painful issues or memories. Bilingual individuals often switch to English when they want to attain some emotional distance from an issue or when they are referring to experiences in this country. During psychological assessment, we lose the richness of information provided through the linguistic switch if the individual can only communicate in one language or if the evalu-ation is done with the help of translators.

The learning of, and interacting with, a second language has processes similar to the developmental stages found in the acquisition of the first language. Clinician assessing Chicanos/Latinos should be able to identify the individual's speech patterns and the emotional stress of language barriers. The individual's attempts to communicate in the second language are not emotionally rewarded as in the acquisition of the first language. These efforts are frequently emotionally painful and discouraging. The use of a second language, or even being exposed to interactions with the dominant language, temporarily changes the linguistic structure of the first language. Interac-tions with the dominant language are defined here as integration of vocabu-lary, expressions, or acquisition of second language survival skills. Hispanics say that once they have lived in the United States, their Spanish is not the same. The changes in sentence structure are temporary and reversible. However, the process of learning and using a second language has emotional consequences that have to be properly identified when determining the individual's psychological and social functioning.

The use of translators in mental status examinations and psychological testing is neither ethical or appropriate. Experience indicates that the likelihood of obtaining the mental status of the translator rather than the client is very high. Vital information is lost in the process of translating. The translator needs clinical skills to evaluate the use of language, including assessment of quality and quantity of speech or descriptions of rate, tone, association, and fluency. Common signs of thought disorders cannot be properly identified through translation unless the translator conveys this information. For example, the translator needs to clearly describe pressured speech, blocking, flight of ideas, loosening of associations, tangentiality, circumstantiality, neologism, clanging, and perseveration.

Neologisms or new words invented are difficult to identify because the interactions with a second language create changes in the individual's speech patterns. The translator and evaluator need to distinguish between a neologism and the linguistic process of second language acquisition. The linguistic changes occur even if there is no fluency in the second language. In addition, certain Hispanic groups use words differently, and the translator needs to be able to identify the context in which the words are used. For example, early in my interactions with the Mexican-American culture, a client described her chief complaint, which I understood as having no one to help her move. She used the word *trastear*. As the director of a mental health unit in a Hispanic nonprofit agency, I could access social services for my clients. I immediately asked for relatives or friends willing or able to help with the problem and began to ask such questions as, "When do you need this done?", "Have you asked other friends or relatives for help?", and so on. I was ready to use the social services of the agency such as transportation for relocation and moves. I was puzzled by her insistent statements that "My mother no me trastea, mi hermano tampoco." At that point, I asked her to define the meaning of the word *trastear*. To my surprise, we were speaking about two different things. I had known the word *trastear* as meaning to move from one house to another. She was using a Spanish–English colloquial expression meaning trust. I was ready to arrange transportation to help her move or relocate and she was asking for help to reestablish trust with her family members. This illustrates that even when two individuals speak fluent Spanish, they still need to be sure they are using words in the same way.

Translators also need to be able to identify and convey the different emotional connotations that the same word can have in English and

Spanish. An example is a word that in English can be used as a complement and in Hispanic culture can be perceived as a negative trait. An
example is the word *ambitious.* In many Hispanic cultural contexts, this
word is used to describe an individual who is motivated by money, is
selfish, and often does not have scruples to accomplish a goal.

Literal translation occurs when there is lack of familiarity with the
culture. Here is an example from my early experience in this country. I
went to a teacher of an introductory psychology class and asked permission *to assist his course.* I was hurt and angry when the teacher stated that
that was not possible until my English was better. When I related the
incident to another teacher, she took the time to check the meaning of
the word *assist* in English and the word *assist* in Spanish. We discovered
that I had not correctly conveyed my request. I had wanted to audit his
course—simply to be present during his lectures. The teacher's response
suggested that he thought that I wanted to be a teaching assistant.

Certain aspects of a cognitive evaluation—such as orientation, attention
and concentration, short-term memory, fund of knowledge, calculations,
and abstract abilities—have a better chance of being accurately assessed
with the help of a professional clinical translator. Common thought content disorders such as hallucinations, delusions, illusions, derealization,
depersonalization, and suicidal and homicidal ideation may accurately
be identified through translation when the translator and the psychologist
or psychiatrist doing the evaluation have enough knowledge about the
Hispanic culture to understand the individual's emotional tone and the
proper context of thought content.

Dramatic life circumstances need to be taken into account when evaluating perceptual distortions. For example, a Central-American political
refugee who entered the United States illegally was beaten and raped. She
reported a vision of the Virgen de Guadalupe consoling and guiding her to
a safe place in the middle of the night. When translated, this could be
diagnosed as a perceptual disturbance or transient hallucinatory episode.
The trauma could be identified as the external stimulus and the hallucinatory experience as being adaptive—a defensive coping mechanism that
protected her psychologically. The belief that the Virgen de Guadalupe was
protecting her is culturally acceptable. Superstitious behaviors and experiences with voices and visions need to be understood in the context of the
individual's background. There are some beliefs that are not necessarily
pathological, although they may result in problematic behaviors. An
example is the belief that an itching on the palm of the hand means that the
person is going to receive money. This is a delightful belief that could be
harmless. It is only culturally problematic or pathological if, based on the
itching of the hand, the person overspends money that has not yet been
received. Descriptions of superstitious beliefs are often confused with signs

of thought disorders, especially when the clinician is not familiar with the cultural context in which the superstitious beliefs occur and does not take the time to explore them. There are many false beliefs that are culturally accepted and transmitted. For example, seeing a black butterfly in the house is a symbol that somebody is going to die. To end an undesirable visit in the house, just put a broom behind the door and the individuals visiting will leave without you having to tell them that it is time to go.

Hispanic culture seems more permissive than other cultures in the use of magical thinking. The structure of the Spanish language allows a degree of exaggeration, minimization, and embellishment that is generally understood by the members of the culture. When the words are translated, it is easy to confuse the presentation with dramatization, grandiosity, or minimization. It also seems that the Spanish language allows a greater degree of emotional catharsis. The informal or nonacademic discourse does not need to be exact or precise. The use of strong adjectives and descriptors is culturally acceptable. Hispanics also seem more passionate in their verbal communication. This cultural characteristic is often confused with aggression.

Assessment of general appearance and behaviors requires an understanding of Hispanic culture and the differences among groups. Grooming, or level of hygiene, and characteristics of clothing could be deceiving. Hispanics take great pride in their physical appearance and often tend to dress formally. It is important to check with other family members the level of energy that the individual has for routine activities and whether somebody helps with reminders for showering or coordinating clothing. Untidiness and uncleanliness are not necessarily, or generally, correlated to socioeconomic status or background. Even Hispanics who are functioning intellectually in the borderline range will constantly have problems when their children are placed in foster care. The children's physical appearance and clothing become the central issue in complaints about care of the children. Observations suggest that non-Hispanic populations tend to accept less formal use of clothing for their children than Hispanics. Female children's long hair is another common problem for Hispanic parents. Some Hispanic subgroups make religious promises related to not cutting the female children's hair until they reach a certain age. This promise is an exchange for a wish to be granted, such as recovering from early childhood illness and so on.

The assessment of judgment or the ability to make sound decisions regarding everyday activities needs to take into account the cultural values of the individual. In the assessment of the individual's history of decision making, one also has to bear in mind the historical and socioeconomic context of those decisions. Hispanics are often described as having poor judgment. A common example is the Hispanic individual who is court ordered to cooperate with treatment or social services. Hispanics tend to miss appointments because they give priority to the needs of relatives and friends, as dictated by cultural values. Although this could happen with non-Hispanic clients as well, there is a difference in the frequency and emotional consequences of giving priority to one's own needs. Clinical experience indicates that this problem with priorities is easily corrected once the root of the behavior is identified and the person is provided with the information needed to function in accordance with the expectations of the dominant culture. In addition, it is necessary to help the client negotiate the conflict that is created by the pressures of social functioning with opposing sets of cultural values.

In the initial assessment, the degree of eye contact and the ability to interact with the interviewer is determined by the individual's mental status, education, and socioeconomic background. Hispanics coming from rural areas or farm lifestyles take longer to establish rapport and trust. Special consideration needs to be made when the individual is used to the oppression of the *patron*, particularly when there is a background history of employment as a live-in maid or similar type of relationship. The word *patron* is used here with the Spanish meaning—a synonym of *master* or *boss*. It could be a sign of disrespect—or being *igualado* to have, in the initial interview, what we call good eye contact. Being *igualado* means to deem equal, to place yourself in the same position of somebody you consider to have a higher status, power, or authority such as a doctor, psychologist, priest, or patron. Cuban individuals who immigrated to this country after 1976 tend to have a less passive or submissive style of interaction. Political and historical processes in Cuba seem to have changed how Cubans presently relate to authority figures and society in general. They generally appear to be more assertive than other Hispanic groups.

There is a Therapeutic Assessment model that attempts to correct deficits or short-comings of traditional psychological assessment. An approach that uses

> psychological test and collaborative assessment method to help clients reconceptualize their lives and move forward in their healing. Research has demonstrated that after a therapeutic assessment, many clients exhibit less distress and have higher self-esteem. In addition valid and usable test data are collected, which may be used for diagnosis, treatment planning, or documentation of change after treatment. (Finn, 1997, p. 6)

The question How is Therapeutic Assessment different from traditional assessments? is answered by Finn (1997) as follows:

> In the therapeutic assessment model, psychological testing is seen as a potential intervention, as well as a method of gathering information about a

client. We involve clients and referring persons in all stages of the assessment process, as collaborators, co-observers, and co-interpreters of certain test results. We always give verbal feedback to clients about test results and provide a written report when desired. At the end of the assessment we solicit written feedback from the clients about their experience of the assessment. (p. 7)

A Therapeutic Assessment model has the potential to provide one alternative to the limited mental health resources available for Hispanics. It combines an identification of the individual's cognitive and personality profile through testing, focuses on questions identified by the referral source and the client, and uses a model of brief therapy for therapeutic interventions. In addition, it has the potential to promote cultural competence "because the goal in Therapeutic Assessment is for the assessor to get in the client's shoes' and 'view the world as the client does' while addressing the client's agenda for the assessment, it also minimizes ethnocentrism and cultural bias as compared to traditional assessment" (Finn, personal communication, 1998).

REFERENCES

Butcher, J. N. (Ed.). (1996). *International adaptations of the MMPI-2: Research and clinical applications*. Minneapolis, MN: University of Minnesota Press.

Butcher, J. N., Dahlstrom, W. G., Graham, J. R., Tellegen, A. M., & Kaemmer, B. (1989). *MMPI–2: Manual for administration and scoring*. Minneapolis: University of Minnesota Press.

Chicano Latin Affairs Council. (1998, July). *Al Dia*. St. Paul, MN: Author.

Chicano Latino Affairs Council. (1998, January). *Bilingual directory*. St. Paul, MN: Department of Administration.

Finn, S. E. (1997, April). *Therapeutic assessments: Using MMPI-2, Rorschach, and other instruments as brief psychotherapy*. Workshop conducted by the Minnesota Rorschach Society.

Office of Minority Health Minnesota. (1997, Spring). *Populations of Color in Minnesota, Health Status Report*. St. Paul, MN: Minnesota Department of Health.

Office of the Ombudsperson for Families. (1995). *Annual report of the Ombudsperson for Spanish speaking families*. St. Paul, MN: Minnesota Department of Human Services.

Pope, S. H., Butcher, J. N., & Seelen, J. (1993). *The MMPI, MMPI-2, and MMPI-A in court: A practical guide for expert witness and attorneys*. Washington, DC: American Psychological Association.

Sendin, C. (1981). *Respuestas populares al test de Rorschach en sujetos españoles* [Popular Rorschach responses from individuals in Spain]. Actas del 10th Congreso Internacional de Rorschach, Washington, DC.

Wechsler, D. (1989). *WISC Escala de Inteligencia de Wechsler para ninos (11th ed.) (Wechsler Intelligence Scale for children)*. Madrid: TEA Ediciones.

24

Assessment Practices With African Americans: Combining Standard Assessment Measures Within an Africentric Orientation

Edward F. Morris
George Fox University

Over the past 25 years, the United States has undergone a dramatic change in the composition of its population. It is estimated that by the year 2000, approximately one third of the population will consist of racial and ethnic minorities (U.S. Bureau of the Census, 1995). As society becomes more diverse, so do the issues of acculturation and adjustment. When the non-Euro-American culture is similar to the dominant culture, the adverse impact of the cultural differences is subtle. However, if there is a significant discrepancy between a person's culture and the dominant culture, the impact on the individual can be emotionally, physically, and economically debilitating. Emotional debilitation can manifest itself within the nonadjusted person as clinical depression, extreme anxiety, severe adjustment problems, relationship difficulties, and substance abuse. Physical debilitation can manifest itself as psychosomatic complaints, gastrointestinal difficulties, headaches, or fatigue. Finally, economic debilitation can be expressed as any significant change in the person's financial or social status that is less than what he or she had been accustomed within his or her dominant community. When such a significant change occurs with one's economic stability, it is not unusual for the individual to experience symptoms of emotional and/or physiological instability. Unfortunately, the necessary systemic changes that are essential to handle the diverse emotional needs of African Americans within the mental health system have been neither comprehensive nor widespread throughout the various communities (Wade & Bernstein, 1991). Although the incidences of mental health problems have increased significantly during the past 20 years within the African-American community, mental health budgets have been slashed, services have been curtailed, and staffs have been reduced to the point where they are barely able to meet the most severe needs of their constituents.

It is the goal of this chapter to provide a synthesized review of the literature as it pertains to current assessment and diagnostic practices with African Americans. Through this process, this writer presents an integrated approach to conceptualizing, evaluating, and diagnosing African Americans that is sensitive to the cultural uniqueness of this particular group. Using an Africentric perspective as the theoretical underpinning, this chapter also examines various clinical, assessment, and diagnostic issues that could enhance the credibility of psychologists who work with African-American clients as well as the efficacy of standard evaluation measures that are used to assess their intra- and interpersonal experiences.

AFRICENTRIC PERSPECTIVE

The Africentric perspective is an ideological model that provides a culturally consistent frame of reference for African Americans. It is based on cultural nuances of the African culture and not on Euro-American standards. It emphasizes humanistic values and the integration of various components of a person's sociocultural experiences. It is based on the seven principles of Nguzo Saba (Karenga, 1989) that exemplify the integrity of the African-American culture. Briefly, these principles are: (a) *Umoja* (unity)—to strive for and maintain unity in the family, community, and culture; (b) *Kujichagulia* (self-determination)—to define and speak for oneself rather than being defined and spoken for by others; (c) *Ujima* (collective work and responsibility)—to build and maintain a community and share problems and accomplishments; (d) *Ujamaa* (cooperative economics)—to build and maintain resources and businesses within the African-American community and to profit from them together; (e) *Nia* (purpose)—to collectively build and develop the community to restore African Americans to their highest level; (f) *Kuumba* (creativity)—to do as much as possible to leave the community more beautiful and beneficial to others; and (g) *Imani* (faith)—to believe with all of one's heart in other African Americans, parents, teachers, and leaders.

ASSESSMENT CONSIDERATIONS IN PROVIDING RESPONSIBLE EVALUATIONS TO AFRICAN-AMERICAN CLIENTS

The number of psychological, cognitive, and educational tests available to evaluators is substantial. *Tests in Print* (Murphy, 1994) listed more than 3,000 available measures currently in print. Despite its overwhelming number, the normative population for these measures is predominantly Euro-American, college-age students, and/or middle class (Jones, 1996; Williams, 1991). The problems that arise as a result of the normative bias are considerable. When African Americans are assessed using these norms, for example, questions can legitimately be raised about cultural bias, validity problems, reliability concerns, and diagnostic certainty. The short- and long-term impact of the usage of these tests on African Americans in educational and vocational settings are equally profound. With inaccurate, invalid, or unreliable information, service providers are at risk for making wrong diagnoses, inappropriate placement decisions, and other disposition errors. For years, numerous individuals and professional organizations have raised questions regarding the appropriateness of standard measures with African Americans. These issues have been debated in professional journals (Gottfredson, 1994; Johnson, 1993; Mio & Iwamasa, 1993; Murray, 1996; Pedersen & Marsella, 1982; Zuckerman, 1990) as well as litigated in courts (*Hobson v. Hanson*, 1967; *Larry P. v. Riles*, 1972; *Marshall v. Georgia*, 1984; *PACE v. Hannon*, 1980). Despite the passionate protest by members of the African-American psychological community and other interested individuals and organizations, the assessment concerns continue.

There are several categories of problems that can impact the assessment of African-American clients. Following is a listing of the major problem areas:

- *Examiner biases:*

Bennett (1986) articulated some of the ill effects of ethnocentrism and stereotyping on the assessment process. He contended that the former problem minimizes or denies cultural differences between the evaluator and the client, whereas the latter problem causes the evaluator to selectively observe negative behaviors of the ethnic–minority client. Combined, these two problem areas adversely impact the examiner's perceptions of the client's performance and behavioral style. If the results of the classic Pygmalion study serve as a guide, evaluators treat clients for whom they have expectations of improvement differently from those for whom they have no such expectations (Rosenthal & Jacobson, 1968). When such negative perceptions are held with African-American clients, they are neither evaluated objectively nor unbiasedly. Although objective tests have a multitude of validity and reliability problems, they are not as vulnerable to examiner bias as projective tests. Standard administration procedures and clearly defined instructions provide some protection to ethnic–minority clients. Conversely, the advantages and disadvantages of projective tests lie in their ambiguity. The major advantage of projective measures lies in the degrees of freedom that are afforded to the clinician to integrate other objective data (e.g., behavioral observations, psychosocial history, genogram, cultural evaluation) into the overall assessment protocol. Projective measures also allow the examiner more latitude to tailor the testing protocol to fit the cultural uniqueness of the individual client. The major disadvantage of projective tests, however, lies in its reliance on the evaluator's worldview and theoretical orientation. If there is congruency between the worldviews of the African-American client and the evaluator, there is a greater chance that the evaluation will be culturally sensitive and diagnostically relevant. However, if the evaluator is neither culturally similar nor culturally sensitive to the influence of the client's culture on his or her emotional development and behavioral symptomotology, there is a greater chance that the evaluation will be clinically inaccurate and diagnostically questionable.

- *Countertransference:*

This particular phenomenon is often considered one of the potential debaucheries of therapy. Undetected, it can exhibit itself as paternalism, overidentification, overconcern, excessive sympathy, indulgence, reactive fear, or inhibition (Messer & Warren, 1995). Within a multicultural context, it can exhibit itself as latent prejudice or racism. Yamato (1993) has indicated that there are four types of racism: aware/blatant racism, aware/covert racism, unaware/unintentional racism, and unaware/self-righteous racism. Although there is a difference between racism and prejudice, the general categories of racism that Yamato identified could apply to individuals who are prejudiced. Being human, service providers can have negative or noncomplimentary feelings and thoughts about certain racial and/or ethnic groups based on perceptions, experiences, or stereotypes. It is extremely difficult to live in a race-conscious society like the United States without being impacted by race-based assumptions, fears, and stereotypes. It is also extremely difficult at times to separate personal from professional feelings. Although not at a conscious level, these noncomplimentary race-based thoughts or feelings can adversely impact the assessment process. Thus, countertransference that is based on unresolved racial issues are projected onto, or communicated to, the African-American client without the evaluator being aware of the interpersonal dynamics or exchange. If the African-American client becomes aware, and responds to, the therapist's projection, his or her behavior might change accordingly. At that point of the assessment process, it becomes difficult, if not impossible, for the evaluator to know which parts of the client's behavior to evaluate. Both the evaluator and assessment measures are evoking conscious and unconscious responses from the client as a result of the bidirectional racial exchange. Unfortunately, the evaluator is more likely to elicit a negative response than the ambiguous test item or measure. Unfortunately, it is the client's reaction to the evaluator's counter-transference that is labeled as *hostile, uncooperative, paranoid,* or *threatening.*

• *Bad person–environment fit:*
The notion of *person–environment fit* is frequently used within the field of community psychology to describe the relative adjustment of individuals within different settings. When community psychologists indicate that there is a good fit, they imply that the individual has made a functional adjustment to a particular situation (Barker, 1974; Moos, 1976). Conversely, when there is a bad fit, either the situation or the individual is nonfunctional, inoperative, or ineffectual. Unfortunately, when there is a bad fit, the results of this interactional exchange can adversely impact the assessment process. Given the bidirectionally of the person–environment fit, it is conceivable that African-American clients can sabotage their own performance during the assessment process if they perceive the testing situation or the evaluator as being threatening, hostile, or uncomfortable. As previously mentioned in this chapter, race can be a significant factor in the therapy and evaluation process. Because race is a major variable that can contribute to either a good fit or bad fit for African Americans in evaluation situations, the testing atmosphere becomes as important as the testing material. The result of a bad fit can be low motivation, test anxiety, and cultural awkwardness. Unfortunately, all of these resultant factors can adversely impact the client's test performance. If the evaluator is insensitive to these cultural issues, then he or she is at risk of misevaluating the effects of the person–environment fit as well as the client's abilities or personality functioning. Unfortunately, the evaluator's inability to discern these interacting factors is frequently the reason that there is a disproportionate number of African-American children in behavioral handicapped placements rather than in more constructive types of placements (e.g., tutorial programs, remediation services, learning disability programs, medication trials).

• *Unproductive test-taking skills and strategies:*
Unproductive test-taking skills and strategies are yet another major area that can adversely impact the assessment process with African-American clients. Sattler (1992) and Kaufman (1979) contended that this issue is particularly problematic for ethnic–minority children. Both of these researchers have indicated that African-American children tend to score

lower on standardized tests than their Euro-American counterparts. Although there is considerable disagreement among researchers (Jensen, 1981; Kaufman, 1979; Mercer, 1973; Oakland & Fiegenbaum, 1979; Reschly, 1978; Reynolds, 1980; Sattler, 1992) regarding the etiology of culturally discrepant scores, there is recognition that culture can impact how different groups perform on standardized tests. Because most standardized tests are based on Eurocentric principles and use predominantly Euro-American items, naturally the tests favor one group over another. The more congruent the person's cultural values and idiosyncrasies are with Eurocentricism or the more he or she understands the rules of Eurocentric thinking, the better the fit between the client's test-taking strategies and skills and those needed to perform well on standardized tests. Numerous researchers contend that standardized tests do not necessarily measure a person's innate abilities, but rather how well he or she does with formal tests that examine formalized education (Bosma, 1972; Gay & Abrahams, 1973; Gerry, 1973; Helms, 1992; Irvine & Carroll, 1980; Miller-Jones, 1989; Newland, 1973; Oakland, 1973; Oakland & Fiegenbaum, 1979; Taylor, 1980). In fact, Mercer (1973) asserted that a particular phenomenon exists among some African-American children where they experience a form of *situational retardation* that occurs only when they are in school or taking a formal test. Outside of school, these same children are able to function at the same competent level as their peers in multiple nonformalized, school-related activities. Similarly, Kaufman (1979) indicated that the ethnic–minority child's performance on certain intelligence tests is to a large extent dependent on the form of relationship established between the examiner and child. Because relationship factors, culture, and environmental influences can significantly impact test results, extreme caution should be exercised when assessing African-American individuals. It is conceivable that the examiner could assess everything but the child's true abilities and/or personality dynamics with Euro-American normed measures. At a minimum, the examiner should take time to (a) establish a culturally respective relationship with the African-American client, (b) assess cultural influences on the client's test-taking strategies, and (c) utilize various emic measures that have been normed on African-Americans as a supplement to, or in place of, existing etic measures.

- *Incongruent thought processes:*

Luria (1976) and Cairns and Walsiner (1982) presented a different perspective on the test-taking strategy issue. They argued that an individual's thought processes are influenced by the types of activities that are predominant within his or her culture. Individuals whose lives are dominated by concrete and practical activities, for example, have a different method of thinking than those whose lives are dominated by abstract, verbal, and theoretical activities. According to Luria (1976), abstract thinking develops through different types of verbally oriented activities and formal education. Conversely, concrete thinking develops through different types of hands-on or practical activities and informal education. Life experiences and education type, therefore, can influence a person's ability to think abstractly. The more diverse the experiences, the more expansive the thought processes; the more formal the education, the greater the use of different categorizations to express ideas and thoughts. Because socioeconomic status (SES) is intimately tied to the depth and breath of education and experiences, individuals who are economically challenged are at a distinct disadvantage when they are part of an environment that places an emphasis on these particular activities. Because a greater percentage of economically challenged individuals are ethnic minorities, such individuals are more inclined to be at the practical end of the thought continuum than at the abstract end. Most standardized tests are based on the individual's ability to think abstractly and be familiar with standard English, therefore most ethnic minorities are always at a disadvantage on such tests. Consequently, most of these individuals do not perform at a level that is reflective of their innate abilities. Rather than change the way in which evaluations are conducted or measures are chosen, most culturally insensitive evaluators penalize ethnic–minority clients for culturally different test-taking strategies that are incongruent with the demands of standardized tests.

From a Eurocentric perspective, Luria is correct in asserting that formal education can assist individuals in making the transition from concrete to abstract thinking. From an Africentric perspective, however, education can come in a variety of forms and situations; it does not have to all come from a formal structure. It can come from elders in a community, pastors in the church, peers on the street, and relatives and nonrelated caregivers. For African-American individuals, the end result of this expanded form of education could be as abstract, intuitive, and complex as those depicted within a formal educational setting. The problem, therefore, may not necessarily be solely with African Americans, but, in part, with current measures' inability to adequately assess this other form of equally complex and intricate thought processes.

When the assessment process is approached from an Africentric perspective, several questions regarding the tests' validity and reliability should be raised by clinicians, diagnosticians, and evaluators. The first series of questions should stem from the relative match of the measure's underlying theoretical orientation and the client's sociocultural experiences. The second series of questions should stem from the relative match of the examiner's conceptual framework and the client's cultural worldview. Finally, the third series of questions should stem from the relative match of the examiner's cultural orientation and the client's cultural orientation. If there are dissimilarities in any of these three domains, more serious questions should be raised about the appropriateness of the usage of certain measures with African Americans as well as the ethics of the examiners when they work with individuals with dissimilar cultural backgrounds. Competency requires a working knowledge of a particular population, an intimate understanding of certain evaluation measures, and a sensitivity to the bidirectionality of cross-cultural interactions. In providing services to African Americans, it is imperative that evaluators strive to be competent in all three of these areas. To do otherwise would be a disservice to the culturally different client and may be unethical.

Following is a list of questions that should be considered before using standard assessment measures with African-American clients:

- In examining the *reliability* of a measure, how dependable is a particular test in examining context-specific behaviors that African Americans have had to adopt as a form of cultural survival and adaptability?
- In examining the *content validity* of a measure: (a) how culturally relevant are the items to African-American individuals, and (b) do they measure the same content area when examined from a cross-cultural perspective?
- In examining the *construct validity* of a measure: (a) does it have the same connotative and denotative meaning with African Americans as it does with Euro-Americans and (b) do the test items reflect the same construct when examined cross-culturally?
- In examining the *concurrent validity* of a particular Eurocentric measure, how do the test scores relate to scores on an already established Africentric measure that examines the same content area?
- In examining the *predictive validity* of a particular measure: (a) does it have the same degree of probability with African Americans as it does with Euro-Americans, and (b) what effect would the person's stage of identity development have on its predictability?
- In examining the *internal validity* of a measure, how much of the measured variable is attributed to the African American's sociocultural experiences, test reactivity, and cultural worldview?
- In examining the *external validity* of a measure, to what extent could you generalize the results to a cultural group that is different in significant and variable ways without factoring those differences in the test construction?
- Is the language of a particular measure equally clear to African Americans as it is to Euro-Americans?

- Is the normative sample of a particular measure representative of the larger multicultural population?

If these questions were used as the criteria for inclusion of assessment measures in an evaluation protocol, most of the instruments that are currently used by evaluators would be inappropriate with African Americans. To use current measures without making necessary modifications to the tests would indicate a blatant disregard for several guiding principles of the Ethics Code. To use the measures without making sufficient qualifying statements and/or interpretations would also indicate a blatant disrespect for a cultural group whose welfare service providers have pledged to protect.

ASSESSMENT RECOMMENDATIONS

If current assessment measures have questionable representativeness, construct consistency, worldview compatibility, and generalizability, they should not be used. To do so without modifications or disclaimers would represent an ethical violation. There are numerous situations, however, when additional information is needed about an African-American client, and the psychosocial interview is insufficient in obtaining the necessary data. Several suggestions have been offered in the literature as a means to obtain the information in a manner that is more consistent with the African-American culture and the Africentric perspective than current assessment tools. As with all assessment tools, there are advantages and disadvantages. Given the choice of using instruments that are culturally inappropriate and practicing in a way that is ethically questionable, the alternative approaches provide a progressive step that honors the integrity of the African-American culture and the assessment process.

The first suggestion is to establish pluralistic norms for current assessment tools (Mercer, 1976). The advantages of this particular approach are better representation of multiple cultural groups, more reliable data, and more valid measures. Although pluralistic norms would create multiple standards so that better between- and within-group comparisons could be made, the disadvantages are such that caution should be exercised in utilizing this approach. As delineated by DeAvila and Havassy (1974), pluralistic norms would (a) lower expectations of African-Americans' performance, (b) reduce African Americans' level of aspiration to succeed if the data were noncomplimentary, (c) have little relevance outside of a specific geographic area or reference group, and (d) provide minimum information regarding the complex reasons for different scores/responses when examined cross-culturally. Another problem, as raised by Dana

(1993), would be nonethnic–minority clinicians' willingness to become culturally competent diagnosticians and evaluators. As Dana (1993, 1994, 1997, 1998a, 1998b) noted on several occasions, it would be a paradigm shift for many clinicians who have been trained from, and operated within, a Eurocentric perspective. For many of these classically trained service providers, they would need to become familiar with the African-American culture, culture-specific assessment measures, racial identity theory, and African-American personality dynamics. Such a task is difficult enough for clinicians and diagnosticians who are part of this particular cultural group. For individuals who are not African American, the task may require perseverance, heightened sensitivity, and ongoing introspection of personal and clinical worldviews.

A second suggestion is to modify current assessment tools (Dana, 1998b; Hilliard & Cummings, 1996; Williams, 1991). With interviews, more open-ended questions should be used with an emphasis on the sociocultural experiences of the ethnic–minority client. With objective and projective measures, the evaluator should test the limits by asking qualifying and/or clarifying questions to discern the impact of cultural experiences on the client's functioning and development. Testing limits not only provides the opportunity for the clinician to go beyond the constraints of the assessment measures, but it also facilitates discussion and increases rapport with the culturally different client. Although less cumbersome than establishing pluralistic norms, this modification approach has some disadvantages when used with African-American clients. With open-ended questions, there is an increased possibility of interviewer bias, which would foster interpretative information filtered through a dissimilar cultural worldview and may be reflective of the evaluator's stereotypes and preconceptions. With objective measures and projective measures, there is the increased possibility of poor reliability and uncertain validity when the evaluator modifies the administration of a particular test.

A third suggestion is to use existing culturally specific tests (Dana, 1998a, 1988b; Lindsey, 1998). The major advantage of this particular approach is that the tests are more culturally consistent and sensitive to the idiosyncrasies of the African-American culture. Also most of the culture-specific measures have been standardized on African Americans, which gives them more validity and reliability than many of the standard Euro-American measures. The shortcoming of this approach is in its assumptive premise. It assumes that African Americans are a monolithic group with little intragroup variability. Although there are numerous sociocultural experiences that bind African Americans and foster a sense of community that is independent of geographic location and familial parameters, differences in SES and racial identity development can cause considerable within-group variability. The other shortcoming of this approach lies in its relative newness. Standardized tests within this country have been around for many decades and have been developed predominantly by Euro-Americans. African Americans are only recently gaining access to public forums in which to publish measures that are more culturally congruent with the African-American experience. Similarly, African Americans are only recently gaining entry to academic arenas in which they can present alternative evaluation measures with better utility for African Americans. With more time, resources, public exposure, and a paradigm shift toward multicultural evaluations, emic-type evaluation measures will become more prominent within the assessment domain. Until that time, it would be prudent for clinicians, diagnosticians, and evaluators to further their education by examining current literature and evaluation measures that focus on African Americans and their sociocultural experiences.

A fourth suggestion is to combine the underpinnings of two conceptual models—Helms' (1990) Racial Identity Development Stages and Dana's (1997, 1998a) Multicultural Assessment-Intervention Model—and develop a hybrid model specifically for African Americans. Helms' model is based on two major premises: (a) all people, regardless of race, go through a stagewise process of developing racial consciousness wherein the final stage is an acceptance of race as a positive aspect of themselves and others; and (b) the process of acquiring an internalized racial consciousness may be similar for African Americans and Euro-Americans. However, the content/theme of the process is likely to be different because of the dissimilar socialization experiences that accompany race in this country. Dana's model is based on three major premises: (a) universal assessment instruments are too insufficiently developed for any meaningful applications in clinical assessment practices with ethnic-minority clients, (b) most standard assessment tests developed in the United States are culture-specific and typically based on Eurocentric standards and worldview, and (c) augmenting current assessment practices by including more culturally relevant information would increase the reliability and integrity of the assessment process as well as improve the diagnostic labels and efficacy of subsequent interventions.

Both positions have been empirically substantiated and have considerable merit in defining cultural experiences of individuals within a multicultural society. The Helms' position, however, lacks the conceptual template that is needed to instruct clinicians and evaluators on how to provide culturally competent assessments and treatment with African Americans. Similarly, Dana's model lacks the specific Africentric focus and instructional template that is needed to assist clinicians and evaluators with provision of services to African Americans. The proposed model attempts to bridge the gaps in these two positions and presents a model that is (a) culturally sensitive to African-American clients who may have Eurocentric or Africentric worldviews, (b) instructive to clinicians and diagnosticians, and (c) practical. Before describing the model, a brief description of Helms' and Dana's models is warranted. The components of Helms' (1990) model are as follows:

- *Preencounter:* In this stage, the person idealizes the Eurocentric world-view and, consequently, denigrates the Africentric worldview. Because the dominant Eurocentric worldview in the United States considers Euro-Americans and their culture as superior to African Americans and their culture, the African-American person who espouses this perspective must find some way to separate him or herself from his or her devalued reference group to minimize the psychological discomfort that arises from the cultural cognitive dissonance.

- *Encounter:* In this stage, the person becomes overwhelmed with race-based affronts and indignities that are either direct (e.g., verbal and/or physical abuse, discrimination) or indirect (e.g., marginalization, absence of representation, ignored, or dismissed). He or she exhausts considerable emotional energy trying to rationalize these occurrences and/or minimizing their implications. At some point during this stage, it becomes extremely difficult for the person to deny the reality of racism in his or her environment. This awareness is usually triggered by a significant race-based incident that touches the person's inner core/spirit and makes salient the social reality that his or her racial identity is determined by Euro-Americans to whom Africentric standards or worldview are irrelevant.

- *Immersion/Emersion:* In this stage, the person physically and emotionally withdraws into the African American's culture and uncritically adopts the Africentric worldview. He or she thinks, feels, and acts in a way that he or she believes to be authentic African American. Moreover, the person evaluates other African Americans on the basis of their conformance to these idealistic cultural standards. Thus, an African-American ascribed identity and an African-American reference-group orientation dominate the person's personality often at the cost of his or her personal identity.

- *Internalization:* In this stage, the person internalizes an African-American identity that is positive and personally relevant (i.e., blending of personal and ascribed identities). African Americans become the primary reference group to which he or she belongs, although the quality and quantity of his or her relationships with non-African Americans are no longer externally determined. By developing a stable African-American identity, the individual can face the world from a position of personal strength and renegotiate his or her positions with respect to Euro-Americans and a Eurocentric society. Although the person rejects racism and similar forms of oppression, he or she is able to reestablish relationships with individual Euro-American associates who merit such relationships and analyze Eurocentricism and the Euro-American culture for its strengths and shortcomings.

The components of Dana's (1997) model are as follows:

- *Cultural orientation*: The extent of influence of the person's culture on his or her personality dynamics, behavioral patterns, and worldview constitutes a person's cultural orientation. It is determined through interviews, formal evaluation, and informal measures. The possible multicultural orientation areas are (a) assimilated—negligible influence from an original culture, (b) marginal—selective influences from both original and host cultures, (c) bicultural—functions comfortably within the original culture and mainstream society, and (d) traditional—maintenance of the original culture and language.
- *Instruments*: Emics (i.e., culture-specific)—assessment instruments that have been conceptualized, designed, constructed, and normed for a particular cultural/racial group. Etics (i.e., universal)—assessment instruments that have been conceptualized, designed, constructed, and normed on a generalized population within a particular area.
- *Formulation*: Clinical formulations and interpretations that incorporate the impact of cross-cultural experiences and their impact on the person's current level of psychological and cognitive functioning.
- *Intervention*: Specific intervention strategies that are congruent with the person's cultural orientation.

The proposed model is based on four major premises: (a) African Americans have unique cultural values, behavioral idiosyncracies, and worldview that are similar in some ways, but radically different in most ways, from Euro-Americans and other ethnic–minority groups; (b) the ongoing experiences and effects of racism and discrimination impact African Americans' personalty dynamics and racial identity development; (c) competent assessment, conceptualization, and intervention requires a working knowledge of paradigm differences between the Eurocentric and Africentric perspectives; and (d) specific information about the African-American culture and the client's worldview can serve to increase the reliability and validity of the assessment process and improve the diagnostic labels and efficacy of subsequent interventions. Table 24.1 is the conceptual template for the proposed Culturally Sensitive Assessment and Treatment Model for African Americans.

TABLE 24.1
Culturally Sensitive Assessment and
Treatment Model for African Americans

Worldview	Predominant Eurocentric	Mostly Eurocentric	Mostly Africentric	Predominant Africentric
Racial Identity Stage	Preencounter	Encounter	Integrated	Immersion/ Emersion
Treatment Goals	Individual actualization	Balance with more individual goals than cultural goals	Balance with more cultural goals than individual goals	Cultural actualization
Assessment Measures (if necessary)	Standard measures	Modified measures with Eurocentric focus	Modified measures with Africentric focus	Culture-specific measures
Conceptual Synthesis	Monocultural (Eurocentric)	Cross-cultural with Eurocentric emphasis	Cross-cultural with Africentric emphasis	Monocultural (Africentric)
Intervention Strategies	Universal strategies	Combined with Eurocentric emphasis	Combined with Africentric emphasis	Culture-specific strategies
Diagnoses	Appropriate	Appropriate with clarification	Appropriate with clarification	Inappropriate

The following is a description of the model's components with suggested questions for further clarification:

• *Worldview*: A person's worldview is his or her conceptualization of the world, interactions among people, philosophy of life, and value systems. In fact, as a philosophy and approach to life, it can be independent of race. It is neither dichotomist nor nominal. Rather, a person's worldview can exist along a continuum and remain context-specific. Despite its flexibility, most people have a predominant worldview that includes overarching characteristics that permeate most of their thoughts, intrapersonal beliefs, and interpersonal relationships. For this particular domain, the evaluator should assess the client's worldview along the Eurocentric–Africentric continuum. In assessing this particular domain, he or she should explore the following areas. Where along the continuum is the client's predominant worldview? What are the predominant value areas that characterize the client's worldview? If the client's worldview is contextual, what are the factors within the various areas that would make it contextual? What are the personal, environmental, and sociocultural influences that contribute to the client's worldview?

- *Racial identity stage*: Based on Helms' stages of racial identity, what would be the client's predominant racial identity stage? What personal experiences, family and peer influences, environmental components, and sociocultural factors have influenced the client's racial identity development? Did the client's racial identity development occur in a stepwise manner? If not, what events caused changes in the developmental pattern?

- *Treatment goals*: What are the primary treatment goals that the client wants to work on while in therapy? Are the goals consistent with the client's worldview (i.e., Eurocentric or Africentric) or a balance of the two perspectives? If somewhat balanced, is there an individualized or a cultural inclination/drift? What specific precipitants (e.g., personal vs. cultural) are prompting the client to work on certain goals?

- *Assessment measures*: The choice of assessment measures should be based on the client's worldview. If the client is predominantly Eurocentric, then standard measures could be used to supplement the clinical interview. If the client is mostly Eurocentric or mostly Africentric in his or her orientation, then standard measures are only appropriate with modifications, disclaimers of the test's cultural limitations, or clarification of cultural differences that may impact the assessment process. If the client is predominantly Africentric, the culture–test mismatch may rule out ethical use of standard measures. With clients who are predominantly or mostly Africentric, the clinician could use various emic (i.e., culture-specific) measures that have been standardized with predominantly African Americans. Most of these measures are listed at the end of this particular section. For further information about the instruments, refer to Jones (1996).

- *Conceptual synthesis*: Based on collected data (i.e., racial identity stage, treatment goals, assessment measures) from the client as well as collaterals, what is the clinician's synthesized conceptualization of the client's intrapersonal experiences, interpersonal interactions, and sociocultural adjustment? Are the treatment goals congruent with the clinical picture that the client presents in therapy? If not, what is causing the incongruity?

- *Intervention strategies*: Based on the client's worldview, what specific intervention strategies should the clinician recommend? For the most efficacious results, the recommendations should be congruent with the worldview. The more Africentric the worldview, the more active the role of the clinician. He or she may need to serve multiple roles as well as multiple functions with the African-American client. Also, the more Africentric the client, the more involvement from the African-American community and its various components. Conversely, the more Eurocentric the client, the more the clinician can rely on standard intervention strategies based on the therapist's orientation and comfort level.

• *Diagnoses*: The appropriateness of the diagnoses should be contingent on the client's worldview. Because the current diagnostic system is Eurocentric in its orientation and emphasis, it would be appropriate in its present form only for clients who are predominately Eurocentric. The more the client drifts from that end of the worldview continuum, the less reliable the diagnosis. Cultural factors, historical issues, race-based experiences, and personality dynamics may become significant variables. Therefore, the current diagnostic system may not accurately represent the complexity of the African-American client's personality structure.

Table 24.2 is a diagram of supplementary areas that should be considered and/or discussed with the client, but not necessarily included in the evaluation.

The following is a description of the model's supplementary components with suggested questions for further clarification:

• *In therapy*: With *most likely* being self-initiated and *least likely* being other-initiated, where would the client fall along this particular continuum? Was the therapy contact self- or other-initiated? If the latter, who was the initiator of services? What were the particular issues that prompted the client to come to therapy? Were the precipitating events of an emergent nature and, thereby, warrant immediate attention?

• *Therapist race preference*: With this particular domain, was the race of the therapist an important issue in the client's consideration of therapy? If racial preference was an important determinant, what were the factors that made it important to the client? Was the therapist's race an important enough factor to determine therapy outcome? If so, what impact did it have on the therapy process?

TABLE 24.2
Culturally Sensitive Assessment and Treatment Model
for African Americans (Supplementary Areas)

Worldview	Predominant Eurocentric	Mostly Eurocentric	Mostly Africentric	Predominant Africentric
In Therapy	Most likely			Least likely
Racial Preference	Euro-American	Either with Euro-American preference	Either with African-American preference	African American
Racial Issues	Client initiated	Client/therapist initiated	Therapist/client initiated	Therapist initiated
Diagnoses	Appropriate	Appropriate with clarification	Appropriate with clarification	Inappropriate

- *Racial issues*: The client's worldview should determine who initiates the discussion about racial issues. Given its sensitive nature, it would probably be more prudent for the client to initiate if his or her worldview is predominantly or mostly Eurocentric. Conversely, if the client's worldview is predominantly or mostly Africentric, then he or she probably would not mind if the evaluator initiated discussion on the topic. Regardless of the client's worldview, caution, sensitivity, and respect should be exercised by the evaluator when discussing this issue. If asked by the client, the evaluator should be open, reflective, and honest about his or her feelings and thoughts. Because of ongoing experiences with Euro-Americans, most African Americans can sense the evaluator's level of sincerity and self-disclosure.

Competent assessment practices with African-American clients require more than a paradigm shift for diagnosticians and evaluators. It warrants increased sensitivity to the subtle nuances of relationship dynamics that exist between African Americans and Euro-Americans; it warrants a heightened understanding of the cultural factors that define the African-American culture; it warrants a knowledge of the intricacies of standard assessment tools so that they can be modified, if necessary, to make them more relevant and culturally sensitive to African Americans as well as maintaining the integrity of the tests. This is not an easy task, but a necessary one when working with African-American clients. By using the proposed model, evaluators should have a starting point in synthesizing the material that would produce an evaluation that captures the African-American culture and sociocultural experiences. Sattler (1992) offered several other suggestions that are particularly applicable to African-American clients and may facilitate the assessment process. He suggests that evaluators should: (a) be thoroughly familiar with the instrument, technique, and methodology used in the emic (i.e., culture-specific) and etic (i.e., universal) assessment measures; (b) be familiar with the ethnocultural traditions of the client and his or her degree of ethnic identity with his or her reference group; (c) take detailed notes of perceptions and experiences during the assessment activities with special attention given to possible ethnocultural biases; (d) whenever possible, use an examiner who is familiar with the ethnocultural background of the client; and (e) participate in culture awareness training to heighten sensitivities to the importance of culture.

Table 24.3 is a listing of culture-specific measures that have been standardized with African Americans. Although not exhaustive, they should provide a starting point when incorporating non-Euro-American measures into the assessment process. For further information, refer to Jones (1996).

TABLE 24.3
Culture-Specific Measures for African Americans

Measures

Infant Measures

  Measuring psychological maltreatment of infants and toddlers

  An experimental procedure and scales for assessing attachment relationships in African
    American

  Observation instruments of toddler and infant experiences

  Developmental Milestones Expectations Scale: An assessment of parents' expectations for
    infants' development

  African-American normative data for the Revised Denver Developmental Screening Test

  Measuring separation-individuation processes

Children: Cognitive Approaches and Measures

  Optimal performer locator for parents and teachers

  The "Who" & the "O": Contextually situated vehicles for the assessment of pupil potential

  Identifying and assessing the gifts and talents of young African-American learners:
    Promising paradigms and practices

  Informal assessment of intellectual ability using Piagetian tasks

Children: Self-Esteem Measures

  Optimal extended self-esteem scales

  The Hare General & Area-Specific (School, Peer, & Home) Self-Esteem Scale

Children: Race-Related Tests and Measures

  Inventory for assessing cultural mistrust in African-American children

  Perceived Racial Stress and Coping Apperception Test

  Development of the Children's Racial Attitude and Preference Test

  Race awareness and racial stereotyping assessment: Cultural (racial) cognition

  Measures of attitudes toward school, physical self, African Americans, Whites, and
    neighborhood

Adolescents and Young Adults Measures

  How I Learn & How My Child Learns Scales

  Assessing achievement motivation in African-American populations: Castenell Achieve-
    ment Motivation Scale

  National study of African-American college students

  Jackson Competency Scales

  Development of the Scale of Racial Socialization for African-American Adolescents

  Social network record

  African-American Male Experiences Measure

Language Assessment and Attitude Measures

  Test of African-American English for teachers of bidialectal students

  African-American English attitude measures for teachers

  African-American English tests for students

Parental Attitudes and Values

  Parental questionnaire on children's behavioral competence

  Parental belief interview

  Ecological Scale of Parental Competence

  Assessing childrearing practices and attitudes of African-American parents during infancy

  African-based childrearing opinion survey: A research instrument for measuring African-
    American cultural values

(Continued)

TABLE 24.3
(Continued)

Measures

Family Structure and Dynamics
  Typology of household structure in the African-American Community
  Development of the African-American family process Q-sort
  Measures of marital quality
  Scales and protocols for assessment of extended family support of single African-American
    mothers
Worldview Measures
  Belief System Analysis Scale and Belief & Behavior Awareness Scale development:
    Measuring and optimal Afrocentric worldview
  Individual/Collective Worldview Scale: A preliminary report
  Comparison of African and European groups utilizing a worldview opinionnaire
Physiological Measures and Neuropsychological Assessments
  Neuropsycological assessment of African Americans: Conceptual and methodological
    considerations
  Physiological measure in studies of African-American populations
Spirituality Measures
  Life Attitude Inventory: Preliminary evaluation of a measure of spiritual orientation
  Exploring spirituality: Development of the Armstrong measure of spirituality
Acculturation, Life Experiences, and Values
  African-American Acculturation Scale: Origin and current status
  Critical Events Inventory: Modification for research with African-American women
  Expressed Values Scale: Assessing traditionalism in lower socioeconomic status African-
    American women
Racial Identity Attitude Measures
  Assessing optimal theory applied to identity development: The OTAID-R instrument
  Milliones' Developmental Inventory of African-American Consciousness
  Introduction to African Self-Consciousness Scale
  Racial Identity Attitude Scale
  Measuring African-American internalization of White stereotypes about African Ameri-
    cans: Nadanolitization Scale
Personality Variables Measures
  Taylor's Measure of Dysphoria, Anxiety, Anger, and Self-Esteem
  Measures of assimilation, pluralism, and marginality
  Cultural Mistrust Inventory: Development, findings, and implications
  Inventory of African-American nationalist ideology
  African-American Personality Questionnaire: A review and critique
  Themes concerning African-American tests
  Cornell Reference Group Inventory: Examination into the relationships among reference
    group orientation, reference group dilemmas, and self-esteem
  Wyatt Sex History Questionnaire
Stress, Racism, and Coping Measures
  John Henryism Scale for Active Coping
  Acculturative Stress Scale: Preliminary findings
  Assessing quality of life: Construction and validation of a scale
  Convergent, discriminant, and concurrent validity of the Perceived Racism Scale: A
    multidimensional assessment of the experience of racism among African Americans
  IRS: Multidimensional measurement of institutional racism

(Continued)

591

TABLE 24.3
(Continued)

Measures

Social Resources and Social Supports Questionnaire: A multidimensional inventory
Social Support Questionnaire for Racial Situations
Two measures of responses to racism: Development of the African-American Nationalism
and Authoritarian Coping Style Scales
Mental Health Delivery Measures
Survey of African-American behavior
Help-seeking questionnaire as a psychotherapeutic intervention with depressed low-in-
come patients in an outpatient clinic
Use of the CAKSI to assess preparedness for delivery of mental health services to African
Americans
Mental health services and treatment outcome questionnaires
Research Program-Based Measures
Naturally occurring psychological expectancies: Theory and measurement in African-
American populations
Use of help resources: A method for studying help-seeking from the National Survey of
African Americans
Concepts and measures in the National Survey of African Americans
Index of psychological well-being among African Americans
Racial stereotypes and self-esteem of African Americans

DIAGNOSTIC CONSIDERATIONS IN PROVIDING
RESPONSIBLE SERVICES TO AFRICAN AMERICANS

It is a difficult challenge to examine diagnostic considerations and behaviors without discussing their cultural context. They are intimately related.
What may be considered abnormal within one context might be considered culturally appropriate and/or justifiable within another context. To
attempt to diagnose the relative abnormality of particular behaviors without considering the cultural context in which they occur is an arduous
task that is fraught with potential errors. Given the importance of culture
in the diagnostic process, it becomes important that the construct *culture*
is clearly defined. The problem, however, is that there is little consensus
among clinicians and researchers regarding its definition. In fact, when
Kluckhohn and Kroeber (1952) attempted to develop a clear and concise
definition, they examined 150 different explanations and concluded that
any effort to develop a single definition of culture is hampered by theoretical and conceptual differences. Since this early attempt to develop an
objectifiable definition of this construct, other researchers have made
similar efforts (Betancourt & Lopez, 1993; Linton, 1945; Marsella &
Kameoka, 1989; Okazaki & Sue, 1995). Unfortunately, they too came to

the same inconclusive determinations. In fact, De la Cancela and So-tomayer (1993) suggested that caution should always be exercised in the use of such terms as *culture, ethnicity,* and *race.* These terms are complex, laden with surplus meaning, subject to politicization, and affected by racism. Dana (1998b) echoed the cautionary note regarding the potential controversy that can result from the misuse or misoperationalization of these constructs.

Despite the lack of consensus on the connotative parameters of culture, ethnicity, and race, increasingly more clinicians are advocating that *culture* and *ethnicity* should replace race as preferred terms within the literature (Yee, Fairchild, Weizmann, & Wyatt, 1993; Zuckerman, 1990). Landrine and Klonoff (1996), in fact, suggested that the profession should have a moratorium on *race* and instead use *culture.* Their rationale for the suggestion is that many ethnic minorities within this country have origins in other countries with strong ethnic bases (e.g., Puerto Rico, Mexico, Cuba). Therefore, they perceive themselves as cultural beings more than they consider themselves a racial status. However, Carter (1995) and Helms (1994) strongly asserted that race should remain of ultimate importance in this country for African Americans. Their rationale is threefold: (a) most African Americans wish to be acknowledged, accepted, and assessed as racial beings, (b) race has become an almost invisible conceptual construct for a significant number of ethnic minorities in this country and to not acknowledge its importance would foster further invisibility, and (c) substituting ethnicity for race contributes to further confusion in racial terminology. With African-American clients, any and all attempts should be made to respect their preferred identity. Because race is of primary importance to African Americans, it should be reflected in treatment strategies, assessment protocols, and diagnostic considerations.

The *Diagnostic and Statistical Manual–IV (DSM–IV;* American Psychiatric Association, 1994) represents a systematic effort to operationally define and provide comprehensive descriptions for specific disorders. Recent changes over the years have incorporated physical, medical problems, and life stressors as factors that could impact individuals' psychosocial functioning and, thereby, diagnoses (Loring & Powell, 1988). Proponents of the system claim that psychiatric disorders are likely to be distributed and manifested in similar patterns throughout the world. Taking a more guarded position, other diagnosticians maintain that Western nosological systems merely provide a convenient framework for detecting and comparing mental disorders found in different cultures. Opponents of the position suggest that psychopathology may change at different times, vary in different circumstances, and not be shared by different cultural or subcultural groups (Tseng & Hsu, 1980). In particular, the latter group feels that the current diagnostic system is a disappointment for culturally sensitive evaluators as well as to culturally different clients (Cervantes & Arroyo, 1994; Dana, 1998b). As highlighted by Akbar (1991), the current diagnostic system fails to include disorders that result from oppression and comprehend the insidiousness of racism on an individual's personal development and behaviors. Dana (1998b) also added that there have been only token attempts to make the diagnostic categories culturally sensitive with ethnic–minority individuals. Out of 840 pages in *DSM–IV* that focus on diagnostic information, only 15 address culture, age, and gender features; within the 15 pages, the cultural material includes inter-cultural variations as well as gender- and age-specific material (Tseng & Hsu, 1980).

As long as there have been diagnoses, there have been controversies. Some clinicians claim that the current diagnostic system is more medically oriented than psychologically oriented. Some clinicians claim that it is more behaviorally oriented than dynamically oriented. Some clinicians claim that it is more quantitatively oriented than qualitatively oriented. Some clinicians claim that it is more psychologically oriented than eco-logically oriented. Some clinicians claim that it is more pathology ori-ented than situationally oriented. More recently, some ethnic–minority diagnosticians claim that it is more culturally myopic than culturally sensitive. The issues regarding diagnoses are multiple and appear to be contingent on discipline, orientation, and worldview. If the primary pur-pose of the diagnostic process is to provide clinicians with a common language, then dissimilar orientations, worldviews, or cultural back-grounds would make this endeavor inconsistent and capricious. In fact, service providers who lack familiarity with particular cultural subgroups are more prone to misdiagnose clients' problems, refer them to emergency or inpatient care when outpatient care would be more appropriate (Lind-sey & Paul, 1989; Snowden & Cheung, 1990), or overpathologize them (Rosenthal, 1987). Also, based on the literature, African Americans are more likely than Euro-Americans to receive more negative evaluations when exhibiting emotional disturbances (Jenkins-Hall & Sacco, 1991), be rated more psychologically impaired (Jones, 1982; Loring & Powell, 1988), receive more chronic diagnoses than acute episodes when experiencing psychotic or affective disorder (Adebimpe, 1981), receive a schizophrenic diagnosis when exhibiting symptoms suggestive of a bipolar affective disorder (Mukherjee et al., 1983; Pavkov, Lewis, & Lycons, 1989), and be perceived as having a simple and uncomplicated psychological compo-sition (Spurlock, 1985). Diagnosing mental illness, therefore, is an inter-pretative process that is highly influenced by cultural factors (Loring & Powell, 1988).

DIAGNOSTIC RECOMMENDATIONS

Understanding African-American clients cross-culturally can be a difficult, but not an impossible, task. Although tried for decades by many service providers, ignoring differences between Euro-American service providers and African-American clients does not work. Such a strategy perpetuates the division that already exists between the clinical community and the African-American community. This particular strategy also exacerbates the underutilization of services by African Americans. To remedy this situation within the mental health field, several suggestions are offered. Westermeyer (1987) suggested understanding the sociocultural background and experiences of clients as a way to distinguish culturally bound behavior from actual aberrant behavior. Similarly, Castillo (1997) suggested culturally relevant guidelines for each disorder as a necessary supplement to the current diagnostic system. Dana (1998a) suggested a more ambitious, and probably more sensitive and sensible, approach. He recommended adopting a multifactor, pluralistic approach in which the cultural frame of reference would enable service providers to (a) understand the contextual nature of culture-specific behaviors and how particular behaviors make sense within each culture, and (b) appreciate cultural values and culture-specific coping patterns that may impact the assessment process, and (c) guard against inappropriate generalizations. Dana also suggested a narrative summary as an assessment and diagnostic alternative for multicultural clients. The narrative would allow better integration of cultural information as well as clarification of idiosyncratic behaviors. Moreover, it bypasses the Eurocentric diagnostic system that would be inappropriate with culturally different clients. Application of the current system to African-American clients with a strong Africentric worldview would be tantamount to forcing a diagnostic system on a cultural group whose behaviors and cultural idiosyncrasies may be more diverse than what the current system could comprehend and incorporate. To force the fit could lead to inaccurate diagnoses, inappropriate dispositions, and incongruent treatment.

Disposition Options and Concluding Thoughts

Cultural matching of clients and clinicians has been widely recommended as a remedy to overcome problems in ethnic–minority use of mental health services (Flaskerud, 1986, Sue & Sue, 1990). Although this suggestion has intuitive appeal, its practicality is questionable when applied to African Americans. There are too few African-American clinicians and diagnosticians to meet the overwhelming needs of African-American clients. The disparity between supply and demand is too great for it to happen with any modicum of success. Because the ideal remedy is not possible, appropriate alternatives should be considered. One alternative is to improve the compatibility or fit between African-American clients and clinical services. This strategy involves utilizing appropriate services and people outside of the agency. However, service providers are typically so agency-bounded that community-based treatment is seen as time-intensive, resource-consuming, and clinically questionable. Interestingly, the community psychology literature contends that long-lasting and effective indigenous services require direct and front-line intervention (Moos, 1976). Such direct services would require not only a change in resource allocation, but also a change in paradigms. The paradigm shift would need to include an appreciation of worldviews congruent with the African-American culture, an appreciation of the richness of the African-American community, and a willingness to change incorrect and derogatory personal assumptions and stereotypes.

The African-American community is rich with resources. There are elders within the community, pastors within the churches, mentors within professional agencies, and significant peers and relatives within the family. Identifying and connecting clients with these resources as an adjunct to or in place of therapy would be an appropriate treatment disposition. Therapy does not have to be within the traditional Westernized model. It can be as effective, if not more efficacious, within an environment in which the client feels comfortable, safe, and familiar. Utilizing community resources provides an effective interface with individuals and resources that could assume the continuation of treatment after it has been officially concluded with the agency. In fact, the therapist does not necessarily have to provide the bulk of the intervention strategies. He or she might be more effective serving as an advocate, intervener, consultant, or professional friend. Effective therapy roles are limited only by the boundaries with which the therapist chooses to adopt and that legal and ethical guidelines allow. In fact, according to Flaskerud (1986), the efficacy of psychotherapy is, among many factors, a function of the extent to which a therapist can communicate in the clients' language and understand their cultural background.

Changing the role of the therapist is one suggestion that has immeasurable possibilities. Another suggestion is to make services more available to the community. There are several studies that have demonstrated the effectiveness of alternative service structure. O'Sullivan, Peterson, and Cox (1989) demonstrated that more effective treatment can be provided by moving clinics to more convenient locations within the community. Hernandez and Schweon (1989) demonstrated that delivering services with a mobile unit increased service utilization. Sue and Morishima (1982) demonstrated that expanding clinic hours increased service access. LeVine and Padilla (1980) suggested incorporating community representatives on the policymaking board as a way to improve relationships and service advocacy. Effective agency involvement is limited only by the priorities with which it operates within a community.

If it is not fiscally possible to change either the services offered or the structure of the agency, one alternative would be to have ongoing cultural sensitivity training of staff by African-American clinicians and diagnosticians. Cultural sensitivity training can work if the recipients of the training are open to consider other perspectives, are willing to relinquish inherent ethnocentric thoughts, and are committed to changing services within the agency to accommodate African-American clients. Its effectiveness has been demonstrated to have a positive effect in changing perceptions (Wade & Bernstein, 1991) and ethnic–minority service utilization (Wu & Windle, 1980). However, if sensitivity training is not part of the infrastructure of the agency and prioritized as a highly valued process, the status quo will be maintained. Unfortunately, it is the status quo that has perpetuated the cultural insensitivity that permeates most service agencies.

Dana (1998b) offered another suggestion that could impact the field of psychology in a more global way. He suggested that the American Psychological Association (APA) revise its ethical guidelines regarding ethnic minorities so that there is more of an emphasis on cultural competence as a prerequisite for clinical practice. With the use of vignettes, clinical examples, and case materials, service providers could begin exchanging conceptual thoughts and intervention strategies with the goal of sensitizing each other to better serve ethnic–minority clients. There is a considerable amount of literature written during the past 25 years that examines various aspects of African-American culture. As a point of ethical integrity, practicum students, externs, interns, and other professionals should be familiar with relevant literature before they work with such clients. To ensure that personal cultural biases do not interfere with the clinical or evaluation process, continual self-examination should be a prerequisite for training programs and State's continuing education requirement. Without APA and State licensure boards taking the lead in implementing various initiatives to ensure cultural competence, the status quo of cultural mediocracy will be maintained. As Pedersen (1995) indicated, "... the weakness of ... the American Psychological Association ... ethical guidelines are that they lack explicit philosophical principles, assume a dominant culture perspective, and generally minimize or trivialize the role of culture in ethical decision making" (p. 42).

Dana (1998b) contended that the profession should take a more assertive position in cultural competence training. His Multicultural Assessment Intervention Model provides a conceptual framework that could achieve this particular goal. He suggested that all ethnic–minority clients should have an acculturation evaluation of their cultural orientation. The evaluation would provide clinical information that would enable clinicians to develop assessment protocols and treatment strategies that are more congruent with their particular orientation. He added that a variety of measures or interview data can facilitate a decision as to whether a client is assimilated, bicultural, marginal, or traditional (Dana, 1993, 1994, 1997). As presented in this writer's model, a similar process could determine whether the African-American client is at the preencounter, encounter, emersion, or integrated stage. Such acculturation information is vital to the efficacy of treatment as well as to the integrity of the evaluation process. Using Dana's model as a conceptual foundation, the following steps are provided as a way to obtain clinically and culturally pertinent information from African-American clients.

• *Comprehensive psychosocial interview:* Examine the basic areas of the client's presenting problems, background information, and mental status. With each of these identified areas, an effort should be made to determine the contextual history of any problem area. Questions that examine the exceptions of the presenting problems would also help discern the issues' contextual value.

1. Explore with the client his or her expectations of therapy or evaluation, experiences with self-disclosing to other people, and feelings about being in a therapy or evaluation situation.
2. Present the goals and parameters of treatment as a collaborative effort where the client is intimately involved in the entire process.
3. If the client is referred, there are some legal entanglements; discuss your role in the process as well as the limits of confidentiality.

• *Cultural identity evaluation:* Use existing cultural identity evaluation measures to assess the client's level of identity or acculturation. Using this information, provide a descriptive elaboration of the client's identity development and how it interacts with presenting problems, psychosocial functioning, and cultural history.

1. Gather information on the client's immediate and extended families, significant relationships within and outside of the community, and involvement with different social groups. A genogram could provide a reasonable tool to assist with this effort.
2. Identify and focus on the relative strengths of the client him or herself as well as the strengths of the family and community.
3. Explore the significance of the presenting problems within the context of other situations where the client had been relatively successful.

4. If appropriate, examine issues revolving around racial identity and affiliation.

• *Psychological evaluation:* As a general rule, the evaluation should always be administered to African-American clients using an acceptable style to gain rapport and encourage optimal performance on the tests. Efforts to be patronizing, condescending, and ethnocentric would not only create an environment that is nonconducive to treatment and evaluations, but could also compromise the integrity of the testing process. If modification/alterations are warranted in the evaluation process, make the corrections during the interpretation and feedback session. The value of making the necessary changes during this phase of the evaluation process is that it (a) maintains the integrity of the tests while allowing the evaluator the opportunity to clarify any incongruent information, (b) incorporates the data into the interpretation, and (c) synthesizes the clinical data with the sociocultural experiences of the client.

1. Refer to the Jones (1996) for culture-specific measures for African Americans.

• *Feedback session:* Every encounter with an African-American client has the potential of being an enriching experience. If the experience is positive, the client will incorporate the new data into his or her cultural information bank and use it to promote mental health services for him or herself and others. If the service is negative, the client will continue his or her apprehension toward mental health services as well as service providers. For the clinician, if the experience is positive, he or she could use the encounter as an opportunity to update his or her perceptions of African-American clients and build on that knowledge base with sensitivity training sessions and workshops.

1. Discuss the therapy or evaluation process with the client. Using the client as a consultant, explore areas in which you could improve as a culturally sensitive clinician or evaluator.

REFERENCES

Adebimpe, V. R. (1981). Hallucinations and delusions in Black psychiatric patients. *Journal of the National Medical Association, 73*(6), 517–519.

Akbar, N. (1991). Mental disorders among African-Americans. In R. G. Jones (Ed.), *Black psychology* (3rd ed., pp. 339–351). Berkeley, CA: Cobb & Henry.

American Psychiatric Association. (1994). *Diagnostic and statistical manual of mental disorders* (4th ed.). Washington, DC: Author.

Barker, R. (1974). The ecological environment. In R. Moos & P. Insel (Eds.), *Issues in social ecology* (pp. 255–266). Palo Alto, CA: National Press Books.

Bennett, M. J. (1986). Toward ethnorelativism: A developmental model of intercultural sensitivity. In R. M. Paige (Ed.), *Cross-cultural orientation: New conceptualizations and applications* (pp. 27–69). Lanham, MD: University Press of America.

Betancourt, H., & Lopez, S. R. (1993). The study of culture, ethnicity, and race in American psychology. *American Psychologist, 48,* 629–637.

Bosma, B. (1972). The NEA testing moratorium. In T. Oakland & B. Phillips (Eds.), *Assessing minority group children* (pp. 304–306). New York: Behavioral Publications.

Cairns, B., & Walsiner, J. (1982). *Culture and science in developmental psychology. Science as Culture Symposium.* Washington, DC: American Psychological Association.

Carter, R. T. (1995). *The influence of race and racial identity in psychotherapy: Toward a racially inclusive model.* New York: Wiley.

Castillo, R. J. (1997). *Culture and mental illness: A client-centered approach.* Pacific Grove, CA: Brooks/Cole.

Cervantes, R. C., & Arroyo, W. (1994). DSM–IV: Implications for Hispanic children and adolescents. *Hispanic Journal of Behavioral Sciences, 16,* 8–27.

Dana, R. H. (1993). *Multicultural assessment perspectives for professional psychology.* Boston: Allyn & Bacon.

Dana, R. H. (1994). Testing and assessment ethics for all persons: A beginning and an agenda. *Professional Psychology: Research and Practice, 25,* 349–354.

Dana, R. H. (1997). Multicultural assessment and cultural identity: An assessment-intervention model. *World Psychology, 3,* 121–141.

Dana, R. H. (1998a). Multicultural assessment of personality and psychopathology in the United States: Still art, not yet science, and controversial. *European Journal of Psychological Assessment, 14*(1), 62–70.

Dana, R. H. (1998b). *Understanding cultural identity in intervention and assessment.* Thousand Oaks, CA: Sage.

DeAvila, E. A., & Havassy, B. (1974). The testing of minority children: A neo-Piagetian approach. *Today's Education, 63*(4), 72–75.

De la Cancela, V., & Sotomayer, G. M. (1993). Rainbow warriors: Reducing institutional racism in mental health. *Journal of Mental Health Counseling, 15,* 55–71.

Flaskerud, J. H. (1986). The effects of culture-compatible intervention on the utilization of mental health services by minority clients. *Community Mental Health Journal, 22,* 127–141.

Gardner, G. (1990). *Working with persons from African American backgrounds.* Paper presented at the Cross-Cultural Psychotherapy Conference, Hahnemann University, Philadelphia.

Gay, G., & Abrahams, R. D. (1973). Does the pot melt, boil, or brew? Black children and White assessment procedures. In T. Oakland & B. Phillips (Eds.), *Assessing minority group children* (pp. 294–303). New York: Behavioral Publications.

Gerry, M. H. (1973). Cultural myopia: The need for a corrective lens. In T. Oakland & B. Phillips (Eds.), *Assessing minority group children* (pp. 307–315). New York: Behavioral Publications.

Gottfredson, L. S. (1994). The science and politics of race-norming. *American Psychologist, 49,* 955–963.

Helms, J. E. (1990). *Black and White racial identity: Theory, research, and practice.* New York: Greenwood.

Helms, J. E. (1992). Why is there no study of cultural equivalence in standardized cognitive ability testing? *American Psychologist, 9,* 1083–1101.

Helms, J. E. (1994). How multiculturalism obscures facial factors in the therapy process: Comments on Ridley et al. (1994), Sodowsky et al. (1994), Ottavi et al. (1994), and Thompson et al. (1994). *Journal of Counseling Psychology, 41*(2), 162–165.

Hernandez, A. H., & Schweon, C. (1989). Mobile mental health team reaches minorities. *Aging, 46,* 12–13.

Hilliard, A. G., & Cummings, W. (1996). The "Who" and the "O": Contextually-situated vehicles for the assessment of pupil potential. In R. Jones (Ed.), *Handbook of tests and measurements for Black populations* (pp. 155–168). Hampton, VA: Cobb & Henry.

Hobson v. Hanson, 269 F. Supp. 401 (DC 1967).

Jenkins-Hall, K., & Sacco, W. P. (1991). Effect of client race and depression on evaluations by White therapists. *Journal of Social and Clinical Psychology, 10,* 322–333.

Jensen, A. R. (1981). *Straight talk about mental tests.* New York: The Free Press.

Johnson, R. (1993). Clinical issues in the use of the *DSM–III–R* with African American children. *Journal of Black Psychology, 19,* 447–460.

Jones, E. E. (1982). Psychotherapists' impressions of treatment outcome as a function of race. *Journal of Clinical Psychology, 38,* 722–731.

Jones, R. (1996). *Handbook of tests and measurements for Black populations* (Vols. 1 & 2). Hampton, VA: Cobb & Henry.

Karenga, M. (1989). *The African-American holiday of Kwanzaa.* Los Angeles, CA: University of Sankore Press.

Kaufman, A. (1979). *Intelligent testing with the WISC–R.* New York: Wiley.

Kluckhohn, C., & Kroeber, T. (1952). *Culture.* New York: Vintage Press.

Landrine, H., & Klonoff, E. A. (1996). *African-American acculturation: Deconstructing race and reviving culture.* Thousand Oaks, CA: Sage.

Larry P. v. Riles, 1306 (N.D. Ca. 1972), No. C-71-2270 RFP (Sept. 25, 1986) (order modifying judgment).

LeVine, E. S., & Padilla, A. M. (1980). *Crossing cultures in therapy.* Monterey, CA: Brooks/Cole.

Lindsey, K. P., & Paul, G. L. (1989). Involuntary commitments to public mental institutions: Issues involving the overrepresentation of Blacks and assessment of relevant functioning. *Psychological Bulletin, 106,* 171–183.

Lindsey, M. L. (1998). Culturally competent assessment of African-American clients. *Journal of Personality Assessment, 70*(1), 43–53.

Linton, R. (1945). *The culture background of personality.* New York: Appleton-Century-Crofts.

Loring, M., & Powell, B. (1988). Gender, race, and DSM–III: A study of objectivity of psychiatric diagnostic behavior. *Journal of Health and Social Behavior, 29,* 1–22.

Luria, A. B. (1976). *Cognitive development: Its cultural and social foundations.* Cambridge, MA: Harvard University Press.

Marsella, A. J., & Kameoka, V. (1989). Ethnocultural issues in the assessment of psychopathology. In S. Wetzler (Ed.), *Measuring mental illness: Psychometric assessment for clinicians* (pp. 231–256). Washington, DC: American Psychiatric Press.

Marshall v. Georgia, No. CV 482-233 (S.D. Ga. 1984).

Mercer, J. R. (1976). Pluralistic diagnosis in the evaluation of Black and Chicano children: A procedure for taking sociocultural variables into account in clinical assessment. In C. A. Hernandez, M. J. Haug, & N. N. Wagner (Eds.), *Chicanos: Social and psychological perspectives* (pp. 183–195). St. Louis: Mosby.

Messer, S. B., & Warren, C. S. (1995). *Models of brief psychodynamic therapy.* New York: Guilford.

Miller-Jones, D. (1989). Culture and testing. *American Psychologist, 44,* 360–366.

Mio, J. S., & Iwamasa, G. (1993). To do, or not to do: That is the question for White cross-cultural researchers. *The Counseling Psychologist, 21,* 197–212.

Moos, R. (1976). *The human context: Environmental determinants of behavior.* New York: Wiley-Interscience.

Mukherjee, S., Shukla, S., Woodle, J., Rosen, A. M., & Olarte, S. (1983). Misdiagnosis of schizophrenia in bipolar patients: A multiethnic comparison. *American Journal of Psychiatry, 140,* 1571–1574.

Murphy, L. L. (1994). *Tests in print IV: An index to tests, test reviews, and the literature on special tests.* Lincoln: University of Nebraska, Buros Institute of Mental Measurement.

Murray, C. B. (1996). Estimating performance: A confirmation bias. *Journal of Black Psychology, 22,* 67–85.

Newland, T. E. (1973). Assumptions underlying psychological testing. In T. Oakland & B. Phillips (Eds.), *Assessing minority group children* (pp. 294–303). New York: Behavioral Publications.

Oakland, T. (1973). Assessing minority group children: Challenges for school psychologists. In T. Oakland & B. Phillips (Eds.), *Assessing minority group children* (pp. 294–303). New York: Behavioral Publications.

Oaklund, T., & Fiegenbaum, D. (1979). Multiple sources of test bias on the WISC–R and Bender Gestalt. *Journal of Consulting and Clinical Psychology, 47*(5), 968–974.

Okazaki, S., & Sue, S. (1995). Methodological issues in assessment research with ethnic minorities. *Psychological Assessment, 7*, 367–375.

O'Sullivan, M. J., Peterson, P. D., & Cox, G. B. (1989). Ethnic populations: Community mental health services ten years later. *American Journal of Community Psychology, 17*, 17–30.

PACE v. Hannon, 506 F. Supp. 831 (N.D. Ill. 1980).

Pavkov, T. W., Lewis, D. A., & Lycons, J. S. (1989). Psychiatric diagnosis and racial bias: An empirical investigation. *Professional Psychology: Research and Practice, 20*, 364–368.

Pedersen, P. B. (1995). Culture-centered ethical guidelines for counselors. In J. G. Ponterotto, J. M. Casas, L. A. Suzuki, & C. M. Alexander (Eds.), *Handbook of multicultural counseling* (pp. 34–49). Thousand Oaks, CA: Sage.

Pedersen, P. B. (1982). The ethical crisis for cross-cultural counseling and therapy. *Professional Psychology, 13*, 492–500.

Reschly, D. (1978). WISC–R factor structures among Anglos, Blacks, Chicanos, and Native Americans. *Journal of Consulting and Clinical Psychology, 46*(3), 417–422.

Reynolds, C. (1980). Differential construct validity of intelligence as popularly measured: Correlations of age with raw scores on the WISC–R for Blacks, Whites, males, and females. *Intelligence, 4*(4), 371–378.

Rosenthal, R. (1987). Pygmalion effects: Existence, magnitude, and social importance. *Educational Researcher*, 37–40.

Rosenthal, R., & Jacobson, L. (1968). *Pygmalion in the classroom: Teacher expectation and pupils' intellectual development.* New York: Holt, Rinehart and Winston.

Sattler, J. M. (1992). *Assessment of children* (3rd ed.). San Diego, CA: Jerome Sattler.

Snowden, L. R., & Cheung, F. K. (1990). Use of inpatient mental health services by members of ethnic minority groups. *American Psychologist, 45*, 347–355.

Spurlock, J. (1985). Assessment and therapeutic intervention of black children. *Journal of the American Academy of Child Psychiatry, 24*, 168–174.

Sue, D. W., & Sue, D. (1990). *Counseling the culturally different: Theory and practice.* New York: Wiley.

Sue, S., & Morishima, J. K. (1982). *The mental health of Asian Americans.* San Francisco: Jossey-Bass.

Taylor, H. F. (1980). *The IQ game.* New Brunswick, NJ: Rutgers University Press.

Tseng, W. S., & Hsu, J. (1980). Minor psychological disturbances of everyday life. In H. C. Triandis & J. C. Draguns (Eds.), *Handbook of cross-cultural psychology* (Vol. 6, pp. 61–98). Boston: Allyn & Bacon.

U.S. Bureau of the Census. (1995). *Statistical abstract of the United States.* Washington, DC: Government Printing Office.

Wade, P., & Bernstein, B. (1991). Culture sensitivity training and counselor's race: Effects on Black female clients' perceptions and attrition. *Journal of Counseling Psychology, 38*, 9–15.

Westermeyer, J. (1987). Clinical considerations in cross-cultural diagnosis. *Hospital and Community Psychiatry, 38*(2), 160–165.

Wu, I., & Windle, C. (1980). Ethnic specificity in the relationship of minority use and staffing of community mental health centers. *Community Mental Health Journal, 15*, 156–168.

Yamato, G. (1993). Something about the subject makes it hard to name. In V. Cyrus (Ed.), *Experiencing race, class, and gender in the United States* (pp. 206–209). Mountain View, CA: Mayfield.

Yee, A. H., Fairchild, H. H., Weizmann, F., & Wyatt, G. E. (1993). Addressing psychology's problems with race. *American Psychologist, 48,* 1132–1140.

Zuckerman, M. (1990). Some dubious premises in research and theory on racial differences: Scientific, social, and ethical issues. *American Psychologist, 45,* 1297–1303.

25

Cultural Identity Description and Cultural Formulation for Hispanics

Israel Cuéllar
Genaro González
University of Texas–Pan American

This chapter reviews the various descriptions and components attributed to the self and self-concept and relates this to identity and its component parts and descriptions—specifically, cultural identity and the cultural self. Cultural identity is viewed as developing within ecological/cultural contexts and is influenced by person interactions between external variables (e.g., physical and cultural environment) and internal variables (biological and psychological). This view is consistent with the biopsychosocial model (Engel, 1977, 1980), Berry's Ecocultural model (Berry, Poortinga, Segall, & Dasen, 1992), and Marsella's interactional model (Marsella & Kameoka, 1989). An example of a cultural formulation is provided to assess specific influences of culture on an individual's behavior and personality. Accuracy of psychological assessment is related to accurate cultural formulation and is viewed as essential and necessary for competent multicultural assessment practices in psychology. Cultural identity is viewed as a lifespan process evolving and changing as the individual moves through the various psychosocial stages of development. This view is consistent with ecological systems theory, which stresses that the person is affected by a range of environmental influences from immediate settings to broad cultural values (Berk, 1998).

Whereas human behavior was once viewed as being determined primarily by biological and psychological factors, these conceptualizations are now regarded as too simplistic (Marsella & Kameoka, 1989). Newer conceptualizations of human behavior place emphasis on cultural and environmental determinants, including social systems and their transactions. The Ecological Transactional Model, based on research on pathology in children and adolescents (Cicchette & Lynch, 1993; Cicchette & Toth, 1998), views the multiple transactions among environmental forces, caregiver characteristics and child characteristics as dynamic, reciprocal contributions that may either exacerbate or decrease the likelihood of specific symptomatology and the emergence of illness. An integration of Marsella's General Interactional Model of human behavior with Cicchetti and Toth's Ecological Transactional Model is shown in Fig. 25.1. Ecological systems theory views the person as developing within a complex system of relationships affected by multiple levels (macrosystem, exosystem, mesosystem, and microsystem) of the surrounding environment (Bronfenbrenner, 1989).

As Dana (1998) noted, most personality conceptualizations have origins in Euro-American personality theories developed largely by male theorists. Multicultural practices have redirected the focus of attention on external, environmental, or social factors and demands on psychological functioning.

The biopsychosocial model (Taylor, 1991) was among the first clinical models that provided a framework for the inclusion of social, group, and cultural elements in explaining psychological functioning. However, clinicians and researchers in their use of the biopsychosocial model often stopped short of cultural inclusion, which generally was represented by the outermost concentric circle in this model. This model placed culture in a distal frame.

Developmental theories like Erickson's (1960) psychosocial theory, Bronfenbrenner's (1993) ecological theory, and Vygotsky's (1978) sociocultural theory over the past 60 years have given renewed and increasing importance to the transactions and influences of social demands, culture, and contexts on behavior, but not always to personality formation. Internal psychological processes are not minimized by ecological models, but rather are expanded in their relations to external environmental influences. Both personality and identity may potentially be influenced by group, social, and cultural processes to the extent that they are formed from interactions with others, result from resolution of conflicts, and are consolidated by commitment to ideals, beliefs, and values.

Cultural identity, being a part of the self and reflected by behaviors and cognition, can also be explained by ecological transactional models. The cultural self is viewed as developing from the dynamic interactions of external and internal characteristics as well as within multilevel systems (macrosystems, exosystems, mesosystems, and microsystems) and from person–situation interactions and transactions. Internal variables such as

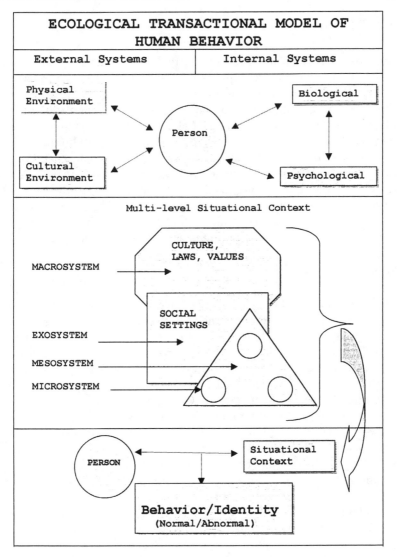

FIG. 25.1. Ecological transactional model of human behavior.

age, gender, and psychological characteristics (including personality) interact with ecological and cultural contexts to formulate the stages of cultural
identity. Ecological transactional models of behavior view culture as a set
of potentiating variables that leads to particular psychological adaptations
or outcomes. Simultaneously, cultural identity is seen as a compensatory
process that can moderate behavioral and psychological outcomes.

CONCEPTUALIZING THE SELF

Who we are as individuals is intimately tied to ethnic and cultural identity. To determine who we are requires first an objectification of the self and second mental comparisons to others. The self is a relational construct whose definition entails the comparison of two objects. William James (1892), the father of American psychology, regarded the self as the difference between how one would like to be (ideal) and who one is. Thus, the relations among the perceptions of what one considers *ideal* and the perceptions of who we are interact to form our *self*. These perceptions, or self-referent thoughts (thought relating to our *selves*), form the basis of our self-worth and self-esteem. Cooley (1902) defined *self-worth* as a direct function of what a person thinks others think of him or her. Again, a relational definition is used to define aspects of the object: self.

Conceptions of Self

The self in Erikson's theory is closely related to identity; to achieve identity is to arrive at a clear notion of who one is. The *self* is often used synonymously with *identity* (LeFrancois, 1996). *Identity*, like self, is a relationally defined concept that develops from perceptions of self in comparison with others and any self-referent conceptualizations that come about from this process. Self-referent cognitions can run a continuum from a strong sense of self at one end to diffuse self-concepts (self-image, self-worth, self-esteem, etc.) at the other end. The ego in psychoanalytic theory is at times used synonymously with Erickson's expression *ego-identity*. A strong sense of self is associated with a healthy self-concept, whereas a diffused, conflicted sense of self is associated with poor psychological outcomes (i.e., psychological maladjustment, psychopathology, and mental illness).

A detailed description of the distinctions that have been logically made between the ego, self-concept, the real self, ego-identity, and personality goes beyond the scope of this chapter (see Rosenberg, 1979, for a description of the nature of the self-concept). An important distinction about these psychological constructs is whether they are formed from human perceptions or if they are part of the innate self (i.e., genetically determined). In Rosenberg's formulation, the total personality is composed in part by the self-concept of the person, and the self-concept is clearly a product of self-perceptions that are in turn largely influenced by social forces. As such, it is greatly affected by culture.

The self has a variety of components (Dana, 1998), but all components of the self are formed from self-referent thoughts and are subject to perceptual influences. Both group and individual identity are components of cultural identity (Dana, 1998). Social or group identity is characterized by those groups, statuses, or categories to which the individual belongs (Rosenberg, 1979). *Cultural identity* is considered as a type of group identity and at times used synonymously with *ethnicity*. *Ethnicity* may be more of an externally applied label, whereas *ethnic identity* appears to be more of an internally applied label. Cultural identity may be either an external or internal dynamic; it is a type of social identity that relates to being a member of a cultural group, a racial group, an ethnic group, or other group, sharing essential cultural features, histories, heritage, or genetics.

Personal identity, also referred to as *individual identity*, is represented by a unique label: the person's name. As Rosenberg described it, personal identity is a type of social identity represented by a single case. Individual identity is the self and is reflected in the personality. Individual identity, or the individual self, has boundaries (Dana, 1998) that vary in permeability, allowing for the selective admission of elements from other cultures. The cultural identity of the person is subject to change or transformation as a function of interactions with other individuals and exposure to elements of other cultures or acculturation processes (see Fig. 25.1). Both synthesized and multiple cultural identities are possibilities.

In a hierarchical structural model, ethnic identity is a part of one's cultural self, and one's cultural self is a part of the self that reflects a constellation of the individual's psychological characteristics—a concept subsumed, according to Rosenberg, under the term *personality*. Although cultural identity is merely a portion of the self, it is viewed in this chapter as being a central component of self because it defines the self based on the values and emotions attached to ethnic group membership. Thus, ethnic identity encompasses many aspects of both cognitive and emotional perceptions.

CONCEPTUALIZING CULTURAL IDENTITY

Cultural identity, like self-concept, is an object of perception and reflection (Rosenberg, 1979); it follows the principle of reflected appraisals and evolves and changes within the contextual environment characterizing the various psychosocial stages of the life span. Likewise, cultural identity involves self-objectification, as Rosenberg emphasized, requiring the individual to "stand out of himself" and "to react to himself as a detached object of observation" (p. 8). Self-concept is the totality of the individual's thoughts and feelings with reference to oneself, whereas the cultural self is a subset of those thoughts and feelings that relate to social and ethnic identities. According to Rosenberg, social identity stems from the groups, status, or categories to which a person is socially recognized as belonging to (e.g., gender, race, ethnic group, religion, family status, legal status, profession, political affiliation, etc.). Tajfel (1981) defined ethnic identity as an aspect of a person's self-concept that derives from his or her knowledge in a social group (ethnic group presumably) together with the value and emotional significance attached to that membership. Ethnic identity requires self-objectification and discovery as one learns more of one's own ethnic group. It develops not unlike other aspects of identity, evolving as one interacts with others and learns more about one's cultural background as well as the sociopolitical history of one's ethnic group.

The term *cultural identity* is not the same as *ethnic identity*. White Euro-Americans may have a strong sense of cultural identity (e.g., identification with U.S. culture) and a diffuse sence of ethnic identity (identification with an ethnic group). Ethnic identity is a complex psychological construct including degrees of cultural orientation (including behaviors, cognition, and affects) and/or identification (behaviors, cognition, and affects) with an ethnic group. It has been described (Dana, 1998; Phinney, 1992; Tajfel, 1981) as including numerous components or aspects of culture. These aspects include self-selected ethnic categories or descriptions for oneself, aspects of cultural/ethnic heritage, ethnic awareness, ethnic loyalty, cultural orientation(s), language preference(s), folk beliefs, customs, folk practices, cultural beliefs, values, worldviews, music preferences, food preferences, and religious beliefs among others. An important element of ethnic identity has to do with how one feels about one's ethnicity and its salience or prominence in forming one's overall identity, self-concept, or personality. Studies of ethnic identity in both adolescents and young adults have found that ethnic identity is more salient for some than for others (Cuéllar, Roberts, Nyberg, & Maldonado, 1997; Phinney & Alipuria, 1990). From these findings, it could be deduced that cultural identity also holds more salience for some than for others.

Ethnic identity is composed of three distinct components: ethnic behaviors, affirmation and belonging, and ethnic identity achievement (Phinney, 1992). Ethnic minorities score higher than a comparison White Euro-American group on the Multigroup Measure of Ethnic Identity Measure (MEIM; Phinney, 1992), suggesting that for minorities ethnic identity is a salient construct. Anglo cultural orientation (White Euro-American orientation) was found to be negatively correlated with ethnic identity, whereas Mexican orientation was positively related to all three components of ethnic identity (Cuéllar et al., 1997). The findings of both Phinney (1992) and Cuéllar et al. (1997) suggest that White Euro-Americans (Scottish, Irish, German, Anglo, and other European origins and ancestral backgrounds) do not appear to have a strong sense of ethnic identity. This indicates low interest, low awareness and little clarity concerning ethnicity or ethnic identity for white Euro-Americans. Ethnicity is not as important to the sense of self for White Euro-Americans as it is for non-White Euro-Americans.

These are not the first findings suggesting that the sense of self is different in distinct cultural groups. Triandis (1994) described two types of cultures: those that emphasize the collective (group) and those cultures where the emphasis is on an individual sense of self. Collectivistic cultures emphasize the views, needs, and goals of the collective. For this reason, an individual who abandons his or her collectivistic self for an individualistic self is often labeled as a *traitor* by his or her traditional ethnic group. In individualistic cultures, the self is independent and holds beliefs and ideas different from the group, making an autonomous person independent from the collective. Markus and Kitayama (1994) noted that in an individualistic culture the self is independent; in a collectivistic culture, the self is interdependent or part of a whole.

How notions of ethnicity and culture are transmitted from one generation to the next is provided by Knight, Bernal, Garza, Cota, and Ocampo (1993). They demonstrated that in ethnic–minority children (Mexican Americans) between 6 and 10 years of age, mothers who were comfortable with their ethnicity were more likely to teach their children about the Mexican culture and influenced their children's ethnic identity.

CULTURAL IDENTITY DESCRIPTIONS

There are as many ways to describe cultural identities as there are theoretical perspectives. The most popular perspectives encompass acculturation theory. Acculturation defined by Redfield, Linton, and Herskovitz (1936) is a process occurring whenever individuals from two distinct cultures come into first-hand contact. These authors defined *acculturation* as a process encompassing all the changes that occur from culture contact in either one or both of the two original cultures as well as the individuals who comprise those cultures. In describing the possible adaptations that result from acculturation, Berry (1980) suggested the following four types of adaptations: traditional, integrated, marginal, and assimilated. Although many other adaptations have been hypothesized and proposed, these four types continue to constitute the foundations of cultural identity descriptions in adaptation to United States or other host culture.

The traditional cultural self continues to hold on to its original culture. Traditionals, as the label implies, retain traditional ideation, customs, orientation, and identity. A distinction has been made between a traditional, who represents a new immigrant being eager to adapt to his or her new culture, versus a traditional, who, for example, has remained for years in the United States and resists adapting or assimilating into the mainstream White Euro-American culture (separationist). The integrated bicultural retains significant traditional cultural orientation but also has adapted to White Euro-American culture. The marginal type is charac-terized by weak identity or orientation to either traditional or White Euro-American culture. A Marginal's commitment is minimal to either of the two major cultures in contact within a given context. These indi-viduals have historically been construed to possess greater risk for psy-chological and/or adaptive dysfunction. The assimilated type does not retain many, if any, cultural referents from his or her traditional culture and has a strong U.S. cultural orientation. The assimilated cultural identity is the only one of the various cultural identities that is thought to be fairly represented by tests normed on U.S. populations (Cuéllar, 1998).

Variants on these cultural typologies are numerous, but some represent important distinctions that sometimes need to be made. Two variants of the integrated type have been described (Cuéllar, Arnold, & Maldonado, 1995; Cuéllar & Roberts, 1997; Felix-Ortiz, Newcomb, & Myers, 1994): a high-bicultural type and a low-integrated bicultural type, distinguishable in the extent or strength to which they endorse two cultures. Although both are bicultural, one type (the high bicultural) may represent a much healthier adaptation than the other (Cuéllar, Roberts, Romero, & Leka, 1998). The low bicultural may be synonymous with the marginal type described earlier and may be thought of as a variant of the marginal type.

Still another descriptive cultural category is represented by the linear concept of acculturation level, represented by five categories (Levels 1–5), with each level representing increasing acculturation toward the U.S. culture. The traditional cultural self is represented by Level 1. Level 2 is a bicultural who is more oriented toward traditional culture than U.S. culture. A Level 3 is a bicultural that is balanced with regard to traditional and U.S. orientation. Level 3 individuals can be either high biculturals or low biculturals. A major limitation of the linear categorization model is that it does not make a distinction between high biculturals and low biculturals as it groups both as Level 3s. Level 4s are biculturals who are more oriented toward U.S. culture than traditional orientation, and Level 5s are represented by the assimilated type.

CULTURAL FORMULATION

Cultural formulations are still very much in the evolving stages. They offer, through better understanding of cultural identity, the potential for identifying assessor bias in conceptualizations of personality and remov-ing ethnocentric dominance characterizing many current training pro-grams in psychology (Dana, 1998).

The initiation of a cultural formulation is recommended at the onset of the clinical diagnostic or the personality assessment process whenever suspected cultural differences may exist between the clinician and patient.

An outline of a cultural formulation, included in Appendix I of *DSM–IV*, has five components: (a) cultural identity of the individual, (b) cultural explanations of the individual's illness, (c) cultural factors related to psychosocial environment and levels of functioning, (d) cultural elements of the relationship between the individual and the clinician, and (e) overall assessment for diagnosis and care.

The authors of *DSM–IV* do not explain these five components or describe how the clinician is to conduct a cultural formulation, suggesting only that the clinician may provide a narrative summary for each of the components. Table 25.1 was constructed to suggest where along the diagnostic assessment process the cultural formulation might be gathered. Table 25.1 compares three different approaches that conduct either a diagnostic or cultural formulation and demonstrates how cultural formulation and diagnostic formulation can be parallel processes. Table 25.2 shows how a cultural formulation might be conducted in conjunction with the diagnostic process. Using the model suggested in *DSM–IV*, an elaboration is provided next for each of the five areas suggested for developing a cultural formulation.

TABLE 25.1
Tasks Required in Conducting a Cultural
Formulation and a Diagnostic Formulation

DSM–IV Components of a Cultural Formulation	*Wing et al. (1980) Points of Reliability Risk in the Diagnostic Process*	*Othmer & Othmer's (1994) Phases of the Clinical Interview*
1. Cultural identity of the patient	1. Defining the symptoms	1. Warm-up and screening
2. Cultural explanations of patient's illness	2. Interviewing the patient	2. Follow-up on preliminary impressions
3. Cultural factors related to psychosocial environment and level of functioning	3. Classify the symptoms	3. Psychiatric history and database
4. Cultural elements of the relationship between the individual and the clinician	4. Including other clinical information	4. Diagnosis and feedback
5. Overall assessment for diagnosis and care contract	5. Including lab findings	5. Prognosis and treatment
	6. Reclassifying the symptoms	
	7. Considering the presence or absence of etiological factors	

TABLE 25.2
Cultural Competence Steps/Skills Required in Cultural
Formulation With Mexican Americans As an Example

Diagnostic Process	Cultural Competence Steps/Skills Required in Cultural Formulation
1. Define symptoms	1. Determine the presence or absence of mental disorder; know culture-bound syndromes; know culture-specific terms such as *embrujado*; look for culturally defined symptoms and clusters representing cases of somatization (i.e., *ataque* or *susto*). Know *DSM–IV* criteria; know cultural norms.
2. Interview the patient	2. Evaluate behavioral style; use patient's first language; use acceptable behavioral style; recognize and respect traditional orientations; know strengths and weaknesses of traditional orientations and identities; be knowledgeable about sociocultural factors that can influence interview outcome; be knowledgeable about sociocultural factors that can influence behavioral observations. Know how to conduct an interview in English and Spanish; assess the cultural identity of the patient; obtain cultural explanations if any about the patient's illness.
3. Classify symptoms	3. Be knowledgeable of *DSM–IV*; have knowledge of which symptoms represent which diagnostic categories, if any; know which symptoms might be reflective of specific sociocultural influences; know culture-bound syndromes for Mexican Americans; same skills and steps as Step 1.
4. Include other clinical information	4. Weigh the psychosocial history obtained from medical records and other mental health providers; weigh its cultural relevance and validity based on the source and knowledge of that source; obtain a history from family members while continuing to filter information based on its source.
5. Include test/lab findings	5. Know what unique diagnostic data are available pertaining to Mexican Americans and specific psychological tests; weigh the value of ordering it and using; know which test data can be moderated by specific sociocultural variables and which specific test data should be moderated; know how to conduct a cultural formulation that includes psychological data.
6. Reclassify the symptoms	6. Weigh the data obtained from all sources; reevaluate diagnostic and cultural formulations based on any new symptoms or patterns that may have emerged from test and other clinical information; examine cultural elements of the relationship between the individual and the clinician; repeat skills and steps listed in Step 3; consider cultural factors that may impact on care as well as diagnosis.
7. Consider the presence or absence of etiological factors	7. In considering presence or absence of etiological factors, it is necessary to weigh the source of information and any cultural filters it may have traversed to get to the interviewer; have knowledge of sociocultural variables associated with specific etiologies; reformulate the diagnostic and cultural formulations based on etiological factors.

Part 1: Cultural Identity of Patient

A modification to the traditional clinical interview is recommended to elicit culturally relevant data for diagnostic purposes, preferably following an eight-step outline developed by Kleinman (1988, 1993). Cultural identity assessment can be done during any of the first three phases of the clinical interview (see Table 25.1). The warm-up and screening, the psychiatric history and database, and the follow-up on preliminary impressions phase seem the most logical points for initiating the cultural formulation. Ethnic identity can be measured formally using an instrument such as Phinney's (1992) Multigroup Ethnic Identity Measure (MEIM). It can also be measured informally by asking the patient questions such as: What is your ethnic background? How important is it to you? How do you feel about your ethnic background?

During Phase 2 of the clinical interview (follow-up on preliminary impressions), the clinician may wish to probe further into areas having possible sociocultural relevance. Cultural dynamics suspected of having an influence on assessment should be explored further at this phase. The interviewer may wish to explore feelings of inferiority, superiority, bitterness, hatred, marginality, and ambivalence with regards to interethnic dynamics. Positive histories of adjustment, adaptation, and interactions with other ethnocultural groups should be noticed as well as negative sociocultural history. Personal experiences may have altered the patient's identity or feelings toward other ethnic groups.

It is possible that information obtained during the cultural assessment may not necessarily have an impact on diagnosis per se but may be significant in therapy. If this is determined to be the case, the clinician may choose to pursue this part of the cultural formulation later when therapy is initiated.

In the case of a Spanish-dominant client, both the language used during the interview and the nature of the presenting symptoms provide clear evidence for a traditional cultural orientation. It might still be helpful to impose a test for cultural orientation. Many tests assessing cultural orientation are now available for use with Hispanics (Cuéllar, Arnold, & Maldonado, 1995; Marin, 1992) and other groups (Sabnani & Ponterotto, 1992). In this instance, it is preferable to infer cultural orientation from interview data using the factorial loadings from standard moderator variables for Mexican-American acculturation such as the Acculturation Rating Scale for Mexican Americans (Cuéllar, Arnold, & Maldonado, 1995; Cuéllar, Harris, & Jasso, 1980) and other tests (see chap. 6, Dana, 1993).

Level of acculturation is part of our ethnic identity and provides meaningful information on the extent to which the patient is embedded in a cultural perspective different from that of the interviewer. With Mexican

Americans, this can be done formally using ARSMA–II (Cuéllar, Arnold, & Maldonado, 1995), which has two orthogonally developed cultural orientation subscales (Mexican Orientation Subscale [MOS] and the Anglo Orientation Subscale [AOS]). Acculturation may also be assessed informally with items such as: Do you speak Spanish? If so, how often? Language proficiency in Spanish has always been a potent indicator of the extent to which a Mexican American is oriented toward the Mexican culture and is generally, but not always, indicative of degree of acculturation toward White Euro-American culture (Cuéllar, Arnold, & Maldonado, 1995; Cuéllar, Arnold, & González, 1995).

Part 2: Cultural Explanations of the Patient's Illness

A subsequent step here is dependent on the assessor's understanding of the health/illness beliefs of traditional Hispanics. *Nervios* probably constitutes a culturally interpreted symptom that appears in a great many Hispanic cultures within the United States and Latin America, often as a culturally acceptable mode of presenting psychosocial distress (Low, 1985). The meaning of each instance of *nervios* can be found in an understanding of the client's cultural history. *Nervios* often follows a psychosocial stressor and is of brief duration, during which a temporary relinquishment of social roles occurs as a result of impulsivity, dissociation, and perceptual disturbances (Oquendo, Horwath, & Martinez, 1992).

Susto is a Mexican-American folk mental condition (Rubel, 1960, 1964) that is believed to be caused by a frightening experience or hassles in everyday life that upset equanimity. In *susto*, the *espirito* or spirit becomes disengaged or dislodged and may be treated by lay persons or *curanderos*, who are culturally sanctioned folk healers. Hexing or *embrujo* may constitute a paranoid symptom or a normal behavior with a culturally acceptable interpretation. Thus, the likelihood of a hexing by a person believed to be a witch must be evaluated as a possible cause of the symptomatology.

Whatever the assessor's decision as to the appropriateness of any of these descriptive labels, consistent with Hispanic health/illness beliefs, these conditions are not considered to be as serious as the psychopathological labels (e.g., Ingham, 1970) that might be provided by mental health professionals using the *DSM–IV*. Folk healers tend to minimize severe psychopathology in contrast to mental health professionals (Arenas, Cross, & Willard, 1980). Assessors of traditional Mexican Americans, for example, need to be informed on the services subsumed under *curanderismo* and available from *curanderos* within their local catchment area (e.g., Hamburger, 1978; Kreisman, 1975).

Cuéllar, Arnold, and González (1995) developed a Folk Belief Subscale that provides an indication of the extent to which Mexican Americans endorse tendencies to rely on traditional folk beliefs and healing practices. This and other scales may be helpful in assessing the degree to which folk illness ideologies may be confounding the clinical picture.

Testing with formal scales and instruments to assess cultural differences between the clinician and the patient is not the only way to obtain pertinent cultural information. Useful information on the patient's illness ideologies may be obtained via the clinical interview by asking the patient a series of questions such as: What do you think is the matter with you? What do you think is causing you to feel this way? What do you think should be done about it? (Kleinman, Eisenberg, & Good, 1978)

Part 3: Cultural Factors Related to Psychosocial Environment and Level of Functioning

The authors of the *DSM–IV* suggest interviewing for culturally relevant interpretations of social stressors, available social supports, and level of functioning and disability. It may be helpful to gather life stress information from significant others, family members, or close friends. The use of a checklist by the assessor would facilitate organizing and interpreting this information (Cervantes, Padilla, & de Snyder, 1991). Asking patients to explain the crucial factors from their experience that are troubling them and why serves as a check-and-balance system to make sure the clinician is not solely imposing his or her priorities, order of importance, or relevance to variables and factors on the patient's illness experience. The importance of eliciting the meaning of symptoms and illness from clients to ascertain cultural interpretations relevant to treatment cannot be overstated.

Part 4: Cultural Elements of the Relationship Between the Individual and the Clinician

This component examines the differences between the interviewer and patient and any problems this may present for diagnosis and treatment. The clinician needs to continuously weigh information obtained during the cultural formulation and compare it to his or her own worldviews and beliefs. Reclassifying symptoms in Wing, Nixon, Cranach, and Strauss' (1980) sixth step requires the clinician to analyze different sets of data or information and come to conclusions based on a reconciliation of that data. Similarly, in Part 4 of developing a cultural formulation, the clinician is required to draw some conclusions about how the information obtained in prior phases of the cultural formulation relates to differences between the patient and the clinician. A referral should be made to another clinician if for whatever reason the clinician feels insufficiently knowledgeable about the particular cultural influences in a case or how these factors impact the patient's illness experience.

Part 5: Overall Assessment for Diagnosis and Care

This aspect of the cultural formulation evaluates "... how cultural considerations specifically influence comprehensive diagnosis and care" (American Psychological Association, 1994, p. 844). An overview of the seven areas where reliability may be jeopardized should be reviewed and weighed by the clinician to determine specifically which cultural influences have what impacts on assessment. It is here where the cultural formulation extends beyond assessment and has relevance in caring for the patient.

Whenever etiology is reformulated, prognosis and course of illness considerations may be dramatically altered. Folk illnesses (i.e., *nervios*, *susto*) are treated in the community by *curanderos* at reasonable cost and with considerable efficacy. Moreover, such treatment is without the stigma and pejorative meaning of psychiatric hospitalization for the patient's family and the traditional Mexican-American community in which they live. Nonetheless, because the patient has already been hospitalized, there are also issues that pertain to responsibility for the patient's crisis by the family, the Mexican-American community, and the psychiatric hospital as representative of the larger White Euro-American society. Protection of the patient from any potential suicide attempt and community persons from uncontrolled and violent behaviors must also be considered.

Other Considerations

Because cultural issues extend beyond the clinician and patient, it is often necessary to examine cultural issues impacting the larger community such as hospital staff, family members, and the patient's community. Communities suffering from abnormally high rates of violence, drugs, posttraumatic stress disorder (PTSD), disorders, suicide rates, crimes, and the like require special consideration of cultural factors and their relations to etiology of illness and its treatment.

Indigenous healers are plentiful in most Hispanic communities and include *curanderos* (folk healers), *sobadores* (massagers), *yerberos* (root doctors), and *es spiritistas* (spiritualists), among others. Indigenous witches such as *brujos* are also an integral part of cultural conceptualizations, beliefs, and schemas in many Hispanic communities. These cultural conceptualizations can and do impact psychodynamics as well as the delivery of mental health services. For example, when, if, and how to integrate the role of a *curandero* are important treatment considerations. If this does not occur when it should, there are a host of ethical issues pertaining to potential discrimination on the basis of culture and subsequent violations of human rights as a result of hospitalization and possibly inappropriate psychiatric interventions (American Psychological Association, 1993; Dana, 1993).

CONCLUSIONS

The assessment of Hispanics is too often attempted without an adequate understanding of clients as cultural beings. The influences of cultural orientation, ethnic identity, and other cultural factors on personality are enormously complex, but can be assessed via the clinical interview, through the use of cultural formulations or through a developing body of culturally relevant scales and instruments. Cultural influences used to be viewed as distal factors, whereas more recent studies suggest that culture is a ubiquitous proximal factor whose influence is central to identity, concept of self, personality, and adaptation. There is an increasing need to assess differences and similarities in our clients because both can have important ramifications on accurate psychological assessment and treatment in an age of increasing multicultural diversity. Investigators and clinicians alike need to have some conceptual framework for recognizing and considering cultural influences on both normal and abnormal behavior as well as its assessment, treatment, and interventions.

REFERENCES

American Psychological Association. (1993). Guidelines for providers of psychological services to ethnic, linguistic and culturally diverse populations. *American Psychologist,* 48(1), 45–48.

American Psychiatric Association. (1994). *Diagnostic and statistical manual of mental disorders* (4th ed.). Washington, DC: Author.

Arenas, S., Cross, H., & Willard, W. (1980). Curanderos and mental health professionals: A comparative study on perceptions of psychopathology. *Hispanic Journal of Behavioral Sciences, 2,* 407–421.

Berk, L. E. (1998). *Development through the lifespan.* Needham Heights, MA: Allyn & Bacon.

Berry, J. W. (1980). Acculturation as variants of adaptation. In A. M. Padilla (Ed.), *Acculturation: Theory, models and some new findings* (pp. 9–25). Boulder, CO: Westview.

Berry, J. W., Poortinga, Y. H., Segall, M. H., & Dasen, P. R. (1992). *Cross-cultural psychology: Research and applications.* Cambridge, England: Cambridge University Press.

Bronfenbrenner, U. (1989). Ecological systems theory. In R. Vasta (Ed.), *Annuals of child development* (Vol. 6, pp. 187–251). Greenwich, CT: JAI Press.

Cervantes, R. C., Padilla, A. M., & de Snyder, N. S. (1991). The Hispanic Stress Inventory: A culturally relevant approach to psychosocial assessment. *A Journal of Consulting and Clinical Psychology, 3,* 438–447.

Cicchette, D., & Lynch, M. (1993). Toward an ecological/transactional model of community violence and child maltreatment: Consequences for children's development. *Psychiatry, 56*, 96–118.

Cicchette, D., & Toth, S. L. (1998). The development of depression in children and adolescents. *American Psychologist, 53*(2), 221–241.

Cooley, C. H. (1902). *Human nature and the social order.* New York: Scribner's.

Cuéllar, I. (1998). Cross-cultural clinical psychological assessment of Hispanic Americans. *Journal of Personality Assessment, 70*(1), 71–86.

Cuéllar, I., Arnold, B., & González, G. (1995). Cognitive referents of acculturation: Assessment of Cultural constructs in Mexican Americans. *Journal of Community Psychology, 23*, 339–356.

Cuéllar, I., Arnold, B., & Maldonado, R. E. (1995). The Acculturation Rating Scale for Mexican Americans-II: A revision of the original ARSMA scale. *Hispanic Journal of Behavioral Sciences, 17*(3), 275–304.

Cuéllar, I., Harris, L. C., & Jasso, R. (1980). An acculturation scale for Mexican American normal and clinical populations. *Hispanic Journal of Behavioral Sciences, 2*(3), 199–217.

Cuéllar, I., & Roberts, R. E. (1997). Relations of depression, acculturation, socioeconomic status in a Latino sample. *Hispanic Journal of Behavioral Sciences, 19*(2), 230–238.

Cuéllar, I., Roberts, R. E., Nyberg, B., & Maldonado, R. E. (1997). Ethnic identity and acculturation in a young adult Mexican Origin Population. *Journal of Community Psychology, 25*(6), 535–549.

Cuéllar, I., Roberts, R. E., Romero, A., & Leka, G. (1998). *A test of Stonequist's Hypothesis.* Manuscript submitted for publication.

Dana, R. H. (1993). *Multicultural assessment perspectives for professional psychology.* Boston: Allyn & Bacon.

Dana, R. H. (1998). *Understanding cultural identity in intervention and assessment.* Thousand Oaks, CA: Sage.

Engel, G. L. (1977). The need for a new medical model: A challenge for biomedicine. *Science, 196*(4286), 129–136.

Engel, G. L. (1980). The clinical application of the biopsychosocial model. *American Journal of Psychiatry, 137*(5), 535–544.

Erickson, E. H. (1960). *Identity, youth and crisis.* New York: Norton.

Felix-Ortiz, M., Newcomb, M. D., & Myers, H. (1994). A multidimensiional measure of cultural identity for Latino and Latina adolescents. In A. M. Padilla (Ed.), *Hispanic psychology: Critical issues in theory and research* (pp. 26–42). Newbury Park, CA: Sage.

Hamburger, S. (1978). Profile of curanderos: A study of Mexican folk practitioners. *International Journal of Social Psychiatry, 24*, 19–25.

Ingham, J. M. (1970). On Mexican folk medicine. *American Anthropologist, 72*, 76–87.

James, W. (1892). *Psychology: The briefer course.* New York: Holt.

Kleinman, A. (1988). *The illness narratives: Suffering, healing, and the human condition.* New York: Basic Books.

Kleinman, A. (1993, January). How culture is important for *DSM–IV?* In *Group on culture and diagnosis, cultural proposals and supporting papers for* DSM–IV (3rd rev., pp. 12–31). Pittsburgh, PA: University of Pittsburgh.

Kleinman, A. M., Eisenberg, L., & Good, B. (1978). Culture, illness, and cure: Clinical lessons from anthropologic and cross-cultural research. *Annals of Internal Medicine, 88*(2), 251–258.

Knight, G. P., Bernal, M. E., Garza, C. A., Cota, M. K., & Ocampo, K. A. (1993). Family socialization and the ethnic identity of Mexican-American children. *Journal of Cross-Cultural Psychology, 24*(1), 99–114.

Kreisman, J. J. (1975). The curandero's apprentice: A therapeutic integration of folk and medical healing. *American Journal of Psychiatry, 132*(1), 81–83.

LeFrancois, G. R. (1996). *The lifespan* (5th ed.). Boston: Wadsworth.

Low, S. M. (1985). Culturally interpreted symptoms or culture-bound syndromes: A cross-cultural review of nerves. *Social Science and Medicine, 21,* 187–196.

Marin, G. (1992). Issues in the measurement of acculturation among Hispanics. In K. F. Geisinger (Ed.), *Psychological testing of Hispanics* (pp. 235–251). Washington, DC: American Psychological Association.

Markus, H. R., & Kitayama, S. (1994). The cultural construction of the self and emotion: Implications for social behavior. In S. Kitayama & H. R. Markus (Eds.), *Emotion and culture: Empirical studies of mutual influence* (pp. 89–130). Washington DC: American Psychological Association.

Marsella, A. J., & Kameoka, V. A. (1989). Ethnocultural issues in the assessment of psychopathology. In S. Wetzler (Ed.), *Measuring mental illness: Psychometric assessment for clinicians* (pp. 229–256). Washington, DC: American Psychiatric Press.

Oquendo, M., Horwath, E., & Martinez, A. (1992). Ataques de nervios: Proposed diagnostic criteria for a culture-specific syndrome. *Culture, Medicine, and Psychiatry, 16,* 367–376.

Othmer, E., & Othmer, S. C. (1994). *The clinical interview using DSM–IV: Vol. 1. Fundamentals.* Washington, DC: American Psychiatric Press.

Phinney, J. S. (1992). The Multigroup Ethnic Identity Measure: A new scale for use with diverse groups. *Journal of Adolescent Research, 7*(2), 156–176.

Phinney, J. S., & Alipuria, L. L. (1990). Ethnic identity in college students from four ethnic groups. *Journal of Adolescence, 13,* 171–183.

Redfield, R., Linton, R., & Herskovitz, M. J. (1936). Memorandum for the study of acculturation. *American Anthropologist, 38,* 149–152.

Rosenberg, M. (1979). *Conceiving the self.* New York: Basic Books.

Rubel, A. J. (1960). Concepts of disease in Mexican-American culture. *American Anthropologist, 62,* 795–814.

Rubel, A. J. (1964). The epidemiology of folk illness: Susto in Hispanic America. *Ethnology, 3,* 368–383.

Sabnani, H. B., & Ponterotto, J. G. (1992). Racial/ethnic minority-specific instrumentation in counseling research: A review, critique, and recommendations. *Measurement and Evaluation in Counseling and Development, 24,* 161–187.

Tajfel, H. (1981). *Human groups and social categories.* New York: Cambridge University Press.

Taylor, S. E. (1991). Health psychology: The science and the field. In A. Monat & R. S. Lazarus (Eds.), *Stress and coping: An anthology* (3rd ed., pp. 62–80). New York: Columbia University Press.

Triandis, H. C. (1994). Culture and social behavior. In W. J. Lonner & R. Malpass (Eds.), *Psychology and culture* (pp. 169–173). Boston: Allyn & Bacon.

Vygotsky, L. S. (1978). *Mind in society: The development of higher psychological processes.* Cambridge, MA: Harvard University Press.

Wing, J., Nixon, J., Cranach, M., & Strauss, A. (1980). *Multivariate statistical methods used in the International Pilot Study of Schizophrenia* (DHHS Pub. No. (ADM) 80-630). Washington, DC: U.S. Government Printing Office.

26

Assessment of Depression Among American Indians and Alaska Natives

Norman G. Dinges
University of Alaska–Anchorage

Mera M. Atlis
University of Minnesota–Minneapolis

Shawna L. Ragan
University of Alaska–Anchorage

The goal of this chapter is to provide a broad overview of some of the key issues involved in conducting culturally competent assessment of depression among American Indians and Alaska Natives. The approach to this task concentrates on three essential areas. First, we briefly summarize some of the fundamental cultural issues regarding the way in which depression is expressed and experienced, as well as the social meaning it carries within local cultural settings. We then review the empirical literature regarding available instruments for assessing depression among Indian and Native clients. Finally, and perhaps most important for the purposes of culturally competent assessment, we attempt to describe important clinical variations in the subjective aspects of the depressive experience among American Indians and Alaska Natives. Here we turn to the growing literature on the use of systematic cultural formulations to inform and enrich clinical understanding of cultural identity, explanatory belief models, the influence of the psychosocial environment, and the relationship between the individual and clinician. In this regard, we are guided by the need for clinicians and clinical researchers to contextualize behavior and emotional experience as a means to avoid the imposition of one's own cultural categories onto another culture for which they lack validity (Lewis-Fernandez & Kleinman, 1994).

BROAD ISSUES CONCERNING CROSS-CULTURAL
ASSESSMENT OF DEPRESSION

The literature on the relationship between culture and depression has identified a number of key issues that are relevant to clinical assessment goals. One of the more typically cited issues concerns the question of the universality (etic) or relativistic (emic) nature of the depressive experience as a recognizable psychopathological entity (Manson, 1995). Etic assumptions that cultural groups are more similar than dissimilar, such as the belief that people have overlapping or coextensive worldviews and similar personality characteristics, are quite common and can obviously limit the clinician's ability to recognize culturally shaped expressions of depression (Dana, 1988).

Although there appears to be empirical support for the presence of depression or depressivelike disorders among diverse human populations, considerable doubt remains about the core and peripheral symptoms as well as its phenomenology among specific cultural groups. Moreover, there is considerable debate over the presence and relative weight of the essential symptom components of clinical depression (e.g., affective, cognitive, somatic, behavioral), as well as their intensity and duration among culturally different groups. Of greatest concern for the clinician is the ease with which the assumption of a universal symptom presentation can lead to under- or overdiagnosing the presence and severity of depression. For example, the accurate assessment of dysphoria as a key symptom of depression may lead to serious diagnostic errors if the emotional lexicon of a specific tribal population expresses sadness, discouragement, or hopelessness in different words than that typically associated with the *Diagnostic and Statistical Manual of Mental Disorders, Fourth Edition* (*DSM–IV*; American Psychiatric Association, 1994). In addition, despite the lack of an equivalent term within a culture for representing depression as either a disease symptom or syndrome, it is important to recognize that it may exist as what anthropologists term an *implicit category*. For example, Manson, Shore, and Bloom (1985) found that 93% of their Hopi informants reported no Hopi equivalent for the Western concept of depression. However, based on diagnostic outcomes using the Schedule for Affective Disorders and Schizophrenia–Lifetime Version (SADS–L), about 50% of the Hopi patient sample had chronic and major depression. One form of Hopi indigenous illness category (*uu nung mo kiw ta*), composed of symptoms of weight loss, psychomotor retardation, disrupted sleep, fatigue, not being likable, trouble thinking clearly, agitation, loss of libido, sinfulness, and shame, appeared to overlap strongly with the Western conceptualization of depression (Manson et al., 1985). This illustrates quite clearly that the lack of an exact equivalent for the term *depression* does not preclude its presence in a given culture.

The concept of the culture-bound syndromes provides an example of a highly relativistic (emic) view of psychopathology that can be equally problematic for the clinician. In this case, the indigenous diagnosis of the depressive experience may be described in such unique cultural features that the clinician may feel inadequate to assess it appropriately. The diagnosis of *anomic depression* among Indian and Native populations is a good example. Derived from the concept of *two-worlds* conflict (e.g., Kluckhohn & Leighton, 1958; Merton, 1968), anomic depression denotes the development of a particular coping style among American Indian and Alaska Native populations as a reaction to cultural and social deprivation in the context of the Indian–White relationship (Topper & Curtis, 1987).

Egocentric versus sociocentric distinctions are also important for clinical assessment purposes. Egocentric views of the self regard it as a self-contained, autonomous entity characterized by a unique configuration of internal attributes and observable behaviors. By contrast, sociocentric views of the self are governed by rules of interdependence with individual interests subordinated to the collective good of the group. Viewed from the egocentric perspective, psychological normality or abnormality such as depression is located within the self and assessment of it is focused on the individual. Viewed from a sociocentric perspective, depression would more appropriately be seen as located in the complex web of interpersonal relationships that define the person, and assessment of it would consequently be focused on understanding the individual's social status, roles, and obligations, as well as the nature of the interactions within the extended family and community. These different ways of conceptualizing and assessing depression may go unrecognized by the clinician because the sociocentrically oriented client may not have available cognitive schemas and expressive emotional vocabulary with which to report their distress to an egocentrically oriented clinician.

Space limitations do not permit more extensive discussion of other broad cultural issues such as mind–body dualism, variations in the expression of affect, and definitions of selfhood that are important to consider in the accurate and appropriate assessment of depression among American Indians and Alaska Natives. We encourage the reader to consult several recent sources for expanded discussion of these and related topics (Allen, 1998; Dinges & Cherry, 1994; Lewis-Fernandez & Kleinman, 1994; Jenkins, Kleinman, & Good, 1991; Kleinman & Good, 1985; Manson, 1995; Shore & Manson, 1981).

DEPRESSION SCREENING INSTRUMENTS

The Center for Epidemiological Studies Depression Scale (CES–D; Radloff, 1977) is one of the most commonly used depression-screening instruments among American Indians and Alaska Natives. Although Radloff found no factor structure differences by gender or ethnicity in the original validation sample of White and African-American adults, the dimensional structure of CES–D differs for American Indian and Alaska Native samples. Three studies investigating the factor structure of CES–D (Baron, Manson, Ackerson, & Brenneman, 1990; Beals, Manson, Keane, & Dick, 1991; Manson et al., 1990) found evidence for a general factor consisting of Depressed Affect and Somatic items (see Table 26.1). The relationship between these two item clusters suggests a high conceptual overlap between the expression of somatic and depressive symptoms, which is consistent with findings by Lichtenberg, Chapelski, and Youngblade (1997). For elderly Great Lakes American Indians, medical burden might be a partial mediator variable between depression and self-reported activities of daily living, indicating the overlapping links among functional abilities, physical illness, and depression. Baron et al. (1990) found that perceived pain and limitations placed on daily activities are related to the reporting of depressive symptoms, which are related through the expression of somatic complaints among elderly American Indians.

CES–D studies among American Indians and Alaska Natives indicate that endorsement rates for depression decline with age, ranging from 58% in adolescents to 32% to 45% in adulthood (see Table 26.1). These rates are generally consistent with CES–D studies in other populations. The rate of depressive symptoms among American Indian and Alaska Native females is also consistent with other findings of gender differences in the prevalence of depression. To illustrate, American Indian and Alaska Native boarding school girls report depressive symptoms at similar levels to those found among adult females. Although Hodge and Kipnis (1996) found no significant differences across gender and age for 1,249 adult Native American multitribal patients, "women scored higher than men, unemployed scored higher than employed, and age exhibited a curvilinear relationship with higher rates found in late adolescence and early adulthood" (p. 91). The few studies that used other depression-screening instruments, such as the Inventory for Diagnosing Depression (Zimmerman & Coryell, 1987) and the Geriatric Depression Scale–Short Form (Olin et al., 1992), also report rates of depressive symptoms similar to findings using the CES–D.

Nonclinical instruments such as CES–D might be used as indicators of general distress (Allen, 1998). Nonetheless, in addition to not allowing for classification into discrete diagnostic categories, investigations of their utility in a two-step psychiatric case-screening procedure yield mixed results (Roberts, 1990). A high false-positive rate is commonly found in CES–D studies among American Indians and Alaska Natives (Baron et al., 1990; Manson et al., 1990). This suggests that the CES–D may be an appropriate screening tool for preventive interventions. However, a high

TABLE 26.1

Assessing Depression Among American Indians and Alaska Natives: CES–D and Other Depression Screening Instruments

Author	Subjects	N	Instruments[a]	Results
		Center for Epidemiological Studies Depression Scale (CES-D)		
Baron et al. (1990)	Older American Indians from Confederated Tribes of Warm Springs' reservations	Total (314): - Females 70% - Males 30%	- CES–D	- 32.2% scored positively for depression (using cutoff score of 16+) - Significantly higher prevalence of depression among females (38% vs. 19%) - Positive relationship among depressive symptomatology, pain, health status, and activities affected
Manson et al. (1990)	Multitribal American Indian boarding school students	Total (179): - Females 54% - Males 46%	- CES–D	- 58% scored positively for depression (using cutoff score of 16+)
Somervell et al. (1993)	Adult American Indians from a Northwest Coast tribe	Total (120): - Females 47% - Males 53%	- CES–D	- 29% scored positively for depression (using cut-off score of 16+) - Persons with a current diagnosis of alcohol abuse or dependence had higher CES-D scores - Subjects with depressive disorders had higher CES–D total scores than those with other disorders. Statistical tests of significance were not performed
Beals et al. (1991)	American Indian college students	Total (605): - Females 62% - Males 38%	- CES–D	- 45% scored positively for depression (using cutoff score of 16+, with 13.3% scoring above 28)

(Continued)

627

TABLE 26.1
(Continued)

Author	Subjects	N	Instruments[a]	Results
Dinges & Duong-Tran (1994)	Multitribal Alaska Native and American Indian boarding school adolescents	Total (291): - Females 57% - Males 43%	- CES–D - Diagnostic Interview Schedule for Children (DISC)	- 41% of adolescents had indications of serious suicide ideation - 30% suicide attempt rate - CES–D clearly contributed to prediction of suicide ideation and suicide attempt
Hodge & Kipnis (1996)	Adult Native American patients at 18 urban and rural Native health clinics in northern California	Total (1,249): - Females 65% - Males 35%	- CES–D	- 42% scored positively for depression (using cutoff 16+, with 15% scoring above 28) - The risk for depressive symptoms among women was higher, although when certain variables such as age and acculturation were controlled the difference was nonsignificant
Lichtenberg et al. (1997)	Elderly Great Lakes American Indians from urban and rural settings	Total (314): - Females 64% - Males 36%.	- CES–D	- Less education, being married, and living in an urban area associated with higher depression scores - Medical burden positively related to depression scores

		Inventory for Diagnosing Depression (IDD)		
Ackerson et al. (1990)	Multitribal American Indian boarding school students	- CES-D (Year 1 only) - IDD (Years 2 & 3 only)	Total (152): - Females 48% - Males 52%	- Scored positively for depression: CES-D (58.1%); IDD (13.8%); IDD when duration is considered (5.3%) - Females had significantly higher median depression scores than the males (6 out of 20 items for CES-D; 1 out of 22 items for IDD)
Wilson et al. (1994)	Adult American Indian (primarily southern Athabascan) outpatients in a Native hospital on a reservation	- IDD	Total (106): - Females 34% - Males 66%	- 20.7% scored positively for depression - Patients with depressive syndrome were more likely to use mental health facilities 1 month after clinic visit
		Other Instruments		
Young (1991)	Native American college students	- Zung's Self-Rating Depression Scale	Total (53)	- Low scorers on Assaultive, Verbal, and Indirect Hostility are more likely to indicate depression and belief in control by powerful others. No association for high scorers.
Ferraro et al. (1997)	Elderly Native Americans from a reservation in a North Central North Dakota	- Geriatric Depression Scale–Short Form	Total (22)	- 23% had symptoms indicative of probable depression - Age and number of medications recently taken positively correlated with depression

[a]Most studies used multiple measures; however, instruments included in this table are related to the assessment of depression.

percentage of false positives warrants the use of higher screening thresholds and another screening diagnostic instrument as an additional criterion.

CLINICAL DIAGNOSTIC ASSESSMENT INSTRUMENTS

Minnesota Multiphasic Personality Inventory

The Minnesota Multiphasic Personality Inventory (MMPI; Hathaway & McKinley, 1940) is one of the most frequently utilized instruments in assessment of American Indian and Alaska Native clients (Todd-Bazemore & Allen, 1994). There are nine studies that used the MMPI with American Indian and Alaska Native samples and reported findings relating to depression (see Table 26.2). Some clinical scale elevations, including Scale 2 (D), are apparent in these studies. However, like findings with other minority populations, no consistent pattern of MMPI findings emerges among American Indians and Alaska Natives (Allen, 1998; Greene, 1987). For example, Pollack and Shore (1980) found that patients with nonpsychotic depression described their symptoms in a manner almost identical to that of schizophrenic patients. However, Butcher, Braswell, and Raney (1983) found that American Indian patients were less pathological than White patients on Scale 7 (Pt) and Scale 8 (Sc), with no differences on other clinical scales such as Scale 2 (D).

Other than the 77 American Indians from an unspecified tribe included in the normative sample, there has been little use of the second edition of the MMPI (MMPI–2; Butcher et al., 1989) with the populations of interest in this chapter. American Indian participants scored higher on most clinical scales in the normative study. However, Graham (1993) concluded that the lack of studies in this area makes it unclear how differences in scale elevations between American Indians and other populations should be interpreted.

Acculturative influences on American Indian clients' responses to MMPI items have been noted (Greene, 1991; Hoffmann, Dana, & Bolton, 1985). For instance, Hoffmann and colleagues (1985) administered the MMPI–168 and the 32-item acculturation scale to 69 Rosebud Sioux and found that Scales 2 (D), 4 (Pd), and 7 (Pt) were most influenced by cultural value orientation and employment in the wage economy. Moreover, Lakota language usage among females, but not males, was significantly correlated with five clinical scales, suggesting that "women who prefer to speak and think their native language are more group-oriented, sociable and open, and naive and uninsightful, but characterized by depression, agitation, and self-derogation" (Hoffmann et al., 1985, p. 252). Better edu-

TABLE 26.2

Assessing Depression Among American Indians and Alaska Natives: Minnesota Multiphasic Personality Inventory (MMPI)

Author	Subjects	N	Instruments[a]	Results
Arthur (1944)	Multitribal high school students and White college applicants and freshmen	Total (345): - White 77% - American Indian 23%	- MMPI[b]	- No significant differences between the two groups for either males or females - Indian girls showed a slightly greater trend toward depression than did the White girls - Girls in both groups showed more of a tendency toward depression than boys
Kline et al. (1973)	Adult male Native American alcoholics in an inpatient treatment program	Total (33)	- MMPI	- Native American alcoholics' profiles appeared to be more elevated and had different configuration than did the profiles of White alcoholics in other studies - The greatest pathology was indicated via elevations on Scale 8 (Sc), whereas the least disturbance was evident in profiles with 2–4 configuration
Mandelzys & Lane (1980)	Adult male Native American inmates admitted to Canadian maximum security prison psychiatric hospital	Total (95)	- MMPI	- With exception of Scales 8 (Sc) and F, profile elevations were consistent with other inmate populations in the United States and Canada - Scale 8 (Sc) and F elevations were markedly elevated for Native offenders in comparison with nonnative offenders
Pollack & Shore (1980)	Adult American Indian patients from Pacific Northwest tribes	Total (142): - Females 52% - Males 48%	- MMPI - Unstructured diagnostic interview (DSM–II)	- At least one diagnosis (37%), Schizophrenia (4%), Nonpsychotic Depression (6%), Situational Reaction (12%), Antisocial-alcoholic (15%) - Patients with Nonpsychotic Depression described their symptomatology in a manner almost identical to that of Schizophrenic patients

(Continued)

TABLE 26.2
(Continued)

Author	Subjects	N	Instruments[a]	Results
Uecker et al. (1980)	American Indian and White veterans enrolled in the alcoholism treatment program	Total (80): - White 50% - American Indian 50%	- MMPI	- No group differences were found for any of the scales - "Indianism" was positively and significantly related to Scale 1 (Hs), Scale 3 (Hy), Scale 7 (Pt), and Scale 8 (Sc) and approached significance at .05 level for Scale 2 (D) - American Indian and White profiles were consistent with mean profiles of alcoholics found in other samples
Butcher et al. (1983)	American Indian and White adult psychiatric inpatients	Total (587): - White 77% - African American 17% - American Indian 6%	- MMPI - Hospital chart review (DSM–III diagnoses) - Assignment into one of six crisis groups based on presenting complaint	- Significant ethnic differences in selection were found among Whites, African Americans, and American Indians for depression-related, aggression-related, and paranoid-type symptoms - No significant differences in rates of classification to a given diagnostic category between African-American and their White matches and between American Indian and their White matches - African Americans had significantly higher elevations on F and Scales 6 (Pa), 8 (Sc), and 9 (Ma) than other ethnic groups - American Indian patients were less pathological as measured by MMPI than the other two groups

Study	Sample	Instrument	Findings
Hoffmann et al. (1985)	Adult Sioux from the Rosebud Indian Reservation in South Dakota	Total (69): - Females 46% - Males 54%	- MMPI-168	- Better educated subjects employed in higher level occupations endorsed fewer MMPI-168 items indicative of depression, agitation, feelings of inadequacy, withdrawal, nonparticipation, and impulsive acting out - For females, Scale 2 (D) positively correlated with Language and Education/Occupation acculturation subscales - For males, Scale 2 (D) positively correlated with Values and Education/Occupation acculturation subscales - Lower degrees of acculturation were associated with higher elevations on MMPI profiles
Bernstein, Teng, Grannemann, & Garbin (1987)	Whites, Hispanics, African Americans and Native Americans from Inmate and Job Applicants' electronic databases	Total (13,433): - White 66% - African American 22% - Hispanic 11% - Native American, males only 1%	- MMPI	- Principal component structure of MMPI did not change across race, sex, and context of testing (inmate vs. job application) with exception of male African-American applicants who resembled male African-American inmates more than they did other applicant groups
Venn (1988)	Native American, Mexican American, and White male alcoholics at an inpatient alcohol rehabilitation facility	Total (545): - Mexican American 3% - White 94% - Native American 3%	- MMPI	- Ethnic variation disappeared when subjects were matched by age and marital status - 2-4 code type was normative among alcoholics of all three ethnic groups

aMost studies used multiple measures, however, instruments included in this table are related to the assessment of depression.
bReported data only on Scales 1 to 4.

cated persons in higher level occupations also endorsed fewer items characteristic of depression, agitation, feelings of inadequacy, withdrawal and nonparticipation, and impulsive acting out (Hoffman et al., 1985), which is consistent with the finding that less acculturated adult American Indians tend to have elevated MMPI profiles (Uecker, Boutillier, & Richardson 1980).

Structured and Semistructured Interviews

The use of structured and semistructured clinical interviews with American Indians and Alaska Natives has only recently received much attention. As illustrated in Table 26.3, the Diagnostic Interview Schedule for Children (DISC; Costello et al., 1984) appears to have received most attention in this population. Dinges and Duong-Tran (1993) conducted DISC interviews in a sample of 416 boarding school American Indian and Alaska Native adolescents. In this quasiclinical sample, co-occuring rates for diagnoses of depression with substance abuse and suicidality significantly exceeded the rates reported for non-Native adolescents. The same study also examined the relationship among stressful life events, depression, and comorbidity. The positive relationship among loss of cultural supports as a stressor, the diagnosis of depression, and attempted suicide provided empirical support for the interpretation that the loss of cultural traditions that support sustained cultural identity may be tied to vulnerability to depression and other forms of dysfunction (Dinges & Duong-Tran, 1993).

Sack, Beiser, Baker-Brown, and Redshirt (1994) conducted a longitudinal study of multitribal adolescents attending school in various reservations across the United States. Among second-grade students, a 1% rate of major depression was comparable to studies in White populations (Sack et al., 1994). Unlike the cross-sectional DISC study of older boarding school adolescents described earlier, Sack and colleagues (1994) found that depressive symptoms declined with age. In the same longitudinal study, when compared to White children, Indian children reported less depressive symptoms but more suicidal ideation. At the same time, teachers viewed Indian children as more depressed. Parents viewed Indian males as more depressed than Indian females, whereas non-Indian females were seen as more depressed than non-Indian males.

Many self-report scales, such as the ones reviewed in the prior section, are developed using assumptions of cross-cultural universality. A number of these instruments have well-developed norms that can provide a clinician with a point of reference as well as advantages of easy administration and scoring. At the same time, etic assessment approaches can constrain the ability to recognize indigenous depressive symptoms of clinical

TABLE 26.3

Assessing Depression Among American Indians and Alaska Natives: Structured and Semistructured Clinical Interviews

Author	Subjects	N	Instruments[a]	Design	Results
Dinges & Duong-Tran (1993)	Multitribal Alaska Native and American Indian boarding school adolescents	Total (416): - Females 52% - Males 48% Age ($M = 16.4$)	- DISC	Cross-sectional	- 24.2% scored positively for depression - Current suicidal ideation (14% of all cases) was the most common additional diagnosis - After the age of 15, comorbidity tends to increase with age - Depression and current suicide ideation was more common for 16- to 18-year-olds than 14- to 15-year-olds - Females had higher percentage of depression and comorbid diagnoses - Overall comorbidity rates for depression with substance abuse and suicidality in this population was higher than reported for non-Native youth
Sack et al. (1994)	2nd-, 4th-, and 6th-grade students in culturally diverse reservation sites in the United States and Canada	Total (973)	- DISC & DISC–P	Longitudinal	- 1% scored positively for depression - Indian children evidenced less depressive symptoms but more suicidal thoughts than did similar non-Indian children - Teachers perceived Indian children as more depressed than non-Indian children - White girls reported greatest number of depressive symptoms, which dropped down with age

(Continued)

TABLE 26.3
(Continued)

Author	Subjects	N	Instruments[a]	Design	Results
Shore et al. (1987)	American Indian patients from three tribal cultures	Total (104)	- Schedule for Affective Disorders and Schizophrenia–Lifetime Version (SADS–L)	Cross-sectional	- Parents reported that non-Indian females show more depressive symptoms than non-Indian males, whereas Indian males were seen as more depressed than Indian females - 82.7% scored positively for depression - Among the Pueblo and Plains Indians, females had almost twice as many confirmed cases of Major Depression as males (females 74.1%, males 25.9%) - Among the Plateau Indians, males had more confirmed cases of depression than Plateau females (females 39%, males 61%) - For all three cultures, 64% had more than one depressive episode (average 3.3 episodes)

[a]Most studies used multiple measures, however, instruments included in this table are related to the assessment of depression.

interest. Additionally, in the interpretation of assessment results, clinicians using any of the instruments described earlier are strongly encouraged to take into account moderator variables such as acculturative status, language usage and fluency, and degree of ethnic identity (Dana, 1993).

CULTURAL CASE FORMULATION APPROACHES
TO THE PHENOMENOLOGY OF DEPRESSION

Several proposals have been made to increase the centrality of culture in making psychiatric diagnoses such as depression. The formation of a Culture and Diagnosis Group to advise the *DSM–IV* task force (Mezzich, 1995) has probably had the most impact to date, albeit less than might be desired. After considering several alternatives, the Culture and Diagnosis Group made a decision to adopt a narrative approach similar to that of the Psychodynamic Formulation (Friedman & Lister, 1987; Perry, Cooper, & Michels, 1987), which provides a complementary narrative to the multiaxial *DSM–IV* diagnosis by following a structured outline of content. A similar outline was developed to provide a systematic narrative description that would represent mental illness from the perspective of the sufferer and his or her primary reference group. This outline was aptly called the Cultural Formulation (Lewis-Fernandez, 1996).

The basic aim of the Cultural Formulation is to provide a unique portrayal of the person and his or her sociocultural environment in a way that provides a more humanized account of suffering such as occurs with depression. The Cultural Formulation is a systematic review of an individual's cultural background, the role of cultural context in the expression and evaluation of symptoms and associated dysfunction, and the effect of cultural differences on the relationship between the individual and clinician. Appendix I of the *DSM–IV* describes the five essential categories comprising the Cultural Formulation (American Psychiatric Association, 1994). A more complete description of the Cultural Formulation can be found in Lewis-Fernandez (1996) and Castillo (1996), and its application to child cases is discussed by Novins et al. (1997).

The cultural identity of the individual characterizes his or her ethnic or cultural reference groups, the degree of involvement with the culture of origin and the host culture, and language abilities, use, and preference, including multilingualism if applicable. The cultural explanations of the individual's illness notes predominant idioms of distress, the local illness categories used to identify the condition, and the meaning and perceived severity of symptoms in relation to cultural norms and the cultural reference group. The cultural elements of the relationship between the individual and clinician indicate the differences in culture and social status between the individual and clinician and any problems that those differences may cause in diagnosis and treatment. Finally, the overall cultural assessment for diagnosis and care is a discussion of how cultural considerations specifically influence comprehensive diagnosis and care. To illustrate the application of these concepts for enhanced understanding of the social and phenomenological aspects of depression, we have provided a series of short vignettes that are summarized from more extensive cultural formulations reported in the literature. The reader is encouraged to consult these case formulations in their entirety (Case 1, O'Nell, 1998; Case 2, Fleming, 1996; Case 3, Wisecarver & Dinges, 1998; Case 4, Topper & Curtis, 1987).

Case 1

Lionel is a 30-year-old American Indian male diagnosed with psychotic depression and alcoholism. He describes feelings of sadness/tearfulness, thoughts of death, and "not caring" about separation from his children and culture. In his tribe, people who are experiencing a severe form of loneliness are likely to be focused on exterior complaints such as interpersonal problems with family, friends, and significant others. Lionel has recently been separated from his current wife and has experienced racism from both non-Indians and his father's family because of his mother's mixed Mexican/Indian heritage. Lionel claims to have a feeling of a *mathematically* based crisis that prompted his separation from family and culture. He has also reported encountering spirits who have tried to "deceive him into dying," and he has claimed to have psychic foreknowledge of his wife's pregnancy and subsequent miscarriage. Although spiritual encounters and prophecy are acceptable in this culture, the morbid quality of his thoughts and his idea of *world mathematics* is both unique and bizarre by local cultural norms and suggestive of a mild psychotic episode.

Discussion. This case illustrates several aspects of the Cultural Formulation. Lionel struggles with his ethnic identity both in terms of how important he views acceptance in tribal and majority White culture and in being the offspring of a father who married a woman from outside his tribe. His psychosocial stressors, although not unlike that of members of other cultures, take on added meaning and weight by dint of the sociocentric nature of his tribal culture. Loneliness as an idiom of distress has quite different and more serious implications for understanding the potential severity of his depression. However, the gender-based behavioral norm of tearful expressions in public would have less symptomatic importance for him than it might in another cultural context. However, the cultural values placed on maturity make it more difficult to assess the increased suicidal potential associated with Lionel's depression because he is likely to deny it. Although spiritual encounters involving prophecy are acceptable by indigenous norms, it is important to recognize that Lionel's delusions are considered bizarre by members of his own culture and thus are not confounded by normative uncertainty.

In assessing Lionel's life stressors, awareness of the cultural norms within which he lives are important to fully comprehend their severity. Lionel's fears of separation, preoccupation with interpersonal relationships, and dependency serve to identify his intense feelings of isolation. Lionel's cultural norms focus on the interdependence of members of their society. His feelings of isolation, "not caring," interpersonal disruptions, and preoccupation with misfortune would indicate that he might be experiencing what his culture terms *loneliness*. Although there are many meanings of *loneliness*, the type that Lionel is experiencing includes a profound and pervasive experience of worthlessness. In his culture, feeling worthless is akin to a sense of complete abandonment, indicating that a person is undeserving of being involved in his society's networks of care. His expression of "not caring" is the most severe form of loneliness. Of note, in this culture, it is quite common for men to express more sadness and tearfulness at community gatherings than women. Knowing this, the clinician should reduce the pathological significance of his statement of crying easily. By contrast, suicide is seen as immature, thus denial of it would be expected from an adult in this culture.

Case 2

Mary is a 24-year-old American Indian female suffering from depression, alcoholism, and childhood trauma. Although Mary had remained sober for a lengthy period, she started drinking again about 9 months after her grandmother's death. A friend suggested she attend a bereavement support group. The non-Indian mental health provider conducting the group mistakenly assumed that Mary was suffering solely from complicated bereavement and did not explore any other possible explanations. Mary felt that members of the non-Indian support group focused more on issues to which she could not relate and did not experience grief in the same way she did. This was particularly evident in the somewhat disbelieving reaction of other group members when Mary reported seeing her grandmother and hearing her voice.

Complicating Mary's clinical picture is her experience, at a very early age, of being sexually abused by an elderly relative. Openly discussing sexual abuse has only recently begun to happen in her community and is nearly inconceivable if the offender is from a high-status family such as Mary's. These factors, coupled with her strongly held value of honoring Indian elders, kept her from disclosing the abuse for many years. Her family has exerted great pressure on her to keep this *shame* hidden, but she has continued dealing with it in the weekly therapy sessions she undertook as an alternative to the bereavement support group.

In Mary's community, experimental alcohol use in the early teens is common. Despite her family's high status, which typically would have precluded her using alcohol, Mary began experimenting in her early teens and quickly developed a deeply ingrained substance abuse pattern. Elders of the tribe believe that teens experiment with and become dependent on intoxicating substances because they do not known who they are as Indians.

Discussion. Mary's case illustrates the need to carefully assess the associated stressors and causal contributions to the expression of depressive symptoms among members of her tribe. Tribal norms structured and guided the experience of her grief in terms of both its length and acceptable forms of expression. For Mary, seeing her grandmother and hearing her voice are culturally appropriate forms of grief symptoms during the required 12-month grieving period for this tribe. However, it would be clinically misleading to use cultural norms regarding grief as an availability heuristic that might mask other sources of depression, such as that associated with Mary's past sexual abuse or the comorbid drinking problems she experienced. The initial clinical presentation of substance abusing behaviors among American Indian and Alaska Native clients is often a distractor from signficant underlying depression. Of equal importance are the norms of nondisclosure about the abusive behaviors of older male tribal members that are likely to lead to considerable suppression of clinically relevant material in the presentation of depressive symptomatology. This case also illustrates cultural explanations of the illness by attributing drinking problems to a failure of youth to understand and identify with their Indian heritage.

Case 3

Anastasia is a 59-year-old Yup'ik female suffering from comorbid physical disease and depression with a history of substance abuse. She currently resides in a metropolitan nursing home far from her home village and is on antidepressant medication, which appears to be minimally effective. For most of her life, since her late teens, Anastasia has been in and out of hospitals for respiratory related illnesses, which contributes to her depression. At the age of 17, she contracted tuberculosis and was sent out of state to an isolation ward where she remained for 2 years; during this time, she bore a son that was conceived with her husband just prior to her hospitalization. While hospitalized, she had little contact with members of her culture and was further isolated from other patients and staff by language barriers. After discharge and returning home, her tuberculosis proved to be a chronic and debilitating illness that forced her to withdraw from the vigorous and active community life of her childhood. Her illness also prevented her from completing the various duties that her culture expected from a woman, wife, and mother. As her illness became more severe, she was able to do less and less and failed to meet the cultural norms of physical hardiness and the women's role in supporting her husband's hunting and fishing activities, as well as seeing to all the needs of her family. These personal inadequacies resulted in a profound sense of worthlessness for Anastasia.

Anastasia reports a constant pain in her abdomen despite reassurance from examining physicians that there is nothing medically wrong. She rejects offers of counseling or therapy because she feels that the clinicians do not help her physical pain. Anastasia considers the nursing home counselors too intrusive and comments that they talk too much, interrupt her frequently, and ask too many questions that are often embarrassing or do not pertain to her physical illness. She has been consistently unresponsive to inquiries about her personal feelings about her illnesses. She does not trust the counselors because they misinterpret her words or use them to probe about personal issues, particularly concerning her childhood and adolescent experiences. Anastasia is sensitive about any attempts to discuss problems concerning her immediate family and considers such topics well beyond the range of acceptable social discourse.

Discussion. Many Yup'ik people, as well as other Alaska Native peoples, are protective of their innermost feelings and share them only with carefully selected friends or family members. This selective disclosure of emotion applies particularly to traumatic emotional experiences that are commonly suppressed and revealed only within a narrative context of long-standing relationships between the discussants. These cultural norms are likely to play a significant role in the clinician–patient relationship and the clinician's ability to elicit depressive symptoms.

Despite decades of experience with health care providers, Anastasia did not feel as if she could share her feelings about her illness with anyone for fear that she would be seen as childish for complaining, which runs counter to the Yup'ik views of selfhood. In the Yup'ik language, Anastasia's illness is described as *upqucilirrtuq*; this refers to an individual who has an overwhelming and complicated accumulation of multiple physical and psychological problems. Although social behaviors or emotions that are uncomfortable, such as complaining too much to others, tend to be suppressed, there is an expressive vocabulary to communicate such conditions. These include such terms as *aliayug* (to be lonely or depressed), *nanikua* (to feel impotent or helpless), *nanikuaq* (to feel abandoned), and *caunritua* (to feel worthless).

In a culture where it is acceptable to discuss physical symptoms but not emotional ones, somatic complaints such as Anastasia's undiagnosed abdominal pains could be a major channel with which to express emotional distress. Illustrating aspects of the relationships between client and clinician are her unsatisfactory experiences with mental health providers due to limited understanding of the impact of her illness on her social role or status and sense of selfhood. In her own eyes and within the norms of her culure, Anastasia never became a "Real Yup'ik Woman," but it is unlikely that failure to attain this status was fully appreciated in understanding her depression.

Case 4

Sam is an adolescent Navajo male living near an agency town. He is suffering from what would be defined by conventional diagnosis as a dysthymic disorder. His mother's family leads a very traditional Navajo lifestyle while his stepfather is a wage worker in the agency town. Sam had become so aggressive toward his younger siblings and matrilineal nieces and nephews that juvenile authorities had become involved and he was facing a possible jail sentence. He displays hostility, depressed mood, and feelings of inadequacy, which are also accompanied by binge drinking with peers and sometimes getting into physical fights. At times Sam's feelings of inadequacy and hopelessness about the future are so strong they border on the delusional. Relations with his parents, siblings, and relatives have become so strained that his family sought help from the local clinic.

Discussion. To appreciate the sociocultural factors that influenced symptom expression, the clinicians reporting this case (Topper & Curtis, 1987) have created a diagnosis they call *synergistic dual anomic depression*. This diagnosis is similar to dysthymic disorder, but the unique combination of the extended family and the economic environments in which agency-town Navajo adolescents are raised warrants its distinction as a culture-specific variety of dysthymic disorder. In the Navajo language, key symptoms of this disorder are described as *ch'íína' bi niilhí'*, which translates as an idiom of distress to "one is being killed by melancholy."

It is important to note that the Navajo explanatory belief model of depression views it as a destructive condition affecting a person physically, socially, emotionally, and spiritually. Its rendering in the Navajo language is akin to dying from melancholy, which carries a powerful emotional force considering the Navajo behavioral taboos regarding death. It also conveys a serious psychological dysfunction exceeding that described by the *DSM–IV* definition of dysthymic disorder. The root of this condition for younger Navajos is found in cultural identity conflicts stemming from the perceived unattainable goal of economic independence in either the traditional or nontraditional Navajo culture, as well as the incompatibility between the goals of establishing a viable personhood in White and Navajo cultures.

In Sam's case, the negotiation of clinical reality involved the use of a variant of extended family therapy to bridge the therapeutic gap between the explanatory belief models of the Western therapists and the treatment needs of an adolescent caught between the developmental demands of two different cultures. The overview of cultural assessment for diagnosis and care that was formulated in this case provides an excellent example of the way in which two Western therapists were able to integrate their explanatory belief models and therapeutic modalities with those of the client and his extended family to achieve a successful treatment outcome.

SUMMARY

This chapter has attempted to describe some key concepts and assessment instruments and provide a sense of the social and phenomenological dimensions involved in the experience of depression among American Indians and Alaska Natives. We have been guided by a growing literature that asserts that

> personality and psychopathology take form in distinct worlds characterized by behavioral environments consisting of consensual orientations to self, objects, space, time, motivations, and moral norms that are culturally constituted, shared to different degrees, and invoked differently in specific situations by members of the social group. (Lewis-Fernandez & Kleinman, 1994, p. 68)

We have succeeded if clinicians are better able to make the concept of culture more central to the challenge of accurate and appropriate assessment of depression among the diversity of clients whom they serve in the future.

REFERENCES

Ackerson, L. M., Dick, R. W., Manson, S. M., & Baron, A. E. (1990). Properties of the inventory to diagnose depression in American Indian adolescents. *Journal of the American Academy of Child and Adolescent Psychiatry, 29*(4), 601–607.

Allen, J. (1998). Personality assessment with American Indians and Alaska Natives. *Journal of Personality Assessment, 70*(1), 17–42.

American Psychiatric Association. (1994). *Diagnostic and statistical manual of mental disorders* (4th ed.). Washington, DC: Author.

Arthur, G. (1944). An experience in examining an Indian twelfth-grade group with the Muliphasic Personlity Inventory. *Mental Hygiene, 25,* 243–250.

Baron, A. E., Manson, S. M., Ackerson, L. M., & Brenneman, D. L. (1990). Depressive symptomatology in older American Indians with chronic disease: Some psychometric considerations. In C. C. Attkisson & J. M. Zich (Eds.), *Depression in primary care screening and detection* (pp. 217–231). New York & London: Routledge.

Beals, J., Manson, S. M., Keane, E. M., & Dick, R. W. (1991). Factorial structure of the center for epidemiological studies—Depression scale among American Indian college students. *Psychological Assessment, 3*(4), 623–627.

Bernstein, I. H., Teng, G., Grannemann, B. D., & Garbin, C. P. (1987). Invariance in the MMPI's component structure. *Journal of Personality Assessment, 51,* 522–531.

Butcher, J. N., Braswell, L., & Raney, D. (1983). A cross-cultural comparison of American Indian, Black, and White inpatients on the MMPI and presenting symptoms. *Journal of Consulting and Clinical Psychology, 51,* 587–594.

Butcher, J. N., Dahlstrom, W. G., Graham, J. R., Tellegen, A., & Kaemmer, B. (1989). *Minnesota Multiphasic Personality Inventory–2 (MMPI–2): Manual for administration and scoring.* Minneapolis: University of Minnesota Press.

Castillo, R. J. (1996). *Culture and mental illness: A client-centered approach.* Pacific Grove: Brooks-Cole.

Costello, A. J., Edelbrook, C., Dulcan, M. K., Kalas, R., & Klarice, S. (1984). *Final report to U.S. National Institute of Mental Health on the diagnostic interview schedule for children.* Unpublished manuscript, University of Pittsburgh.

Dana, R. H. (1988). Culturally diverse groups and MMPI interpretation. *Professional Psychology: Research and Practice, 19,* 490–495.

Dana, R. H. (1993). *Multicultural assessment perspectives for professional psychology.* Boston: Allyn & Bacon.

Dinges, N. G., & Cherry, D. (1994). Symptom expression and the use of mental health services among American ethnic minorities. In J. F. Aponte, R. Y. Rivers, & J. Wohl (Eds.), *Psychological interventions and cultural diversity* (pp. 40–56). Boston: Allyn & Bacon.

Dinges, N. G., & Duong-Tran, Q. (1993). Stressful life events and co-occuring depression substance abuse and suicidality among American Indian and Alaska Native adolescents. *Culture, Medicine and Psychiatry, 16,* 487–502.

Dinges, N. G., & Duong-Tran, Q. (1994). Suicide ideation and suicide attempt among American Indian and Alaska Native boarding school students. *American Indian and Alaska Native Mental Health Research, 4*(Mono), 167–188.

Ferraro, F. R., Bercier, B., & Chelminski, I. (1997). Geriatric Depression Scale–Short Form (GDS–SF) performance in Native American elderly adults. *Clinical Gerontologist, 18*(1), 52–55.

Fleming, C. M. (1996). Cultural formulation of psychiatric diagnosis: An American Indian woman suffering from depression, alcoholism, and childhood trauma. *Culture, Medicine, and Psychiatry, 20,* 145–154.

Friedman, R. S., & Lister, P. (1987). The current status of psychodynamic formulation. *Psychiatry, 50*(2), 126–141.

Graham, J. R. (1993). *MMPI–2: Assessing personality and psychopathology.* New York: Oxford University Press.

Greene, R. L. (1987). Ethnicity and MMPI performance: A review. *Journal of Consulting and Clinical Psychology, 55*(4), 497–512.

Greene, R. L. (1991). *MMPI–2/MMPI: An interpretive manual*. Needham, MA: Simon & Schuster.

Hathaway, R. H., & McKinley, J. S. (1940). A multiphasic personality schedule (Minnesota): 1. Construction of the schedule. *Journal of Psychology, 10*, 249–254.

Hodge, F. S., & Kipnis, P. (1996). Demoralization: A useful concept for case management with Native Americans. In P. Manoleas (Ed.), *The cross-cultural practice of clinical case management in mental health* (pp. 79–98). Binghamton, NY: The Haworth Press, Inc.

Hoffmann, T., Dana, R., & Bolton, B. (1985). Measured acculturation and MMPI–168 performance of Native American adults. *Journal of Cross-Cultural Psychology, 16*, 243–256.

Jenkins, J., Kleinman, A., & Good, B. J. (1991). Cross-cultural studies of depression. In J. Baker & A. Kleinman (Eds.), *Psychosocial aspects of depression* (pp. 67–99). Hillsdale, NJ: Lawrence Erlbaum Associates.

Kleinman, A., & Good, B. (Eds.). (1985). *Culture and depression: Studies in the anthropology and cross-cultural psychiatry of affect and disorder*. Berkeley, CA: University of California Press.

Kline, J. A., Rozynko, V. V., Flint, G., & Roberts, A. C. (1973). Personality characteristics of male Native American patients. *International Journal of the Addictions, 8*, 729–732.

Kluckhohn, C., & Leighton, D. (1958). *The Navajo*. New York: Doubleday.

Lewis-Fernandez, R. (1996). Cultural formulation of psychiatric diagnosis. *Culture, Medicine and Psychiatry, 20*, 133–144.

Lewis-Fernandez, R., & Kleinman, A. (1994). Culture, personality, and psychopathology. *Journal of Abnormal Psychology, 103*, 67–71.

Lichtenberg, P. A., Chapelski, E. E., & Youngblade, L. M. (1997). The effect of depression on functional abilities among Great Lakes American Indians. *The Journal of Applied Gerontology, 16*, 235–248.

Mandelzys, N., & Lane, E. B. (1980). The validity of the MMPI as it pertains to Canadian native inmates. *Canadian Journal of Criminology, 22*, 188–196.

Manson, S. M. (1995). Culture and major depression: Current challenges in the diagnosis of mood disorders. *Cultural Psychiatry, 18*(3), 487–501.

Manson, S. M., Ackerson, L. M., Dick, R. W., Baron, A. E., & Fleming, C. M. (1990). Depressive symptoms among American Indian adolescents: Psychometric characteristics of the Center for Epidemiological Studies depression scale (CES–D). *Psychological Assessment, 2*(3), 231–237.

Manson, S. M., Shore, J. H., & Bloom, J. D. (1985). The depressive experience in American Indian communities: A challenge for psychiatric theory and diagnosis. In A. Kleinman & B. Good (Eds.), *Culture and depression: Studies in the anthropology and cross-cultural psychiatry of affect and disorder* (pp. 331–368). Berkeley, CA: University of California Press.

Merton, R. K. (1968). *Social theory and social structure*. New York: The Free Press.

Mezzich, J. E. (1995). Cultural formulation and comprehensive diagnosis: Clinical and research perspectives. *The Psychiatric Clinics of North America: Cultural Psychiatry, 18*(3), 649–658.

Novins, D. K., Bechtold, D. W., Sack, W. H., Thomson, J., Carter, D. R., & Manson, S. M. (1997). The *DSM–IV* outline for cultural formulation: A critical demonstration with American Indian children. *Journal of the American Academy of Child and Adolescent Psychiatry, 36*(9), 1244–1251.

Olin, J. T., Schneider, L. S., Eaton, E. M., Zemansky, M. F., & Pollock, V. E. (1992). The Geriatric Depression Scale and the Beck Depression Inventory as screening instruments in an older adult outpatient population. *Psychological Assessment, 4*, 190–192.

O'Nell, T. D. (1998). Cultural formulation of psychiatric diagnosis: Psychotic depresion and alcoholism in an American Indian man. *Culture, Medicine, and Psychiatry, 22*, 123–136.

Perry, S., Cooper, A. M., & Michels, R. (1987). The psychodynamic formulation. *The American Journal of Psychiatry, 144*(5), 543–550.

Pollack, D., & Shore, J. H. (1980). Validity of the MMPI with Native Americans. *American Journal of Psychiatry, 137,* 946–950.

Radloff, L. S. (1977). The CES–D scale: A self-report depression scale for research in general population. *Applied Psychological Measurement, 1,* 385–401.

Roberts, R. E. (1990). Special population issues in screening for depression. In J. M. Zich (Ed.), *Depression in primary care: Screening and detection* (pp. 183–216). New York: Routledge.

Sack, W. H., Beiser, M., Baker-Brown, G., & Redshirt, R. (1994). Depressive and suicidal symptoms in Indian school children: Findings from the Flower of Two Soils. *American Indian and Alaska Native Mental Health Research,* 4(Mono), 81–96.

Shore, J. H., & Manson, S. M. (1981). Cross-cultural studies of depression among American Indians and Alaska Natives. *White Cloud Journal, 2,* 5–12.

Shore, J. H., Spero, M. M., Bloom, J. D., Keepers, G., & Neligh, G. (1987). A pilot study of depression among American Indian patients with research diagnostic criteria. *Journal of the National Center,* 1(2), 4–15.

Somervell, P. D., Beals, J., Kinzie, J. D., Boehnlein, J., Leung, P., & Manson, S. M. (1993). Use of the CES–D in an American Indian Village. *Culture, Medicine and Psychiatry, 16,* 503–517.

Todd-Bazemore, E., & Allen, J. (1994, April). *Psychological assessment with Native Americans.* Paper presented at the midwinter meeting of the Society for Personality Assessment, Chicago.

Topper, M. D., & Curtis, J. (1987). Extended family therapy: A clinical approach to the treatment of synergistic dual anomic depression among Navajo agency-town adolescents. *Journal of Community Psychology, 15,* 334–348.

Uecker, A. E., Boutillier, L. R., & Richardson, E. H. (1980). "Indianism" and MMPI scores of men alcoholics. *Journal of Studies on Alcohol, 41,* 357–362.

Venn, J. (1988). MMPI profiles of Native, Mexican, and Caucasian-American male alcoholics. *Psychological Reports, 62,* 427–432.

Wilson, C., Civic, D., & Glass, D. (1994). Prevalence and correlates of depressive syndromes among adults visiting an Indian Health Service primary care clinic. *American Indian and Alaska Native Mental Health Research, 6,* 1–12.

Wisecarver, M., & Dinges, N. G. (1998). *Cultural formulation of psychiatric diagnosis: Co-morbid depression, substance abuse and physical disease.* Manuscript under review.

Young, T. J. (1991). Locus of control, depression, and anger among Native Americans. *The Journal of Social Psychology,* 131(4), 583–584.

Zimmerman, M., & Coryell, W. (1987). The Inventory to Diagnose Depression (IDD): A self-report scale to diagnose major depressive disorder. *Journal of Consulting and Clinical Psychology,* 55(1), 55–59.

27

Assessment Issues With Jewish Clients

Peter F. Langman
Jewish Family Service of the Lehigh Valley, Allentown, PA

The psychological assessment of Jews in the United States did not get off to an auspicious start. Early in the century, Henry Goddard tested Jewish immigrants as they came through Ellis Island and concluded that 83% were "feeble-minded," with 76% being "morons" and 7% "imbeciles" (Goddard, 1917). Such research was used to document the undesirability of Jews to justify closing the doors of immigration. This is a good example of how not to do multicultural assessment.

Goddard was not alone among psychologists and psychiatrists in pathologizing Jews. Galton and Pearson both believed that Jews were "inferior" (Hirsch, 1976; see also Kamin, 1974). In fact, a belief in unusually high rates of psychopathology among Jews existed long before formal assessments appeared in the field. Major figures such as Kraepelin, Charcot, Krafft-Ebing, and Binswanger supported the notion that Jews were more mentally ill than non-Jews (Gilman, 1993), and Jung believed that the Jewish unconscious was inferior to the Aryan unconscious (Adams & Sherry, 1991). These views were often related to a belief in the *degeneracy* of Jews. At times, however, they were the result of an awareness of the impact of oppression on Jews.

This leads to a delicate issue in multicultural assessment. On one hand, discussions of psychopathology among a particular culture may be seen as stereotyping or pathologizing that group. Historically, Jews have been the victims of such stereotyping and pathologizing. On the other hand, it may be that certain psychological problems are more common within particular cultures. Throughout this century, there have been legitimate attempts at comparing the rates of psychiatric diagnoses among Jews and other groups (Sanua, 1992).

Although intergroup comparisons are interesting for the potential light they can shed on the psychology of different cultures, the primary focus here is on the assessment of individuals. To accurately assess individuals, however, it is necessary to be familiar with their culture and its norms. Thus, the first half of this chapter briefly reviews Jewish cultural diversity, Jewish attitudes toward suffering and help-seeking, and Jewish identity issues (due to space limitations, this discussion is brief; for more detail on all these topics, see Langman, 1999). The second half of the chapter discusses specific concerns related to the assessment of Jewish clients. Assessment in this context refers both to standardized testing as well as the information gained from psychosocial histories, clinical interviews, observations of clients, and any other information that is used in understanding, evaluating, and diagnosing clients.

BACKGROUND INFORMATION

Jewish Diversity

Jewishness is not simply a religious identification, but a cultural one as well. Many Jews reject Judaism as a religion, but maintain a strong sense of Jewishness. This double nature of Jewishness has research implications in terms of who constitutes an appropriate comparison group to Jews. There are studies that focus on religion and compare Jews to Protestants and Catholics. In other studies, the focus is on Jewishness as an ethnicity, and Jewish Americans are compared to Irish Americans and Italian Americans. Focusing on religion ignores race and ethnicity, putting African-American Baptists and WASPs into the same group based on their common Protestant Christianity. Focusing on ethnicity ignores the influence of Judaism and every other religion and denomination.

The problem of defining Jewishness is exacerbated by the religious, ethnic, and racial diversity of Jews. Jews, in fact, constitute a multicultural group within themselves. During the course of history, Jews have lived in many of the world's nations. Through intermarriage, conversion, and adoption, there have been Jews of every race. Jews in China look Chinese, Jews in India look Indian, and Jews in Ethiopia look Ethiopian. In addition, Jews and Jewish culture are influenced by the cultures in which they live. Thus, there is no such thing as Jewish culture, but rather a multitude of Jewish cultures.

The primary geographical and cultural division of Jews is that between Ashkenazic and Sephardic Jews. Ashkenazic Jews have their roots in central and eastern Europe. Their native language is Yiddish, which is a Germanic language written with the Hebrew alphabet. Sephardic Jews have their roots in Spain and Portugal. Following the expulsion of Jews from Spain in 1492, however, they traveled throughout the Mediterranean as well as into northern Europe and even the New World. Their native language is known as Ladino, Judezmo, or Judeo-Spanish, which is a form of Spanish written with the Hebrew alphabet.

A third category of Jews is known as Mizrachim. They have ancient roots in North Africa and the Middle East in countries such as Iran, Iraq, Yemen, and Egypt. Since the founding of Israel in 1948, however, most of these populations have fled or been driven out.

One issue in assessment is language. Jews in the United States may come from France, Argentina, Russia, Israel, or almost anywhere. If they are recent immigrants, they might have little or no knowledge of English. Even if they do know English, it cannot be assumed that any standardized test will be valid for them.

The vast majority of Jews in the United States, however, are Ashkenazic Jews who know English as a first language. Within this group, the most important cultural dimension is religiosity. For assessment purposes, it is important to distinguish Orthodox and Hasidic Jews from Reform, Reconstructionist, Conservative, and unaffiliated Jews. The terminology used here includes *Orthodox* (which includes Hasidic Jews) and *non-Orthodox* (which includes the rest). This is not ideal, but it serves.

Non-Orthodox Jews. Most Jews in the United States are not Orthodox, and many Jews are not affiliated with any congregation. The non-Orthodox affiliations include Reform, Reconstructionist, and Conservative. Although blanket statements are bound to be inaccurate to some extent, they are hard to avoid in writing on cultural groups. Keeping this in mind, it can be said that Reform, Reconstructionist, and Conservative Jews are more assimilated than Orthodox Jews. They typically do not distinguish themselves by dress or appearance and are less likely to adhere to the observances that define traditional Judaism.

Orthodox Jews. Orthodox Jews believe that the *Torah* (the first five books of the Bible) are God's word. Therefore, the commandments contained there and interpreted in the Talmud cannot be ignored or changed. There are three areas in particular that define Orthodox observance: following the laws of kashrut (keeping kosher), refraining from work on the Sabbath (Friday night to Saturday night), and maintaining the laws of family purity, which regulate physical and sexual contact between husband and wife.

Sabbath observance means a ceasing of all work activities, as well as attendance at services. On the sabbath, Orthodox Jews will not drive a car or turn on anything that will use electricity because of the prohibition against work. This prohibition includes the making of fire, and combustion engines and electricity have been interpreted as falling within this prohibition. Keeping kosher involves not eating particular meats (pork, shellfish, etc.), as well as not eating milk products and meat together. The laws of family purity require immersions in a *mikveh* (ritual bath) at prescribed intervals (see Donin, 1991).

Hasidic Jews are the most traditional segment of Orthodoxy. Their roots are in eastern Europe, the birthplace of Hasidism in the 18th century. Hasids are known by the name of the town in which their sect began: the Bobover began in Bobov, the Lubavitcher in Lubavitch, and so on. Each sect has a rebbe as its spiritual leader. The rebbe is consulted by his followers for virtually anything and everything—from what job to take, to whom they should marry, to medical and psychological concerns.

The daily language among Hasidim is Yiddish, and this is the first language the children learn. The children later learn English during their secular schooling and Hebrew during their religious schooling. Most Hasids do not own a television set or watch movies—not because they reject technology, but because of moral objections. Modesty is an important element in Hasidic culture, and popular culture is thus avoided because of its constant violation of modesty. Secular culture in general is avoided because it is a threat to the values of Hasidic life. This attitude toward the secular world is not monolithic, however. Despite their similarities, there are important differences among the sects. Some are quite insular and avoid secular education as much as possible. Others are more involved in the secular world, participating in higher education and entering various professions.

Attitudes Toward Suffering and Help-Seeking

Attitudes toward suffering and help-seeking among Jews often differ from those found in people of other cultural groups. In addition, these attitudes often vary among different groups of Jews. This section provides an overview of these differences.

Non-Orthodox Jews. The attitudes toward suffering and help-seeking among this group of Jews tend to differ dramatically from those of other minorities, as well as differing from the attitudes of many European American cultures. Whereas many cultures emphasize suffering alone and in silence, this is not the case in Jewish culture. For example, Zborowski (1969) compared how pain was dealt with by patients of different cultural groups in the United States, including Jewish, Irish, Italian, and WASP patients. Jewish patients tended to be much more open and expressive of their pain, especially compared with the Irish and WASP patients. WASP patients were reluctant to express pain because this was seen as useless. They also preferred to be self-reliant and take pain "like a man." Their way of coping was to be stoic and hide or deny their pain, often avoiding seeking medical attention until their conditions had become quite serious.

Regarding the patients of Irish descent, Zborowski found that they tended to emphasize stoicism and self-control, believing that "there was a certain amount of honor . . . in refusing to admit that you had pain" (p. 197). Like the WASPs, they believed that there was no point in talking about their pain, and they also tended to avoid seeking medical attention.

Unlike the Irish and WASP patients in Zborowski's study, Jewish patients tended to value emotional expressiveness. They communicated their pain and viewed this both as a release and a way to maintain social connectedness. The lack of such expression was seen as harmful: "Failure to achieve catharsis is bad, for it is dangerous to retain what should be expressed" (Zborowski & Herzog, 1995, p. 328).

Jewish patients also tended to speak freely of their personal concerns: "They seem to look forward to the opportunity to talk about their pain, illness, anxieties, intrafamily relationships, and so on. They seem happy to find a listener with whom they can share their feelings, worries, and opinions" (Zborowski, 1969, p. 98). Compared with groups who tended to put off seeking medical help, Jews tended to respond immediately to physical discomfort. This was summed up by one patient who said, "Of course, when I don't feel well I go to the doctor. We don't wait" (p. 120).

This willingness to talk about pain and consult an expert tends to characterize Jewish attitudes toward psychotherapy. Herz and Rosen (1982) noted that when Jews have an emotional problem, they seek professional help. Data collected decades ago found that Jews were more favorably inclined toward psychotherapy and more likely to utilize it than were Protestants and Catholics (Srole, Langner, Michael, Opler, & Rennie, 1962).

A study by McGoldrick and Rohrbaugh (1987) questioned mental health professionals of different ethnic groups about their family attitudes toward a variety of topics. Jews differed from other groups on a number of items relevant to the discussion of suffering. Jews scored higher than other groups on the following items: "Talking about one's problems was considered the best way to cure them," "Suffering could be born more easily when expressed and shared," and "You really got attention when you were sick." Jews scored lower on the item "Complaining about problems was bad form." In comparison, WASPs scored higher than Jews on "Suffering was to be borne in silence," and Irish scored higher than Jews on "Suffering was to be done alone."

Shandler (1979) compared American German Jews to American East European Jews (both groups fall within the category of Ashkenazic Jews) and found that "the German group had statistically a more significant positive attitude toward psychotherapy than did the East European group" (p. 1078). Other relevant studies include Croog (1961), Mechanic (1963), and Suchman (1964).

Russian Jews. Although Russian Jews who come to the United States are both Ashkenazic and non-Orthodox, they constitute a particular cultural group. Russian Jews tend to be highly suspicious of mental health professionals for a variety of reasons. First of all, it is difficult for Russian Jews to believe that community agencies are not part of the national government and that mental health professionals "are not government officials to be feared, disbelieved, and avoided" (Brodsky, 1988, p. 132). In addition, mental health problems were severely stigmatized in Russia. Also, under the Soviet regime, political nonconformity was viewed as a mental problem that was treated with "forced commitment to mental hospitals" (Brodsky, 1988, p. 133). As a result, psychiatry was viewed as an extension of the oppressive government.

Russian Jews tend to deny the presence of psychological problems (Goldstein, 1979). They blame external factors or present with somatic complaints. Russian culture has been described as lacking in psychological mindedness to the point of having psychophobia (Kohn, Flaherty, & Levav, 1989). Goldstein (1984) reported a focus on external circumstances, somatizing, lack of introspection, and unfamiliarity with talking about personal matters among Russian Jews.

The behavior of Russian Jews in the area of physical health and medical care also deserves attention. In the Russian medical system, patients were often not informed of why operations were done, and it was considered presumptuous for patients to ask questions (Wheat, Brownstein, & Kvitash, 1983); patients expected to be told what to do. The common practice in the United States for nurses or physicians to smile when meeting patients can be misinterpreted by Russian Jews as ridicule. In Russia, health is serious business and "Illness is not something to smile about" (Wheat, Brownstein, & Kvitash, 1983, p. 902).

In response to the inadequate medical care in Russia, patients often exaggerated their symptoms in an effort to get quicker appointments and better care. Bribery and manipulation were simply seen as survival skills, and Russian patients often do not understand why such practices are frowned on in this country. In addition, "Russian patients firmly believe that all drugs are a poison in some way. They will stop using them at the first resolution of symptoms" (Wheat, Brownstein, & Kvitash, 1983, p. 902). All of these attitudes and practices can have implications for psychiatric assessment.

Orthodox Jews. Speaking broadly, Orthodox and Hasidic Jews have a positive attitude toward seeking medical attention. Heilman (1992) noted of Hasidic Jews that, "They went to the physician straight away if they had problems" (p. 74). According to Landau (1993), there are some extremely religious Jews who still use folk remedies, but generally they keep up with the latest advances in modern medicine and "zealously take care of their health as a matter of religious duty" (p. 47). Rabinowicz (1996) noted that historically there has been occasional ambivalence among Hasidics toward medicine due to a tendency to believe that healing was in the hands of God or that the proper intervention would be made by their rebbe. This attitude is still found among Bratslav Hasidics, who are "suspicious of medicine in general and psychiatry in particular" (Witztum, Greenberg, & Buchbinder, 1990, p. 128).

The Orthodox/Hasidic attitude toward psychological treatment is quite different than that of non-Orthodox Jews. Wikler (1986) noted that "Orthodox clients do not enter treatment easily" (p. 118; see also Paradis, Friedman, Hatch, & Ackerman, 1997). Whereas more assimilated Jews tend to be open to using therapy, Orthodox clients often avoid seeking help from mental health professionals. Wikler identified two causes of this avoidance: the association of therapy with insanity, and the risk of jeopardizing people's marriage prospects. In Orthodox communities, family background plays an important role in choosing marriage partners. If a person is known to be in therapy, this could keep him or her from finding a spouse. In addition, if any family member is in therapy, this could also limit marriage opportunities.

As a result, confidentiality is of paramount importance. The risk of entering therapy is even greater in Orthodox communities because they tend to be small and closely knit. Wikler (1986) emphasized:

> Mental health practitioners who treat Orthodox Jewish clients must always be aware of the enormous resistance these clients overcame and the enormous risk they took in entering treatment. Their concern with confidentiality, which could be seen as paranoid, therefore, needs to be understood within the context of the social risk involved. (p. 118)

Jewish Identity Issues

Having noted the diversity among Jews, any discussion of Jewish identity is bound to be problematic. Obviously, there can be no such thing as a single Jewish identity. Nonetheless, Jews in the United States often experience similar issues in regard to being Jewish. Because most of the research on Jewish identity has been on non-Orthodox Jews, this is the group that is focused on here. This does not mean that Orthodox Jews never face any of the same issues. However, given the difficulties in speaking of Jewish identity, it is best to avoid making unwarranted generalizations.

There are two major issues in Jewish identity: internalized antisemitism and fear of visibility. Internalized antisemitism has parallels among other minority cultures in internalized racism or prejudice and attempts to disidentify from one's culture. In the case of Jews, it is common for Jews to attempt to minimize or deny the extent of their Jewishness. This can include essentially disowning Judaism as a religion and denigrating those who practice it. As stated by Lewin (1948), "The feeling of inferiority of the Jew is but an indication of the fact that he sees things Jewish with the eyes of the unfriendly majority" (p. 198). In other words, many Jews believe in the negative evaluation of Jewishness that is prevalent in the dominant culture and thus disidentify from their Jewish heritage.

The second major issue is the fear of visibility as Jews. The centuries of persecution of Jews have left their mark on Jews today in the form of fear—even terror—at the thought of being visibly Jewish in public. A few quotes provide illustrations of this dynamic. Lopate (1989) referred to "The old fear of making ourselves too visible, drawing too much attention to Jewish things in a world that will never be anything but anti-Semitic" (p. 296). Gilman (1991) identified the desire to become invisible and noted that, "This may well account for the self-imposed invisibility of Jews as Jews in certain social and political contexts. For visibility brings with it true risk" (p. 236). Himmelfarb (1987) mentioned the need for "keeping a low profile, not making waves—prudence at the expense of self-respect" (p. 6).

What might sound like paranoia to a non-Jewish clinician might be perfectly normal in American Jewish culture. Jews might be afraid to wear a yarmulke (head covering) in public, use Yiddish or Hebrew words in conversation, wear a Star-of-David necklace or clothes with Hebrew writing, and do anything that would reveal their Jewishness. One psychologist referred to "what, for Jews, is the most feared question: 'Are you Jewish?'" (Weinrach, 1990, p. 548). This is a feared question because Jews have no way of knowing what will happen if they answer it truthfully. Some Jews lie, saying, "No, I'm not Jewish." As Himmelfarb commented, it is a matter of prudence at the expense of self-respect. Historically, Jews have been killed just because they were Jews, and even if the world appears to be safe, the fear endures.

The Assessment of Jewish Identity.   A common concern in studies of Jewish identity is with the possible connection between Jewishness and mental health or self-esteem. Klein (1977) conducted a multifaceted study of Jewish identity, alienation, and self-esteem. Although some of her results confirmed a connection among a positive Jewish identity, high self-esteem, and low alienation, other results did not show the same connections.

Sanua (1962) reviewed the literature on Jewish identity and mental health and found no consistent trends. Sanua (1963) cited two studies that address the question of Jewish identity and mental health. One was a study of Jewish identity among psychiatric and nonpsychiatric populations that found no differences in Jewish identity between the two groups. The other was a study of possible connections between anxiety and levels of Orthodox and Hasidic observance. This study found no correlation between religious practice and anxiety. In fact, it was not religious observance but marginality that was related to anxiety. A study by Fernando (1975) found that depressed Jews were less religious than nondepressed Jews. Sarnoff (1951) found that Jews who are high on internalized antisemitism tend to be "insecure, chronically anxious individuals" (p. 214).

An intriguing study by Sanua (1959) explored Jewish identity and psychological adjustment across three generations of Jews in America. He found that objective personality assessment indicated that each successive generation became more adjusted, whereas projective assessment indicated that each successive generation became more maladjusted. Sanua suggested that "the foreign-born are least adjusted 'socially' while the third generation appears to have the greatest 'inner maladjustment' " (p. 454). It seems that the immigrants knew who they were internally but had a hard time adjusting to a new culture, whereas the third generation was well adjusted to the culture but no longer had strong internal identities.

Taken together, these studies demonstrate the difficulty in making any definitive statements about Jewish identity and mental health. Some studies find a correlation between aspects of Jewish identity and psychopathology, whereas other studies do not.

Zemlick's (1977) study using personal construct theory captured many of the nuances of Jewish identity. For example, an Israeli male had his ideal self "more closely aligned with ideal persons in general than ideal Jewish persons" (p. 58). A Jew who described himself as Conservative scored as being opposed to Conservative Jews. One subject defined all his ideals in opposition to Jewish role figures; he also defined Gentiles as related to all Jewish figures and most closely related to Orthodox Jews. Finally, in regard to one subject, Zemlick wrote:

> In contrast to her statement at the time of interview, that the ideal Jewish woman was not related to her ideal self, structurally this does not appear to be a true representation. Her ideal self is seen as similar and even more closely tied to the ideal Jewish persons than to ideal persons in general. It is she who appears rather incongruent with her ideals. (p. 78)

Zemlick's work demonstrates the complexities of Jewish identity and the need for more idiographic work in this area.

ISSUES IN ASSESSMENT

Antisemitism

The outspoken antisemitism of psychologists and other professionals that existed in the late 19th and early 20th centuries appears to have vanished. This does not mean, however, that the field is now free of biases and stereotypes. Individuals are still prone to be influenced by prejudice in evaluating their clients. Bloombaum, Yamamoto, and James (1968) studied therapists' attitudes toward Jews and other minorities and rated over 20% of the therapists' responses as highly stereotypical and nearly 80% of their responses as containing "subtle stereotypic attitudes" (p. 99).

Pearce (1994) reported on two studies that reveal the impact of stereotypes. One study involved counseling students and the other nursing students. In both studies, the students were given case histories that were identical except for the ethnicity of the client, which appeared as Asian, Jewish, White, or West Indian. Thus, the only difference in the cases was the single word used to identify the client's ethnicity. The students read the case descriptions and rated the clients on a series of semantic differentials (strong–weak, warm–cold, etc.) with a rating scale from 1 to 11.

The results of the counseling students' responses found that three categories comparing Whites and Jews were significantly different. Regarding the extent to which the clients were perceived as warm (1) versus cold (11), the White client was viewed as more warm (3.33) and the Jewish client was seen as more cold (8.00). The ratings of friendly (11) versus hostile (1) showed that the White client was viewed as more friendly (9.33) and the Jewish client was seen as more hostile (5.00). The ratings of helpful (1) versus obstructive (11) found that the White client was viewed as more helpful (3.66) and the Jewish client was seen as more obstructive (6.00). It is worth noting again that nothing in the client descriptions was different except the one-word ethnic label.

Among the nursing students, the White client was viewed as more strong, flexible, sincere, and kind; the Jewish client was seen as weaker, more rigid, less sincere, and less kind. This study also asked if the client's problems were caused by the client or by external circumstances. The White client was seen as a victim of circumstance more than the other clients.

These studies reveal the extent to which people in the helping professions are influenced by prejudice. Their perceptions of clients were skewed by ethnic bias, as were their conceptualizations of the source of the client's difficulties. Professionals must be aware of their own attitudes toward Jews and the potential impact that their own beliefs and attitudes can have on their assessment. This is true for both non-Jews and Jews. There are many sources of intergroup antagonism with the Jewish community, and such antagonism can affect assessment. A nonreligious Jew may look down on Jews who are intensely religious and vice versa. All professionals need to explore their own attitudes toward Jews and Jewishness to prevent bias in their assessments.

The Question of Validity

Although objective and projective instruments have been used frequently with Jewish populations, most studies do not examine the validity of an instrument for a particular Jewish population. A few relevant studies are examined.

Dayan (1959) used the MMPI with Orthodox Jews attending Yeshiva University and found significantly elevated scores on the Hypochondriasis, Depression, Hysteria, Psychopathic Deviate, Male/Female, Psychasthenia, and Schizophrenia scales. In another study of Orthodox college students, Levinson (1962) found elevated scores on every scale of the MMPI except Social Introversion. He stated that, "the present MMPI norms are not functional in this subculture" (p. 27). Although the MMPI has been revised since 1962, and although the current generation of Orthodox Jews may differ from that of 1962, this research demonstrates the potential problems in using standardized tests among particular populations of Jews. As noted by Dana (1993), "The MMPI can only be used if the assessee is similar on relevant demographic variables to the standardization population and speaks English as a first language" (p. 175).

Why Jews had elevated scores in these studies is not known. One possibility is that if the MMPI were normed on a population that tended to be noncommunicative of emotions and personal difficulties, the Jewish tendency to be more expressive might lead to elevated scores. Another possibility is that Jews tend to read the items differently and thus respond differently. This seems likely among Orthodox students who are trained extensively in the interpretation of texts. Levinson (1962) concluded that, "because in the subcultural matrix of traditional values internalized by these students the meaning of the items and scales are different for them than for the general population, validation and interpretation of these must, therefore, be arrived at anew" (p. 26).

On a related note, two studies (Gynther, Gray, & Strauss, 1970; Strauss, Gynther, & Kneff, 1971) examined the influence of religious affiliation

(Protestant, Catholic, Jewish) on the endorsement of MMPI items relating to religion. Both studies found that Jews responded differently to the items than did Catholics and Protestants. This is hardly surprising because the MMPI contained items referring to going to church, belief in the second coming of Christ, belief in miracles performed by Jesus, and so on. Thus, rather than reflecting individual personality and psychopathology, Jewish responses to such items are largely determined by their identity. In addition, it should not be assumed that a rejection of such items has the same meaning for Jews and Christians. The use of such religion-specific items in standardized testing is problematic for clients from other religious backgrounds.

In a study of first-year college students, Jews had significant differences from Catholics and Protestants on several MMPI subscales (Bohrnstedt, Borgatta, & Evans, 1968). Among both males and females, Jews scored higher on the Depression, Hysteria, and Psychopathic Deviate scales. Both Jewish men and women also scored as more feminine than non-Jewish men and women. Jewish males were lower on Social Introversion than non-Jewish males. There were also differences on the validity scales. Although all of the scores were within normal limits, this study demonstrated the existence of differences between assimilated Jews and non-Jews.

Another test whose validity for Orthodox Jews has been examined is the Goodenough–Harris Drawing Test. Although this test is used for the assessment of intelligence and not personality, other drawing tests such as Draw-A-Person and House-Tree-Person are used for personality assessment. The issues raised by the use of the Goodenough–Harris test are relevant for other drawing tests.

A study of Jewish children's responses on the Goodenough–Harris test found that Jewish children scored below the norms for their chronological ages (Levinson & Block, 1977). The researchers concluded that the test may be used for this population "provided appropriate norms are developed" (p. 157).

Another study using the Goodenough–Harris test compared 40 different cultural groups. Of the 40, Orthodox Jewish students in Brooklyn ranked 10th in intelligence and Hasidic Jews in Brooklyn ranked 33rd (Dennis, 1966). How is this difference to be explained? After all, both groups are Orthodox, Ashkenazic Jews living in the same city. Dennis suggested that the ancient prohibition against the making of images, as well as the minimal contact with modern culture (television, movies, magazines, etc.), account for the poor quality of drawings among the Hasids. In addition, some of the Hasids stated that they had never drawn a man before. Obviously, a child's first drawing of a person cannot be compared to that of a child who has been drawing human figures for several years.

Religiosity

Perhaps the largest cultural gap that is likely to exist between professional and client is religion. Sevensky (1984) noted that the general population is more religious than mental health professionals. Thus, there is commonly a significant difference between client and therapist in degree of religiosity—whether Jewish, Christian, or other religion.

Religiosity and Countertransference. There are a number of issues to explore regarding religiosity and assessment. First, religiosity should never be viewed as a sign of psychopathology. Starting with Freud, there has been a tendency to view religious devotion as a form of neurosis. Spero (1996) recommended that clinicians explore their own religious attitudes. Is a clinician uncomfortable when clients discuss religion? Has a therapist resolved his or her own religious identity and beliefs? What specific aspects of religion or religious experience are most challenging to work with? Clinicians who are not self-aware may have negative reactions to religious clients that would bias their assessments.

This is especially likely in cases of more exotic religiosity, such as reports of being chased by demons or angels (Bilu, 1979; Witztum, Buchbinder, & van der Hart, 1990) or being visited in dreams by ancient Jewish holy men (Bilu & Abramovitch, 1985). Such reports need to be considered within the context of the client's religious culture. Having acknowledged this, however, it is important to realize that when such Jews come for treatment, they "are no longer adjusted or adapted to their own milieu, and they deviate considerably from the norms of their own subculture" (Shimrat, 1979, p. 163). In other words, the fact that Jews from highly religious and insulated subcultures seek help from professionals who are outside of the subculture indicates the presence of severe disturbance.

Healthy Versus Unhealthy Religiosity. In working with Orthodox clients, it is important to differentiate between healthy versus pathological religiosity (Spero, 1996). For clinicians to be able to do this, they need some knowledge of the religious practice and lifestyle in a particular Orthodox community. Spero presented a list of points to consider in distinguishing healthy or mature religiosity from unhealthy or immature religiosity.

One warning sign of unhealthy religiosity is when clients have experienced a sudden, rapid increase or change in their religious behavior or identity, especially if this has involved cutting themselves off from significant people in their lives. Related to this is a history of major religious crises and/or changes in religious identity or practice.

Another warning sign is seen in clients who adopt religious practices that are unusually strict and go beyond the norm for a given community. This might be related to a number of other symptoms, including shame, self-hatred, the need to be vilified, and obsessing about sin and guilt. As mentioned earlier, to distinguish an obsession about sin and guilt from normal religiosity requires knowledge of communal practices.

Misunderstanding Religious Behavior. Spero (1983) provided a good example of why it is important to know something about Orthodox culture. He reported on an Orthodox Jew who was hospitalized and at one point was expected to participate in a group activity that included watching television. When he refused, his behavior was seen as a "significant regression, suggesting . . . paranoid ideas regarding strange influences in the TV" (p. 287). The staff tried to get him to watch television and was prepared to use peer pressure if necessary. In fact, the client was not at all psychotic. In his culture, the content of television was considered to be immoral. "In the client's circles, watching television was, in fact, considered *asur* (forbidden) by contemporary rabbinic ban" (p. 288).

This example demonstrates the necessity of considering the cultural context of behavior before diagnosing and treating clients. A similar situation could arise in a hospital with Orthodox clients who refuse to eat; rather than being suicidal or anorexic, they are probably following their religious guidelines for not eating food that is not kosher. Another behavior that is important to be aware of is that Orthodox Jews do not permit physical contact between members of the opposite sex other than one's spouse and children. Therefore, an Orthodox client who does not shake the hand of a clinician of the opposite sex is acting in accordance with Orthodox culture. This behavior could easily lead to misunderstandings with therapists, staff, or other clients.

Religiosity and Diagnosis. A study by Draper, Meyer, Parzen, and Samuelson (1965) demonstrated the utility of religiosity in assessment. Inpatients and outpatients were interviewed on their religious beliefs and experiences, and this material was then presented anonymously to a team of psychiatrists. Using this religious material, the team was able in virtually every case to determine whether the patient was neurotic or psychotic and identified the correct diagnosis in 92% of the cases. In addition to providing sufficient information for accurate diagnosis, the religious material "also offered keys to the understanding of certain patients' current conflicts that were not easily grasped from the available clinical data" (p. 205). The researchers concluded that

a patient's religious and philosophical views present as useful an avenue for psychiatric diagnosis as any other personal facet of his life. The rich source that religious material offers dynamically qualifies it as another royal road to the unconscious. (p. 206)

What this study indicates is that psychopathology manifests itself in religiosity. Thus, a disturbed psyche is likely to contain disturbed religiosity, and professionals who are open to exploring religious issues with clients can gain important information about the client's mental dynamics. What the study did not attempt, however, was to see whether a clinical team could distinguish healthy religiosity from unhealthy religiosity. Because the participants in the research were known to be clients, the clinical team knew they were dealing with a disturbed population.

Religiosity and Delusions. Although the literature on religious delusions has focused largely on Christians, Jews also have religious delusions (Clark, 1980). Clark made an interesting point in understanding the differences in Jewish and Christian views of the messiah. A Christian who claims to be the messiah is also claiming to be God. A Jew who claims to be the messiah, however, is making no such claim. In Judaism, the messiah is described as a mortal, not a divine, figure. Thus, a Jewish client's claim to be the messiah is less grandiose and perhaps less aberrant.

A study of messianic psychotic patients (Perez, 1977) found neither Jews nor Muslims who believed that they were God. Neither did any believe that they had died and been resurrected. Both of these delusions occur among Christians. Perez concluded that, generally speaking, even psychosis "does not succeed in going beyond the limits of the ethnic-religious identity of the patient" (p. 367). In two severe cases of paranoid schizophrenia, however, Jewish patients developed delusions that included material from Christianity and/or Islam. The presence of such delusional content occurred when "the individual identity destruction is very deep" (p. 369), and thus may be useful in diagnosis.

Religiosity and Obsessive–Compulsive Behavior. Many aspects of Jewish religious practice may be difficult to distinguish from pathological ritualistic behaviors (Paradis, Friedman, Hatch, & Ackerman, 1997). Paradis et al. provided guidelines in distinguishing normal ritual behavior from abnormal behavior. First, does the behavior exceed what is required by religious law? Second, does the behavior have a narrow or trivial focus? In other words, does the client's concern with religious behavior actually ignore the full range of religious practice and concentrate on one narrow area? Third, does the behavior interfere with other domains such as work, prayer, and family life? It may be necessary to consult with a knowledgeable professional or rabbi to determine the extent to which a particular behavior deviates from the group's norm.

Religious Barriers to Assessment. There are three aspects of traditional Judaism that may interfere with gathering information from orthodox clients, whether in clinical interviews or standardized testing: the commandment to honor your father and your mother, *lashon hara* (the prohibition against evil speech or gossip), and modesty.

The commandment to honor your parents may keep clients from saying anything that would reflect badly on their mother or father. Obviously, this may mean that they withhold relevant information. This should not be seen as resistance or denial, but rather understood as adhering to an important value. In some cases, it may be necessary to have the clients consult with their rabbi to get permission to speak to mental health professionals.

The prohibition regarding evil speech includes anything that might take away from someone's good name. This not only refers to rumors, but to things that are true as well. There are strict guidelines on when it is permitted to speak badly of someone. Clients may not know if it is permitted to violate the prohibition in the context of therapy or assessment and again may need to consult with a rabbi.

The third barrier is modesty. Modesty not only refers to how one dresses, but to all areas of life, including speech. For example, even speaking of sexuality is usually off limits. Schindler (1983) reported that in reference to sex one Hasidic client stated that, "We don't talk about that openly and we don't use that word," and another client said, "Only prostitutes talk about that" (p. 58). Even when help is sought with sexual problems, it may be difficult to assess what the presenting complaint is because of the veiled way it is referred to. There is such silence regarding sexuality that many Hasidic teenage boys and girls do not know how pregnancy occurs (Goshen-Gottstein, 1984).

Modesty cannot only be an issue in interviews and questionnaires, but in other forms of assessment too. With the Rorschach, for example, clients may not report anything that would be immodest. On the Draw-A-Person test, clients may refrain from participating. Spero (1985) reported on a client who drew a male figure without any hesitation, but who became visibly upset when asked to draw a female figure. The client said, "Why do I have to draw a woman? It's disgusting, to say the least!" (p. 100) and asked if the request were modest. In Spero's view, the client's reaction was not a matter of principle, but was a reflection of the client's own issues. This, however, may not be an easy distinction to make.

Another potential problem is that, for some Orthodox Jews, modesty forbids a man and woman to be alone in a closed room (unless they are husband and wife). Although some Jews may waive this principle in cases of medical and psychological services, others may adhere to it. There are two ways to handle this problem. One is to keep the office door slightly open to avoid being alone in a closed room. Another solution is to have a third party sit in on the session. The third party could be a second therapist or a person who accompanies the client, whether friend, relative, spouse, or rabbi. Although having a person sit in on the session may appear to be a barrier, Heilman and Witztum (1994) found it useful to have a chaperon from the client's culture be present and act as an intermediary as well as an important source of information (see also Witztum, Greenberg, & Buchbinder, 1990).

In these situations, it is possible that when clients object to particular procedures, religiosity is being used as a mask for resistance—as a justification for not revealing particular information. This cannot be assumed, however, and needs to be handled with sensitivity and perhaps with consultation of a rabbi (by the client and/or professional).

A related issue that perhaps is more cultural than religious is found in the difficulty that highly religious Jews often have in acknowledging undesirable aspects of themselves (Ostrov, 1976). Feelings related to anger and sexuality may be perceived as sinful and thus denied or repressed. This lack of awareness or inability to articulate any undesirable impulses in themselves may make assessment of such clients difficult.

Cultural Differences and Psychopathology

There are three issues to be addressed in this section. The first is the extent to which particular diagnoses are, or are not, found among various populations of Jews. The second is the extent to which depression manifests differently among Jews. The third is the manner in which people in different cultures respond to particular symptoms of schizophrenia.

Epidemiology. Sanua (1992) conducted a comprehensive review of epidemiological studies of Jews and mental illness. Caution must be used in interpreting the results of these studies because of the many factors that are difficult to control for (income, education, rural vs. urban, etc.). In addition, if Jews tend to be more open to seeking psychological help, they may well be overrepresented in clinical populations.

Although Sanua found many contradictory results, a few trends appear fairly consistently. Jews, compared with other populations, tend to have lower rates of psychoses, alcoholism, and organic dysfunction such as senile dementia. Jews, however, tend to have higher rates of neuroses such as mood and anxiety disorders. Schizophrenia appears more common in non-Jews, but manic–depressive psychosis is more common in Jews. Within schizophrenia, Jews tend to have more hebephrenic, catatonic, or simple schizophrenia than paranoid schizophrenia. In Israel, Sephardic Jews manifested more schizophrenia, but Ashkenazic Jews had more depression. A study of Israeli Jews (Skea, Draguns, & Phillips, 1969) found that psychopathology in Asian (Mizrachi) Jews "appeared to be directed outward rather than inward and expressed through action rather than thought" (p. 35). Psychopathology among Ashkenazim, however, "is that of affective and intrapsychic disturbance" (p. 36).

Enough research has been conducted to indicate that there are indeed cultural differences in the manifestation of psychopathology between Jews and non-Jews, as well as within Jewish populations. In the view of Skea, Draguns, and Phillips (1969), "Psychopathology represents a caricature, or a reduction to absurdity, of adaptive patterns prevalent within a social milieu" (p. 39).

Variations in the Manifestation of Depression. Dana (1993) noted that in depression, "There are cultural differences in mood, symptoms, and the expression of somatic complaints" (p. 179). The way that depression manifests among Jews, as well as the meaning of depression in Jewish culture, has received attention in the literature. In a study comparing depressed Jews to depressed non-Jews, Fernando (1966) found that Jews tended to be more hypochondriachal than non-Jews. However, Jews expressed less guilt and self-blame or "intropunitiveness." Fernando concluded that "a tendency to blame oneself when depressed is a trait with cultural differences" (p. 995).

Similar results were obtained in a study by Ball and Clare (1990). In this study, hypochondriasis was found in 80% of depressed Jews, compared with 30% of depressed non-Jews. Also, although guilt was found in 48% of the Jews, it was reported by 92% of the non-Jews. Another significant difference was in the amount of tension the participants reported, with Jews reporting significantly more than non-Jews.

A study of Russian Jewish immigrants found that they tended to score low on depression but high on somatization (Kohn, Flaherty, & Levan, 1989). The authors also found a high degree of demoralization. They concluded that the "high rate of somatization and demoralization found among the older Soviet-Jewish immigrants is an expression of depression in this population" (p. 357). These studies suggest that in diagnosing depression among Jews it may be important to realize that symptoms can differ from those found among non-Jews.

At the theoretical level, Frost (1992) questioned "whether secular, desacralized psychological concepts (such as depression) can convey the insights or therapeutic opportunities implicit in spiritual concepts such as the Hasidic concept of melancholy" (p. 72). In Frost's view, melancholy is different from depression. He argued that, although "depression is an abnormal ('negative') condition that demands treatment; melancholy is an authentic response ('positive') to accurate perceptions of life experiences that are incongruous" (pp. 81–82). Thus, "the melancholy of the Hasidic masters must be distinguished from depression, as well as from that type of 'sadness' that connotes deadness of soul, passive withdrawal, emotional defeat" (p. 84). In Frost's view, what may be perceived as clinical depression may in fact be spiritual melancholy—a condition that is not in need of treatment.

This view is challenged to some extent by Loewenthal (1992). She argued that in Judaism neither depression nor melancholy is seen as a positive or desirable state; people suffering from these states are expected to take action to promote change. However, Loewenthal stated that, "depression and melancholy are seen as presenting opportunities for spiritual struggles that are of the essence in the inner religious life" (p. 107). Thus, regardless of whether clients are viewed as depressed or melancholy, professionals should be aware of the potential spiritual issues involved in the condition.

Culture and Complaints of Schizophrenia. A study by Wylan and Mintz (1976) found that, although the actual symptoms experienced by Jewish and Irish schizophrenics were the same, Jewish families complained about different symptoms than Irish families. The authors noted that, "specific types of symptoms determine generally whether or not a person will be labelled deviant by members of his society" (p. 94). What they found was that Irish families tended to be more tolerant of deviant thinking, but complained about the patient's deviant emotionality. Jewish families tolerated the deviant emotionality but complained about the deviant thinking. Also, Jewish families tolerated what was perceived as laziness, but Irish families complained about this.

Thus, in collecting information from families on schizophrenic relatives, it can be important to understand that the symptoms that Jewish families focus on may be different than those focused on by families from other cultures; in addition, these complaints may not represent the full clinical picture, but only those symptoms that are least tolerable.

CONCLUSION

This chapter has sought to increase knowledge of Jewish cultures to sensitize clinicians to the issues involved in assessing Jewish clients. Jewish diversity, Jewish attitudes toward suffering and help-seeking, and Jewish identity issues were discussed to provide a foundation to the understanding of Jews as a cultural (and multicultural) group. In addition, particular issues in the assessment of Jews were addressed. These issues included the need for awareness of possible antisemitic bias toward Jewish

clients, the question of the validity of standardized tests for Jewish subgroups, and the many facets of Jewish religiosity that may challenge
clinicians in their assessment of Jews.

REFERENCES

Adams, M., & Sherry, J. (1991). Significant words and events. In A. Maidenbaum & S. Martin
    (Eds.), *Lingering shadows: Jungians, Freudians, and anti-Semitism* (pp. 357–396). Boston:
    Shambhala.
Ball, R., & Clare, A. (1990). Symptoms and social adjustment in Jewish depressives. *British
    Journal of Psychiatry, 156,* 379–383.
Bilu, Y. (1979). Demonic explanations of disease among Moroccan Jews in Israel. *Culture,
    Medicine and Psychiatry, 3,* 363–380.
Bilu, Y., & Abramovitch, H. (1985). In search of the Saddiq: Visitational dreams among
    Moroccan Jews in Israel. *Psychiatry, 48,* 83–92.
Bloombaum, M., Yamamoto, J., & James, Q. (1968). Cultural stereotyping among psycho-
    therapists. *Journal of Consulting and Clinical Psychology, 32,* 99.
Bohrnstedt, G., Borgatta, E., & Evans, R. (1968). Religious affiliation, religiosity, and MMPI
    scores. *Journal for the Scientific Study of Religion, 7,* 255–258.
Brodsky, B. (1988). Mental health attitudes and practices of Soviet Jewish immigrants. *Health
    and Social Work, 13,* 130–136.
Clark, R. (1980). Religious delusions among Jews. *American Journal of Psychotherapy, 34,* 62–71.
Croog, S. (1961). Ethnic origins, educational level, and responses to a health questionnaire.
    Human Organization, 20, 65–69.
Dana, R. (1993). *Multicultural assessment perspectives for professional psychology.* Boston: Allyn
    & Bacon.
Dayan, S. (1959). *A comparative study of the personality structure of male and female college
    freshman of traditional background.* Unpublished dissertation, Yeshiva University, New
    York.
Dennis, W. (1966). Goodenough scores, art experience, and modernization. *Journal of Social
    Psychology, 68,* 211–228.
Donin, H. (1991). *To be a Jew: A guide to Jewish observance in contemporary life.* New York:
    Basic Books.
Draper, E., Meyer, G., Parzen, Z., & Samuelson, G. (1965). On the diagnostic value of religious
    ideation. *Archives of General Psychiatry, 13,* 202–207.
Fernando, S. (1966). Depressive illness in Jews and non-Jews. *British Journal of Psychiatry,
    112,* 991–996.
Fernando, S. (1975). A cross-cultural study of some familial and social factors in depressive
    illness. *British Journal of Psychiatry, 127,* 45–53.
Frost, C. (1992). *Melancholy* as an alternative to the psychological label of *depression.*
    International Journal for the Psychology of Religion, 2, 71–85.
Gilman, S. (1991). *The Jew's body.* New York: Routledge, Chapman, Hall.
Gilman, S. (1993). *Freud, race, and gender.* Princeton, NJ: Princeton University Press.
Goddard, H. (1917). Mental tests and the immigrant. *Journal of Delinquency, 2,* 243–277.
Goldstein, E. (1979). Psychological adaptations of Soviet immigrants. *American Journal of
    Psychoanalysis, 39,* 257–263.
Goldstein, E. (1984). "Homo Sovieticus" in transition: Psychoanalysis and problems of social
    adjustment. *Journal of the American Academy of Psychoanalysis, 12,* 115–126.

Goshen-Gottstein, E. (1984). Growing up in "Geula": Socialization and family living in an ultra-Orthodox Jewish subculture. *Israel Journal of Psychiatry and Related Sciences, 21*, 37–55.

Gynther, M., Gray, B., & Strauss, M. (1970). Effects of religious affiliations, religious involvement, and sex on the social desirability ratings of MMPI religion items. *Journal of Consulting and Clinical Psychology, 34*, 338–342.

Heilman, S. (1992). *Defenders of the faith: Inside ultra-Orthodox Jewry.* New York: Schocken.

Heilman, S., & Witztum, E. (1994). Patients, chaperons and healers: Enlarging the therapeutic encounter. *Social Science and Medicine, 39*, 133–143.

Herz, F. M., & Rosen, E. J. (1982). Jewish families. In M. McGoldrick, J. K. Pearce, & J. Giordano (Eds.), *Ethnicity and family therapy* (pp. 364–392). New York: Guilford.

Himmelfarb, M. (1987). Jewish perceptions of the new assertiveness of religion in American life. In R. Neuhaus (Ed.), *Jews in Unsecular America* (pp. 1–7). Grand Rapids, MI: Eerdmans.

Hirsch, J. (1976). Behavior-genetic analysis and its biosocial consequences. In N. Block & G. Dworkin (Eds.), *The IQ controversy: Critical readings* (pp. 156–178). New York: Random House.

Kamin, L. (1974). *The science and politics of IQ.* New York: Wiley.

Klein, J. (1977). *Jewish identity and self-esteem.* Unpublished dissertation, Wright Institute Graduate School.

Kohn, R., Flaherty, J., & Levav, I. (1989). Somatic symptoms among older Soviet immigrants: An exploratory study. *International Journal of Social Psychiatry, 35*, 350–360.

Landau, D. (1993). *Piety and power: The world of Jewish fundamentalism.* London: Secker & Warburg.

Langman, P. (1999). *Jewish issues in multiculturalism: A handbook for educators and clinicians.* Northvale, NJ: Jason Aronson.

Levinson, B. (1962). The MMPI in a Jewish traditional setting. *Journal of Genetic Psychology, 101*, 25–42.

Levinson, B., & Block, Z. (1977). Goodenough–Harris drawings of Jewish children of Orthodox background. *Psychological Reports, 41*, 155–158.

Lewin, K. (1948). Self-hatred among Jews. In G. Lewin (Ed.), *Resolving social conflicts: Selected papers on group dynamics* (pp. 186–200). New York: Harper & Row.

Loewenthal, K. (1992). Melancholy, depression, and Judaism. *International Journal for the Psychology of Religion, 2*, 101–108.

Lopate, P. (1989). Resistance to the Holocaust. In D. Rosenberg (Ed.), *Testimony: Contemporary writers make the Holocaust personal* (pp. 285–308). New York: Random House.

McGoldrick, M., & Rohrbaugh, M. (1987). Researching ethnic family stereotypes. *Family Process, 26*, 89–99.

Mechanic, D. (1963). Religion, religiosity, and illness behavior: The special case of the Jews. *Human Organization, 22*, 202–208.

Ostrov, S. (1976). A family therapist's approach to working with an Orthodox Jewish clientele. *Journal of Jewish Communal Service, 53*, 147–154.

Paradis, C., Friedman, S., Hatch, M., & Ackerman, R. (1997). Orthodox Jews. In S. Friedman (Ed.), *Cultural issues in the treatment of anxiety* (pp. 130–153). New York: Guilford.

Pearce, A. (1994). Investigating biases in trainee counsellors' attitudes to clients from different cultures. *British Journal of Guidance and Counselling, 22*, 417–428.

Perez, L. (1977). The messianic psychotic patient. *Israel Annals of Psychiatry and Related Disciplines, 15*, 364–374.

Rabinowicz, T. (Ed.). (1996). *The Encyclopedia of Hasidism.* Northvale, NJ: Jason Aronson.

Sarnoff, I. (1951). Identification with the aggressor: Some personality correlates of anti-Semitism among Jews. *Journal of Personality, 20*, 199–217.

Sanua, V. (1959). Differences in personality adjustment among different generations of American Jews and non-Jews. In M. Opler (Ed.), *Culture and mental health* (pp. 443–466). New York: Macmillan.

Sanua, V. (1962). Minority status among Jews and their psychological adjustment. *Jewish Journal of Sociology, 4,* 242–253.

Sanua, V. (1963). Social science research relevant to American Jewish education. *Jewish Education, 33,* 162–175.

Sanua, V. (1992). Mental illness and other forms of psychiatric deviance among contemporary Jewry. *Transcultural Psychiatric Research Review, 29,* 197–233.

Schindler, R. (1983). Counseling Hassidic couples: The cultural dimension. *Journal of Psychology and Judaism, 8,* 52–61.

Sevensky, R. (1984). Religion, psychology, and mental health. *American Journal of Psychotherapy, 38,* 73–86.

Shandler, M. (1979). A study of the attitudes toward psychotherapy of American German Jews and selected gropus of American East European Jews. *Dissertation Abstracts International, 40*(2-A), 1078–1079.

Shimrat, N. (1979). Sociocultural and psychodynamic characteristics of ultraorthodox psychiatric Jewish patients. *International Journal of Social Psychiatry, 25,* 157–166.

Skea, S., Draguns, J., & Phillips, L. (1969). Ethnic characteristics of psychiatric symptomatology within and across regional groupings: A study of an Israeli child guidance clinic population. *Israel Annals of Psychiatry and Related Disciplines, 7,* 31–42.

Spero, M. (1983). Religious patients in psychotherapy: Comments on Mester & Klein (1981) The Young Jewish Revivalist. *British Journal of Medical Psychology, 56,* 287–291.

Spero, M. (1985). The clinical significance of Orthodox Jewish cultural content in idiographic responses to diagnostic psychological tests. *Journal of Psychology and Judaism, 9,* 86–113.

Spero, M. (1996). Diagnostic guidelines for psychotherapy of the religious patient. In M. Spero (Ed.), *Psychotherapy of the religous patient* (pp. 19–60). Northvale, NJ: Jason Aronson.

Srole, L., Langner, T., Michael, S., Opler, M. K., & Rennie, T. A. (1962). *Mental health in the metropolis: Midtown Manhattan Study* (Vol. 1). New York: McGraw-Hill.

Strauss, M., Gynther, M., & Kneff, D. (1971). Psychiatric patients' responses to MMPI religion items. *Journal of Personality Assessment, 35,* 282–284.

Suchman, E. (1964). Sociomedical variations among ethnic groups. *American Journal of Sociology, 70,* 319–331.

Weinrach, S. (1990). A psychosocial look at the Jewish dilemma. *Journal of Counseling and Development, 68,* 548–549.

Wheat, M., Brownstein, H., & Kvitash, V. (1983). Aspects of medical care of Soviety Jewish emigres. *Western Journal of Medicine, 139,* 900–904.

Wikler, M. (1986). Pathways to treatment: How Orthodox Jews enter therapy. *Social Casework: The Journal of Contemporary Social Work, 67,* 113–118.

Witztum, E., Buchbinder, J., & van der Hart, O. (1990). Summoning a punishing angel: Treatment of a depressed patient with dissociative features. *Bulletin of the Menninger Clinic, 54,* 524–537.

Witztum, E., Greenberg, D., & Buchbinder, J. (1990). "A very narrow bridge": Diagnosis and management of mental illness among Bratslav Hasidim. *Psychotherapy, 27,* 124–131.

Wylan, L., & Mintz, N. (1976). Ethnic differences in family attitudes toward psychotic manifestations, with implications for treatment programmes. *International Journal of Social Psychiatry, 22,* 86–95.

Zborowski, M. (1969). *People in pain.* San Francisco, CA: Jossey-Bass.

Zborowski, M., & Herzog, E. (1995). *Life is with people: The culture of the shtetl.* New York: Schocken. (Originally published in 1952)

Zemlick, S. (1977). *An Intrapersonal Definition of Jewish Identity and Self-concept.* Unpublished doctoral dissertation, California School of Professional Psychology, San Diego, CA.

28

Teaching Culturally Informed Psychological Assessment

Steven Regeser López
University of California–Los Angeles

I am both delighted and concerned about the development of multicultural assessment. I am delighted because psychology is now beginning to take notice of culture. The developments in multicultural assessment reflect the growing interest in the psychological study of culture (e.g., Markus & Kitayama, 1991). I am concerned, however, that our efforts to advance an understanding of culture are based on narrow conceptualizations. Culture is a complex, dynamic phenomenon that is grounded in social and historical contexts (Jenkins & Karno, 1992). Developing measures of psychological variables such as stress or anxiety for specific ethnic groups or deriving global acculturation measures based on loosely associated behavioral indexes (language, food, and music preferences) will not capture culture's richness.

In this chapter, I argue that, as we consider psychological assessment for our culturally diverse world, we be guided by processes (see also Greenfield, 1997). Given that culture is dynamic and ever-changing, our assessment approaches also have to be dynamic and respectful of change. In my instruction, I attempt to teach graduate students a process—a way of knowing. Specifically, I teach them ways to assess how culture relates to some behavior or set of behaviors. Identifying culture's role cannot be accomplished with the administration of a given instrument with a specific norm. Multiple perspectives are needed that integrate multiple tests and observations. By adopting this view, I believe that a clinician or researcher can begin to learn the role that culture plays or does not play in specific behavior in specific contexts.

In my teaching of culturally informed assessment, I am guided by three principles. Each contributes to demonstrating the importance of process. First of all, I try to provide a strong conceptual base to culture. I do this by tying issues of culture to key conceptual tools offered by mainstream psychology. A key component of these conceptual tools is thinking critically about what is and is not culture. Second, I try to foster active student participation through the use of key illustrations and exercises. Finally, I apply the conceptual tools to actual clinical cases. Adherence to each of these principles helps me demonstrate the process nature of culturally informed assessment.

At UCLA, I am one of three professors responsible for the clinical core course of psychological assessment. I share this honor with my colleagues Tom Bradbury and Rena Repetti. Our main goal is to teach first year doctoral students in clinical psychology basic principles of assessment that can be applied to research as well as clinical endeavors. Professor Bradbury is the main instructor and covers the significant conceptual issues of assessment, such as hypothetical constructs (MacCorquodale & Meehl, 1948) and clinical versus statistical inference (Dawes, Faust, & Meehl, 1989). Professor Repetti addresses issues concerning the assessment of children and families, and I address issues of culture, race, and ethnicity. We provide a 10-week course that includes a weekly lab meeting.[1] The class focuses on the principles of assessment, whereas the lab addresses applied issues, including the introduction of standard psychological assessment tools (e.g., the clinical interview, WAIS–III, WPPSI, MMPI–2). In this chapter, I present my contribution to this class. Although the course concerns general psychological assessment, I believe that the approach I use can be applied to courses in more specific domains, including personality and psychodiagnostic assessment.

CONCEPTUAL GROUNDEDNESS

When Professor Bradbury and I first taught this course 7 years ago, we agreed that issues of culture, race, and ethnicity should be well integrated throughout the course, not relegated to the end, akin to a special topic. We wanted to communicate clearly to students that issues of culture, race, and ethnicity were essential to assessment. To accomplish this, we made a concerted effort to ground the different cultural-related topics with significant principles or aspects of assessment. For example, the discussion

---

[1]Following the core course, students are required to take an additional quarter of assessment that exposes them to a wider range of assessment tools and provides them with more testing experience.

of the definition of culture, race and ethnicity is associated with the discussion of construct validation. Also, the study of test bias follows the presentation of cognitive-intellectual assessment and personality assessment. In addition, the influence of culture, race, or ethnicity in clinical judgment is tied to the presentation of clinical versus statistical inference. This conceptual organization allows us as instructors to integrate the discussion of key aspects of assessment with the discussion of culture and related topics (for a similar perspective, see Fiske, 1995).

There are clear advantages to this conceptual approach. Students who have had little exposure to culturally related issues learn that they too can enter into a scholarly discussion of culture by applying some of the key concepts from class. Concepts such as construct validity (Cronbach & Meehl, 1955), divergent and convergent validity (Campbell & Fiske, 1959), and the distinction between mediators and moderators (Baron & Kenny, 1986) are critical to understanding how culture, race, and ethnicity relate to human behavior. For other students who have a great interest in cultural topics, they learn that the application of mainstream psychology's rich conceptual tools can contribute significantly to the discussion of these issues. In fact, using these tools can enhance their thinking about the role of cultural factors in human behavior (see also Clark, 1987).

The psychological study of culture, race, and ethnicity is political in nature. Historically, our field has either ignored these issues or has examined them in a discriminatory manner (Betancourt & López, 1993; Graham, 1992; Guthrie, 1976). Ascribing the low cognitive-intellectual functioning of racial and ethnic–minority groups to biological factors is one example of such discriminatory treatment (see Guthrie, 1976, for a review). Because of the political nature of culture, race, and ethnicity, some students shy away from an in-depth discussion of these topics. Given the importance of culture, race, and ethnicity in our society, it is critical that all students learn to contribute to the discussion of such issues. Addressing them from a conceptual base and tying the discussion to mainstream psychology communicates to students that these politically charged topics are and can be part of an academic discourse.

Conceptual groundedness also refers to thinking critically about culture, race, and ethnicity. A key theme of our course is: How do we know what we know? We want our students to be critical consumers of assessment data in both research and clinical contexts. I present two main conceptual points throughout the course to help students think critically about culturally related topics. First, I strongly encourage students to go beyond or *unpack* the molar concepts of culture, race, and ethnicity by hypothesizing what matters about culture, race, and ethnicity. This enables them to test specific cultural hypotheses. Second, I urge them to generate and test alternative hypotheses. This two-pronged approach can guard against misapplying cultural notions while enhancing the under-standing of culture's role in specific instances.

Let us consider a case to illustrate the value of assessing specific cultural notions. A college student from an immigrant family seeks help from a psychology training clinic because he is doing poorly in his coursework. During the initial interview, he responds only minimally to the inter-viewer's questions. To understand the client's reticence and nondisclosing behavior, it would be wise for the student–clinician to consider the pos-sible role of culture. However, it is important that the clinician specify what about his interaction style might be cultural in nature. This reticence might suggest the client's respect for authority. Perhaps the college stu-dent believes that he should listen to the authority figure—in this case, the clinician—instead of speaking on his own. The reticence could also be a language issue. The client may have limited English fluency. By specifying the possible cultural factor, the clinician is now in a position to test whether this style is indeed cultural in nature. The therapist can then assess how the college student is with other authority figures (e.g., the student's parents). The therapist can also ask the client and significant others how they consider his nondisclosing style. Do they think it is appropriate behavior in the initial phases of therapy, perhaps as a show of respect? To test the language hypothesis, the clinician can directly assess the client's English fluency through the use of language measures (e.g., Woodcock & Muñoz, 1993). The important point is that as students consider cultural factors they need to formulate specific cultural notions that can be tested directly.

The second component of this critical thinking approach that I present to students is the importance of generating and testing alternative hypothe-ses. In the case of the reticent college student, it may be that he is socially withdrawn, highly suspicious, or lacking in basic social skills. Observing him over time, with others (family members or in a group therapy setting), will provide additional evidence to test both a cultural hypothesis—he shows respect for authority—or the alternative hypothesis—he has a clinical problem. By collecting both evidence for and against the specific cultural hypothesis, the examiner reduces the likelihood of simply confirm-ing a preferred hypothesis. Moreover, the psychologist is in a position to advance an understanding of the actual role of culture in the given context.

I refer to this critical thinking approach as *shifting cultural lenses*—a concept I borrowed from Kleinman and Kleinman (1991). They argued that the clinician (and researcher) should move between lay systems of meaning and professional systems of meaning to make sense of behavioral observations. In other words, the clinician should shift between the client's specific cultural set of meanings and the clinician's own set of meanings. This is captured in their quote about the ethnographer's mission:

> The ethnographer's focus moves back and forth. The task is to interpret patterns of meaning within situations understood in experience-near categories; yet, ethnographers also bring with them a liberating distance that comes from their own experience-near categories and their existential appreciation of shared human conditions. . . . Getting at mediating psychological processes requires that eventually we shift to the view from afar—we cannot otherwise abstract universalizing processes from the particularizing content of ethnopsychological meaning—but to understand actual situations we must use both lenses. (Kleinman & Kleinman, 1991, p. 278)

By entertaining specific cultural hypotheses (e.g., respect for authority) and alternative hypotheses (e.g., suspiciousness), one is shifting cultural lenses from the possible lenses of the client to the lenses of the professional. I have found that the idea of shifting cultural lenses to be a most useful heuristic in teaching students how to incorporate both a healthy appreciation of alternative cultural meanings and a critical approach to the role of culture.

ILLUSTRATIONS AND EXERCISES

The more I teach this course, the more interested I have become in presenting key ideas through the use of metaphors and exercises rather than through the readings and discussion of the specific passages from which these key ideas originated. In my section of the course, we do both. However, I find myself looking for ways to translate these abstract ideas in ways that make sense to the student—in ways that get close to the students actually experiencing the ideas. Accordingly, I try to use illustrations and exercises to begin the discussion of key sections of the course. Having presented the illustration or exercise, we then move into a more academic discussion of the ideas presented in the readings. In this section, I present an important illustration and two exercises that I find useful.

Shifting Cultural Lenses: Turn Signals on Mexican Highways

To illustrate the notion of shifting cultural lenses, I draw on one of my many lessons gained from driving the highways of Mexico. The lesson is straightforward—turn signals have multiple meanings. I first describe this example and then discuss how I apply it.

In Mexico, one has the option of traveling on public highways (*libre*) or toll roads (*cuota*). The public roads typically have only two lanes, one each for opposing traffic. The toll roads generally have four lanes, two lanes on each side of a concrete barrier. Because of the considerable fee to drive on the toll roads, most motorists prefer the public roads. The advantage of the public highways is that there is no fee, whereas the disadvantage is that, with a slow-moving vehicle and no passing lanes, traffic can accumulate quickly (see Fig. 28.1). Drivers who do not want to be delayed cross over to the opposing lane when possible. In the event there is no oncoming traffic, they accelerate to pass the slower vehicle. This can be quite dangerous because the visibility of the driver intending to pass is often blocked by the vehicle in front of him or by the lay of the road (e.g., hills or curves).

To assist in passing each other safely, Mexican drivers—particularly professional drivers—have developed a simple but effective form of signaling motorists who wish to pass. When there is oncoming traffic, the driver in front turns on the right-hand turn signal; the intended message is: "Don't pass, there are cars approaching." When the same driver sees that there is no oncoming traffic, he signals to the motorist waiting to pass by turning on the left-hand turn signal. This means that there are no cars approaching and the driver can pass safely. Interestingly, some trucks and other large vehicles have rear mud flaps with the words *Alto* and *Siga*. *Alto*, which means stop, is placed below the right-hand turn signal, and *Siga*, which means continue, is placed below the left-hand turn signal (see Fig. 28.2). These mud flaps reflect the alternative meanings. The other possible meaning of the turn signal, like in the United States, is that it indicates an upcoming turn. The challenge for the driver behind a slow-moving vehicle is to figure out the intended meaning of the turn signal.

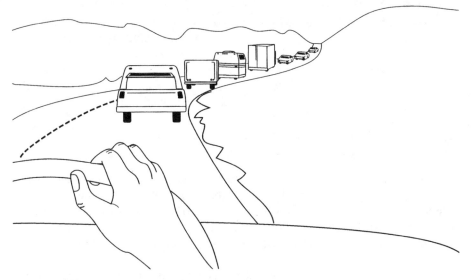

FIG. 28.1. Driving behind a number of motor vehicles on a public road in Mexico.

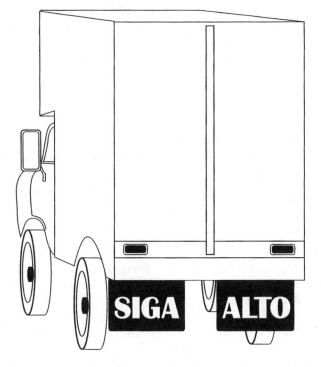

FIG. 28.2. Mud flaps indicating to pass (*siga*) and not to pass (*alto*).

After presenting this background to the students, I then ask them how they might know which set of meanings to use—the meanings associated with turning or with the status of oncoming traffic. Little by little, the students begin to identify ways to discern which meaning to apply. One student might comment, "If you were behind a truck for a long time and then all of sudden he turns on the left blinker, it could mean that you should pass. To be sure you might first check for oncoming traffic and if it is clear then it means to pass." Another student might say, "If you are traveling in a hilly area on a winding road with no obvious cross roads ahead then it probably means to pass." Eventually the students understand the main idea—that they have to look to the context to consider what meaning to apply. In other words, the meaning is tied to the cues in the specific context.

I then translate this concrete example into more conceptual terms. In discerning the appropriate meaning, one must first entertain both sets of meanings or apply both sets of cultural lenses. Then one collects data to test both sets of meaning. What evidence is there that the flickering light means that a turn is forthcoming? What data are available that suggest I can pass? Ultimately, one weights the available evidence and then chooses the course of action that is most appropriate. It is important to note that whatever decision is made there usually exists some degree of uncertainty. He or she makes decisions and takes action, not knowing for sure what the blinking taillight actually means. By collecting evidence to test the two possible meanings, the driver attempts to reduce uncertainty.

Application to Clinical Judgment

One of the first exercises that I use in class as a prelude to presenting the notion of shifting cultural lenses is to have the students make clinical judgments of an enacted clinical interview. The main purpose of this exercise is to have students experience and learn the possible risks in attributing a patient's behavior to his or her cultural background. This exercise combines two brief lectures, observation of a client in an enacted interview, an evaluation of the clients' presenting problems, and a group discussion.

At the beginning of this exercise, I present a one-sided minilecture of the role of culture and psychopathology. I argue that culture has largely been ignored in the study of psychopathology and that it plays a most important role. (This is a one-sided view because I do not point out the evidence that mental illness is universal, e.g., Murphy, 1976.) I then refer to two excellent examples of how culture is related to psychopathology. The first concerns how culture can influence the expression of mania among Amish bipolar patients (Egeland, Hostetter, & Eshleman, 1983); the second addresses how culture is related to the expression of internalizing and externalizing disorders in children (Weisz, 1989). My main point is that culture matters. My intention is to prime the students' view of how important culture is to increase the likelihood that they implicate culture in their judgments of the enacted case.

I then introduce the client to the students as Mrs. Ramirez, a 26-year-old married Mexican woman living in Los Angeles with no children. Following the introduction, I present a videotape of the enacted clinical interview; it lasts about 12 minutes. Joseph Nuñez, a former student, and I developed the videotaped interview for research purposes some years ago. The presenting problems were based on an actual patient of an outpatient clinic. In responding to the clinician's questions Mrs. Ramirez presents multiple problems including some physical problems (numbness in the jaw), problems with her marriage (her husband sometimes leaves and does not return until the next day), and depressive symptoms (loss of interest in usual activities).

Following the videotape, I instruct students to make a series of clinical judgments regarding the severity of the client's problems (e.g., marital adjustment, depression, somatization, and physical problem), the likelihood of benefiting from therapy, and their degree of interest in wanting to serve as her therapist. In fact, I ask them to make two sets of ratings on the identical dimensions. For the first set of ratings, I instruct them to assume that the presenting problems are related to the patient's (Mexican) cultural background. On completing those ratings, I then ask them to rate the client again, this time assuming that her presenting problems had nothing at all to do with her cultural background. In all, I attempt to manipulate the students' attributions of the presenting problems to the client's cultural background.

After they complete their ratings, we then discuss whether their judgments were influenced by taking or failing to take culture into account. Invariably some students volunteer that their ratings changed. For example, a student might say that when she took culture into account, she viewed the patient as suffering from less marital distress because her husband's involvement in extramarital relationships may be more acceptable for women of Mexican origin. On further inquiry, the student might make some reference to *machismo* or traditional marital roles. Another student might comment that when he believed culture played a significant role he thought Mrs. Ramirez would be less likely to suffer from an actual physical disorder. He might refer to the notion that Latinos, particularly women, tend to express psychological distress as physical distress—a cultural notion he has read about. Many students are comfortable in sharing their ratings and discussing the possible cultural influences on the presenting problems. Not all students have different ratings across the two conditions.

After time is allotted for discussing the students' impressions I then turn to relevant literature concerning the cultural basis of presenting problems of Latinos. I refer to the literature on traditional marital roles (Cromwell & Ruiz, 1979) and somatization (Escobar et al., 1987). I argue that the best available data do not support the view that Mexican Americans adhere to *machismo* and traditional marital roles and that somatization is not as prominent among Mexican Americans as some clinical writings suggest. I point out that there is little empirical support for many of the cultural notions that clinicians might have for Mexican origin patients. Furthermore, I argue that Mexican origin people are quite heterogeneous in terms of their cultural beliefs, norms, and practices. Finally, I caution them that imposing their notions of what is and is not culture can be detrimental to their clients. Having a husband who is involved in extramarital relationships, for example, can be most distressing to many Mexican women and may not at all be part of her cultural world. Assuming that men's extramarital relations is culturally acceptable behavior is strictly an assumption. This then leads to a discussion of how we know some behavior is cultural in nature, which sets the foundation for a discussion of shifting cultural lenses. In my view, what makes this exercise most useful is that the students actually consider how culture plays a role in a given clinical context, and they observe first hand how their cultural considerations or that of their peers can affect their clinical judgment.

To carry out this exercise, instructors could choose their own clinical case or draw one from some pertinent clinical writing. The point is to select a case that pulls for cultural stereotypes—ideally ones for which there is research to suggest that the stereotypes are true or false. Ultimately, the critical question becomes whether a given cultural notion applies to a specific individual.

Language and Assessment

One of the factors that is overlooked in the assessment of culturally diverse people is the role of language. Language is a most significant factor when the client or patient does not speak English. The evaluator will likely be limited in the tests that can be used. Also, the clinician may have to use an interpreter. Whatever approach used will be fraught with considerable difficulty. Language is also a concern for bilingual individuals, especially those for whom English is their nondominant language. The likelihood for misunderstandings and miscommunications is great, which could then lead to significant errors in assessment.

Language in clinical assessment has not received the attention it deserves in the research literature. Perhaps the most often cited research is that concerning the assessment of bilingual patients. Some authors have concluded that when assessing bilingual patients in their native language more pathology is observed than when assessed in English (Del Castillo, 1970; Price & Cuellar, 1981). Others have found the opposite; when interviewed in the patient's native language, less pathology is observed than when evaluated in a second language (Marcos, Urcuyo, Kesselman, & Alpert, 1976). Given these apparently contradictory findings, it is not clear how language influences the evaluation of bilingual patients. In fact, a recent, more rigorous study failed to clarify the specific role of language (Malgady & Costantino, 1998). Nevertheless, these observations suggest that language matters, perhaps in more than one way.

As an exercise to communicate the importance of language, I interview a student volunteer who speaks a second language. Typically the student is a native speaker, but students who learned a second language even with a low level of mastery have contributed to successful exercises. Usually I interview the student in English first. This way everyone can understand the content of the second interview which is conducted in a second language. Given that I speak Spanish and students more likely know Spanish as a second language, at least in Los Angeles, the second interview has generally been carried out in Spanish. However, I have conducted a makeshift interview in Mandarin and Taiwanese. I simply ask the questions in English and the person responds in his or her other language. Although not as fluid as when both the interviewer and interviewee speak the same language this modified format has still proved useful. During the interview, I typically address recent activities in the person's life (e.g., What did you do during the quarter break?) and touch on instances of both positive and negative affect (e.g., Tell me one thing that you really liked [did not like] during the break).

After the interview, I ask the interviewees whether they noticed any differences in their responses given the language of the interview. Usually they are able to point out some important difference in their behavior as a function of the two language conditions. The main point of the exercise is to have the students' peers (taking the role of the clinical rater) watch for any differences in the content or process of the two interviews. Students might point out that in the dominant language there is more elaboration or that in the second language there is more or less gesturing with the hands. We then discuss the implications these differences can have for actual clinical evaluations (perceiving more or less pathology). Although removed from the clinical setting, the exercise is a fun and engaging way to communicate the importance of language.

This exercise also provides an opportunity to apply the notion of shifting cultural lenses to another context. Students sometimes ask what language should be used in assessing bilingual patients. The dominant language is likely to be the best language for assessment purposes. There is likely to be less *noise* in evaluating someone when using their dominant or primary language. However, there are three important issues to consider with regard to the dominant language. First, identifying the dominant language requires systematic evaluation. Relying solely on people's self-report of their language competence can be problematic as discrepancies can exist in reported and actual language competency. Woodstock and Muñoz (1993) provide a most useful language assessment battery covering many domains for those who speak English and Spanish. Second, psychological functioning may be related to the language spoken by bilingual persons (Marcos & Alpert, 1976). In other words, there may be differences in people's functioning given the language they speak. Third, the depth of vocabulary may vary by the social domains being assessed. For example, for immigrant children, English language vocabulary may be more developed in academic contexts whereas their native language may be more developed in family contexts. Thus, assessments carried out in both languages can shed important light on a person's functioning. Evaluating persons in both languages is consistent with the idea of shifting cultural lenses and allows the examiner to capture more fully a person's level of psychological functioning (see López, 1997; Velasquez et al., 1997, for other examples).

Summary

I have presented one illustration and two exercises that I use in teaching students how to integrate a cultural perspective in assessment. I have found that the notion of *shifting cultural lenses* serves as a useful metaphor. Each subsequent exercise, with regard to clinical judgment, language, cognitive-intellectual functioning, and personality functioning, applies that basic notion to the specific content areas. Thus, not only is the idea of using local sets of meanings and professional sets of meaning reinforced, but students are also taught how to apply that basic idea to specific assessment domains.

A CLINICAL CASE

In addition to the conceptual basis and the illustrations and exercises, I draw on some of the assessments I have conducted or some of my previous students have conducted to teach students how to integrate a cultural perspective. My primary assessment background has been in the domain of cognitive-intellectual assessment (López & Taussig, 1991). However, I have carried out some personality assessment in the past. In this section, I first summarize the key issues that I raise in class with regard to potential cultural biases of the MMPI–2. This provides some background to the approach taken in the case that then follows. I present this case in our course to illustrate the idea of shifting cultural lenses with personality and psychodiagnostic assessment tests. This assessment took place 15 years ago when I was just developing my ideas regarding culture and assessment. Furthermore, the use of the MMPI is now dated given the development of the MMPI–2. Nevertheless, I believe that the general principles addressed with this case not only apply when using the MMPI–2, but also serve to point out how such an assessment can be improved given our understanding of culture and assessment today.

Potential Cultural Biases

The research literature largely indicates that there is no evidence for racial (African American–White) biases of the MMPI and MMPI–2. (The research regarding Latinos and Asian Americans is much more limited.)[2] There

---

[2]Although there is a growing body of research regarding African Americans, Latinos, and Asians (for Latinos, see Velasquez, Ayala, & Mendoza, 1998), most of the studies do not address whether the tests are biased for a given ethnic group. The identification of group differences does not necessarily reflect biases.

are three major reviews that support this view (Dahlstrom, Lachar, & Dahlstrom, 1986; Greene, 1987; Pritchard & Rosenblatt, 1980) as well as recent studies of the MMPI–2 (Ben-Porath, Shondrick, & Stafford, 1995; Timbrook & Graham, 1994). Although not everyone shares the view that there is little to no evidence of racial bias (Gynther & Green, 1980), it is hard to ignore the consistent conclusions drawn from carefully conducted reviews.

The lack of evidence for bias, however, does not mean that there is no bias or that for a given individual cultural factors play no role (see Malgady, 1996). As noted in the key reviews, there are few validity studies to test for possible racial biases. Furthermore, the normative sample of the MMPI–2 differs in many ways from the racial/ethnic distribution within the United States. Although the proportion of African Americans in the normative sample is similar to that of the U.S. population, the educational level of African Americans within the normative sample is considerably higher than that of African Americans in the United States. Also, the proportion of Asian Americans and Latinos in the normative sample is disturbingly low. Given both the lack of evidence of racial bias and these and other limitations with the normative sample and research literature, I encourage students to take the stance suggested by Dahlstrom et al. (1986):

> ... the best procedure would seem to be to accept the pattern of results generated by the standard scales on the basic MMMPI profile, male or female, and, when the pattern is markedly deviant, to take special pains to explore in detail the life circumstances of that individual in order to understand as fully as possible the nature and degree of his or her problems and demands. (p. 204)

Dahlstrom and colleagues also pointed out that psychologists should consider other possible reasons for test invalidity, including poor or careless reading of the items, impulsive answering, and other factors that can affect the meaning of the scores. The comments by Dahlstrom et al. indicate that they are open to possible biases in the use of the MMPI, although systematic biases due to race, ethnicity, or culture have not been found.

Their recommendations "to take special pains to explore in detail the life circumstances of that individual" are consistent with my view of testing specific cultural hypotheses for a given individual. In terms of shifting cultural lenses, a psychologist can use the U.S. norms as one set of lenses from which to ascribe meaning to a given individual's MMPI–2 test scores. By examining the life circumstances of a given patient in detail the psychologist is entertaining the possibility of applying another set of lenses from which to ascribe meaning to the same MMPI–2 test scores. Perhaps the pattern of scores reflect special life circumstances, cultural or otherwise, that require alternative meanings. The goal of the psychologist then is to determine what set of meanings is the valid one for a given individual. This process of considering two sets of meaning in interpreting MMPI test scores are discussed in the following case for which I served as the clinical supervisor.

Psychosis or Cultural Factors?

Sung[3] is a 30-year-old, single Korean-American male who was born in Korea and, at the age of 20, immigrated to the United States with his family. At the time of treatment, he was living with his parents in Korea-town. He has two sisters, ages 31 and 39. Sung sought treatment at a psychology training clinic because he was feeling depressed about having recently been placed on academic probation in college. He was feeling lethargic, sometimes to the extent of not getting out of bed. He was eating more than usual and occasionally had difficulty falling asleep.

As part of his initial screening, Sung completed the MMPI. The test responses revealed an elevated profile for many of the clinical scales, with the D, Pt, and Sc being the highest. In consulting established interpretive sources, the student–therapist learned that this profile was apparently valid and associated with a seriously disturbed individual—someone who likely held delusional beliefs, among other psychotic symptoms. These findings were seemingly inconsistent with the therapist's initial evaluation, in which no evidence of psychosis was noted either at the time or in the past.

In trying to understand this discrepancy, the student–therapist considered the possibility that language and cultural factors may have contributed to this specific profile. To examine this possibility, the therapist identified the items that led to the specific scale elevations and then asked the client to elaborate his responses further. During this inquiry, Sung indicated that he misunderstood several items, such as believing that people were plotting against him. Considering his responses to this questioning and the fact that English is his second language, she believed linguistic factors contributed significantly to the elevated scores. That is, he may have misunderstood the content of several items. On other occasions, cultural factors appeared to play a role. For example, he indicated that he got into trouble for his sexual behavior. He stated that on two occasions he had been to a woman's house without his parents' knowledge. For Sung, this was shameful behavior. For both the student–therapist and myself, this behavior was not inappropriate behavior for a single adult. Thus, the critical item inquiry raised the possibility that the elevated

---

[3]Sung is not the client's real name.

scales may have been a function of linguistic and cultural factors rather than psychosis.

In addition to testing the possible role of linguistic and cultural factors, the student therapist tested the alternative hypothesis that Sung was psychotic. She did this by administering the psychosis section of the Present State Examination (PSE)—a semistructured diagnostic clinical interview (Wing, Cooper, & Sartorius, 1974), which is widely recognized as one of the most thorough clinical assessment tools of psychosis. In response to the many questions taken from the PSE, Sung convincingly denied having any specific hallucinations or delusions within the last 3 months. (At the time, I was an experienced PSE interviewer and trained the student–therapist to carry out the noted section of the interview. I also observed her administration of the psychosis section of the PSE.) Together the critical item inquiry and the further assessment of psychosis led the therapist and me to believe that the obtained MMPI profile, which suggested psychosis, was probably a function of linguistic and cultural factors.

The treatment goals were to address his depression using Beck's (1976) cognitive therapy. After 4 weeks of treatment, Sung discontinued therapy because he said he did not like the homework component. Two months later, he returned to the clinic to resume therapy. After a period of several weeks, Sung began to deteriorate, seemingly precipitated by the mugging of his sister. After that incident, Yung began to express beliefs that people from his former place of employment were plotting against him and had been *bugging* his house. Furthermore, he indicated that they knew what he was thinking and had told half of Los Angeles about him. Once we learned of his deterioration, working in conjunction with his family, we referred him to a day treatment program where he was treated for his psychosis.

I like to present this case to my class because it raises a number of issues. From the perspective of a culturally informed approach, this case has merit. We considered the hypothesis that the pattern of scores reflected cultural and linguistic factors. It is important to note that we did not assume that the MMPI interpretation was inappropriate; we simply considered the hypothesis that culture or language played a role. Furthermore, we articulated a somewhat specific cultural hypothesis that Sung's may have misunderstood some of the test questions due to linguistic and cultural factors. Therefore, we were in a position to test directly this hypothesis. We then took steps to test both the linguistic/cultural hypothesis and the competing hypothesis that he was psychotic. This approach reflects both shifting cultural lenses and taking *special pains* to explore the individual's circumstances when the pattern of scores are markedly deviant. Thus, by systematically evaluating the linguistic/cultural and alternative hypotheses, we carried out the assessment from a responsible cultural perspective.

An alternative view is that we erred in our evaluation, as suggested by Sung later becoming psychotic. Had we accepted the MMPI findings at face value, we may have been in a position to recognize the underlying psychosis and refer him for treatment at an earlier stage of the illness. From this point of view, reviewing the critical items and finding that Sung ascribed different meanings to a series of items than what we thought were the intended meanings may have been misleading, particularly given that the items were from the clinical scales. Because the clinical scales are empirically rather than rationally or conceptually derived, it is hard to know why endorsing specific items in particular ways is related to certain psychological functioning (Butcher, Graham, Williams, & Ben-Porath, 1990). Thus, the alternative view is that undertaking the critical item inquiry may have clouded rather than clarified the clinical picture.

In retrospect, the culturally informed assessment was limited in two important ways. First, Sung did not want us to contact his family. He believed that such contact might bring shame to his family. The family's perspective could have been helpful in many ways to discern cultural and language issues from psychosis. For example, they could have provided a historical context to Sung's presenting problems. Second, the process of considering the cultural and alternative hypotheses was limited by the use of a single method of assessment. Both the critical item inquiry and PSE were based on the patient's self-report. Drawing from Campbell and Fiske's notion of using multiple methods to assess multiple traits, it would have been valuable to have used other methods. For example, were I to supervise this case today, I would have addressed the language hypothesis more rigorously. I would have requested that Sung's English language fluency be directly assessed using language tests. Furthermore, I may have requested that he complete the Korean language version of the MMPI–2 after having completed the English language version. Also, the content scales of the MMPI–2 would have been useful. These additional steps could have proved useful in determining whether language-based misunderstandings were responsible, at least in part, for the scale elevations when the MMPI was administered in English. To assess further for psychosis, I would also consider having someone administer the Rorschach or another projective measure. Together the use of the projective test, the language fluency test, the MMPI–2 in his native language, and the content scales would provide a more rigorous test of both the language and psychosis hypotheses particularly because the different tests draw from diverse methods.

Presenting actual cases provides a rich opportunity for students to translate the conceptual ideas presented in class into actual practice. In my course, they learn the practical steps of shifting cultural lenses. Furthermore, by reviewing cases, students have an opportunity to evaluate the strengths and weaknesses of a given assessment and discuss ways to improve such evaluations. The next step is for students to carry out their own assessments under supervision, which they begin to do in our class and build on in subsequent training.

CONCLUSION

Culturally informed assessment is a process—a way of thinking critically about the role of culture in human behavior. Teaching a responsible cultural perspective can take many forms. My strategy is to establish a firm conceptual base, engage students in key ideas through exercises and illustrations, and demonstrate steps to follow in actual clinical cases. I have found that these pedagogical tools help students develop a perspective that is both respectful and critical of culture's role in human behavior. Such a perspective is needed in the assessment of culturally diverse people. It is those psychologists who can present evidence for and against cultural interpretations who will be in the strongest position to convince others when culture matters most.

ACKNOWLEDGMENTS

I would like to thank Tom Bradbury, Rena Repetti, and Roberto Velasquez for their helpful comments on an earlier draft. The preparation of this manuscript was supported, in part, by an NIH, Fogarty International Center, Minority International Research Training grant to UCLA–Instituto Mexicano de Psiquiatria.

REFERENCES

Baron, R. M., & Kenny, D. A. (1986). The moderator-mediator variable distinction in social psychological research: Conceptual, strategic, and statistical considerations. *Journal of Personality and Social Psychology, 51*, 1173–1182.

Beck, A. (1976). *Cognitive theory and the emotional disorders.* New York: International Universities Press.

Ben-Porath, Y. S., Shondrick, D. D., & Stafford, K. P. (1995). MMPI–2 and race in a forensic diagnostic sample. *Criminal Justice and Behavior, 22*, 19–32.

Betancourt, H., & López, S. R. (1993). The study of culture, race, and ethnicity in American psychology. *American Psychologist, 48*, 629–637.

Butcher, J. N., Graham, J. R., Williams, C. L., & Ben-Porath, Y. S. (1990). *Development and use of the MMPI–2 content scales.* Minneapolis: University of Minnesota Press.

Campbell, D. T., & Fiske, D. W. (1959). Convergent and discriminant validation by the multitrait-multimethod matrix. *Psychological Bulletin, 56*, 81–105.

LÓPEZ

Clark, L. A. (1987). Mutual relevance of mainstream and cross-cultural psychology. *Journal of Consulting and Clinical Psychology, 55,* 461–470.

Cromwell, R. E., & Ruiz, R. E. (1979). The myth of macho dominance in decision making within Mexican and Chicano families. *Hispanic Journal of Behavioral Sciences, 1,* 355–373.

Cronbach, L. J., & Meehl, P. E. (1955). Construct validity in psychological tests. *Psychological Bulletin, 52,* 281–302.

Dahlstrom, W. G., Lachar, D., & Dahlstrom, L. E. (1986). *MMPI patterns of American minorities.* Minnesota: University of Minnesota Press.

Dawes, R. M., Faust, D., & Meehl, P. E. (1989). Clinical versus actuarial judgment. *Science, 243,* 1668–1674.

Del Castillo, J. C. (1970). The influences of language upon symptomatology in foreign-born patients. *American Journal of Psychiatry, 127,* 160–162.

Egeland, J. A., Hostetter, A. M., & Eshleman, S. K., III. (1983). Amish study: III. The impact of cultural factors on diagnosis of bipolar illness. *American Journal of Psychiatry, 140,* 67–71.

Escobar, J. I., Burnam, A., Karno, M., Forsythe, A., & Golding, J. (1987). Somatization in the community. *Archives of General Psychiatry, 44,* 713–718.

Fiske, A. P. (1995). The cultural dimensions of psychological research: Method effects imply cultural mediation. In P. E. Shrout & S. T. Fiske (Eds.), *Personality research methods, and theory: A festschrift honoring Donald W. Fiske* (pp. 271–294). Hillsdale, NJ: Lawrence Erlbaum Associates.

Graham, S. (1992). Most of the subjects were white and middle class: Trends in published research on African Americans in selected APA journals, 1970–1989. *American Psychologist, 47,* 629–639.

Greene, R. L. (1987). Ethnicity and MMPI performance: A review. *Journal of Consulting and Clinical Psychology, 55,* 497–512.

Greenfield, P. M. (1997). Culture as process: Empirical methods for cultural psychology. In J. W. Berry, Y. H. Poortinga, & J. Pandey (Eds.), *Handbook of cross-cultural psychology: Theory and method* (Vol. 1, 2nd ed., pp. 301–346). Boston: Allyn & Bacon.

Guthrie, R. V. (1976). *Even the rat was white: A historical view of psychology.* New York: Harper & Row.

Gynther, M. D., & Green, S. B. (1980). Accuracy may make a difference, but does a difference make for accuracy?: A response to Pritchard and Rosenblatt. *Journal of Consulting and Clinical Psychology, 48,* 268–272.

Jenkins, J. H., & Karno, M. (1992). The meaning of expressed emotion: Theoretical issues raised by cross-cultural research. *American Journal of Psychiatry, 149,* 9–21.

Kleinman, A., & Kleinman, J. (1991). Suffering and its professional transformation: Toward an ethnography of interpersonal experience. *Culture, Psychiatry, and Medicine, 15,* 275–301.

López, S. R. (1997). Cultural competence in psychotherapy: A guide for clinicians and their supervisors. In C. E. Watkins, Jr. (Ed.), *Handbook of psychotherapy supervision* (pp. 570–588). New York: Wiley.

López, S. R., & Taussig, I. M. (1991). Cognitive-intellectual functioning of impaired and nonimpaired Spanish-speaking elderly: Implications for culturally sensitive assessment. *Psychological Assessment, 3,* 448–454.

MacCorquodale, K., & Meehl, P. E. (1948). On a distinction between hypothetical constructs and intervening variables. *Psychological Review, 55,* 95–107.

Malgady, R. G. (1996). The question of cultural bias in assessment and diagnosis of ethnic minority clients: Let's reject the null hypothesis. *Professional Psychology: Research and Practice, 27,* 73–77.

Malgady, R. G., & Costantino, G. (1998). Symptom severity in bilingual Hispanics as a function of clinician ethnicity and language of interview. *Psychological Assessment, 10,* 120–128.

Marcos, L. R., & Alpert, M. (1976). Strategies and risks in psychotherapy with bilingual patients: The phenomenon of language independence. *American Journal of Psychiatry, 133,* 1275–1278.

Marcos, L. R., Urcuyo, L., Kesselman, M., & Alpert, M. (1976). The language barrier in evaluating Spanish-American patients. *Archives of General Psychiatry, 29,* 655–659.

Markus, H. R., & Kitayama, S. (1991). Culture and the self: Implications for cognition, emotion, and motivation. *Psychological Review, 98,* 224–253.

Murphy, J. M. (1976). Psychiatric labeling in cross-cultural perspective. *Science, 191,* 1019–1028.

Price, C. S., & Cuellar, I. (1981). Effects of language and related variables on the expression of psychopathology in Mexican American psychiatric patients. *Hispanic Journal of Behavioral Sciences, 3,* 145–160.

Pritchard, D. A., & Rosenblatt, A. (1980). Racial bias in the MMPI: A methodological review. *Journal of Consulting and Clinical Psychology, 48,* 263–267.

Timbrook, R. E., & Graham, J. R. (1994). Ethnic differences on the MMPI–2? *Psychological Assessment, 6,* 212–217.

Velasquez, R. J., Ayala, G. X., & Mendoza, S. A. (1998). *Psychodiagnostic assessment of U.S. Latinos: MMPI, MMPI-2, MMPI-A results.* Lansing, MI: Julian Samora Research Institute, Michigan State University.

Velasquez, R. J., Gonzales, M., Butcher, J. N., Castillo-Canez, I., Apodaca, J. X., & Chavira, D. (1997). Use of the MMPI–2 with Chicanos: Strategies for counselors. *Journal of Multicultural Counseling and Development, 25,* 107–120.

Weisz, J. R. (1989). Culture and the development of child psychopathology: Lessons from Thailand. In D. Cicchetti (Ed.), *The emergence of a discipline: Rochester symposium on developmental psychopathology* (Vol. 1, pp. 89–117). Hillsdale, NJ: Lawrence Erlbaum Associates.

Wing, J. K., Cooper, J. E., & Sartorius, N. (1974). *The description and classification of psychiatric symptoms: An instructional manual for the PSE and CATEGO system.* London: Cambridge University Press.

Woodstock, R. W., & Muñoz, A. F. (1993). *Language survey.* Chicago: Riverside.

Author Index

Subject Index